Windows –

Advanced Programming Design

This book is dedicated to my wife Fio (Fizz Mozz) my wonderful lady and most definitely 'a babe', for all the years she's put up with me – even when she shouldn't have. For love, love, love and then even more love.

Without you there'd simply be no point to my doing anything - This is for you.

(P.S. Thanks for the clubs).

Windows –
Advanced Programming
Design

Peter J. Morris

NEW·TECH

Newtech
An imprint of Butterworth-Heinemann Ltd
Linacre House, Jordan Hill, Oxford OX2 8DP

℞ A member of the Reed Elsevier group

OXFORD LONDON BOSTON
MUNICH NEW DELHI SINGAPORE SIDNEY
TOKYO TORONTO WELLINGTON

First published in1993
©Peter J . Morris

NOTICE

The author and the publisher have used their best efforts to prepare this book, including the
computer examples contained in it. The computer examples have been tested. The author and
the publisher make no warranty, implicit or explicit, about the documentation. The author and
the publisher will not be liable under any circumstances for any direct or indirect damages
arising from any use, direct or indirect, of the documentation or computer examples contained
in this book

TRADEMARKS / REGISTERED TRADEMARKS

Computer hardware and software brand names and company names mentioned in this book
are protected by their respective trademarks and are acknowledged

British Library Cataloguing in Publication Data
A catalogue record for this book is available from the British Library

Library of Congress Cataloguing in Publication Data
A catalogue record for this book is available from the Library of Congress

ISBN O 7506 0636 3

Typeset by Jan Bridges, Advanced Resources
Printed and bound in Great Britain by Martins of Berwick

Contents

The return of the shell

Appendices   857

Index   899

This book owes much to many both involved in its creation and its inspiration. I would like to thank the people in both parts –

*F*izz Mozz,

*K*aren Field (slugger), for always encouraging and looking out for me, and for being the best looking techie I ever saw – it was a pleasure Kaz (Hi Will & Ed),

*E*veryone at The Mandelbrot Set for being so completely wierd,

*Q*A People and staff,

*B*rian and Dennis for all the glue I used,

*R*PF,

*N*CC1701 & NCC1701D – Crews and Captains,

*R*obin Rigby for the hotline and the 'big guitar' playing at lab time!,

*A*dion (I know that) Jennery for some good days and pink encounters – Oh yes, and for dragging me out of that ditch late one night!,

*T*he 'Computer Guy', Mark Taylor (markta) for helpful input are you using 4 yet?,

*M*artin Dunsmuir – brief but highly interesting,

*B*onnie Cohen Boca,

*K*irk Bates (and Vanessa), for many things – technical, spirtual, social, for not tying his shoelaces, for the 'space' when I needed it for all my stuff, for all the exchanges, etc etc – what's the latest (dangling pointer) direction Kirk?,

*M*ozart, U2 and Jan Hammer for some good ol' toons,

*P*hillip Spencer, (call me Phil – I've optimised my name), for neat tricks with the left side of the brain, for telling me all about how sane XOR looks through an alcoholic haze in Boca, for jug-ing! and for objectism insights ++,

*N*igel Thompson, (nigelt The King of Carnation), for encouragement and especially for the good old days Tatyan's The C Court, the weekends etc How's it going Niggle?,

*M*ike and Ali – much more than just good friends – say n' more, say n' more, know wot I mean, know wot I mean- eh?!,

*B*ob Bridges (Hi Jan), for support, for teaching me so much C and objectism over the years (just when you thought it was safe...), for helping me with my Air Nav, and for all the great stories that have nothing to do with computing at all – 'Did I ever tell you about the time I learnt to ski? It was in a car park in Iran of all places!',

*A*ndrew Marshall, for many bright sparks in Boca, 'should be easy - just do ...',

*S*teve Baker, for helping me with the 'other' OO language, stress relief, and to whom the remark 'I hope someone blows you away' is always welcome!,

*L*in Brown, for showing me the difference between drivability and userability – and for being a foodie in CA.,

*T*he P1201.1 group, in fact, for all the standards guys 'n gals I've ever worked with for everything,

*p*hilba, for showing me the hallowed ground,

xii

Mike (the cheese-burger) Cheeseman and James, 'Hello mate' Watt for saying 'Come on down' (seems like a life time ago),

The Windows Development Team (new and old (1594)), for the magic,

billg, for the Windows Development Team,

bill and ted for the adventure (can never find one that works dam it!),

BC, for being inside when I wasn't,

G. Dwight Flinkerbusch, for being a good ol' boy,

Ben Matharu (and Jan), for sharing some of his insights with me, the room, and all the interesting VxD jawin' we did in various bars around London (pass t' bottle on the left hand top down parser),

The author of 'Juggling for the Complete Klutz',

Jon Bentley, for 'the pearls',

Dick (but my name's ?????? (we know who you are)) Popeye for being such a complete hoser,

Feargle Dearle, for you know what,

Bob G (Hi Doc), for helpful info,

Susie Hubber for letting me try some of this stuff out at an earlier time,

Mark Sunner and Mark Williams (Mark squared) for being some of the 'good guys', and being 'in there' at an earlier time – how's it goin' dudes,

ex-students for the 5s in particular!,

Mark (the B*****d) Sewell, for providing me with essential stimulants when I needed them,

Hi Helen, William & Katie,

Jon Burn – simply a good techie dude who was always ready to hear me out and discuss Windows prog-ing over a smoke and a coke!

APJ, RA, SW and esp. JG – just thanks,

Mike Cash, for not putting me under pressure when I was writing and taking way too long,

The Ladies and Gentlemen of Compuserve,

Others, that have slipped my mind (they know who they are),

and lastly to all those dudes that understand it – 'Thanks for the shirt' – it's magic!

To you all – a heart felt 'THANKS'...
Remember. The secret's to keep banging the rocks together.

Be forever excellent to each other and – Party on Dudes.

Introduction

Hello

Hello. I'm currently sitting several miles up in the air (37,000 ft or so, or about 7 miles) somewhere over the Atlantic Ocean en route for the USA from England. I'm actually on my way to West Palm Beach, (just in case you didn't know – West Palm's in Florida). Today I'm taking the long route – it goes via Toronto, Philadelphia and eventually, to West Palm Beach.

Let me introduce myself and tell you why I'm here (talking to you) and explain the connection between transatlantic flights and a book on programming Microsoft's Windows.

I'm on my way to Florida from the UK to co-teach a *migration* course (migration from Windows to OS/2 Presentation Manager) for IBM at Boca Raton which is just down the road from West Palm Beach. You might be wondering why I'm going all the way to Canada in order to get to Florida? Well, we're currently just over a week into what's been called the *Gulf War* and to be honest, I don't really relish the idea of taking either a US or UK carrier to Florida over all that water, hence my current lofty position (you'll be able to get some idea as to how long it's taken to write this book now)! What else could date this book's beginning? Well Windows 3.0's not been out long, the current edition of Slow-S-2 is 1.3, the world is using DOS 4 and the current version of Microsoft's 'C' compiler is version 6, that should do it!

As is customary on these long flights you have to get well stocked up with reading materials, personal computers, walkmans and anything else mildly entertaining in order to speed the crossing – I'm told that Valium also works well! My reading material, as usual for us computer bods, is primarily of a technical nature; it includes various magazines and a couple of books. In fact within the last 30 minutes I've just finished one of the books and that's why I'm making such a spectacle of myself in the cabin of this 747 by hammering on this PC's keyboard. Let me explain further (by the way the PC's an Olivetti M15 and I don't own a walkman!).

The book I've just finished was one of the very latest Windows 3.0 programming books and it's the third I've read on the new version of Windows (that's 3.0 remember). It's from a reputable publisher and was written by some people that seem to know what they're doing, so what's the problem then? Well, its like this –

I have been involved with Windows programming (and other stuff!) for some time, and I occasionally teach 'C' based Windows' SDK programming. Most of the people I teach, and have taught, are usually interested in exploring out of their depth (as students do) and find that they're not being stretched by the current commercial book offerings in the MS Windows area – they've long given up searching out explanations in the SDK manuals of course! They are also interested in reading *normal* stuff that quite frankly I've never seen explored to depth in a current book on Windows (their most common *wish list* is coming up). I guess when it comes right down to it I'm disappointed in the current Windows 3 books available, mainly because – to a large degree – they're all the same.

One more time

They all explain pretty much the same stuff, to the same depth, using the same design. That design is coded in the same old code, in the same old way and in the same old language etc etc etc and I've just reached the point (half an hour or so ago) where I've decided to write a book on the subject of Microsoft Windows programming myself. And here it is! Well it's a start anyway!

I'm hoping that it'll break new ground in that it will cover some of the stuff that I'm always getting asked about by both new and experienced Windows' programmers alike. I'm equally hopeful at this early stage (Gulp!) that it'll go to new depths in areas fundamental to successful Windows' programming. It'll analyse design issues, take a good look at the coding used in *old* Windows' applications. It'll attempt (note *attempt!*) to use totally unambiguous terms. It'll cover the object oriented goals and engineering constructions employed in Windows and it'll look at some (discuss briefly) of the other languages that may be used in the creation of Windows' applications, and of course when it's done, and I'm asked 'How can my library's WEP possibly get called before its initialisation routine does?' I'll be able to point the questioner at a book on the subject and make a buck!

My first book

This is my first full blown Windows book and I'm determined to get it right – please feed back comments to me directly; my email address is at the end of the book. I intend to keep both you and I on the right track by ensuring, through detailed explanation, that you understand my position (not the current elevated one in this plane!) (this will aid you to see the direction of the book), the book layout, typographic conventions etc that will be used throughout.

My aims

I've already stated that I sometimes teach Windows' Programming professionally and that just like your parents, I think I know what's best for you! If you think about it every author must think this otherwise they wouldn't be writing a book at all. An author's responsibilities in writing such a book as this are in the simplest case to teach you the reader the fundamentals of the subject under discussion. In my case, that's not the – Windows' Application Programming interface or API; I want to show you how to make that API work for you rather than against you! Inevitably however authors will teach you a whole lot more that you might not want to know or perhaps I should say, should be shielded from. For example, every book I've ever seen on Windows' programming uses the same programming model as every other one, they'll teach you therefore all about this model by example, and of course you'll design your applications in the same way and code them as you've been taught, remember, as a reader you must assume that the author knows best – now the bad news! I'm also going to use this model as it is a de-facto standard (more's the pity), but I will give you an alternative in just a little while! As most of these other books cover the same old stuff (in the main (should that be WINMAIN?)), you'll also learn to use only a small subset of the functionality of the API, but we're getting ahead here a little, so let's slow down a bit and let me simply state my aims in this book, after all that is the title of this section – and the in – flight movie's about to start!

I'll explore the programming model used, we'll discuss the model and both its good and bad points. We'll then decide to change the model slightly and we'll further agree on fairly large coding changes, of course you'll have to agree as I can't really reason this out with you, as you're reading this book without me, this is called a perk of the job I think ! Here's some of the things coming up to whet your appetite (please note that there may or may not be complete chapters covering this stuff, ie. some of this stuff is implicit and appears as a kinda side bar to other detailed chapters) –

- Advanced Debugging
- Advanced Dialog Boxes, Dynamic Dialog Boxes and Message Boxes
- Advanced Custom Control building
- Advanced Messaging System Information and Concepts
- Advanced Memory Management
- OOT – OOD/OOP etc
- Advanced Dynamic Linking
- Advanced Inter-task Communications
- Application Design
- Coding Practices and Standards in GUIs
- Windows I/O
- Windows' Languages
- Win32
- Advanced Windowing
- Advanced Miscellaneous 'Stuff'
- Useful Appendices

and the list goes on and on.

Please note that this list is not my original list; that earlier list contained the following in addition to what was listed above :

- Writing Help Files (There's something on this in the Miscellaneous chapter)
- Writing TSR's and Windows Virtual Device Drivers (VxDs) (mention is made of each of these in the text however)
- Undocumented Internals of Windows (These have now been covered to a great depth in another book – see book list in the appendix)
- Communications I/O under Windows (whole books now covering the subject)
- Designing C++ class libraries for Windows (ditto)
- Writing 3.1 Screen Savers
- Extending Drag 'n Drop to apps like the File Manager
- Do it yourself Drag 'n Drop
- Multi-Media Extensions and API
- A Whole Chapter on Tips and Tricks and undocumented features (learnt when I worked elsewhere!)

I just threw that in 'cos I feel, now that it's done, that I should've done more!

However two, or is that three, things created the earlier list.

1) It would have been too big and books that are too big don't get sold – they get made smaller (or into two volumes), this leads on to

2) Each *important* chapter would not have had as much space allocated for it, this leads us on to

3) I asked the people that matter, that's you, what you'd like to see in an Advanced Windows' Programming book – I got more than I bargained for, I was inundated with suggestions and in some cases pleas.

The end result was that essentially you apparently, in the main, want in-depth stuff on old stuff – you know dialog boxes and all that stuff etc and would rather have seldom used stuff produced as separate books – maybe a single book dedicated to a particular subject (we're actually seeing this happen now). Well this is your book; I took your advice (thanks to anyone that gave advice) and here it is – other books to follow? No way – it took me two and a half years to write this one and my wife is looking forward to my going to the local store with her at weekends to help with getting the groceries!
.... Perhaps I should think of writing another!!

I'm also going to provide you with, I hope, useful succinct examples! I don't know about you but I often find that an example can be so complex that its complexity essentially, and almost purposely, obscures many, or all, of the concepts being explained. For example, when you read about building custom controls, usually the example given will be like way over the top; the control will probably be quite ostentatious and will require, for example, some complex GDI calls in order to draw itself – I've seen custom controls that ought to be in a section on the GDI many a time! A custom control is just a Windows' class used for specialised I/O – and that's it. You'll also find that these flash controls don't really mimic a Windows' standard control, ie. they don't, for example, pass their parent's WM_CTLCOLOR messages, nor do they interact with the dialog box manager when the dialog box manager is trying to figure out what kinda control they really are and what kinda keyboard input they require (push button, list box, static kinda controls or what!). Now wouldn't it be more useful to see a real boring control that has the appearance of, say, a black square, but that really does have everything? Well I think so, and I hope you do too because I just love black square controls! My custom control section promises just that; advanced stuff on controls – not on GDI! Please note that most of the code used in this book is available from me directly (and nowhere else) – a limited number of copies of the code are available (limited because I want to tidy up my machine!) so first come first serve – please note that if you request the code via electronic mail that there's no charge for it.

☐ What you'll need

It's a good time to discuss what you're going to need to not only follow this book though, but to code with sanity for Windows (current and future versions).

You'll need a knowledge of 'C' and a 'C' compiler for all but the discussion on alternative languages – for that you'll need an open mind – period!. Don't be put off if you haven't as far, as you're concerned, a good knowledge of 'C' (if you can read the code in chapter 1 you're pretty much OK, if you can't, you're not – simple. See the references in there to some good books on the subject).

'C' and the Windows' API work like wood and nails do when you build a shack. The wood is the real stuff you're interested in, it provides the functionality and most of the form, but to do so it must be stuck together firmly using nails or perhaps glue (!). Let me just say here and now that to use 'C' as a form of glue is rather like using plastic explosive when you should be using clay! The wood's the stuff in which we're interested, because the glue is simple glue and anyway, given that you understand how to build a shack, you could choose the adherent of your choice – anything from plastic explosive to dry paper.

All the code in this book (apart from the chapter on other languages etc) has been developed using Microsoft 'C'/C++ 7.00a or Visual C++ 1.0. Of course you'll need the Windows' Software Development Kit or SDK (if you've got the full 'C'7 you'll already have this), guess where you get that from! Make sure it's complete and yours

– don't let it wander away, nail it to the desk or something! To follow through with debugging to the full, you're going to need a 386 based machine, lastly, especially if you're an old hand wanting just the advanced stuff, you're going to need to refer to the index and contents pages to find just the sections you're interested in, for the novice, you'll have to perhaps re-think entirely how you design and visualise your code in order to get the most from this book.

NOTE

This book doesn't intend to cover stuff well covered in other books on this subject. In particular its not going to paraphrase the *Programmers' Learning Guide* [sic] which comes with the SDK, by the way, keep this handy! If you're a novice, this book will bring you quickly up to speed on the programming model used in Windows and the Windows' architecture, bear this in mind, you might want to read through the Programmers' Learning Guide or Overview in parallel with this book if you find the going at all tough. By the way, if you have an earlier *Programmers' Learning Guide (3.0), Programmer's Reference, Volume 1: Overview (3.1)*, keep it around, it'll come in handy sooner rather than later. I have a saying that's worth repeating right here, – *A document discarded as valueless will become vital shortly after the garbage is collected.* How often have we all seen this come true!

☐ **'C'**

All the main code in this book is going to be written in 'C' (some alternative languages/methods are mentioned in the *Miscellaneous* chapter.

Let me state here that in my opinion 'C' is not the right language, more on this in a moment. I'm using it here because you're probably using it already, if you're not, I apologise to you, after all, you're quite sane and we're all mad (us 'C' – Windows' Programmers that is).

☐ **'C' why**

Why use 'C' then? To be honest, until Microsoft start truly supporting other languages we're stuck with 'C'. Why so? Because all of Microsoft's Windows support is geared up for 'C', so are the SDK examples and Learning Aids as are all the most popular available books. As an example consider the poor sod using Visual Basic. Most of their programming can be done under VB directly but sooner or later they'll need a DLL or VBX control that doesn't exist, ie. they'll have to write it – how? Typically by using 'C'.

All I'll say at the moment is – remember the open mind you're keeping? Well keep it wide open in this area when we get to looking at other languages better suited to the job of gluing together Windows' APIs (or even hiding them altogether). I have used Microsoft 'C' as it is still by far the most popular when it comes to Windows' programming. *The book went to press about a month after Visual C++ 1.0 was released – typical, I test my code primarily under what's going to be (by the time you get this book) an old version of the compiler! As stated above however, I have re-compiled under Visual C++ 1.0 (using it as a 'C' compiler) and everything's OK —Phew!*

☐ A history lesson

OK, OK, OK!, enough you cry, I'll buy it, now get on with it.

Your wish is my command.

It would be useful, as a scene setter, to start with a brief history of Windows (everyone else has done this so why shouldn't I?) –

☐ Windows – The early years

Windows (the actual system) has many good, and some, bad points as do some Windows' components like the CUA guide etc. The first good point that springs to my mind about the system is that Windows has now been around for many years. This is good as it means (perhaps I should say, 'should mean') that the product is well debugged and is therefore presumably in a stable condition. Unfortunately, due to the current climate and the great IBM – MS (I wonder if both companies will have survived as single entities by the time this book is published) wars, products tend to get pushed out of the doors rather too quickly. Too quickly for the people using, and writing code for them that is! The software industry is just about the only industry in existence where you pay for a repair, Oh, I'm sorry, shouldn't I call that an upgrade! Often an *upgrade* is no more than a bug fix – would you expect to have to pay for a bug to be put right in say your digital dishwasher!? Most of the time I'd like to have a version of a compiler that is thoroughly debugged rather than one that suffers from a whole new class of bugs due to its hasty development and the addition of even more bells and whistles!

☐ Windows 1

Microsoft launched Windows 1 towards the end of 1985. As far as I know it shipped as 1.01, 1.03 & 1.04 (some people are still using and developing using this version by the way - seriously!).

> The actual launch was a brilliantly stage managed affair – After many delays Microsoft called a press conference at that year's – Comdex Fall show held in Las Vegas.
>
> The whole thing was billed as the 'Microsoft tries to save face over the demise of its long awaited "Windows" product' which up until this time had been the subject of much media and MS hype. Everyone was convinced that Microsoft were going to admit defeat at the event and were going to drop their 'Windows' GUI or at least announce yet another delay.
>
> However during the press conference the doors burst open to reveal heaps of shrink wrapped copies of Windows 1.01, one for each attendee to take away. There were many *Cheshire Cat* smiles to be seen among the Microsoft people attending.
>
> Apparently, those journalist that chose not to show up thinking that Microsoft were simply going to announce that it was pulling out of the GUI

> business were seen later that evening trying to buy a copy of Windows off anyone who had one for basically any price. Can you imagine having to explain to your editor just why you missed such an important event!

Windows was quite an innovative product for the PC and its clones and drew lots of attention, something like a freak does in a circus perhaps? To most it was different and intriguing and promised much; whole new metaphors and acronyms for example!

I have some tape recordings of one of the first *Windows Development Seminars* given by Microsoft in New York, it's dated June 5,6 1986, they still get listened to occasionally as well. You can still hear, even though this is some 6 months or so after the launch, the excitement and mystery surrounding the new product in both the voices of the Microsoft personnel and the audience alike.

Windows 1 was mainly lacking in the memory department; don't get me wrong here, the memory management was a pretty good emulation of what was to be called the Intel 86 series of processors protect mode addressing mechanism and worked very well indeed (albeit minus the protection!), what was lacking was quantity, not quality. It's interesting to note that John Pollock in a talk on memory management (on the tapes mentioned above) mentions the i86 protect mode (only available on some of the Intel chips) and that some interesting problems with the Windows 1 memory management scheme simply go away when using that mode. The man was right!

Windows 1 introduced some terminology that we'll have to get into sooner or later so let's make it sooner and mention something here about window types.

Windows 1 had three types of window. The definition of window here by the way is the logical one. It means a rectangular visual object materialised on the screen and managed by a window manager (WM), the WM is part of Windows and may not be changed. You'll see later in the book that there are many more re-definitions of *window*!

A common window is made up of several bits. If we look at the window opposite (this is HeapWalk's main window (see chapter on debugging for more on what HeapWalker is)), we'll notice the following with just a little help –

The area covered in text is called the client area. This part of the window can be thought of as your piece of paper if you like, after all a window in Windows is really meant to be an imitation of a piece of paper on a desktop. Your application performs most of its input and output (I/O) from, and to, this section of any of its windows.

The rest of the window, everything apart from the client area that is, is called collectively the non-client area! This includes the title bar at the top of the window, the window shown has a title, it's HeapWalker – (Main Heap). Below this comes the *menu bar* or *action rail*. Until Windows 3 all your menuing was traditionally carried out through this menu bar, even now, post Win 3, most of your menuing will be done through this non-client area artefact.

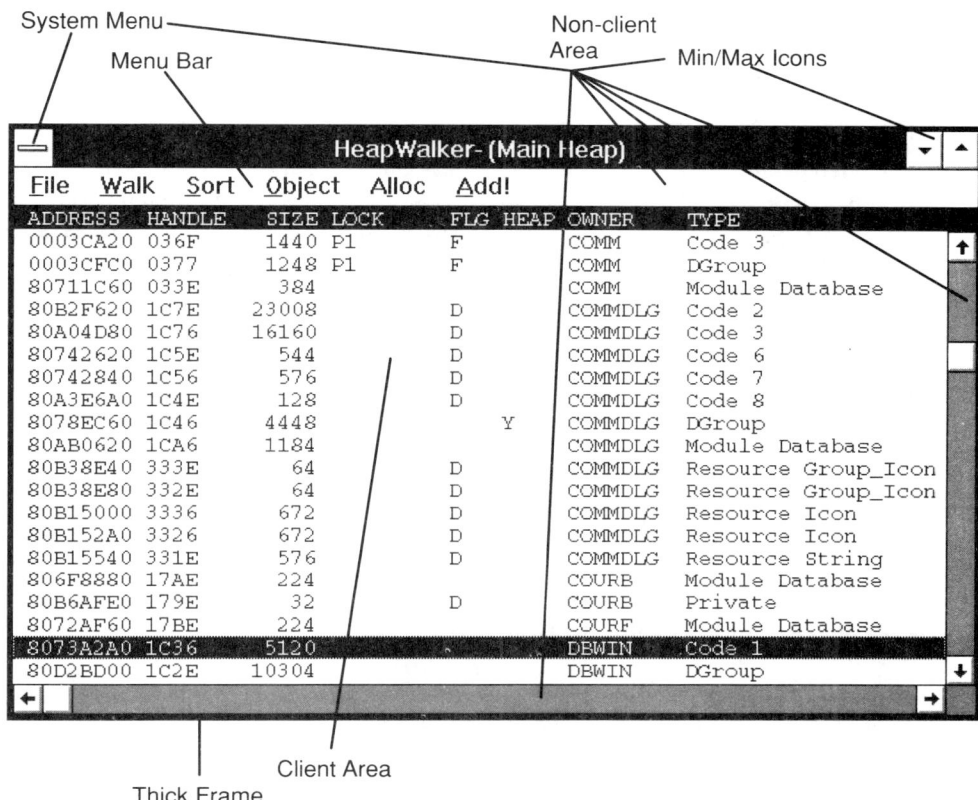

System Menu

Menu Bar

Non-client Area

Min/Max Icons

Thick Frame

Client Area

Around the edge of the window is a frame, this is called a thickframe (sometimes also called a resizing frame) and it can be used to resize/reposition the window in both X and Y. By resizing the frame it's possible to move the window to any location on the desktop. You can also move the window by clicking on, and then dragging, the title bar, or by selecting *Move* from the system menu.

If we leave the scroll bars just for now, the only things left to discuss are to the right and left of the title bar. To the right you'll find two arrows. One points up, the other down. These are called the maximise and minimise icons respectively. If you click the down arrow you minimise the window; minimise is sometimes called more accurately iconise (it's also called *close* on some systems – close means something else in Windows (unless you're using CloseWindow()!)). If you click the up arrow, the window is maximised or zoomed so that the title bar, menu bar and client areas fill the desktop entirely. This is your way of saying, 'look, I want to focus all my attention on this window OK?'! You'll notice when you do this that the up arrow changes to an up & down arrow which we now call a restore icon! If you click this icon you'll put the window back in its pre-maximised state with regard to its size and location. You can also zoom (maximise) and restore a window by double clicking its title bar; 'not a lot people know that', as Michael Caine might say! To the left of the title is what's known as the *system menu* sometime called the system menu icon. This is really here for the mouseless user. You activate it by clicking on it once (I hope you're *with mouse*, if not we'll get to how you're meant to access this in a moment). You'll see that it contains a series of menu items – move, resize, zoom, minimize, close, restore and switch to. They're pretty obvious in their use. Look at the system menu graphic again. What does it mean – what does that dash, or whatever it is meant to be, *say to* the user? A student once told me it looked like a filing cabinet drawer and that by clicking on it you opened it and could see inside. That's not bad, this student must have had a rather good imagination though because most people look at it and say, 'I haven't a clue'! It's meant to look like the space bar on the keyboard! OK you say, I'll believe you. Hit the space bar. Did you select the menu? No, you have to hold the Alt key down and hit the space bar in order to select it!

I find myself at this point saying, 'is this intuitive?' and of course the answer is no – a real world paper based user wouldn't have a clue. The nice thing about this though is that once you've learned this, *interface manipulation*, it's not only foolproof* but it's the same for all Windows applications – intuitive or not, in fact it's the same for all PM & CUA applications too. I hope that that's covered the majority of the make up of an MS Windows window, at least for now?

*One of Murphy's Corollaries says – 'It's impossible to make anything foolproof because fools are so ingenious'.

☐ Tiled windows

The first type of window that Windows 1 provided the programmer with was called a *tiled* window. You may also hear this referred to as a *top level window* and so it is, however the second type of window that Windows 1 gave us is also a top level window so we'll stick to the formal MS term for this type of window ie. Tiled.

Tiled was meant to be analogous to say a floor tile, rather than a roof tile, because windows of this sort could slide up to one another and indeed, touch each other, but they couldn't be overlapped, like a roof tile. When a Windows 1 application started it was supposed to create a tiled window. All the tiled windows on the desktop (the screen) always filled the entire available screen or desktop real estate apart from a small section at the bottom of the screen called the icon rail.

So if we only have one tiled window it will fill almost all of the entire screen. If you then ran another application at this point, and that too created a tiled window, your first tiled window was resized by the Windows' WM to accommodate the second. You can perhaps see a problem here? If the first window formed part of say a text editor program, and let's say that with the window filling the desktop we see 80 columns of text, what will happen when we run the second application? Should we now see 40 columns of text as the window now has only half the space it previously had? Should the application resize the text using a smaller font size so that we can still see 80 columns of text? Should the application rejustify the text leaving the font size the same to accommodate the incoming window? I'll come back to this in a moment. You lucky non-Windows 1.x users can get a feel for what it was like to use Windows however by say using the *Tile* option on the Program Manager, or better still, and of course if you have it, open about five documents in Word for Windows and select *Window; Arrange All!*

☐ The desktop

Remember that GUIs are meant to model the desktop metaphor, in other words, this new graphical wonder should mimic, as far as is possible, a real desktop.

Well let's just think what we usually do with a real desktop before once again returning to the problem posed above.

If we feel the desk is getting a little overcrowded we generally stack, or overlap, the bits of paper etc that are making it messy, alternatively we might file them away in a draw or on a shelf. We also bring that important piece of paper on which we want to focus our attention to the top of the pile as and when we need it. Could we do this to our Windows' 1 graphic windows? No, well not easily anyway. If the real desktop gets too full we start stacking stuff on the floor. Can we do this in Windows 1? No. Do we usually *tile* our papers? Again, no. You can see that Windows didn't (doesn't) really act like a real desktop. We can of course get Windows' applications to perform feats that we aren't able to do on the real desk in a similar fashion, but then again, a real desk doesn't claim to follow the MS Windows windowing metaphor (well the last one I asked didn't anyway!).

Back to the resized Windows' application. The answer as to what the first application should do was really up to the programmer or designer of the application to decide. This is fine but leads to inconsistency across different applications, as different applications of course do things differently! The desktop real estate in Windows 1 was limited to the number of usable tiled windows it could accommodate, after all you probably don't want to use a text editor with a main window say half an inch wide in X and Y do you (all you W4W users who followed the example above)?! You can, I think, begin to see the limitations. Tiled windows in Windows 2 and later behave differently to this as we'll see in a moment.

☐ Popup windows

Windows' second type of window was, and is currently a *popup* window. A popup usually *pops up* in the form of a dialog box! Hence its name. They don't have to be dialog boxes they may be top level windows and more importantly, especially for Windows 1, they can overlap other windows (the desktop itself is a popup window). The behaviour of a popup in an application is dictated essentially by the programmer. They may be related to other windows managed by the window manager or not. They'll behave and interact in a particular way with other windows on the screen depending on whether or not the window they're interacting with is related to it or not, popups so related were/are sometimes erroneously (in the MS Windows sense) called *child windows*. More on this in the windowing chapter. Popups are not normally resized automatically by the window manager which is convenient for managing complex output screens. Popups can appear, and be placed anywhere on the (or even off for that matter) the desktop.

☐ Child windows

The last type of window we have to look at is the *child* window. This type of window, like the popup, is available in all versions of Windows. In some ways a child window isn't a window at all! A child window is a sub-division of some donor window's client area that is managed and treated in most ways like a real window. It's really important that you take on board that last definition so I'll re-phrase it and repeat it. A child window is formed from, and is really part of, another window's client area. Once you have this firmly grasped you'll easily accept the fact that a child window cannot be moved outside of its donor window's client area (note that logically it can – what I mean by this is that a user cannot drag a child outside of a parent). The donor is called the parent of the child window, and as we already know, the child window is called a child of the donor! Again, much more on this in the windowing chapter later.

☐ Windows 2

Then there was Windows 2. or, If nobody uses it, there's a reason!'

Windows 2 shipped as far as I know as 2.03, 2.10 & 2.11 (2.1X was also called Windows 286, there was also a Windows 386 version of version 2.1X)

Windows 2, released late in 1987, changed some of the Windows stuff covered above. For a start more memory was made available to applications via EMS, this created more interest in Windows obviously as now bigger, and a greater quantity of Windows applications could run under it. As well as making available EMS memory (this caused more trouble than it was worth in my opinion) Windows could also access approximately 50Kb more memory than that available to DOS on a 286 or 386 machine. This is why the product was called *286*, it didn't require a 286, but if you had one, you got the extra memory. Doesn't sound like much does it, 50Kb, but it made all the difference. These are usually considered to be the main changes between versions 1 and 2.

In my opinion though the main change came with the introduction of *overlapped* windows.

☐ Overlapped windows

Overlapped windows are essentially like popups (they are not the same thing however). They can overlap other windows, they can go anywhere on the screen, they are not resized by the window manager etc. They also behave more like real pieces of paper than the tiled windows that they replace.

To make this clear let's just list the types of window we have so far – Overlapped, popup and child. We still actually have tiled windows although they don't work like the Windows 1 tiled windows anymore, in fact they behave just like overlapped windows, the two things are now the same exactly. Sorry to keep repeating this but, more on this in the windowing chapter.

☐ **Windows 286/386 or**
Anytime things appear to be going better, you've overlooked something!

Windows 286 is simply a renamed Windows 2, and Windows 386, a product which caused 2 to be renamed 286 added the virtual 8086 capability of the 30386 chip to the list of Windows' features allowing DOS applications to be pre-emptively multi-tasked alongside Windows applications – I'll cover tasking in various places later.

☐ **Windows 3 or**
To do it right plan to throw one (or two) away – you will anyway

Windows 3.0 was launched as the main part of a very enjoyable and multi million dollar extravaganza on May 22nd in New York. I know this because I was lucky enough to be there and fell about at the spontaneity of Bill's 'Why there's Paul Allen' joke with everyone else (I wonder if it was really a joke)!

It provided the following basic enhancements over Windows 2. These first ones are primarily aimed at the user but we should review them quickly and as you'll see below when we discuss the new important features from the view of the programmer, there is some overlap.

For the user – The now famous, you either love it or you hate it, 3D front end that isn't quite! A different colour scheme on the front end which was intended to make the product more appealing. Three important new applications :– The Program Manager which is very like the PM Desktop Manager, The File Manager, and the Task List (at this time the MSDOS Executive still came in the box). An application standard Help Manager; A better set-up program which for the best part runs in Windows itself! A redesigned Control Panel, a Print Manager, a proportional system font, better and more standard applications, and lastly a symbol font.

For the programmer – The standard application Help Manager. Windows' new ability to run the 286, and up, processors in protect mode giving access to extended memory. Virtual memory when run on a 386 equipped machine. Working as a DOS extender and DPMI server to non-Windows' applications running in DOS boxes (DPMI in standard mode didn't work too well). The Palette Manager for handling colour requests between colour intensive applications. The proportional system font. DIBs or Device Independent Bitmaps. Device independent icons and cursors. Nested menus. Real popup menus. A new dialog box control called a combo box. Improved functionality for most existing controls. Extensive *Owner Draw* capability provided throughout Windows. An improved API (yet more functions!) Enhancements to

DLLs. Better network awareness. Better printer drivers and more that elude me for the moment, but are probably unimportant.

One very important note here. If you've been using Windows 2 for programming put your hand up. If you put your hand up, now put it down and put it up again if you've read the *Installation and Update Guide*. Not many hands up in the air I bet. This guide is very important, it covers some things that are covered nowhere else in the entire SDK notes, guides or readme files. So for now simply find it and keep it near, you might be using it later! You might do the same with the rest of the manuals by the way. I find that I have to keep them at my fingertips all the time; I have a set at home, one at work and one in the car! Only kidding (about work!)!

All of these improvements are talked abut more fully in the rest of the book, see the index for more information on any given subject.

☐ Windows 3.1 or how to remove UAEs!

Windows 3.1 shipped in May 1991 and is, at the time or writing, the current version of Windows. It's faster and more stable than 3.0. The UAE (Unrecoverable Application Error) has been replaced generally with a GPF (General Protection Fault) dialog (Have you heard the one about a UME? IBM's OS/2 suffers from these – UME stands for Unrecoverable Marketing Error!). A general protection fault means that an application has attempted to access memory with either incorrect rights to the memory or more commonly that the memory simply doesn't belong to the task accessing it – programmers call GPFs *trap Ds* (D in decimal is 13 – the number awarded to such a general protection exception by the silicon).

3.1 is more stable due to the way error checking is carried out on passed parameters (to the Windows' API). Whereas in 3.0 Windows believed you, 3.1 doesn't. For example if you passed 3.0 an invalid window handle, say 0, it would treat the value as a valid window handle. This might have caused Windows to incorrectly address or change internal tables. The result was that the system would/could become unstable, thus the message about restarting Windows in order to stabilise the system. In 3.1 this would not happen as the passed window handle would be checked for validity before any further action was taken with it. The result – no erroneous changes to Windows' internals and a more stable system. To add this extra error checking, and yet increase the overall speed of Windows has taken a lot of work. (Most apps – even the famous ones – still pass erroneous information to the APIs, see the debugging chapter for more on this).

Real mode support has been removed, now all Windows' applications must run in either 286 standard mode or 386 enhanced mode – no EMS memory, Yea, way t'go.

The popular press slated off the 3.0 File Manager, 3.1 has a new one - so far the press are happy with it – the *press* amaze me; they find some excuse for not liking anything; I'm waiting for the next gem!

Some new applications have been added, <u>very important</u> – a new game called Mine Sweeper has appeared.

For the support engineer/programmer a diagnostic application called Dr. Watson has been included (why wasn't it called Holmes? Dr. Watson was usually portrayed as a bubbling idiot! I can only think that as Dr. Watson (the character) was Holmes' chronicler, Dr. Watson (the application) is Windows' fault chronicler?).

True Type fonts have been added. A True Type font is an outline font, ie. it is not a bit pattern (raster font) but a description a little like a vector font.

Generally 3.1 is a flash 3.0 though.

The Windows' SDK has been improved yet again, more tools, old tools acting a little differently etc The new debugging tools and libraries are better than ever, in fact if anything the debug libs are a little too much as we'll see.

☐ Events *drive* programs

To fully appreciate an event driven architecture we must first define *mode*. Before I talk about what a mode is, let's see what the experts say –

The IBM's CUA (Common User Access) guide says this about Modes –

> Users are in a mode whenever they must cancel what they are doing before they can do something else or when the same action has different results in different situations.
>
> Modes force users to focus on the way an application works, instead of on the task they want to complete. Modes therefore, interfere with the users' ability to use their conceptual model of how the application should work. It is not always possible to design a modeless application; however, you should make modes an exception and limit them to the smallest possible scope.
>
> Whenever users are in a mode, you should make it obvious by providing good visual cues. The method for ending the mode should be easy to learn and remember.

Isn't an expert defined as – *ex* = has been, *spert* (or spurt) = a drip under pressure?

Most DOS applications enforce *modes* on the user of them – they are *Modal* therefore. It is more difficult to work with modes (in a modal way) than without them (called modeless operation). We as humans work mostly in a modeless way; for example. I'm at this moment writing this page and at the same time I'm waiting for some visitors to arrive. If they arrive, let's say mid sentence, I can easily switch from writing this page to answering the door and dealing with my guests without giving a moment's thought to the PC, Word for Windows or anything else for that matter. Again, think how you work, you're writing some code and suddenly decide to call someone up on the telephone to ask a technical question, Microsoft perhaps? You MIGHT get half way through this and decide to keep them waiting for a change, ask them to hold, and go and get a cup of coffee or do some more juggling practice! You get the point –

you always work best when you're truly mode-less

Remember this because you not only work better like this, but so does your user base. Make your applications as modeless as possible. Applications such as Microsoft's Visual Basic (VB) encourage modeless application development – well done.

Some things we do are modal of course, the modality of such a task usually signals that the task is critical and cannot be disturbed for fear of loss of life etc. For example, you wouldn't get half way into overtaking someone on the freeway then suddenly start reading *Juggling for the Complete Klutz* or *Penguin Dreams and Stranger Things* (Hi Opus) would you?

OK if modes are bad, and DOS applications are in the main modal, how can we get around it (DOS & modes)? One way to do this in a computer system is to implement a message or event based system like Windows.

In such a system user actions result in an event being picked up by the system. The system passes the event to an appropriate application for processing. Here it's the user that's in control, not the application.

User are Biological Event Dispatchers

For example, I can in the middle of hitting keys, which generate events, which are fed into Word for Windows', move the cursor to say the Program Manager and click it. I have decided to interrupt the writing of the book to say review the state of my diary. I did this because, as I was typing, I suddenly remembered I'd arranged to meet someone for lunch tomorrow and wondered if I'd put this fact in my diary. This is a typical thing for a human to do and it's particularly pleasing to find that you're allowed to switch like this if you're also a computer user, as is the case if you're using Windows or PM (we'll see where this falls flat on its face a little later).

Events are usually, and more popularly, called messages in Windows. I actually prefer the first term as the term message in Windows' programming has at least three different definitions! I'll use the latter though as it's more popular and point out the meaning as and when it changes however.

Messages come from one of four places, the user, the system, other applications or the same application. Messages go to one of three places, a task, a window or all windows.

The technical definition of a message for now is a 16 bit unsigned integer that specifies an event type (the new 3.1 type UINT is used). Event types can have symbolic names in Windows and <u>most</u> do. For example the event represented by the value 0x0111 hex or 273 decimal doesn't mean much to us as human programmers but its symbolic identifier of *WM_COMMAND* does, doesn't it? Don't worry if it doesn't, it will soon. For now I'll simply say that WM_COMMAND messages usually mean to an application that some menu item has been chosen off one of its menus. Another message might have the identifier WM_KEYDOWN, this message tells us that the user has pressed down a key on the keyboard. This is a new way to receive input isn't it? Your traditional programs use getcha() or some other such macro or function to read keys from the keyboard, they have to be expecting them of course and have probably put the user into a mode while they're waiting for them! Here the system informs the program that the user has pressed a key automatically. getcha() is not really at fault here by the way, it's just the way it's written. If getcha() could be interfaced to an event dispatcher it too could be just as friendly as Windows (there are libraries for Windows' applications that allow them to use functions such as getcha(), look out for them if you're a big user of STDIO and want to simply port a DOS based application into Windows. One such library ships with Microsoft's Quick 'C' for Windows).

Generally messages are queued and delivered to your application in pretty much the same order as they occurred. It's up to your application to poll its task queue on a regular basis to see if any messages are pending for it. The queue you'll be dealing with is commonly called the *application queue,* you'll see in a moment why this term is wrong.

Let's just change one thing here. I've been using application or program up until now to mean your running application, sounds sensible. Well, I'm going to change that now for the rest of the book. From now on your running application will be called a task.

☐ Tasks

A task is many things in Windows. You'll find lots of different definitions of it like – *A task is anything with its own stack* (not really so although a task always has access to a stack). *Windows is a task*, again, in the strict sense, not so.

A task is a process that Windows regards as a separately running application that may be scheduled to execute by the Windows' scheduler. A dynamic link library is not a task simply because it is not scheduled, nor can it, without the aid of a calling task use or access a stack. It contains executable, non-taskable code only. When library code is executing, Windows considers it to be your task that is currently running, not the library (the task that called the library is *your* task). We hear a lot of talk about the *application queue* in the SDK documentation, let me also tidy this up here and now. The application queue should really be called the task queue as each task gets its own queue. Every instance of an application is a separate task from another instance, each gets its own *task queue.*

Not all messages are queued and must be retrieved in this way, in actual fact Windows 3 queues very few messages in your application task queue. Basically, only input messages must be queued (even this might change in Windows-NT).

☐ Conventions

OK, that's really all I intend to say about Windows for now. The rest of this chapter is directed towards some of the conventions used throughout this book, this includes typographic and syntactic notations used in code fragments. We ought to look at these now.

Firstly – you either love it or you hate it. What ('C' maybe?)? Hungarian Notation (I'll call it HG or HN from here on in) that's what. Well I sort of love it and use it in this book to a small degree. It's used by professional Windows and PM – OS/2 programmers the world over and there are probably as many variants of HG as there are programmers! So, let's look at it in some detail, in fact many pages of detail, and let you form your own opinion as to its worth! Perhaps I should say that I'll use a short form Hungarian Notation right here before I frighten you off with the long form. What are these short and long forms? Read on.

HG was devised by an ex-Xerox Parc and Microsoft computer scientist named Charles Simonyi. Born in Budapest in 1948, Charles is so far most widely known for a form of notation derivation called *Hungarian Notation* (also called more correctly *type algebra)*, which I think is rather sad as he has made many significant contributions to computer science. Charles defines Hungarian notation as a set of conventions that controls the naming of all quantities in a program. Note the use of *all* here.

If you look closely at any non-Windows program you'll find that most of it is names. Usually those names say very little or more usually nothing at all about the data item to which they relate and this is fine in small programs.

HG has little to do, on the face of it, with multiple name space restrictions where for example in larger programs the name space can get polluted between say two teams of programmers working on different modules of the same project causing name collisions. In a situation like this its usual to find the project leaders meeting to agree on a naming style or convention for each of the groups so that one can use *1_Main_loop* and the other *2_Main_loop* for example without getting problems when different modules are brought together in a final assembly and test phase (they might also prefix their routine names with a module name). HG can be useful here also but let's just consider it for the moment as a *stand alone file* convention.

HG has two forms called *short form* and *long form*, I'll explain both in a moment but first let's have a look at some HG.

consider the HG free code –

```
SomeFunc(...)
{
        int x;
        float y;
        ...
        y=3.142;
        x=y;          /* assign to x the value of y          */

        if(x==3.142)
        {
                /* code here never done                    */
        }
}
```

Here it's not certain, at the time of the assignment (and without having the convenience of looking back at the data definitions), whether the assignment is between two objects of the same type or not.

In the example *x* will not be promoted to a float before the assignment and will hold the value 3.0 should it be required within the expression for further evaluation. It's an *integer* after all! When we now test x against 3.142 in the conditional expression it's promoted to a float. Here it will be 3.0 and so it will never equal 3.142. This is a serious bug and is made obvious by the size of the code fragment and its simplicity, but just imagine if this were a 50 line function and that the defining declarations of both x & y were off the top of the screen. It harder to see isn't it? The bug can be partly fixed by promoting the integer to a float within the expression. See the following examples. In the second one the cast to float is required to be bound to x. :-

```
{
    int x;
    float a,b;
    a=3.142;
    b=(x=a);          /* error, x and therefore b is 3 (3.0) */
    printf('%f\n'b);  /* prints 3.0                          */
    printf('%d\n',x); /* prints 3                            */
}


{
    int x;
    float a,b;
    a=3.142;
    b=((float)x=a);   /* OK, x and therefore b is 3.142      */
    printf('%f\n'b);  /* prints 3.142                        */
    printf('%d\n',x); /* prints 3                            */
}
```

```
SomeFunc(...)
{
    int nX;
    float fY;
    ...
    fY=3.142;
    nX=fY;                  /* assign to nX the value of fY     */

    if(nX==3.142)


    {
                            /* code here never done            */
    }
}
```

Now the bug is still here, but the code is clearer. Well it will be once you're told that identifiers prefixed with an *n* are of type integer while those prefixed with an *f* are of type floating point. Now, whenever you are in your code and see two different identifier prefixes across either side of an assignment operator (with no casts), you'll know that there'll be implicit promotion/demotion and possible problems with the assignment.

It might also be useful to say something about the usage of these variables. After all *X* and *Y* doesn't say much to me – how about you?! We could also say something about the variable's storage class, their visibility or scope, the life of the object, maybe something exact about the data type. We might also consider using HG as a suffix in order to prevent naming collisions etc. Long form HG is loosely defined as the variety of HG that *says* everything it can about an identifier, ie. a long form identifier would include information about scope, storage class, size/distance of the item etc etc; short form is what we'd probably call the *normal* form, ie. it's the form you're probably used to seeing in existing Windows' code.

So, we could end up with enormous identifiers, here's a automatic constant pointer to a constant character written in *semi* long-form HG – WOW!:

```
auto const * char const   pCocCoAuMainWindowTitle;
```

Microsoft C, and its linker, recognise only (only!) 31 characters (ANSI specification for the compiler) in identifiers (extra characters are discarded) and we've already seen just how long some of these *long form* names can get! It's easily possible to get over 31 characters of HG (which could easily be duplicated in another identifier) before you get to the usage part, which has a better chance of being unique. So why not put the usage first. Follow this with an underscore, and follow that with the HG?!

I also like to state explicitly the storage class of all my data objects so I guess the code should now look like this

```
SomeFunc(...)
{
    auto int LoopCounter_Au_Bl_usn;
    static float FloatResult_St_Bl_f_Ap;
    ...
    FloatResult_St_Bl_f_Ap=3.142;
    LoopCounter_Au_Bl_usn=FloatResult_St_Bl_f_Ap;
    /* assign to LoopCounter FloatResult's value */

    etc
}
```

Here

Au	means	auto
St	means	static
Ap	means	application life
Bl	means	block scope
usn	means	unsigned short integer
f	means	float

OK, you can see the problem. Too much HG gets unreadable (and almost un-write-able)! In fact now you can see why it's called Hungarian Notation; it's nothing to do with the nationality of Dr. Simonyi, its simply because people react to it by saying, 'the code looks so unreadable it might as well be written in Hungarian'! This sounds bad for HG!

Many have tried to work on a combined short-form-long-form HG, or put another way – how to make the long form a shorter form! One approach is to code certain standard data types with a single uppercase letter. for example, a common data type used throughout your application might be an automatic unsigned short integer which has of course block scope and life. The full long form would be – Usage_Au_Bl_usn. Well we could substitute say a Z for the Au_Bl_usn part and simple write Usage_Z for the identifier. Well it does look shorter, and it's certainly easier to write, but is it any more readable now than before? No. In practice it's even harder to read now as you've got to know what a Z means before you can even have a hope! A sensible short code for this Au_Bl_usn would be fine – if you can find one.

HG can be used elsewhere in your code, how about this –

```
HTASK hTask;
hTask=CheckInstance(GetWindowTask(hWnd));
```

Here the letter *h* says that the object is a generic handle. Obviously therefore the function CheckInstance must return a handle mustn't it? No way. Maybe it's defined like this –

```
BOOL CheckInstance(HANDLE hTask)
{
    return GetCurrentTask() == hTask ? TRUE : FALSE;
}
```

Now we can see that the function does in fact return a BOOL. This could be typedef'd as an unsigned int and so might HANDLE and we'd never get any warnings about this assignment from a 'C' compiler, even with function prototypes, as there's no type checking across *derived from the same root type* types in 'C' (Is it too early to get into the *Why you shouldn't use 'C' stuff yet?*). How about if we were to change the name of the function a little to include information about the type of data item it returns to callers? Now we have this -

```
hInstance=bCheckInstance(GetWindowTask(hWnd));
```

and we can see the problem with the code more easily. What we'd <u>probably</u> like to see is –

```
hInstance=hCheckInstance(GetWindowTask(hWnd));
```

Taking this further there's another problem. We don't know anything about passed parameters from the function's name, and after all it expects a HANDLE but could get passed a BOOL with similar consequences as before – error. Maybe we should do this then –

```
hInstance=h_hCheckInstance(GetWindowTask(hWnd));
```

Here we're saying that the function returns a handle (it's nearest to the object to which the assignment is taking place) and takes a single handle as a parameter. Are you going to buy this at this stage? No, of course you're not because if we were to take a Windows' API with a decent(!) list of passed parameters like for example the function CreateFont() and name extend it in this way we'd get this –

```
hf_n_n_n_n_b_b_b_b_b_b_b_b_lpszCreateFont(.parameters in here.)
```

The function returns a HANDLE to a FONT (HFONT thus hf), and is passed four integers, eight bytes (unsigned char) and a long pointer to a string that's zero terminated! The name looks like a joke (it is) and we haven't said whether or not the integers are signed/short etc yet!!

It is possible, with long, or full, form HG to even say, in the identifiers used, whether or not integral, or typedef'd types are involved, and when using pointers, who should free the memory to which a pointer points (if anyone needs or has to).

OK, you're now saying that this sounds good in small doses but it can't be really useful to me, can it? One of the worst things about 'C' isn't 'C', its the typical linker it uses. The linker can cause problems that simply can't occur when you're using HG in your source code this way. Let me explain. Those of you used to using a C++ translator may recognise, to some degree, these strange looking names. What we've been using here is a form of name mangling or, as they are sometimes caled, decorated names! C++ translators typically mangle names (you think these are bad?!) to promote in the main, type safe linking, we've just done the same in 'C'! Even variadic functions can have mangled names, simply pick a letter or perhaps word that means (to you) *and the rest!*

Type safe linking is what 'C' doesn't have (or is that the linker!). For example I can call a function called *func* in module *a* passing it 5 integers, and define it in module *b* as taking 5 doubles. Resulting errors? Nothing – from the compiler of course. The compiler knows only about the module it's compiling. Nothing – from the linker. It doesn't check the return type, or the types of passed parameters!

What, you don't believe me, well *check this out* –

module *a*

```
// Declaration.
extern void func(double,double,double,double,double);
void main(void)
{
    func(1.1,1.2,1.3,1.4,1.5);
    return;
            }
```

module *b*

```
// Definition.
void func(int a,int b,int c,int d,int e)
{
    return;
}
```

Compile and link these two modules. Apart from the unreferenced formal parameters in module b, this will compile and link at – W4 just fine!

If we re-wrote the code using the rather strange HG naming used above, it'd look something like this –

module *a*

```
extern void v_d_d_d_d_d_func(double,double,double,double,double);
void main(void)
{
    v_d_d_d_d_d_func(1.1,1.2,1.3,1.4,1.5);
    return;
}
```

module *b*

```
void v_n_n_n_n_n_func(int a, int b, int c, int d, int e)
{
    return;
}
```

Again, we still get the unreferenced formal parameters but now the code won't link. We get an unresolved external of –

```
error L2029: '_v_d_d_d_d_d_func' : unresolved external
```

I guess now we could say the only problem with this, and 'C', is that the compiler doesn't generate these names for you. Well that's good. If you can't see why, start the HG section above again!

Before I declare my colours, let's look at another case where HG sounds great but is in fact, hard to effectively use: Arrays.

Most Windows' programmers who use HG declare arrays and character pointers like this –

```
auto char szAuBuffer[100];
auto char * szAuP;
```

Now szBuffer can be confused with the scalar variable szP in an assignment like this–

```
szAuBuffer=szAuP;        /* error - assigning to rvalue!!    */
```

I prefer to use the HG prefix *ca* for character array and would declare the array like this instead (you'll notice that the pointer is also sized in this new declaration) –

```
auto char caAuBuffer[100];
auto char NEAR * npszAuP;

npszAuP=caAuBuffer;      /* OK! */
```

OK. So what can go wrong here. Well how about this –

```
caAuBuffer[300]=*npszAuP;                /* ouch!   */
```

There's nothing in the array name that states its size, hey, *all quantities* remember. How about this –

```
ca_100_AuBuffer[100]=*npszAuP;  /* ouch again! */
```

Here I've inserted the array's defined size into it's name, but ouch, assigning to element *100* isn't a good idea as the array will begin at *0* and end at *99*. In so doing, I've stepped off the end of the array bounds! (Are you sure it's too early to talk about 'C' yet?).

Many HG users use symbolic names to define array sizes and include the symbolic name in the array name like so –

```
auto char ca_BUFF_AuBuffer[BUFF];
...
ca_BUFF_AuBuffer[50]=*npszAuP; /* OK? who knows! */
```

Here, its up to you to look up the symbolic BUFF in order to find the array's size. I've even seen this for arrays by the way –

```
#define B99 100
auto char caB99AuBuffer[B99];
/* now        */
caB99AuBuffer[99]='x';  /* OK!! */
```

Using this scheme you can once more check the array bounds as you're writing the code (after all 'C' won't do it. Ever!) but you've got to have very strict access rights to the define in order to prevent errors when someone defines B99 to be 50 (Don't laugh, it's easily done).

So is HG a good idea? In my opinion, a resounding Yes; but, too much of a good thing can cause more trouble than it's worth. This can also be said about languages - Bjarne Stroustrup says at the beginning of chapter 6 on operator overloading in his first book on C++ Here be Dragons!. Maybe he uses HG as well!

Short Form HG says that identifiers should start with a letter(s) identifying the data type of the object to which they relate (in Hungary the family name is always written before the given name), capital letters are usually used to separate the two.

Data types are always written in lowercase: *sn* = signed integer. Modifiers and storage class designators are always two letters. The first letter is always in uppercase, the second is in lower. The same rule applies to scope. You add/leave out whatever you like. If you don't like putting in *Au* for automatic - leave it out. 'C' allows us to write declarations in many ways, for example:

```
signed integer const auto x = 10;
```

or

```
auto const signed integer x = 10;
```

Which is correct? Both.

The second is the most popular and I use it here.

☐ Coding standards

My firm, TMS uses a variety of conventions as part of their 'C' coding standard (the standard actually covers C++ and *generic* languages); the standard is also targeted at Windows' developers. If you're interested in obtaining TMS's coding standards contact me directly please.

☐ Conventions and standards used

So, this is the conventions section. I'm going to use a short form HG throughout this book, I'll also use a `fixed pitched font` when we look at code. Text in Bold is usually important. *Italic text* is a softer form of bold, ie. its importance is less than bold text. Underlined text is usually critical. Bold and underlined text is life threatening!

All the examples in this book have all the necessary files laid out locally to one another unless otherwise stated. Every example has been tested and will compile using MSC 7.00a, warning level 4, no warnings, no errors (this actually doesn't mean a great deal – after all this is 'C' and you can usually cast away your blues!). A couple of warnings have been *turned off* here and there by using a #pragma; these warnings are about using a double slash comment ('//'), and not referencing a function's formal parameters (see the #pragma statement in the headers). The link stage sometimes involves using LINK.EXE (not a link executed by cl). Make was NMAKE.EXE shipped with the 'C'7 compiler. Where make files are shown they are usually not those generated by PWB (I can't understand them – nor do I use PWB) – they are hand-rolled.

One last note on the choice of the compiler – Yes I know that there are many 'C' compilers around (now) that can produce the necessary far function prologs and epilogs so as to enable them to produce Windows' binaries, but Microsoft's 'C' compiler is regarded by most Windows' developers as the one they'd use given the choice and enough money. Also it's the most prolific in the world of Windows' programming currently, I therefore owe it to the majority of you to code here using Microsoft's compiler – so don't get on my back OK!

One last thing before we get in to chapter 1, you'll need to read chapter 2 to fully understand some of the concepts introduced in chapter 1! I'm very sorry about this but I couldn't help it. Adele Goldberg and David Robson put the case well in their book Smalltalk-80 The Language. They state that some of the terms used in their early chapters are defined in terms of themselves! It's therefore essential that you understand the terms used in order to understand the term you're reading about; this of course means that you must first understand the current term as the term that you don't understand is defined in terms of the current term! The bottom line is that you must therefore know everything, before knowing anything!

OK, There's nothing more to be said –

so let's do it!

Chapter 1

T h e   S h e l l

☐ The Shell

OK, we're on our way. Lets start coding.

If you're new to Windows, this is really your chapter. I'm going to go a long way towards bringing you up to speed in this chapter. Even if you're an old hand at Windows coding you might want to scan this chapter to see how I write code here (and consider why); you might also like to ask yourself about how you write code and compare your own against that presented here.

In the next chapter (2) we're going to re-invent and re-write the SHELL1 application introduced and discussed in this chapter.

We're going to start our look at the code with a look at the *minimum application*. The code is given here for the tradition a *Hello World* DOS and Windows applications, complete with all the bugs (in the Windows case that's lots – most of which are implicit, or at the very least, those which will show up later).

☐ The standard code

Let me also say here that I don't like the *de facto* coding technique used by the majority of Windows' programmers, and that I <u>generally</u> don't use it. The *de facto* standard is like that found in the majority of Windows' applications; a very good example of it is found in the SDK samples. The Windows' application we'll be looking at in this chapter does however use this *de facto* standard, I'm going to change this in the next chapter when we'll look at this *code shell* once more. You may therefore want to go straight to that chapter now, it's up to you, I just want to make it clear that most of what you're about to see will change in the next chapter. If you're new to Windows don't be tempted to skip chapter 1, stay and read this chapter through. The way I write code probably, and quite naturally, differs from the way most people write code; after all we're all individuals. As I've said, I normally don't code to the normal de facto standard as I think it lacks quite a lot and prefer to do my own thing; I realise however that the majority of Windows' programmers out there use the *standard* style and so I have chosen to use that style in the rest of this book – all apart from chapter 2 that is. The actual shell used in the remainder of this book is taken from the SDK example *generic*.

The coding style used by the majority of Windows' programmers, whilst in my view being fundamentally flawed, is nevertheless a standard, and there's a lot to be said for standards, they're *standard* for starters, or put another way û they're <u>always</u> not acceptable by some people or in some situations – consider a general coding standard; how many people do you know that agree with a coding standard! Seriously, one must consider the implications of changing anything, no matter how unacceptable it is to you personally, if it's already a standard, particularly if you're going to publish, or if you like, put another way – **True wisdom consists of knowing when to avoid perfection**. Well, I considered using my *standard* code throughout this book but in the end decided against it for the reasons outlined earlier – the *generic* standard is *de facto* and I should stick to it here.

Let's just consider how this standard got to be a standard in the first place? Well the standard Windows GUI application code can probably be traced back to before Microsoft's Windows but the precise Windows' standard code of course comes from Microsoft. Some of the first Microsoft Windows' applications are usually attributed to a guy called Mark Taylor. Mark wrote the first resource compiler and a number of the first *Microsoft Windows* applications ever written like the calculator and the game Reversi (actually Mark wrote the *drawing* code in Reversi) that has shipped with all version of Windows so far. Mark, I suspect, used the classic coding model used for an event driven system, changed it a little and hey presto – *The Standard Windows* Code came into being. You can just hear a conversation at Microsoft between Mark and, say, a new member of the Windows' applications team.

New Man: 'Hey man, this Windows stuff sounds real neat, how do I go about coding a Windows app, like show me some code will ya dude?' (a good proportion of all MS staff speak like this).

Mark: 'Sure, here's some code from one of my first applications, take a look at it, and if you like, modify it to fit your application'.

New Man: 'Sounds like a good way to get productive like quickly, OK, I'll do it'.

This method of *cut and paste* has been used by Windows' programmers from that hypothetical day to this. For example, if you want an *About* dialog, simple, cut one out of one of the SDK examples, after all they're all written using the same coding style. Anyway, what are the alternatives? 1. Start again or 2. Modify. I believe that radical modification is bad – **Once a job is fouled up, anything done to improve it only makes it worse,** so I must be saying start again right? I can just hear you now – 'But I can't, I have to get this out of the door by yesterday' (this means you'll certainly be driven to cut and paste)! The SDK examples of course are what everyone has always learnt from, and they of course teach by example. All the SDK paper based example code is the same, as are most of the books on Windows' programming – they've all seen, and used, the *standard code*. Well as I've said I normally don't.

The *standard* Windows application is presented here in typically standard code. I have left out of the standard application, as we'll see shortly, any exception checking or handling, that's usually the standard to which standard applications are written (Exception checking is typically the exception!)! I've also left in a lot of literal data (something's that's not a good idea in Windows' applications) etc. Please don't look at the first Windows' application presented here as an indication of either my personal coding standards or coding technique, see chapter 2 and later for that and feel free to criticise it.

Before we see the Windows' code lets see how this standard application looks in 'C' when written for say, DOS.

The standard 'C' application that everyone knows and probably learns first of all looks something like this –

☐ The 'C' hello world program

⊞ Cshell.c :

```
#include <stdio.h>>
void main(void);
void main(void)
{
        printf('Hello World\n');
}
```

⊞ Makefile :

```
all : cshell.exe
cshell.obj : cshell.c
        cl -c -W4 -WX cshell.c
cshell.exe : cshell.obj
        cl cshell
```

I *made* (make'd!) the application using *NMAKE* i.e. nmake<CR>. The *all* target isn't needed if you want to turn the make file upside down giving cshell.exe and its dependents as the target but I prefer to read the make file in this order and so the dummy's required to make all of the application. I also hate the make files produced by tools like the Programmer's Workbench (just thought I'd chuck that in!).

I hope we're <u>ALL</u> happy with this small 'C' application that simply calls the standard library stream function *printf* to output the string *Hello World*. The make file compiles the 'C' source to object code using *cl*, later cl is exec'd again to do the link (it executes the linker to do the actual job). If you're used to using a *real* LINK fine but you might want to explore using the cl engine to do the link for you, you'll find it has some advantages. If you're not happy with this application stop reading this book now and panic a little. You'll need to read up on 'C' to fully understand the vast majority of the code presented in this book.

Some good books on 'C' and how to use it are :–

- The 'C' Programming Language Second Edition by Kernighan & Ritchie.
- The 'C' Puzzle Book by Alan R. Feuer.
- The 'C' Answer Book Second Edition by Tondo and Gimpel.
- The Standard 'C' Library by P. J. Plauger.
- C Traps & Pitfalls by Andrew Koenig.

All of these books except the last are published by Prentice Hall, the last is published by Addison Wesley. By the way, there is a potential bug in the code above, can you spot it? If the answer's no, then read Andrew Koenig's excellent book.

OK. Lets look at the Windows app that essentially does the same thing as the standard 'C' hello world application (or does it, see the text at the end of the chapter for a comparison?). Again it was made by typing nmake.

☐ The Windows' hello world program

Complex problems have uncomplicated understandable wrong answers.

Shell1.c:
```c
/*
** Just about the minimum Windows' 'hello world' application. The code in
** here is pretty bad, for example there's minimalist commenting, it uses
** old Windows' types, doesn't include the STRICT define and has no excep-
** tion testing at all! The application is explained in the main text.
*/


#include <windows.h>

/*
** Turn off unref formal param warning.
** Note that C7 has a pragma for doing
** this also.
*/
#define NO_W4_URFP_WARN(x) ((x)=(x))

void PASCAL WinMain(HANDLE,HANDLE,LPSTR,int);
LONG FAR PASCAL MainWndProc(HWND,unsigned int,WORD,LONG);

void PASCAL WinMain
(
    HANDLE      hInstance
  , HANDLE      hPrevInstance
  , LPSTR       lpszCmdLine
  , int         nCmdShow
)
{
    auto HWND hWnd;
    auto MSG msg;
    auto char * pszClassName = "shell"'; /* used in WNDCLASS and CreateWindow.*/
```

```
NO_W4_URFP_WARN(lpszCmdLine);

if(hPrevInstance == (HANDLE)NULL)/* first instance? */
{
   auto WNDCLASS wc;                 /* detail class 'pClassName'. */
   wc.style          = CS_HREDRAW | CS_VREDRAW;
   wc.lpfnWndProc    = MainWndProc;
   wc.cbClsExtra     = (int)NULL;
   wc.cbWndExtra     = (int)NULL;
   wc.hInstance      = hInstance;
   wc.hIcon          = (HANDLE)NULL;
   wc.hCursor        = LoadCursor((HANDLE)NULL,IDC_ARROW);
   wc.hbrBackground  = COLOR_WINDOW + 1;
   wc.lpszMenuName   = (LPSTR)NULL;
   wc.lpszClassName  = pszClassName;
   RegisterClass(&wc);               /* register it with Windows. */
}

hWnd = CreateWindow(pszClassName    /* derive a window from it.  */
                   ,pszClassName
                   ,WS_OVERLAPPEDWINDOW
                   ,CW_USEDEFAULT
                   ,(int)NULL
                   ,CW_USEDEFAULT
                   ,(int)NULL
                   ,(HWND)NULL
                   ,(HMENU)NULL
                   ,hInstance
                   ,(LPSTR)NULL
                   );

 ShowWindow(hWnd,nCmdShow);     /* show it to the world and paint */
 UpdateWindow(hWnd);            /* 'hello world'.                 */

                               /* now wait to die. */

 while(GetMessage(&msg,(HWND)NULL,(WORD)NULL,(WORD)NULL) != FALSE)
 {
    TranslateMessage(&msg);
    DispatchMessage(&msg);
 }
}


LONG FAR PASCAL MainWndProc(HWND hWnd,unsigned int nMessage,WORD
wParam,LONG lParam)
{
   auto PAINTSTRUCT ps;

                                    /* used in PAINT case. */
   auto char * pszText = 'Hello World';
   auto RECT   rc;

   switch(nMessage)
   {
      case WM_DESTROY:
         PostQuitMessage((WORD)NULL); /* main window dead so kill task. */
         break;
      case WM_PAINT:
         GetClientRect(hWnd,&rc);
         BeginPaint(hWnd,&ps);
         DrawText(
                 ps.hdc
                ,pszText
                ,-1
```

```
                ,&rc
                ,DT_SINGLELINE |
                DT_CENTER      |
                DT_VCENTER
                );
            EndPaint(hWnd,&ps);
            break;
        default:
            return DefWindowProc(hWnd,nMessage,wParam,lParam);
    }
    return 0L;
}
```

Makefile:

```
1 all : shell1.exe
2 shell1.obj : shell1.c
3       cl -c -Gsw -Zp -W4 -D NOCOMM shell1.c
4 shell1.res : shell1.rc
5       rc -r shell1.rc
6 shell1.exe : shell1.obj shell1.def shell1.res
7       cl shell1.obj /link /NOD /ALIGN:16 libw.lib+slibcew.lib, shell1.def
8       rc shell1.res shell1.exe
```

Shell1.def :

```
1 NAME SHELL1
2 DESCRIPTION 'shell1 - basic-badly written Windows application by petermor'

3 EXETYPE WINDOWS
4 DATA PRELOAD MOVEABLE MULTIPLE
5 CODE PRELOAD MOVEABLE DISCARDABLE
6 STUB 'WINSTUB.EXE'
7 HEAPSIZE                    5120
8 STACKSIZE                   5120
9 EXPORTS
10        MAINWNDPROC @1
```

Shell1.rc :

```
1 /* A 'sod all' resource script. */
```

I'm sure you'll agree with me in saying that the Windows's code looks strange to say the least – there's also a lot of it! The good news is that it's very straightforward. Once again, if you're in anyway unsure about the 'C' here refer to the books listed earlier. If you're unsure about the Windows' stuff, and still feel the same once you've read through this chapter, refer to the SDK documentation for further explanation – *Guide To Programming, Volume 1: Overview.*

OK. Lets take it to bits and see what it does and why.

We'll start with the 'C' file – SHELL1.C. You'll first notice that there's the mandatory WINDOWS.H include – seems like a good place to start. This header contains (most) all the function prototypes, manifest constants and typedefs used in Windows' programming. It's over 152Kb in size! That's some header; you might also see windowsx.h – this is a header added with the 3.1 SDK and provides useful macros and message crackers, more on these later. I'd recommend that you read WINDOWS.H right through; for that matter I'd recommend, if you haven't already done so, reading all the headers you use regularly. I have WINDOWS.H printed out and refer to the printout a lot. I also have it automatically included into a read only edit buffer whenever I start coding for Windows – do the same, it's very useful although you shouldn't read it in bed – you'll get a reputation!

The next thing I'd point out is that I next predeclare two functions. The first WinMain is the only fixed name function there is in a Windows' application (excluding the Windows' API of course). It's analogous to *main* in normal 'C' programming. It defines a function entry point to the Windows startup code just like main does for your standard 'C' or PM application. You don't have to *predeclare* this function as you don't use it before the compiler sees the new style function definition. This new style definition is sometimes called a prototype and it acts as a predeclaration for the function. The next function predeclared is called a *window procedure* it probably ought to be called a window function but that's another matter. A window procedure, or wndproc, looks after, in its simplest sense, a window created by your Windows' task. You might have a similar piece of 'C' code that looks after some aspect of a text window in your conventional 'C' programs. Well this is something like one of those routines. We'll see how it fits into the picture in more detail soon.

☐ WinMain

The code really starts with WinMain. WinMain is declared as returning a void in this program, if you've seen code for Windows' applications previously you'll probably be used to seeing this function defined as returning an int. Well there's nothing wrong with that and it 's fine if you've spawned a Windows' application and want 'o know how it terminated (even then it's not as simple in actual use as it sounds) but most Windows' applications are executed by Windows. They therefore *return* to Windows when they exit. Windows doesn't make use of the int value potentially returned by any application it spawns so it simply gets in the way, I've therefore removed it just as you would in a DOS 'C' application by declaring the entry point as returning nothing – *void*. If you compile this application using your 3.1 SDK it should compile, as previously stated, with no warnings or errors; however, if you define STRICT to get the *new* strict type checking feature you'll find that it will generate at least one error. The error is due to WinMain having been prototyped in WINDOWS.H as returning an int.

You'll further see that WinMain is declared PASCAL. This means that it has the PASCAL calling and naming conventions as do all but one of the Windows APIs you might call. Giving a function that's non-variadic (unknown number and type of parameters) the PASCAL calling convention is usually a good idea as it's called and returned from a little faster for a start. If the function is called from more than one location it'll also cut down on the size of the code in the calling module. More on this a little later.

A brief aside on what happens at start-up

When Windows starts an application, it doesn't, despite popular belief, actually call WinMain but instead calls a startup routine supplied with the application by the compiler and linker called __astart; this routine in turn calls various other functions (which until recently have remained undocumented) to initialise the task further. The startup routine is responsible for initializing the application, making the call to WinMain, and, once the application is through, exiting the application via a DOS interrupt.

When Windows first calls the startup routine, the processor registers have the following values:

- AX　　Zero.
- BX　　Specifies the size, in bytes, of the stack as specified in the .def file.
- CX　　Specifies the size, in bytes, of the heap as specified in the .def file.
- DI　　A handle identifying the new application instance.
- SI　　A handle identifying the previous application instance.
- BP　　Zero.
- ES　　The segment address of the program segment prefix (PSP).
- DS　　The segment address of the automatic data segment for the application.
- SS　　Same as the DS register (SS equals DS).
- SP　　The offset to the first byte of the application stack.

The first thing that the *real* starup routine does is to initiase the task. It does this by calling a function called InitTask(). InitTask() returns values that are ultimately passed on to WinMain. The InitTask function initializes the task by setting registers, setting up the command line, and initializing the task's local heap. InitTask() returns 1 (success) or 0 (failure) in the AX register and fills the CX, DX, ES:BX, SI, and DI registers with information about the new task. The contents of these registers are :

- CX　　The stack limit, in bytes.
- DI　　The instance handle for the new task. Passed to WinMain.
- DX　　The nCmdShow parameter. Passed to WinMain.
- ES　　The segment address of the program segment prefix (PSP) for the new task.
  ES:BX The 32-bit address of the command line. Passed to WinMain.
- SI　　The instance handle for the previous instance of the application. Passed to WinMain.

The function has no parameters. InitTask also copies the top, minimum, and bottom address offsets of the stack to the 16 bytes of reserved memory at the beginning of the automatic data segment for the application (pStackTop, pStackBot, pStackMin). These bytes are defined in the startup code itself and are called rsrvptrs.

Next the event queue is flushed by making a call to WaitEvent(); this clears the event that started the task. Next the task's message queue is initialised by making a call to InitApp(). The function takes the task's instance handle as a parameter and returns 1 in AX if it's successful or 0 if it failed. Next the task's WinMain entry point is called and your programs runs. Next, after WinMain has exited, the application is terminated by making a call to DOS via INT21 function 4Ch. If you've ever written your own function in a Windows' application called InitApp(), WaitEvent() or InitTask() etc û and wondered why the app wouldn't start you now know the answer!

For a more detailed discussion of this subject refer to the Volume 1: Overview.

WinMain is passed four parameters, although I only use three in the code. There are two objects of type HANDLE which are called respectively hInstance and hPrevInstance, an object of type LPSTR called lpszCmdLine and an int called nCmdShow. From the preface and its discussion of Hungarian Notation (HG) we'll be able to decrypt one of these types, LPSTR lpszCmdLine. HG says that the type information in an identifier normally proceeds the use description (which starts with a single upper case letter) and is in lower case. lpsz - means long pointer to a string that's zero terminated. The usage part says that this is a pointer to our command line arguments. Note that this is not the same as the conventional argc argv that we're used to seeing from the normal 'C' startup code. More on these (argc argv) later. OK, that's one formal parameter taken care of, now what about the others. The first two, the HANDLE types, are called instance handles.

☐ Instance handles

Every Windows' task (a task running under Windows) is a single *instance* of an application (or *tasked executable* module). To explain these instance handles more fully let's first consider a task running under DOS (An instance handle identifies a task's DS).

DOS allows only a single task (non-TSR) to run at any one time. For example, if you run say WordStar, you can say that there's a single instance of this task running. It's impossible to run a second copy or instance of WordStar because DOS prior to DOS 5 didn't have any provision for doing so. Windows is a multi-tasking operating system (It's hard to justify calling it an application running on top of DOS these days) that allows task instancing, i.e. multiple instances of the same application to run, apparently to the user, simultaneously (even DOS 5.0 doesn't do this). Some older multi-tasking operating systems only allowed single instances of a task to run, but would allow different tasks (albeit single instances of them) to run simultaneously. Windows not only allows different applications to run simultaneously, but also allows more than one instance of each application.

Windows is efficient at using memory and we'll look at this efficiency in many areas before this book is out. One area in which Windows is very good at utilising available memory is in its handling of multiple instances of an application, and we should take a quick look at this now to understand instance handles more fully.

☐ Something about code and stuff

Under Windows the code that makes up the control logic portion of your application is labelled *read only, executable*. If the code is read only it means that no instance may modify it, this is called non-self modifying code or sometimes pure code. Each instance of your application could therefore execute the same code when it runs. Or put another way – the code becomes shareable between all instances because it cannot be altered by any instance.

Windows allows all instances of an application to share common code in this way. Each instance, when tasked, would be executing different parts of the same binary of course so the CS (code segment register, or, pointer to the base of the current code segment) and IP (the instruction pointer within CS) register may change for each instance as it's tasked in by Windows (CS will change if the code segment changes for any instance within a multi-code-segmented task, and IP will point to the next instruction to be executed by that instance within the context of CS and the task ID). This is handled by the Windows' tasker and is transparent to any task. How about data then? Could each instance share a common data segment(s)? The answer is probably not. Each instance of your application will want to work on its own dynamic data, of course each might want to share some common resources but that's a matter for later.

Each instance gets its own DS (data segment pointer) and Windows has to *fix up* a common instance of code with different instances of data for related tasks (instances of the same application) as each is tasked by Windows. This leads us to a very important question – how does Windows know which DS to bind to a CS,IP when any of a number of instances might be executing this common application code? The answer lies in the instance handle.

Under Windows when an instance of an application is run it's given an instance id or handle. This, as we have seen, is called hInstance in the code above; it's the first formal parameter passed to WinMain. hInstance is a unique number that identifies *this instance* of this application from every other task running under Windows (Windows also uses task handles that more properly do the same thing, more on these later in the book). The type of the object is HANDLE and so the identifier starts with an *h*. Handles are used to get a grip on something and so the name given to the type becomes obvious. If you're an American you're used to saying things like, 'hold on, lets see if I can get a handle on this' in every day speech, but Europeans etc typically aren't, so the explanation's necessary!

WinMain is also passed the instance handle of the previous instance of the application – hPrevInstance (hInstance for the instance previous to this instance). What values might these two formal parameters hold then when consecutive instances of an application are started?

Lets say that you plan to run two copies of SHELL1. The first invocation might result in WinMain being called with hInstance equal to 0xAAAA and hPrevInstance will be set to 0x0000. Finding 0 in hPrevInstance means you're the first instance, if you had a previous instance, you'd have it's hInstance value here instead of zero. We'll ignore the other parameters for now. Lets say we start another instance. It might get called with hInstance equal to 0xBBBB and hPrevInstance will have the value given to the previous instance as its instance handle, i.e. 0xAAAA in this example. Remember that 0 (zero) means *not a valid value* or in this case, *no previous instance.*

OK, hInstance identifies *us* (it's sometimes called an *us* handle) but why should I need hPrevInstance? Well, We use it typically for a couple of things 1. detecting whether or not we're the first instance of this application (hPrevInstance == 0), this is important as we'll see shortly, and 2. for communicating between instances; this is called inter-instance communication (IIC). Both uses of hPrevInstance and functions like GetInstanceData() may become obsolete and non-functional in future versions of Windows. I'll explain those remarks in the next chapter, but for now let's press on to the next and last parameter.

The only parameter left to discuss is nCmdShow. The value of this variable will be either SW_SHOWNORMAL or SW_SHOWMINNOACTIVE. Both of these are defined in WINDOWS.H and I'll return to them and nCmdShow a little later in this chapter.

Well, we're past the first line of the function's definition! Lets see what's next.

We now declare three auto variables. One's of type HWND which means a *handle to a window* type, the next is of type MSG, this is a message structure, and the last is a char pointer which is initialised to point to the zero terminated string *shell1*. A handle to a window is used to tag an existing window, the value of the handle is decided by the window manager. Windows passes this unique value (within the session) to an application whenever a window is successfully created for it. A message structure contains details of a Windows' event. Remember that we're event driven. MSG is of type *message structure* and it's common to see any identifier defining a single instanciation of a structure type either taking simply the lower case name of the type (as here - msg) or, if the structure's type name is formed of more than one word, the first character of each word, again in lower case (i.e. PAINSTRUCT ps;). You'll see how these variables are used shortly.

Next we see a macro which is used for turning off a compiler warning that is issued by the Microsoft 'C' compiler (MSC 6 and onwards) about unreferenced formal parameters (in 'C'7 we could use a #pragma to do that same thing – in fact we will from the next chapter on). We don't use lpszCmdLine but as we have coded the function with lpszCmdLine as a formal parameter we'll pull one of these off the stack when WinMain is called. As we don't then use it within the function the compiler warns us. You'll get quite a few of these warnings whilst programming for Windows as you'll often have a function definition pressed upon you and may elect not to use all or some of that function's formal parameters. This macro gets rid of the warnings. Its name û NO_W4_URFP_WARN says 'no W4 unreferenced formal parameter warnings', you might like to shorten it down a little! It would be preferable in my mind to have defined the macro like this by the way –

```
#define NO_W4_URFP_WARN(x) ((x)==(x))
```

Unfortunately the compiler spots that this statement has no effect and issues a warning to that effect instead! Another way to get rid of the original warning is to do this –

```
ret type func (type UnWanted1, type UnWanted2)
{
    return ret type
    /* get rid of W4 warning - don't use formal parameters*/
    if(UnWanted | Unwanted2);
}
```

The compiler doesn't notice that this statement also has no effect and is in actual fact not even reached due to the return statement on the line above if! You'll find that the compiler's optimiser doesn't produce code for any of these so it's obviously not the optimiser that reports the fact that the statement has no effect! Most *current* compilers allow you to turn off warnings about unreferenced parameters and 'C'7 is no exception. We'll see the pragma that does this in a little while.

Onward –

Now we get to the first real piece of code. We check to see if this (this instance) is the first instance of the application by checking the value of hPrevInstance against NULL.

NULL is defined in WINDOWS.H as *0* by the way and so all the casts you'll see throughout this code on NULL are not actually required. I put them in so that you will be able to see the actual types involved more easily.

The ANSI 'C' standard defines NULL as 0, 0L or (void *)0 , the standard 'C'6 or 'C'7 headers define it as (void *)0, ie. zero cast to a void pointer, WINDOWS.H defines it, for historical reasons, as *0*. The C6/C7 and windows headers have conditional compilation on the definition of NULL, i.e. –

```
#ifndef NULL            /* or #if !defined NULL */
#if (_MSC_VER >= 600)   /* MSC 6 or later       */
```

```
#define NULL    ((void *)0)

#ifndef NULL              /* or #if !defined NULL */
#if (_MSC_VER >= 600)     /* MSC 6 or later        */
#define NULL    ((void *)0)

                          /* tiny, small or medium model */
#elif (defined(M_I86SM) || defined(M_I86MM))
#define NULL    0
#else                     /* large, compact, huge        */
#define NULL    0L
#endif
#endif
```

so include WINDOWS.H before any 'C'7 or windows header if you want to use NULL as an integer and don't want casts everywhere.

NOTE: Some programmers prefer to not use NULL as they believe this should be a pointer type but define ZERO as *0* and use that instead –

```
#if (defined(M_I86SM) || defined(M_I86MM))
#define ZERO 0
#else
#define ZERO 0L
#endif
```

You'll remember that hPrevInstance is equal to NULL if this instance (the instance checking its hPrevInstance parameter) is the first instance of the application.

If this expression is evaluated TRUE we carry out the statements in the compound statement, else we go straight on.

☐ Application initialisation

If this is the first instance we must carry out some initialisation that is good for the entire application. This is sometimes called *first instance initialisation* in error. This initialisation should be called *Application Initialisation* and it's done by the first instance (thus the confusion with first instance initialisation), we'll see in a little while that instance initialisation infers something else.

The application initialisation that we must carry out in SHELL1 is called class registration. This is a typical example of a facet of application initialisation (until Win 32 that is!).

☐ Classes

Every window in Windows belongs to a *class* of window. A class defines some basic attributes of any window derived from it. For example, a class may define a class menu. This menu is used by every window that is derived from the class. As is apparent – many windows may be derived from the same class although within an application it's typical to find that each application window is derived from a unique class. The most important attribute that a class defines by far is the *window procedure* or the wndproc for the class – it might have been preferable to have called this a *class window procedure*. The wndproc attribute of the class defines the routine that is to handle, or look after, every window derived from the class. Windows may be thought of as instances, or instanciations, of a class. So a class is an abstract entity whereas a window is a class incarnate if you like. It's a lot like saying that given the declaration int x,y; that both x and y and instanciations of the class or data type *integer.*

Windows has some built in *standard* classes (called global classes) from which you build all the push buttons, edit fields, dialog boxes etc that you see in most Windows' applications. These standard classes exist when Windows starts up. New classes have to be created as and when they are needed. We need a new window class in SHELL1 as we want to build, and present, a window to our users into which we want to write *Hello World*. We must therefore build a class as we need to have the window processed by a wndproc with the necessary *Hello World* writing functionality.

Classes may be shareable amongst all tasks and so we only want to do this once, create a class that is. All subsequent instances (tasks) can use the class created by the first instance (task) (note that a private class (non – CS_GLOBALCLASS) is still shareable by other tasks just as long as they're instances of the task registering the class). Classes may be shared amongst all tasks remember (not redefinitions of Windows' global classes). This may not be desirable and so the default is to make the class private to instances of the application that created the class. You may change this by using the *class style* attribute – CS_GLOBALCLASS (Windows 3.X only). Another way of stating the same thing is to say that by default classes are private to the application that creates them.

The Windows' class is embodied, as far as the application is concerned, in a data structure called a WNDCLASS. It's typedef'd in WINDOWS.H version 3.0 like this –

```
typedef struct tagWNDCLASS
{
    WORD                            style;
    LONG (FAR PASCAL *              lpfnWndProc)();
    int                             cbClsExtra;
    int                             cbWndExtra;
    HANDLE                          hInstance;
    HICON                           hIcon;
    HCURSOR                         hCursor;
    HBRUSH                          hbrBackground;
    LPSTR                           lpszMenuName;
    LPSTR                           lpszClassName;
}   WNDCLASS;
```

and like this in WINDOWS.H version 3.1

```
typedef struct tag1WNDCLASS
{
    UINT                           style;
    WNDPROC                        lpfnWndProc;
    int                            cbClsExtra;
    int                            cbWndExtra;
    HINSTANCE                      hInstance;
    HICON                          hIcon;
    HCURSOR                        hCursor;
    HBRUSH                         hbrBackground;
    LPCSTR                         lpszMenuName;
    LPCSTR                         lpszClassName;
}   WNDCLASS;
```

The structure member names have stayed the same but most of the types have changed. Depending upon whether or not you have defined STRICT to the compiler these new types will or will not cause a problem to this or any other *old* code. In WINDOWS.H for the 3.1 SDK there is a lot of conditional compilation based on STRICT. For example, let's consider the type HBRUSH. This used to be the same as a good ol generic HANDLE, note that now it isn't if you use STRICT. HBRUSH is defined like this in the 3.1 WINDOWS.H.

```
DECLARE_HANDLE(HBRUSH);
```

DECLARE_HANDLE() is a macro defined like this.

```
#ifdef STRICT
typedef const void NEAR*        HANDLE;
#define DECLARE_HANDLE(name) struct name##__ { int unused; }; \
                             typedef const struct name##__ NEAR* name
#else   /* NOT STRICT */
typedef UINT                    HANDLE;
#define DECLARE_HANDLE(name)    typedef UINT name
#endif  /* STRICT */
```

The macro (for STRICT) first creates a struct with the name HBRUSH__ which has one member called unused which is of type int. Next a typedef is put in place which creates a structure pointer to the struct HBRUSH__, the type name in the typdef is HBRUSH, if I expand the macro here you'll see what it looks like to the compiler.

```
struct HBRUSH__
{
    int unused;
};
typedef const struct HBRUSH__ NEAR * HBRUSH;
```

So as you can see, either an HBRUSH is a UINT (not STRICT) or a pointer to a constant structure called *HBRUSH__*'

Note that the for a declaration of, say, HBRUSH hMyBrush, that the object name, hMyBrush doesn't appear in the macro expansion – this is good. Moreover, the type name HBRUSH is also left in place as it becomes a new type, ie. even if you view the code after preprocessing the declaration will look the same.

Getting back to the WNDCLASS, please note that the *tag* on this, and most Microsoft structure declarations, isn't required and may be misleading. That is It's possible to instanciate a WNDCLASS using one of two ways from this declaration û WNDCLASS x; or struct tag1WNDCLASS x; Why do they do this? I just don't know. Leave the tag off; it doesn't do anything (unless you want to reference the structure from within the structure that is, you may want to do this if fabricating a linked list of structure types for example) for you.

Lets look at the members of a WNDCLASS (using the 3.0 one for now) one by one now.

For more detailed information of this data structure refer to the index in this book and section 7 page 62 of volume 2 of the SDK reference for the Windows 3.0 and Chapter 3 page 425 of volume 3 of the SDK reference for Windows 3.1.

☐ class style

Defines some aspects of how a window derived from a class will behave. All the available styles are defined beginning with *CS_* (class style). For example – CS_GLO-BALCLASS, we already know about, it's detailed above. CS_NOCLOSE, means that you want to inhibit the close system menu item on any system menu in any window derived from the class. We'll be looking at more class styles in various chapters, you may want to refer to the index to track down any class style you're particularly interested in. Note that some class style attributes are acted upon by a class object and others are acted upon by Windows. For example CS_SAVEBITS.

☐ lpfnWndProc

This is the address of a subroutine that will be the window procedure for the class and therefore of course all windows derived from it.

☐ cbClsExtra
cbWndExtra

These two members are used to specify an amount of memory (in bytes) that will be awarded, and made private to, a class (accessible by any task with access to an instance of the class) or window (accessible by any task with access to the window's handle). The class data isn't, unfortunately, accessible to the class; it's only accessible to an instance of the class or, if you prefer, a window. It's sometimes used for inter-window communications. We'll see how these two fields may be used later to provide a means of data abstraction and encapsulation that is available to a window later (the terms used here are explained in the next chapter).

☐ **hInstance**

Identifies the instance of the application creating the class (this may be a dynamic link library's instance or module handle), instance handles have been explained above – libraries later.

☐ **hIcon**

Identifies an icon resource that may be used by all windows of the class when they become iconic or minimised.

☐ **hCursor**

As above but for a cursor resource; nothing to do with the iconised state of a window (resources will be covered in more detail later in this chapter).

☐ **hbrBackground**

hbr means *handle to a brush*. This member identifies a colour to be used by Windows whenever it needs to paint in the background of any window derived from the class. You may see this set to – GetStockObject(WHITE_BRUSH) (see the GetStockBrush macro in windowsx.h also) in many code examples. This is not good as it sets the background of the window to white, period! What happens if the user wants to change the window background using the control panel? Well every window except yours changes colour if you use the stock object call above, I've used COLOR_WIN-DOW+1. This tells Windows to use whatever colour the user's selected for the client area part of your window; if the user changes the client area colour while your application is running, the background of your window will change to reflect the new choice. In my example the text *Hello World* will also be output. You might want to change your background to something other then white to see what happens to the text output by SHELL1. NOTE : COLOR_WINDOW+1 is not a brush, ie. you can't do SelectObject(hDC, COLOR_WINDOW+1)!

☐ **lpszMenuName**

This names a menu resource to use in all windows of the class just like the hIcon & hCursor members named resources, more on resources soon.

☐ **lpszClassName**

This member is very important as it names the class. You'll need to know the name of your class in order to derive a window from it later, the required datatype is a zero terminated string (an integer can be used instead of a string providing that it is first turned into a zero terminated string using either the MAKEINTRESOURCE or MAKEINTATOM macros provided in WINDOWS.H.

```
wc.lpszClassName = MAKEINTATOM(0x5000);
CreateWindow(
             MAKEINTATOM(0x5000)
             ....
             );
```

MAKEINTATOM is a macro :

```
#define MAKEINTATOM(i)  ((LPCSTR)MAKELP(0,(i)))
```

MAKELP is also a macro :

```
#define MAKELPARAM(low,high)              ((LPARAM)MAKELONG(low,high))
```

Guess what? MAKELONG is also a macro!

```
#define MAKELONG(low,high) ((LONG)(((WORD)(low))|(((DWORD)((WORD)(high))) << 16)))
```

What does all this look like when it's expanded? :

```
(LPCSTR)((void _far*)((long)(((WORD)(((0x5000))))|(((DWORD)((WORD)((0)))) <<
16))))),
```

Looks a bit odd? What's going on here? Well Windows treats any zero terminated string whose selector or DS value is zero as an integer ID, it uses this ID – the value of the address of the string (literally) to identify a class. Here we are casting a WORD (unsigned integer) into a DWORD (double word or unsigned long integer û 32 bits) then casting that into a far pointer to a character (char far *). This means that we have a far data pointer whose selector or DS value (upper 16 bits) is zero (casting the integer to a char *, say, would have created a valid far data pointer (DS:????) which is not what we want. If we had simply cast the integer to a LPSTR we might have got a compiler warning). Windows checks for this (a zero DS) then uses the value of the lower 16 bits as a class ID. This actually allows Windows to save some memory, ie. it is able to store just two bytes to identify a class with rather than a whole string (in USER's data segment), even if the string were hashed or condensed in some way (which it isn't) you'd still see a saving here. All the Windows system classes are defined in this way (0x8000 and up); we'll see more on the system classes elsewhere in this book.

☐ **Registering your class**

So we've filled in our WNDCLASS now let's create a class. We do this, or cause this to be done, by calling the Windows' RegisterClass() routine. This routine returns a BOOL (TRUE or FALSE) which is the indication of class creation success or failure. You can see from the code that I don't test it! I will do in the future examples. We pass RegisterClass the address of our WNDCLASS data structure which is located on our stack as it was declared *automatic*. Note that in 3.1 this API returns an ATOM, atoms identify strings. A BOOL is an int, an ATOM is a UINT (unsigned int), note that the compiler doesn't warn you about assigning from one to the other normally.

Once we've done this you'll notice that the *first* and *subsequent* instance routes join forces to perform the instance initialisation part of the overall task initialisation. Typically, instance initialisation means creating a window, showing it, then waiting around to service the task.

☐ Window creation

This is the first part of a task's typical instance initialisation.

Window creation may be achieved by making a call to the Windows' CreateWindow() (see CreateWindowEx() also) function. This routine returns a window handle or tag that identifies our new window from every other one in the system. If that handle has the value *0*, the creation has not taken place, i.e. the function returned its indication of failure. We may use any valid handle to directly manipulate the window, or better still, to have it manipulated by the window manager, in the future. We use the window handle returned in subsequent calls to some other Windows' routines. You'll notice again that I don't test hWnd against 0 in order to detect and exception – I just assume it works! That's fine for now. If I had have put all the correct exception handling code in SHELL1 it would have been twice as long and four times more difficult to read!

CreateWindow() is passed eleven parameters!. These are explained below.

☐ Classname

Lets Windows know from which existing class we'd like to derive a window.

☐ Caption

Defines a property that is used by the window to display a title for the window should the window have a title bar. Even if the window doesn't have a title the window remembers its caption. Defining a caption for a window without a title bar is therefore not an error and we will see where Windows does this for some of its own windows later. Our window has a caption, and a title bar and so the window will show the word *shell1* in its title bar. Caption properties may be used to store more or less arbitrary data even if the window doesn't implicitly use the data (if you've seen the *tag* property in Visual Basic controls you've seen an example of this). For example you could store data in a child window's caption property instead of using window words – of course you probably don't want to display arbitrary data!

☐ Window style

Windows just like classes have style attributes. For a window these typically fine tune its appearance and behaviour. Our window has the style given by the manifest constant WS_OVERLAPPEDWINDOW. If we look this style up in WINDOWS.H we find that it is a composite style and that it is made up of the following single styles bitwise OR'ed together –

```
WS_OVERLAPPED           main window style
WS_CAPTION              window has a caption
WS_SYSMENU              window has a system menu
WS_THICKFRAME           window has a resizing frame
WS_MINIMIZEBOX          window has minimize icon
WS_MAXIMIZEBOX          window has maximize icon
```

Interestingly, there's a little duplication here. WS_OVERLAPPED implies a *main type* of window with a caption bar. Therefore the WS_CAPTION isn't needed. If you remove it by say using the bitwise exclusive OR (^) operator or the bitwise AND (&) and NOT (~) operators on the style thus –

```
wc.style = WS_OVERLAPPEDWINDOW ^ WS_CAPTION;
wc.style = WS_OVERLAPPEDWINDOW & ~WS_CAPTION;
```

you'll find that the caption is not removed from the visible window. On a 'C' note, be careful here with precedence. &, ~ and ^ all have a higher precedence than |, so for example the following isn't the same as the code above –

```
wc.style =
      WS_OVERLAPPED               |
      WS_CAPTION                  |
      WS_SYSMENU                  |
      WS_THICKFRAME               |
      WS_MINIMIZEBOX              |
      WS_MAXIMIZEBOX             ^          WS_CAPTION
```

The ^ binds the WS_MAXIMIZEBOX with WS_CAPTION and not with the combined style for the overlapped window. To cure it use parentheses. Also, note that the ^ method above will act as a toggle for the bit, whereas the & ~ combination will always have the result that the bit will not be set. Our own (TMS's) coding standards state that all bitwise operations should be parenthesized by the way to avoid problems with their precedence.

WS_OVERLAPPED is defined as 0L. WS_TILED is defined (yes û it's still defined!) as WS_OVERLAPPED, tiled windows are overlapped windows therefore. See WINDOWS.H or the CreateWindow() section of volume 1 of the SDK v3.0 reference, or volume 2 of the SDK v3.1 reference for a full list of window styles. Again, some of these window style bits are used by the class object, others are used by Windows – for example WS_POPUP is used by Windows to determine the window type.

☐ **Initial position**

Defines just where the window will be placed on the desktop by the window manager. The fields in the example are filled in with the following –

```
Initial X position                CW_USEDEFAULT
```

```
Initial Y position                    0
Initial Width                         CW_USEDEFAULT
Initial Height                        0
```

As we have used *CW_USEDEFAULT* for both initial X and initial width the window manager chose just where to place the window on the desktop. It will also choose an initial Y and initial height for our window. As this is the case, and because the initial Y field may be used for something else, we usually set initial Y and initial height to 0 or NULL at this time.

If 0, or NULL, is given the window manager sets the width and height of the window so that the window touches the right hand, and bottom, edges of the desktop, or put another way – the width is given by wX – oX and the height by hY – oY, where wX is the width of the desktop, hY is the height of the desktop, oX is the X offset of the window (initial X position) and oY is the Y offset of the window (initial Y position). Or put another way wX = oX + window width, hY = oY + window height.

The units here by the way are device units or pixels. The origin is relative (for the moment) to the top left hand corner of the screen. If you had a VGA display (640 * 480) you could position the window precisely in the middle of the desktop by using say –

```
640 / 3        //initial X
480 / 3        //initial Y
640 / 3        //initial width
480 / 3        //initial height
```

So you'll see therefore that the width and height if given are relative to the window origin. I'll show you a way to determine the resolution of your display later so that you may do this sort of thing on any display.

☐ Parent window

Specifies whether or not this window is related to another window. Related windows behave in a particular way when certain actions are carried out on the window to which they are related or when the screen positions of the two related windows coincide. All related windows are commonly called child windows this is a big error. More on this later. Our main window doesn't have a parent (or an owner) and so this field is set to NULL.

☐ Menu

You'll recall that we had the opportunity to define a class menu in the WNDCLASS data structure and that I said that if we had done this that every window derived from the class would be equipped with this class menu? Well during window creation we have an opportunity to change the menu that will be attached to our window by setting this parameter to be a valid menu handle. This could be done all sorts of ways and I'll cover menus and these various ways in great detail later in the book. For now

I've set this parameter to NULL indicating that no menu is attached to this window (As we have no class menu. If we had, NULL would mean – *use the class menu*).

□ hInstance

Is what it was for the class; the instance handle of the creating module.

□ lpParams

This last parameter may be used to pass information to any window as it is created and provides for a certain amount of data abstraction in the process. We'll look at it later, for now note that it too is set to NULL and is therefore not used.

Having created our window we now need to show it to our user.

□ Showing windows

When CreateWindow() returns, the window is not automatically shown, nor is it explicitly shown by the window procedure during the creation process. It exists but is not made visible by the window manager. To force the window manager to show the window we use the ShowWindow() routine. The whole window apart from the application's client area output is usually made visible by this call. It is possible though to use this routine to un-show or hide a window. The routine places a WM_PAINT (and others) message into our task's queue. This, when it gets delivered, is our code's chance to paint in the client area of the window. Windows cannot paint in the foreground of the client area as it doesn't know what we'd like to display there! It does know however what colour the background should be (hbrBackground in the class structure), it uses this colour to *erase* the window's client area by painting in the background of the client area.

By the way, if you set hbrBackground to NULL you'll have to erase the background of your window yourself whenever it needs doing. You'll know when this is as Windows will pass you a WM_ERASEBKGND message. You can also detect this by testing the fErase member of a PAINTSTRUCT parsed by a BeginPaint() call.

We can force this WM_PAINT message to be delivered straight away by calling UpdateWindow(). This causes our wndproc to handle a WM_PAINT message and in so doing to paint in the client area of the window.

ShowWindow() takes two parameters, our window handle, hWnd, and an indication of how we'd like the window shown, nCmdShow. The latter comes from the user via Windows and is passed to a task via the fourth formal parameter to WinMain. If the user holds down the shift key then say double clicks on shell1.exe using the file manager, shell1 will be started in an iconic state, nCmdShow will be SW_SHOWMINNOACTIVE as defined in WINDOWS.H. It will not become active and input focus remains with the file manager. Input focus is a the term used to specify which window takes input from

This is not recommended as the user will expect to be able to control the initial state of the main window, and when they find they cannot, they'll rebel!

When these two routines are through we have a visible, painted window on the desktop ready to go.

☐ Looking for messages

We now enter what's called a message polling loop.

Firstly lets look at that MSG structure as it's declared and typedef'd in WINDOWS.H 3.0 & 3.1 respectively.

```
typedef struct tagMSG
{
    HWND                hwnd;
    WORD                message;
    WORD                wParam;
    LONG                lParam;
    DWORD               time;
    POINT               pt;
} MSG;

typedef struct tagMSG
{
    HWND                hwnd;
    UINT                message;
    WPARAM              wParam;
    LPARAM              lParam;
    DWORD               time;
    POINT               pt;
} MSG;
```

Again, it's type name differences only.

For now, let's just talk about the first four members of this structure, hwnd, message, wParam and lParam.

<u>hwnd</u> identifies the window to which an event took place, or should affect. Of course in our application we only have one window and so this member will always have the same value as that returned by CreateWindow() (in one case it won't, I'll explain further down).

<u>message</u> identifies the event type. This member is usually referred to as *the message*. This can get confusing as we now have two definitions of message { the structure, and now the event type. Event types usually have symbolic names defined in WIN-DOWS.H such as WM_PAINT (window needs repainting), WM_SIZE (the window has been resized), WM_CLOSE (the window wants to be closed or removed) etc.

DOWS.H such as WM_PAINT (window needs repainting), WM_SIZE (the window has been resized), WM_CLOSE (the window wants to be closed or removed) etc. Notice also that this *odd* member missed out on <u>any</u> HG – why not uMessage or wMessage? Of course it's too late to change its name now!

<u>wParam</u> is, from it's HG a WORD sized thing on the face of it that may contain extra useful information for some events. A WORD is a signed int. In 3.1 a new type called a WPARAM has been defined, and the type has changed just a little bit. WPARAM is a UINT so just the sign of the wParam changes from 3.0 to 3.1 – no big deal.

The same is true for <u>lParam</u>, but please note that it's a LONG in 3.0 and a LPARAM (defined as a LONG, which is defined as a signed long – no change between 3.0 and 3.1) in 3.1. Let me give you an example of how the wParam & lParam aid the message member in detailing an event.

If the user moves the mouse cursor over the client area of our window this will cause mouse events to be placed into our task message queue, we'll retrieve them using GetMessage() which is talked about below. If we were to break up the message structure and look at the parts we've talked about so far, we would find that the message member has the value WM_MOUSEMOVE as defined in WINDOWS.H. That the wParam contains a bitmap (not a picture!) which details the state of the mouse's and some keyboard keys, whether the left mouse button was down (at the time of the move) for example. That the lParam treated as a DWORD (double word) type contains information regarding the position of the cursor's hot spot after the move (the one pixel point that identifies the cursor's position), its client area relative X value in device units is in the low order word whilst the Y is in the high. Not exactly intuitive is it? We'll see later in the book when we look at object libraries that this can be made very obvious and intuitive if we try. Now more on how we pull these events off our queue.

You'll remember that our task is event driven and that by and large events come from the user or the system. Well we need some way of finding out if and when those events take place. If an event does take place to our window, say the user moves the mouse cursor over it, Windows will place an event detailing this into our task message queue. The event in this case has the name WM_MOUSEMOVE. We therefore need to test on a regular basis to see if there's an event in our task message queue. We do this usually by calling the routine GetMessage(). GetMessage() returns with a message if one exists. Once a message has been retrieved, we call TranslateMessage() and DispatchMessage() passing to these two functions the address of the MSG (message) structure declared as an automatic at the top of WinMain. The MSG structure will have been filled in by the GetMessage() routine with the necessary event information.

This seems a little odd doesn't it? Why call Windows simply in order to re-call Windows a moment later? Or put another way. Why call Windows, surely, Windows could call our wndproc directly when there's something for it to do?

Well you're right. Windows could do the latter and it would be possible to build in an implicit GetMessage() call to the message handling wndproc relatively simply. There's many reasons why this isn't done. Some of the major ones are to do with the flexibility of Windows and will be covered later. For the meantime lets ask again why I need to call Windows in order for it to call my wndproc. This is necessary in order for Windows to multitask Windows' tasks. It works like this –

☐ Pre-emptive versus non pre-emptive scheduling

Currently (it will change in Windows 32 for DOS & NT) Windows employs a non-pre-emptive scheduling system. This means that its not the operating system (Windows) that decides when to run one task or another. No, its up to the tasks themselves to voluntarily give up the processor to Windows when they're through with it, tasks may even task other tasks themselves bypassing Windows. Each task runs until it passes control of the CPU back to Windows. This is different from say OS/2 where the operating system magically regains control from any task on a regular basis irrespective of whether or not that task wants the CPU or not (this is not as black and white as it sounds, as, under OS/2, a task may retain the processor for as long as it requires it under certain circumstances. This has led many in the past to ask if OS/2 is all it's cracked up to be (in the scheduling area)). OS/2's scheduler is called pre-emptive, which loosely means that something pre-empts, or beats, something else before it has the chance to act upon some aspect of the program, like a pre-emptive strike etc. OK, we're non-pre-emptive so as we need to give up the processor to Windows this must mean that we must call the Windows' scheduler itself on a regular basis. <u>Correct!</u>

SHELL1 calls Windows' scheduler via the call to GetMessage(). This indicates that its ready to give up the processor if it doesn't have any more events to process in its task message queue. Windows at this time searches the task's queue to see if there's anything to be done. If the SHELL1 task has an event to process, Windows fills in the MSG structure to which the task has passed it a long pointer and returns TRUE to the caller (GetMessage() returns TRUE). If there aren't any events waiting in the task's queue Windows may pass control to any other task that does have events in its task message queue (that task must have been waiting all this time in a GetMessage() (or something like it) call of course. It will now get a return from that call). When that task is through with processing its events there may be no events in any task's queue. As the Windows scheduler has control (the last scheduled task yielded control to Windows by calling GetMessage()) it simply keeps control until an event needs to be processed by a task, at which time that task gets a return from its GetMessage() call and can process the event. Simple isn't it!

I'm sure you'll agree that it does explain something of why we have to call Windows?

How then do we quit? Do we simply call exit when we're ready to terminate or what? What you <u>have</u> to do is cause the message polling loop to exit and with what I've told you so far this would be a mean feat unless you're to use a break statement or sage() returns TRUE else it doesn't return. Well that's not always absolutely true! GetMessage() doesn't return an indication of whether or not there's a message to process, as I've said, the very fact that it's returned shows us that fact, it actually returns an indication of whether or not the message type being retrieved from Windows is, or is not, of type WM_QUIT, phew! Simply, this means that if the message member of the structure is WM_QUIT (message == WM_QUIT) then GetMessage() returns FALSE else it returns TRUE (when it returns). Therefore we can see that when GetMessage() returns FALSE our loop exits and so does, in SHELL1, the task.

I noted earlier that there was one case when the *hwnd* member of the MSG structure, parsed by GetMessage(), didn't contain a valid window handle. Well this is the case; where the message being retrieved is a WM_QUIT message. In this case the hwnd member will be set to zero. This is because the message is actually posted to the task, and not to any window that the task builds or maintains. DispatchMessage() ignores the WM_QUIT message should you ever try to pass it on for processing by say calling

```
for (;;)       /* forever */
{
    GetMessage(&msg,NULL,0,0);
    DispatchMessage(&msg);
/* if it's a QUIT, then quit
** after passing on the message
*/
    if(msg.message == WM_QUIT)
      {
            exit(msg.wParam);
      }
}
```

DispatchMessage() whenever a message is retrieved; you could do this by fabricating a *real* infinite loop like this for example –

So how do we get a WM_QUIT message in our task message queue? It's done in the wndproc, MainWndProc, usually in the WM_DESTROY case and we'll discuss it shortly.

TranslateMessage() does what its name suggests, it translates a message. The messages it translates are raw, uncooked, keyboard messages. It turns them into another type of keyboard message.

We have reached the stage in our application where we now have to pass, or cause to have passed, the event to our wndproc. We do this by calling DispatchMessage(). Windows then calls our wndproc and passes the four parts of the MSG structure examined above as actual parameters to that function. Note that we haven't said which function to call, we simply say *process this* and pass Windows the address of the message structure, Windows figures out which wndproc to call. Again as we only which function to call, we simply say *process this* and pass Windows the address of the message structure, Windows figures out which wndproc to call. Again as we only have one, it's not hard to figure out, but as you'll see later we may have many windows in our application and we pull messages for all of these windows off the single task message queue. We never have to tell DispatchMessage() which wndproc to call, it still figures it out and passes to that function the first four parts of the message structure.

DispatchMessage() calls the wndproc just as if you had called it (don't try calling your WndProcs as functions though û it may or may not work!). In other words as a sub-routine call. Therefore DispatchMessage() doesn't return until the wndproc finishes processing the message which has been dispatched to it. DispatchMessage() returns a LONG, so does a wndproc under 3.0; under 3.1 they return an LRESULT which conveniently is a LONG. DispatchMessage() returns the result of processing the message in the wndproc. As you can see we don't make any use of this as yet. Microsoft should really have defined DispatchMessage() as returning an LRESULT of course – this one, and some, slipped through the net. See the *Miscellaneous* Chapter for more on this subject.

☐ The WinProc

You'll notice that MainWndProc is declared as returning a LONG and that calls to it are resolved by FAR reference. Also, the function, just like WinMain, has the PASCAL calling and naming conventions. I've already mentioned the LONG (or LRESULT) returned by this routine and it will come up again and again in the future so I won't say any more about it for now. It's a FAR function because it's called by Windows and Windows doesn't live in our CS (code segment) therefore in order to call our wndproc both CS and IP (the instruction pointer) must change. This is what's referred to as a far call. It's PASCAL because Windows calls it as a PASCAL function. See also the brief discussion on PASCAL in the section on WinMain above and further references to PASCAL in the index.

The function declares two autos. One is a structure called a PAINSTRUCT, the other a character pointer which is initialised to point to the string constant *Hello World.*

The wndproc is really one large switch statement or jump table. You'll remember, it's called to handle a class window message. You're passed the window handle of the window (*hwnd* structure member – *hWnd* formal parameter) to which the event has taken place – the actual instance of the class if you like. A message ID (*message* structure member – *nMessage* formal parameter (this is in keeping with the type associated with message IDs in 3.0, ie. they were WORD values. WORD was a signed int) detailing the event type, and the parameter members (*wParam* and *lParam* at both ends)). The wndproc switches on the event type (nMessage). This wndproc handles explicitly only two event types, one's called WM_DESTROY, the other WM_PAINT. a DESTROY is passed to the wndproc when the window given in hWnd has been destroyed by Windows and has been removed from the desktop by the window manager. A PAINT is passed to the wndproc when the window given in hWnd needs to re-paint some or all of its client area.

You'll notice a default to the switch statement. The wndproc is in reality passed many messages in which it is simply not interested. This fact (your wndproc's indifference to most of the messages being passed to it) MUST be signalled to Windows so that it might process some of these messages for you. You do this by calling DefWindow-Proc() (usually called the *default window procedure*) and passing to it all unwanted events. If you're used to other windowing systems, such as X based systems, you'll find handling these un-requested messages an initial chore but nothing more.

If the wndproc handles an event it should return 0L (a LONG zero) to the caller (this isn't a must as it's mostly ignored at the moment – see table below), if on the other hand it doesn't handle an event it must return the result of calling the default window procedure, which is also usually zero.

Below are two lists of all the current documented WM_? messages that your window procedures may be passed (I've included their real values as well). The first list is shown sorted on message name, the second on message ID. Additionally, in the first list those <u>messages shown with an asterisk are those that are significant to DefWindowProc()</u>.

List 1. Window Messages Sorted By Name.					
WM_ACTIVATE	0x0006	*	WM_MENUSELECT	0x011F	
WM_ACTIVATEAPP	0x001C		WM_MOUSEACTIVATE	0x0021	*
WM_ASKCBFORMATNAME	0x030C		WM_MOUSEMOVE	0x0200	
WM_CANCELMODE	0x001F	*	WM_MOVE	0x0003	
WM_CHANGECBCHAIN	0x030D		WM_NCACTIVATE	0x0086	*
WM_CHAR	0x0102		WM_NCCALCSIZE	0x0083	*
WM_CHARTOITEM	0x002F	*	WM_NCCREATE	0x0081	*
WM_CHILDACTIVATE	0x0022		WM_NCDESTROY	0x0082	*
WM_CLEAR	0x0303		WM_NCHITTEST	0x0084	*
WM_CLOSE	0x0010	*	WM_NCLBUTTONDBLCLK	0x00A3	*
WM_COMMAND	0x0111		WM_NCLBUTTONDOWN	0x00A1	*
WM_COMPACTING	0x0041		WM_NCLBUTTONUP	0x00A2	*
WM_COMPAREITEM	0x0039		WM_NCMBUTTONDBLCLK	0x00A9	
WM_COPY	0x0301		WM_NCMBUTTONDOWN	0x00A7	
WM_CREATE	0x0001		WM_NCMBUTTONUP	0x00A8	
WM_CTLCOLOR	0x0019	*	WM_NCMOUSEMOVE	0x00A0	*
WM_CUT	0x0300		WM_NCPAINT	0x0085	*
WM_DEADCHAR	0x0103		WM_NCRBUTTONDBLCLK	0x00A6	
WM_DELETEITEM	0x002D		WM_NCRBUTTONDOWN	0x00A4	
WM_DESTROY	0x0002		WM_NCRBUTTONUP	0x00A5	
WM_DESTROYCLIPBOARD	0x0307		WM_NEXTDLGCTL	0x0028	
WM_DEVMODECHANGE	0x001B		WM_NULL	0x0000	
WM_DRAWCLIPBOARD	0x0308		WM_PAINT	0x000F	*
WM_DRAWITEM	0x002B	*	WM_PAINTCLIPBOARD	0x0309	
WM_ENABLE	0x000A		WM_PAINTICON	0x0026	*
WM_ENDSESSION	0x0016		WM_PALETTECHANGED	0x0311	
WM_ENTERIDLE	0x0121		WM_PALETTEISCHANGING	0x0310	

WM_ERASEBKGND	0x0014 *	WM_PARENTNOTIFY	0x0210
WM_FONTCHANGE	0x001D	WM_PASTE	0x0302
WM_GETDLGCODE	0x0087	WM_QUERYDRAGICON	0x0037
WM_GETFONT	0x0031	WM_QUERYENDSESSION	0x0011 *
WM_GETMINMAXINFO	0x0024	WM_QUERYNEWPALETTE	0x030F
WM_GETTEXT	0x000D *	WM_QUERYOPEN	0x0013 *
WM_GETTEXTLENGTH	0x000E *	WM_QUEUESYNC	0x0023
WM_HSCROLL	0x0114	WM_QUIT	0x0012
WM_HSCROLLCLIPBOARD	0x030E	WM_RBUTTONDBLCLK	0x0206
WM_ICONERASEBKGND	0x0027 *	WM_RBUTTONDOWN	0x0204
WM_INITDIALOG	0x0110	WM_RBUTTONUP	0x0205
WM_INITMENU	0x0116	WM_RENDERALLFORMATS	0x0306
WM_INITMENUPOPUP	0x0117	WM_RENDERFORMAT	0x0305
WM_KEYDOWN	0x0100 *	WM_SETCURSOR	0x0020 *
WM_KEYUP	0x0101 *	WM_SETFOCUS	0x0007
WM_KILLFOCUS	0x0008	WM_SETFONT	0x0030
WM_LBUTTONDBLCLK	0x0203	WM_SETREDRAW	0x000B *
WM_LBUTTONDOWN	0x0201	WM_SETTEXT	0x000C *
WM_LBUTTONUP	0x0202	WM_SHOWWINDOW	0x0018 *
WM_MBUTTONDBLCLK	0x0209	WM_SIZE	0x0005
WM_MBUTTONDOWN	0x0207	WM_SIZECLIPBOARD	0x030B
WM_MBUTTONUP	0x0208	WM_SPOOLERSTATUS	0x002A
WM_MDIACTIVATE	0x0222	WM_SYSCHAR	0x0106 *
WM_MDICASCADE	0x0227	WM_SYSCOLORCHANGE	0x0015
WM_MDICREATE	0x0220	WM_SYSCOMMAND	0x0112 *
WM_MDIDESTROY	0x0221	WM_SYSDEADCHAR	0x0107
WM_MDIGETACTIVE	0x0229	WM_SYSKEYDOWN	0x0104 *
WM_MDIICONARRANGE	0x0228	WM_SYSKEYUP	0x0105 *
WM_MDIMAXIMIZE	0x0225	WM_TIMECHANGE	0x001E
WM_MDINEXT	0x0224	WM_TIMER	0x0113
WM_MDIRESTORE	0x0223	WM_UNDO	0x0304
WM_MDISETMENU	0x0230	WM_VKEYTOITEM	0x002E *
WM_MDITILE	0x0226	WM_VSCROLL	0x0115
WM_MEASUREITEM	0x002C	WM_VSCROLLCLIPBOARD	0x030A
WM_MENUCHAR	0x0120	WM_WININICHANGE	0x001A

List 2. Window Messages Sorted By Value.

WM_NULL	0x0000	WM_NCRBUTTONDBLCLK	0x00A6
WM_CREATE	0x0001	WM_NCMBUTTONUP	0x00A8
WM_DESTROY	0x0002	WM_NCMBUTTONDBLCLK	0x00A9
WM_MOVE	0x0003	WM_KEYDOWN	0x0100
WM_SIZE	0x0005	WM_KEYUP	0x0101
WM_ACTIVATE	0x0006	WM_CHAR	0x0102
WM_SETFOCUS	0x0007	WM_DEADCHAR	0x0103
WM_KILLFOCUS	0x0008	WM_SYSKEYDOWN	0x0104
WM_ENABLE	0x000A	WM_SYSKEYUP	0x0105
WM_SETREDRAW	0x000B	WM_SYSCHAR	0x0106
WM_SETTEXT	0x000C	WM_SYSDEADCHAR	0x0107
WM_GETTEXT	0x000D	WM_INITDIALOG	0x0110
WM_GETTEXTLENGTH	0x000E	WM_COMMAND	0x0111
WM_PAINT	0x000F	WM_SYSCOMMAND	0x0112
WM_CLOSE	0x0010	WM_TIMER	0x0113
WM_QUERYENDSESSION	0x0011	WM_HSCROLL	0x0114
WM_QUIT	0x0012	WM_VSCROLL	0x0115

WM_QUERYOPEN	0x0013	WM_INITMENU	0x0116
WM_ERASEBKGND	0x0014	WM_INITMENUPOPUP	0x0117
WM_SYSCOLORCHANGE	0x0015	WM_MENUSELECT	0x011F
WM_ENDSESSION	0x0016	WM_MENUCHAR	0x0120
WM_SHOWWINDOW	0x0018	WM_ENTERIDLE	0x0121
WM_CTLCOLOR	0x0019	WM_MOUSEMOVE	0x0200
WM_WININICHANGE	0x001A	WM_LBUTTONDOWN	0x0201
WM_DEVMODECHANGE	0x001B	WM_LBUTTONUP	0x0202
WM_ACTIVATEAPP	0x001C	WM_LBUTTONDBLCLK	0x0203
WM_FONTCHANGE	0x001D	WM_RBUTTONDOWN	0x0204
WM_TIMECHANGE	0x001E	WM_RBUTTONUP	0x0205
WM_CANCELMODE	0x001F	WM_RBUTTONDBLCLK	0x0206
WM_SETCURSOR	0x0020	WM_MBUTTONDOWN	0x0207
WM_MOUSEACTIVATE	0x0021	WM_MBUTTONUP	0x0208
WM_CHILDACTIVATE	0x0022	WM_MBUTTONDBLCLK	0x0209
WM_QUEUESYNC	0x0023	WM_PARENTNOTIFY	0x0210
WM_GETMINMAXINFO	0x0024	WM_MDICREATE	0x0220
WM_PAINTICON	0x0026	WM_MDIDESTROY	0x0221
WM_ICONERASEBKGND	0x0027	WM_MDIACTIVATE	0x0222
WM_NEXTDLGCTL	0x0028	WM_MDIRESTORE	0x0223
WM_SPOOLERSTATUS	0x002A	WM_MDINEXT	0x0224
WM_DRAWITEM	0x002B	WM_MDIMAXIMIZE	0x0225
WM_MEASUREITEM	0x002C	WM_MDITILE	0x0226
WM_DELETEITEM	0x002D	WM_MDICASCADE	0x0227
WM_VKEYTOITEM	0x002E	WM_MDIICONARRANGE	0x0228
WM_CHARTOITEM	0x002F	WM_MDIGETACTIVE	0x0229
WM_SETFONT	0x0030	WM_MDISETMENU	0x0230
WM_GETFONT	0x0031	WM_CUT	0x0300
WM_QUERYDRAGICON	0x0037	WM_COPY	0x0301
WM_COMPAREITEM	0x0039	WM_PASTE	0x0302
WM_COMPACTING	0x0041	WM_CLEAR	0x0303
WM_NCCREATE	0x0081	WM_UNDO	0x0304
WM_NCDESTROY	0x0082	WM_RENDERFORMAT	0x0305
WM_NCCALCSIZE	0x0083	WM_RENDERALLFORMATS	0x0306
WM_NCHITTEST	0x0084	WM_DESTROYCLIPBOARD	0x0307
WM_NCPAINT	0x0085	WM_DRAWCLIPBOARD	0x0308
WM_NCACTIVATE	0x0086	WM_PAINTCLIPBOARD	0x0309
WM_GETDLGCODE	0x0087	WM_VSCROLLCLIPBOARD	0x030A
WM_NCMOUSEMOVE	0x00A0	WM_SIZECLIPBOARD	0x030B
WM_NCLBUTTONDOWN	0x00A1	WM_ASKCBFORMATNAME	0x030C
WM_NCLBUTTONUP	0x00A2	WM_CHANGECBCHAIN	0x030D
WM_NCLBUTTONDBLCLK	0x00A3	WM_HSCROLLCLIPBOARD	0x030E
WM_NCRBUTTONDOWN	0x00A4	WM_QUERYNEWPALETTE	0x030F
WM_NCRBUTTONUP	0x00A5	WM_PALETTEISCHANGING	0x0310
WM_NCMBUTTONDOWN	0x00A7	WM_PALETTECHANGED	0x0311

This list is Windows 3.0 complete, 3.1 adds some more. See the later chapter on DLLs for a complete list.

How does SHELL1 handle DESTROY and PAINT. For the DESTROY we are choosing to terminate the task. We do this by getting the GetMessage() call to return FALSE. This you'll remember comes about by retrieving a WM_QUIT message from the task message queue. All we need do then is place a WM_QUIT message in our queue. This is accomplished using PostQuitMessage(). The parameter, here given as 0, will be in the wParam of the WM_QUIT message when it is retrieved from the queue. This may be passed back to some caller or even used for some other means in WinMain (we declared WinMain as a *void* so don't try returning it from WinMain – exit() is fine of course)! After we call this PostQuitMessage() routine we encounter a break statement which breaks us out of the switch. We then return 0L which you'll remember signals that we've processed the WM_DESTROY message. For the PAINT we simply want to output some text on the window. We'll get a paint message if any section of our window needs repairing and therefore repainting. We'll get our first one when we call UpdateWindow() in WinMain remember. In response to the PAINT we initialise two structures. A RECT, by using the very sociable Windows' routine GetClientRect() (Get The Customer Wrecked (smashed)), and a PAINSTRUCT structure by passing its address to Windows' BeginPaint() routine. The RECT holds the size of the client area of the window specified by hWnd. The PAINTSTRUCT holds all sorts of interesting stuff but for now let me just say we're after the hdc or, handle to a device context, member of it. We use the hdc member of the PAINSTRUCT – ps.hdc in a call to a text painting routine called DrawText(). The hdc member of ps gives us the necessary permissions and tools needed for painting onto the window. The Draw-Text() routine allows us to do some funky stuff like always drawing text in the center of a given rectangle. The text length is given as -1, this only works for 0 terminated strings such as those native to 'C'. We ask DrawText() to center our text both vertically and horizontally within our client area by using the flags begining with DT_. Finally we free up any resources Windows may have allocated internally for us for the painting operation by signalling to it that we've finished painting by calling End-Paint(); we then break and return 0L as before. Paint messages are called, more accurately, expose messages or events on some GUIs as a window procedure will only be called to process one when some of its client area is both invalid and exposed. For example if your window is obscured by another window you'll not recieve a paint message; when the window becomes un-obscured (or exposed), it will get a paint message. It is not totally accurate to say therefore that you'll get a paint when some or all of the window's client area becomes invalid.

One last bit of information, the messages received by our window as it's created are as follows. You'll see that there are quite a few of them. Listed from left to right are the window handle of the window, the message received, the wParam value and lastly the lParam value. Note that this list was not produced using SPY, rather a slightly modified version of the shell application was used to produce this it, stay tuned to see how it was done.

```
5048  WM_GETMINMAXINFO     0000  062507A4
5048  WM_NCCREATE          0000  15751F8C
5048  WM_NCCALCSIZE        0000  15751F72
5048  WM_CREATE            0000  15751F8C
5048  WM_SHOWWINDOW        0001  00000000
5048  WM_SETVISIBLE        0001  00000000
5048  WM_QUERYNEWPALETTE   0000  00000000
5048  WM_ACTIVATEAPP       0001  000004B5
5048  WM_NCACTIVATE        0001  00001394
```

```
5048 WM_GETTEXT        004F 15751DA0
5048 WM_ACTIVATE       0001 00001394
5048 WM_SETFOCUS       1744 00000000
5048 WM_NCPAINT        0B82 00000000
5048 WM_SYNCPAINT      0005 00000001
5048 WM_ERASEBKGND     0866 00000000
5048 WM_SIZE           0000 02270380
5048 WM_MOVE           0000 0097007C
5048 WM_PAINT          0000 00000000
```

After writing about the Windows' code another old and mildly amusing saying pops into my mind, it's this –

Whenever you set out to do something, something else must be done first.

There'll be of course much more on all this later in the book. For now give yourself a pat on the back and get yourself a coffee, I am!

Lets take a quick look at the other files in SHELL1

☐ MAKEFILE

The make file is in nmake or nmk format. Line 1 says make *all*. This can be anything – it's called a pseudotarget. It's needed because unlike old make (MS MAKE), the new makes (NMK & NMAKE) don't evaluate targets in the make file sequentially like MAKE used to. The new format is to build only the first target, and before it, any of it's dependents. Therefore in MAKEFILE NMAKE wants to build *all*, this depends upon SHELL1.EXE, to build SHELL1.EXE NMAKE evaluates the SHELL1.EXE target and it's dependents and so on. You get the same result if you turn your old make files upside down (if you wrote them following popular conventions).

To build shell1.exe we might need to build shell1.obj. This is done by invoking the 'C' compiler on line 3 of the make file. The flags are -c (compile only, no link) -Gsw (generate no stack probes and Windows' full far function prologue and epilogue sequences) -Zp (pack structures on byte boundaries (packed)) -W4 (highest warning level available) -D NOCOMM (define symbol NOCOMM to the preprocessor. This prevents lots of WINDOWS.H -W4 warnings about bit field types - WINDOWS.H 3.0 and earlier defines a structure with bit field members of type BYTE, which is typedef'd as an unsigned char. This isn't legal ANSI 'C', hence the warnings, WINDOWS.H 3.1 changes the type to UINT – no warnings). We'll look at a different set of compiler flags in the next chapter and from that point onwards.

Shell1.rc is another source code file. Not a 'C' language file but a resource language file. We use the resource language to define and add resources to our executable. These resources are loadable at run time by any task and are defined as read only discardable data items. Anything can be a resource, and in a round about way, even code can be a resource which is loaded and executed at run time. Typical resources are ICONs, CURSORs, BITMAPs, STRINGTABLE, MENUs and DIALOGs. I'll go into more on these resources throughout the book but you should read the section on the resource language in the SDK reference volume 2, chapter 8 to become fully conversant with it.

☐ The resource compilation

We need to compile the resource script (.RC file) using the resource compiler (RC.EXE). You'll learn much more about resources as you cover future chapters.

The resource compiler is the application that *marks* your Windows' application with a version number, i.e. whether or not this application runs under Windows 1, 2 or 3.0 or 3.1. You'll see from the resource script file that we don't actually have any resources and that the resource file simply contains a rather 'C' looking comment. We'll that's there so that the resource compiler modifies the executable with the resource/Windows version which in our case will be 3. If we didn't do this Windows would assume, wrongly, that it's a Windows 1 executable. You can confirm this by missing out the last *rc* invocation – *rc ?????.res ?????.exe* and then running your application under Windows. You'll find that Windows tells you that this application was written for an earlier version of Windows.

We compile the resources with just one switch on line 5, -r. This switch means compile the resources to a file, called a res (resource) file, and do nothing more with them. Res files have the extension .RES. By default the resource compiler would have compiled the resources in shell1.rc then would have tried to add them to shell1.exe. We build this first shell1.exe using the linker so we don't want that to happen yet, not until after the link is complete. You'll see on line 8 that the resource compiler is re-run to add the resources to the executable built by the linker.

☐ The link

Talking of the link, this is done using the cl engine again. This is just the way I prefer to do it, I find it easier and reckon that it has some advantages over the regular LINK used by so many Windows' programmers. More on these soon. The linker is exec'd with the following significant switches /NOD (no default library search as we want to link with the Windows libraries only), /ALIGN:16 (align the executable on 16 byte boundaries. This makes sense for any application with many segments – it causes the loading of the application to take a little longer (maybe) but reduces the size of the executable on disk considerably, the default is 512), /NOI (no ignore case, causes the linker to distinguish between lower and upper case characters in the object module, or a case sensitive link if you prefer). This last switch is implicit and is put on whenever you use cl to exec the linker as is the /FARCALL switch. We also identify the libraries LIBW.LIB and SLIBCEW.LIB as those to which we'd like to link. LIBW.LIB is the Windows API import library. It doesn't contain code (well not much anyway) and is used in dynamic linking. We'll return to import libraries in the chapter on dynamic linking. SLIBCEW.LIB contains the standard 'C' library small (S) model routines for Windows applications.

☐ Module definition file

The last file to look at is the def or definition file.

Line 1 defines the name of the module, it should be the same as the executable name, so mine is SHELL1. It can be left out in which case the linker assumes the name is that of the executable. NAME identifies this as an application, SHELL1 maybe used to identify the module when exporting functions.

Line 2 gives a module description. Text given here between single quotes is embedded in the module and usually, for applications, contains information regarding copyright etc.

Line 3 defines this module as WINDOWS aware, options are OS2 or UNKNOWN, as we're a Windows' application it's set to WINDOWS of course.

Next, on lines 4 and 5 we define the behaviour of all our CODE and non-resource DATA. Our code is MOVEABLE or relocatable in memory, is PRELOADed prior to being called, and DISCARDABLE should Windows require the space occupied by our single code segment. Our data is again PRELOADed into memory before any access is attempted and again the data segment may be MOVEABLE or relocated around memory by Windows. Data (apart from read only resources and read only

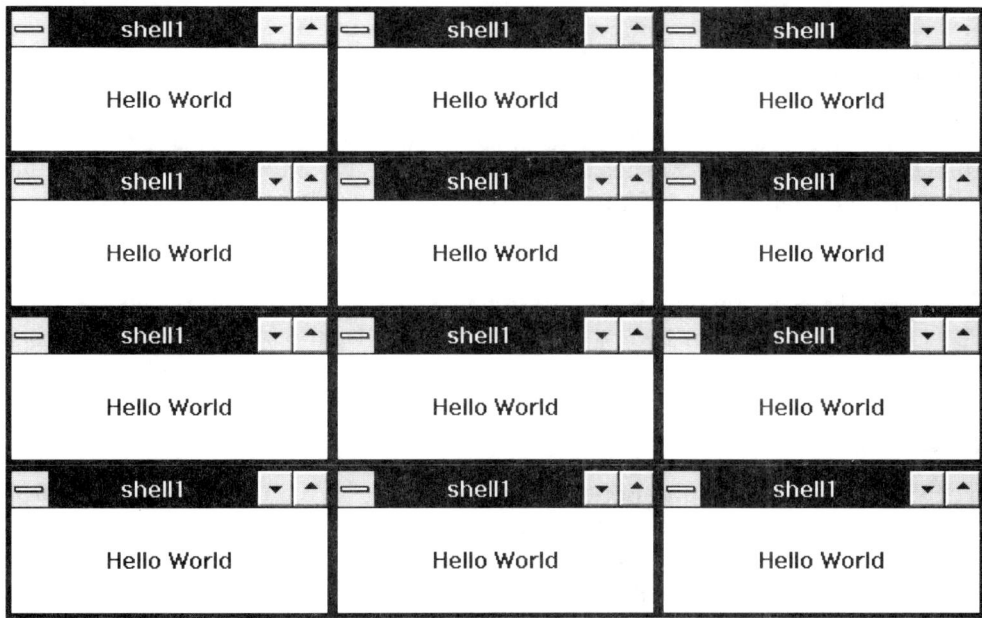

code (executable data)) is never discarded from memory even in 386 Enhanced mode so you'll not see the DISCARDABLE flag set against the DATA directive. Our data is flagged as MULTIPLE which means that we'd like a new data segment for each instance of our application. Instances of Windows applications share code but work on unique data (unless provisions are made for sharing data).

Lastly on lines 9 and 10 we define all the entry points into our application apart from WinMain (an entry point is potentially any FAR function although to successfully work as a entry point some code in the function's prologue and epilogue sequences needs to be changed, more on this much later). MAINWNDPROC is such a FAR function that is OK to call from outside our application by Windows. The @1 defines the location of the function's name in the applications name table. You'll see also later that when we export functions from dynamic link libraries it is better to use these ordinals rather than the function names as they, the ordinals, conserve space. The ordinal is not required and if omitted will be assigned a default ordinal value.

The difference

OK so why so much code in the Windows version? Well we've got to really consider not simply the code and the issue of why there's more in a Windows' application, we've really got to consider the environments targeted by each of the applications we've seen – cshell & shell1 and the level of functionality and usability offered by each. After we've looked at each application's environment briefly, reconsider whether you still regard the Windows' application as large (code wise)?

DOS

The DOS environment, and in particular the display, is well catered for in the 'C' runtimes. Consider printf which is the function we used in cshell to output *Hello World*. Printf outputs a formatted text string to *stdout* (standard out) which DOS directs to the CON device. The cshell application is the only application using that part of the screen to which it directs its output. Note that we don't have to specify where the text should be output, we don't get the choice with a simple printf call and we of course accept the default or current (cursor) position imposed by the device, its driver and DOS. Obviously another difference between the two applications is that the DOS application runs for a very short time, it simply outputs its text then terminates. Note also that when it terminates it, or DOS, doesn't tidy up the screen!

Windows

The Windows' coded application gets a lot more support than does the DOS application. For example you'll notice that you can have practically any number (instances) of SHELL1 running. Each Instance outputs its text using DrawText() to the same logical co-ordinate. You'll gather with a little observation that each identical co-ordinate can map to some other area of the physical screen. For example look at the snapshot below.

This shows many instances of SHELL1 running. Each thinks that it owns all of the display. Windows manages each window and maintains for each a personal universe for it into which it draws. You'll notice also that you're able to move any window to anywhere on the display. You're even able to cover up, then re-expose any particular instance which immediately tidies itself up by once more re-painting its window with the text *Hello World*. You can zoom, minimize, move, resize, close and even select the task list by using the window's system menu. All in all not bad for such a small piece of code!

Well as I said when this chapter began, this chapter was to bring you up to speed (maybe it's half speed). I hope you found it interesting and that you now have some understanding of how Windows works? I've shielded you (believe it or not) from quite a lot of detail in this chapter. The detail will be added during the rest of the book.

In the next chapter we'll re-write the SHELL application a little (lot) differently giving good emphasis on coding standards and design and of course all that that entails – extensibility, data abstraction, code re-use etc, see you there.

Chapter 2

The return of the shell

☐ The shell (from hell) – again

The code towards the end of this chapter is a kinda *generic* re-write. I've never really liked the way most Windows' apps are written, as in I don't think much of the examples to which they're written, and thought that I'd *do* a bit of a job on it here. Generic's pretty grimy and hasn't changed much since it appeared in source form with the very first SDKs – you can tell this if you look closely at it!

The *generic* app is however <u>meant</u> to be very basic; it serves a lot of people as a good first step to writing Windows' code. Unfortunately a lot of people have taken that code, changed it very little and are using it as the basis of all their current Windows work -honest, I've met some of *em!*

The shell code presented below is not meant to be a replacement for generic (Typically every new solution causes a whole new class of problems); it's really a kind of conversation piece. I hope that when you look through it you'll find a lot to appreciate in it -you might also find a load of stuff that you hate and strongly disagree with. This is quite natural and is encouraged. I'm really hoping that it'll make you think about the way we write our code -period.

☐ The current standard hasn't been designed

A design should say all sorts of things to the user of the design (the programmer). If you don't have access to the design you should be able to deduce all sorts of things from the code which has been coded to the design. Unfortunately you can't do the latter with regard to Windows' code very often, if at all.

Design can be quite subtle or, totally obvious.

For example, I don't like 'C' (for writing Windows programs) but I recognise as a programmer that it was a well designed computer language. What evidence is there for saying that? One easy example is that arrays in 'C' are addressed by subscripts starting at 0. This suggests to me that Brian and Dennis recognised that for programmers, asymmetric loop bounds were easier to read, understand and debug etc (also, as an array's name evaluates to the address of the first item in that array, if you add offset zero to the array name you therefore get to the first item in it (array + 0), using zero as a subscript now seems totally obvious), it makes sense therefore to start your array index at 0; a subtle one I think. As another example, when you look at a car you can tell, to some extent, what category of car it is by examining visually its design. A sports car will look sleek and have a low centre of gravity, it'll probably have wide tyres and be painted red etc; an obvious one I think. You can say the same about all sorts of things we come in contact with daily so why not the majority of code – the embodiment of design surely; or the design or blueprint itself perhaps?

I can find nothing formally on *The standard Windows Application Design* and the typical code we see coded to it. It *says* to me therefore, very little (nothing in fact) about the window object and its relationships to other instantiations of a class, or other related (by class) windows or indeed anything about those windows related by parent (or more properly -root). It says nothing about operating system or system considerations , whether or not re-entrancy or recursion for example is desirable, is a problem, or for that matter, can even occur. It says nothing about inter-task communication (ITC, or IPC for inter process communication if you prefer), efficiency or optimisation. It says nothing about portability, memory model, modularity or granularity. It does nothing to encourage data abstraction or to promote extensibility or code re-use explicitly. In short, as a design, and role model, it says and does very little of which we can be proud. We certainly oughtn't, without question, emulate it, simply because, like the old adage says, it happens to be there!

Perhaps I'm being a little harsh on the poor old design, and am putting too much of a burden on it. I should perhaps be swayed towards reading the documentation and code itself if I believed that I might find an explanation there, but I can't usually.

Most programmers, it seems, pay very little attention to design these days, they simply start with the coding and WinMain() and address design issues as and when they get in the way or cramp someone's style! They usually manifest themselves in terms I've heard described many times as this environment makes it difficult to program an easy solution and the like. I'm not saying that there aren't difficult to program for environments, not at all, I've worked in some myself over the years. No, I'm saying study the paradigm to which you are forced to code in the greatest detail before, and as you code your application, and <u>do</u> the design up front (the sooner you start to code the longer the app will take to complete).

☐ Object based design begins here

> Apology:
>
> When I first finished this chapter I re-read it (as you do); then I read it to some of my colleagues (as you may do); they read it to some friends (as you don't normally do at all), my colleagues and their friends called me up and said 'What?!'. On advice I then chopped and changed some of the definitions used in this section as apparently no-one exposed to it in its original form could follow it at one sitting (some of these are OOP (object

> oriented people!) and have been for years!). One of my colleagues gave me a quote which I'll use here but not before I say that I've hopefully made this section much more readable today, and to say that if you have trouble understanding <u>objectism</u> to read a book dedicated to the subject without delay (the 'C'7 introduction to C++ (which also includes an introduction to Object Oriented Design) is a good place to start). The quote is very apt – not in terms of my annotation (I hope?), but in terms of the ideas put forward in these following definitions; when you're reading this stuff remember one important piece of information there's nothing <u>really</u> new here, Oh yes, the quote –
> **'Any simple idea will be worded in the most complicated way and repeated** *n* **times. Minor changes will of course be made during each iteration'!** Anon.

Windows is a thoroughly object oriented GUI, and it should be reasonably clear by now that Windows' programs should also be explicitly object oriented, if for no other reason then simply to *fit in* with the way the system works. OK, so where do we start with objects? Again, with design.

☐ Terms before use

To fully appreciate a good object oriented design we must first become conversant with some of the popular object oriented terms and their definitions and relate these where appropriate to Windows – we'll start by doing just that.

Where there are differences between some common OO (object oriented) terms and definitions within programming languages or designs I have chosen to adopt the definition and term used in C++ as I believe that this language will become the accepted OO language for now and for the foreseeable future. To fully understand this language see The Annotated C++ Reference Manual by Stroustrup and Ellis, published by Addison Wesley and Programming in C++ by Dewhurst and Stark, published by Prentice Hall. I should also say a big thank you to the Smalltalk language (and its derivatives). Smalltalk was developed by the SCG (Software Concepts Group) at Xerox PARC (where else), and was influenced by the Simula language as was C++; *object orientation* as I see it therefore, owes everything to the designers and developers of these languages and environments.

☐ What is object oriented programming?

Using stepwise refinement is a good (as any) way of defining object oriented programming. Therefore – object oriented programming is programming implemented by passing messages to objects. Problem solving in an OOP (object oriented programming) way therefore involves learning about – objects and messages. To fully support objects and message passing, a language should support the following -abstraction, encapsulation, class definition and instancing (object definition and creation); message passing, inheritance and polymorphism. Now all we need to do in order to better understand the model is to define those terms.

☐ Class

Really the abstract definition of a type. A lot of C++ bods say that a C++ class (an object definition) is not directly comparable to a Windows' class – I disagree in the main as a Windows' class defines an true object (or data type) just as much as a C−+ one does.

A true data type, or <u>class</u>, implies more than the term *data type*, which is the common imprecise way to name a type in C, implies. Kernighan and Ritchie fully understand this and state in their book (either edition) that – <u>It must be emphasised that a typedef declaration does not create a new type in any sense; it merely adds a new name for some existing type</u>. *Type* should imply not only a data structure but also a set of allowable operations on that data structure. The *data* part I'll call state to differentiate between it and ordinary data, while the operations or functions that may modify the *state* I'll call methods, again to keep a method from becoming an ordinary function definition. The ability to bind both state and method in this way is called encapsulation, i.e. state and method are tightly coupled or encapsulated in a definition of a true type. The ideal of encapsulation is very closely related to the concept of an object. An object can be thought of as being an instance of a class, which in turn defines a type as described above.

For example, in 'C' we often call, or think of, a typedef as a new type, after all the term used implies *define a new type* –

```
typedef struct
{
    unsigned  long    int    lDayMonthYear;
    unsigned  short   int    nHours;
    unsigned  short   int    nMins;
    unsigned  short   int    nSecs;
}DATE;
```

This typedef defines a data structure of *pseudo type* DATE. It does <u>not</u> truly define a DATE type however because, as has been previously stated, a true type defines not only a data structure but the operations permitted on that data structure (it might be argued that the operations allowed are the same as for the individual members. This is true by and large when individual members are accessed only). *struct* notation is a convenient way to alias a group of intrinsic types, and the operations allowed on them (which are the same on a per member basis as they are of course for the intrinsic type), under another name and absolutely nothing more.

In case the difference is still not clear, consider the following illegal use of three DATE objects (as typedef'd above) in 'C'.

```
auto DATE a,b,c;

a.lDayMonthYear=0L;
a.nHours=12;
a.Mins=45;
a.nSecs = 10;

a.LdayMonthYear=0L;
a.nHours=1;
a.Mins=10;
b.nSeconds = 20;


/*
** add the two objects together to total
** their seconds, put result in c.
*/

c = a + b;    /* illegal operation on fake 'type' */
```

Here I'm trying to add two times (in the shape of two DATES) together and of course 'C' has no way to know just what that means (I've no way in 'C' to specify what + means when it's applied to two DATEs). I've defined a conveniently named holding area of DATA for each DATE object (the sizeof(DATE)), but I haven't said what can be done with one or more DATEs in terms of their processing. In C, I can take the address of a struct, pass it by value to a function, and do structure assignment, i.e. assign a to b for example; but I cannot add two DATEs together. To do this in 'C' I'd have to assign individual members –

```
c.nSecs = a.nSecs + b.nSecs;
```

In 'C' you'd probably hide this assignment by providing a function that does it –

```
int nAddDates(DATE d1,DATE d2)
{
    return d1.nSecs + d2.nSecs;
}
```

The name of the function *nAddDates* helps considerably with its meaning within a block of code but I'm sure you'll agree that it isn't as clear as c = a + b;. In fact the function above doesn't add two dates, it simply adds seconds (and doesn't adjust minutes etc as may be required if this were a *real* example) -it's too easy to be misleading here.

An object oriented language like C++ or Smalltalk however would allow us to define a true DATE type that would permit the addition of two objects (and the initialisation of a third using the result of the addition) of type DATE as shown above (or indeed, anything else we'd like to do with a DATE or two, or three ...).

So a class is usually an abstract paradigm of data (state) plus some operations (methods) to process or change that state.

This is just like a *real* integral 'C' type like a *char* for example. A *char* defines an amount of data, usually 8 bits, and a set of mathematical operations that are allowed to modify that data item. The mathematical operations are carried out on the char type by binding an instance of a char type to one or more allowable operators.

```
static char x,y,z;

x='A';
y='B';

z=x+y; /* no problem, '+' allowed on 'char' */

or

char a='Y';

a++;   /* send a '++' message to the char type and bind it to */
       /* instance 'a' -or if you prefer -invoke the '++'      */
       /* method of the char type and bind it to instance 'a'  */
```

By the way I'm not in favour of using the pure mathematical operators on a char object (except where it really makes sense like printing out a character set etc).

A Windows' class is something not too unlike this example of an abstract data type. It's an abstract data structure that combines both *data* members (state) and the operations (methods) to modify that state. The methods are defined in the class's window procedure as is most of the data usually. We'll see a better way to define a window's data soon. Messages are passed to the object's class wndproc and when this wndproc is called, it's bound in the context of the call to an instance of a class (visually, a window – internally, just some instance data), if you're used to C++ or Smalltalk, you might like to think of a window's handle as either *this* or *self*. Using the text above (in the comments and modifying it slightly) we can pass a *PAINT* message to the window type (class) and bind it to instance x (any window of that class). Of course a class, just like our abstract type *int*, doesn't exist in any real sense until we create, or derive, a window from it by using say CreateWindow(). This leads us into what an *object* is.

☐ Object

An object may be thought of as an instance of a class. This is analogous to *int* being a class, and *int x*, where x names an instance of an int, being an object of type int. x can be passed any *int* type message (like + add for example) therefore, x identifies not only an area of memory but also, implicitly, a set of allowable operations on that area of memory. It would be nice to create a window in Windows with a similar construct would it not –

WINDOW w;

int identifies a type of integer whilst WINDOW of course is too ambiguous for our use, a window is not as primitive as an int. ints can be initialised thus – int x = 10; and so can our window. For example, we could tell the window where it will be on the desktop via some initialisation data. However our window is a far more complex beast than an int and has many more *properties* to be considered when it's initialised than an int does.

Because 'C' doesn't support an intrinsic *WINDOW type*, we can't use the statement above (we could perhaps use a struct typedef'd and an initialiser list), so we use a function call to the Windows' API instead, which does know how to instanciate a WINDOW type object – CreateWindow() is used in other words. The parameters to the function can be thought of as a set on construction information. This is very much like creating an instance of a C++ object which has an appropriate constructor.

Of course, we know that for now we *instanciate* a window with CreateWindow() typically and that we *say* what type of window we'd like (and the operations permitted on it) by specifying a set of identifying parameters in the CreateWindow() call, in particular we pass to the API the classname, or type, of the object we wish to create. In this way, using CreateWindow() to create a variety of objects, we're using CreateWindow() as a kind of generic object allocator – much like we'd use the *new* operator in C++, ie. one method can be used to create any number of different objects, the object name, just like in C++, is given by passing CreateWindow() a classname, ie. we're saying – 'Hey instanciate an object of type ????? for me' whenever we use it.

Of course, the class has already defined some characteristics of any instance of itself, like its class style attribute, its class menu and its class cursor etc. (This data is shared by all instances of the class and in this way is analogous to a static member of a C++ class, or a class variable in Smalltalk). We'll see that this is more of a convenience than a must and that most of this may be specified, or overridden in the instanciation of the class, or window, instead. Of course, another facet of an object is that you may have, on the face of it, any number of them. You can instanciate an int after all as much as you like, just as long as you have enough unique identifiers to use, so why not a Windows' class? Each instanciation of an int is an *int* type, each instanciation of a window is a *lpszClassname* type. Each instanciation of an int uses the same internal micro-code when say 1 is added to it; windows belonging to the same class also share common micro-code in this way. The code in question is, of course, the code contained within a wndproc that defines the way a window responds to any given message. In conventional languages, objects are created implicitly as well as explicitly as shown above. Consider the following 'C' statement where x is of type integer: x = 2 + 3; This code may create an anonymous object of type integer which holds the value 5 (2 + 3), the value in this nameless object is then applied to the object called x. The anonymous object lives for the expression, or if you like dies when the statement terminator (;) is crossed. In C++ this can be a problem as programmer defined objects get created automatically on the fly like this. Here Windows differs. In Windows, no significant window can be implicitly created like this (not unless you use a call to CreateWindow() as part of the general evaluation of an expression – which of course we don't!). The closest we get to anonymous objects in Windows' programming probably occurs when we create a dialog box which contains implicitly anonymous objects (like static controls), ie. anonymous objects are created as a side effect of, say, calling DialogBox(). We could also say, that since DialogBox() doesn't return before these objects are destroyed, that they exist just until the statement separator is reached – Windows that exist during expression evaluation!?

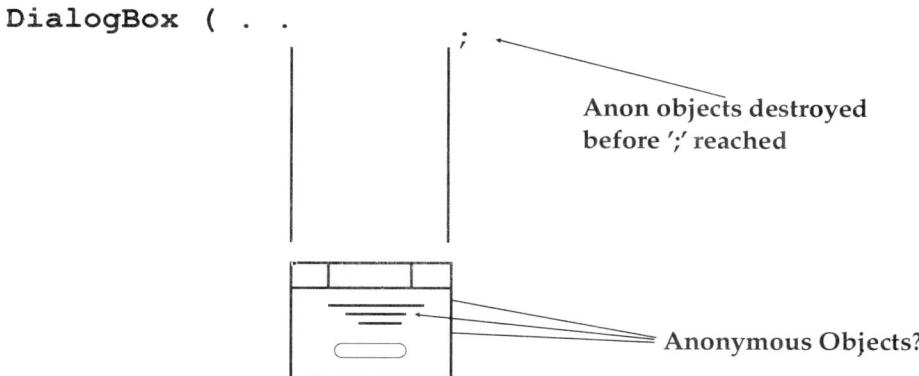

DialogBox (. .

Anon objects destroyed before ';' reached

Anonymous Objects?

Message

Messages usually cause, for an instance or object, a change in the state or behaviour of the object processing the message. For example, in the paragraph above, I talked about adding one to an int; we'd describe this in terms of objectism by saying that an instance of an int was passed a + (add message (binary message)) message and a parameter of 1, or another object of type int (the amount to be added to the instance receiving the message). The + message causes the + method to be executed which will have the effect of adding one to the integer. A message is the mechanism that forces an object to do some work then. In Windows, a message passed to a window, or class wndproc, or instance, usually causes some work to be carried out for the instance (methods do not necessarily need to be bound to an instance – I'll explain this later). For example, we can ask a window to repaint itself by passing it a WM_PAINT message. The window will respond to this message by repainting its client area. In terms of Windows then, we can think of a message as a function call to the class wndproc. That call will be bound in context to an instance of the class (or a window). Evaluating the message by way of a message identifier means executing a method of the object.

☐ Polymorphism late binding

1. Polymorphism – *'Exhibiting polymorphic or polymorphous behaviour.'*
   Polymorphic – *'Having many varieties. Multiform. Assuming many forms.'*

2. Late Bound –*'Not known at present time. Decided later.'*

From 1 above – Each form may be thought of as a variant of some, or a *kinda* (*kind of*) basic form. Aircraft are polymorphous. They appear in a variety of guises, (helicopters, stealth bombers, Concord) but all are essentially aircraft.

From 2 above – A pointer to a function which will point to say an interrupt handler is said to be late bound if it is set to point at the interrupt handler at run time and not at compile time. We don't know what will happen when we call the routine to which the pointer points until it points somewhere! At compile time, we couldn't say whether or not it points to a valid address as it's only set later, at run time.

We've just noted that some aspects of our class are known at compile time, like its cursor etc. This is an example of an early bound property of the class (the property is known (its name at least) at compile time). As we bind the rest of a class definition with a wndproc, the wndproc may be thought of as early bound also. You'll remember that a wndproc is a message handler and that messages are handled by methods. We can therefore say that the methods required to handle the set of messages handled by a given class are also early bound to our instance. All of our window's behaviour, therefore, is known at compile time.

If our class window procedure is caused to modify this default behaviour at run-time, this is called a late bound property of the class (not known at compile time). For example – if we can change the method executed when a particular message is passed to our window, then that method is said to be late bound (not known at compile time) and the message is said to be polymorphic.

Late binding is an aid to inheritance and to the issues of sub-classing and super-classing which are all coming up so I'll come back to this soon. For now, think of late binding as a way for an object, or instance of a class, to respond in a different way to say another instance of the same class, if at run-time, some means was found to alter or modify some of the class methods, of a given instantiation or window. (In Windows, this can be done both for an individual window (instantiation of the class) or indeed, for the class as a whole).

In all cases, the object to which a message is passed is treated as an early bound object (in the context of the message being passed to it. In other words, the message passer always assumes that the object's response to the message will be to invoke the early bound message handling method specified in the class definition). The class of the object being sent the message will appear somewhere in the hierarchy of classes from which the window is derived (this need not be at the same actual level (equivalent) from which the window has been derived), the object responds to the message in a polymorphic way, which means, in terms of its *actual* type (the class from which it is actually derived) which is, as just stated, not necessarily in the context of the class to which the message was passed.

This means that such a system may be extended by deriving a new class from an old. The new class (when made object) exhibits new or different behaviour from the old (this type of object is sometimes called a *kinda*). The code passing messages to this new object however may remain ignorant of the new type. Messages may be passed to the new type in the context of the old type. The new type responds as a new type thing, and not as an old type thing.

Another classical (but long) way of describing this feature is to state that –

If an instanciation can change its behaviour, and will therefore act slightly differently from another instanciation of the same class, given the right impetus, and if we were to ask each instanciation to respond to a class message, and that if each instanciation were to respond to the message correctly (in terms of its own identity), that the message handling is late bound or polymorphic in the class and is handled not in the context of the class but in the context of the type of the instance.

☐ Inheritance

The ability to modify the functionality of a class (and therefore an instance of it). Inheritance works two ways, up, or down.

An upwards inheritance mechanism is called a sub-classing mechanism. A sub class is said to be derived from a super class and changes the state or functionality of any instanciations of itself only (this is called a *derived class* in the ANSI C++ X3J16 base document). A downwards inheritance mechanism is called a super-classing mechanism. A *super class* change changes the functionality of all instanciations of the class being derived from the class (this is called a base class in the ANSI C++ X3J16 base document). Another way to think of this is to traverse the hierarchy a step downwards then to apply a sub-class. Windows uses the same term – *subclass* in both cases. I stated earlier that the *class* doesn't exist in any real sense; it might be helpful here to say that just like in C++ and Smalltalk, it is possible to communicate with the abstract class, and for the class to access private data without there being an instance of the class (a window) present.

Windows' applications can super, or sub-class any existing class or window. This isn't done the same as for most OO languages (thinking of Windows code in terms of a language). For example, in C++ it is not possible to subclass an object directly; only a class may be sub-classed. It is therefore not possible to change the behaviour of existing objects in C++ by using a pure sub-classing mechanism. The same is true of Smalltalk. To subclass means to derive a new class (subclass) from an existing super-class. The changes are only evident when the new class is instanciated in the form of an object. This *new* object will usually then exhibit some modified behaviour.

> Note: It is possible to achieve a sub-classed state in both languages by changing the type of an object (objects capable of doing this are called *self metamorphic*). In C++ this would be done correctly with the aid of a cast whilst in Smalltalk it would be done by providing a class method to coerce the instance into some other type.

Inheritance is useful as an extensibility or inheritance tool primarily. For example, say we have a class that when instanciated produces an edit field. Say we'd like the facilities of an edit field in some new class, its ability to use the clipboard etc, but want our new class to permit numeric entry only. Well there's not such a class (numeric entry) in Windows but there is a general purpose edit field available that will allow any input. Do we have to write our own specialised edit class then, when all we want is to change in a minor way the functionality of a standard class? The answer is no. We sub-class either the class (sub-class), or an instanciation (a window) of the class (change the type – self metamorphorsize) and add (you may prefer *remove* here) functionality and in so doing, re-use all that standard class's code and ability etc. Sub-classing doesn't necessarily define a new class, whereas super-classing usually does.

☐ Data abstraction

This is an easy one you're probably pleased to hear!

In true objectism it's usual that only a method of an object can modify an object's state. The data is abstracted away from outside influence if you like. More rarely, but just as valid, is the idea of *hiding* away some of an object's methods, making them only available to other methods in the class. Both these properties limit the ability of an programmer to arbitrary tinker with an object's implementation detail, or put another way, to prevent that programmer's code from becoming dependant upon it (remember that traditionally one of your constants might be someone else's variable – hide it!). Class data, whether it be instance, ie. window, or real, ie. class words (or in C++ -static class data) can normally only be modified by messages passed by the event dispatcher to a window instance; these messages, which map to class methods, may be either external, ie. they are sent by the system or some other window object with internal knowledge of our window (a kinda friend window maybe), or by the object itself, ie. the object causes a method (message handler) to get hit by passing itself a message. If this message is a *private* message the message is analogous to calling a private method of the object (and indeed could be alternatively implemented as a private function rather than as a message handler). This means that should the designer and implementor of a class change, say, the internals (either state or method) of a class, that there is a reduced, or even zero possibility that those changes will affect the client code that instanciates and uses the class. Data abstraction is a great development tool. The classic example of this is in creating and using a stack.

☐ The stack is to general abstraction as factor finding is to recursion

Let's say that we want to build an operating system, shouldn't take long! One of the first data structures we'll need is probably a stack. Now, wouldn't it be nice if we could simply, as the designers and implementors of the stack, allow our users, those members of the teams building other parts of the operating system, access to any number of stacks via, say, a couple of methods called *push* and *pop*. We could then implement our stack very quickly using say an array of integers or *words* for the moment. Of course an array probably isn't good enough for our needs (over doing things is harmful in all cases, even when it comes to efficiency) and at some later date we'll of course want to rework our stack so that it's truly dynamic by, say, using a doubly linked list of word bearing structures allocated as needed by the stack or by some other such means. Of course, we'd hate to find that once we'd done this work, we'd broken everybody's code! We'd of course examine just how this sorry state of affairs could have come about and would of course find that nearly everyone, instead of using *push* and *pop*, accessed our array of words directly in order to save the function call overhead incurred going through the procedural interface to the stack! After all, we can't really prevent them from doing this with a conventional program-ming language such as C, or at least – not very easily.

If 'C' supported pure data abstraction, as C++ does, we could have hidden the implementation from our users and guaranteed that if and when we changed the implementation, we'd not have broken our Users' code in the process of doing so. Don't forget that data abstraction implies method abstraction. We could have hidden to all but other methods of the stack class, a method which say yielded the address of the first free element of the stack, or perhaps a method giving access to the stack pointer.

It's easy to provide this level of abstraction in Windows' programming, if only we try.

We could even imagine creating a *stack* window whose job it is to store and retrieve stack data, ie. data items owned by the stack window (as they're said to be on the stack). The window could be created, say, from the *stack* class. Any stack object derived from it, ie. a window created from the stack class, would, according to the stack class definition, export or make visible some stack type methods (message handlers) called, say, WM_PUSH, WM_POP etc. These public interface methods would use message parameters to actually transport data to and from the stack object window, ie. the actual data being pushed etc would be passed via wParam say. The stack might use internal methods (WM_USER type messages) to manage its internal state and of course would store stack data in some non-disclosed class defined way.

Anyone wanting to use a stack simply instanciates a window of class stack and sends/post WM_PUSH and WM_POP messages to it to get it to do some useful work. Should the implementor at some time change the way that a stack object internally stores data they may do so without causing any client code (apps using the stack) to be modified, ie. the stacks external or exported public interface methods remain the same.

We could even, up front, consider making any stack object a stack based container class rather than a pure stack (where every object stored is the same size), ie. why not have the stack store anything in a *first in last out* way. We could perhaps have stated that a WM_PUSH message's lParam point to the data to be stored and that its wParam should specify the actual size of the data pointed to by lParam. When someone pops something we could set the message's lParam to point to the data (the stack object will have allocated the space for the object) and set wParam to the objects size?

We could go further, why not create two classes – one's a container type class, the other's a sub-class of it, ie. it is a kinda container, called a stack object!?

Here's a question – Would you expect a stack window to show itself or should it remain hidden? Well there's no definitive answer; it's up to the designer. However I'd argue that at sometime it would be handy to have a stack window show itself – it could even provide its user with dialog boxes and menus. Think how useful it would be to see a stack, no more guessing what was on it, what's the next thing to come off it etc – Wow what a debugging aid!

Let's take a rest and look at some code. Here's the re-written shell talked about earlier – maybe I should have written a container and stack instead – Ho hum.

The shell consists of a number of files :

d	Debug file.
about.dlg	About box definition.
pragma.h	Pragmas used in application.
proto.h	Function prototypes.
wshl.h	Main header file.
def.h	Windows' defines (removes WINDOWS.H).
wshldef.h	WSHL.C header to include parts of WINDOWS.H.
miscdef.h	MISC.C header to include parts of WINDOWS.H.
dlgdef.h	DIALOG.C header to include parts of WINDOWS.H.
initdef.h	INIT.C header to include parts of WINDOWS.H.
wshl.c	Main source file and 'app' routines.
misc.c	Misc routines.
dialog.c	Dialog box routines.
init.c	Initialisaton routines.
makefile	Makefile.
wshl.ico	Application Icon file.
wshl.rc	Resource script.
wshl.def	Module definition file.

The 'Shell' Files.

Wshl.c :

```
/*H***********************************************************
*
* Main source file for WSHL. Contains WINMAIN, main wndproc handler,
* message loop, and event handlers for main wndproc.
*
*H*/


#include "pragma.h"        /* These headers need to */
#include "def.h"           /* be   included   before */
#include "wshldef.h"       /* WINDOWS.H.          */

#include <windows.h>
#include <stdio.h>
#include <string.h>

#include "wshl.h"
#include "proto.h"


PRIVATE HACCEL hAccel;     /* File scope (PRIVATE) accelerator handle. */

/*F*
**
**  FUNCTION:    lAboutCommandHandler
**
**  DESCRIPTION: Handles IDM_ABOUT WM_COMMAND message.
**
**  PASSED:      HWND       -Window handle of window      -hWnd
**               UINT       -Message                      -uMessage
**               WPARAM     -Message wParam               -wParam -IDM_ABOUT
**               LPARAM     -Message lParam               -lParam
**
**  RETURNS:     LRESULT    -Indication of whether or not message was handled.
**
*F*/
LRESULT NP lABOUTCommandHandler
(
  HWND     hWnd
 ,UINT     uMessage
 ,WPARAM   wParam
 ,LPARAM   lParam
)
{
  auto  FARPROC    lpprocBDIALOGPROC;
  auto  HINSTANCE  hInst;
  auto  PSTR       pcDialogName;
  auto  BOOL       bErrOccurred    = FALSE;

  bErrOccurred = FALSE;


  hInst = HINSTFROMHWND(hWnd);

  pcDialogName = pcGetString(IDS_TEMPLATE, hInst);

  if(pcDialogName != 0)
  {
      lpprocBDIALOGPROC = MakeProcInstance((FARPROC)BDIALOGPROC, hInst);
```

```
        if(lpprocBDIALOGPROC != 0)
        {
            if(DialogBox(
                        hInst
                        ,pcDialogName
                        ,hWnd
                        , (DLGPROC)lpprocBDIALOGPROC
                        ) == -1
                )
            {
                bErrOccurred = TRUE;
            }
            (VOID)FreeProcInstance(lpprocBDIALOGPROC);
        }

        if(bReleaseString(pcDialogName) == FALSE)
        {
            vReportError(hWnd,IDS_ERR_RELEASESTRING, hInst);
        }
    }
    else  /* Couldn't load string. */
    {
        bErrOccurred = TRUE;
    }

    if(bErrOccurred == TRUE)
    {
        vReportError(hWnd,IDS_ERR_DIALOG, hInst);
    }

    return W_HANDLED;
}




/*F*
**
**   FUNCTION:     lCommandHandler
**
**   DESCRIPTION: Handles a WM_COMMAND message for a window.
**
**   PASSED:       HWND      -Window handle of window      -hWnd
**                 UINT      -Message                      -uMessage
**                 WPARAM    -Message wParam               -wParam
**                 LPARAM    -Message lParam               -lParam
**
**   RETURNS:      LRESULT   -Indication of whether or not message was handled.
**
*F*/
LRESULT NP lCommandHandler
(
  HWND     hWnd
 ,UINT     uMessage
 ,WPARAM   wParam
 ,LPARAM   lParam
)
{
  auto  LRESULT   lResult;
```

```
    switch(wParam)
    {
        case IDM_ABOUT:
            lResult = lABOUTCommandHandler(hWnd, uMessage, wParam, lParam);
            break;

        default:
            break;
    }


    return lResult;
}




/*F*
**
**   FUNCTION:     lCreateHandler
**
**   DESCRIPTION: Handles a WM_CREATE message for a window.
**
**   PASSED:      HWND       -Windows handle of window       -hWnd
**                UINT       -Message                        -uMessage
**                WPARAM     -Message wParam                 -wParam
**                LPARAM     -Message lParam                 -lParam
**
**   RETURNS:     LRESULT    -Indication of whether or not message was handled.
**
*F*/
LRESULT NP lCreateHandler
(
  HWND      hWnd
 ,UINT      uMessage
 ,WPARAM    wParam
 ,LPARAM    lParam
)
{
    auto int        nCmdShow;
    auto PSTR       pcAccelName;
    auto HINSTANCE  hInst;

    nCmdShow = *((int FAR *) (((LPCREATESTRUCT)lParam) -> lpCreateParams));

    hInst = HINSTFROMHWND(hWnd);

    /* Load accelerator table. */

    if((pcAccelName = pcGetString(IDS_ACCELNAME, hInst)) != NULL)
    {
        if((hAccel = LoadAccelerators(hInst ,pcAccelName)) == NULL)
        {
            vReportError(0, IDS_ERR_ACCELERATORS, hInst);
        }

        if(bReleaseString(pcAccelName) != TRUE)
        {
            vReportError(0, IDS_ERR_RELEASESTRING, hInst);
        }
    }
```

```
   else
   {
       vReportError(0, IDS_ERR_LOADSTRING, hInst);
   }

   (VOID)ShowWindow(hWnd,nCmdShow);
   (VOID)UpdateWindow(hWnd);

   /* Return -1 if accelerator table could not be loaded. */

   return hAccel ? W_HANDLED : (LRESULT)-1;
}




/*F*
**
**   FUNCTION:    lDefaultHandler
**
**   DESCRIPTION: Handles all messages for a window not handled by other
**                handlers.
**
**   PASSED:      HWND      -Windows handle of window      -hWnd
**                UINT      -Message                       -uMessage
**                WPARAM    -Message wParam                -wParam
**                LPARAM    -Message lParam                -lParam
**
**   RETURNS:     LRESULT   -Indication of whether or not message was handled.
**
*F*/
LRESULT NP lDefaultHandler
(
   HWND      hWnd
  ,UINT      uMessage
  ,WPARAM    wParam
  ,LPARAM    lParam
)
{
   return DefWindowProc(hWnd,uMessage,wParam,lParam);
}




/*F*
**
**   FUNCTION:    lDestroyHandler
**
**   DESCRIPTION: Handles a WM_DESTROY message for a window.
**
**   PASSED:      HWND      -Windows handle of window      -hWnd
**                UINT      -Message                       -uMessage
**                WPARAM    -Message wParam                -wParam
**                LPARAM    -Message lParam                -lParam
**
**   RETURNS:     LRESULT   -Indication of whether or not message was handled.
**
```

```
*F*/
LRESULT NP  lDestroyHandler
(
    HWND     hWnd
   ,UINT     uMessage
   ,WPARAM   wParam
   ,LPARAM   lParam
)
{
    (VOID)PostQuitMessage(0);

    return W_HANDLED;
}


/*F*
**
**   FUNCTION:     LMAINWNDPROC
**
**   DESCRIPTION:  Handles all messages for a window.
**
**   PASSED:       HWND       -Windows handle of window     -hWnd
**                 UINT       -Message                      -uMessage
**                 WPARAM     -Message wParam               -wParam
**                 LPARAM     -Message lParam               -lParam
**
**   RETURNS:      LRESULT    -Indication of whether or not message was handled.
**
*F*/
LRESULT  __export CALLBACK LMAINWNDPROC
(
    HWND     hWnd
   ,UINT     uMessage
   ,WPARAM   wParam
   ,LPARAM   lParam
)
{
    auto LRESULT    lResult;

    switch(uMessage)
    {
        case WM_COMMAND:
            lResult = lCommandHandler(hWnd,uMessage,wParam,lParam);
            break;

        case WM_CREATE:
            lResult = lCreateHandler(hWnd,uMessage,wParam,lParam);
            break;

        case WM_DESTROY:
            lResult = lDestroyHandler(hWnd,uMessage,wParam,lParam);
            break;

        default:
            lResult = lDefaultHandler(hWnd,uMessage,wParam,lParam);
            break;
    }

    return lResult;
}
```

```
/*F*
**
**   FUNCTION:    nExecInst
**
**   DESCRIPTION: Message poller for application.
**
**   PASSED:      VOID
**
**   RETURNS:     int  -parameter passed to PostQuitMessage().
**
*F*/
int NP nExecInst(VOID)
{
   auto  MSG   msg;

   while(GetMessage(&msg, (HWND)NULL, 0, 0))
   {
       if(!TranslateAccelerator(msg.hwnd, hAccel, &msg))
       {
           (VOID)TranslateMessage(&msg);
           (VOID)DispatchMessage(&msg);
       }
   }

   return msg.wParam;
}




/*F*
**
**   FUNCTION:    WINMAIN
**
**   DESCRIPTION: Application entry point.
**
**   PASSED:      HINSTANCE  -Instance handle for this instance      -hInst
**                HINSTANCE  -Instance handle for previous instance -hPrevInst
**                LPSTR      -Command line args if any               -lpszCmdLine
**                int        -How the window should be shown         -nCmdShow
**
**   RETURNS:     int        -Parameter passed to PostQuitMessage if app
**                            starts OK else 0.
*F*/

int PASCAL WINMAIN
(
   HINSTANCE     hInst
  ,HINSTANCE     hPrevInst
  ,LPSTR         lpszCmdLine
  ,int           nCmdShow
)
{
   return bInit(hInst,hPrevInst,lpszCmdLine,nCmdShow) ? nExecInst() : 0;
}

/****************************************************************************
*******************************************EOF******************************
```

Init.c :

```c
/*H********************************************************************
*
* This source file is used to initialise the app and the instance.
*
*H*/


#include "pragma.h"        /* These headers need to */
#include "def.h"           /* be  included    before */
#include "initdef.h"       /* WINDOWS.H.            */

#include<windows.h>

#include<string.h>         /* For memset. */

#include"wshl.h"
#include"proto.h"




/*F*
**
**    FUNCTION:    bInit
**
**    DESCRIPTION: Causes appropriate initialisation to be carried out for
the
**                 task depending on the value of hPrevInst.
**
**    PASSED:      HINSTANCE -Our instance handle                -hInst.
**                 HINSTANCE -Our previous instance's handle     -hPrevInst.
**                 LPSTR     -Command line arguments             -lpszCmdLine.
**                 int       -How the first/main window is shown -wCmdShow.
**
**    RETURNS:     BOOL      -Indication of success.             -bResult.
**
*F*/
BOOL FP bInit
(
  HINSTANCE     hInst
 ,HINSTANCE     hPrevInst
 ,LPSTR         lpszCmdLine
 ,int           nCmdShow
)
{
   auto BOOL bResult = TRUE;  /* Overall result of function. Set to TRUE. */

   /****************************************************************
    *
    * If no previous instance then initialise application then, if the
    * application was initialised -initialise the instance, else just
    * initialise the instance. Note that testing hPrevInst will not be
    * sufficient in  the  future -FindWindow() using  a class name is
    * recommended.
    *
    */
```

```
   switch((UINT)hPrevInst)
   {
       case NO_PREVIOUS_INSTANCE:
           bResult = bInitApp(hInst);
           break;

       default:
           break;
   }

   return bResult ?  bResult = bInitInst(hInst,nCmdShow) : FALSE;
}




/*F*
**
**  FUNCTION:    bInitApp
**
**  DESCRIPTION: Initialises the application by registering a new class.
**
**  PASSED:      HINSTANCE -Our instance handle    -hInst.
**
**  RETURNS:     BOOL       -Indication of success. -bResult.
**
*F*/
BOOL NP bInitApp(HINSTANCE hInst)
{
   auto  WNDCLASS wcClass;
   auto  BOOL     bResult              = FALSE;
   auto  PSTR     pcClassName;

   /*
   ** First retrieve class name from string table.
   */

   if((pcClassName = pcGetString(IDS_SHELLCLASS, hInst)) != 0)
   {
       auto char cClassName[STRINGTAB];

       lstrcpyn(cClassName, pcClassName ,lstrlen(pcClassName) + 1);

       if(bReleaseString(pcClassName) == TRUE)
       {
          memset(&wcClass, 0x0, sizeof(WNDCLASS));

          wcClass.style          = CS_HREDRAW | CS_VREDRAW;
          wcClass.lpfnWndProc     = (WNDPROC)LMAINWNDPROC;
          wcClass.hInstance       = hInst;
          wcClass.hIcon           = LoadIcon(
                                            hInst
                                            ,MAKEINTRESOURCE(IDI_SHELLICON)
                                            );
          wcClass.hCursor         = LoadCursor(
                                               (HINSTANCE)NULL
                                               ,IDC_ARROW
                                               );
          wcClass.hbrBackground   = (HBRUSH)USER_COLOR;
```

```
                wcClass.lpszMenuName     = MAKEINTRESOURCE(IDM_SHELLMENU);
                wcClass.lpszClassName    = &cClassName[0];

                bResult = (BOOL)RegisterClass(&wcClass);
            }
        }
    else /* Couldn't load the classname string! */
    {
        vReportError(0, IDS_ERR_LOADSTRING, hInst);
    }

    return !!bResult; /* Make sure that a 1 or 0 is returned. */
}


/*F*
**
**  FUNCTION:    bInitInst
**
**  DESCRIPTION: Initialises this task or instance by creating our
**               main window.
**
**  PASSED:      HINSTANCE -Our instance handle              -hInst.
**               int       -How our main window should be shown -nCmdShow
**
**  RETURNS:     BOOL      -Indication of success            -bResult.
**
*F*/
BOOL NP bInitInst(HINSTANCE hInst, int nCmdShow)
{
    auto PSTR pcClassName;              /* The name of our window class. */
    auto PSTR pcCaption;               /* The caption for the window.   */
    auto BOOL bResult     = FALSE;     /* The overall function result.  */

    /*
    ** Retrieve the class and caption names.
    */

    if((pcClassName = pcGetString(IDS_SHELLCLASS,   hInst)) != 0 &&
       (pcCaption   = pcGetString(IDS_SHELLCAPTION, hInst)) != 0
      )
    {
        auto char cClassName[STRINGTAB];
        auto char cCaption[STRINGTAB];

        (VOID)lstrcpyn(cClassName, pcClassName ,lstrlen(pcClassName) + 1);
        (VOID)lstrcpyn(cCaption, pcCaption ,lstrlen(pcCaption) + 1);

        if(bReleaseString(pcClassName) == TRUE &&
           bReleaseString(pcCaption) == TRUE)
        {
            auto HWND hWnd;

            hWnd = CreateWindow(
                            cClassName           /* Class name.  */
                            ,cCaption            /* Caption.     */
                            ,WS_OVERLAPPEDWINDOW /* Styles used. */
                            ,CW_USEDEFAULT       /* Top X pos.   */
```

```
                                    ,0                      /* Top Y pos.  */
                                    ,CW_USEDEFAULT          /* Width.      */
                                    ,0                      /* Height.     */
                                    , (HWND)NULL            /* Owner.      */
                                    , (HMENU)NULL           /* Menu.       */
                                    ,hInst                  /* Inst handle. */
                                    , (LPSTR) (NPSTR) &nCmdShow /* How to show. */
                                    );

            bResult = !!hWnd;
        }
        else
        {
            vReportError(0, IDS_ERR_RELEASESTRING, hInst);
        }
    }
    else /* Didn't load string(s)? */
    {
        if(pcClassName != 0)
        {
            if(bReleaseString(pcClassName) == FALSE)
            {
                vReportError(0, IDS_ERR_RELEASESTRING, hInst);
            }
        }

        if(pcCaption != 0)
        {
            if(bReleaseString(pcCaption) == FALSE)
            {
                vReportError(0, IDS_ERR_RELEASESTRING, hInst);
            }
        }

        vReportError(0, IDS_ERR_LOADSTRING, hInst);
    }

    return !!bResult; /* Make sure that a 1 or 0 is returned. */
}


/*****************************************************************************
                                    EOF
*****************************************************************************/
```

Dialog.c :

```
/*H*************************************************************************
*
* This file contains functions to handle wshl's dialog box
*
*H*/



#include "pragma.h"        /* These headers need to */
#include "def.h"           /* be  included    before */
#include "dlgdef.h"        /* WINDOWS.H.            */
```

```
#include <windows.h>

#include "wshl.h"
#include "proto.h"




/*F*
**
**   FUNCTION:     bCommandHandler
**
**   DESCRIPTION: Handles a WM_COMMAND message for a dialog box.
**
**   PASSED:       HWND      -Window handle of dialog box  -hDlg
**                 UINT      -Message                      -uMessage
**                 WPARAM    -Message wParam               -wParam
**                 LPARAM    -Message lParam               -lParam
**
**   RETURNS:      BOOL      -Indication of whether or not message was handled.
**
*F*/
BOOL NP bCommandHandler
(
   HWND     hDlg
  ,UINT     uMessage
  ,WPARAM   wParam
  ,LPARAM   lParam
)
{
   /*
   ** As long as it's a button click -close down the dialog.
   */

   if(HIWORD((DWORD)lParam) == BN_CLICKED)
   {
      (VOID)EndDialog(hDlg,(int)wParam);
   }

   return D_HANDLED;
}




/*F*
**
**   FUNCTION:     bDefaultHandler
**
**   DESCRIPTION: Handles all messages for a dialog box not handled by other
**               handlers.
**
**   PASSED:       HWND      -Window handle of dialog box  -hDlg
**                 UINT      -Message                      -uMessage
**                 WPARAM    -Message wParam               -wParam
**                 LPARAM    -Message lParam               -lParam
**
```

```
**   RETURNS:       BOOL       -Indication of whether or not message was handled.
**
*F*/
BOOL NP bDefaultHandler
(
   HWND     hDlg
  ,UINT     uMessage
  ,WPARAM   wParam
  ,LPARAM   lParam
)
{
   return D_NOTHANDLED;
}




/*F*
**
**   FUNCTION:     bInitDialogHandler
**
**   DESCRIPTION: Handles a WM_INITDIALOG message for a dialog box.
**
**   PASSED:       HWND       -Window handle of dialog box   -hDlg
**                 UINT       -Message                       -uMessage
**                 WPARAM     -Message wParam                -wParam
**                 LPARAM     -Message lParam                -lParam
**
**   RETURNS:      BOOL       -Indication of whether or not message was handled.
**
*F*/
BOOL NP bInitDialogHandler
(
   HWND     hDlg
  ,UINT     uMessage
  ,WPARAM   wParam
  ,LPARAM   lParam
)
{
   return D_HANDLED;
}




/*F*
**
**   FUNCTION:     BDIALOGPROC
**
**   DESCRIPTION: Handles a dialog box.
**
**   PASSED:       HWND       -Window handle of dialog box   -hDlg
**                 UINT       -Message                       -uMessage
**                 WPARAM     -Message wParam                -wParam
**                 LPARAM     -Message lParam                -lParam
**
**   RETURNS:      BOOL       -Indication of whether or not message was handled.
**                                                          -bResult.
```

```
**
*F*/
BOOL __export CALLBACK BDIALOGPROC(HWND hDlg,UINT uMessage,WPARAM
wParam,LPARAM lParam)
{
    auto BOOL bResult;      /* Holds result of function. */

    /*
    ** Switch on message and call appropriate handler.
    ** bDefaultHandler used to service those messages
    ** in which we're not explicitly interested.
    */

    switch(uMessage)
    {
        case WM_INITDIALOG:
            bResult = bInitDialogHandler(hDlg,uMessage,wParam,lParam);
            break;

        case WM_COMMAND:
            bResult = bCommandHandler(hDlg,uMessage,wParam,lParam);
            break;

        default:
            bResult = bDefaultHandler(hDlg,uMessage,wParam,lParam);
            break;
    }

    return bResult;
}



/*************************************************************************
                                EOF
*************************************************************************/
```

Misc.c :

```
/*H*********************************************************************
*
* This file contains functions to load strings from a stringtable
* and report errors to the user.
*
*H*/


#include "pragma.h"          /* These headers need to */
#include "def.h"             /* be  included   before */
#include "miscdef.h"         /* WINDOWS.H.            */

#include <windows.h>

#include "wshl.h"
#include "proto.h"
```

```
/*F*
**
**  FUNCTION:    pcGetString
**
**  DESCRIPTION: Retrieves a string from a string table.
**
**  PASSED:      UINT      -The ID of the string to be retrieved -uString
**               HINSTANCE -Our instance handle                  -hInst
**
**  RETURNS:     PSTR -A pointer to the string if successful else a 0
pointer.
**
*F*/
PSTR FP pcGetString(UINT uStringID,HINSTANCE hInst)
{
   auto LOCALHANDLE hString  = 0;
   auto PSTR        pcString = NULL;

   /*
   ** Allocate memory of size max string size (STRINGTAB) and lock it.
   **
   */

   if((hString = LocalAlloc(LMEM_ZEROINIT, STRINGTAB)) != NULL &&
      (pcString = LocalLock(hString)) != NULL)
   {
      auto int nStringLen;

      /*
      ** Load the string specified by uStringID and keep length.
      ** If length  is 0 it failed.  If length is > 0 reallocate
      ** local  memory  large  enough  just  to  hold the string
      ** and its 0 terminator.
      */

      nStringLen = LoadString(hInst,uStringID,pcString,STRINGTAB);

      if(nStringLen != 0)
      {
          /* Now reallocate to smallest possible size. */

          hString = LocalReAlloc(hString,nStringLen,LMEM_ZEROINIT);
      }
      else

      /*
      ** Allocated and locked memory but couldn't load string,
      ** unlock and free memory.
      */

      {
         /************************************************************
          *
          * Makes sense to test in pairs like this because if unlock
          * fails we don't attempt a localfree -this is good as it
          * couldn't work!
          *
          */

         if(LocalUnlock(hString) != NULL || LocalFree(hString) != NULL)
```

```
              {
                    vReportError(0, IDS_ERR_FREEMEM, hInst);
              }
              pcString = NULL;        /* Set string pointer to NULL. */
        }
    }
    else                        /* Couldn't allocate or lock local memory. */
    {
        vReportError(0, IDS_ERR_ALLOCMEM, hInst);

        if(hString != NULL)     /* If we allocated we need to free. */
        {
            if(LocalFree(hString) != NULL)
            {
                vReportError(0, IDS_ERR_FREEMEM, hInst);
            }
        }
    }

    return pcString; /* Either a pointer to the load string or NULL. */
}



/*F*
**
**  FUNCTION:    bReleaseString
**
**  DESCRIPTION: Releases a string from locally allocated memory.
**
**  PASSED:      PSTR -A pointer to the string -pcString
**
**  RETURNS:     BOOL -Indication of success. TRUE if successful else FALSE.
**
*F*/
BOOL FP bReleaseString(PSTR pcString)
{
    auto HLOCAL hString;
    auto BOOL   bResult = FALSE;

    if(pcString != NULL)
    {
        /*
        ** Get a local handle to the object pointed to by pcString.
        */

        hString = LocalHandle((VOID NEAR *)pcString);

        if(hString != 0)
        {
            if(LocalUnlock(hString) == 0)
            {
                if(LocalFree(hString) == 0)
                {
                    bResult = TRUE;
                }
            }
        }
    }
}
```

```
   return bResult;
}




/*F*
**
**   FUNCTION:    vReportError
**
**   DESCRIPTION: Cause a MessageBox with error information to be displayed.
**
**   PASSED: HWND -A window handle for the message box to use -hWnd
**           WORD -An error code (see WSHL.H)                 -wErrorCode
**           HINSTANCE -Instance handle                        -hInst
**
**   RETURNS:     VOID.
**
*F*/
VOID FP vReportError(HWND hWnd, WORD wErrorCode, HINSTANCE hInst)
{
   auto PSTR pcErrorMsg;
   auto PSTR pcErrorBoxTitle;

   /**************************************************
    *
    * If the window handle passed is invalid, use 0.
    *
    */

   if(IsWindow(hWnd) == 0)
   {
       hWnd = 0;
   }

   /**************************************************
    *
    * If the problem's with either GetString or
    * ReleaseString use static error text.
    *
    */

   if(wErrorCode == IDS_ERR_LOADSTRING ||
      wErrorCode == IDS_ERR_RELEASESTRING)
   {
       vShowError(hWnd, 0, 0);
   }
   else
   {
       /* Load the error box caption and main text. */

       pcErrorBoxTitle = pcGetString(IDS_ERR_TITLE, hInst);
       pcErrorMsg = pcGetString(wErrorCode, hInst);

       /****************************************************
        *
        * If one or both GetStrings failed release any string
```

```
         *  that  may  have  been  allocated  then  recurse  to
         *  function and  report  error.  Also  report error if
         *  couldn't free any allocated string.
         *
         */

         if(pcErrorBoxTitle == 0 || pcErrorMsg == 0)
         {
             if(pcErrorBoxTitle != 0)
             {
                 if(bReleaseString(pcErrorBoxTitle) == FALSE)
                 {
                     vReportError(hWnd, IDS_ERR_RELEASESTRING, hInst);
                 }
             }

             if(pcErrorMsg != 0)
             {
                 if(bReleaseString(pcErrorMsg) == FALSE)
                 {
                     vReportError(hWnd, IDS_ERR_RELEASESTRING, hInst);
                 }
             }

             vReportError(hWnd, IDS_ERR_LOADSTRING, hInst);
         }
         else  /* Both error strings loaded OK. */
         {
             vShowError(hWnd, pcErrorBoxTitle, pcErrorMsg);

             if(bReleaseString(pcErrorBoxTitle) == FALSE ||
                bReleaseString(pcErrorMsg)       == FALSE )
             {
                 vReportError(hWnd, IDS_ERR_RELEASESTRING, hInst);
             }
         }
    }

    return;
}




/*F*
**
**   FUNCTION:    vShowError. Used by vReportError.
**
**   DESCRIPTION: Cause a MessageBox with error information to be displayed.
**
**   PASSED:      HWND -A window handle for the message box to use -hWnd
**                PSTR -A pointer to the text used in the message box's caption
**                      -pcTitle
**                PSTR -A pointer to the text used in the message box itself
**                      -pcErrorMsg
**   RETURNS:     VOID.
**
*F*/
VOID NP vShowError(HWND hWnd, PSTR pcTitle, PSTR pcErrorMsg)
```

```
{
   if(pcTitle == 0 || pcErrorMsg == 0)
   {
       pcTitle = NULL;
       pcErrorMsg = "Error Loading or Releasing String Resources!";
   }

   (VOID)MessageBox(
                   hWnd
                   ,pcErrorMsg
                   ,pcTitle
                   ,MB_OK
                   );
   return;
}




/****************************************************************************
                                    EOF
****************************************************************************/
```

Def.h :

```
/****************************************************************************

  Contains a list of defines that are used in WINDOWS.H to   selectively
  include & exclude WINDOWS.H stuff. Each 'C' file includes this header.
  This list of defines is complete -ie. it  means  exclude  just about
  everything in WINDOWS.H!

  Each 'C' file also has its own 'redef' type header which contains a list
  of #undefs that that 'C' file requires in order to  access  the stuff in
  WINDOWS.H that it needs.

****************************************************************************/



#define NOKERNEL
#define NOGDI
#define NOUSER
#define NOSOUND
#define NOCOMM
#define NODRIVERS
#define NOMINMAX
#define NOLOGERROR
#define NOPROFILER
#define NOMEMMGR
#define NOLFILEIO
#define NOOPENFILE
#define NORESOURCE
#define NOATOM
#define NOLANGUAGE
#define NOLSTRING
```

```
#define NODBCS
#define NOKEYBOARDINFO
#define NOGDICAPMASKS
#define NOCOLOR
#define NOGDIOBJ
#define NODRAWTEXT
#define NOTEXTMETRIC
#define NOSCALABLEFONT
#define NOBITMAP
#define NORASTEROPS
#define NOMETAFILE
#define NOSYSMETRICS
#define NOSYSTEMPARAMSINFO
#define NOMSG
#define NOWINSTYLES
#define NOWINOFFSETS
#define NOSHOWWINDOW
#define NODEFERWINDOWPOS
#define NOVIRTUALKEYCODES
#define NOKEYSTATES
#define NOWH
#define NOMENUS
#define NOSCROLL
#define NOCLIPBOARD
#define NOICONS
#define NOMB
#define NOSYSCOMMANDS
#define NOMDI
#define NOCTLMGR
#define NOWINMESSAGES
#define NOHELP


/**********************************************************************
                               EOF
**********************************************************************/
```

Dlfdef.h :

```
/**********************************************************************

 WINDOWS.H undefines to include WINDOWS.H stuff required by the 'C' source
 code that includes this header -see def.h for more information.

**********************************************************************/



#undef NOUSER
#undef NOCTLMGR



/**********************************************************************
                               EOF
**********************************************************************/
```

Initdef.h :

```
/*****************************************************************************

   WINDOWS.H undefines to include WINDOWS.H stuff required by the 'C' source
   code that includes this header -see def.h for more information.

   *****************************************************************************/




#undef NOKERNEL
#undef NOGDI
#undef NOUSER
#undef NOWINSTYLES
#undef NOCOLOR
#undef NOLSTRING




/*****************************************************************************
                                    EOF
   *****************************************************************************/
```

Miscdef.h

```
/*****************************************************************************
   WINDOWS.H undefines to include WINDOWS.H stuff required by the 'C' source
   code that includes this header -see def.h for more information.

   *****************************************************************************/




#undef NOKERNEL
#undef NOUSER
#undef NOMEMMGR
#undef NOMB




/*****************************************************************************
                                    EOF
   *****************************************************************************/
```

Pragma.h :

```
/*****************************************************************

 This file is included into each 'C' source file. It turns off two MSC7
 warnings:

   1. Unreferenced formal parameters (C4100).
   2. Non standard extension used (C4001).

 The second is used to remove warnings about double slash comment.

 *****************************************************************/




#pragma warning(disable:4100)
#pragma warning(disable:4001)




/*****************************************************************
                                EOF
 *****************************************************************/
```

Proto.h :

```
/*****************************************************************

 Prototypes for functions defined in all modules.

 *****************************************************************/




/* init.c */
BOOL FP  bInit         (HINSTANCE,HINSTANCE,LPSTR,int);
BOOL NP  bInitApp      (HINSTANCE);
BOOL NP  bInitInst     (HINSTANCE,int);




/* wshl.c */
LRESULT NP lCommandHandler        (HWND,UINT,WPARAM,LPARAM);
LRESULT NP lCreateHandler         (HWND,UINT,WPARAM,LPARAM);
LRESULT NP lDefaultHandler        (HWND,UINT,WPARAM,LPARAM);
LRESULT NP lDestroyHandler        (HWND,UINT,WPARAM,LPARAM);
LRESULT NP lABOUTCommandHandler   (HWND,UINT,WPARAM,LPARAM);
FWNDPROC   LMAINWNDPROC;
int     NP nExecInst(void);




/* dialog.c */
BOOL NP  bCommandHandler          (HWND,UINT,WPARAM,LPARAM);
BOOL NP  bDefaultHandler          (HWND,UINT,WPARAM,LPARAM);
```

```
BOOL NP   bInitDialogHandler   (HWND,UINT,WPARAM,LPARAM);
FDLGPROC BDIALOGPROC;


/* misc.c */
BOOL FP   bReleaseString       (PSTR);
PSTR FP   pcGetString          (UINT,HINSTANCE);
void FP   vReportError         (HWND,WORD,HINSTANCE);
void NP   vShowError           (HWND,PSTR,PSTR);



********************************************************************************

                                  EOF
******************************************************************************/
```

Wshl.h :

```
/******************************************************************************

  Main include file for 'winshell'.

******************************************************************************/



/*
** Due to the resource compiler not liking it, some #defines are not
** parenthesised here.
*/

#define NO_PREVIOUS_INSTANCE     (0)

#define W_HANDLED                ((LRESULT)0)/* WndProc handled message.  */
#define D_HANDLED                (TRUE)      /* DlgProc handled message.  */
#define D_NOTHANDLED             (FALSE)     /* DlgProc NOT handled code.  */

#define STRINGTAB                (256)       /* LoadString buffer size.   */

#define IDM_ABOUT                (100)       /* About box menu item ID.   */

#define IDI_SHELLICON            1000        /* Resource ID of icon.      */
#define IDM_SHELLMENU            1010        /* Resource ID of menu.      */

#define IDS_SHELLCLASS           (1020)      /* Classname string ID.      */
#define IDS_SHELLCAPTION         (1030)      /* Window caption string ID. */
#define IDS_TEMPLATE             (1050)      /* Dialog template string ID. */

#define IDS_ERR_DIALOG           (1060)
#define IDS_ERR_LOADSTRING       (1070)
#define IDS_ERR_RELEASESTRING    (1080)
#define IDS_ERR_TITLE            (1090)
#define IDS_ERR_DEFAULT          (1100)
#define IDS_ERR_ALLOCMEM         (1110)
#define IDS_ERR_FREEMEM          (1120)
```

```
#define IDS_ERR_ACCELERATORS     (1130)

#define IDS_ACCELNAME            (1140)

                                 /* Macro to get a HINSTANCE from a HWND.  */
                                 /* There's also  an  equivalent macro in  */
                                 /* WINDOWSX.H */

#define HINSTFROMHWND(X)         (HINSTANCE)GetWindowWord((X),GWW_HINSTANCE)

                                 /* Window color to use.                   */

#define USER_COLOR               (COLOR_WINDOW + 1)

                                 /* WndProc & DlgProc types.               */

typedef LRESULT (__export CALLBACK FWNDPROC)(HWND, UINT, WPARAM, LPARAM);
typedef BOOL    (__export CALLBACK FDLGPROC)(HWND, UINT, WPARAM, LPARAM);


#define PRIVATE static


#define NP NEAR PASCAL
#define FP FAR  PASCAL


/*******************************************************************************
                                   EOF
*******************************************************************************/
```

Wshldef.h :

```
/*******************************************************************************

 WINDOWS.H undefines to include WINDOWS.H stuff required by the 'C' source
 code that includes this header -see def.h for more information.

*******************************************************************************/




#undef NOKERNEL
#undef NOUSER
#undef NOCTLMGR
#undef NOMSG
#undef NOMB
#undef NOWINOFFSETS




*******************************************************************************
                                   EOF
*******************************************************************************/
```

About.dlg :

```
ABOUT DIALOG LOADONCALL MOVEABLE DISCARDABLE 95, 42, 172, 80

CAPTION "About Shell ..."

STYLE WS_BORDER | WS_CAPTION | WS_SYSMENU | WS_POPUP | DS_MODALFRAME

BEGIN

    CONTROL "'Windows -Advanced Programming and Design'"
            ,-1
            ,"static"
            ,SS_CENTER | WS_CHILD
            ,3
            ,24
            ,164
            ,8

    CONTROL "By petermor"
            ,-1
            ,"static"
            ,SS_CENTER | WS_CHILD
            ,44
            ,40
            ,96
            ,8

    CONTROL IDI_SHELLICON
            ,-1
            ,"static"
            ,SS_ICON | WS_CHILD
            ,12
            ,48
            ,20
            ,16

    CONTROL "OK"
            ,IDOK
            ,"button"
            ,BS_PUSHBUTTON | WS_TABSTOP | WS_CHILD
            ,76
            ,56
            ,32
            ,16

END
```

Makefile :

```
#*****************************************************************************
#
# Makefile for SHELL1.EXE
#
#*****************************************************************************

#
# Decide whether or not to include debug information
```

```
#

!IFDEF DEBUG
CCDEB=-Zi
LKDEBUG= /CO /M
CCDEB1=> $*.err
!ELSE
CCDEB=
LKDEBUG=
CCDEB1=
!ENDIF

#
# Macros
#

LIBS=libw.lib mlibcew.lib
OBJS=wshl.obj+misc.obj+init.obj+dialog.obj

LINK=link /NOD /NOI $(LKDEBUG)
CC=cl -DSTRICT -NT$*_TEXT -W4 -WX -GA2s -AM -Od -Zpe -c $(CCDEB) $*.c
$(CCDEB1)

C_DEPEND  =  $*.c makefile wshl.h proto.h def.h pragma.h
RC_DEPEND =  $*.rc makefile $*.h about.dlg $*.ico


TYPE=type $*.err | more

#
# Commands
#

all : wshl.exe

wshl.res : $(RC_DEPEND)
        rc -v -r $*.rc

wshl.obj : $(C_DEPEND) wshldef.h
        cnest < $*.c
        $(CC)
!IFDEF DEBUG
        $(TYPE)
!ENDIF

init.obj : $(C_DEPEND) initdef.h
        cnest < $*.c
        $(CC)
!IFDEF DEBUG
        $(TYPE)
!ENDIF

dialog.obj : $(C_DEPEND) dlgdef.h
        cnest < $*.c
        $(CC)
!IFDEF DEBUG
        $(TYPE)
!ENDIF
```

```
misc.obj : $(C_DEPEND)  miscdef.h
        cnest < $*.c
        $(CC)
!IFDEF DEBUG
        $(TYPE)
!ENDIF

wshl.exe : $*.obj misc.obj init.obj dialog.obj $*.res $*.def
        $(LINK) $(OBJS),$@,$*.map,$(LIBS),$*.def
        rc -v -t $*.res $*.exe
!IFDEF DEBUG
        mapsym wshl.map
!ENDIF



#/*****************************************************************************
#                                  EOF
#*****************************************************************************/
```

Wshl.def :

```
NAME            WSHL            WINDOWAPI

PROTMODE

EXETYPE         WINDOWS 3.1

STUB            'WINSTUB.EXE'

DESCRIPTION     'New Shell (C) 1993 petermor.'

CODE            MOVEABLE LOADONCALL DISCARDABLE
DATA            MOVEABLE PRELOAD    MULTIPLE

SEGMENTS
                _TEXT        PRELOAD    MOVEABLE DISCARDABLE
                MISC_TEXT    LOADONCALL MOVEABLE DISCARDABLE
                INIT_TEXT    LOADONCALL MOVEABLE DISCARDABLE
                WSHL_TEXT    PRELOAD    MOVEABLE DISCARDABLE
                DIALOG_TEXT  LOADONCALL MOVEABLE DISCARDABLE

STACKSIZE       5000
HEAPSIZE        256



;*****************************************************************************
;                                  EOF
;*****************************************************************************
```

Wshl.rc :

```
/* resources for 'WinShell' */

#include<windows.h>
#include"wshl.h"
```

```
/*
** Icon shown in dialog box and when main window iconic.
*/
IDI_SHELLICON ICON WSHL.ICO


/*
** Menu containing one dropdown menu with one item.
*/
IDM_SHELLMENU MENU
BEGIN
    POPUP "&Help"
    BEGIN
        MENUITEM "&About WinShell ...",IDM_ABOUT
    END
END


/*
** String table.
*/
STRINGTABLE LOADONCALL MOVEABLE DISCARDABLE
BEGIN
    IDS_SHELLCLASS,         "WinShellClass"
    IDS_SHELLCAPTION,       "WinShellCaption"
    IDS_TEMPLATE,           "ABOUT"

    IDS_ACCELNAME,          "ACCEL"

    IDS_ERR_ALLOCMEM,       "Error Allocating Memory From Heap!"
    IDS_ERR_FREEMEM,        "Error Freeing Memory From Heap!"
    IDS_ERR_TITLE,          "An Error Has Occurred!"
    IDS_ERR_DIALOG,         "Dialog Box Couldn't Be Created!"
    IDS_ERR_DEFAULT,        "A Truly Radical and Weird Thing's Just Happened
                             To Me!"
    IDS_ERR_ACCELERATORS,   "Cannot Load Accelerators!"
END


/*
** Accelerators.
*/
ACCEL ACCELERATORS
BEGIN
        "^A",IDM_ABOUT
END


/*
** Include dialog box template.
*/
rcinclude about.dlg



/********************************************************************
                              EOF
********************************************************************/
```

D :

```
"DEBUG="
```

This shell, which is based on one I usually use as the foundation of all my new Windows' apps, is slightly bigger than generic! It <u>tries</u> to do most things properly which really any shell type of application should – after all you'll *inherit* and build upon it in future applications so it'd better be right! For example, it tries always to check function return values to see if they've failed – it also tries to cope with those failures as best it can.

It keeps most of its static string data in a resource for two reasons –

1   so that it consumes as little non-discardable memory as possible,

2   so that its string data is kept in one piece and can be modified easily

– you don't have to go about the app looking for strings, they're in the string table. One string isn't – it's the one for handling errors loading strings! This is a form of encapsulation. The data is being held locally in a string type object called a string table. Access to it is restricted – LoadString() is the only realistic way to get at the data.

The app is built by either entering nmake or nmake @d; @d builds a debugging version of the app by defining the symbol DEBUG to nmake.

We could argue that because the app is built in separate source code modules that it is in some ways object oriented, ie. each module has a well defined interface in its external entry points, ie. the functions that it makes available to other units. The data associated with each unit is private to the unit, to access it or change it, you need to go via a function that interfaces the caller with the data structures maintained in the called unit. In a similar the window class contains private data that is accessed through, and by, Windows' messages.

Using the *module* as a encapsulation method is fine with me as long as the module, or resulting object module or library is generic – surely the shell modules are just that? One of the problems with modules is that they often use global data as inter-function communication transport. For example we often see HINSTANCE hInst declared in applications as a way of *sharing* hInst between interested functions within the module. Also of course if the item is not declared static then the said item has external linkage, ie. it may be used by other modules indiscriminately – this is similar to *exports*. It is sometimes overly difficult to manipulate and access such useful items without making them global! However, the global item may still be effectively hidden by surrounding it by a static function :

```
static HINSTANCE hGetSethInst(HINSTANCE hInstance)
{
  static HINSTANCE hInst;

  if(hInstance != NULL)
    {
        hInst = hInstance;
    }

  return hInst;
}
```

Here the data item hInst serves the same purpose as the *normal* global variable. However this one is isolated, or abstracted away behind a function. To use hInst we need to set it – typically this is done in WinMain

```
...WinMain(...)
{
    ...
   hInst = hInstance;
    ...
}
```

Well the same can be done to our *private* hInst.

```
..WinMain(...)
{
    ...
   hGetSethInst(hInstance);
    ...
}
```

When we want our instance handle we can get it via a call to hGetSethInst() like so :

```
   ...
   DialogBox(
            hGetSethInst(NULL)
            ,"AboutBox"
            ,hWnd
            ,About
            );
   ...
```

Note that the function hGetSethInst() is also private, ie. it has internal linkage due to the use of the static key word!.

Now I'm not suggesting that you hide all you global data away behind a function wrapper (although you could do worse) but at least remember that you can. Generally I'd say

- Minimise the amount of global data you have.
- Any global data that can be should be marked static.
- Consider using functions to hide data.

What else is object oriented about this 'C' based program? Well, I guess we could say that its header mechanism is a little object oriented. To speed up compilation, the shell defines all those things that cause the compiler to discard most of WINDOWS.H. WINDOWS.H uses #defines to achieve conditional inclusion of most of itself :

For example, if you define NOMEMMGR you loose this little lot :

```
#ifndef NOMEMMGR

/* Global Memory Flags */

#define GMEM_FIXED                            0x0000
#define GMEM_MOVEABLE            0x0002
#define GMEM_NOCOMPACT           0x0010
#define GMEM_NODISCARD           0x0020
#define GMEM_ZEROINIT            0x0040
#define GMEM_MODIFY                           0x0080
#define GMEM_DISCARDABLE         0x0100
#define GMEM_NOT_BANKED          0x1000
#define GMEM_SHARE                            0x2000
#define GMEM_DDESHARE            0x2000
#define GMEM_NOTIFY                           0x4000
#define GMEM_LOWER               GMEM_NOT_BANKED

#define GHND                  (GMEM_MOVEABLE | GMEM_ZEROINIT)
#define GPTR                  (GMEM_FIXED | GMEM_ZEROINIT)

#define GlobalDiscard(h)      GlobalReAlloc(h, 0L, GMEM_MOVEABLE)

HGLOBAL WINAPI GlobalAlloc(UINT, DWORD);
HGLOBAL WINAPI GlobalReAlloc(HGLOBAL, DWORD, UINT);
HGLOBAL WINAPI GlobalFree(HGLOBAL);

DWORD   WINAPI GlobalDosAlloc(DWORD);
UINT    WINAPI GlobalDosFree(UINT);

#ifdef STRICT
void FAR* WINAPI GlobalLock(HGLOBAL);
#else
char FAR* WINAPI GlobalLock(HGLOBAL);
#endif

BOOL    WINAPI GlobalUnlock(HGLOBAL);
```

```
DWORD    WINAPI GlobalSize(HGLOBAL);
DWORD    WINAPI GlobalHandle(UINT);


/* GlobalFlags return flags (in addition to GMEM_DISCARDABLE) */
#define GMEM_DISCARDED       0x4000
#define GMEM_LOCKCOUNT       0x00FF
UINT     WINAPI GlobalFlags(HGLOBAL);


#ifdef STRICT
void FAR* WINAPI GlobalWire(HGLOBAL);
#else
char FAR* WINAPI GlobalWire(HGLOBAL);
#endif


BOOL     WINAPI GlobalUnWire(HGLOBAL);

UINT     WINAPI GlobalPageLock(HGLOBAL);
UINT     WINAPI GlobalPageUnlock(HGLOBAL);


void     WINAPI GlobalFix(HGLOBAL);
void     WINAPI GlobalUnfix(HGLOBAL);


HGLOBAL WINAPI GlobalLRUNewest(HGLOBAL);
HGLOBAL WINAPI GlobalLRUOldest(HGLOBAL);


DWORD    WINAPI GlobalCompact(DWORD);


#ifdef STRICT
typedef BOOL (CALLBACK* GNOTIFYPROC)(HGLOBAL);
#else
typedef FARPROC GNOTIFYPROC;
#endif


void     WINAPI GlobalNotify(GNOTIFYPROC);

HGLOBAL WINAPI LockSegment(UINT);
void     WINAPI UnlockSegment(UINT);


#define LockData(dummy)      LockSegment((UINT)-1)
#define UnlockData(dummy)    UnlockSegment((UINT)-1)

UINT     WINAPI AllocSelector(UINT);
UINT     WINAPI FreeSelector(UINT);
UINT     WINAPI AllocDStoCSAlias(UINT);
UINT     WINAPI PrestoChangoSelector(UINT sourceSel, UINT destSel);
DWORD    WINAPI GetSelectorBase(UINT);
UINT     WINAPI SetSelectorBase(UINT, DWORD);
DWORD    WINAPI GetSelectorLimit(UINT);
UINT     WINAPI SetSelectorLimit(UINT, DWORD);


void     WINAPI LimitEmsPages(DWORD);


void     WINAPI ValidateFreeSpaces(void);


/* Low system memory notification message */
```

```
#define WM_COMPACTING          0x0041


/***** Local Memory Management */

/* Local Memory Flags */
#define LMEM_FIXED                             0x0000
#define LMEM_MOVEABLE           0x0002
#define LMEM_NOCOMPACT          0x0010
#define LMEM_NODISCARD          0x0020
#define LMEM_ZEROINIT           0x0040
#define LMEM_MODIFY                            0x0080
#define LMEM_DISCARDABLE        0x0F00

#define LHND                  (LMEM_MOVEABLE | LMEM_ZEROINIT)
#define LPTR                  (LMEM_FIXED | LMEM_ZEROINIT)

#define NONZEROLHND           (LMEM_MOVEABLE)
#define NONZEROLPTR           (LMEM_FIXED)


#define LocalDiscard(h)       LocalReAlloc(h, 0, LMEM_MOVEABLE)


HLOCAL  WINAPI LocalAlloc(UINT, UINT);
HLOCAL  WINAPI LocalReAlloc(HLOCAL, UINT, UINT);
HLOCAL  WINAPI LocalFree(HLOCAL);

#ifdef STRICT
void NEAR* WINAPI LocalLock(HLOCAL);
#else
char NEAR* WINAPI LocalLock(HLOCAL);
#endif

BOOL    WINAPI LocalUnlock(HLOCAL);

UINT    WINAPI LocalSize(HLOCAL);
#ifdef STRICT
HLOCAL  WINAPI LocalHandle(void NEAR*);
#else
HLOCAL  WINAPI LocalHandle(UINT);
#endif

/* LocalFlags return flags (in addition to LMEM_DISCARDABLE) */
#define LMEM_DISCARDED        0x4000
#define LMEM_LOCKCOUNT        0x00FF

UINT    WINAPI LocalFlags(HLOCAL);

BOOL    WINAPI LocalInit(UINT, UINT, UINT);
UINT    WINAPI LocalCompact(UINT);
UINT    WINAPI LocalShrink(HLOCAL, UINT);

#endif  /* NOMEMMGR */
```

Quite a lot. If you don't need memory management functions, why cause the compiler grief by including all this stuff? The approach taken in the shell is to exclude everything from WINDOWS.H and to then re-include, by using #undef-ines in the specific module's header, only those bits that it requires. You won't believe just how much faster everything compiles! Are you convinced that the header that excludes everything is a generally useful thing therefore, ie. an object of sorts? Well OK, it doesn't seem to display any inheritance mechanism. This could be cured however by making that file a special case of, say, WINDOWS.H. It could do that by including WINDOWS.H itself. Now all my source code modules don't have to include WIN-DOWS.H as well as DEF.H, all they need to do is include DEF.H as it is a kinda WINDOWS.H – the difference is that DEF.H defines a different but related object. Of course, this won't actually work here because, in between including DEF.H and WINDOWS.H, we have to undef all the stuff we need in WINDOWS.H – else we'll get basically nothing included! However, we could have still got somewhere by building specific headers with a little more thought. Let's take one of those headers that undefs stuff, say, DLGDEF.H. This header just contains :

```
#undef NOUSER
#undef NOCTLMGR
```

We could have re-written this to be :

```
#include "def.h"        /* Get rid of everything. */

#undef NOUSER           /* Put some stuff back in. */
#undef NOCTLMGR

#include <windows.h> /* See the result! */
```

Now we'd only need to include DLGDEF.H in dialog.c instead of WINDOWS.H, DEF.H and DLGDEF.H – Inheritance?

Another object oriented *thing* might be the way in which the app handles messages, ie. it passes them to message handlers (a technique made more trendy by the inclusion of message crackers in WINDOWSX.H).

Each window in a Windows' application is handled by a class window procedure. Each class window procedure is a sub-classing function! A standard window can be described as being of type *DefWindowProc* class, ie. a standard window is a window whose behaviour is defined by DefWindowProc() (You can even give DefWindow-Proc as the address of your class call-back in the WNDCLASS structure if you like!). Your window differs from a DefWindowProc class window because you handle certain messages differently to DefWindowProc(). Those messages you don't handle (and maybe those the you do) are passed on to DefWindowProc() however so that the base class object can do some default handling with them – sounds very much like a sub-classing exercise to me! So due to our using DefWindowProc() we are kinda saying that we inherit some kind of standard window class and modify it. Keeping our message handling out of the actual window procedure code therefore is good for productivity! The code we write as Windows' programmers is inherently object oriented to some *programmer defined* degree and many of the benefits of using a pure object oriented language like code re-use, abstraction (data and functional), inheritance and polymorphism are available to you by using 'C' and the Windows' system correctly – don't forget it!

☐ Moving on

Well, I hope this chapter has got you thinking – hopefully not that I'm a weird programmer! Has it brought out any question marks over the way you write your code; has it shown you anything that you think's useful – I hope so?

I now invite you to read once again the opening page of this chapter and figure out what my shell design says to you about what can and can't be done in Windows.

> By the way, the comments at the top of each module and those that begin each function might look a little weird. The ones that begin each module begin with /*H* – this means header comment. The function comments begin with /*F*. Each comment ends with the corresponding *H*/ or *F*/! We have a small in-house tool here for extracting these comments from source listings – it provides you with the comment and the line numbers for the comments – it helps us find a particular function and helps document the code as well. It's so useful that I couldn't resist including it for you. One snag, it's written using the UNIX utility lex –those of you with lex (even a PC version), should have no trouble building it, those of you without lex can't build it – period! If you haven't got lex get it off Compuserve or something – you won't be sorry. The lex source listing's provided in the appendices. Oh, one other thing; CNEST (as shown in the make files) is yet another small utility we use that checks for nested comments in the code. This is not included as most modern compilers will now check this for you.

It's time to move on – scrap my Wshl shell, revert to the de-facto standard, forget generally about objectism and do some *normal* stuff.

Chapter 3

D i a l o g   B o x e s

☐ **MessageBox!**

The standard MessageBox() will be first for analysis in this chapter, after all, a message box is a *real* dialog box.

Dialog boxes are built from the Windows class *called* #32770 (also know as WC_DIA-LOG in WINDOWS.H), Maybe I should re-phrase that as there are dialog boxes in applications which are not built from this class. Take Microsoft's Word for Windows for example. Its dialogs are built from a class called bosa_sdm_Microsoft (it must mean something to someone)! Usually these *abnormal* classes add extra behaviour to the dialog that is not available with the standard dialog class. Back to the normal dialog built by a call to MessageBox() however.

The prototype for MessageBox() is :

```
int WINAPI MessageBox(HWND, LPCSTR, LPCSTR, UINT);
```

WINAPI is a macro defined as _far _pascal (any mention of __export etc was left out as in the PC (IBDA) world this is a Microsoft extension and would cause non-Microsoft compilers a hard time in understanding WINDOWS.H).

The parameters are a window handle defining the owner window for the message box, two long pointers to constant 'C' type strings, and an unsigned integer which is used for defining just how the message box looks and behaves. This last parameter is the most interesting.

WINDOWS.H defines several () MB_ ??????? constants that can be used/combined here, they are currently :

```
#define MB_OK                    0x0000
#define MB_OKCANCEL              0x0001
#define MB_ABORTRETRYIGNORE      0x0002
#define MB_YESNOCANCEL           0x0003
#define MB_YESNO                 0x0004
#define MB_RETRYCANCEL           0x0005
#define MB_TYPEMASK              0x000F  ?
```

```
#define MB_ICONHAND                 0x0010
#define MB_ICONQUESTION             0x0020
#define MB_ICONEXCLAMATION          0x0030
#define MB_ICONASTERISK             0x0040
#define MB_ICONMASK                 0x00F0 ?

#define MB_ICONINFORMATION          MB_ICONASTERISK
#define MB_ICONSTOP                 MB_ICONHAND

#define MB_DEFBUTTON1               0x0000
#define MB_DEFBUTTON2               0x0100
#define MB_DEFBUTTON3               0x0200
#define MB_DEFMASK                  0x0F00 ?

#define MB_APPLMODAL                0x0000
#define MB_SYSTEMMODAL              0x1000
#define MB_TASKMODAL                0x2000

#define MB_NOFOCUS                  0x8000 ?
```

The styles defined above fall into four styles :

- Button configuration
- Icon configuration
- Default button configuration
- Mode state configuration

The styles with the question marks placed beside them are not documented.

The first three (mask type styles) may be used to produce a bitmap mask of the first three items listed above. The last one, MB_NOFOCUS, does nothing! It is used *internally* to produce a *hard modal message box* and was left in WINDOWS.H apparently by accident!

To build a message box you simply pick from the list a set of required properties and call MessageBox() :

```
MessageBox(
        hWnd
       ,"This text appears in the box"
       ,"This is the caption"
       ,MB_ABORTRETRYIGNORE | MB_DEFBUTTON3 | MB_ICONHAND | MB_APPLMODAL
       )
```

The function returns a value which details which button from those requested was pressed.

The code above produces this box :

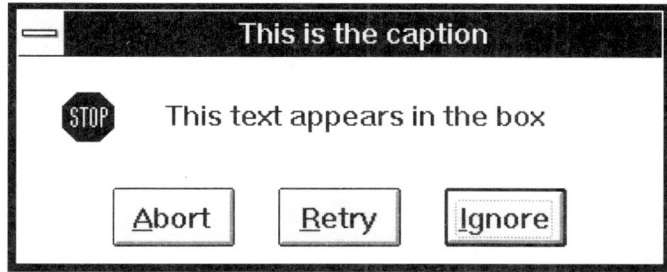

The MB_DEFBUTTON3 specifies that the third button should have the focus when the box is shown. The message box instructs its caller as to which button was pressed by passing back a value that identifies a button eg. IDIGNORE; the box is dismissed when a button is pressed. MessageBox() therefore doesn't return to the caller until after the message box is dismissed.

The biggest problem with this very useful function is that there is no documented way to configure the message box in some way other than the default way. For example, say you wanted to remove the box's system menu, display a custom icon in the box, change the ordering of the controls (ie. say you wanted *Yes No* as *No Yes*), or even include a *Help* button? If you wanted to do any of these things you'd normally have to use a modal dialog rather than a message box. We'll see soon how you can actually change a message box and additionally, towards the end of the chapter, we'll see a DLL that provides a message box replacement which is entirely configurable! For now let's consider modes.

☐ Modal States

MessageBox() supports, explicitly, three of the possible modal states of operation in Windows. The ones it supports are :

- Application Modal,
- Task Modal
- System Modal.

These are explained further below. The modal state that MessageBox() does not support is no mode, ie. modeless operation.

Application Modal.

An application modal message box is just like a standard modal dialog box. The box does not allow the window to which it is attached, through what MessageBox() calls *parentage*, to process user input, ie. it may process messages passed to its window procedure but not direct user input. However, only the *parent* window is thus affected. This means that if you have a main overlapping window, which in turn creates a popup window, which in turn creates an application modal message box (the popup is the parent, or owner, of the message box), you may not activate the popup but may activate the overlapped window!

This is not what many programmers expect, nevertheless, it is what the standard modal dialog and message box have always done/allowed. This was a bug (or was it a feature) noticed in some earlier version of Windows that for message boxes got fixed in Windows 3.0 (fix by addition). What is normally expected of course is *Task Modality.*

Task Modal.

The task modal message box prevents the user from re-activating any top-level (overlapping and popup) windows within the *task* that called MessageBox(). This is usually what you want as default behaviour. You call MessageBox() a little differently if you want this sort of message box. You set the hWndParent parameter to 0 and use the MB_TASKMODAL style. This produces a message box that, if you like is what *application modal* should have been. MB_TASKMODAL was added in Windows 3.0.

Unfortunately, there's no way to produce a modal dialog box (via DialogBox() et al) that acts like a task modal message box. We'll see how this can be done later. Let's now take a look at what's often called the *bad news* modal state.

System Modal.

System modal is what some Windows' programmers call the *S**t has hit the fan* modal state. It prevents the user from using any window, and therefore any task, in the system apart from the system modal message box window. You must respond to this message box before anything else in the system can continue working (well almost – See the later discussion on System Modal states!).

Modeless.

The modal state that MessageBox() lacks to make it complete is modeless, ie. one that allows the user to carry on using the *parent* window (and associated task) whilst the message box exists. There is a way to get a modeless message box however; you create it MB_APPLMODAL (pronounced *apple modal)* and set the hWndParent parameter to NULL or zero! This may be undocumented behaviour but it's sure handy!

It's not like calling CreateDialog() however, ie. a call to message box like this :

```
MessageBox(0, "Contents", "Caption", MB_OK | MB_APPLMODAL);
```

does not return immediately but blocks. However the task and all of its windows can continue to receive messages. Be careful of re-entrancy problems when using a modeless message box! One *different* aspect of producing a message box like this is that the message box, and its caption, now show up in the Task-list etc. Playing around with the MB_ mode based flags produces even more varieties – try some out!

It is rumoured that the message box displayed as system modal is not a *real* message box at all but a bitmap; this may or may not be the case – it's hard to determine also because when the system modal message box is present everything else stops (including the current task's timers), you cannot therefore, within a normal application, say, walk the window manager's list of windows to see if there's another one added to it for the message box!

Question: When is a system modal dialog *not* (as Wayne & Garth might say)?

Answer: When it's a dialog box created using DialogBox() etc.

☐ **Dialog Boxes.**

Let's continue our discussion on modal states before getting into dialog boxes too far.

Dialog boxes come in three modal flavours. Modeless, system modal or modal. Modeless and system modal are both pretty obvious (we'll see in a moment that system modal can be different from a message box's system modal however) but what the heck does modal mean, ie. is it *task modal* or *apple modal*?

Dialog boxes are, in message box speak, APPLMODAL. ie. they prevent you from working with the dialog's immediate *parent*, but DO allow you to switch to other top-level windows etc within the task. This behaviour is usually not what you want. Programmers typically want functionality like message box's TASKMODAL from a modal dialog box. The good news is that a task modal state may be imposed upon an application modal dialog quite easily. The code below may be used to create true task modal dialog boxes.

The following code enables/disables all the top level windows in the task that uses it (remember that a child window will become disabled if its parent does – eventually then this parent must be a top-level window. This code therefore will disable <u>all</u> the windows in any task that uses it).

It is written a little like EnableWindow(), in that EnableWindow() is used to enable or disable a window – you just enable one disabled! You pass it a window handle of a window in the task. This window handle is used to identify the task. Most importantly, It is also excluded from being disabled (a task with all its windows disabled isn't useful!). The second parameter is TRUE or FALSE. FALSE means disable, TRUE means enable.

The idea here is that you call this function from your dialog box call-back/handler function passing it the window handle of the dialog box. The function bundles the passed parameters into an LPARAM and calls a standard function called EnumTaskWindows(). This function enumerates all the top-level windows in the task identified by its first parameter. It uses another function called EnumWindows() to do this. We get our task ID by calling GetWindowTask(), using the passed window handle as a parameter. The second parameter to EnumTaskWindows() is the address of a call-back function (or thunk) that will be called repeatedly. You will be safe if you create this *address* using MakeProcInstance(). You can omit this if you're using the

MSC 7 compiler with the -GA (prot mode only) switch and the __export function qualifier. Here's the function :

```
BOOL bMakeDialogTaskModal(HWND hDlg, BOOL bCondition)
{
    return EnumTaskWindows(
                        GetWindowTask(hDlg)
                        ,bEnumProc
                        , (LPARAM)MAKELONG(hDlg, bCondition)
                        );
}
```

The call-back function unpacks the window handle of the window to exclude, and the required disable state of all the task windows – TRUE or FALSE. It then checks the enumerated window handle against the one to exclude. If the handles don't match, the window is disabled/enabled according to bCondition :

```
BOOL CALLBACK bEnumProc(HWND hWnd, LPARAM lUserInfo)
{
    auto BOOL bCondition;
    auto HWND hWndExclude;

    bCondition  = HIWORD(lUserInfo);
    hWndExclude = LOWORD(lUserInfo);

    if(hWnd != hWndExclude)
    {
        EnableWindow(hWnd, bCondition);
    }

    return TRUE;
}
```

Note that although the function (EnumTaskWindows()) is documented as enumerating *all* the windows in a given task, it doesn't! It enumerates only the top level windows in the task. Note that this kind of caper can also be accomplished through using APIs such as GetWindow() etc but that those APIs are not, potentially, as safe as EnumTaskWindows(). As the footnote in the reference says;

'The EnumTaskWindows function is reliable even when the application causes odd side-effects, whereas an application that uses a GetWindow loop risks being caught in an infinite loop or referencing a handle to a window that has been destroyed'!

The nice thing about GetWindow() however is that you don't need a call-back and all that goes with it. Typical code, using GetWindow() etc, to produce the same effect as the code above might look like this (the following code uses macros defined in WINDOWSX.H) :

```
VOID vMakeDialogTaskModal(HWND hDlg, BOOL bCondition)
{
    auto HWND hWnd;

    if((hWnd = GetFirstSibling(hDlg) != NULL)
    {
        do
        {
            if(hWnd != hDlg)
            {
                EnableWindow(hWnd, bCondition);
            }
        }
        while((hWnd = GetNextSibling(hWnd)) != NULL);
    }

    return VOID_RETURN;
}
```

Or, if you prefer for loops :

```
VOID vMakeDialogTaskModal(HWND hDlg, BOOL bCondition)
{
    auto HWND hWnd;

    for(
        hWnd = GetFirstSibling(hDlg)
        ;hWnd
        ;hWnd = GetNextSibling(hWnd)
        )
    {
        if(hWnd != hDlg)
        {
            EnableWindow(hWnd, bCondition);
        }
    }

    return VOID_RETURN
}
```

By using any of the functions above we now have available to us (the dialog users) all currently available (imaginable) modal states, however, some are still a little involved to create!

To create a modeless dialog requires some extra effort for two reasons. The first is that when you create a modeless dialog the API call used to create it returns immediately, ie. it doesn't block but allows you to carry on processing messages. This side-effect requires some extra work as the creation, and processing of the actions which result from user input in the box, are no longer in sync with its creation – as is the case when creating modal dialogs. Think about the modal case. Wouldn't it be nice to create a modeless dialog that blocks on the call to create it, but that still allows queued messages to arrive for further processing, ie. create, maintain/process, tidy up like a modal dialog? The second reason modeless dialogs are more effort is that the main message loop of the application has to be altered in order to support the keyboard interface normally provided by the dialog box manager, ie. so that the tab key etc works as it does when a modal dialog is active (IsDialogMessage() is a DM entry point). There is another little bit to the tale. Modeless dialogs also require explicit destruction by calling the DestroyWindow() API, again another difference to the modal case.

We'll go through modeless dialog creation the documented way in detail soon, but first let's do it the undocumented way by using DialogBox() instead of CreateDialog()!

The normal way to create a modal dialog is :

```
nRes = DialogBox(hInst,  "AboutBox",  hWndOwner,  fpsrProcAbout);
```

The parameters are :

Your instance handle, the dialog template resource name, the window handle of the parent window and lastly the address (or thunk) of some call-back function that will process messages sent to it by the dialog manager.

The function blocks until the dialog box is closed down and then returns some meaningful value to the caller of DialogBox(). A value of -1 is returned by the dialog box manager if the dialog cannot be created. OK, here's how to create a modeless dialog box the quick way (you may have thought of what follows already after reading the stuff above about modeless message boxes – if you did, have a banana!):

```
nRes = DialogBox(hInst,  "AboutBox",  NULL,  fpsrProcAbout);
```

The only thing that has changed is that the given *parent* window handle is set to NULL! This creates what seems to be a modeless dialog. The position of the dialog is now <u>not</u> relative to one of your windows (hWndOwner earlier) as you haven't specified an owner! The owner is now implicitly the desktop window (Well sorta)! The DialogBox() call still block but does not disable your application's ability to retrieve and process messages in its task queue (the dialog box manager also looks after servicing your task queue and calling IsDialogMessage()). The box produced is a modeless dialog that requires no special modifications, ie. your main message loop is as it was before, the call you use is the same as before, the box is handled in a synchronous manner as before but to all observers it's modeless!

A *modeless* dialog box created in this way does behave differently in terms of its Z order however, ie. as a non-child of the main window it is now free to descend below the would-be parent; it does in fact now act just like an un-owned WS_OVERLAPPED window; this may, or may not be desirable! Also, as in the MessageBox() case, a modeless dialog created in this way also appears in the Task-list.

There's actually another way to produce more or less the same effect, ie. a modeless dialog, but this time leave the normal Z order intact (also it does not appear in the Task-list)! What you do is re-enable the parent window in the WM_INITDIALOG case of the dialog's call-back function; this time the resulting dialog is parented to its normal window but doesn't disable it! The result is a parented modeless dialog, ie. one that stays on top of, or higher in the Z order than, its parent (this also leaves the call to DialogBox() totally legal). Again, as before, the main window, and all the others in the task, can continue to be worked with. This also produces a modeless dialog that behaves correctly when its parent is iconised etc – all in all, it's a very good imitation of a real modeless dialog.

I actually prefer this latter type of pseudo modeless dialog over a real modeless dialog for several reasons (some of these can be applied to the earlier version also). The first is that I just don't like the way that CreateDialog...() calls return immediately – you may however? I prefer the modal model in that the API blocks (doesn't return) until the dialog's closed down; I like the consistency here (I also like using the same APIs to build and destroy my dialogs).. I often have more than one modeless dialog visible at any one time; having to modify the main message loop to cater for two or more modeless dialogs can be pain in the butt (see simple solution to this later). Maintaining the correct parentage is important (unless you fancy the dialog as an OVERLAPPED window approach?) as it saves you having to deal with positioning/visibility properties of the dialog (including the unparented dialog appearing in the Task-List). The latter method is also safer in that the *parent* parameter is indeed another window since the value inserted into the call identifies a *real* window; all you're doing is re-enabling the parent. The latter method also saves you having to call that loathsome IsDialog-Message() subroutine – yuk! By the way, this technique also requires, potentially a little modification to your dialog templates. For example, try the *preferred* method above (enabling the parent) on the *generic* sample application provided with the SDK - it won't work! The resultant dialog box seems to be unaffected!!

The dialog template in generic has the style :

```
STYLE DS_MODALFRAME | WS_CAPTION | WS_SYSMENU
```

and that's the problem. If you take a look at the dialog window with a tool like SPY you'll find that the dialog window produced is actually a WS_OVERLAPPED window and not a POPUP – you can see this from the snapshot shown below!

> There's nothing to stop you from adding/changing the window styles assigned to the main dialog window by changing the dialog template.
>
> You can for example create a dialog box that's a child window by removing WS_POPUP/WS_OVERLAPPED (if they're given) and inserting WS_CHILD (an application that does this appears later in this chapter).

This will create a child window dialog which in turn has child windows of its own – its controls. Do not create a child window dialog that doesn't have a parent, ie. don't put 0 or NULL in as the parent window parameter; child windows need a parent and the dialog box manager will refuse to create such a dialog – also, don't create a modal dialog that's a child window; the dialog box manager disables the parent of any modal dialog, this in turn causes any child windows (of the parent) to be disabled – now what!

You can if you want parent the child dialog to the desktop (give the parent window handle as GetDesktopWindow()); you'll have to also include the window style WS_CLIPSIBLINGS if you don't want to draw over any other window that gets in the way of the dialog. All top level windows are children (not necessarily child) windows of the desktop!

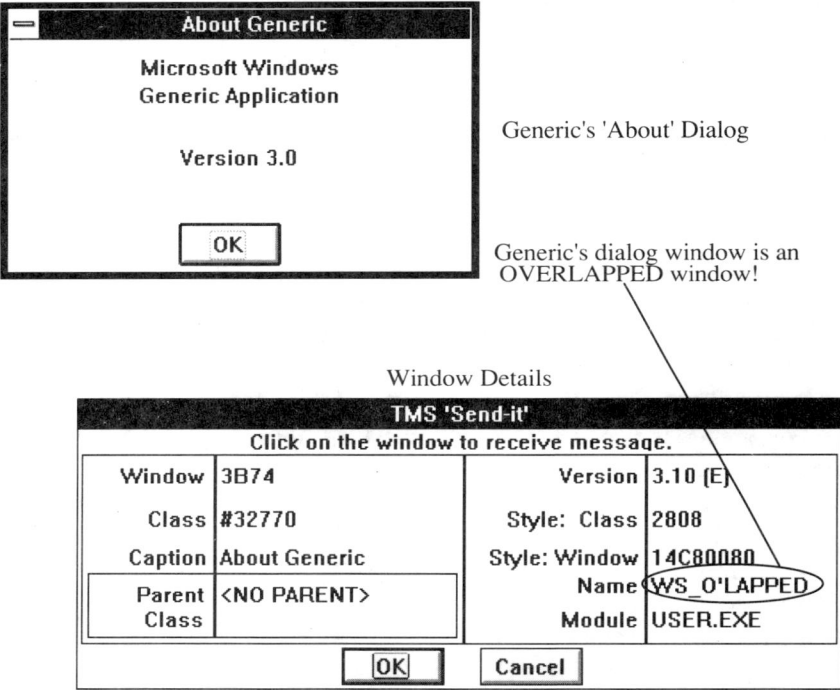

Generic's 'About' Dialog

Generic's dialog window is an OVERLAPPED window!

Window Details

The app used to find the window's details in the snapshot above was TMS Send-it, an application that works with SPY to test a window's responses to messages, ie. whereas SPY spys on messages driving a window, Send-it is a messaging source – it causes messages to be passed to a window.

To create a modeless dialog using DialogBox() in generic you'll need to alter the dialog template in generic's .rc file by adding the WS_POPUP constant into this style like so:

STYLE DS_MODALFRAME | WS_CAPTION | WS_SYSMENU | WS_POPUP

I said earlier that an HWND of NULL implied that the dialog was parented to the desktop window (as might be shown by examining HWND_DESKTOP in WINDOWS.H). This is not really the case as a modal dialog parented to the desktop proper (using the GetDesktopWindow() API) will produce a somewhat different dialog still. Well, not really a different dialog, but one that is different in its behaviour. For example, a modal dialog re-parented to the desktop window can cause mouse based input to be ignored (keyboard usually unaffected)!

System Modality and Dialog boxes

You may create a system modal dialog box in one of two ways (three if you think of MessageBox() with the MB_SYSTEMMODAL style (see qualifier below however and section on SysErrorBox() later)), by using the dialog style of DS_SYSMODAL or by using the Windows' function SetSysModalWindow(). The two methods are identical. There isn't really any equivalent to SetSysModalWindowNOT() so if you have dialog templates that may be either system or task/application modal give them the style of DS_MODAL frame and make them system modal in the WM_INITDIALOG case of your call-back/handler :

```
case WM_INITDIALOG:
    SetSysModalWindow(hDlg);
    break;
```

System modal message boxes are not the same as system modal dialog boxes. They're close, but definitely not the same. For example, say you set a timer going for the *parent* window of the dialog/message box. If you create a system modal message box, timer events for the *parent* will be stopped. However, if you create a system modal dialog using either DS_SYSMODAL or SetSysModalWindow() they will continue to arrive as though nothing has happened (however they will not be delivered to any other window (or call-back) in any other task. For example, watch the clock. It will stop while the system modal whatever exists)! The two things are very obviously different therefore. The *Exit Windows* dialog box is a *real* dialog and not a message box. The dialog is system modal. It would be nice if the message box function gave you the same amount of control over the appearance of the resulting box as the SetSysModal-Window() API does when used with a *real* dialog box. I guess that's why the last dialog you ever see in Windows is a *real* dialog!

By the way, none of the weird dialogs built above (or later) cause the debug libraries to complain, it's reasonable that they don't as you're not doing anything that's wrong or undocumented. The MessageBox() documentation states that if the window handle given is NULL then the message box is not parented; that justifies MessageBox(). As a message box is a dialog box, ie. it is created using a DialogBox() call, and as therefore the window handle given for *the owner window* is whatever we pass to MessageBox(), DialogBox() should not complain either?

How To Alter MessageBox()!

I said earlier that one of the biggest problems with MessageBox() was the apparent impossibility of changing the captions on the buttons within the message box main window, and this is true.

I have wanted to change these captions so much before that I decided to re-write the MessageBox() function and add not only an extra button but more functionality still. That *new box* is shown later in this chapter.

The *re-write* approach does cure all known problems, if you get it right that is; however, the re-write, depending upon what it is you're re-writing, takes time, and that's its drawback of course. What you really want is code reuse as preached by Object Oriented Technology (OOT). Often I've found myself compelled to re-write some API or another just to find at some later date that there's another, quicker, way of doing it, and that's what I'm about to show you; another way to create custom message boxes without having to re-write the MessageBox() API – Of course, it can't be as good (or better) than a re-write can it?

The key to this technique lies in two pieces of Windows' behaviour that may change at some future time. The first is, as discussed previously, the ability to create modeless message boxes, ie. one parented to a *NULL* window. The other piece of Windows' behaviour that this relies on is that the SetWindowWord() function continues to allow the use of GWW_HWNDPARENT. This constant is normally reserved for use with the GetWindowWord() function. Using SetWindowWord() with GWW_HWNDPAR-ENT allows us to re-parent any window (don't confuse this with SetParent() will you!). Armed with these two pieces of behaviour, we can now customise a message box completely!

When a message box is produced two major things happen, the first is that, according to the type of message box, a window, or windows, in the application are disabled. The second is that the message box code (really the DialogBox code) takes over polling the task's message queue; if any are found it dispatches them normally. Of course, disabled windows cannot receive user input events like (mouse or keyboard).

If we bring up a modeless dialog the first part, ie. the disabling of a window or windows within the task does not occur. The message box window is still associated with the task but not with any of the windows in the task. The call still blocks; that is to say the original thread of execution remains within the message box call, but other threads (loosely using the term) may be created to process user input, ie. because the message box code is polling for messages which are transmitted to the task, and because it (the message box) hasn't disabled any windows within the task, the task windows can still process user input (queued) messages. Thus although the message box is visible, the task's other windows can accept user input in the form of mouse and/or keyboard messages. This means that if we *post* ourselves (some owner window) a message before we create the modeless message box, this message will be retrieved from the task queue and delivered by the MessageBox()/DialogBox() code internally making calls to GetMessage(). Also, due to the way in which WM_PAINT messages are processed, we can say that this posted message will definitely be processed before the message box and its controls are painted.

A message box is created entirely before it starts polling for messages, this means that all the message box's child window controls etc have also been created – so if the message we post to ourselves contains details of, say, what captions we'd like in the message box controls, these captions (or whatever) may be *set* before the message box etc paints itself (the message will be processed before the WM_PAINT messages are sent to the controls and main message box window. We can therefore change the box and/or the controls contained within it prior to them becoming visible). All we need to do then, to produce a *real* message box, is re-parent the message box window to our main window and disable the main window!

Sounds like a lot I know but it's really simple to do. In the following code, I have elected to do most of the work during the processing of the *private message* posted to the task before the message box call is made. Further, I've chosen to do this processing in a functional replacement to DefWindowProc(); I've also chosen to use GetWindow() (instead of the WINDOWSX.H macros (used in this chapter already) to reveal as much as possible about the mechanics of what's going on.

The main thing we don't normally have control over (that we'd like to have control over) in a message box is the captions used in the buttons; that's all that this code will allow you to customise, but if you wanted to, say, reposition the message box you could do that equally easily using this code.

OK, you're ready for the code right? Well here it is :

First we need the following typedef and function prototypes :

```
/*
** Replacement to MessageBox() API. Calls MessageBox() internally.
*/
int  NewMessageBox(HWND ,LPCSTR, LPCSTR, LPCSTR, LPCSTR, LPCSTR, UINT);

/*
** Replacement to DefWindowProc() API.
*/
LRESULT NewDefWindowProc(HWND, UINT, WPARAM, LPARAM);

/*
** 'New' MessageBox() control caption details.
*/
typedef struct
{
   LPCSTR Caption;
   LPCSTR Button1;
   LPCSTR Button2;
   LPCSTR Button3;
} BOX_INFO;
```

The function NewMessageBox creates a message box that may have its button captions modified. The function NewDefWindowProc replaces calls to DefWindow-Proc for the window (or class of windows) to which the *new* message box is parented. This function processes only one message explicitly, that's our private message that's posted before the real MessageBox() function is called. The type *BOX_INFO* allows us to pass four parameters by using the LPARAM of the *private message* as a pointer to a BOX_INFO. The type is a structure that contains pointers to the message box's title bar caption and the captions of up to three buttons (maximum of three buttons only in a standard message box).

Now the code for producing this message box :

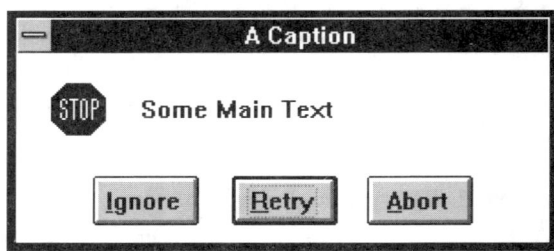

his is the standard MB_ABORTRETRYIGNORE box but with the buttons reversed! Also, the box has the MB_ICONSTOP and MB_DEFBUTTON2 styles.

First the code to create the message box in response to, say, a menu selection :

```
nRes = NewMessageBox(
                    hWnd
                    ,"Some Main Text"
                    ,"A Caption"
                    ,"&Ignore"
                    ,"&Retry"
                    ,"&Abort"
                    , MB_ABORTRETRYIGNORE | MB_ICONSTOP | MB_DEFBUTTON2
                    );
```

This call produces the message box pictured above. You may now see the meaning of the extra LPCSTR parameters used in a NewMessageBox call, they detail the button captions.

The NewMessageBox code looks like this :

```
int NewMessageBox
(
   HWND    hWndParent
  ,LPCSTR MainText
  ,LPCSTR Caption
```

```
    ,LPCSTR  Button1Caption
    ,LPCSTR  Button2Caption
    ,LPCSTR  Button3Caption
    ,UINT    Style
)
{
    static UINT      uNewMessage; /* Holds new message ID.         */
    auto   BOX_INFO  info;        /* Box configuration info.       */
    auto   int       nReturn;     /* Result of 'real' message box. */

      /*
      ** Fill in BOX_INFO with essential passed data.
      */
    info.Button1 = Button1Caption;
    info.Button2 = Button2Caption;
    info.Button3 = Button3Caption;
    info.Caption = Caption;

      /*
      ** Create private communication message if required.
      */
    if(uNewMessage == 0)
    {
    uNewMessage = RegisterWindowMessage("NewMessageBox");
    }

      /***************************************************
       * Post the main  window our  message, include with it
       * a pointer to BOX_INFO structure containing required
       * button captions etc.  Processing this  message dis-
       * ables the main window in NewDefWindowProc.
       */

    PostMessage(hWndParent, uNewMessage, 0,(LPARAM)(BOX_INFO FAR *)&info);

    /*
    ** Now call up 'real' message box. NewMessageBox processing
    ** is blocked here until MessageBox() returns.
    */
    nReturn = MessageBox(NULL, MainText, Caption, Style);

    /*
    ** Re-enable window before returning. It will have been
    ** disabled by the NewDefWindowProc() message handler.
    */
    EnableWindow(hWndParent, TRUE);

    /*
    ** Return MessageBox() result to caller.
    */
    return nReturn;
}
```

The function's parameters are :

- HWND - Window handle of parent window.
- LPCSTR- The text that will appear inside the message box.
- LPCSTR- The text that will appear in the message box's caption.
- LPCSTR- The text to appear in the first button control of the message box.
- LPCSTR- The text to appear in the second button control of the message box.
- LPCSTR- The text to appear in the third button control of the message box.
- UINT- MessageBox() styles defining ICON number of buttons etc.

This code fills in the BOX_INFO type (info) with the requested main window caption and all the requested button captions, a NULL pointer specifies that a button caption is not required. The first NULL pointer button caption signals the end of all new button captions. It then registers a Windows' message. The RegisterWindowMessage() API returns an ID somewhere in the range 0xC000 to 0xFFFF, any further call to RegisterWindowMessage() with the same string will result in the same ID being returned. This message is then posted to the window designated as being, in MessageBox() speak, the parent window of the message box. The message's LPARAM is set to be a 32 bit long pointer to the BOX_INFO type (info).

When the NewMessageBox function returns the message box will have been dismissed, the function, like the MessageBox() function it replaces, returns an indication of which button was selected. Lastly, the main window is re-enabled (it is disabled in the handling of the private message in the DefWindowProc() replacement code).

The actual message box will be created in the MessageBox() call. Before it is painted our private message will be pulled from the task's message queue and dispatched to our main window. The main window's WndProc will not handle this message explicitly so it would normally be passed to the default window procedure – it too would not normally handle it and so it would, in effect, be thrown away!

To prevent this we replace the normal call to DefWindowProc() with a call to NewDefWindowProc, this new function will handle the private message. Alternatively, code could be inserted into the *normal* part of the WndProc to handle this private message (indeed this would increase the speed of default message handling). I have chosen to do it like this for two reasons. Firstly to encourage you to put this code into a DLL, you would then always call NewDefWindowProc instead of DefWindowProc(). Secondly to simply show you how easy it is to modify some existing Windows' function. DefWindowProc() is an obvious candidate for modification as most Windows' programmers are usually familiar with the source code for it; there are others to which you don't have the source however which are equally easy to modify in this way.

Here is the *new* DefWindowProc code :

```
LRESULT NewDefWindowProc
(
   HWND    hWnd               /* Message to this window.         */
  ,UINT    message            /* The message ID.                */
  ,WPARAM wParam              /* The WPARAM parameter.          */
  ,LPARAM lParam              /* The LPARAM parameter.          */
)
{
   static  UINT uNewMessage;   /* Holds private message ID. */

   /*
   ** If not yet set uNewMessage do it now.
   */
   if(uNewMessage == 0)
   {
       uNewMessage = RegisterWindowMessage("NewMessageBox");
   }

   /*
   ** Is message our private message?
   */
   if(message == uNewMessage)
   {
       auto HWND hWndMess; /* Message box window handle. */


       /*
       ** Find message box window.
       */
       hWndMess = FindWindow("#32770", ((BOX_INFO FAR *)lParam)->Caption);

       /*
       ** If we found it?
       */
       if(hWndMess != NULL)
       {
           /*
           ** hWnd for each control in box.
           */
           auto HWND    hWndControl;

           /*
           ** Used to walk BOX_INFO captions.
           */
           auto UINT    uLoop;

           /*
           ** Caption to use on control.
           */
           auto LPCSTR lpstrControlCaption;

           uLoop = 0;  /* Set offset (loop counter) to 0. */

           /*************************************************************
            * Search through window list for controls in message box,
            * also  check to see control caption pointer is not NULL.
```

```
              * When a control is found  we make  sure that it is not a
              * static (control ID  ==  -1), if  it  is  not  we set its
              * caption  according  to  ControlCaption which is  set to
              * point to each non-NULL passed control caption.
              */

             for(
                 hWndControl = GetTopWindow(hWndMess)
                 ;hWndControl &&
                 (lpstrControlCaption = *(&((BOX_INFO FAR *)lParam)->
                 Button1 + uLoop))
                 != NULL
                 ;hWndControl = GetWindow(hWndControl, GW_HWNDNEXT)
                 )
             {
                 if(GetWindowWord(hWndControl, GWW_ID) == -1)
                 {
                     continue; /* Static control so ignore it. */
                 }
                 else
                 {
                     /*
                     ** Got a button so set caption.
                     */
                     SetWindowText(hWndControl, lpstrControlCaption);

                      /*
                      ** Inc offset to get next caption.
                      */
                      uLoop++;
                 }
             }

             /* Finished setting captions.   */

             /*
             ** Re-parent message box.
             */
             SetWindowWord(hWndMess, GWW_HWNDPARENT, (WORD)hWnd);

             /*
             ** Disable the main window.
             */
             EnableWindow(hWnd, FALSE);
         }
         else
         {
             MessageBox(hWnd,"Cannot Find MessageBox!", NULL, MB_OK);
         }
     }
     else
     {
         /*
         ** Not our private message so pass it on to Windows.
         */
         return DefWindowProc(hWnd, message, wParam, lParam);
     }
}
```

The first thing this function does is test whether or not the message being received is the *private message,* note that it uses a static variable to ensure that the call to RegisterWindowMessage() is done only once, further calls to the function are not required.

The next thing that's done is that the message box is located, that is to say that its window andle is retrieved. Note that the class name #32770 is given as well as the message box's caption in order to minimise the possibility of finding the wrong window (this could still happen if there was another message box in the system with the same caption!)!

```
hWndMess = FindWindow("#32770", ((BOX_INFO FAR *)lParam)->Caption);
```

Having found the message box's window, we now find the message box's control windows using this for loop :

```
for(
    hWndControl = Get TopWindow(hWndMess)
    ;hWndControl &&
    (lpstrControlCaption = *(&((BOX_INFO FAR *)lParam)->
    Button1 + uLoop))
    != NULL
    'hWndControl = GetWindow(hWndControl, GW_HWNDNEXT)
    )
```

Each iteration is conditional on two things, 1 – that we have found another control window, and 2 – that we have another control caption in the BOX_INFO structure pointed to by the lParam. This is required to prevent the remainder of the function using a NULL pointer as a valid character pointer in the case where the style regarding the number of required buttons does not match the number of captions given. For example if the MB_ ABORTRETRYIGNORE style was given but only two captions defined in the BOX_INFO structure we would want to leave the third button's caption alone - this can be a really useful feature (see below).

Having found a control we check to see that its ID is NOT -1. In message boxes, static controls have the ID of -1, we don't want to change the caption of the icon etc so we ignore any control that has an ID of -1. We could have checked to see if the class name of the control was BUTTON but this would have taken a little longer (string compare etc).

Having found a button control (only buttons left when the statics have gone), and having a non-NULL pointer as a candidate caption, we set the caption of the button found using SetWindowText(). I usually use the message version of an API if one is available as it's quicker, ie. a SendMessage() with WM_SETTEXT in this case (a call to SetWindowText() results in a call to SendMessage() so why not call SendMessage() in the first place!). This caption setting lark is continued until either of the two conditions detailed above are false, ie. we run out of controls or run out of captions! Lastly, the message box window is re-parented to the main window which is then disabled. Note that this technique of re-parenting causes the resultant message box's caption to be removed from the Task-List.

The result is a *real* message box but with modified button captions. You might find it useful if you use this code, to define yourself some extra ID??? and MB_????? constants, for example :

```
#define MB_ONEBUTTON              0x0000
#define MB_TWOBUTTON              0x0001
#define MB_THREEBUTTON            0x0002
```

The values used here refer to :

```
#define MB_OK                     0x0000
#define MB_OKCANCEL               0x0001
#define MB_ABORTRETRYIGNORE       0x0002
```

Essentially, what you're saying is give me one, two or three buttons and ignore the captions on them. You can also use the function with existing captions, ie. if you use, say, MB_YESNOCANCEL but give only one caption in the call to NewMessageBox (must be the first caption) of, say, *Hello*, the message box produced will look like this:

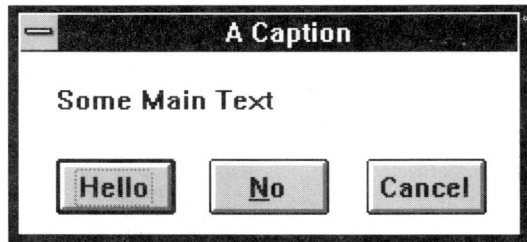

The call would look like this :

```
nRes = NewMessageBox(
                hWnd
                ,"Some Main Text"
                ,"A Caption"
                ,"Hello"
                ,NULL
                ,NULL
                ,MB_YESNOCANCEL
                );
```

Note that the *&* was omitted from *Hello*, the result is a button that is not selectable using the Alt key.

You could, using this technique, change anything about the message box's appearance.

For example, you'll notice that message boxes left align their internal text, well perhaps you want it centred? Or, perhaps you want your company's logo displayed in the message box - whatever, you can now do it. Although the *alignment* option above probably sounds easier than perhaps displaying your company's logo - it isn't! The message box code creates, for the box's internal text, a single static control. These controls display their window captions; you'd change the text displayed with, say, SetWindowText(). The control is resized so that it is just large enough to hold the text, further the static style given for the control is SS_LEFT which means that the text is shown left aligned like so :

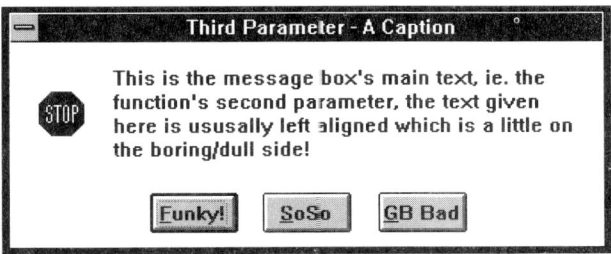

Wouldn't it just be fab to show the text centred like so? :

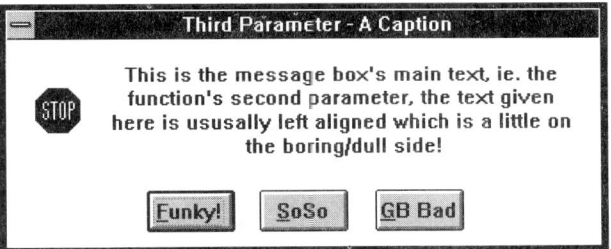

This was done by changing the static text control so that its window style was changed by adding the style SS_CENTER, the code is very simple – made more so by the predictability of the standard message box controls, it looks something like this :

```
if(GetWindowWord(hWndControl, GWW_ID) == -1)
{
    auto DWORD dwStyle;

    dwStyle = GetWindowLong(hWndControl, GWL_STYLE);

    if((dwStyle & SS_ICON) == 0)
    {
        SetWindowLong(hWndControl, GWL_STYLE , (dwStyle | SS_CENTER) & ~SS_LEFT);
    }

    continue; /* Static control so igrore it. */
}
else
    ...
```

A company logo (or a floppy disk in the following example) could be shown more easily if the logo were held in an ICON format. All you'd do is add the ICON to your resources and at some convenient time create a new static class child window (of the message box main window) to hold the icon. Something like this :

```
CreateWindow(
             "static"
             ,"LOGO"
             ,WS_CHILD | SS_ICON | WS_VISIBLE
             ,nTop
             ,nLeft
             ,0
             ,0
             ,hWndMess
             ,-1
             ,GetWindowWord(hWnd, GWW_HINSTANCE)
             ,0
             );
```

This bit of code creates a new message box control; the control's an ICON type static control. These controls are automatically sized to accommodate the icon represented by their captions so the width and height are set to zero. The icon, *LOGO* is defined in our resources and so the instance handle given for the HINSTANCE parameter is derived from the parent window handle hWnd. The control is parented to the message box window hWndMess and given the control ID of -1 as is in keeping with the convention. The resultant message box might now look like this :

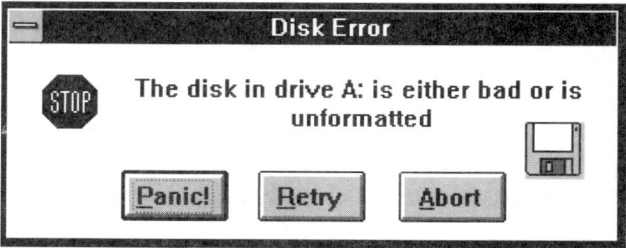

Note that the *Panic* button is the default!

How about getting rid of the box's system menu? :

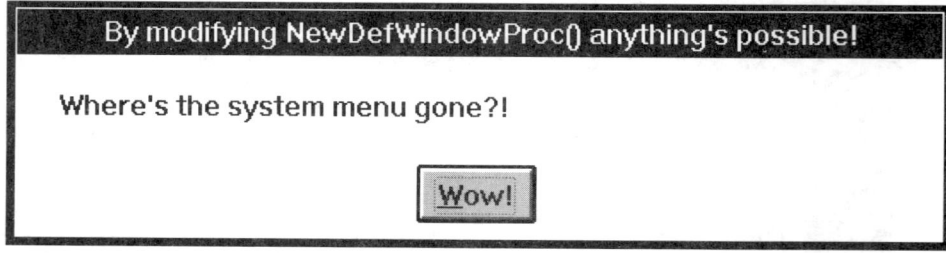

All this required was the following (in bold code) to be inserted into NewDefWindowProc:

```
if(hWndMess != NULL)
{
    /*
    ** hWnd for each control in box.
    */
    auto HWND    hWndControl;

    /*
    ** Used to walk BOX_INFO captions.
    */
    auto UINT    uLoop;

    /*
    ** Caption to use on control.
    */
    auto LPCSTR lpstrControlCaption;

    /*
    ** Now remove the system menu from the box!
    */
    SetWindowLong(
                hWndMess
                ,GWL_STYLE
                ,GetWindowLong(hWndMess, GWL_STYLE) & ~WS_SYSMENU
                );

    uLoop = 0;  /* Set offset (loop counter) to 0. */

    ...
    ...
```

We'll look at the *total replacement* for MessageBox() later but for now, on to *real* dialog boxes.

☐ Dialog Boxes Proper

Modal first. The current APIs to create a modal dialog are :

```
DialogBox()
DialogBoxParam()
DialogBoxIndirect()
DialogBoxIndirectParam()
```

All calls to the functions shown above result in a call to an API that creates a modeless dialog - CreateDialogIndirectParam(). Any dialog created with one of these functions is destroyed using EndDialog().

However, please note that EndDialog() doesn't really destroy the dialog box; also note that when you call this function, any code following it is executed. EndDialog() actually sets an internal flag that says, 'When you next get control kill this window'!

The dialog window is still a window even after this API is called, all it does is hide the window and set that internal flag; you can even re-show the window if you wish! Once you return to the dialog box manager, however, the window is destroyed.

Modal dialogs are the easiest dialogs to create, they are therefore the most prevalent kind of dialog box as most programmers usually take the easiest route when building dialogs. They are not usually the *best* or most suitable dialog box though.

As was stated earlier in this book You're at your best when you're modeless. Human beings are, by and large, single tasking modeless creatures, your users will feel more at home in a world such as Windows if your applications are also modeless. Creating modeless dialogs isn't hard – I'm sure you've all created one at some time – so why don't you use them whenever you can? For example, why should an *About Box* be modal? Most of them are! The question you should ask yourself when building a dialog is, 'should my user be able to continue to use the application even when this dialog box is present?'. The answer, almost all of the time, is 'yes they should'. Again, think of the About Box.

A refinement to this exists, why not destroy dialogs like About Boxes when they become inactive windows? For an About Box this approach is ideal. The user calls forth the box, notes its contents and decides to go back to the main window in your application. As the About Box becomes inactive you arrange for it to be destroyed – result = happy punter, happy Windows, tidy desktop (nice house, nice tea). OK, what's the downside, there must be one? The downside is that users don't expect to have About Boxes etc behaving intelligently like this and it may disturb them (most user are *disturbed* if you ask me!). If you like, the old ways are the bad ways but at least they're predictable and de facto! Also, such dialogs must be, of course, non task or application modal if the parent is to be activated whilst the dialog's up!

Dialog boxes are normally created in response to some user input, they want to check a document's spelling or want to peek at the about box. Sometimes however, they are created by the system (again usually after some user input) or by the application, say, to inform the user that they haven't saved their work in the last ten minutes. Wherever they are created, and due to whatever circumstances, dialogs should be maintained, by and large, by the dialog call-back function that traditionally looks after them.

The call-back function is not the same as the call-back used to maintain a window however, the former is *called back* from an existing WndProc while the latter *is* a WndProc.

The diagram overleaf shows the relationship which exists between a user supplied call-back and the Windows' dialog box manager, or, DM. Note that the class (and window) call-back is also supplied as an integral part of the dialog box manager, the call-back function's nothing more than a sub-classing function of sorts, as is DefDlgProc() as it is a sub-class of DefWindowProc() which in terms of object orientation describes the *standard window* behaviour. These sub-class procs change that standard behaviour in some way. I often describe object oriented programming as *programming by describing the differences,* this window procedure chain I think is a good example of that statement. The difference between a *standard class behaviour* (DefWindowProc() processing alone) and *your* class is that your class window procedure handles more events than the standard class's window procedure does (DefWindowProc()); your class also probably handles some of the standard class's events or messages differently, sometimes passing them on to the default class window procedure for processing and sometimes not. A sub-classing function, when applied, demonstrates the notion of late-binding, or polymorphism and may be applied to *class* as well as *instance* objects (there'll be more on this DM -> call-back relationship later in this chapter). The source for DefDlgProc() is supplied with the MS SDK and is included in the appendix to this book; you'll find it useful as a reference when reading the next couple of sections.

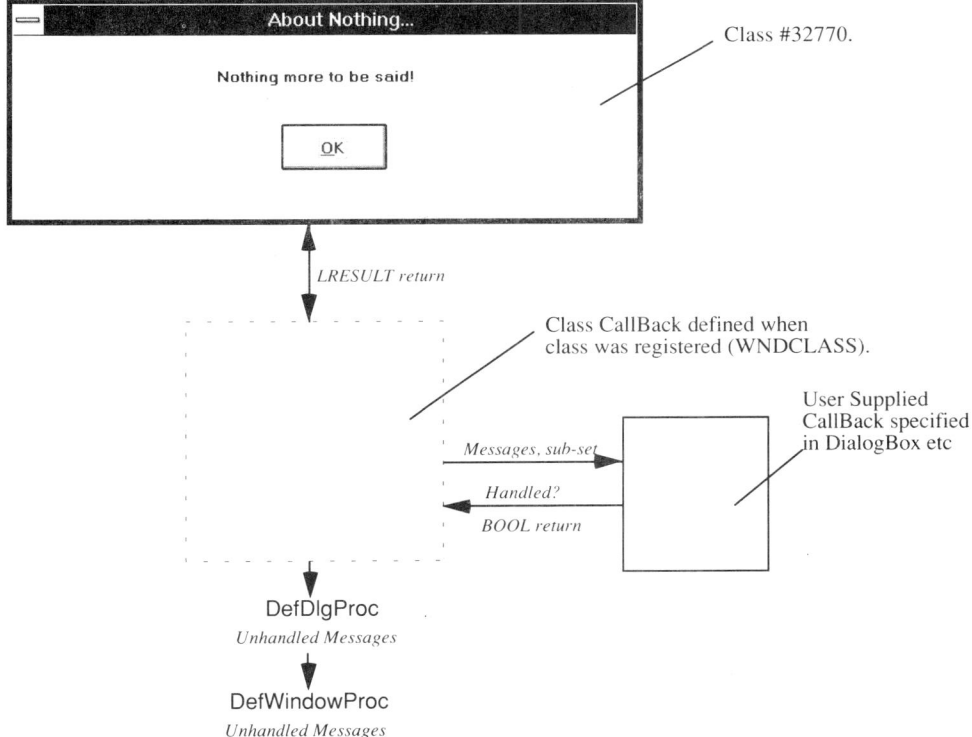

It is possible to have a dialog box built from another class than #32770. The easiest way to arrange for this is to supply a class name as part of the dialog box template. Dialog box templates are usually defined within the application's resources, they, like all resources, are made up of read only data and as such, unlike dynamic data, may be discarded from the global heap when the space they occupy is required by the system (it is possible to create resources that are read/write also).

☐ The Dialog Resource

The dialog resource (as pertaining to how it is defined to the resource compiler) is defined as follows :

```
NameID DIALOG [load-option] [mem-option] x, y, width, height
BEGIN
    control-statements
    .
    .
    .
END
```

The options for [mem-option] are FIXED MOVEABLE DISCARDABLE. Be careful not to specify something like FIXED and DISCARDABLE together. The resource compiler doesn't treat these as mutually exclusive - the result is a discardable resource – always!

Having a resource fixed in memory is sometimes very handy as it can allow you to modify the resource as a memory image (AccessResource() can be used to change a resources physical disk image although the method is not documented – turn the read only file handle into a read/write and DO IT!); talking of memory images of resources...

☐ Dialog Templates in Memory

It usually makes sense for dialogs to be labelled LOADONCALL and MOVEABLE/ DISCARDABLE; however, specifying that a resource is FIXED allows you to modify the resource on the fly.

You can get hold of the resource in a number of ways : FindResource(), LoadResource(), LockResource(), FreeResource() and AccessResource().

For example, to turn Generic's about box into this :

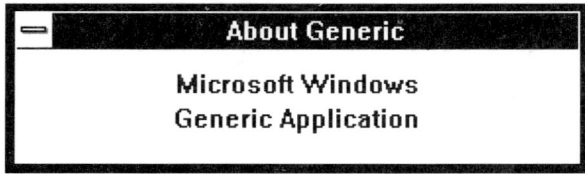

This is what you could do.

First you find and load the required resource :

```
auto HRSRC      hRes;
auto HINSTANCE  hInst;

hInst = GetWindowWord(hWnd, GWW_HINSTANCE);
```

```
hRes = FindResource(hInst, "AboutBox", RT_DIALOG);

if(hRes != NULL)
{
    auto HGLOBAL hGlob;

    hGlob = LoadResource(hInst, hRes);
```

Then you lock it to get its address :

```
if(hGlob != NULL)
{
    auto LPDLGTEMPLATE lpDlgT;

    lpDlgT = (DLGTEMPLATE FAR *)LockResource(hGlob);
```

Now you modify and show the dialog :

```
lpDlgT->dtCY = 30;

(void)DialogBoxIndirect(hInst, hGlob, hWnd, About);
```

Lastly, you free the resource :

```
(void)FreeResource(hGlob);
```

The interesting bit here is contained within the type LPDLGTEMPLATE, or long pointer to a DLGTEMPLATE. This poor structure is not actually documented in WINDOWS.H (under 3.1 or 3.0), nor is it defined in the 3.1 Programmer's Reference (volume 3). You can find the documentation on this resource type (3.1 version only) in volume 4 chapter 7 section 7.6. If you're using the 3.0 SDK you'll find it in volume 2 in section 7 page 31. Interestingly, but not really that surprisingly, the structures used to define this resource have changed between 3.0 and 3.1!

In version 3.0 of the SDK this structure is one of three which are all closely related to each other, they are DLGTEMPLATE, DLGITEMTEMPLATE and a FONTINFO. As I've said, they were documented in the 3.0 documentation but not in the 3.0 WINDOWS.H, in fact they couldn't have been as the typedef'd structures described in the documentation contain illegal 'C'! They look more or less like this in the docs however:

```
typedef struct
{
    DWORD           dtStyle;
    BYTE            dtItemCount;
    WORD            dyX;
    WORD            dtY;
    WORD            dtCX;
    WORD            dtCY;
    char            dtMenuName          [ ];
```

```
        char              dtClassName              [ ];
        char              dtCaptionText            [ ];
} DLGTEMPLATE;

typedef struct
{
        WORD              ditX;
        WORD              ditY;
        WORD              ditCX;
        WORD              ditCY;
        WORD              ditID;
        DWORD             ditStyle;
        char              ditClassName             [ ];
        char              ditCaptionText           [ ];
        BYTE              ditInfo;
        LPSTR             ditData;
} DLGITEMTEMPLATE;

typedef struct
{
        WORD              fiPointSize;
        char              fiTypeFace  [ ];
} FONTINFO;
```

The 'C' problem with these structure/types is that they contain uninitialised arrays of char, ie. the arrays defined within these types are not dimensioned (the empty square brackets mean that the array has 0 members or elements – obviously illegal).

However, MSC 7 does allow you to specify such an array as the last member of a structure (can't remember if C6 allowed this!), but it will not allow you to specify more than one, even if they are both at the end of the structure, or to have one as anything other the last member. This means that both the DLGTEMPLATE and DLGITEMTEMPLATE above are illegal! OK, so what about the 3.1 SDK? Well still illegal 'C' I'm afraid. These three structures are now replaced by two; they look like this :

```
struct DialogBoxHeader
{
        DWORD             lStyle;
        BYTE              bNumberOfItems;
        WORD              x;
        WORD              y;
        WORD              cx;
        WORD              cy;
        char              szMenuName  [ ];
        char              szClassName [ ];
        WORD              wPintSize
        char              szFaceName  [ ];
}
```

```
struct ControlData
{
    WORD        x;
    WORD        y;
    WORD        cx;
    WORD        cy;
    WORD        wID;
    DWORD       lStyle;
    union
    {
            BYTE        class;
            char        szClass     [ ];
    } classID;
    char        szText      [ ];
}
```

What's changed? Well now the old FONTINFO type, or struct, is an integral part of the DialogBoxHeader structure; it's only used however if the lStyle member of the DialogBoxHeader structure is set to DS_SETFONT, ie. if the dialog box is to use a font other than the standard one. The old FONTINFO type was really the same thing. The DLGTEMPLATE type was followed in memory by a FONTINFO type *if* the dialog box style included DS_SETFONT, so all in all not a big change. There is another change however. The control structure ControlData does not now include the members *ditInfo* and *ditData* as shown in the DLGITEMTEMPLATE. Well what were these members and can you still use them even though they're not defined? These members were used to pass *type* (or class) specific data to controls of a particular type as they were created as *control members* of a dialog box.

Let's say that you have your own type of control that looks like a regular push button, except that the caption of such a button can be aligned differently to that of a standard push button, aligned top left etc. You further want to include some of these controls in your dialog box. This is fine, all you have to do is design your dialog with the dialog editor substituting, say, ordinary push-button for your custom push buttons (does anyone really define new custom control DLLs?) .

A short digression on how to do this follows before we continue with dynamic dialog boxes:

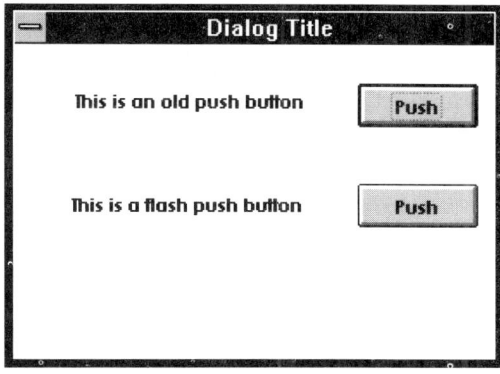

You could have substituted any old thing, say, a black rectangle if you'd liked but as a *Super* push button is obviously something like a regular boring push-button it made sense to choose push buttons. Once this is done you save the template and create a .dlg file which will now look something like this :

```
IDC_OLDBUTTON DIALOG 32, 29, 160, 100
STYLE DS_MODALFRAME | WS_POPUP | WS_VISIBLE | WS_CAPTION |
WS_SYSMENU
CAPTION "Dialog Title"
FONT 8, "Century Gothic"
BEGIN
    CONTROL   "This is an old push button", -1, "Static",
WS_GROUP, 20, 14, 91, 9
    CONTROL   "Push", IDC_OLDBUTTON, "Button", WS_TABSTOP, 114,
12, 40, 14
    CONTROL   "This is a flash push button", -1, "Static",
WS_GROUP, 19, 47, 89, 8
    CONTROL   "Push", IDC_NEWBUTTON, "Button", WS_TABSTOP, 114,
44, 40, 14
END
```

If you take a close look at the contents of the CONTROL statement you'll notice that there's a strong correlation between the information supplied in a CreateWindow() call. What's missing? Three things :

1 The window handle of a parent window; remember that controls are usually created as child windows (implicit when using CreateWindow() indirectly like this) and that every child must have a parent.

2 The instance handle of the instance of the application wishing to create the dialog/child controls.

3 Creation parameter information (the last parameter to CreateWindow()).

Of the three the only one that's *really* missing is the last; the other two can only be resolved at run-time and are assigned by the dialog box manager, after all, it's the dialog box manager that creates the dialog box top level window so it's only the dialog box manager that knows the window handle to use as a parent window handle for the controls.

The dialog box itself of course will *probably* required a parent (owner would be better here), and that is passed to the dialog box manager by you when you call any of the dialog box creation functions; the same is true for the instance handle of the instance of the application requiring the dialog box. Control windows are created in the order they appear in the template - this fact may sometime be very useful to know.

You might want to set the captions of all the *new* push buttons to, say, *New* – this will make them a little easier to spot. Once you've done this you now edit the .dlg file replacing the class name of button for whatever your new button's class name is; then you run the resource compiler over it to make a new .res file. Once that is done you're practically through. If you now re-run the dialog editor and re-open your .res file (the new one) you'll find this :

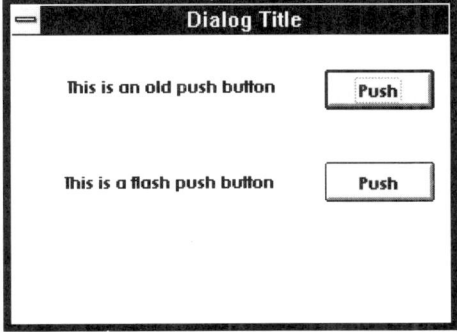

The dialog editor's replaced the unknown class with a class called DlgCustom (the 3.0 SDK dialog editor does something very similar). You can now edit this new control defining style attributes for it etc.

Remember that some attribute codes are filtered by windows; for example WS_VISIBLE is not directly used by the control class but is filtered by the window manager -which in turn makes the window visible of course. More on this sort of stuff in the chapter on window types.

Once you've configured your styles etc you're ready to add the freshly saved .dlg file to your resources proper. As long as the control class has been registered by your application, or some other module if the class is global, before the dialog box is loaded your new control will be part of your dialog box :

End of Digression.

OK, back to indirect dialogs. The new control, we'll call it a window of class Flash-PushButton, can be passed initialisation information via a CreateWindow() call. This data is passed in the last parameter and is received within the class window procedure, for a given instance of a *FlashPushButton*, via a CREATESTRUCT pointed to by the lParam of either the WM_NCCREATE or WM_CREATE messages. The lpCreateParams member of the CREATSTRUCT is used to actually get a hold of the initialisation data.

Now it would be nice, or it may even be a requirement, to pass some sort of data to a *FlashPushButton* when it is created. The dialog box manager creates, via CreateWindowEx(), not only the dialog box window but also each control in the dialog box. Of course the dialog box manager doesn't know that your control class requires a little something extra passed to it as it is created, can't do it, and therefore fails to properly initialise your new control(s).

The ditInfo and ditData members were added (supposedly) to allow this kind of initialisation to take place. The ditInfo parameter was set to the size (in bytes) of the ditData member (0 if ditData didn't exist). The data (the memory following sizeof(ditInfo) + ditInfo) was passed to the control via the CREATESTRUCT member as previously mentioned. If the ditInfo was zero it meant that no private data followed it, ie. no private data to send to the window procedure. it was really a good idea – it's a pity it didn't work too well!

These members have been removed from the resource definition (which as I said is still not even legal in terms of the 'C' used) and so we must assume that although they worked before, that they may disappear in the future – Pity as now there's no documented way to pass CREATESTRUCT creation data to the control. The only way to pass private data to a class of window that is to be used as a control, as well as a non-control window, is to pass it via some private message which is delivered sometime after the actual window has been created. I guess there are some other ways; like using the window style bits, or using some sort of code in the window's caption – a good idea especially if the window does not display a caption. All of these measures however are not as clean nor as OO as the CREATESTRUCT method. If you think of WM_CREATE handling as being analogous to, say, the execution of a C++ constructor it really is the place to initialise the object.

Instances of these objects/types are created, either by loading an existing dialog resource or by creating them anew using the global heap, and passed to the relevant dialog creation function. The diagram opposite shows the ordering in memory.

Some programmers use these *dynamic* subroutines to modify existing dialog resources, others use them when they build up entire new dialog resources from scratch using the global heap. The easiest way is with a compromise however.

Building a template dynamically would be simplicity itself if it were not for one small detail that makes the whole process more messy than in my opinion it's worth; that small detail is to do with those empty character arrays. These arrays are *in line* members of the structure, that is to say that these structures are truly *dynamic* in that their size is not fixed.

What you're suppose to do is add the relevant string into the structure tagging any remaining elements on behind the last zero byte of the 'C' string. This makes assignment to later members much more complex as you have to work out where you're up to currently by doing some pretty messy pointer computations - yuk. Why oh why didn't they change these members to be of type LPCSTR, ie. pointers to

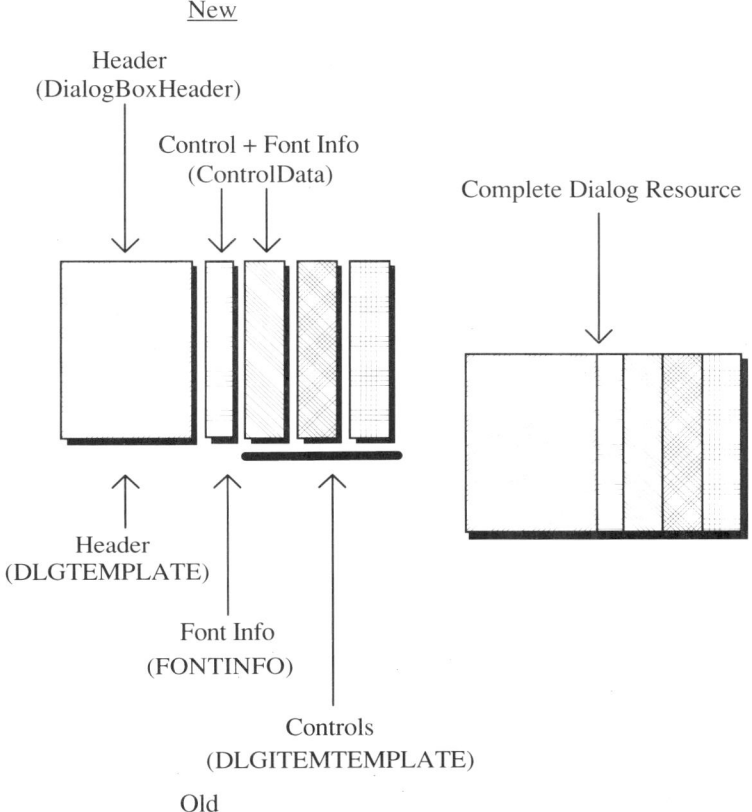

New

Header
(DialogBoxHeader)

Control + Font Info
(ControlData)

Complete Dialog Resource

Header
(DLGTEMPLATE)

Font Info
(FONTINFO)

Controls
(DLGITEMTEMPLATE)

Old

character arrays, this would have meant that the structures used to describe a dialog box would have been of a fixed size – much nicer, oh well!

The template for Generic's dialog box as a memory object looks like this when viewed using heap walker :

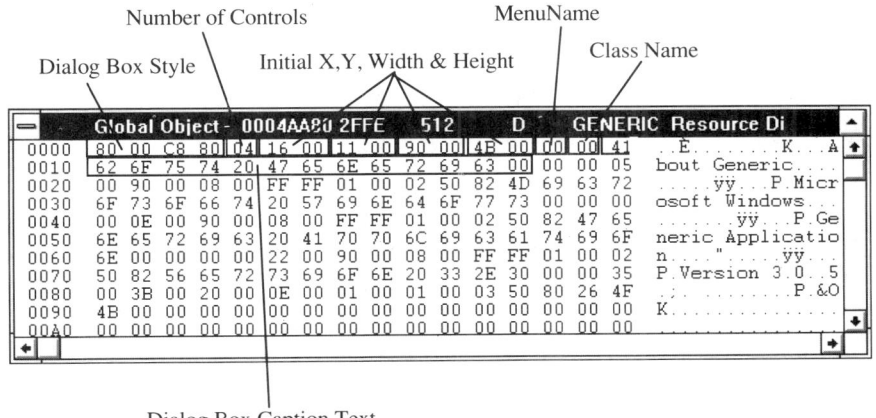

Number of Controls

Dialog Box Style

Initial X,Y, Width & Height

MenuName

Class Name

Dialog Box Caption Text

Initial X,Y, Width & Height

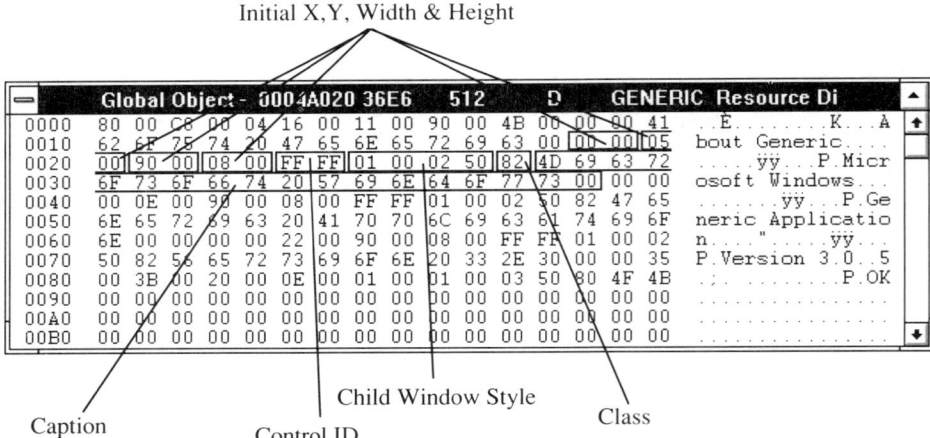

Child Window Style

Caption

Control ID

Class

IDOK

Class IDs

These three heap walker snap shots show the same dialog box resource. Things of general interest, that are not already labelled, are shown in the last picture.

The first snapshot shows the format, internally, of the dialog box header. Note the in-line strings; further note that if a string is not given that a NULL string terminator must still be given, ie. although we haven't got a menu or a special class specified that we've still got two 'C' string terminators.

The second snapshot shows the format of the first child control in the resource; this is a static control. Note that the class name may be specified by a single byte. The hexadecimal value of this byte will be either 0x80 for a button, 0x81 for an edit control, 0x82 for a static control, 0x83 for a list box, 0x84 for a scroll bar or 0x85 for a combo box. This also holds for 3.0 by the way.

If we alter the dialog resource in the .dlg giving a new class name, a menu name and a custom control class we will see how this has changed :

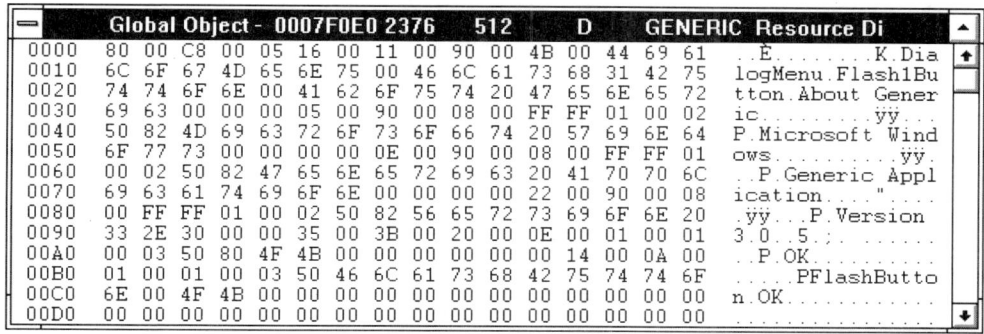

The format is not equivalent to the formats of the DLGTEMPLATE etc used above; for example note that both the menu and class names come before the dialog caption. This doesn't really matter, it's just mildly interesting, Windows obviously moves things about a bit!

All the dynamic structures and types shown earlier contain these in-line empty arrays. When ever I build a dynamic dialog, which is not very often, I use one of the following two methods. First I create a DLGTEMPLATE type that does not include the arrays :

```c
typedef struct
{
    DWORD           dtStyle;
    BYTE            dtItemCount;
    WORD            dyX;
    WORD            dtY;
    WORD            dtCX;
    WORD            dtCY;
} DLGTEMPLATE;
```

I then use character pointers in place of the arrays.

```c
char *              dtMenuName;
char *              dtClassName;
char *              dtCaptionText;
```

The same goes for the DLGITEMTEMPLATE and FONTINFO :

```c
typedef struct
{
    WORD            ditX;
    WORD            ditY;
    WORD            ditCX;
    WORD            ditCY;
    WORD            ditID;
    DWORD           ditStyle;
} DLGITEMTEMPLATE;
```

```
char *                      ditClassName;
char *                /     ditCaptionText;


typedef struct
{
    WORD                    fiPointSize;
} FONTINFO;

char            *           fiTypeFace;
```

Each structure is filled in and copied to a global memory block :

```
auto HGLOBAL            hGlob;
auto DLGTEMPLATE        tDlgTemplate;
auto VOID FAR *         lpDialogData;

tDlgTemplate.dtStyle = WS_POPUP | DSMODALFRAME...
...

hGlob = GlobalAlloc(
                    GMEM_???
                    ,sizeof(DLGTEMPLATE) +
                    sizeof(FONTINFO) +
                    sizeof(DLGITEMTEMPLATE) * uControls +
                    lstrlen(lpszCaption)  +
                    lstrlen(lpszClass) ... etc
                    );

lpDialogData = GlobalLock(hGlob);

_fmemcpy(lpDialogData, &tDlgTemplate, sizeof(DLGTEMPLATE));

//etc for all strings and other structures types.
```

I'm sure you get the idea? Pretty tedious stuff although nicely variable (see example application later in this chapter for a variation on this theme).

The other way I have created dynamic dialogs is to have a dummy dialog as a resource which contains a default set of the stuff you might want. You load that resource, lock it down and modify it to create your required dialog box. Again the only fly in the ointment is those darn in-line character arrays. If the dummy dialog has a caption of say 10 characters life is made real simple if your required caption has ten characters also, if it has either less or more then you've got to shuffle memory about again. I once saw someone else use this technique, their dummy template contained large empty (spaces) strings for captions, they then overwrote these empty captions in the loaded resource and null terminated them, they ended up with window captions that were left aligned etc so the exercise didn't really work. We'll see how untidy all this gets in practice a little later in this chapter (example application).

OK, we've talked through the template stuff so let's carry on with Modal dialogs.

☐ Modal Dialogs

The standard modal dialog is created with either DialogBox() or DialogBoxParam(). The latter enables the user to pass information to the dialog call-back via the WM_INIT-DIALOG message's LPARAM parameter. The call-back function is defined as :

```
BOOL __export CALLBACK BDIALOGPROC(HWND,UINT,WPARAM,LPARAM);
```

The function returns a BOOL type (via its return value), and is flagged as exported. The function's labelled CALLBACK which is FAR PASCAL and its *parameter set* is the same as for a window procedure.

We'll start creating a dialog box now!

The dialog will be application modal and mimic the input box (InputBox$()) function in Microsoft's Visual Basic. In case you haven't seen Visual Basic's InputBox$ here it is:

Visual Basic's Input Box

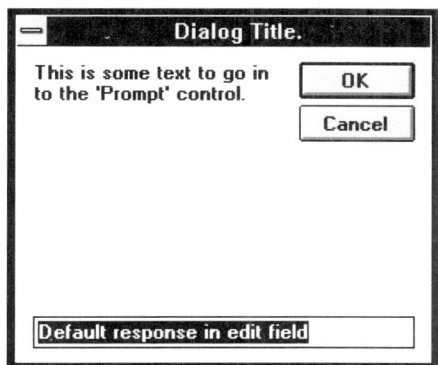

The InputBox$ function, for that it what it is, has the following form:

InputBox$(prompt$[,title$ [,default$ [,xpos%, ypos%]]]). Those identifiers ending with a $ are string arguments, whereas those ending with a % are integer arguments. The arguments specify the following :

> promtp$ The text that will appear inside the box, that's This is some text to go in to the 'Prompt' control. in the diagram above.

> title$ -   The dialog box's caption.

> default$-   The text that will appear in the edit control at the bottom of the box, Default response in Edit field in the diagram above.

> xpos%/ypos%-   Positioning information, ie. a point which identifies the upper top left corner of the input box.

The Visual Basic InputBox$ is variadic, ie. it can take a variable number of arguments, the minimum being one – prompt$ I'll not duplicate all of this functionality in my 'C' based InputBox for two reasons, 1. Most users of InputBox use all but the last two parameters, ie. they omit the positioning information, and 2. Implementing my 'C' based routine to be a variadic function will increase the amount of code required to produce what is after all a very simple dialog box; when I read programming books I usually want to see the minimum amount of code required to animate a concept, I hope you feel this way too!? If the user presses the OK button the function returns a string which is a copy of that entered into the edit control. Here's the Visual Basic code :

```
Sub DoInputBox ()

Dim Msg      As String
Dim Title    As String
Dim Default  As String
Dim Response As String

    Msg      = "This is some text to go in to the 'Prompt' control."
    Title    = "Dialog Title."
    Default  = "Default response in edit field"
    Response = InputBox$(Msg$, Title$, Default$)

    '...

    MsgBox Response, 0, "This was in edit -"
End Sub
```

This code creates an InputBox, and when the box is dismissed creates a message box which details the string returned from the InputBox's edit control.

The Visual Basic InputBox$ function creates a standard, class #32770, or WC_DIA-LOG, modal dialog box and of course this dialog box contains some child window controls (a pretty useless dialog would result if one didn't!). The controls are :

An edit control (style 0x50010000, ID 101). A static control (style 0x50000000, ID 101). Two push buttons, one labelled OK, the other Cancel. Here's a diagram with the controls marked –

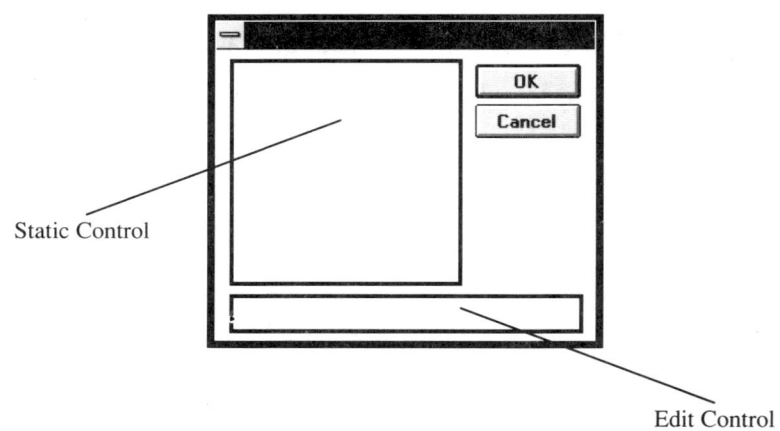

Static Control

Edit Control

The dialog doesn't resize etc like that produced by MessageBox() and always looks the same. The Visual Basic Language Reference says that the static control (used for displaying the main text) can display about 255 characters depending upon the size of the font used; this is because it doesn't get resized, ultimately the text would simply over flow the control and get clipped therefore. Other functionality described in the reference is that when the user presses the cancel button the function returns an empty string, ie. "". When the box is first displayed, the default text in the edit control is highlighted, this control has to have the focus to do that so it is focused by the function.

Here's my InputBox :

You'll notice, that although they are a little differently shaped, that they are basically the same thing; indeed the controls even have the same child IDs!

Although the function used to create this InputBox is non-variadic, the dialog does have some extra functionality. The edit control used in my dialog box has a different style – 0x50010080, just in case you haven't got WINDOWS.H in memory, the extra 80 is this :

```
#define ES_AUTOHSCROLL    0x00000080L
```

My edit control allows the user to enter more text into the edit control by scrolling text already entered to the left. The standard Visual Basic InputBox only allows as much text to be entered as will fit into the control; although this is somewhat more useful it does mean that a little extra work has to be done to handle this functionality in terms of the 'C' code. The InputBox above was produced with the following call :

```
auto int        nRes;
auto char       carBuff[255];

nRes = InputBox(
            hWnd
            ,"This is some text to go in to the 'Prompt' control."
```

```
               ,"Dialog Title"
               ,"Default response in edit field"
               ,&carBuff[0]
               ,sizeof(carBuff)
               );
```

```
MessageBox(hWnd, &carBuff[0], "Entered Text", MB_OK);
```

You'll notice that this code is smaller than the equivalent Visual Basic code above? This is 8pt, that was 10!

My InputBox can be described like this :

int InputBox(*hWnd, lpszPrompt, lpszTitle, lpszDefault, lpszBuff, uSize*)

HWND *hWnd*;	/* Handle to owner window.	*/
LPCSTR *lpszPrompt*;	/* The main text that appears inside the box.	*/
LPCSTR *lpszTitle*;	/* The box's caption text.	*/
LPCSTR *lpszDefault*;	/* The text originally shown in the dialog's edit control.	*/
LPSTR *lpszBuff*;	/* A pointer to a buffer that receives the users answer.	*/
UINT *uSize*;	/* The size of the buffer pointer to by lpszBuff.	*/

The InputBox function creates a dialog box which is used to solicit a response from the user to some question posed in the box.

Parameters

hWnd

Identifies the parent window for the InputBox.

lpszPrompt

A long pointer to a constant character string. The string pointed to becomes the main text used in the box, this text forms the question to which the user responds.

lpszTitle

A long pointer to a constant character string. The string pointed to becomes the caption text used in the InputBox.

lpszDefault

A long pointer to a constant character string. The string pointed to is shown highlighted in the InputBox's edit control as soon as it becomes visible.

lpszBuff

A long pointer to a character string or buffer. The buffer pointed to receives the contents of the edit control, or an empty string, when the InputBox is closed down. If the user presses the OK button the buffer contains the edit control text; if the user presses the Cancel button the buffer will contain an empty string.

Return Value

nRes

The result of using InputBox. nRes will be one of the following : –1 The input box could not be produced, this code will be returned if any of the parameters are illegal. IDOK (1) if the user pressed the OK button. IDCANCEL (2) if the user pressed the Cancel button.

Comments

If the passed default text is longer than the provided return buffer then the default text is truncated to the length of the return buffer. Any truncation of the displayed default text does not effect the buffer used to pass the default text to the function.

The edit control accepts text input up to the number of characters specified by the length of the return buffer.

An InputBox is always centred on the screen.

The InputBox function blocks.

All we need to do now is take a look at the code. First a list of manifest constants, types and prototypes :

```
int          NEAR PASCAL InputBox(HWND, LPCSTR, LPCSTR, LPCSTR, LPSTR, UINT);
BOOL __export  FAR  PASCAL bInputBoxProc(HWND, UINT, WPARAM, LPARAM);

/*
** Dialog defines.
                       */
#define EC_INPUTBOX   101
#define SC_INPUTBOX   102
#define IDD_INPUTBOX 42


typedef struct

{
   LPCSTR  lpszPrompt;
   LPCSTR  lpszTitle;
   LPCSTR  lpszEditDefault;
   LPSTR   lpszResult;
   UINT    uSizeofResultBuff;
} INPUTBOXINFO;
```

Now the dialog template used for the input box :

```
IDD_INPUTBOX DIALOG 0, 0, 124, 143
STYLE          DS_MODALFRAME | WS_POPUP | WS_VISIBLE | WS_CAPTION | WS_SYSMENU
CAPTION        ""
FONT           8, "MS Sans Serif"
BEGIN

  CONTROL        /* Prompt control. */
                 ""
                 ,SC_INPUTBOX
                 ,"Static"
                 ,WS_GROUP
                 ,4
                 ,11
                 ,77
                 ,108


  CONTROL        /* Edit control. */
                 ""
                 ,EC_INPUTBOX
                 ,"Edit"
                 ,ES_AUTOHSCROLL | WS_BORDER | WS_TABSTOP
                 ,4
                 ,125
                 ,117
                 ,14


  CONTROL        /* Cancel button. */
                 "&Cancel"
                 ,IDCANCEL
                 ,"Button"
                 ,WS_TABSTOP
                 ,84
                 ,25
                 ,37
                 ,14


  CONTROL        /* Ok Button. */
                 "&OK"
                 ,IDOK
                 ,"Button"
                 ,WS_TABSTOP
                 ,84
                 ,5
                 ,37
                 ,14

END
```

The InputBox function uses an INPUTBOXINFO struct to pass initialisation information to the dialog procedure bInputBoxProc. The InputBox dialog box is created using

DialogBoxParam()); a pointer to a INPUTBOXINFO structure is passed into the dialog's WM_INITDIALOG message handler via that message's lParam.

The input box function looks like this :

```
int  InputBox
(
   HWND     hWndOwner          /* Who's gonna own the InputBox?     */
  ,LPCSTR   lpszPrompt         /* Pointer to static ctrl text.      */
  ,LPCSTR   lpszTitle          /* Pointer to dialog caption text.   */
  ,LPCSTR   lpszEditDefault    /* Pointer to edit ctrl default text. */
  ,LPSTR    lpszResult         /* Pointer to buffer for result.     */
  ,UINT     uSizeofResultBuff  /* Sizeof result buffer.             */
)
{
   auto INPUTBOXINFO ibi;               /* Passed to dialog box proc. */
   auto int          nDialogResult;     /* Dialog box result.         */

   /*
   ** Make sure we've got a valid window handle for the owner.
   */
   if(IsWindow(hWndOwner) == NULL)
   {
       return -1;
   }

   /*
   ** Fill in INPUTBOXINFO struct with passed parameters.
   */
   ibi.lpszPrompt      = lpszPrompt;
   ibi.lpszTitle       = lpszTitle;
   ibi.lpszEditDefault = lpszEditDefault;
   ibi.lpszResult      = lpszResult;
   ibi.uSizeofResultBuff = uSizeofResultBuff;

   /*
   ** Do the dialog box! Pass struct via WM_INITDIALOG's lParam.
   */
   nDialogResult = DialogBoxParam(
                               GetWindowWord(hWndOwner, GWW_HINSTANCE)
                               ,MAKEINTRESOURCE(IDD_INPUTBOX)
                               ,hWndOwner
                               , (DLGPROC)bInputBoxProc
                               , (LPARAM)(INPUTBOXINFO FAR *)&ibi
                               );

   /*
   ** Handle dialog return result. -1 means either that the DM
   ** couldn't produce the box or that a passed parameter was invalid.
   */
   if(nDialogResult == -1)
   {
       MessageBox(hWndOwner, "Couldn't produce input box!", NULL, MB_OK);
   }

   return nDialogResult;
}
```

The code is short and well documented so there is little for me to add.

Note that the dialog resource is taken from the resources of the owner window; that is why the code returns -1 (fail) if the passed window handle is not a window (unlike DialogBox() etc). If this function were placed into a DLL the instance handle used above (GetWindowWord(hWndOwner, GWW_HINSTANCE)) derived from the owner window handle would have to be replaced with the instance (or module) handle of the DLL; in that case it would be possible to create modeless InputBoxes using the NULL parent window handle technique discussed earlier; typically however, such a box would impose a modal state on its owner, after all the program is asking for something that it requires before continuing.

The code for the InputBox call-back function looks like this :

```
BOOL __export CALLBACK bInputBoxProc
(
    HWND      hDlg        /* Dialog box main window handle.  */
    ,UINT     uMessage    /* Message.                        */
    ,WPARAM   wParam      /* WPARAM sized message parameter. */
    ,LPARAM   lParam      /* LPARAM sized message parameter. */
)
{
    /*
    ** Holds the address of the buffer
    ** into which the entered text is
    ** returned. Must be 'static'.
    */
    static LPSTR lpszReturnBuffer;


    /*
    ** Holds the size of the buffer
    ** into which the entered text is
    ** returned. Must be 'static'.
    */
    static UINT  uSizeofResultBuff;


    switch(uMessage)
    {
            /*
            ** The lParam of this message points to an INPUTBOXINFO struct
            */
        case WM_INITDIALOG:
            {
                auto HWND    hWndEditControl;   /* The dialog's edit ctrl. */
                auto HWND    hWndStaticControl; /* The dialog's static ctrl.*/
                auto LPCSTR  lpszPrompt;        /* Pointer to static ctrl text.*/
                auto LPCSTR  lpszTitle;         /* Pointer to dialog caption. */
                auto LPCSTR  lpszEditDefault;   /* Pointer to edit ctrl default text.*/
```

```
auto RECT    rs;                    /* For centring dialog box.*/
auto int     nXOrg;                 /* For centring dialog box.*/
auto int     nYOrg;                 /* For centring dialog box.*/

/*
** Set up various text pointers from INPUTBOXINFO struct.
*/
lpszPrompt        = ((INPUTBOXINFO FAR *)lParam)-> lpszPrompt;
lpszTitle         = ((INPUTBOXINFO FAR *)lParam)-> lpszTitle;
lpszEditDefault   = ((INPUTBOXINFO FAR *)lParam)-> lpszEditDefault;
lpszReturnBuffer  = ((INPUTBOXINFO FAR *)lParam)-> lpszResult;
uSizeofResultBuff = ((INPUTBOXINFO FAR *)lParam)-> uSizeofResultBuff;

/*
** Get required ctrl window handles.
*/
hWndEditControl   = GetDlgItem(hDlg, EC_INPUTBOX);
hWndStaticControl = GetDlgItem(hDlg, SC_INPUTBOX);

/*
** Check that  all is OK to  proceed?  If something's
** wrong terminate the dialog. We need a  break after
** the  EndDialog()  as  the  function  DOES  return.
** If we terminate we return 0xFFFF which will signal
** the caller that something's wrong.
*/
if(
   hWndEditControl     == NULL     ||
   hWndStaticControl   == NULL     ||
   lpszPrompt          == NULL     ||
   lpszTitle           == NULL     ||
   lpszEditDefault     == NULL     ||
   lpszReturnBuffer    == NULL     ||
   uSizeofResultBuff   == 0
   )
 {
   EndDialog(hDlg, -1);
   break;
 }

/*
** If  edit ctrl's given  default  text  is  longer than
** the sizeof the caller's result buffer,  adjust the size
** of the default text (as we can't adjust the size of the
** callers buffer.  It makes  no sense  to allow the edit
** ctrl  to  contain  default  text  that  is longer than
** can fit into the caller's buffer).
*/
if((UINT)lstrlen(lpszEditDefault) > uSizeofResultBuff)
{
   *((LPSTR)lpszEditDefault + uSizeofResultBuff - 1) =  '\0';
}

/*
** Set limit on text ctrl to match sizeof caller's
** buffer.
*/
SendMessage(
```

```
                hWndEditControl
                ,EM_LIMITTEXT
                , (WPARAM) uSizeofResultBuff - 1
                , (LPARAM) 0
                );

/*
** Set the caller's default text into the edit ctrl,
** note that although the EM_LIMITTEXT message has been
** processed by the ctrl already that it is still
** possible to input more text into the ctrl than
** the EM_LIMITTEXT permits - this is not desirable of
** course. We don't need to worry however coz we have
** already (possibly) adjusted the size of the default
** text in-line with the caller's buffer size - the
** caller's buffer size is what the EM_LIMITTEXT is set
** to so we're all OK.
*/
SendMessage(
                hWndEditControl
                ,WM_SETTEXT
                , (WPARAM) 0
                , (LPARAM) lpszEditDefault
                );

/*
** Now select ALL the text in the ctrl.
*/
SendMessage(
                hWndEditControl
                ,EM_SETSEL
                , (WPARAM) 0
                ,MAKELPARAM(0,-1)
                );

/*
** EDIT CONTROL INIT COMPLETE. Now set up the dialog's
** caption.
*/
SendMessage(
                hDlg
                ,WM_SETTEXT
                , (WPARAM) 0
                , (LPARAM) lpszTitle
                );

/*
** Now set up the static ctrl's caption.
*/
SendMessage(
                hWndStaticControl
                ,WM_SETTEXT
                , (WPARAM) 0
                , (LPARAM) lpszPrompt
                );

/*
** Centre the dialog.
```

```
        */
        GetWindowRect(hDlg, &rs);

        nXOrg = GetSystemMetrics(SM_CXSCREEN);
        nXOrg = (nXOrg / 2) - ((rs.right - rs.left) / 2);

        nYOrg = GetSystemMetrics(SM_CYSCREEN);
        nYOrg = (nYOrg / 2) - ((rs.bottom - rs.top) / 2);

        MoveWindow(
                  hDlg
                 ,nXOrg
                 ,nYOrg
                 ,rs.right - rs.left
                 ,rs.bottom - rs.top
                 ,FALSE
                 );


        /*
        ** Last bit, set the focus to the edit ctrl.
        */
        SetFocus(hWndEditControl);

        return FALSE; /* Say we've set the focus. */

        break;
    }

case WM_COMMAND:

    /*
    ** Input from  dialog ctrls. The  only  stuff  we're
    ** interested in  is notifications  from buttons, in
    ** particular  - we're only interested in 'clicks'.
    */
    if(HIWORD(lParam) == BN_CLICKED)
    {
        auto HWND hWndEditControl; /* The dialog's edit ctrl. */

        /*
        ** Signal end of dialog and cause it to be hidden. Pass
        ** back ID of button (OK or CANCEL).
        */
        EndDialog(hDlg,wParam);

        /*
        ** Get edit ctrl window handle.
        */
        if((hWndEditControl = GetDlgItem(hDlg, EC_INPUTBOX))!= NULL)
        {
            /*
            ** If the user cancelled reset text in edit to "".
            */
            if(wParam == IDCANCEL)
            {
                SendMessage(
                            hWndEditControl
```

```
                                  ,WM_SETTEXT
                                  , (WPARAM) 0
                                  , (LPARAM) (LPSTR) (NPSTR) ""
                                  );
            }

            /*
            ** If the user pressed OK get text from edit ctrl
            ** into caller's buffer.
            */
            SendMessage(
                         hWndEditControl
                        ,WM_GETTEXT
                        , (WPARAM) uSizeofResultBuff
                        , (LPARAM) lpszReturnBuffer
                        );
          }
        }
        break;

    default:

        /*
        ** Let WC_DIALOG class proc handle everything else.
        */
        return FALSE;
    }

    /*
    ** Get here from 'break'.
    */
    return TRUE;
}
```

Again, the code is well commented and needs little in the way of explanation.

Note that I have used SendMessage() instead of SetWindowText(), as was noted earlier, the former is faster than using SetWindowText(). Also, note that EndDialog() is called in the WM_COMMAND handler before any interrogation of the box's controls is performed. Is this OK? Haven't those controls been destroyed before I use them? No they haven't.

EndDialog() doesn't destroy the dialog box or its child window controls, it just hides them. I did it like this mainly in case the user presses the cancel button. If they press the cancel button the edit field text is set to "", ie. nothing. To stop the user seeing this happen, albeit in a flash, I first hide the dialog box by calling EndDialog(). Also, the call to SetFocus() is currently redundant as the edit control is the first control, given in the template, that has the WS_TABSTOP style, the dialog box manager will set the keyboard focus to this control even if the WM_INITDIALOG handler above returned TRUE. I left it in just in case I ever rearranged the control order given in the template. Another way to have set the focus to the edit control having first tested whether or not this was necessary would be to use GetNextDlgTabItem(), if the handle returned by this is not a handle to the edit control then we use SetFocus() , you probably wouldn't want to do this but here goes :

```
{
    // End of WM_INITDIALOG handler.

    auto BOOL bSetFocus;

    if(hWndEditControl != GetNextDlgTabItem(hDlg, GetTopWindow(hDlg), FALSE))
    {
        SetFocus(hWndEditControl);
        bSetFocus = FALSE;
    }
    else
    {
        bSetFocus = TRUE;
    }

    return bSetFocus; /* Say we've set the focus? */
}
```

A typical call to the InputBox function might look like this :

```
auto int       nRes;
auto char      carBuff[255];

/*
** Call InputBox() and wait for return. Function blocks remember.
*/
nRes = InputBox(
            hWnd
            ,"This is some text to go in to the 'Prompt' control."
            ,"Dialog Title"
            ,"Default response in edit field"
            ,&carBuff[0]
            ,sizeof(carBuff)
            );

/*
** What did the user do?
*/
switch(nRes)
{
    case -1:
        MessageBox(hWnd, carBuff, "Error creating box", MB_OK);
        break;

    case IDOK:
        MessageBox(hWnd, carBuff, "User pressed OK", MB_OK);
        break;

    case IDCANCEL:
        MessageBox(hWnd, "User quit, title should be empty?", carBuff, MB_OK);
        break;
}
```

☐ The Dialog Manager re-visited

Before we take a look a modeless dialogs let's just re-visit the dialog manager -> dialog call-back relationship. The dialog box call-back function provided by you, despite popular belief, gets all normal Windows' message for the dialog box window (as passed on to it by the Dialog Box Manager).

The dialog box window is derived from class #32770, or, if you prefer, class WC_DIALOG (this is defined in WINDOWS.H). The WC_DIALOG class is pre-registered when Windows starts up, as are the standard control classes etc. The class call-back function given (lpfnWndProc member of WNDCLASS) is DefDlgProc(). When you create a window from class WC_DIALOG the *standard* window procedure for the window will be DefDlgProc(). How does your call-back then get called?

By DefDlgProc(). The class call-back function tests to see if there was a call-back defined when the dialog box was created, if there is, that call-back is then called to handle the message passed to DefDlgProc() by Windows. If that call-back returns FALSE, ie. it didn't handle the message then DefDlgProc() must check to see if it handles it; ultimately, if it doesn't handle it will pass it on to DefWindowProc() to see if it should be handled there. The piece of code that checks this out in DefDlgProc() looks like this :

```
//
// Call the dialog proc if it exists
//
if(((PDLG)hwnd)->lpfnDlg == NULL ||
        !(result = CallDlgProc(hwnd, message, wParam, lParam)))
{
```

The code uses a 'C' sequence point (the logical OR operator) to handle both the testing and calling of any user supplied call-back. The code above first checks to see if the dialog window, which is hwnd above, has a call-back defined for it :

```
if(((PDLG)hwnd->lpfnDlg == NULL ...
```

lpfnDlg is your call-back's address. If this is NULL the other half of the logical OR doesn't get evaluated - the *if* condition evaluates to FALSE. However, if the dialog does have a call-back defined the other half of the OR has to be evaluated in order to determine the result of the overall conditional expression being tested by the *if* :

```
|| !(result = CallDlgProc(hwnd, message, wParam, lParam)))
```

In other words, the call-back function is called to handle the message. Whatever the call-back returns *is* the result of the evaluation of this part of the expression and, therefore, the entire *if* expression being tested.

Only if the *if* evaluates to FALSE does DefDlgProc() processes the message further.

One of the nice things I liked (notice past tense!) about IBM's Presentation Manager was the ability to create simple dialogs (with only one button – About boxes etc) without using a call-back function. What you'd do was give the address of Win-DefDlgProc() (somewhat the same as DefDlgProc) as the call-back for the dialog. You can't do this in Windows. If you were to give the address of DefDlgProc() as the address of your call-back think what would happen. DefDlgProc() gets called to handle message X, it sees if you've given the address of a call-back and, if you have, calls that to handle the message. DefDlgProc() now gets re-entered as you gave its address as that of your call-back. The code once again checks to see if there's a call-back defined for this window and if there is it calls it! On and on – recursion is not the stack's best friend!

You can create a dialog box without a call-back however! You pass NULL as the address of your call-back (although this is not documented under the normal dialog creation functions it is OK to do this). Now DefDlgProc() does all your message processing! Unfortunately, there's no special handling in either DefDlgProc() or DefWindowProc() of a WM_COMMAND message, ie. the message you'd receive from your About box's *OK* button. This means that the dialog seemingly ignores the OK button, result – near immortality for the dialog box!

It would be nice if DefDlgProc() had some default handling for WM_COMMAND so that we could build simple dialogs without using a call-back function. Such a dialog box would not normally therefore contain buttons etc but it might contain, say, a load of static controls into which you wanted to set some text from time to time, maybe giving the user some sort of status information. Of course, this sort of dialog ought to be modeless! You'd destroy the dialog with DestroyWindow() or EndDialog() depending upon its type.

Where does WM_INITDIALOG come from?

This is tied in with the existence, or not, of a call-back function. WM_INITDIALOG is not a *real* message, ie. it is not sent or posted to the window (although it could be sent). Your call-back is called by the dialog creation function when it has created the dialog window (before the child window controls are created). The dialog creation function causes CreateWindow() to be called, this sends all the normal creation messages to the class procedure (listed below), when that CreateWindow() returns, the dialog creation function sets into the dialog window's words (discussed more below) the address of the call-back function you specified in the dialog creation function. The dialog creation function then calls DefDlgProc() with the WM_INIT-DIALOG message ID (and any *param* you may be passing if you're using the *Param* versions of the dialog creation functions) which in turn passes it on to your call-back. Up until this time all the messages received by DefDlgProc() were not passed on to your call-back because you hadn't got one (as far as DefDlgProc() was concerned). One last point, the dialog creation function only passes a WM_INITDIALOG message to DefDlgProc() if you did specify a call-back function address in the creation function, if you didn't do this the dialog creation function does not pass it on to DefDlgProc() – there'd be no point, so it doesn't bother!

None of these first four messages
get sent to the call-back.

Messages received by the call-back.

```
1F98 WM_GETMINMAXINFO     0000 07BF0730
F98 WM_NCCREATE           0000 117716CC
F98 WM_NCCALCSIZE         0000 117716BA
F98 WM_CREATE             0000 117716CC
1F98 WM_INITDIALOG        20EC 00000000      1F98 WM_INITDIALOG        20EC 00000000
1F98 WM_WINDOWPOSCHANGING 0000 1177164C      F98 WM_WINDOWPOSCHANGING 0000 1177164C
1F98 WM_NCACTIVATE        0001 00001F58      F98 WM_NCACTIVATE         0001 00001F58
1F98 WM_ACTIVATE          0001 00001F58      F98 WM_ACTIVATE           0001 00001F58
1F98 WM_CTLCOLOR          0B9E 000320EC      F98 WM_CTLCOLOR           0B9E 000320EC
1F98 WM_SHOWWINDOW        0001 00000000      F98 WM_SHOWWINDOW         0001 00000000
1F98 WM_WINDOWPOSCHANGING 0000 11771758      F98 WM_WINDOWPOSCHANGING 0000 11771758
1F98 WM_NCPAINT           0001 00000000      F98 WM_NCPAINT            0001 00000000
1F98 WM_GETTEXT           004F 11771540      1F98 WM_GETTEXT           004F 11771540
F98 WM_ERASEBKGND         0B96 00000000      F98 WM_ERASEBKGND         0B96 00000000
F98 WM_CTLCOLOR           0B96 00041F98      F98 WM_CTLCOLOR           0B96 00041F98
F98 WM_WINDOWPOSCHANGED   0000 11771770      F98 WM_WINDOWPOSCHANGED   0000 11771770
F98 WM_SIZE               0000 00960120      F98 WM_SIZE               0000 00960120
F98 WM_MOVE               0000 00BA009D      F98 WM_MOVE               0000 00BA009D
F98 WM_PAINT              0000 00000000      F98 WM_PAINT              0000 00000000
F98 WM_CTLCOLOR           0B96 00061FF8      F98 WM_CTLCOLOR           0B96 00061FF8
F98 WM_CTLCOLOR           0B96 0006205C      F98 WM_CTLCOLOR           0B96 0006205C
F98 WM_CTLCOLOR           0B96 000620A4      F98 WM_CTLCOLOR           0B96 000620A4
F98 WM_CTLCOLOR           0B96 000320EC      F98 WM_CTLCOLOR           0B96 000320EC
F98 WM_COMMAND            0001 000020EC      F98 WM_COMMAND            0001 000020EC
F98 WM_CTLCOLOR           0B96 000320EC      F98 WM_CTLCOLOR           0B96 000320EC
F98 WM_SETFOCUS           20EC 00000000      F98 WM_SETFOCUS           20EC 00000000
F98 WM_WINDOWPOSCHANGING  0000 117714AC      F98 WM_WINDOWPOSCHANGING 0000 117714AC
F98 WM_WINDOWPOSCHANGED   0000 117714C4      F98 WM_WINDOWPOSCHANGED   0000 117714C4
F98 WM_NCACTIVATE         0000 00001F58      F98 WM_NCACTIVATE         0000 00001F58
F98 WM_ACTIVATE           0000 00001F58      F98 WM_ACTIVATE           0000 00001F58
F98 WM_KILLFOCUS          1F58 00000000      F98 WM_KILLFOCUS          1F58 00000000
F98 WM_DESTROY            0000 00000000      F98 WM_DESTROY            0000 00000000
F98 WM_NCDESTROY          0000 00000000      F98 WM_NCDESTROY          0000 00000000
```

These two message lists are nearly identical, they were created using a DLL shown later in the book. The one on the left is recorded from DefDlgProc() whilst the one on the right is recorded from a call-back function. As you can see, DefDlgProc() gets four extra messages (the rest are exactly the same) which are all sent to the procedure as a result of calling CreateWindow(). If you were to *doctor* the call-back address stored in the window words of the dialog window before the switch statement (and test for the existence of the call-back) by inserting the address of the call-back, the call-back would get called with exactly the same set of messages as DefDlgProc()!

You can create dialogs from an application defined class if you wish.

There are two ways of doing this, either by specifying a CLASS statement in your dialog box template(s) or by super classing the WC_DIALOG class.

When you insert a CLASS statement into your dialog resource you're instructing Windows' DM to create a main dialog window from the class you specified rather than have it use WC_DIALOG, a similar sort of thing was shown earlier using controls of private classes. All dialog templates, that need to be created from this private class must have the CLASS statement included as part of their DIALOG resource :

```
IDD_MAINDIALOG DIALOG [Load/Memory Options etc] Position and Size.
CLASS "ClassName"
BEGIN
    CONTROL ...
END
```

This template says that the main dialog window must be built from class *ClassName*; of course, this class should be pre-registered with Windows before the dialog box is requested or else the DialogBox(), or whatever, call will fail (see section at the end of this chapter on reasons why dialog box creation functions might fail).

Another way to do the same thing is to super class the WC_DIALOG class (#32770). The best way to do this is as follows :

First you extract existing information about this class from Windows –

```
auto WNDCLASS wc;

GetClassInfo(NULL, "#32770", &wc);

wc.lpfnWndProc = NewDefDlgProc;
wc.hInstance   = hInstance;

if(RegisterClass(&wc) == 0)
{
    return FALSE;
}
```

Despite what the documentation says, GetClassInfo() does return the instance handle, class name and menu name used in the original RegisterClass() call. We simply change the instance handle and lpfnWndProc members to be our instance handle and the address of a *New* DefDlgProc called in this case NewDefDlgProc (very creative you know!). We then register the class - note that the class is still #32770!

Note, that against popular belief, the RegisterClass() function does not fail at this point. It is perfectly OK (and documented) to have a private class override a global class; all this code does is, for this task, redefine the #32770 class as being local. Note that we don't need to remember the original class call-back address - we know this, it's good old DefDlgProc().

No Dialog box template requires altering now, all requests for an instance of WC_DIALOG will result in just that, an instance of the local class WC_DIALOG, in other words NewDefDlgProc() will now handle all dialog boxes built in this task (as long as they DO NOT use the DIALOG statement in their definitions!). It is still possible to use a call-back function with such a dialog box, the order in which each function gets control now looks like this :

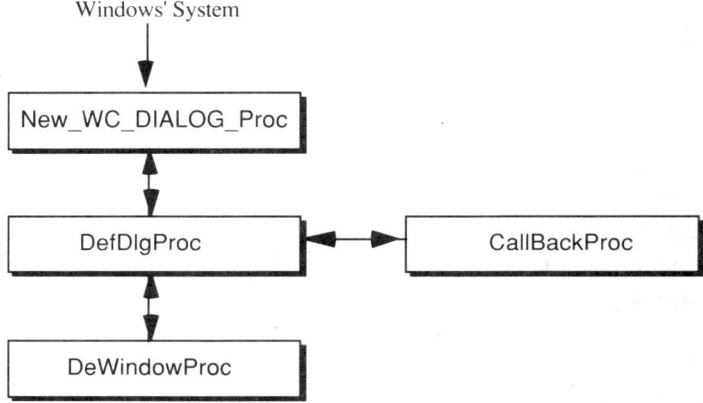

NewDefDlgProc needs to call the old DefDlgProc() as is normal in sub/super classing models. A do nothing NewDefDlgProc simply returns DefDlgProc() :

```
LRESULT __export CALLBACK NewDefDlgProc
(
    HWND     hWnd
   ,UINT     uMessage
   ,WPARAM   wParam
   ,LPARAM   lParam
)
    return DefDlgProc(hWnd, uMessage, wParam, lParam);
}
```

If anyone runs SPY over a dialog box from this class it will also look exactly the same as the global class WC_DIALOG in all but window procedure address. The class name, style etc were taken from the original so they must be the same! In case you're interested the original WNDCLASS used by Windows to register the dialog would have looked like this (constant members shown only).

```
auto WNDCLASS wc;

wc.style          = CS_DBLCLKS | CS_SAVEBITS | CS_BYTEALIGNWINDOW;
wc.lpfnWndProc    = Whatever;
wc.cbClsExtra     = 0;
wc.cbWndExtra     = DLGWINDOWEXTRA;
wc.hInstance      = Whatever;
wc.hIcon          = NULL;      // Add an ICON to a dialog class?
wc.hCursor        = LoadCursor(NULL, IDC_ARROW);
wc.hbrBackground  = NULL;
wc.lpszMenuName   = NULL;
wc.lpszClassName  = WC_DIALOG;
```

One of the best reasons to use your own WC_DIALOG class is to modify a common dialog attribute. For example, say you wanted to add a common icon to your dialogs? You wouldn't believe some of the ways people have dreamt up to do this! By using this method you simply add the icon handle to your WC_DIALOG class definition and that's it. All the dialogs in your task now have an icon – simple, no extra code, no modifications required to the dialog template.

One last thing about using your own dialog WndProc. Don't call DefWindowProc() if you'll ultimately call DefDlgProc(). Remember that DefDlgProc() calls DefWindow-Proc() to process any message it doesn't itself handle – result, some messages might be handled twice by DefWindowProc() - OOPS!

DLGWINDOWEXTRA

DLGWINDOWEXTRA is defined as 30 in WINDOWS.H; all dialog classes require this much data reserved in the window words of any dialog window. You, and Windows DM use these window words. Three further related defines are defined (as defines are!) in WINDOWS.H. DWL_DLGPROC, DWL_MSGRESULT and DWL_USER.

DWL_MSGRESULT

This offset is used to force DefDlgProc() to respond in some fixed way to the message being processed in your call-back function.

For example, You might want DefDlgProc() to return some other value than (LRE-SULT)0 even though you handle a particular message in your dialog call-back. For example, if you want to take control of the cursor displayed by one of your child window controls you'll have to persuade DefDlgProc() to return TRUE to the WM_SETCURSOR message passed to you, via DefDlgProc(), by DefWindowProc() processing messages that are not handled by a control class. If you return TRUE from the dialog call-back, ie. you handled the message, DefDlgProc() will normally return

0, ie. the message's been handled – not we want. If we return FALSE, which is the only other value we can really return, DefDlgProc() will pass the message on to DefWindowProc() for default processing – again, not what we want. What we need to do is somehow get DefDlgProc() to return TRUE when the dialog call-back does.

Well one way to do this is by using DWL_MSGRESULT.

Taking the WM_SETCURSOR example above, when you handle the message in the call-back function do the following :

```c
/*
** Makes the cursor used by the OK button appear to be the 'stock' IDC_UPAR-
ROW.
*/
BOOL __export CALLBACK About
(
    HWND    hDlg
    ,UINT    uMessage
    ,WPARAM  wParam
    ,LPARAM  lParam
)
{
    switch(uMessage)
    {
        case WM_SETCURSOR:

            /*
            ** If the control causing the WM_SETCURSOR is the OK
            ** button then set the cursor.
            */
            if((HWND)wParam == GetDlgItem(hDlg, IDOK))
            {
                /*
                ** Use a stock cursor.
                */
                SetCursor(LoadCursor(NULL, IDC_UPARROW));

                /*
                ** Set window words - DefDlgProc() returns whatever we
                ** put in here IF the call-back also returns TRUE.
                */
                SetWindowLong(
                            hDlg
                            ,DWL_MSGRESULT
                            ,(LRESULT)TRUE
                            );
                /*
                ** Return TRUE - DefDlgProc() will then return TRUE as
                ** that's the value in the dialog's words.
                */
                return TRUE;
            }
            break;

        case WM_INITDIALOG:
            return TRUE;
```

```
    case WM_COMMAND:
        if(wParam == IDOK || wParam == IDCANCEL)
        {
            EndDialog(hDlg, TRUE);
            return TRUE;
        }
        break;
    }

    return FALSE;
}
```

The code to DefDlgProc() that handles this is shown below. As you can see from the comment, this bit of code only gets hit if we returned TRUE from the call-back. If the message is a *special* message then DefDlgProc() returns whatever the call-back returned. For example, WM_CTLCOLOR is a *special* message. Otherwise DefDlgProc() returns the value in its words addressed by DWL_MSGRESULT - it actually uses a cast on the window handle to get to the words! The words are set to zero whenever DefDlgProc() is called (see top of DefDlgProc() code below).

```
/*
** We get here if the dialog call-back returned a value other than FALSE.
*/
ReturnIt:
    // These messages are special cased in an unusual way: the return value
    // of the dialog function is not BOOL fProcessed, but instead it's the
    // return value of these messages.
    //
    if (message == WM_CTLCOLOR      ||
        message == WM_COMPAREITEM   ||
        message == WM_VKEYTOITEM    ||
        message == WM_CHARTOITEM    ||
        message == WM_QUERYDRAGICON ||
        message == WM_INITDIALOG)
    {

        /*
        ** Special message - return whatever the call-back returned.
        */
        return((LRESULT)(DWORD)result);
    }

    /*
    ** Not a special message - return whatever's contained in the words.
    */
    return(((PDLG)hwnd)->resultWP);
}
```

As was noted above, there are some messages passed to the call-back that are *special* in that the value returned from the call-back IS passed back from DefDlgProc(). The messages treated as special like this are :

- **WM_CTLCOLOR**
- **WM_COMPAREITEM**
- **WM_VKEYTOITEM**
- **WM_CHARTOITEM**
- **WM_QUERYDRAGICON**
- **WM_INITDIALOG**

Just to re-cap.

If the call-back returns FALSE then either DefDlgProc() or DefWindowProc() handles the message.

If the call-back returns TRUE then DefDlgProc() returns either the value of DWL_MSGRESULT (which is zero) or whatever the call-back returned if the message is a *special* message.

If the call-back returns TRUE and sets the dialog window's DWL_MSGRESULT words, then DefDlgProc() either returns the value of the words or the value returned from the call-back if the message is a *special* message. You obviously don't therefore set the words if the message you're handling is one in the list above, ie. the window's words are ignored by DefDlgProc() in the case of a *special* message.

Here's the DefDlgProc() code that re-sets the dialog window's words upon entry.

```
LRESULT WINAPI DefDlgProc(....)
{
...
/*
** Set up DWL_MSGRESULT to zero.
*/
(()hwnd -> resultWP = 0L;      // Reset DWL_MSGRESULT window words.
result = FALSE; // Set default result.

if(((PDLG)hwnd -> lpfnDialog == NULL ||
   !(result = CallDlgProc(hwnd, message, wParam, lParam)))
{
   //Either no dialog call-back OR dialog call-back returned FALSE,
   //either way, we must not handle this message.
   ...
   ...
}
```

Now you can see that if our call-back returned TRUE when it handled a WM_SETCURSOR message that DefDlgProc() would return 0 as resultWP was set to 0 on function entry. If we returned FALSE from the call-back DefDlgProc() would return whatever DefWindowProc() returns. If we return TRUE from handling one of the *special message* listed above DefDlgProc() will return TRUE (as an LRESULT) also. So if we want to be sure of what DefDlgProc() will return we handle the message in the call-back, set up the dialog's window words to hold the required result, and return TRUE. DefDlgProc() will now return (as long as it isn't a *special message)* whatever we put into the dialog window words (return (((PDLG)hwnd -> resultWP);

There's another way to return whatever you want (even for a special message). Super-class WC_DIALOG as detailed earlier, ie. as your new class call-back gets the message before DefDlgProc() you can return any value you want!

DWL_DEFPROC

This section of the dialog's window words holds the address, if any, of the dialog call-back function. You can change the call-back on the fly by setting these words to *point* to another call-back:

```
SetWindowLong(hDlg, DWL_DEFPROC, (DWORD)NewAboutProc);
```

or

```
SetWindowLong(hDlg, DWL_DEFPROC, (DWORD)0);
```

to remove any call-back handling temporarily.

The following code allows a common dialog to be processed by two separate dialog call-back functions - yes I know it's not exactly a thrilling example but it IS an example OK! The dialog affected looks like this initially :

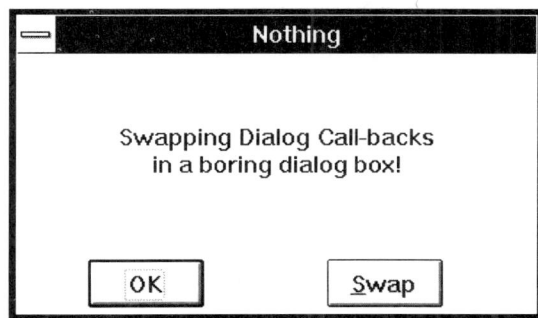

See the comments following the code snippets for some explanation.

```
LRESULT __export CALLBACK MainWndProc
(
   HWND     hWnd
  ,UINT     uMessage
  ,WPARAM   wParam
  ,LPARAM   lParam
)
{

   switch(uMessage)
   {
   case WM_COMMAND:
       switch(wParam)
       {
         case IDM_DIALOG:
            {
               auto HINSTANCE hInst;

               hInst = (HINSTANCE)GetWindowWord(hWnd, GWW_HINSTANCE);

               /* Create dialog box here.  Name CallBack1 as handler.*/
               DialogBox(hInst,"DialogBox", hWnd, (DLGPROC)CallBack1);
            }
            break;
       }
       break;

   case WM_DESTROY:
       PostQuitMessage(0);
       break;

   default:
       return DefWindowProc(hWnd, uMessage, wParam, lParam);
   }

   return (LRESULT)0;
}



/*
** First dialog call-back.
** Initial dialog handler function.
*/
BOOL __export CALLBACK CallBack1
(
   HWND     hDlg
  ,UINT     uMessage
  ,WPARAM   wParam
  ,LPARAM   lParam
)
{
   switch(uMessage)
   {
      case UM_SWAPPROC:
            SetWindowLong(
                             hDlg
                            ,DWL_DLGPROC
                            ,(LONG)CallBack2
```

```
                                );
                PostMessage(hDlg, WM_USER, 0, 0);
                break;

        case WM_USER:
                SetWindowText(hDlg, "CallBack1 processing");
                break;

        case WM_INITDIALOG:
                return TRUE;

        case WM_COMMAND:
                switch(wParam)
                {
                    case IDOK:
                    case IDCANCEL:
                        EndDialog(hDlg, TRUE);
                        return TRUE;
                        break;

                    case IDSWAP:
                        PostMessage(hDlg, UM_SWAPPROC, 0, 0);
                        return TRUE;
                        break;
                }
                break;
    }

    return FALSE;
}


/*
** Second dialog call-back
** Almost the same as CallBack1 above!
*/
BOOL __export CALLBACK CallBack2
(
   HWND     hDlg
  ,UINT     uMessage
  ,WPARAM   wParam
  ,LPARAM   lParam
)
{
   switch(uMessage)
   {
       case UM_SWAPPROC:
            SetWindowLong(
                          hDlg
                         ,DWL_DLGPROC
                         ,(LONG)CallBack1
                         );

            PostMessage(hDlg, WM_USER, 0, 0);
            break;
```

```
        case WM_USER:
              SetWindowText(hDlg, "CallBack2 processing");
              break;


        case WM_INITDIALOG:
              return TRUE;


        case WM_COMMAND:
              switch(wParam)
              {
                  case IDOK:
                  case IDCANCEL:
                      EndDialog(hDlg, TRUE);
                      return TRUE;
                      break;


                  case IDSWAP:
                      PostMessage(hDlg, UM_SWAPPROC, 0, 0);
                      return TRUE;
                      break;
              }
              break;
    }

    return FALSE;
}



#define UM_SWAPPROC (WM_USER  + 1)
#define IDSWAP       101


DialogBox DIALOG 56, 31, 144, 75
STYLE DS_MODALFRAME | WS_CAPTION | WS_SYSMENU
CAPTION "Nothing"
BEGIN
    CONTROL
            "Swapping Dialog Call-backs"
            ,-1
            ,"Static"
            ,SS_CENTER |
            WS_GROUP
            ,0, 20, 144, 8


    CONTROL
            "in a boring dialog box!"
            ,-1
            ,"Static"
            ,SS_CENTER |
            WS_GROUP
            ,0, 28, 144, 8
```

```
CONTROL
        "OK"
        , IDOK
        , "Button"
        , BS_DEFPUSHBUTTON |
        WS_GROUP          |
        WS_TABSTOP
        ,20, 59, 32, 14

CONTROL
        "&Swap"
        , IDSWAP
        , "Button"
        , WS_GROUP |
        WS_TABSTOP
        ,86, 59, 32, 14
END
```

In the code above a dialog box is created which uses CallBack1 as its initial handler. If the user selects the *Swap* button in the dialog, the CallBack1 handler sets the address of the call-back to CallBack2, via a call to SetWindowLong(DWL_DLGPROC, ...), and posts the dialog window a WM_USER message. At this time the call-back which handles the dialog will have been switched to CallBack2 so it's that function that gets the WM_USER message. When it receives it it sets the caption of the dialog box to *CallBack2 Processing'*.

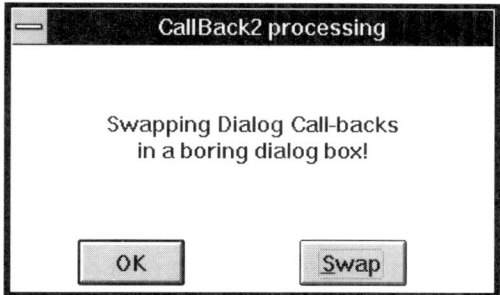

If the user now re-selects the *Swap* button, the call-back handler is switched by CallBack2 back to CallBack1 which will now set the caption of the box to *CallBack1 Processing*.

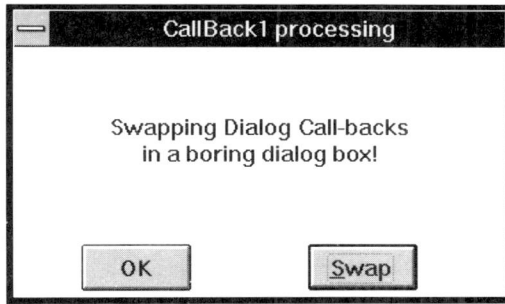

You can even change another task's dialog to use a call-back in your task if you like! This may seem un-useful but can be very handy – it's one of those things that you have to be aware of and then think about for a while before you can see where it'd be useful! For example, being able to change call-backs on the fly like this can help break multi-state dialog processing into separate functional blocks of code.

See the section just below on getting DefDlgProc() to process messages for you for another simple example of how it might be useful.

DWL_USER

The name of this offset is interesting; USER refers to you – the programmer user AND USER – the Windows' module. The first four bytes from DWL_USER are for you – the programmer. You can put anything you like into these bytes.

For example when using modeless dialogs you might want to store, say, a global memory handle in here, each modeless dialog (multiple instances of the same dialog are handled by the same call-back) could allocate some global heap space at WM_INITDIALOG time and store the memory handle in these words with SetWin-dowLong(hDlg, DWL_USER, (DWORD) hGlobMemHandle);. Note that I didn't use SetWindowWord() here – handles in Win32 are 32 bits, this code will work for both Win 3.x and Win32 therefore. When the call-back procedure wants access to this global memory it accesses it through its window words, ie. hGlobMemHandle = GetWin-dowLong(hDlg, DWL_USER);. This makes the global memory handle both persistent and multiply instanced, ie. each window has its own persistent object. A *static* would be persistent but shared by all users of the function, an *auto* would be multiply instanced but would not be persistent – both desirable qualities and both are supplied through the use of this mechanism.

DWL_????

You'll notice that DLGWINDOWEXTRA extends some way past the area addressed by DWL_USER. The rest of the offset is for the USER module!

This area contains stuff which is put there and maintained by USER, its contents is not documented but I'll give you a taste. Offset DWL_USER + 8 contains a WORD value (use GetWindowWord() to get it) that identifies the window handle of the dialog control (if any) that will receive the input focus when the dialog box receives focus. It is only set when the dialog (or its controls) are not focused. Another one, DWL_USER + 14 identifies a WORD that holds two things – the ID of the default push-button (if any) in the dialog, and the *result* of a modal dialog (the value of the second parameter to EndDialog(), ie. when EndDialog() is called the value in the second parameter is inserted into the window's words).

Despite my tempting you, do not fool with these words/longs; undocumented things have a habit of disappearing, or at least changing in some subtle way from time to time! If you want more words/longs, either super class the dialog class, or define your own class and add the required number of words to DLGWINDOWEXTRA, you could then forget DWL_USER and use all this extra space you requested instead – use DLGWINDOWEXTRA as an offset to get at them.

There's more on using window/class words, and the standard classes elsewhere in this book; use the index to locate whatever you're interested in. But before you go, just one point to note; whenever you access window or class words it's usually a good idea to check that you're not about to access an *out of range* word or long by first checking how many words were allotted to the window and the class. You can do this by checking the class members addressed by offsets GCW_CBWNDEXTRA and GCW_CBCLSEXTRA – you could even write a macro or a function to check it for you:

```
WORD wSWW(HWND hWnd, int nOffset, WORD wNewWord)
{
    auto WORD wResult;

    wResult = 0;

    if(IsWindow(hWnd) != FALSE)
    {
        if((WORD)nOffset <= (GetClassWord(hWnd, GCW_CBWNDEXTRA) -
sizeof(WORD)))
        {
            wResult = SetWindowWord(hWnd, nOffset, wNewWord);
        }
        else
        {
            MessageBox(hWnd, "Set window word fail!", "Illegal Offset", MB_OK);
        }
    }

    return wResult;
}

LONG wSWL(HWND hWnd, int nOffset, LONG lNewLong)
{
    auto LONG lResult;

    lResult = 0;

    if(IsWindow(hWnd) != FALSE)
    {
        if((WORD)nOffset <= (GetClassWord(hWnd, GCW_CBWNDEXTRA) -
sizeof(LONG)))
        {
            lResult = SetWindowLong(hWnd, nOffset, lNewLong);
        }
        else
        {
            MessageBox(hWnd, "Set window long fail!", "Illegal Offset", MB_OK);
        }
    }

    return lResult;
}
```

The two functions above check that when using window words that the actual words accessed are in fact allocated in the class. Windows 3.1 does check that you are not trying to access words that are not allocated and returns false if such an access is attempted, however, the functions above actually inform you that such an illegal access has been attempted without you having to check the return value from SetWindow????() or check on DBWIN's display; also, as of 3.1 legal extra words are initialised to 0 anyway, and as the SetWindow????() functions return 0 for failure, or the contents of the old WORD or LONG that is being replaced, it is possible that when setting window words for the first time, or setting one that previously held 0, that the result of SetWindow????() may be confusing, ie. it will be zero. The functions above ignore (do not test) the return value, they test to see if the words exist before any attempt to access them is made. You can write the *get* side of window word access and all of the class word access functions!

☐ Getting default processing before custom processing

In ordinary window procedures you can call DefWindowProc() before performing customised processing on a message, ie. you can get Windows to process the message before you do. With dialog call-backs this is more difficult, ie. you do not normally call DefDlgProc() from your dialog call-back; you instead return TRUE or FALSE. In other words you have to have handled the *message* in your dialog call-back and return FALSE to DefDlgProc() before you can get any default processing from DefDlgProc() and DefWindowProc()! The answer seems to be that you should call DefDlgProc() from your call-back before handling the message in the call-back right? Well there's one very good reason why you shouldn't call DefDlgProc() from your call-back for a given message – it'll kill your app! Recall that your call-back function is called from DefDlgProc().

Remember the DefDlgProc() code shown previously :

```
LRESULT WINAPI DefDlgProc(....)
{
...
((PDLG)hwnd -> resultWP = 0L; // Reset DWL_MSGRESULT window words.
result = FALSE; // Set default result.

if(((PDLG)hwnd -> lpfnDialog == NULL ||
   !(result = CallDlgProc(hwnd, message, wParam, lParam)))
{
   //Either no dialog call-back OR dialog call-back returned FALSE,
   //either way, we must not handle this message.

}
```

DefDlgProc() checks to see if there's a call-back provided for hwnd and if there is it is called via CallDlgProc()! This in turn would cause your code to call DefDlgProc() – recursion – death!!

There are two ways in which you can call DefDlgProc() from your call-back without suffering these effects.

- Use a static flag in your call-back to test for re-entrancy and return FALSE from your call-back if recursion is detected.
- Set the address of your dialog window's call-back to NULL (see DWL_DEFPROC above).

By using either of these techniques you can safely call DefDlgProc() before you process the dialog message in some custom way. Here's an example of each method taken from a modified generic.c (each method is explained after both code examples are shown). The code fragments below are used to draw weird captions in a dialog window at WM_NCPAINT time by drawing in the dialog window AFTER DefDlgProc() and DefWindowProc() have been used to draw the non-client area of the window.

First using a flag to protect against re-entrancy :

```
BOOL   __export CALLBACK About
(
    HWND      hDlg
   ,UINT      uMessage
   ,WPARAM    wParam
   ,LPARAM    lParam
)
{
    /*
    ** Re-entrancy check flag.
    */
    static BOOL bEntered;
    auto   BOOL bResult;


    /*
    ** If already in call-back return FALSE to get DefDlgProc()
    ** to process message.
    */
    if(bEntered == TRUE)
    {
        return FALSE;
    }
    /*
    ** Not already entered so set flag.
    */
    else
    {
        bEntered = TRUE;
    }

    switch(uMessage)
    {
        case WM_ACTIVATE:
            if(wParam == WA_INACTIVE)
            {
```

```
                    break;
               }                                 // FALL THRU.
     case WM_NCPAINT:
          {
               auto HDC     hDC;
               auto HBRUSH  hBrush;
               auto HPEN    hPen;
               auto RECT    rsWindow;
               auto RECT    rsClient;
               auto RECT    rsWorking;
               auto int     nBorderWidth;
               auto int     nBorderHeight;
               auto int     nWindowWidth;
               auto int     nWindowHeight;
               auto int     nClientWidth;
               auto int     nClientHeight;


               /*
               ** Get DefDlgProc() to process WM_NCPAINT first. This
               ** will cause DefDlgProc() to call us again to see if
               ** we handle the  message -  the re-entrancy trap set
               ** above will return FALSE making DefDlgProc() handle
               ** the paint message.  Eventually  it  will return to
               ** here at which time we can  paint 'after' the  non-
               ** client area is all painted!
               */
               DefDlgProc(hDlg, uMessage, wParam, lParam);

               /********* Do our WM_NCPAINT stuff here *********/

               /*
               ** Get client area size info and work out
               ** width and height of client area.
               */
               GetClientRect(hDlg, &rsClient);
               nClientWidth = rsClient.right;
               nClientHeight = rsClient.bottom;

               /*
               ** Get window area size info and work out
               ** width and height of entire window.
               */
               GetWindowRect(hDlg, &rsWindow);
               nWindowWidth = rsWindow.right - rsWindow.left;
               nWindowHeight = rsWindow.bottom - rsWindow.top;

               /*
               ** Work out border width and height.
               */
               nBorderWidth  = (nWindowWidth - nClientWidth) / 2;
               nBorderHeight = (
                              nWindowHeight -
                              nClientHeight -
                              GetSystemMetrics(SM_CYCAPTION)
                              ) / 2;

               /*
```

```
** Get Window DC so we can draw in NC part.
*/
hDC = GetWindowDC(hDlg);


/*
** Create brush and pen for drawing in caption.
*/
hBrush = CreateSolidBrush(RGB(0,255,0));
hPen = CreatePen(PS_SOLID, 0, RGB(0, 255, 0));


/*
** Select 'em into DC.
*/
hBrush = SelectObject(hDC, hBrush);
hPen = SelectObject(hDC, hPen);


/*
** Work out where caption is and set co-ords into
** rsWorking RECT.
*/
rsWorking.left    = nBorderWidth +
                    GetSystemMetrics(SM_CXSIZE) ;

rsWorking.top     = nBorderHeight;

rsWorking.right   = nWindowWidth -
                    nBorderWidth;

rsWorking.bottom  = GetSystemMetrics(SM_CYCAPTION) +
                    nBorderHeight;


/*
** Flood fill caption area.
*/
Rectangle(
        hDC
        ,rsWorking.left
        ,rsWorking.top
        ,rsWorking.right
        ,rsWorking.bottom
        );


/*
** Adjust rect for text output.
*/
InflateRect(&rsWorking, -1, -1);


/*
** Select see-thru text.
*/
SetBkMode(hDC, TRANSPARENT);


/*
** Draw caption text.
*/
DrawText(
        hDC
        ,"Hello There!!"
```

```
                            ,-1
                            ,&rsWorking
                            ,DT_SINGLELINE |
                             DT_LEFT        |
                             DT_VCENTER
                            );

                /*
                ** Clean up.
                */
                DeleteObject(SelectObject(hDC, hBrush));
                DeleteObject(SelectObject(hDC, hPen));
                ReleaseDC(hDlg, hDC);

                bResult = TRUE;
            }
            break;

        case WM_COMMAND:
            if(wParam == IDOK || wParam == IDCANCEL)
            {
                EndDialog(hDlg, TRUE);
                bResult = TRUE;
            }
            break;

        default:
            bResult = FALSE;
            break;
    }

    /*
    ** About to exit so re-set flag.
    */
    bEntered = FALSE;

    /*
    ** Return result of handling message.
    */
    return bResult;
}
```

and now one using the DLW_DLGPROC method :

```
BOOL __export CALLBACK About
(
   HWND    hDlg
  ,UINT    uMessage
  ,WPARAM  wParam
  ,LPARAM  lParam
)
{
   auto    BOOL bResult;
```

```
/*
** Address of old call-back proc.
*/
auto   FARPROC lpDialogProc;


/*
** Set call-back addr to NULL - we'll not
** be called by DefDlgProc() ever again!
*/
lpDialogProc = (FARPROC)SetWindowLong(hDlg, DWL_DLGPROC, NULL);

switch(uMessage)
{
    case WM_ACTIVATE:
        if(wParam == WA_INACTIVE)
        {
            break;
        }                                    // FALL THRU.
    case WM_NCPAINT:
        {
            auto HDC     hDC;
            auto HBRUSH  hBrush;
            auto HPEN    hPen;
            auto RECT    rsWindow;
            auto RECT    rsClient;
            auto RECT    rsWorking;
            auto int     nBorderWidth;
            auto int     nBorderHeight;
            auto int     nWindowWidth;
            auto int     nWindowHeight;
            auto int     nClientWidth;
            auto int     nClientHeight;


            /*
            ** Get DefDlgProc() to process WM_NCPAINT first. This
            ** will cause DefDlgProc() to call us again to see if
            ** we handle the  message -  we can't be called again
            ** as we've set our call-back addr to NULL.
            ** Eventually  it  will   return to here at which time
            ** we can  paint 'after'  the  non-client  area is all
            ** painted!
            */
            DefDlgProc(hDlg,  uMessage,  wParam,  lParam);

            /********* Do our WM_NCPAINT stuff here *********/

            /*
            ** Get client area size info and work out
            ** width and height of client area.
            */
            GetClientRect(hDlg, &rsClient);
            nClientWidth = rsClient.right;
            nClientHeight = rsClient.bottom;

            /*
            ** Get window area size info and work out
```

```
** width and height of entire window.
*/
GetWindowRect(hDlg, &rsWindow);
nWindowWidth = rsWindow.right - rsWindow.left;
nWindowHeight = rsWindow.bottom - rsWindow.top;


/*
** Work out border width and height.
*/
nBorderWidth  = (nWindowWidth - nClientWidth) / 2;
nBorderHeight = (
                  nWindowHeight -
                  nClientHeight -
                  GetSystemMetrics(SM_CYCAPTION)
                ) / 2;


/*
** Get Window DC so we can draw in NC part.
*/
hDC = GetWindowDC(hDlg);


/*
** Create brush and pen for drawing in caption.
*/
hBrush = CreateSolidBrush(RGB(0,255,0));
hPen = CreatePen(PS_SOLID, 0, RGB(0, 255, 0));


/*
** Select 'em into DC.
*/
hBrush = SelectObject(hDC, hBrush);
hPen = SelectObject(hDC, hPen);


/*
** Work out where caption is and set co-ords into
** rsWorking RECT.
*/
rsWorking.left   = nBorderWidth +
                   GetSystemMetrics(SM_CXSIZE) ;

rsWorking.top    = nBorderHeight;

rsWorking.right  = nWindowWidth -
                   nBorderWidth;

rsWorking.bottom = GetSystemMetrics(SM_CYCAPTION) +
                   nBorderHeight;

/*
** Flood fill caption area.
*/
Rectangle(
         hDC
        ,rsWorking.left
        ,rsWorking.top
        ,rsWorking.right
        ,rsWorking.bottom
        );
```

```
                /*
                ** Adjust rect for text output.
                */
                InflateRect(&rsWorking, -1, -1);

                /*
                ** Select see-thru text.
                */
                SetBkMode(hDC, TRANSPARENT);

                /*
                ** Draw caption text.
                */
                DrawText(
                        hDC
                        ,"Hello There!!"
                        ,-1
                        ,&rsWorking
                        ,DT_SINGLELINE |
                        DT_LEFT        |
                        DT_VCENTER
                        );

                /*
                ** Clean up.
                */
                DeleteObject(SelectObject(hDC, hBrush));
                DeleteObject(SelectObject(hDC, hPen));
                ReleaseDC(hDlg, hDC);

                bResult = TRUE;
            }
            break;

        case WM_COMMAND:
            if(wParam == IDOK || wParam == IDCANCEL)
            {
                EndDialog(hDlg, TRUE);
                bResult = TRUE;
            }
            break;

        default:
            bResult = FALSE;
            break;
    }

    SetWindowLong(hDlg, DWL_DLGPROC, (LONG)lpDialogProc);

    /*
    ** Return result of handling message.
    */
    return bResult;
}
```

Each example above does exactly the same thing – paint in the non-client area of the dialog window <u>after</u> Windows has painted it in some default way, ie.<u> after</u> DefDlgProc() has handled the WM_NCPAINT message itself. The result is a dialog box whose caption is coloured green and has left aligned text displayed in it (see also the windowing chapter for a way to change caption text) :

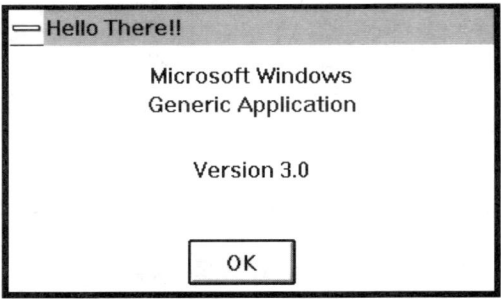

The first code example uses a re-entrancy, static storage class, flag to check that the call-back is not called by the call we make to DefDlgProc() within the call-back. Without this check we'd cause DefDlgProc() to call us again, we in return call it and so on – death through recursion! Whenever the call-back is called we set bEntered to TRUE, whenever we leave it, we re-set it to FALSE. If we get called in between, ie. whilst it is FALSE, we return FALSE from the call-back. Remember that the call-back is called from the code at the start of DefDlgProc().

Originally, the WM_NCPAINT message gets passed to DefDlgProc() (it's the class wndproc remember). DefDlgProc() tests to see if we have a dialog call-back function and if we have it calls it to see if it wants to process the message. When we handle the WM_NCPAINT message in the call-back we've already set bEntered to TRUE and now call DefDlgProc(). DefDlgProc() calls us again to see if we want to handle the message. We reply by returning FALSE (as bEntered is TRUE) instructing the DM to do the non-client area painting. It paints the non-client area and then returns to the original call we made to DefDlgProc(). We are now in our WM_NCPAINT case <u>after</u> Windows has done its default painting. We now paint the caption green and draw some left aligned text in there and return TRUE indicating that we handled the message. The return here is to the original call to the call-back. DefDlgProc() now just simply returns to its caller, the DM, without handling the message. The effect is that DefDlgProc() gets two WM_NCPAINT messages to deal with. The second one comes from the call-back handling the first one. The second one is processed by DefDlgProc() etc and the first one is handled by the call-back. Remember however that the first WM_NCPAINT message in is the one that is used to paint last!

The second method is easier to do as it doesn't require a bEntered flag to be defined or checked. Whenever the call-back is called we set the call-back's address, as registered with DialogBox() or whatever, to NULL using SetWindowLong(hDlg, DWL_DLGPROC, NULL). We keep the old value in an automatic variable. Once again, originally, the WM_NCPAINT message gets passed to DefDlgProc() (it's the class wndproc remember). DefDlgProc() tests to see if we have a dialog call-back function and if we have it calls it to see if it wants to process the message. When we handle a WM_NCPAINT we call DefDlgProc(); remember that at this stage that our call-back address is set to NULL. DefDlgProc() checks to see if we've got a call-back registered and finds that we haven't, ie. `if(((PDLG)hwnd -> lpfnDialog == NULL...)` is TRUE! DefDlgProc() now attempts to handle the message itself; in this case it paints in the non-client area for us. Eventually, DefDlgProc() has to return to our original call to it and we take that opportunity to paint our green caption etc. Lastly, before we exit the call-back we re-set the call-back's address from the automatic we used to store it in earlier! Once again, the effect is that DefDlgProc() gets two WM_NCPAINT messages to deal with. The second one comes from the call-back handling the first one. The second one is processed by DefDlgProc() and the first one is handled by the call-back.

Actually, there is another way to do this kind of thing but it's not as synchronous as the two ways shown above. It is however easier to do than either of them!

All you have to do is to post yourself a WM_USER message from your WM_NCPAINT case! When you get passed a WM_NCPAINT message you post yourself a WM_USER message and return FALSE. DefDlgProc() now causes the non-client area to be painted in the default way and returns control to Windows. At this point your WM_USER message is delivered. Upon receipt of the WM_USER message you paint in your non-client area! Once again you're painting in something that's just been painted by Windows and the DM. This last method, whilst working quite well, can cause a bit more of a flickering effect when the new caption is painted. It also cannot of course make use of any information passed within the original message as that message's been handled and its parameters made invalid.

Enough about the DM etc for now, on to modeless dialog boxes.

☐ Modeless Dialog Boxes

The standard modeless dialog box is created with one of the following functions :

```
CreateDialog
CreateDialogIndirect
CreateDialogParam
CreateDialogIndirectParam
```

The indirect versions allow you to dynamically build a dialog box from scratch, or to load an existing dialog box template, change it, then build it (see example of indirect modeless later in this chapter). The Param versions allow you to pass initialisation information to the dialog box via the WM_INITDIALOG message's lParam.

Modeless dialog boxes do not enter their own modal loop as modal dialog boxes do (the modal loop is maintained within USER by the way), nor do they disable any windows in the task creating the dialog box. To are basically simple POPUP or OVERLAPPED windows with some special characteristics.

Modeless dialog boxes are controlled by the DM and interpret certain key sequences specially, for example, when a modeless dialog box is the active window pressing the TAB key will (probably) move the input focus from one control in the box to another (the next one which includes the WS_TABSTOP style), or as another example; pressing the enter key produces a WM_KEY DOWN message (containing VK_RETURN) which is then turned in to a WM_COMMAND message with its wParam set to IDOK. This keyboard interface is managed by a DM function called IsDialogMessage() that must, for modeless dialogs, be called explicitly:

```
BOOL    WINAPI IsDialogMessage(HWND, MSG FAR*);
```

The function takes a window handle and a pointer to a message structure (this function is discussed in great detail later in this chapter). It tests to see whether the message contained with the message structure is *for* the modeless dialog box whose handle is given as the function's first parameter. If the message is for the dialog box, the message is dispatched within IsDialogMessage(), and handled by the dialog box (or DM). When the DM or dialog box has handled the message IsDialogMessage() returns TRUE, i.e. its indication that the message has been handled. If the function returns FALSE, the message was nothing to do with the dialog box and it should therefore be processed further.

Typically a *global* window handle is kept to hold the handle(s) of a modeless dialog that is active within the task, the call to IsDialogMessage() is done before the message is either translated or dispatched by TranslateMessage() or DispatchMessage(), a typical set-up looks like this :

```
// Global Window Handle.
HWND hWndModeless = NULL;

while(GetMessage(&msg, NULL, 0, 0) == TRUE)
{
   if(hWndModeless == NULL || IsDialogMessage(hWndModeless, &msg) == FALSE)
   {
       TranslateMessage(&msg);
       DispatchMessage(&msg);
   }
}
```

Here the modeless dialog(s) in our task are identified by the global window handle hWndModeless. When one is active, its window handle gets put into hWndModeless. In our main message loop (modeless dialogs do not have their own message polling loop as modal ones do - they therefore receive their messages through the main loop) we test to see whether or not a modeless dialog exists (hWndModeless == NULL), if that part of this expression is TRUE, ie. no modeless dialog exists the right hand half of the expression is not evaluated. If on the other hand a modeless dialog does exist (hWndModeless == NULL equals FALSE), we need to test the right hand half of the expression to see if the overall expression will evaluate to TRUE or FALSE. Doing so means we now test to see if the message is for our modeless dialog. If IsDialogMessage() returns FALSE, the message wasn't for the dialog; we need to process it further now in the compound statement - Translate & Dispatch. If the message was for the modeless dialog we will have dispatched it by calling the IsDialogMessage() function, and that function will, when the message has been processed, return TRUE. TRUE == FALSE is FALSE, the overall evaluation of the expression is FALSE – we don't do the compound statement. Typical modeless dialog creation looks something like this:

```
case IDM_MODELESSABOUT:
    hWndModeless = CreateDialog(
                                hInst
                              , "AboutBox"
                              , hWnd
                              , About
                              );
    if(hWndModeless == NULL)
    {
        MessageBox(hWnd, "Can't create modeless dialog!", NULL, MB_OK);
    }
    break;
```

This code is taken from a modified generic.

The dialog destruction looks like this :

```
case WM_COMMAND:
    if (wParam == IDOK || wParam == IDCANCEL)
    {
        if(GetParent(LOWORD(lParam)) == hWndModeless)
        {
          hWndModeless = (DestroyWindow(hWndModeless) != NULL);
        }
        else
        {
            EndDialog(hDlg, TRUE);
        }

        return TRUE;
    }
    break;
```

Again, taken from a modified generic *About* function.

Here we test hWndModeless against the parent of the control causing the WM_COMMAND to see if they're the same, if they are we destroy the modeless dialog as the user has either pressed the OK button or the enter key. If the two handles are not the same we call EndDialog() as the dialog box must be active (generic has a modal dialog already and this dialog call-back is handling both dialogs!).

As a modeless dialog allows you to access any window's menus etc we must (normally) prevent another copy of the dialog being created (we'll see soon how to allow this). Our modeless dialog above is created from a menu selection (IDM_MODELESSABOUT), all we need to do is disable that menu item until the dialog is destroyed.

```
case IDM_MODELESSABOUT:
    hWndModeless = CreateDialog(
                            hInst
                            ,"AboutBox"
                            ,hWnd
                            ,About
                            );
    if(hWndModeless == NULL)
    {
        MessageBox(hWnd, "Can't create modeless dialog!", NULL, MB_OK);
    }
    else
    {
        EnableMenuItem(
                    GetMenu(hWnd)
                    ,IDM_MODELESSABOUT
                    ,MF_BYCOMMAND | MF_DISABLED | MF_GRAYED
                    );
    }
    break;
```

And re-enable it when the dialog gets destroyed :

```
EnableMenuItem(
            GetMenu(GetWindow(hDlg, GW_OWNER))
            ,IDM_MODELESSABOUT
            ,MF_BYCOMMAND | MF_ENABLED
            );
```

Note that in the last code snippet I used GetWindow() to get a window handle to the dialog's main window, I couldn't use GetParent() because by default in 3.1 dialog boxes are overlapped windows, ie. windows that cannot have a parent. They do have an owner, or can do, and that is what our dialog is, an owned overlapped window. This sounds great, GetParent() fails, but a GetOwner() works fine, don't let the accuracy get to you here coz unfortunately GetWindowWord(hDlg, GWW_HWNDPARENT) will also work! You can now see that a GetParent() doesn't necessarily map down to a GetWindowWord() or a GetWindow()!

It is possible to have IsDialogMessage() look after your entire window set with only a few weirdnesses, ie. you can replace TranslateMessage() and DispatchMessage() with a single IsDialogMessage(msg.hwnd, &msg). All messages are thus dispatched by a single IsDialogMessage() call, of course it will also insist upon translating, in a dialog manager(y) kinda way, a certain number of messages, for example, say good-bye to WM_CHAR messages, see your WM_KEY DOWN - VK_RETURN turn into a WM_COMMAND message etc.

I said somewhere earlier in this chapter that it was hard and sometimes messy to maintain several modeless dialogs at once as it required possibly many checks on the various hWndModelessDialog1 etc handles? Well this can be done, many simultaneous modeless dialogs, more easily like this :

As before use one global window handle. This will do for the any number of modeless dialogs. Use the same message loop as before also - no change in the main code. Now there's one small change in the single, or multiple, dialog call-backs; the change is that you must now handle the WM_ACTIVATE message :

```
case   WM_ACTIVATE:
      switch(wParam)
      {
                  case WA_INACTIVE:
                      hWndModeless = NULL;
                      break;

                  case WA_ACTIVE:            /* FALL THROUGH. */
                  case WA_CLICKACTIVE:
                      hWndModeless = hDlg;
                      break
      }
      break;
```

hWndModeless will now always contain either NULL, when no dialog is active, or the window handle of the active modeless dialog box. Remember, only keyboard input is important with regard to IsDialogMessage(), an inactive modeless dialog will still receive mouse/system/private messages through the main message loop.

☐ Using The Dialog Editor To Create Main Windows

There are really two ways of using the dialog box editor, and a dialog box, as a main window. This is highly desirable if you have a main window which contains numerous controls such as edit fields, buttons, and labels etc.

Creating a main window as a dialog box allows you to make a saving on calling CreateWindow() etc. The first way we'll look at doing this is creating a child window dialog box. This child window dialog will be a child of a main overlapping window, here's what the two windows look like when they're shown together :

As you can see, we have a main window with a minimise box and a menu. The inside of that window's client area is entirely taken up with a child window dialog box. The dialog contains 39 control windows, and, as the caption says, can you imagine creating this the hard way using CreateWindow()?!

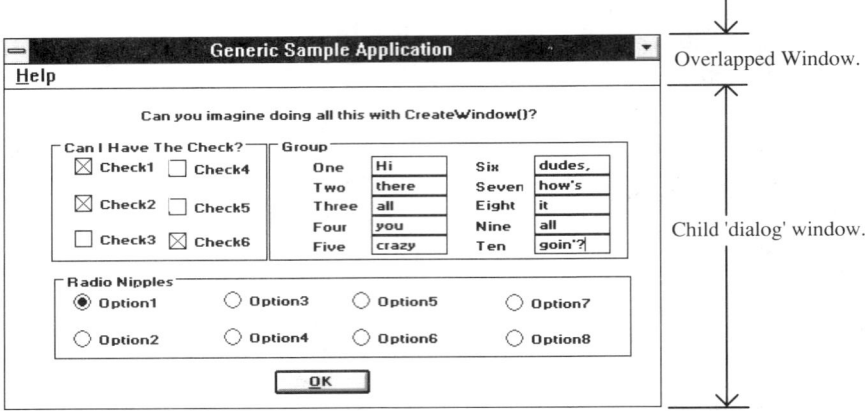

Overlapped Window.

Child 'dialog' window.

As you can see from the picture below, I've again modified the generic application; generic is still there, in fact its modal *About* box still works even though it's handled by the same call-back function that's handling the modeless child dialog :

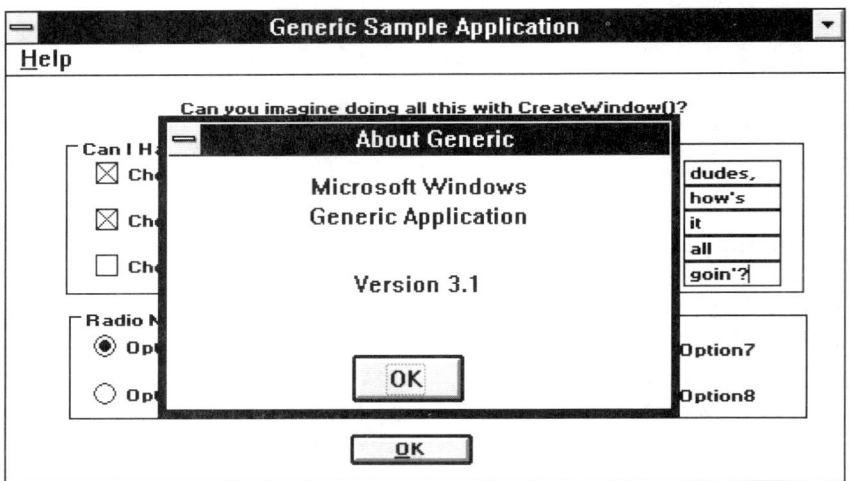

One other advantage to building a dialog/main window like this is that the window (both of them!) may be made iconic easily.

The standard dialog class does not have an icon associated with it (see earlier discussion on the dialog class) and so dialog boxes show NULL (see through) icons when they're made iconic. It is quite easy to super class the WC_DIALOG class and add an icon but this way is more fun! The main window has an icon, so iconising the window, which is the main window and not the dialog it appears to be, hides the child and shows the main window's icon. The menu is handled by a different window procedure than the one that handles control input. You may say that's nice but I'd disagree. I'd prefer it if the same function handled all user input to what after all appears to be one window, you can then in that one function pass the command input to a single handler whose job in life is to handle command input to one window - I guess we could pass on WM_COMMAND messages resulting from menu actions to the dialog handler (yuk!)?

Let's look at what needed to be done to generic to create the result above.

Firstly the dialog template; not the whole thing, just the header (the control content is irrelevant).

```
MAINDIALOG DIALOG 0, 0, 269, 187
STYLE WS_BORDER | WS_CHILD | WS_VISIBLE
FONT 6, "MS Dialog"
BEGIN
    ... CONTROL statements in here.
END
```

The only thing of interest that I'd point out here is that the style of the dialog's WS_BORDER | WS_CHILD | WS_VISIBLE. You could change the border around and see practically no effect in the main application. The important style change is WS_CHILD, the WS_VISIBLE just saves us having to call ShowWindow() in the code.

Let's look at the important parts of the main code :

Again, we have a global variable called hWndModeless defined and the regular modeless dialog loop :

```
HWND hWndModeless = NULL;

while (GetMessage(&msg, NULL, 0, 0))
{
    if(hWndModeless == NULL || IsDialogMessage(hWndModeless,&msg) == FALSE)
    {
        TranslateMessage(&msg);
        DispatchMessage(&msg);
    }
}
```

CreateWindow() for the main window is now followed by a CreateDialog() for the child dialog window :

```
hWnd = CreateWindow(
                  "GenericWClass"
                 ,"Generic Sample Application"
                 ,WS_OVERLAPPED |
                  WS_CAPTION    |
                  WS_SYSMENU    |
                  WS_BORDER     |
                  WS_MINIMIZEBOX
                 ,CW_USEDEFAULT
                 ,0
                 ,CW_USEDEFAULT
                 ,0
                 ,NULL
```

```
                           ,NULL
                           ,hInstance
                           ,NULL
                           );

if(hWnd == NULL)
{
   return FALSE;
}

hWndModeless = CreateDialog(
                             hInstance
                            ,"MainDialog"
                            ,hWnd
                            ,About
                            );

if(hWndModeless == NULL)
{
   MessageBox(0, "Couldn't create modeless dialog box!", NULL, MB_OK);
   return FALSE;
}
```

You can see that in this case we're also using *About* as the dialog call-back. This only works, with the supplied minimal effort given to it here, because the child dialog has minimal functionality.

The main window window procedure has one extra case statement. If our main window gets the focus it passes it on to the child modeless dialog box window. The dialog manager will then set the focus to a control.

```
case WM_SETFOCUS:
     SetFocus(hWndModeless);
     break;
```

Here's the complete *About* call-back function, it's pretty well documented so I won't add any further comment on it :

```
BOOL __export CALLBACK About
(
   HWND           hDlg
  ,UINT           message
  ,WPARAM         wParam
  ,LPARAM         lParam
)
{
   static BOOL bFirst = TRUE; /* Initialisation flag. */

   switch(message)
   {
      case WM_INITDIALOG:

           /*
           ** bFirst is TRUE if WM_INITDIALOG only ever called once.
           */
```

```
if(bFirst == TRUE)
{
    /*
    ** Various ints initialised with GetSystemMetrics().
    */
    auto int  nScreenWidth;
    auto int  nScreenHeight;
    auto int  nBorderWidth;
    auto int  nBorderHeight;
    auto int  nMenuHeight;
    auto int  nCaptionHeight;


    /*
    ** Hold dialog's and main window dimensions.
    */
    auto RECT rsDialog;
    auto RECT rsMainWindow;

    nScreenWidth   = GetSystemMetrics(SM_CXSCREEN);
    nScreenHeight  = GetSystemMetrics(SM_CYSCREEN);
    nBorderWidth   = GetSystemMetrics(SM_CXBORDER);
    nBorderHeight  = GetSystemMetrics(SM_CYBORDER);
    nMenuHeight    = GetSystemMetrics(SM_CYMENU);
    nCaptionHeight = GetSystemMetrics(SM_CYCAPTION);

    /*
    ** Get the screen position of the child dialog box.
    */
    GetWindowRect(hDlg, &rsDialog);

    /*
    ** Move the main window so that it is centred in the
    ** middle of the screen and is as wide and as high as
    ** the child dialog - take into  account the sizes of
    ** the main window's menu and caption.
    */
    MoveWindow(
            GetParent(hDlg)
            ,(nScreenWidth -
            (rsDialog.right - rsDialog.left) -
            (nBorderWidth * 2)) / 2
            ,(nScreenHeight -
            (rsDialog.bottom - rsDialog.top) -
            (nBorderHeight * 2)) / 2
            ,rsDialog.right - rsDialog.left
            ,rsDialog.bottom -
            rsDialog.top +
            nCaptionHeight +
            nMenuHeight
            ,FALSE
            );

    /*
    ** Now find out where the main window's client area
    ** origin (0,0) is relative to the screen.
    */
    GetClientRect(GetParent(hDlg), &rsMainWindow);
    ClientToScreen(GetParent(hDlg), (LPPOINT)rsMainWindow.left);
```

```
            /*
            ** Now move the child dialog to that location.
            */
            MoveWindow(
                     hDlg
                     ,rsMainWindow.left  - nBorderWidth
                     ,rsMainWindow.top   - nBorderHeight
                     ,rsDialog.right     - rsDialog.left
                     ,rsDialog.bottom    - rsDialog.top
                     ,FALSE
                     );

            /*
            ** Ensure that only modeless dialog adjusted.
            */
            bFirst = FALSE;
        }
        return TRUE;

case WM_COMMAND:

        /*
        ** Both dialogs (modal and modeless) have only one
        ** button and each is IDOK ID. Only close down the
        ** dialog  (either) if the COMMAND message is from
        ** the OK button.
        */
        if (wParam == IDOK && HIWORD(lParam) == BN_CLICKED)
        {
            /*
            ** Determine whether or not it's the modeless
            ** dialog that's closing.
            */
            if(GetParent(LOWORD(lParam)) == hWndModeless)
            {
                /*
                ** Modeless dialog closing so close the app.
                ** No need to  destroy the dialog as it's a
                ** child and will  get killed  as the parent
                ** dies.
                */
                SendMessage(
                           GetParent(hDlg)
                           ,WM_SYSCOMMAND
                           ,SC_CLOSE
                           ,0
                           );
            }
            else
            {
                /*
                ** Modal dialog closing so just close that dialog.
                */
                EndDialog(hDlg, wParam);
            }

            return TRUE;
```

```
            }
            break;
    }

    return FALSE;
}
```

And that's it. Now let's look at doing this another way. Actually using a dialog box as a main window. Before we go do this, let me just say that there are many ways to do this trick either using a private dialog class, a super classed WC_DIALOG, or simply by using the existing dialog class. I've decided to use the existing dialog class as it's simpler than the other methods and gives exactly the same results (minus not being able to iconise the window).

I've modified generic again here – don't you think that piece of code is in a state!? The first thing I did with it was to strip out all the comments using a lex script! I have added those that I think have something to say! P.S. – I haven't imposed my style too much on this piece of code so I apologise for the inconsistency.

```c
#define STRICT
#include "windows.h"
#include "generic.h"

#pragma warning(disable:4100)
#pragma warning(disable:4001)

int PASCAL WinMain
(
  HINSTANCE hInstance
 ,HINSTANCE hPrevInstance
 ,LPSTR     lpCmdLine
 ,int       nCmdShow
)
{
    auto MSG  msg;

    /*
    ** Window handle of modeless dialog.
    */
    auto HWND hWndModeless;

    /*
    ** Create the main window dialog.
    */
    if((hWndModeless = CreateDialog(hInstance, "AboutBox", 0, (DLGPROC)About))
       == NULL
      )
    {
        return 1;
    }

    /*
```

```
    ** Show and paint it.
    */
    ShowWindow(hWndModeless, SW_SHOWNORMAL);
    UpdateWindow(hWndModeless);

    /*
    ** Process messages. left in NULL as you might want to add
    ** more windows to this application.
    */
    while(GetMessage(&msg, NULL, 0, 0))
    {
        if(
            hWndModeless == NULL ||
            IsDialogMessage(hWndModeless, &msg) == FALSE
          )
        {
            /*
            ** With only this 'dialog' window in the application
            ** we should NEVER get to here.
            */
            TranslateMessage(&msg);
            DispatchMessage(&msg);
        }
    }

    return msg.wParam;
}


/*
** The only other function in  the application - the dialog call-back;
** this gets every  message except  those  four described earlier that
** are sent before the call-back address is inserted into the window's
** words. NOTE : WM_INITDIALOG is not necessarily  the first message a
** dialog call-back receives - it can get a WM_SETFONT first.
*/
BOOL __export CALLBACK About
(
    HWND     hDlg
   ,UINT     uMessage
   ,WPARAM   wParam
   ,LPARAM   lParam
)
{
    switch(uMessage)
    {
        case WM_INITDIALOG:

            /*
            ** Set focus according to WS_TABSTOP.
            */
            return TRUE;

        case WM_COMMAND:
            /*
            ** Either OK button, or 'Close' selected.
            */
            if(wParam == IDOK || wParam == IDCANCEL)
```

```
                {
                    EndDialog(hDlg, TRUE);

                    /*
                    ** Need to end the application here if we've no
                    ** other windows!
                    */
                    PostQuitMessage(0);

                    return TRUE;
                }
            break;
        }

    return FALSE;
}
```

That's it. This application using the following dialog box template :

```
ABOUTBOX DIALOG PRELOAD 56, 31, 195, 145
STYLE WS_BORDER | WS_POPUP | WS_CAPTION | WS_SYSMENU
CAPTION "This Is A Dialog Box"
FONT 12, "Architect"
MENU DialogMenu
BEGIN
    CONTROL
                    "Modeless Dialog Box as Main Window"
                    ,-1
                    ,"Static"
                    ,SS_CENTER | WS_GROUP
                    ,0, 5, 144, 8

    CONTROL         "&OK"
                    ,IDOK
                    ,"Button"
                    ,WS_GROUP | WS_TABSTOP
                    ,99, 54, 40, 14

    CONTROL         "Push1"
                    ,202
                    ,"Button"
                    ,WS_GROUP | WS_TABSTOP
                    ,149, 6, 40, 14

    CONTROL         "Push2"
                    ,203
                    ,"Button"
                    ,0x0000
                    ,149, 23, 40, 14

    CONTROL         "Push3"
                    ,204
                    ,"Button"
                    ,0x0000
                    ,149, 40, 40, 14
```

```
CONTROL          "Push4"
                 ,205
                 ,"Button"
                 ,0x0000
                 ,149, 57, 40, 14

CONTROL          "Push5"
                 ,206
                 ,"Button"
                 ,0x0000
                 ,149, 74, 40, 14

CONTROL          "Push6"
                 ,207
                 ,"Button"
                 ,0x0000
                 ,149, 91, 40, 14

CONTROL          "Push7"
                 ,208
                 ,"Button"
                 ,0x0000
                 ,149, 108, 40, 14

CONTROL          "Push8"
                 ,209
                 ,"Button"
                 ,0x0000
                 ,149, 125, 40, 14

CONTROL          "Options"
                 ,201
                 ,"Button"
                 ,BS_GROUPBOX
                 ,9, 15, 81, 125

CONTROL          "Check 8"
                 ,210
                 ,"Button"
                 ,BS_AUTOCHECKBOX
                 ,13, 126, 62, 10

CONTROL          "Check 7"
                 ,211
                 ,"Button"
                 ,BS_AUTOCHECKBOX
                 ,13, 112, 62, 10

CONTROL          "Check 6"
                 ,212
                 ,"Button"
                 ,BS_AUTOCHECKBOX
                 ,13, 98, 62, 10

CONTROL          "Check 5"
                 ,213
                 ,"Button"
```

```
                         ,BS_AUTOCHECKBOX
                         ,13, 84, 62, 10

      CONTROL            "Check 4"
                         ,214
                         ,"Button"
                         ,BS_AUTOCHECKBOX
                         ,13, 70, 62, 10

      CONTROL            "Check 3"
                         ,215
                         ,"Button"
                         ,BS_AUTOCHECKBOX
                         ,13, 56, 62, 10

      CONTROL            "Check 2"
                         ,216
                         ,"Button"
                         ,BS_AUTOCHECKBOX
                         ,13, 42, 62, 10

      CONTROL            "Check 1"
                         ,217
                         ,"Button"
                         ,BS_AUTOCHECKBOX | WS_TABSTOP
                         ,13, 29, 62, 10
END
```

The only things of note in here are that the dialog has a menu and that to accommodate that we have to use the WS_BORDER style instead of DS_MODALFRAME.

The application looks like this when it's run :

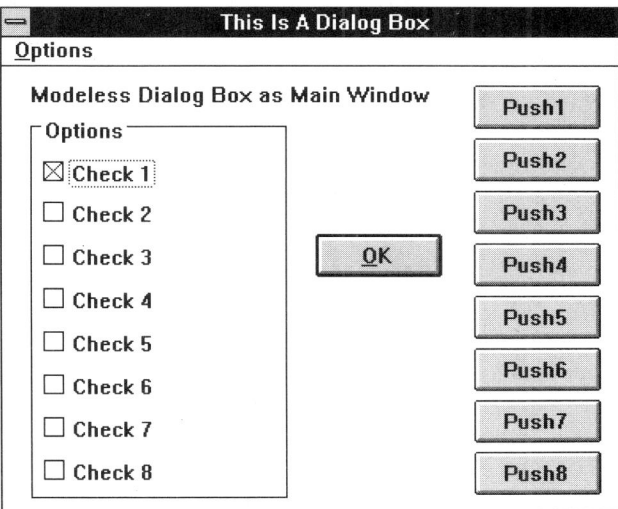

Pretty boring huh?

Note that this dialog cannot really have a minimize box as if it were iconised it would get a NULL icon. We've already see how easy it is to super class the WC_DIALOG class to easily *fit* an icon to it – nuf said?

OK, let's do something else – how about a dialog that expands? You see these in lots of Microsoft applets, like the printer selection dialog.

This kind of dialog is meant to present two views of itself; the non-expanded, or contracted one is the *easy* view, whilst the expanded one is the *advanced* view, again, I've not been too fussy about the look of this example dialog.

It looks like this in the *easy* view mode :

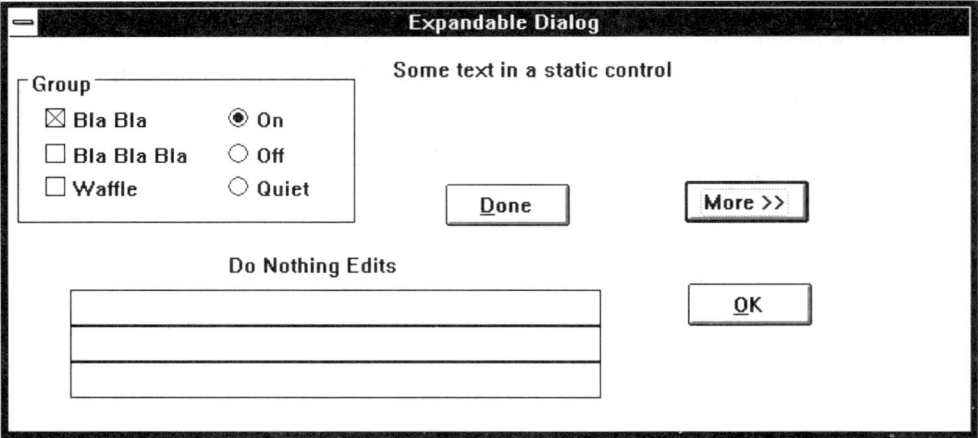

and like this when expanded to the *advanced* view:

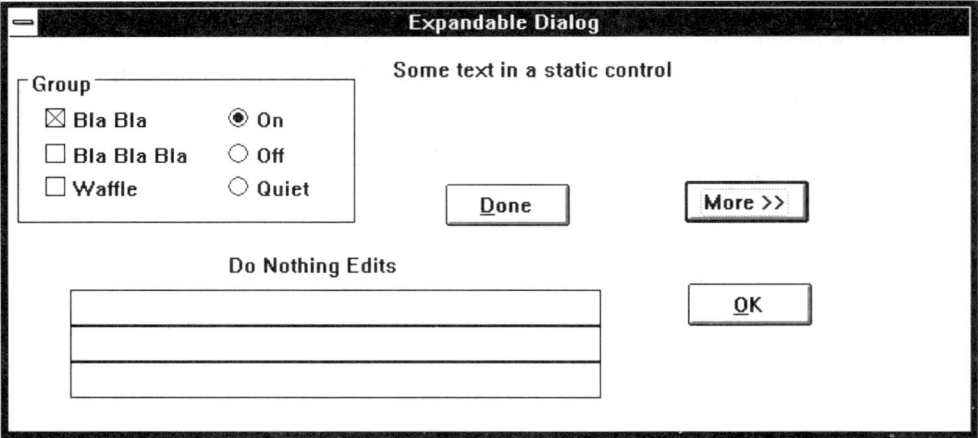

Told you it wasn't too grand to look at!

Before we look at the code, let's look at the dialog template as viewed from the 3.1 dialog editor :

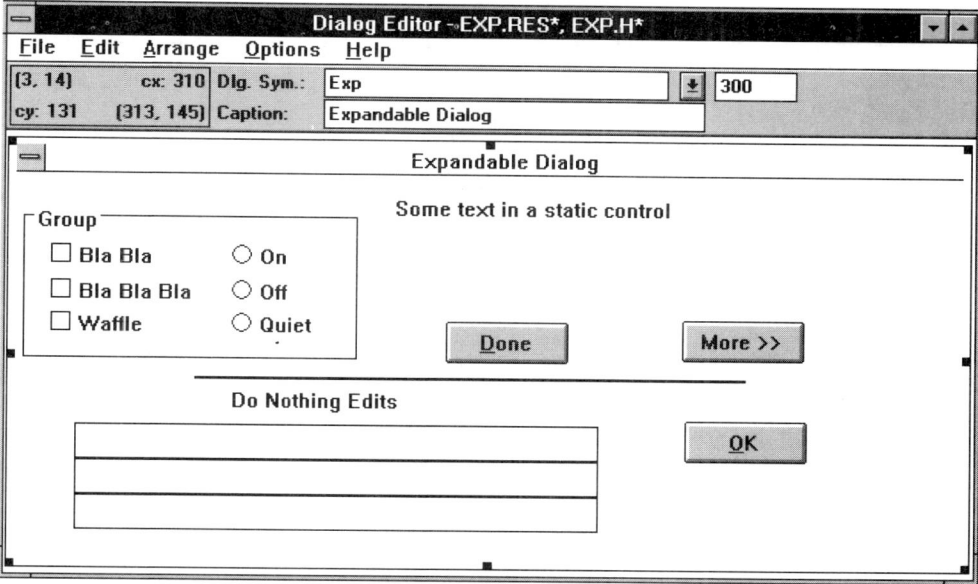

The single thing of note here is the horizontal black line in the centre of the dialog box. This is a static *black rectangle* control, it's ID is IDC_LINE. It is used to position the point at which the expansion or contraction takes place.

This dialog's a normal application (APPLMODAL) dialog, it doesn't have a menu or any other stuff to get in the way of the code example either; the main bit of code is the dialog call-back function, other than that, there's just one other purpose built function to examine. Here's the call-back :

```
BOOL __export CALLBACK DialogProc
(
    HWND      hDlg
   ,UINT      uMessage
   ,WPARAM    wParam
   ,LPARAM    lParam
)
{
    /*
    ** Holds the original, and shrunken height of the dialog box.
    */
    static UINT uOriginalHeight;
    static UINT uShrunkenHeight;

    /*
    ** Indicates whether or not the dialog is
    ** currently expanded or contracted. We
    ** initially show it contracted so it's
    ** set to FALSE explicitly.
    */
    static BOOL bExpanded = FALSE;

    switch(uMessage)
```

```
{

    case WM_INITDIALOG:
        {
            /*
            ** Used to hold the device based positions of
            ** the dialog window and the line control.
            */
            auto RECT rsDlg;
            auto RECT rsLine;

            /*
            ** Get the device based position of the dialog window,
            ** work out its original height.
            */
            GetWindowRect(hDlg, &rsDlg);
            uOriginalHeight = rsDlg.bottom - rsDlg.top;

            /*
            ** Get the device based position of the line control,
            ** work out the dialog's shrunken height.
            */
            GetWindowRect(GetDlgItem(hDlg, IDC_LINE), &rsLine);
            uShrunkenHeight = rsLine.top - rsDlg.top;

            /*
            ** Shrink the window and hide the line control.
            */
            MoveWindow(
                        hDlg
                       ,rsDlg.left
                       ,rsDlg.top
                       ,rsDlg.right - rsDlg.left
                       ,uShrunkenHeight
                       ,FALSE
                       );

            ShowWindow(GetDlgItem(hDlg, IDC_LINE), SW_HIDE);

            /*
            ** Disable controls that are now hidden.
            ** Enable controls that are visible.
            */
            UpdateControlState(hDlg);
        }
        break;

    case WM_COMMAND:
        switch(wParam)
        {
            case IDOK:
                /*
                ** Either 'OK' or 'Done' pressed - we don't
                ** care which - close the dialog.
                */
                EndDialog(hDlg, TRUE);
                break;
```

```
                    /*
                    ** Either contracting OR expanding...
                    */
                case IDC_MORE:
                    {
                        /*
                        ** Dialog's current device position.
                        */
                        auto RECT rsDlg;

                        /*
                        ** Find out where the dialog is on the screen.
                        */
                        GetWindowRect(hDlg, &rsDlg);

                        /*
                        ** Expand or contract it as required.
                        */
                        MoveWindow(
                                hDlg
                                ,rsDlg.left
                                ,rsDlg.top
                                ,rsDlg.right - rsDlg.left
                                ,bExpanded ? uShrunkenHeight : uOriginalHeight
                                ,TRUE
                                );

                        /*
                        ** Toggle expanded/contracted state.
                        */
                        bExpanded = bExpanded == FALSE;

                        /*
                        ** Disable controls that are now hidden.
                        ** Enable controls that are visible.
                        */
                        UpdateControlState(hDlg);
                    }
                break;
                /*
                ** User hit Esc or Close off system menu.
                */
                case IDCANCEL:
                    EndDialog(hDlg, FALSE);
                    break;
            }
            break;

        default:
            return FALSE;

    }
    return TRUE;
}
```

The code is well commented so I'll not spend much time here discussing it.

The function UpdateControlState is coming up; its job is to enable/disable the dialog controls depending upon whether or not they're visible, ie. within the *shown* area of the dialog box window.

The work goes on in WM_INITDIALOG. the line control is made invisible, ShowWindow(GetDlgItem(hDlg, IDC_LINE), SW_HIDE); and the dialog window, which is created as it appears in the dialog editor, is contracted so as its height is governed by the position of the line, ie. its bottom is positioned to be the same as the line's top. Both the dialog's original, and contracted height, once computed, are maintained in static variables.

```
/*
** Get unshrunken, or expanded height and keep in static
*/
GetWindowRect(hDlg, &rsDlg);
uOriginalHeight = rsDlg.bottom - rsDlg.top;

/*
** Get the device based position of the line control,
** work out the dialog's shrunken height.
*/
GetWindowRect(GetDlgItem(hDlg, IDC_LINE), &rsLine);
uShrunkenHeight = rsLine.top - rsDlg.top;

/*
** Shrink the window.
*/
MoveWindow(
        hDlg
        ,rsDlg.left
        ,rsDlg.top
        ,rsDlg.right - rsDlg.left
        ,uShrunkenHeight
        ,FALSE
        );
```

Once the dialog is contracted UpdateControlState is called to disable any control that is not within the visible portion of the dialog window.

```
UpdateControlState(hDlg);
```

When the *More* >> button is pressed the dialog expands or contracts accordingly, again UpdateControlState is called to handle enabling/disabling the visible/obscured control windows. Note that the dialog's device relative position is not maintained in WM_INITDIALOG but is calculated each time that the *More>>* button is pressed. This is to accommodate movements in the dialog's screen position.

The UpdateControlState function looks like this :

```
VOID UpdateControlState(HWND hDlg)
{
   /*
   ** Device position of dialog.
   */
   auto RECT rsDialog;


   /*
   ** Device position of control.
   */
   auto RECT rsControl;


   /*
   ** Window handle of control.
   */
   auto HWND hWndControl;


   /*
   ** Get the device based position of the dialog window.
   */
   GetWindowRect(hDlg, &rsDialog);


   /*
   ** Walk window manager's list of windows for
   ** control windows within dialog window.
   */
   for(
      hWndControl = GetTopWindow(hDlg)
     ;hWndControl
     ;hWndControl = GetWindow(hWndControl, GW_HWNDNEXT)
      )
   {

      /*
      ** Get the device based position of this control.
      */
      GetWindowRect(hWndControl, &rsControl);


      /*
      ** This bit could be used to form an 'new' API called
      ** RectInRect(). We check to see if the control's
      ** device based rectangle is in the dialog's device
      ** based rectangle  - A test for the control's 'top'
      ** point would have done, but what the hell! If the
      ** control's not in the dialog's rect we disable it.
      */
      EnableWindow(
               hWndControl
              ,PtInRect(
                  &rsDialog
                  ,RECTPOINT_TO_POINT(rsControl.left)) &&
               PtInRect(
                  &rsDialog
```

```
                      ,RECTPOINT_TO_POINT(rsControl.right)) ?
             TRUE : FALSE
             );

   }


   return VOID_RETURN;
}
```

This function could really be two. The first could be used to walk the window manager's list of child windows for a dialog box, and the other could be used to test whether or not the whole of one rectangle was inside another. The function walks through all the control windows and tests to see if they're device based rectangle (position) is within the dialog's device based rectangle (position). If the control is outside of the dialog, it's disabled.

Why do we bother disabling/enabling controls like this? The controls need to be disabled so that they can't be tabbed to, ie. if the dialog window was just shrunk you'd still be able to tab to the hidden controls – this might cause the user some confusion as the focus seems to disappear! RECT_TO_POINT is a macro, it's used, as its name suggests, to turn a rectangle into a point.

```
/*
** Turns a RECT point into a POINT.
*/
#define RECTPOINT_TO_POINT(x) (*((LPPOINT)(&x)))
```

OK, the next thing we ought to do is get around to creating a dialog box on the fly using an *Indirect* version of one of these dialog creation functions.

Here's the complete code for an application to do just that. The application builds a modeless dialog box on the fly. What's more, the built dialog contains a custom control (not a flash one – looks a little like Windows 2.1 button!). Also, this custom control is passed creation data via the a CREATSTRUCT structure during WM_CREATE message processing.

Here's what the finished dialog looks like :

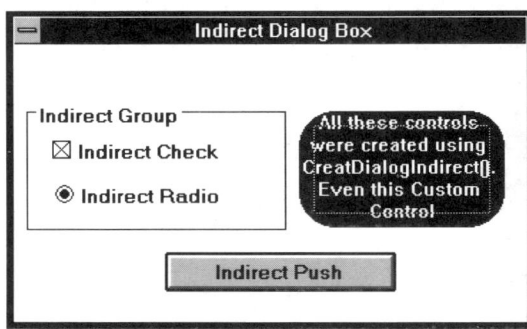

Here you can see that the custom control has the focus (dotted line drawn within it). The text drawn within it is its window caption – just like, say, a regular button control. When the control is created, its window caption is just *Custom Control*. *The remainder of the caption is passed as creation data. The control builds a new caption by concatenating the two pieces of text – you can see the result.*

Well here's the code, the 'C' first :

```c
#define STRICT

#include <windows.h>
#include <memory.h>

/*
** Unref formal parameters warning OFF.
*/
#pragma warning(disable:4100)

/*
** Dialog box menu item ID.
*/
#define IDM_BOX          100

/*
** Default child window control styles.
*/
#define DEF WS_VISIBLE | WS_CHILD

/*
** Control IDs for the RADIO, CHECK, and CUSTOM buttons.
*/
#define IDC_RADIO  102
#define IDC_CHECK  103
#define IDC_CUSTOM 104

/*
** General buffer size.
*/
#define BUFF_SIZE  255


/************************* Function prototypes.***************************/

/*
** Handles 'new' custom control.
*/
LRESULT  __export FAR PASCAL ControlWindowProc
(
   HWND
  ,UINT
  ,WPARAM
  ,LPARAM
);

/*
** Handles application main window.
```

```
*/
LRESULT __export FAR PASCAL MainWindowProc
(
    HWND
   ,UINT
   ,WPARAM
   ,LPARAM
);

/*
** Handles dynamic dialog box - call-back.
*/
BOOL __export CALLBACK DialogBoxCallBack
(
    HWND
   ,UINT
   ,WPARAM
   ,LPARAM
);

/*
** Builds dynamic dialog template.
*/
BOOL bBuildAndDisplayDialogBox      (HWND);

/*
** Registers application window classes and creates main window.
*/
BOOL InitialiseDlgBox               (HINSTANCE, int);

/*
** Sets/Gets modeless dialog's window handle.
*/
HWND AccesshWndModeless             (HWND);

/*
** Write passed date to global heap object.
*/
BOOL bWriteMem                      (HGLOBAL, int, NPSTR, int);

/*
** Main dialog window structure.
*/
typedef struct
{
  DWORD     dtStyle;
  BYTE      dtItemCount;
  WORD      dtX;
  WORD      dtY;
  WORD      dtCX;
  WORD      dtCY;
  char      dtMenuName[1];
  char      dtClassName[1];
  char      dtCaptionText[1];
} DLGTEMPLATE;

/*
** Dialog font structure.
*/
```

```
*/
typedef struct
{
   WORD      fiPointSize;
   char      fiTypeFace[1];
} FONTINFO;

/*
** Dialog control window structure.
*/
typedef struct
{
  WORD      ditX;
  WORD      ditY;
  WORD      ditCX;
  WORD      ditCY;
  WORD      ditID;
  DWORD     ditStyle;
  char      ditClassName;
  char      ditCaptionText[1];
} DIALOGITEMTEMPLATE;

/*
** Normal WINMAIN
*/
int PASCAL WinMain
(
   HINSTANCE     hInstance
  ,HINSTANCE     hPrevInstance
  ,LPSTR         lpszCmdLine
  ,int           nCmdShow
)
{
   /*
   ** Message structure - filled in by GetMessage().
   */
   auto MSG  msg;

   /*
   ** Register main window, and custom control window
   ** classes, create main window.
   */
   if(InitialiseDlgBox(hInstance, nCmdShow) == FALSE)
   {
       return 1;
   }

   /*
   ** Message loop incorporating IsDialogMessage test.
   */
   while(GetMessage(&msg, NULL, 0, 0))
   {
       if((AccesshWndModeless(NULL) == NULL) ||
           IsDialogMessage(AccesshWndModeless(NULL), &msg
          ) == FALSE
          )
       {
           TranslateMessage(&msg);
```

```
            DispatchMessage(&msg);
        }
    }

    /*
    ** Return WM_QUIT wParam value.
    */
    return msg.wParam;
}

/*
** Get/sets dialog window handle.
*/
HWND AccesshWndModeless(HWND hWnd)
{
    /*
    ** Holds the window handle (or NULL) of the
    ** modeless dialog.
    */
    static HWND hWndModeless = NULL;

    switch((UINT)hWnd)
    {
        case NULL:
            break;

        case -1:
            hWndModeless = NULL;
            break;

        default:
            hWndModeless = hWnd;
            break;
    }

    return hWndModeless;
}

/*
** Build dynamic dialog box template, all controls - including
** custom control, create modeless dialog box if all OK.
*/
BOOL InitialiseDlgBox(HINSTANCE hInstance, int nCmdShow)
{
    /*
    ** Class registration structure.
    */
    auto WNDCLASS    wc;

    /*
    ** Window handle for main window.
    */
    auto HWND        hWnd;

    /*
    ** Register the main window's class.
    */
    wc.lpszClassName = (LPSTR) "DialogBoxMainWindow";
```

```
wc.hInstance       = hInstance;
wc.lpfnWndProc     = (WNDPROC)MainWindowProc;
wc.hCursor         = LoadCursor(NULL, IDC_ARROW);
wc.hIcon           = LoadIcon(NULL, IDI_APPLICATION);
wc.lpszMenuName    = "DialogBoxMenu";
wc.hbrBackground   = (HBRUSH)(COLOR_WINDOW + 1);
wc.style           = CS_HREDRAW | CS_VREDRAW;
wc.cbClsExtra      = 0;
wc.cbWndExtra      = 0;

if(RegisterClass(&wc) == 0)
{
    return FALSE;
}


/*
** Register the custom control class.
*/
wc.lpszClassName   = "NewControl";
wc.hInstance       = hInstance;
wc.lpfnWndProc     = (WNDPROC)ControlWindowProc;
wc.hCursor         = LoadCursor(NULL, IDC_ARROW);
wc.hIcon           = NULL;
wc.lpszMenuName    = NULL;
wc.hbrBackground   = (HBRUSH)(COLOR_WINDOW + 1);
wc.style           = 0;
wc.cbClsExtra      = 0;
wc.cbWndExtra      = 0;


if(RegisterClass(&wc) == 0)
{
    return FALSE;
}

/*
** Create main window.
*/
hWnd = CreateWindow(
                    "DialogBoxMainWindow"
                    ,"Indirect Dialog Box & Standard\\Custom Controls"
                    ,WS_OVERLAPPEDWINDOW
                    ,CW_USEDEFAULT
                    ,0
                    ,CW_USEDEFAULT
                    ,0
                    ,NULL
                    ,NULL
                    ,hInstance
                    ,0
                    );

if(hWnd == NULL)
{
    return FALSE;
}
```

```
   /*
   ** Show and update main window.
   */
   ShowWindow(hWnd, nCmdShow);
   UpdateWindow(hWnd);

   return TRUE;
}

/*
** Main window WndProc.
*/
LRESULT __export FAR PASCAL MainWindowProc
(
   HWND     hWnd
  ,UINT     uMessage
  ,WPARAM   wParam
  ,LPARAM   lParam
)
{
   switch(uMessage)
   {
      case WM_COMMAND:
         switch(wParam)
         {
            /*
            ** Build and display dynamic dialog box.
            */
            case IDM_BOX:
               if(bBuildAndDisplayDialogBox(hWnd) != FALSE)
               {
                  /*
                  ** Disable menu item as dialog is up.
                  */
                  EnableMenuItem(
                              GetMenu(hWnd)
                             ,IDM_BOX
                             ,MF_GRAYED | MF_DISABLED
                             );
               }
               break;

            default:
               return DefWindowProc(hWnd,uMessage, wParam, lParam);
               break;
         }
         break;

      case WM_DESTROY:
         PostQuitMessage(0);
         break;

      default:
         return DefWindowProc(hWnd, uMessage, wParam, lParam);
         break;
   }

   return (LRESULT)0;
```

```
}


/*
** Builds and displays dynamic dialog box.
*/
BOOL bBuildAndDisplayDialogBox(HWND hWnd)
{
   /*
   ** Main dialog window template.
   */
   auto DLGTEMPLATE          dtHeader;

   /*
   ** Control template. One of these
   ** required for each dialog control.
   */
   auto DIALOGITEMTEMPLATE   ditItem;

   /*
   ** Font info for dialog.
   */
   auto FONTINFO             fiFont;

   /*
   ** Global memory handle - dialog template lives in here.
   */
   auto HGLOBAL              hDialogTemplate;

   /*
   ** Address of template memory.
   */
   auto VOID FAR *           lpDialogTemplate;

   /*
   ** Holds offset into global memory for data write.
   */
   auto int                  nByteCount;

   /*
   ** Used to hold any textual data, eg. control caption text.
   */
   auto char                 carBuffer[BUFF_SIZE];

   /*
   ** Get dialog box template memory - just get
   ** enough for header first.
   */
   if((hDialogTemplate = GlobalAlloc(
                                       GMEM_MOVEABLE
                                      ,sizeof(DLGTEMPLATE)
                                      )
      ) == NULL
     )
   {
      return FALSE;
   }
```

```
/*
** Reset offset.
*/
nByteCount = 0;

/***********************************************************
 *
 * Main dialog window template item to be added first.
 *
 */

/*
** Set required style, note that DS_SETFONT is used,
** this header must therefore be followed by a FONTINFO.
*/
dtHeader.dtStyle          = DS_SETFONT    |
                            DS_MODALFRAME |
                            WS_POPUP      |
                            WS_VISIBLE    |
                            WS_CAPTION    |
                            WS_SYSMENU;

dtHeader.dtItemCount      = 5;      /* Number of controls. */

/*
** Dialog position. Really ignore as it's centred later.
*/
dtHeader.dtX              = 0;
dtHeader.dtY              = 0;

/*
** Width and height of dialog window.
*/
dtHeader.dtCX             = 160;
dtHeader.dtCY             = 100;

/*
** No dialog menu or private class name, set
** to NULL terminated strings that are just
** the NULL big, ie. put NULL in them.
*/
dtHeader.dtMenuName[0]    = 0;
dtHeader.dtClassName[0]   = 0;

/*
** Write it out to global memory, '-1' is used because we
** didn't fill in CaptionText and this is 1 byte big.
*/
if(bWriteMem(
            hDialogTemplate
           ,nByteCount
           , (NPSTR)&dtHeader
           ,sizeof(DLGTEMPLATE) - 1
           ) == FALSE
  )
{
    return FALSE;
```

```
}
/*
** Inc off set accordingly.
*/
nByteCount += sizeof(DLGTEMPLATE) - 1;

/*
** Write caption text into buffer.
*/
lstrcpy(&carBuffer[0],"Indirect Dialog Box");

/*
** Write it up. +1 for NULL, lstrlen() doesn't include
** NULL byte at end of string.
*/
if(bWriteMem(
               hDialogTemplate
             ,nByteCount
             ,&carBuffer[0]
             ,lstrlen((LPCSTR)&carBuffer[0]) + 1
             ) == FALSE
  )
{
    return FALSE;
}

/*
** Inc off set accordingly.
*/
nByteCount += lstrlen((LPCSTR)&carBuffer[0]) + 1;

/*************************************************************
*
* Add fontinfo item next as DS_SETFONT was used.
*
*/

/*
** Smallish font.
*/
fiFont.fiPointSize = 10;

/*
** Write it up.
*/
if(bWriteMem(
               hDialogTemplate
             ,nByteCount
             , (NPSTR)&fiFont
             ,sizeof(FONTINFO) - 1
             ) == FALSE
  )
{
    return FALSE;
}

/*
** Inc off set accordingly.
```

```
*/
nByteCount += sizeof(FONTINFO) - 1;


/*
** Copy face name to buffer.
*/
lstrcpy(&carBuffer[0], "Ms Sans Serif");


/*
** Write it up.
*/
if(bWriteMem(
              hDialogTemplate
            ,nByteCount
            ,&carBuffer[0]
            ,lstrlen((LPCSTR)&carBuffer[0]) + 1
            ) == FALSE
   )
{
    return FALSE;
}


/*
** Inc off set accordingly.
*/
nByteCount += lstrlen((LPCSTR)&carBuffer[0]) + 1;



/************************************************************
*
* Add first control item next.
*
*/


/*
** Dialog window relative initial X and Y.
*/
ditItem.ditX    = 47;
ditItem.ditY    = 75;


/*
** Width and height.
*/
ditItem.ditCX   = 72;
ditItem.ditCY   = 14;


/*
** ID - this is the OK button.
*/
ditItem.ditID   = IDOK;


/*
** Button style.
*/
ditItem.ditStyle = BS_DEFPUSHBUTTON | WS_TABSTOP | DEF;


/*
** Use 3.1 documented, and 3.0 undocumented short classname
```

```
** for button control.
*/
ditItem.ditClassName = (char)0x80;

/*
** Write it up. '-1' cos we didn't use caption text
** member and this is 1 byte big.
*/
if(bWriteMem(
            hDialogTemplate
           ,nByteCount
           ,(NPSTR)&ditItem
           ,sizeof(DIALOGITEMTEMPLATE) - 1
           ) == FALSE
   )
{
   return FALSE;
}

/*
** Inc off set accordingly.
*/
nByteCount += sizeof(DIALOGITEMTEMPLATE) - 1;

/*
** Copy required button caption text to buffer.
*/
lstrcpy(&carBuffer[0], "Indirect Push");

/*
** Write it up.
*/
if(bWriteMem(
            hDialogTemplate
           ,nByteCount
           ,&carBuffer[0]
           ,lstrlen((LPCSTR)&carBuffer[0]) + 1
           ) == FALSE
   )
{
  return FALSE;
}

/*
** Inc off set accordingly.
*/
nByteCount += lstrlen((LPCSTR)&carBuffer[0]) + 1;

/*
** (in 3.0 docs this next bit is dtilInfo). Set
** to zero as no control extra info to be passed.
*/
carBuffer[0] = 0;

/*
** Write it up.
*/
if(bWriteMem(
```

```
                    hDialogTemplate
                    ,nByteCount
                    ,&carBuffer[0]
                    ,1
                    ) == FALSE
    )
{
  return FALSE;
}


/*
** Inc off set accordingly.
*/
nByteCount += 1;

/***************************************************************
*
* Add second control item next. No further commentary
* till we get to the custom control. This is the
* Radio Button.
*
*/

ditItem.ditX     = 13;
ditItem.ditY     = 49;
ditItem.ditCX    = 65;
ditItem.ditCY    = 10;
ditItem.ditID    = IDC_RADIO;
ditItem.ditStyle = BS_AUTORADIOBUTTON | WS_GROUP | DEF;
ditItem.ditClassName = (char)0x80;

if(bWriteMem(
              hDialogTemplate
              ,nByteCount
              ,(NPSTR)&ditItem
              ,sizeof(DIALOGITEMTEMPLATE) - 1
              ) == FALSE
  )
{
    return FALSE;
}

nByteCount += sizeof(DIALOGITEMTEMPLATE) - 1;

lstrcpy(&carBuffer[0], "Indirect Radio");

if(bWriteMem(
              hDialogTemplate
              ,nByteCount
              ,&carBuffer[0]
              ,lstrlen((LPCSTR)&carBuffer[0]) + 1
              ) == FALSE
  )
{
  return FALSE;
}

nByteCount += lstrlen((LPCSTR)&carBuffer[0]) + 1;
```

```
  carBuffer[0] = 0;

if(bWriteMem(
             hDialogTemplate
            ,nByteCount
            ,&carBuffer[0]
            ,1
            ) == FALSE
  )
{
  return FALSE;
}
nByteCount += 1;

/**************************************************************
*
* Add third control item next. No further commentary
* till we get to the custom control. This is the
* Check Box.
*
*/

ditItem.ditX      = 12;
ditItem.ditY      = 33;
ditItem.ditCX     = 64;
ditItem.ditCY     = 10;
ditItem.ditID     = IDC_CHECK;
ditItem.ditStyle = BS_AUTOCHECKBOX | WS_TABSTOP | DEF;
ditItem.ditClassName = (char)0x80;

if(bWriteMem(
             hDialogTemplate
            ,nByteCount
            ,(NPSTR)&ditItem
            ,sizeof(DIALOGITEMTEMPLATE) - 1
            ) == FALSE
  )
{
    return FALSE;
}

nByteCount += sizeof(DIALOGITEMTEMPLATE) - 1;

lstrcpy(&carBuffer[0], "Indirect Check");

if(bWriteMem(
             hDialogTemplate
            ,nByteCount
            ,&carBuffer[0]
            ,lstrlen((LPCSTR)&carBuffer[0]) + 1
            ) == FALSE
  )
{
  return FALSE;
}

nByteCount += lstrlen((LPCSTR)&carBuffer[0]) + 1;
```

```
carBuffer[0] = 0;

if(bWriteMem(
            hDialogTemplate
           ,nByteCount
           ,&carBuffer[0]
           ,1
           ) == FALSE
  )
{
  return FALSE;
}
nByteCount += 1;

/***************************************************************
 *
 * Add fourth control item next. No further commentary
 * till we get to the custom control. This is the
 * Group Box.
 *
 */

ditItem.ditX     = 4;
ditItem.ditY     = 20;
ditItem.ditCX    = 81;
ditItem.ditCY    = 47;
ditItem.ditID    = 104;
ditItem.ditStyle = BS_GROUPBOX | WS_GROUP | DEF;
ditItem.ditClassName = (char)0x80;

if(bWriteMem(
            hDialogTemplate
           ,nByteCount
           ,(NPSTR)&ditItem
           ,sizeof(DIALOGITEMTEMPLATE) - 1
           ) == FALSE
  )
{
   return FALSE;
}

nByteCount += sizeof(DIALOGITEMTEMPLATE) - 1;

lstrcpy(&carBuffer[0], "Indirect Group");

if(bWriteMem(
            hDialogTemplate
           ,nByteCount
           ,&carBuffer[0]
           ,lstrlen((LPCSTR)&carBuffer[0]) + 1
           ) == FALSE
  )
{
  return FALSE;
}

nByteCount += lstrlen((LPCSTR)&carBuffer[0]) + 1;
```

```
  carBuffer[0] = 0;

  if(bWriteMem(
                hDialogTemplate
                ,nByteCount
                ,&carBuffer[0]
                ,1
                ) == FALSE
     )
  {
    return FALSE;
  }
  nByteCount += 1;

  /*************************************************************
  *
  * Add fifth control item next. This is a custom control,
  * see the control's WndProc for more details on its
  * functionality. Commentary cut down in here to just the
  * interesting stuff.
  *
  */

  ditItem.ditX    = 89;
  ditItem.ditY    = 24;
  ditItem.ditCX   = 64;
  ditItem.ditCY   = 42;

  /*
  ** Custom ID.
  */
  ditItem.ditID    = IDC_CUSTOM;
  ditItem.ditStyle = WS_TABSTOP | DEF;

  /*
  ** Classname identifier set to 0x0 - no standard classname
  ** for custom control, has to be full textual name. See
  ** below for how this is amended.
  */
  ditItem.ditClassName = 0x0;

  /*
  ** Write it up MINUS 1 byte, we effectively lose the
  ** 0x0 classname by doing this.
  */
  if(bWriteMem(
                hDialogTemplate
                ,nByteCount
                ,(NPSTR)&ditItem
                ,sizeof(DIALOGITEMTEMPLATE) - 1 - 1
                ) == FALSE
     )
  {
      return FALSE;
  }

  /*
  ** Inc offset MINUS 1 also.
```

```
*/
nByteCount += sizeof(DIALOGITEMTEMPLATE) - 1 - 1;

/*
** Copy custom control classname into buffer.
*/
lstrcpy(&carBuffer[0], "NewControl");

/*
** And write it up.
*/
if(bWriteMem(
            hDialogTemplate
          ,nByteCount
          ,&carBuffer[0]
          ,lstrlen((LPCSTR)&carBuffer[0]) + 1
          ) == FALSE
  )
{
    return FALSE;
}

nByteCount += lstrlen((LPCSTR)&carBuffer[0]) + 1;

/*
** Custom control caption text - used in
** custom control WM_CREATE handling.
*/
lstrcpy(&carBuffer[0], "Custom Control");

if(bWriteMem(
            hDialogTemplate
          ,nByteCount
          ,&carBuffer[0]
          ,lstrlen((LPCSTR)&carBuffer[0]) + 1
          ) == FALSE
  )
{
    return FALSE;
}

nByteCount += lstrlen((LPCSTR)&carBuffer[0]) + 1;

/*
** Now as we're using a custom control, let's
** pass it some creation information - a text
** string is passed here.
*/
{
    /*
    ** Data to be passed to control.
    */
    auto NPSTR npC = "All these controls were created "
                    "using CreatDialogIndirect(). Even "
                    "this ";

    /*
    ** Fill in ditInfo with size of data, '+1' for string's
```

```
        ** NULL terminator.
        */
        carBuffer[0] = (char)(lstrlen(npC) + 1);


        /*
        ** Write it up.
        */
        if(bWriteMem(
                    hDialogTemplate
                    ,nByteCount
                    ,&carBuffer[0]
                    ,1
                    ) == FALSE
          )
        {
            return FALSE;
        }


        /*
        ** Add one to offset.
        */
        nByteCount += 1;


        /*
        ** Now copy data in buffer and copy it up also.
        */
        lstrcpy(&carBuffer[0], npC);

        if(bWriteMem(
                    hDialogTemplate
                    ,nByteCount
                    ,&carBuffer[0]
                    ,lstrlen(npC) + 1
                    ) == FALSE
        )
        {
        return FALSE;
        }


        /*
        ** Final inc  to offset. nByteCount now holds
        ** complete dialog size - we don't use it any
        ** further here.
        */
        nByteCount += lstrlen(npC) + 1;
}


/*
** CreateDialogIndirectParam() requires pointer to
** template  memory. We pass  this  pointer to the
** dialog  callback  also so that  it can free the
** memory when the dialog's thru.
*/
lpDialogTemplate = GlobalLock(hDialogTemplate);


/*
** Create modeless dialog - store its window handle.
```

```
    */
    AccesshWndModeless(CreateDialogIndirectParam(
                                                (HINSTANCE)
                                                GetWindowWord(
                                                            hWnd
                                                            ,GWW_HINSTANCE
                                                            )
                                                ,lpDialogTemplate
                                                ,hWnd
                                                ,(DLGPROC)DialogBoxCallBack
                                                ,(LPARAM)lpDialogTemplate
                                                )
                    );

    /*
    ** Check to see if DM complained.
    */
    if(AccesshWndModeless(NULL) == (HWND)-1)
    {
        MessageBox(
                    hWnd
                    ,"Failed to create dialog!"
                    ,NULL
                    ,MB_OK
                    );

        /*
        ** If we couldn't create it, free the template.
        */
        GlobalUnlock(hDialogTemplate);
        GlobalFree(hDialogTemplate);

        return TRUE;
    }
}

/*
** Dialog box call-back function.
*/
BOOL __export CALLBACK DialogBoxCallBack
(
    HWND      hDlg
   ,UINT      uMessage
   ,WPARAM    wParam
   ,LPARAM    lParam
)
{
    /*
    ** Holds the global memory handle of the dialog box
    ** template - destroyed when the dialog's destroyed.
    */
    static  HGLOBAL      hDialogTemplate;

    switch(uMessage)
    {
        case WM_INITDIALOG:
            {
                auto VOID FAR * lpDialogTemplate; /* Addr of dlg template.
```

```
*/
            auto RECT           rsWindow;       /* Dialog window rect.   */
            auto int            nXOrg;          /* X pos for dialog wnd. */
            auto int            nYOrg;          /* Y pos for dialog wnd. */


            /*
            ** Get global template handle from template
            ** pointer - use SELECTOF() to do it.
            */
            lpDialogTemplate = (VOID FAR *)lParam;
            hDialogTemplate  = (HGLOBAL)
LOWORD(GlobalHandle(SELECTOROF(lpDialogTemplate)));

            /*
            ** Position dialog box in centre of screen.
            */
            GetWindowRect(hDlg, &rsWindow);

            nXOrg = GetSystemMetrics(SM_CXSCREEN);
            nXOrg = (nXOrg /2) - ((rsWindow.right - rsWindow.left) / 2);

            nYOrg = GetSystemMetrics(SM_CYSCREEN);
            nYOrg = (nYOrg /2) - ((rsWindow.bottom - rsWindow.top) / 2);

            MoveWindow(
                    hDlg
                   ,nXOrg
                   ,nYOrg
                   ,rsWindow.right - rsWindow.left
                   ,rsWindow.bottom - rsWindow.top
                   ,FALSE
                   );
        }
        /*
        ** Set focus to first with WS_TABSTOP.
        */
        return TRUE;
        break;

    case WM_COMMAND:
        switch(wParam)
        {
            /*
            ** Either system menu 'close', IDOK or Custom click.
            */
            case IDOK:
            case IDCANCEL:
            case IDC_CUSTOM:

                /*
                ** Re-enable modeless menu item.
                */
                EnableMenuItem(
                            GetMenu(GetParent(hDlg))
                           ,IDM_BOX
```

```
                                        ,MF_ENABLED | MF_BYCOMMAND
                                    );

                    /*
                    ** Destroy our window.
                    */
                    DestroyWindow(hDlg);
                    break;

                default:
                    return TRUE;

            }
            break;

        case WM_DESTROY:

            /*
            ** Re-set modeless dialog handle.
            */
            AccesshWndModeless((HWND)-1);

            /*
            ** Free up template global heap object.
            */
            if(hDialogTemplate == NULL          ||
               GlobalUnlock(hDialogTemplate) ||
               GlobalFree(hDialogTemplate)
              )
            {
              MessageBox(0, "Failed to release dialog template!", NULL, MB_OK);
            }
            break;


        default:
            return FALSE;
    }

    return TRUE;
}




/*
** Writes pSrce data into hData after offset wOffset, item is wSize big.
*/
BOOL bWriteMem(HGLOBAL hData, int nOffset, NPSTR npcSrce, int nSize)
{
    /*
    ** Locked template long pointer.
    */
    auto LPBYTE lpDest;


    /*
    ** Always does this. Resize global memory object to
```

```
    ** accommodate new npcSrce data.
    */
    if(nOffset + nSize > (LONG)GlobalSize(hData))
    {
        if((hData = GlobalReAlloc(
                                    hData
                                  ,nOffset + nSize
                                  ,GMEM_MOVEABLE
                                  )
           ) == NULL
          )
        {
            (VOID)GlobalFree(hData);
        }
    }

    if((lpDest = GlobalLock(hData)) != NULL)
    {
        /*
        ** Get to end of last write.
        */
        lpDest += nOffset;

        /*
        ** Write new data into template.
        */
        _fmemcpy(lpDest, npcSrce, nSize);

        /*
        ** Unlock it to be friendly.
        */
        GlobalUnlock(hData);

        return TRUE;
    }
    else
    {

        return FALSE;
    }
}


/*
** Handles the custom control.
*/
LRESULT __export FAR PASCAL ControlWindowProc
(
   HWND     hWnd
  ,UINT     uMessage
  ,WPARAM   wParam
  ,LPARAM   lParam
)
{
    switch(uMessage)
    {
        case WM_CREATE:
            {
```

```c
    /*
    ** What was passed as creation data.
    */
    auto LPSTR  lpszCreationString;

    /*
    ** Local memory used to set window's caption text.
    */
    auto HLOCAL hLocalMem;

    /*
    ** Get creation data, should be pointer to a longish string.
    */
    lpszCreationString =

    (LPSTR)(((LPCREATESTRUCT)lParam)->lpCreateParams);

    /*
    ** Allocate some space for it and the current caption.
    */
    if((hLocalMem = LocalAlloc(
                            LMEM_MOVEABLE | LMEM_ZEROINIT
                            ,GetWindowTextLength(hWnd)    +
                            1                             +
                            lstrlen(lpszCreationString)
                            )
      ) == NULL
     )
    {
        return (LRESULT)0;
    }
    else
    {
        /*
        ** Points to local buffer.
        */
        auto VOID NEAR * npvMem;

        if((npvMem = LocalLock(hLocalMem)) == NULL)
        {
            (VOID)LocalFree(hLocalMem);

            return (LRESULT)0;
        }
        else
        {
            /*
            ** Copy creation data into buffer.
            */
            lstrcpy(npvMem, lpszCreationString);

            /*
            ** Get window text into the same buffer.
            */
            GetWindowText(
                        hWnd
                        ,(NPSTR)npvMem + lstrlen(npvMem)
                        ,GetWindowTextLength(hWnd) + 1
```

```
                                        );

                        /*
                        ** Now re-set the caption of the window to be
                        ** the buffer text - ie. concatenate original
                        ** caption and passed creation data string to
                        ** form new and exciting caption!
                        */
                        SetWindowText(hWnd, npvMem);

                        (VOID)LocalUnlock(hLocalMem);
                        (VOID)LocalFree(hLocalMem);
                    }
                }

                /*
                ** Make the radio button and check box look a little
                ** more like they might do something.
                */
                CheckDlgButton(GetParent(hWnd), IDC_RADIO, 1);
                CheckDlgButton(GetParent(hWnd), IDC_CHECK, 1);

            }
            break;

            /*
            ** This stuff draws/removes a focus rectangle in the
            **  custom control  so that  it looks  a little more
            ** like a control when it gets the focus.
            */
        case WM_KILLFOCUS:
        case WM_SETFOCUS:
            {
                /*
                ** Used for manipulating the control's appearance.
                */
                auto HDC   hDC;

                /*
                ** Required to ensure that focus rect is drawn
                ** OK if control is  partially covered and un-
                ** covered.
                */
                UpdateWindow(GetParent(hWnd));
                UpdateWindow(hWnd);

                if((hDC = GetDC(hWnd)) == NULL)
                {
                    break;
                }
                else
                {
                    /*
                    ** Holds the client area rectangle.
                    */
                    auto RECT rsClient;

                    /*
```

```
                    ** Get rectangle.
                    */
                    GetClientRect(hWnd, &rsClient);

                    /*
                    ** Shrink it by 10 pels in width and height.
                    */
                    InflateRect(&rsClient, -10, -10);

                    /*
                    ** Draw focus rect in.
                    */
                    DrawFocusRect(hDC, &rsClient);

                    ReleaseDC(hWnd, hDC);
                }

            }
            break;

        /*
        ** If we get a LBUTTON down set focus to ourselves.
        */
    case WM_LBUTTONDOWN:
        SetFocus(hWnd);
        break;

        /*
        ** If we get an up, post WM_COMMAND message to parent
        ** which will close  down dialog box. Don't bother to
        ** see if we had a LBUTTONDOWN first though - this is
        ** just a demo.
        */
    case WM_LBUTTONUP:
        PostMessage(
                    GetParent(hWnd)
                    ,WM_COMMAND
                    ,GetWindowWord(hWnd, GWW_ID)
                    ,MAKELPARAM(hWnd, BN_CLICKED)
                    );
        break;

    case WM_PAINT:
        {
            /*
            ** Holds control window caption text.
            */
            auto HLOCAL        hLocalMem;

            /*
            ** Alloc enough memory for caption text.
            */
            if((hLocalMem = LocalAlloc(
                                        LMEM_MOVEABLE | LMEM_ZEROINIT
                                        ,GetWindowTextLength(hWnd)   +
                                        1
                                        )
                ) == NULL
```

```
            )
        {
            return DefWindowProc(hWnd, uMessage, wParam, lParam);
        }
    else
        {
            auto VOID NEAR *  npvMem;    /* Pointer to caption text.*/
            auto RECT         rsClient;  /* Client rectangle.       */
            auto HDC          hDC;       /* Cache DC.               */
            auto PAINTSTRUCT  ps;        /* Required for BeginPaint. */
            auto HBRUSH       hbr;       /* New background colour.   */


            /*
            ** Lock mem.
            */
            if((npvMem = LocalLock(hLocalMem)) == NULL)
            {
                (VOID)LocalFree(hLocalMem);


                return DefWindowProc(hWnd, uMessage, wParam, lParam);
            }
            else
            {
                /*
                ** Get controls caption into mem.
                */
                GetWindowText(hWnd, npvMem, GetWindowTextLength(hWnd) + 1);


                /*
                ** Get client size for DrawText().
                */
                GetClientRect(hWnd, &rsClient);


                /*
                ** Get cache DC.
                */
                hDC = BeginPaint(hWnd, &ps);


                /*
                ** Boring white text.
                */
                SetTextColor(hDC, RGB(255,255,255));


                /*
                ** Exciting see-thru white text!
                */
                SetBkMode(hDC, TRANSPARENT);

                /*
                ** Boring gray brush.
                */
```

```
                        hbr = SelectObject(hDC, GetStockObject(BLACK_BRUSH));

                        /*
                        ** Make ourselves look round.
                        */
                        RoundRect(
                                hDC
                                ,rsClient.left
                                ,rsClient.top
                                ,rsClient.right
                                ,rsClient.bottom
                                ,50
                                ,50
                                );

                        /*
                        ** Draw in window caption text.
                        */
                        DrawText(
                                hDC
                                ,npvMem
                                ,-1
                                ,&rsClient
                                ,DT_CENTER | DT_WORDBREAK
                                );

                        /*
                        ** Not really needed... Restore DC.
                        */
                        hbr = SelectObject(hDC, hbr);

                        EndPaint(hWnd, &ps);

                        (VOID)LocalUnlock(hLocalMem);
                        (VOID)LocalFree(hLocalMem);

                        /*
                        ** If we're focused need to get the focus rect
                        ** drawn in OK.
                        */
                        if(GetFocus() == hWnd)
                        {
                            SendMessage(hWnd, WM_SETFOCUS, 0, 0);
                        }
                    }
                }
            }
            break;

        default:
            return DefWindowProc(hWnd, uMessage, wParam, lParam);
            break;
    }

    return (LRESULT)0;
}
```

The .rc file :

```
#define IDM_BOX              100

DialogBoxMenu MENU
BEGIN
  POPUP "&Options"
  BEGIN
       MENUITEM "Modeless...", IDM_BOX
  END
END
```

The .def file :

```
NAME              IND

WINDOWAPI

EXETYPE           WINDOWS 3.1

PROTMODE

STUB              'WINSTUB.EXE'
DESCRIPTION       'Indirect Dialog box with custom control.'

CODE              PRELOAD MOVEABLE DISCARDABLE
DATA              PRELOAD MOVEABLE MULTIPLE

HEAPSIZE          2000
STACKSIZE         5120

EXPORTS
                  DIALOGBOXCALLBACK        @1
                  MAINWINDOWPROC           @2
                  CONTROLWINDOWPROC        @3
```

Again, I feel that the code is well documented and that it shouldn't need me to annotate it here to any great detail. Just a couple of things though.

Notice that all but the custom control uses the *short* class name as documented in the 3.1 Programmer's Reference Volume 4 (Page 93). This saves quite a lot of fiddling about – as you can see from the other places in the code where text has to be appended to the memory area.

On the following page is the template as viewed with Heap Walker.

Also, this code fragment is BIG, don't you think, yet it builds such a simple dialog box with just five controls! However, don't be put off because if you were really going to do this sort of thing most of the static data used in the example would come from disk files, or user input – the overall effect is that the code is shortened considerably.

The Dynamic Dialog Resource

```
┌─┬──────────────────────────────────────────────────────────────────┬─┐
│─│      Global Object - 00050920 1456      288          IND  Private │▲│
├─┴──────────────────────────────────────────────────────────────────┼─┤
│0000  C0 00 C8 90 05 00 00 00 00 A0 00 64 00 00 00 49  À.È.......d...I │▲│
│0010  6E 64 69 72 65 63 74 20 44 69 61 6C 6F 67 20 42  ndirect Dialog B│ │
│0020  6F 78 00 0A 00 4D 73 20 53 61 6E 73 20 53 65 72  ox...Ms Sans Ser│ │
│0030  69 66 00 2F 00 4B 00 48 00 0E 00 01 00 01 00 01  if./.K.H........│ │
│0040  50 80 49 6E 64 69 72 65 63 74 20 50 75 73 68 00  P.Indirect Push.│ │
│0050  00 0D 00 31 00 41 00 0A 00 66 00 09 00 02 50 80  ...1.A...f....P.│ │
│0060  49 6E 64 69 72 65 63 74 20 52 61 64 69 6F 00 00  Indirect Radio..│ │
│0070  0C 00 21 00 40 00 0A 00 67 00 03 00 01 50 80 49  ..!.@...g....P.I│ │
│0080  6E 64 69 72 65 63 74 20 43 68 65 63 6B 00 00 04  ndirect Check...│ │
│0090  00 14 00 51 00 2F 00 68 00 07 00 02 50 80 49 6E  ...Q./.h....P.In│ │
│00A0  64 69 72 65 63 74 20 47 72 6F 75 70 00 00 59 00  direct Group..Y.│ │
│00B0  18 00 40 00 2A 00 68 00 00 00 01 50 4E 65 77 43  ..@.*.h....PNewC│ │
│00C0  6F 6E 74 72 6F 6C 00 43 75 73 74 6F 6D 20 43 6F  ontrol.Custom Co│ │
│00D0  6E 74 72 6F 6C 00 48 41 6C 6C 20 74 68 65 73 65  ntrol.HAll these│ │
│00E0  20 63 6F 6E 74 72 6F 6C 73 20 77 65 72 65 20 63   controls were c│ │
│00F0  72 65 61 74 65 64 20 75 73 69 6E 67 20 43 72 65  reated using Cre│ │
│0100  61 74 44 69 61 6C 6F 67 49 6E 64 69 72 65 63 74  atDialogIndirect│▼│
└──────────────────────────────────────────────────────────────────────┘
```

          ditInfo   Control ID   Class Name

        ditData (Start)

Most of the work in this app is done in bBuildAndDisplayDialogBox, ie. this is the function that creates the dynamic dialog box. It also contains most of the app's code – ie. it's BIG by itself.

The function starts by creating some global memory into which the dialog template will be inserted. After this the dialog's dialog header in inserted into the global memory object. Each *extra* item is also written up to the global memory object – in fact the entire function's taken up with essentially five calls to a function that writes the data for each control to the global memory object. The function that does the writing is called bWriteMem :

```
BOOL bWriteMem(HGLOBAL hData, int nOffset, NPSTR npcSrce, int
nSize)
{
    auto LPBYTE lpDest;

    if(nOffset + nSize > (LONG)GlobalSize(hData))
    {
        if((hData = GlobalReAlloc(
                            hData
                            ,nOffset + nSize
                            , GMEM_MOVEABLE
                            )
            ) == NULL
          )
        {
            (VOID)GlobalFree(hData);
        }
    }

    if((lpDest = GlobalLock(hData)) != NULL)
```

```
        {
            lpDest += nOffset;

            _fmemcpy(lpDest, npcSrce, nSize);

            GlobalUnlock(hData);

            return TRUE;
        }
        else
        {

            return FALSE;
        }
    }
```

This function is passed the following :

- The memory handle (to the global heap object)
- The offset into the memory item at which to write the passed data.
- The data to be written up.
- The size of the data.

The function re-allocates the global object, locks it, then writes up the data to it using the _fmemcpy() function taken from the Microsoft *standard* 'C' library. The last data written up to the global heap object is the custom control.

Once the template is built the dialog's created using CreateDialogIndirectParam(). The *address* of the global heap object is passed to the dialog call-back via the lParam of the WM_INITDIALOG message, ie. the *Param* part of CreateDialogIndirectParam() contains the address of the dialog template :

```
AccesshWndModeless(CreateDialogIndirectParam(
                                        (HINSTANCE)
                                        GetWindowWord(
                                                hWnd
                                                ,GWW_HINSTANCE
                                                )
                                        ,lpDialogTemplate
                                        ,hWnd
                                        ,(DLGPROC)DialogBoxCallBack
                                        ,(LPARAM)lpDialogTemplate
                                        )
                );
```

The call-back uses the pointer to get a handle to the dialog template and stores this in a static variable within the call-back. The call-back uses the handle to destroy the global heap object containing the template whenever the dialog's closed down, ie. the dialog's template is built afresh whenever it's required and destroyed when the dialog is.

```
    ...
    ...
    case WM_INITDIALOG:
```

```
lpDialogTemplate = (VOID FAR *)lParam;
hDialogTemplate  = (HGLOBAL)

LOWORD(GlobalHandle(SELECTOROF(lpDialogTemplate)));
...
...
...
case WM_DESTROY:

    /*
    ** Re-set modeless dialog handle.
    */
    AccesshWndModeless((HWND)-1);

    /*
    ** Free up template global heap object.
    */
    if(hDialogTemplate == NULL       ||
       GlobalUnlock(hDialogTemplate) ||
       GlobalFree(hDialogTemplate)
      )
    {
       MessageBox(0, "Failed to release dialog template!", NULL, MB_OK);
    }
    break;
```

The custom control is passed some creation data via the CREATESTRUCT structure that the lParam of a WM_CREATE message points to. The actual data passed in this example is a pointer to a string of text. The control's WndProc – ControlWndProc, retrieves this data and combines it with the control's existing caption. The rest of the WndProc() makes the control act something like a *real* control window (See control chapter for more precise information and a better example of how to build a control).

☐ Dialog Failure

Before getting on to the standard, or common dialogs, let's just have a quick discussion on why a dialog box creation function might fail.

The dialog box manager returns -1 if it cannot create a modal dialog, and a NULL window handle (not -1 as it says in the 3.0 docs) if it cannot create a modeless dialog. Actually modal dialogs are ultimately created by using CreateDialogIndirectParam() – DialogBox() etc. ultimately call this function.

The dialog manager will return these error codes if the dialog box resource cannot be accessed or used; here are some reasons as to why this might happen.

1   The application uses up all its allocated file handles.

2   The value given for HINSTANCE is incorrect.

3   Windows doesn't have adequate system resources to complete the task.

4   The dialog resource name is wrong.

5. A private dialog class does not call DefDlgProc() with messages that it does not handle OR does not return the result of calling DefDlgProc()

6. A string in the dialog resource begins with ASCII character 255.

Now just a little more detail.

1   A resource is a disk file first and foremost to Windows. It has to open the a *new* file each time a resource is loaded. The default number of handles allocated to a task is 20. Use SetHandleCount() to up this to a maximum of 255.

2   HINSTANCE identifies the module, as a disk file, from which the resource is to be loaded. Giving Windows an incorrect instance handle will therefore always cause dialog creation to fail.

3   This is particularly important with regard to USER's heap. Each control, and the main dialog box window, is of course a window; each requires USER to maintain a window structure for it in its heap. If USER doesn't have enough heap space available internally the dialog box manager initiated CreateWindow() calls will fail.

4   Pretty obvious this one I guess. Give the wrong name for the resource and the DM cannot find the dialog box template.

5   You must call DefDlgProc() in any private dialog class; this is as fundamental to the DM working correctly as not calling DefWindowProc() is to the window manager. You must also normally return the result of calling DefDlgProc().

6   The ASCII code 255 is used by Windows to specify that a string is referenced as an ordinal number rather than a string. If a string therefore starts with ASCII code 255 only an ordinals worth of data is read from the string. The remainder of the string is now treated as something else - if this doesn't screw things up then the item addressed by ordinal will almost certainly screw things up!

Just some things to check on if this ever happens to you.

☐ Impersonating Dialogs

Before we finish this section on modeless dialogs and talk about the common dialogs let me just say that it is often necessary to mimic a modal dialog with a modeless one. You should remember this fact particularly if you create dialogs from dialogs. It is possible sometimes to find that something's broken; for example, if you create a modeless dialog as a *child* of a modal dialog, you'll find that the tab key no longer moves the input focus around control groups. This is because a modal dialog has its own message polling loop and that loop does not include the functionality of your main message polling loop for a modeless dialog, ie. it doesn't include a call to IsDialogMessage()!

A modeless dialog may be made modal quite easily – just disable its parent window (don't do this if the dialog is a true child window). The pseudo modal dialog now has its message processing done by your main loop. Any modeless dialog created as a child of that *modal* now uses IsDialogMessage()) processing.

OK, the common dialogs.

☐ Common Dialogs

The common dialogs are well overdue. These complex *widgets* should have been in from the start (of 3.0 at least) for two reasons.

The first, and most important is that Windows was designed to present a common look and feel to all Windows' applications; if they all look and feel the same, the user has no trouble getting to grips with them. One very common area where applications didn't look the same was in the area of presenting a common dialog interface to common operations. For example, although most applications open a disk file, the dialog used to request the file's name and location was bound to be inconsistent between applications to some (often large) degree!

The second reason they're a good idea is programmer biased. Some of these common dialogs were not trivial to knock up when you <u>had</u> to do them yourself! Can you imagine building the font selection or colour selection dialogs – man, these are not noddy bits of code, also, have you seen all those nice folder type graphics in the file open etc dialogs, they're nice and present an interface that is in keeping with that produced by the file manager – uses are happy navigating the file system using these dialogs coz they've already learned what to do with them by using the file manager.

The common dialogs do with a simple function call what used to take forever when you had to do it yourself; there are 7, or is that 6 common dialogs as the *Print* common dialog uses the dialog box in the printer driver of the currently selected printer to do most of its work – it does simplify the calling interface to it so I guess we should count it?

The only non-modal common dialog is the *Find* dialog, it's a pity really as I can see where these would be useful as modeless dialogs – you can however apply the techniques I discussed at the beginning of this chapter to make them modeless if you want to.

The COMMDLG.DLL library provides the following common dialogs :

- Color
- Font

- Open
- SaveAs
- Print
- Print Set-up
- Find

See the Programmer's Reference Volume 1 for a fuller description of these.

The common dialog DLL allows these standard dialogs to be modified and provides two ways in which this may be achieved. The first is by changing the templates used by the DLL. This allows you to override the standard template with your own.

The standard templates are provided in the \windev\samples\commdlg directory and any defines they use are defined in \windev\include\dlgs.h.

The second way in which these dialogs may be customised is through the provision of a *hook function*. A hook function is a lot like a normal dialog call-back function but with a couple of minor differences, we'll look at them at little later.

For now, let's build a common dialog. I'm going to use just the *FileOpen* dialog in the remainder of this section – if I were to cover all the dialogs, we'd need another volume of this book (this chapter is already on the BIG side)! We'll build two applications; the first builds a normal FileOpen dialog that can be used to start applications. The second application will then be modified so that the dialog box displays additional information about a selected file's size, we'll also centre the dialog, and provide a *No Help Available* message box which is produced when the dialog's help button is selected – we'll also be adding a Help button therefore. To do these last three things we'll need to modify the dialog's template and provide a hook function.

The standard FileOpen dialog box requires that you instanciate and fill in an OPEN-FILENAME structure and call the function GetOpenFileName(). The structure looks like this (it's defined in COMMDLG.H) :

```
typedef struct tagOFN
{
    DWORD       lStructSize;
    HWND        hwndOwner;
    HINSTANCE   hInstance;
    LPCSTR      lpstrFilter;
    LPSTR       lpstrCustomFilter;
    DWORD       nMaxCustFilter;
    DWORD       nFilterIndex;
    LPSTR       lpstrFile;
    DWORD       nMaxFile;
    LPSTR       lpstrFileTitle;
    DWORD       nMaxFileTitle;
    LPCSTR      lpstrInitialDir;
    LPCSTR      lpstrTitle;
    DWORD       Flags;
```

```
    UINT       nFileOffset;
    UINT       nFileExtension;
    LPCSTR     lpstrDefExt;
    LPARAM     lCustData;
    UINT       (CALLBACK *lpfnHook)(HWND, UINT, WPARAM, LPARAM);
    LPCSTR     lpTemplateName;
}   OPENFILENAME;
typedef OPENFILENAME FAR* LPOPENFILENAME;
```

The function GetOpenFileName is also prototyped in COMMDLG.H -

```
BOOL     WINAPI GetOpenFileName(OPENFILENAME FAR*);
```

OK, this is the first application, again I've used generic as a starting point and will just show the changes made to it here (rather than the whole thing) :

New headers to include.

```
#include <commdlg.h>
#include <stdlib.h>
#include <string.h>
#include <cderr.h>
```

Turn off silly warnings.

```
#pragma warning(disable:4100)
#pragma warning(disable:4001)
```

WinMain() etc in here

```
    . . .
```

New MainWndProc
```
LRESULT __export CALLBACK MainWndProc
(
   HWND     hWnd
  ,UINT     uMessage
  ,WPARAM   wParam
  ,LPARAM   lParam
)
{
    auto FARPROC lpProcAbout;

    switch(uMessage)
    {
    case WM_COMMAND:
        switch(wParam)
        {
          case IDM_ABOUT:
              lpProcAbout = MakeProcInstance((FARPROC)About, hInst);
```

```
        DialogBox(hInst,"AboutBox", hWnd, lpProcAbout);

        FreeProcInstance(lpProcAbout);
        break;


case IDM_FO:
    {
        /*
        ** Passed to GetOpenFileName().
        */


        auto OPENFILENAME    ofn;
        /*
        ** Holds the default file extension on input
        ** and the full name of any selected file on
        ** output.
        */

        auto char           carFileNameBuffer   [_MAX_PATH];


        /*
        ** The directory that GetOpenFileName()
        ** should use when the dialog is produced.
        */

        auto char           carInitialDirBuffer [_MAX_PATH];


        /*
        ** Holds the string IDS_FILTERSTRING loaded
        ** from resources. Used to specify file
        ** types and extensions.
        */


        auto char           carFilterBuffer     [MISC_BUFF];
        /*
        ** Points to carFilterBuffer. Used in parsing.
        */
        auto NPSTR          npcStringBuffer;
        /*
        ** Our application's instance handle.
        */
        auto HINSTANCE      hInstance;



        /*
        ** Get instance handle for LoadString().
        */
        hInstance = GetWindowWord(hWnd, GWW_HINSTANCE);
```

```
/*
**
*/
if(LoadString(
             hInstance
             ,IDS_FILTERSTRING
             ,&carFilterBuffer[0]
             ,sizeof(carFilterBuffer)
             ) == 0
  )
{
    /*
    ** Report any error loading string.
    */
    MessageBox(
             hWnd
             ,"Failed to load string resource!"
             ,NULL
             ,MB_OK
             );

    break;
}

/*
** Process filter string so that it becomes
** a series of NULL terminated strings.
*/
npcStringBuffer = &carFilterBuffer[0];

while(strtok(npcStringBuffer,"|") != NULL)
{
    /*
    ** To keep strtok() going.
    */
    npcStringBuffer = NULL;
}

/*
** Contains default file extension on input,
** and the  full  name of  the selected file
** on output.
*/
lstrcpy(&carFileNameBuffer[0], "*.EXE");

/*
** Start looking in the Windows' directory.
*/
GetWindowsDirectory(&carInitialDirBuffer[0], _MAX_PATH);

/*
** Clean ofn as it is auto and we might miss something.
*/
memset(&ofn, 0x0, sizeof(ofn));

/*
** Fill it in and DoIt!
*/
```

```
ofn.lStructSize            = sizeof(ofn);
ofn.hwndOwner              = hWnd;
ofn.hInstance              = NULL;
ofn.lpstrFilter            = &carFilterBuffer[0];
ofn.lpstrCustomFilter      = NULL;
ofn.nMaxCustFilter         = 0;
ofn.lpstrFile              = &carFileNameBuffer[0];
ofn.nMaxFile               = _MAX_PATH;
ofn.lpstrFileTitle         = NULL;
ofn.nMaxFileTitle          = 0;
ofn.lpstrInitialDir        = &carInitialDirBuffer[0];
ofn.lpstrTitle             = "Select Program To Run";
ofn.Flags                  = OFN_FILEMUSTEXIST |
                             OFN_PATHMUSTEXIST |
                             OFN_HIDEREADONLY;
ofn.nFileOffset            = 0;
ofn.nFileExtension         = 0;
ofn.lpstrDefExt            = NULL;
ofn.lCustData              = 0;
ofn.lpfnHook               = NULL;
ofn.lpTemplateName         = NULL;

if(GetOpenFileName(&ofn) != FALSE)
{
    /*
    ** Got a filename - so try and exec it. Don't bother
    ** reporting error as Windows does a good job of this
    ** already.
    */
    WinExec(&carFileNameBuffer[0], SW_SHOWNORMAL);
}
else
{
    /*
    ** Holds error code.
    */
    auto DWORD dwErrorCode;

    /*
    ** Get error code, if it's zero the user pressed
    ** cancel button.
    */
    if((dwErrorCode = CommDlgExtendedError()) != 0)
    {
        /*
        ** Error! Check it out...
        */
        switch(dwErrorCode)
        {
            case CDERR_DIALOGFAILURE:
            case CDERR_GENERALCODES:
            case CDERR_STRUCTSIZE:
            case CDERR_INITIALIZATION:
            case CDERR_NOTEMPLATE:
            case CDERR_NOHINSTANCE:
            case CDERR_LOADSTRFAILURE:
            case CDERR_FINDRESFAILURE:
            case CDERR_LOADRESFAILURE:
```

```
                            case CDERR_LOCKRESFAILURE:
                            case CDERR_MEMALLOCFAILURE:
                            case CDERR_MEMLOCKFAILURE:
                            case CDERR_NOHOOK:
                            case CDERR_REGISTERMSGFAIL:
                            case PDERR_PRINTERCODES:
                            case PDERR_SETUPFAILURE:
                            case PDERR_PARSEFAILURE:
                            case PDERR_RETDEFFAILURE:
                            case PDERR_LOADDRVFAILURE:
                            case PDERR_GETDEVMODEFAIL:
                            case PDERR_INITFAILURE:
                            case PDERR_NODEVICES:
                            case PDERR_NODEFAULTPRN:
                            case PDERR_DNDMMISMATCH:
                            case PDERR_CREATEICFAILURE:
                            case PDERR_PRINTERNOTFOUND:
                            case PDERR_DEFAULTDIFFERENT:
                            case CFERR_CHOOSEFONTCODES:
                            case CFERR_NOFONTS:
                            case CFERR_MAXLESSTHANMIN:
                            case FNERR_FILENAMECODES:
                            case FNERR_SUBCLASSFAILURE:
                            case FNERR_INVALIDFILENAME:
                            case FNERR_BUFFERTOOSMALL:
                            case FRERR_FINDREPLACECODES:
                            case FRERR_BUFFERLENGTHZERO:
                            case CCERR_CHOOSECOLORCODES:
                                /*
                                ** For any CD error just report
                                ** failure.
                                */
                                MessageBox(
                                        hWnd
                                        ,"Common Dialog Failure!"
                                        ,NULL
                                        ,MB_OK
                                        );
                                break;

                            default:
                                /*
                                ** Undocumented error.
                                */
                                MessageBox(
                                        hWnd
                                        ,"Unknown Common Dialog Failure!"
                                        ,NULL
                                        ,MB_OK
                                        );
                                break;
                    } /* End switch(dwErrorCode) */
                } /* dwErrorCode != 0 */
            } /* Else of - GetOpenFileName() != FALSE */
        } /* End case IDM_FO */
        break;
} /* WM_COMMAND, switch(wParam) */
```

```
        break;

    case WM_DESTROY:
        PostQuitMessage(0);
        break;

    default:
        return DefWindowProc(hWnd, uMessage, wParam, lParam);
    }

    return (LRESULT)0;
}
```

The code above produces this dialog :

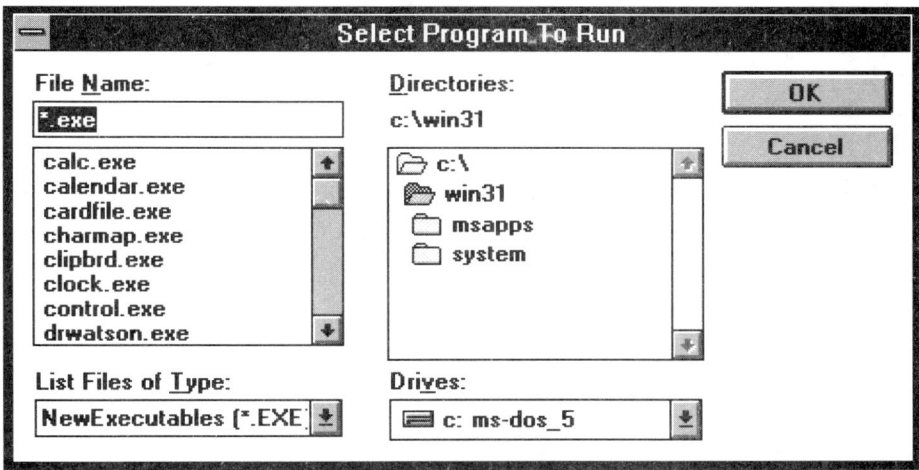

The code is well commented and should be read through to fully understand the mechanism of calling up and using a common dialog.

By double clicking, or otherwise selecting, a file in the left most list box then clicking OK, the file in the *File Name* edit field is exec'd.

The buffer carFileNameBuffer holds, on input to GetOpenFileName(), the default file extension shown in the edit field; on output (return of GetOpenFileName() it holds the fully qualified path name of the selected file, ie. the one to exec.

If GetOpenFileName() returns FALSE we have to test whether or not the user pressed *Cancel* or if some *real* fault occurred. We do this by calling CommDlgExtendedError(). This function returns 0 if there was no error or, if there was a *real* error, some error code. All the common dialog error codes are unique, ie. none of them are repeated across the whole of the common dialogs, I therefore used the complete list of possible common dialog error codes in my switch on any real error code that may be returned from CommDlgExtendedError() – you might like to cut this list down to contain just those pertinent to the actual common dialog used. See the Programmer's overview for a list.

The filter string looks like this :

```
STRINGTABLE
BEGIN
  IDS_FILTERSTRING, "NewExecutables (*.EXE)|*.EXE|Old Executables (*.COM)|*.COM|"
END
```

The string is loaded using LoadString() and parsed into several NULL terminated strings using strtok. strtok replaces any | with a NULL so it's quite convenient.

This is what's changed in generic.h :

```
#define IDM_FO 200
#define IDS_FILTERSTRING 1
#define MISC_BUFF 255
...
LRESULT __export CALLBACK MainWndProc(HWND, UINT, WPARAM, LPARAM);
```

IDM_FO is the ID of a new menu item used for selecting a file to run, ID_FILTER-STRING is the ID of the string above, and MISC_BUFF is the size of the buffer into which the string is read. The definition of MainWndProc has changed to reflect the new 3.1 types etc.

Let's now look at the same dialog box modified to display file size information on the selected file :

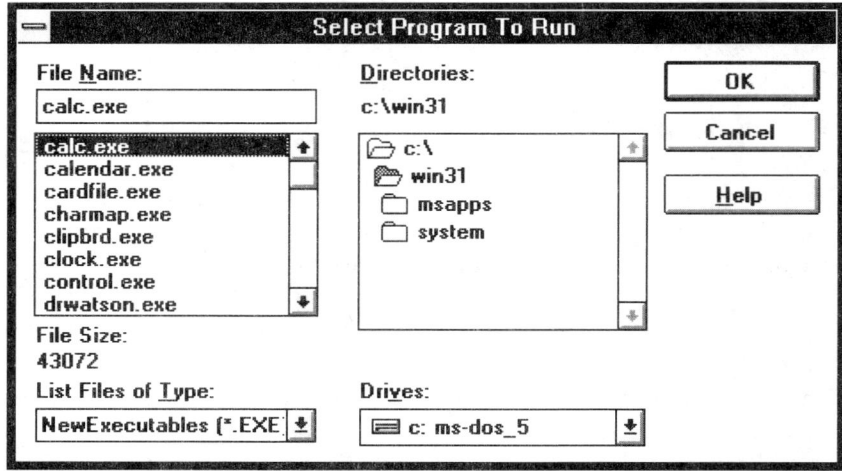

Here you can see that two new items have appeared. The first is positioned just under the first list box – File Size:. The second is the addition of a *Help* button.

This dialog gives the user feedback on the size of the selected file – not particularly useful in a *Run* dialog, but it will give you some idea as to how these dialogs may be altered. Again the overall changes to generic are shown below, the string table is the same as for the pervious example and is not repeated here.

New stuff at top of 'C' code.

```c
#include <commdlg.h>
#include <stdlib.h>
#include <string.h>
#include <cderr.h>
#include "dlgs.h"               /* defines for common dialogs. */
#include <io.h>                 /* used for _filelength etc.    */

#pragma warning(disable:4100)
#pragma warning(disable:4001)

...


LRESULT __export CALLBACK MainWndProc
(
   HWND     hWnd
  ,UINT     uMessage
  ,WPARAM   wParam
  ,LPARAM   lParam
)
{
    auto FARPROC lpProcAbout;

    /*
    ** Holds Window's message for 'Open File' CD help button.
    */
    static UINT CD_HELPMSG;

    switch(uMessage)
    {
    case WM_CREATE:
        /*
        ** Register 'CD Help' message with Windows, doesn't
        ** matter if we do this before CDs do.
        */
        CD_HELPMSG = RegisterWindowMessage(HELPMSGSTRING);
        break;

    case WM_COMMAND:
        switch(wParam)
        {
          case IDM_ABOUT:
              lpProcAbout = MakeProcInstance((FARPROC)About, hInst);

              DialogBox(hInst,"AboutBox", hWnd, lpProcAbout);
```

```
            FreeProcInstance(lpProcAbout);
            break;
    case IDM_FO:
        {
            /*
            ** Passed to GetOpenFileName().
            */
            auto OPENFILENAME    ofn;

            /*
            ** Holds the default file extension on input and
            ** the full name of any selected file on output.
            */
            auto char           carFileNameBuffer    [_MAX_PATH];

            /*
            ** The directory that GetOpenFileName() should use
            ** when the dialog is produced.
            */
            auto char           carInitialDirBuffer [_MAX_PATH];

            /*
            ** Holds the string IDS_FILTERSTRING loaded from
            ** resources. Used to specify file types and
            ** extensions.
            */
            auto char           carFilterBuffer      [MISC_BUFF];

            /*
            ** Points to carFilterBuffer. Used in parsing.
            */
            auto NPSTR          npcStringBuffer;

            /*
            ** Our application's instance handle.
            */
            auto HINSTANCE      hInstance;

            /*
            ** Get instance handle for LoadString().
            */
            hInstance = GetWindowWord(hWnd, GWW_HINSTANCE);

            /*
            ** Load filter string.
            */
            if(LoadString(
                        hInstance
                        ,IDS_FILTERSTRING
                        ,&carFilterBuffer[0]
                        ,sizeof(carFilterBuffer)
                        ) == 0
                )
                {
                    /*
                    ** Report any error loading string.
                    */
```

```
            MessageBox(
                       hWnd
                       ,"Failed to load string resource!"
                       ,NULL
                       ,MB_OK
                       );

        break;
}


/*
** Process filter string so that it becomes
** a series of NULL terminated strings.
*/
npcStringBuffer = &carFilterBuffer[0];

while(strtok(npcStringBuffer,"|") != NULL)
{
    /*
    ** To keep strtok() going.
    */
    npcStringBuffer = NULL;
}

/*
** Set default extension.
*/
lstrcpy(&carFileNameBuffer[0], "*.EXE");

/*
** Start looking in the Windows' directory.
*/
GetWindowsDirectory(&carInitialDirBuffer[0], _MAX_PATH);

/*
** Clean ofn as it is 'auto' and we might miss something.
*/
memset(&ofn, 0x0, sizeof(ofn));

/*
** Fill it in and DoIt!
*/
ofn.lStructSize          = sizeof(ofn);
ofn.hwndOwner            = hWnd;
ofn.hInstance            = hInstance;
ofn.lpstrFilter          = &carFilterBuffer[0];
ofn.lpstrCustomFilter    = NULL;
ofn.nMaxCustFilter       = 0;
ofn.lpstrFile            = &carFileNameBuffer[0];
ofn.nMaxFile             = _MAX_PATH;
ofn.lpstrFileTitle       = NULL;
ofn.nMaxFileTitle        = 0;
ofn.lpstrInitialDir      = &carInitialDirBuffer[0];
ofn.lpstrTitle           = "Select Program To Run";
ofn.Flags                = OFN_FILEMUSTEXIST  |
                           OFN_PATHMUSTEXIST  |
                           OFN_HIDEREADONLY   |
                           OFN_SHOWHELP       |
```

```
                                        OFN_ENABLETEMPLATE|
                                        OFN_ENABLEHOOK;
ofn.nFileOffset          = 0;
ofn.nFileExtension       = 0;
ofn.lpstrDefExt          = NULL;
ofn.lCustData            = 0;
ofn.lpfnHook             = (HOOK)bCDHookProc;
ofn.lpTemplateName       = MAKEINTRESOURCE(FILEOPENORD);


if(GetOpenFileName(&ofn) != FALSE)
{
    /*
    ** Got a filename - so try and exec it. Don't bother
    ** reporting error as Windows does a good job of this
    ** already.
    */
    WinExec(&carFileNameBuffer[0], SW_SHOWNORMAL);
}
/*
** User either pressed cancel or we had some' real' error.
*/
else
{
    /*
    ** Holds error code.
    */
    auto DWORD dwErrorCode;

    /*
    ** Get error code, if it's zero the user pressed
    ** cancel button.
    */
    if((dwErrorCode = CommDlgExtendedError()) != 0)
    {
        /*
        ** Error! Check it out...
        */
        switch(dwErrorCode)
        {
            case CDERR_DIALOGFAILURE:
            case CDERR_GENERALCODES:
            case CDERR_STRUCTSIZE:
            case CDERR_INITIALIZATION:
            case CDERR_NOTEMPLATE:
            case CDERR_NOHINSTANCE:
            case CDERR_LOADSTRFAILURE:
            case CDERR_FINDRESFAILURE:
            case CDERR_LOADRESFAILURE:
            case CDERR_LOCKRESFAILURE:
            case CDERR_MEMALLOCFAILURE:
            case CDERR_MEMLOCKFAILURE:
            case CDERR_NOHOOK:
            case CDERR_REGISTERMSGFAIL:
            case PDERR_PRINTERCODES:
            case PDERR_SETUPFAILURE:
            case PDERR_PARSEFAILURE:
            case PDERR_RETDEFFAILURE:
```

```
                            case PDERR_LOADDRVFAILURE:
                            case PDERR_GETDEVMODEFAIL:
                            case PDERR_INITFAILURE:
                            case PDERR_NODEVICES:
                            case PDERR_NODEFAULTPRN:
                            case PDERR_DNDMMISMATCH:
                            case PDERR_CREATEICFAILURE:
                            case PDERR_PRINTERNOTFOUND:
                            case PDERR_DEFAULTDIFFERENT:
                            case CFERR_CHOOSEFONTCODES:
                            case CFERR_NOFONTS:
                            case CFERR_MAXLESSTHANMIN:
                            case FNERR_FILENAMECODES:
                            case FNERR_SUBCLASSFAILURE:
                            case FNERR_INVALIDFILENAME:
                            case FNERR_BUFFERTOOSMALL:
                            case FRERR_FINDREPLACECODES:
                            case FRERR_BUFFERLENGTHZERO:
                            case CCERR_CHOOSECOLORCODES:
                                /*
                                ** For any CD error just report
                                ** failure.
                                */
                                MessageBox(
                                        hWnd
                                        ,"Common Dialog Failure!"
                                        ,NULL
                                        ,MB_OK
                                        );
                                break;

                            default:
                                /*
                                ** Undocumented error.
                                */
                                MessageBox(
                                        hWnd
                                        ,"Unknown Common Dialog Failure!"
                                        ,NULL
                                        ,MB_OK
                                        );
                                break;
                        } /* End switch(dwErrorCode) */
                    } /* dwErrorCode != 0 */
                } /* Else of - GetOpenFileName() != FALSE */
            } /* End case IDM_FO */
            break;
        } /* WM_COMMAND, switch(wParam) */
        break;

    case WM_DESTROY:
        PostQuitMessage(0);
        break;

    default:
    /*
    ** See if message is help message from 'File Open' CD.
```

```
    */
    if(uMessage == CD_HELPMSG)
    {
        /*
        ** Yes it is so report help required.
        */
        MessageBox(hWnd, "CD Help Selected", NULL, MB_OK);
    }
    else
        return DefWindowProc(hWnd, uMessage, wParam, lParam);
    }

    return (LRESULT)0;
}




/*
** 'File Open' CD hook function - see OPENFILENAME
** ofn.lpfnHook above. Called by common dialog DLL.
*/
BOOL __export CALLBACK bCDHookProc
(
    HWND     hDlg
   ,UINT     uMessage
   ,WPARAM   wParam
   ,LPARAM   lParam
)
{
    /*
    ** In here we use  the ofn.lpstrFile pointer to get a buffer
    ** to work with. Although this ofn member specifies on input
    ** the  default file extension, and  holds the selected file
    ** name on output, it's not  used during message processing.
    ** It makes sense to use it then  as it 's already allocated
    ** and BIG.
    */
    static LPSTR lpFileNameBuffer;

    switch(uMessage)
    {
        case WM_DESTROY:
            /*
            ** Reset local static pointer initialised from ofn.lpstrFile.
            */
            lpFileNameBuffer = NULL;
            break;

        case WM_INITDIALOG:
            {
                /*
                ** This compound statement centres the CD.
                */

                /*
                ** Holds the CD window's window position.
```

```
            */
            auto RECT rsWindow;


        /*
        ** Holds GetSystemMetrics() stuff about screen size.
        */
        auto int  nXOrg;
        auto int  nYOrg;


        /*
        ** Get CD main window device position.
        */
        GetWindowRect(hDlg, &rsWindow);


        /*
        ** Work out given its width and height, and the width
        ** and height of the screen - just where the dialog's
        ** window should be placed to centre it.
        */
        nXOrg = GetSystemMetrics(SM_CXSCREEN);
        nXOrg = (nXOrg /2) - ((rsWindow.right - rsWindow.left) / 2);

        nYOrg = GetSystemMetrics(SM_CYSCREEN);
        nYOrg = (nYOrg /2) - ((rsWindow.bottom - rsWindow.top) / 2);


        /*
        ** Centre it.
        */
        MoveWindow(
                    hDlg
                    ,nXOrg
                    ,nYOrg
                    ,rsWindow.right - rsWindow.left
                    ,rsWindow.bottom - rsWindow.top
                    ,FALSE
                    );
        }


    /*
    ** Set up local static pointer to pointer to carFileNameBuffer.
    */
    lpFileNameBuffer = (LPSTR)((LPOPENFILENAME)lParam)->lpstrFile;


    /*
    ** Set our new static control's text to 'No Size'.
    */
    SetWindowText(GetDlgItem(hDlg, IDC_FILESIZE),"No Size");
    break;

case WM_COMMAND:
    switch(wParam)
    {
        /*
        ** If the edit control that holds the current filename (or
        ** wild card) changes we want to  find out which  file is
        ** currently selected (if any) and determine its file size.
        ** We'll put that file size into our new static control.
        */
```

```
/*
** The edit control into which the selected file name
** is input.
*/
case edt1:
    /*
    ** If it's changed (by a selection in either lst1 or
    ** direct editing, AND we have a buffer pointer...
    */
    if(HIWORD(lParam) == EN_CHANGE && lpFileNameBuffer != NULL)
    {
        /*
        ** Used for getting file size info.
        */
        auto HFILE hFile;

        /*
        ** Get the current path from the static stc1.
        */
        GetWindowText(
                    GetDlgItem(hDlg, stc1)
                    ,lpFileNameBuffer
                    ,_MAX_PATH
                    );

        /*
        ** If the path's not a root directory add a backslash
        ** to it.
        */
        if(*(_fstrrchr(lpFileNameBuffer, (int)92) + 1) != NULL)
        {
            lstrcat(lpFileNameBuffer, "\\");
        }

        /*
        ** Now append the edt1 control's text.
        */
        GetWindowText(
                    GetDlgItem(hDlg, edt1)
                    ,lpFileNameBuffer + lstrlen(lpFileNameBuffer)
                    ,_MAX_PATH - lstrlen(lpFileNameBuffer)
                    );

        /*
        ** Open the file.
        */
        if((hFile = _lopen(lpFileNameBuffer, READ)) != HFILE_ERROR)
        {
            /*
            ** Holds file size.
            */
            auto long lFileLength = 0;

            /*
            ** Get file's size.
            */
            lFileLength = _filelength((int)hFile);
```

```
                        /*
                        ** Overwrite file name with file size.
                        */
                        wsprintf(lpFileNameBuffer, "%ld",lFileLength);

                        /*
                        ** Finished with the file so close it.
                        */
                        _lclose(hFile);
                    }
                    else
                    {
                        /*
                        ** File doesn't exist (probably due to editing).
                        */
                        wsprintf(lpFileNameBuffer, "%s",(LPSTR)"No Size");
                    }

                    /*
                    ** Put file size into new control.
                    */
                    SetWindowText(
                                GetDlgItem(hDlg, IDC_FILESIZE)
                                ,lpFileNameBuffer
                                );
                }
                break;

            default:
                break;
            }
            break;
    }

    return FALSE;
}
```

New .rc file stuff :

```
  #include "dlgs.h"
  ...

  rcinclude dlgs.dlg
```

dlgs.dlg :

```
DLGINCLUDE RCDATA DISCARDABLE
BEGIN
    "DLGS.H\0" /* Embedded .H file name for dialog editor. */
END

/* New (modified) File Open dialog box template. */
```

```
FILEOPENORD DIALOG 36, 24, 264, 148
STYLE DS_MODALFRAME | WS_POPUP | WS_CAPTION | WS_SYSMENU
CAPTION "Open"
FONT 8, "Helv"
BEGIN
    CONTROL         "File &Name:"
                    ,stc3
                    ,"Static"
                    ,WS_GROUP
                    ,6, 6, 76, 9

    CONTROL         ""
                    ,edt1
                    ,"Edit"
                    ,ES_AUTOHSCROLL |
                    ES_OEMCONVERT  |
                    WS_BORDER      |
                    WS_TABSTOP
                    ,6, 16, 90, 12

    CONTROL         ""
                    ,lst1
                    ,"ListBox"
                    ,LBS_NOTIFY            |
                    LBS_SORT              |
                    LBS_OWNERDRAWFIXED    |
                    LBS_HASSTRINGS        |
                    LBS_DISABLENOSCROLL   |
                    WS_BORDER             |
                    WS_VSCROLL            |
                    WS_TABSTOP,
                    6, 32, 90, 68

    CONTROL         "&Directories:"
                    ,-1
                    ,"Static"
                    ,WS_GROUP
                    ,110, 6, 92, 9

    CONTROL         ""
                    ,stc1
                    ,"Static"
                    ,SS_NOPREFIX |
                    WS_GROUP
                    ,110, 18, 92, 9

    CONTROL         ""
                    ,lst2
                    ,"ListBox"
                    ,LBS_NOTIFY           |
                    LBS_SORT             |
                    LBS_OWNERDRAWFIXED   |
                    LBS_HASSTRINGS       |
                    LBS_DISABLENOSCROLL  |
                    WS_BORDER            |
                    WS_VSCROLL           |
```

```
                        WS_TABSTOP,


CONTROL                 "List Files of &Type:"
                        ,stc2
                        ,"Static"
                        ,WS_GROUP
                        ,6, 119, 90, 9

CONTROL                 ""
                        ,cmb1
                        ,"ComboBox"
                        ,CBS_DROPDOWNLIST |
                        CBS_AUTOHSCROLL   |
                        WS_BORDER         |
                        WS_VSCROLL        |
                        WS_TABSTOP,
                        6, 129, 90, 36

CONTROL                 "Dri&ves:"
                        ,stc4
                        ,"Static"
                        ,WS_GROUP
                        ,110, 119, 92, 9
CONTROL                 ""
                        ,cmb2
                        ,"ComboBox"
                        ,CBS_DROPDOWNLIST   |
                        CBS_OWNERDRAWFIXED |
                        CBS_AUTOHSCROLL    |
                        CBS_SORT           |
                        CBS_HASSTRINGS     |
                        WS_BORDER          |
                        WS_VSCROLL         |
                        WS_TABSTOP,
                        110, 129, 92, 68

CONTROL                 "OK"
                        ,IDOK
                        ,"Button"
                        ,BS_DEFPUSHBUTTON |
                        WS_GROUP          |
                        WS_TABSTOP
                        ,208, 6, 50, 14

CONTROL                 "Cancel"
                        ,IDCANCEL
                        ,"Button"
                        ,WS_GROUP  |
                        WS_TABSTOP
                        ,208, 24, 50, 14

CONTROL                 "&Help"
                        ,psh15
                        ,"Button"
                        ,WS_GROUP  |
                        WS_TABSTOP
                        ,208, 46, 50, 14
```

```
CONTROL          "&Read Only"
                 ,chx1
                 ,"Button"
                 ,BS_AUTOCHECKBOX |
                  WS_GROUP         |
                  WS_TABSTOP
                 ,208, 68, 50, 12

/* NEW controls added in here. */
CONTROL          "File Size:"
                 ,-1
                 ,"Static"
                 ,WS_GROUP
                 , 6, 99, 94, 8

CONTROL          ""
                 ,IDC_FILESIZE
                 ,"Static"
                 ,WS_GROUP
                 ,6, 108, 92, 8
END
```

New additions to generic.h :

```
typedef UINT (CALLBACK * HOOK)(HWND, UINT, WPARAM, LPARAM);

BOOL __export CALLBACK bCDHookProc(HWND  ,UINT  ,WPARAM, LPARAM);
```

The main window procedure registers a Windows' message in its WM_CREATE handler. The message is defined by HELPMSGSTRING (defined in COMMDLG.H). This message – CD_HELPMSG is used at the bottom of the window procedure, just before the call to DefWindowProc(), to see if the common dialog help button was pressed. The common dialogs pass this message to the window procedure of the owning window when the help button is pressed – you must therefore always give an hwndOwner in the OPENFILENAME structure.

The ofn structure has these changes (from the earlier example) :

```
ofn.Flags                   = OFN_FILEMUSTEXIST |
                              OFN_PATHMUSTEXIST |
                              OFN_HIDEREADONLY  |
                              OFN_SHOWHELP      |
                              OFN_ENABLETEMPLATE|
                              OFN_ENABLEHOOK;
...
...

ofn.lCustData               = 0;
ofn.lpfnHook                = (HOOK)bCDHookProc;
```

```
ofn.lpTemplateName        = MAKEINTRESOURCE(FILEOPENORD);
```

We want the *Help* button, the *new* template, and the hook options enabled. The hook function's address is given in lpfnHook. The new dialog box resource ID is given in lpTemplateName.

The template's been altered using the dialog box editor. Two new controls were added; one is just used to label the other and is uninteresting, the other is also a static control but is used to display the size of the selected file (if any - No Size if no legal file selected). The control' ID is IDC_FILESIZE (both the extra controls are shown bold in the template above).

The address of the ofn structure is passed to the hook proc as the lParam of the WM_INITDIALOG message it receives. I get the address of carFileNameBuffer by accessing the lpstrFile member of the OPENFILESTRUCT member, the address is held in a static variable and is reset when the hook proc gets a WM_DESTROY message. Also the dialog box is centred, and IDC_FILESIZE's caption is set to *No Size* in the WM_INITDIALOG message handler.

Now all we do is wait till the contents of the edit control (edt1) changes. When it does, signalled by a EN_CHANGE notification message, we build up a path/filename from the static control stc1 and the edit control edt1. We may have to insert a \ in between these two if the static holds a root directory name. Having done that we open the file, get its file size, close it, then update the new control (IDC_FILESIZE) with the file's size. If the file cannot be opened we insert some default text instead – this will probably be due to the user editing the edit field text; for example if they remove the last *e* from generic.exe we will fail to open the file as it's called generic.ex.

Throughout our processing we use the carFileNameBuffer as a general buffer, remember this buffer is filled by the common dialog procedure when it returns and holds the default file extension on input to the GetOpenFileName() function. During the life of the dialog however it is not used by the common dialog code, it makes sense therefore to use it ourselves.

Note that Hook functions do not call EndDialog(), doing so can be *bad* (Ghost Busters)!

There are many levels of *Bad*. 'Hey don't touch that dial', 'Why not', 'Coz it'll be bad'. Bad's like *nice* – it needs refinement. Some Windows' programmer's call things that are <u>really bad</u> Ghost Buster's bad after the great film of the same name. Bad is described in the film as { 'Try to imagine all life as you know it stopping simultaneously and every molecule in your body exploding at the speed of light' – or something like that! But, as they go on to say, 'There's definitely a very slim chance you'll survive'!! Pay heed to any *Ghost Buster's Bad* warning.

Well we've got time for just one more dialog box example. The last dialog example is the biggest and as code speaks louder than written words (especially if it's well commented) I'll not talk about it for a long time.

The last example is really a message box replacement ++, although to be honest, it doesn't do quite all that the standard message box dialog does, for example, as it is implemented, my message box cannot impose a task modal state on the caller (you saw earlier however that it was pretty easy to do this). This *new* message box is really designed to replace MessageBox() in one special case – error reporting.

There probably ought to be some common dialog for error reporting as it's one of those things that most applications do – but do differently! For example, most applications use a simple message box for reporting errors, well how do you include a *Help* button in such a dialog (yea, I know I did this when we looked at modifying *real* message boxes earlier, but let's say you want Abort Retry Ignore and Help – ie. four buttons, now what)? How can you get more than three buttons, how can you change the text on those buttons, how can you add F1 key help support etc etc. The dialog which follows is designed to cure all this and to present a set of standard errors between applications. For example, wouldn't it be nice to have a standard *FILE_READ_ERROR* across all your applications and call one function to present a standard interface (and help) to that error? Well, with this dialog, you can.

The dialog's part of a dynamic link library (there's another chapter on DLLs so the technicalities of DLLs won't be covered here) and that DLL has its own string table resource that contains *error definition strings*. These strings define a dialog box configuration for a set of standard errors; they're a little like a dialog template/control statements in dialog resources. When an application wants to report a standard error, it calls a DLL function and passes it a standard error ID – the DLL builds up what looks pretty much like a message box and displays the error – consistency!

Also, an application might have a unique error that it wants to report, ie. one that is not part of the *standard error* set. If that application can define its own string table resource it calls the same function as above - passes the error string identifier, which is a string table ID, and has the DLL load the error definition string from its (the caller's) string table. The DLL builds the error box as before to present the error information – more consistency!!

Lastly, for those applications that either do not, or cannot build string tables (Visual Basic etc) another DLL function is provided which can accept a dynamic error definition string. From this it builds up the required error box as before.

> We actually use this library for, primarily, the reason given above, ie. to promote a set of error reporting standards – in other words, it's not just a demo app, this one's <u>really</u> useful and is used professionally! You also might want to consider making a small change to it if you're using a network. We actually use a modified version of the library that not only

reports errors in a standard and consistent way but that also logs any reported error to a centrally held *log* file. The log file is analysed by 5 parsers that break it down and produce meaningful statistics about possible problem areas in code we develop and test in-house, in other words, we don't have to rely on the users reporting errors – we get 'em automatically and can act on them before the users even suspect a problem in the code!

To give you a feel for the way this works and looks here are a couple of snapshots of error boxes in use by 1. A traditional 'C' application generic; and 2. a Visual Basic application :

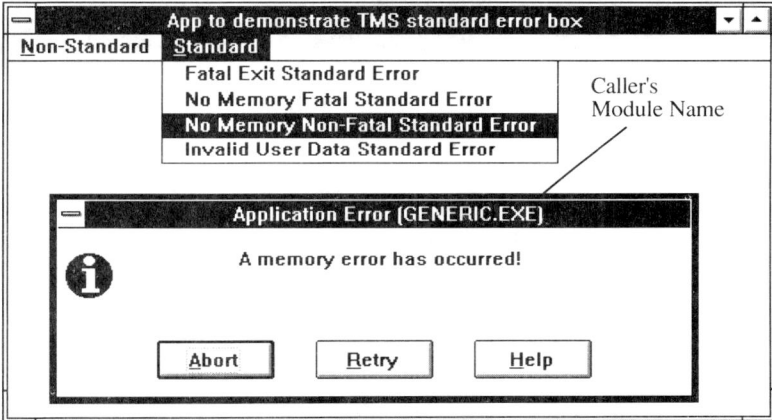

Here we see a modified generic application generating a standard error; <u>this error will be presented in exactly the same form from any application that uses the error box library</u>. The error box code sub-classes the push buttons to add F1 help support, ie. hitting F1 is the same as pressing the *Help* button (if there is one). A non-standard error might look like this :

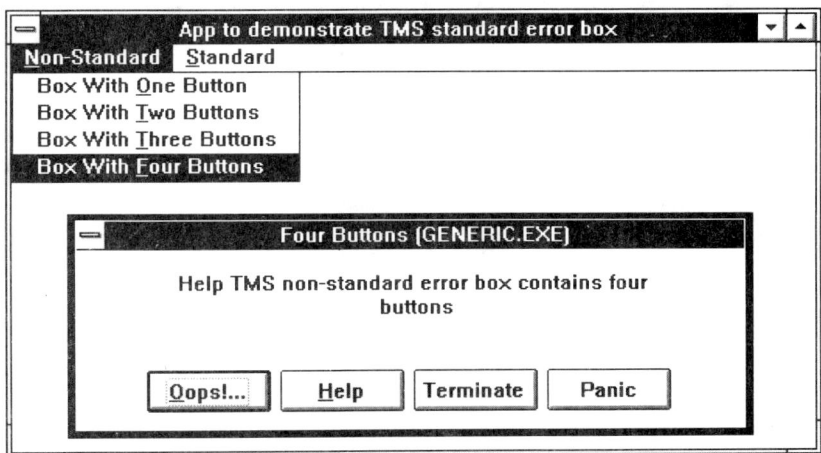

The application here defines this error in its own string table, the previous error is defined within the string table of the DLL. Notice that the module name of the calling application is added to the box's caption. A Visual Basic (VB) application may use standard and non-standard errors too, however, it must use a string parameter in the case of a non-standard error as you cannot add strings to a VB application's string table resource. Here's a Visual Basic application using the error box library :

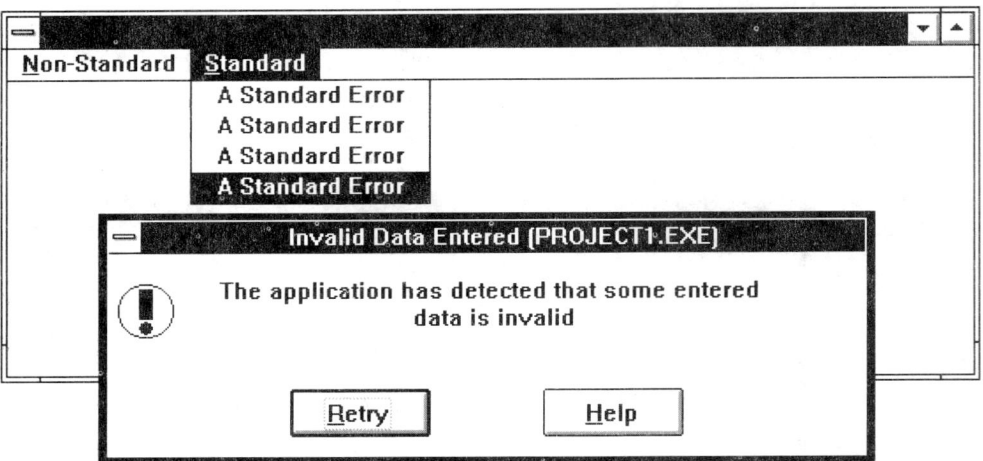

The menu item Non-Standard produces this box :

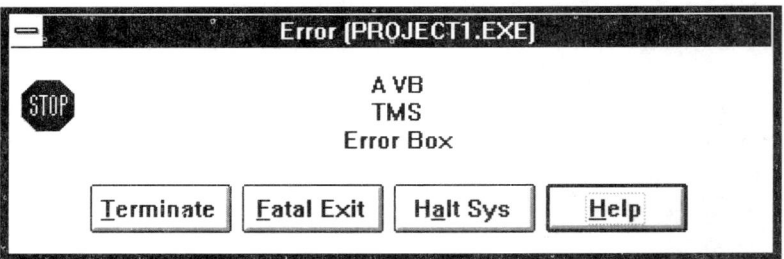

I'm sure you get the idea by now?

Let's take a peek at a VB and a 'C' based error definition string (Note that in the text below and to follow each string is shown split up over several lines – normally each string would not contain line feeds etc). The VB one first :

```
Global Const MYERR1 = "
                    %Error
                    %A VB\nTMS\nError Box
                    %4
                    %&Terminate
                    %&Fatal Exit
                    %H&alt Sys
                    %&Help
```

```
                                   %stop
                                   %4
                                   %modal
                                   "
```

The 'C' based one :

```
STRINGTABLE
BEGIN

  TMSERR_FATALEXIT,
      "
      %Application Error+
      %An error has occurred in the application and the program will terminate+
      %2+
      %&OK+
      %&Help+
      %+
      %+
      %stop+
      %1+
      %modal
      "
END
```

An error string is typically made up of an error box title, error box main text, the number of the push buttons (2 above), button caption text (for up to four buttons), an icon name, the id of the button that will be the default (1 above) and a modal state.

Each part of the definition string begins with a percent sign and typically ends with a plus sign. The percent is used as a token delimiter and the plus as a signal that the end of the field, or sub-string, has been reached; the latter is there purely to allow definition strings to be formatted tidily in a string table resource. The error box can display any standard icon, or a NULL icon. NULL icons are identified by using an icon name that doesn't exist, typically this is *nothing*.

The error box creates a custom control to display the icon. This control mimics the *static* icon control found in standard messages boxes etc and is pretty much uninteresting, we'll talk about controls in another chapter and towards the end of this chapter which should be soon!

Here's the code for the error box DLL (complete) and for the modified generic application that exercises the DLL code :

First the error box code :

tmserror.c

```c
#include "pragma.h"

#define STRICT      /* Requests the strictest type checking in WINDOWS.H */

#include "windows.h"
#include "TMSerror.h"
#include "TMSerr.h"
#include <string.h>
#include <stdlib.h>


/*
** Saves library's instance handle.
*/
HINSTANCE FAR hRetModInst(HINSTANCE hInst)
{
   /*
   ** Holds DLL's module handle for life of DLL.
   */
   static HINSTANCE hInstance;

   /*
   ** If hInst is NOT zero update h.
   */
   if(hInst != 0)
   {
      hInstance = hInst;
   }

   /*
   ** Any caller gets back module handle.
   */
   return hInstance;
}

/*
** Allows new control's classname to be accessed from anywhere without
** using global data.
*/
LPCSTR FAR lpszClassName(VOID)
{
   /*
   ** Just return pointer to classname.
   */
   return &"TMSStatic"[0];
}

/*
** Library's entry point.
*/
BOOL CALLBACK LibMain
(
   HINSTANCE    hModule
  ,WORD         wDataSeg
  ,WORD         wHeapSize
  ,LPSTR        lpszCmdLine
```

```
)
{
    /*
    ** New Icon class WNDCLASS.
    */
    auto WNDCLASS wc;

    /*
    ** Clean it.
    */
    _fmemset(&wc, 0, sizeof(WNDCLASS));

    /*
    ** Remove LibEntry() outstanding lock.
    */
    if(wHeapSize != 0)
    {
        UnlockData(0);
    }

    /*
    ** Save the DLL's instance handle.
    */
    hRetModInst((HINSTANCE)hModule);

    /*
    ** Initialise to new ICON class.
    */
    wc.style         = 0;
    wc.lpfnWndProc   = (WNDPROC)lTMSStaticClassWndProc;
    wc.hInstance     = hRetModInst(NULL);
    wc.hbrBackground = (HBRUSH)(COLOR_WINDOW + 1);
    wc.lpszClassName = lpszClassName(VOID_ARG);
    wc.hIcon         = 0;
    wc.hCursor       = 0;
    wc.lpszMenuName  = 0;
    wc.cbClsExtra    = 0;
    wc.cbWndExtra    = 0;

    /*
    ** Register it.
    */
    if(RegisterClass(&wc) == 0)
    {
        /*
        ** Don't let DLL start if it can't register class.
        */
        return FALSE;
    }
    else
    {
        return TRUE;
    }
}

/*
** New 'Error Box's' Callback function.
*/
```

```
BOOL CALLBACK __export bTMSMessageBoxProc
(
   HWND hWndDialog
  ,UINT uMessage
  ,WPARAM wParam
  ,LPARAM lParam
)
{

   switch(uMessage)
    {
      /*
      ** UM_ICONNAME is defined in the file's .H file as WM_USER + 10
      ** we receive  one of these  from our  bLoadAndParse  routine.
      ** We  set the  icon's window  text to  be the  name passed by
      ** bLoadAndParse.  The icon's wndproc gets a WM_SETTEXT message
      ** due to this. The lParam  of that  message points to the text
      ** passed in the SetDlgItemText() function used below.
      **
      ** The wndproc then  compares that  text against known standard
      ** icon  names and  if a  match is found the  icon is loaded and
      ** painted in. If such  a name is not found no icon is painted.
      */
      case UM_ICONNAME:
          SetDlgItemText(hWndDialog, IDD_ICON, (LPSTR)lParam);
          break;

      /*
      ** Sent by bLoadAndParse. The wParam contains the ID of the control
      ** that is to become the default pushbutton in the dialog.
      */
      case UM_SETDEFAULTPB:
          SendMessage(hWndDialog, DM_SETDEFID, wParam, 0);
          SetFocus(GetDlgItem(hWndDialog, wParam));
          break;

      /*
      ** Sent by bLoadAndParse. Informs us whether or not we're modal or
      ** system modal. The only visual clue is that 'Move' is greyed out
      ** in the box's system menu.
      */
      case UM_USERMODE:
          switch(lParam)
            {
              case SYSMODAL:
                  /*
                  ** Definition  string  says  we're  sys  modal, use
                  ** SetSysModal() window - nicer than MessageBox()'s
                  ** system modal state.
                  */
                  SetSysModalWindow(hWndDialog);
                  break;

              case MODAL:
                  /*
                  ** Already APPL modal so do nothing.  Could implement
                  ** a TASKMODAL case in here to make it even more like
                  ** MessageBox()'s dialog box.
                  */
```

```
                    break;
         }
         break;

case WM_INITDIALOG:
     {
         /*
         ** As this is big put it into our DS as we might trash the
         ** caller's stack otherwise. Re-entrancy isn't a problem as
         ** the buffer is used entirely during the handling of this
         ** single message.
         */
         static  char  pcStringBuffer[MAX_DEFSTRINGLEN];

         /*
         ** Basic loop counter.
         */
         auto    UINT  uLoop;

         /*
         ** Holds the module handle of the module from which
         ** definition strings are taken. For a VB app that will
         ** always be this library's  module handle. If the caller
         ** can have string resources then the module handle will be
         ** the instance handle of that app. Passed in in lParam.
         */
         auto    HMODULE  hMod;

         /*
         ** Holds the error string ID - TMSSTDERROR etc. Passed in in
         ** lParam.
         */
         auto    UINT     uType;

         /*
         ** Holds dialog box system menu.
         */
         auto    HMENU    hMenu;

         /*
         ** Centre the dialog box.
         */
         lSetDlgPos(hWndDialog);

         /*
         ** Get error type (ID). It's 0 if this is a dynamic error box.
         */
         uType = ((PACKET *)LOWORD(lParam))->unType;

         /*
         ** Being called from wTMS_SimpleErrorBox?
         */
         if(uType == 0)
         {
             /*
             ** Definition string length.
             */
             auto UINT len;
```

```
            /*
            ** Copy the passed format string into pcStringBuffer.
            ** Make sure that size isn't exceeded.
            */
            len = min(
                    sizeof(pcStringBuffer)
                    ,lstrlen((LPCSTR)((PACKET *)LOWORD(lParam))->lpDefString)
                    );

            _fstrncpy(
                        pcStringBuffer
                        ,(LPSTR)((PACKET *)LOWORD(lParam))->lpDefString, len
                        );
        }


    /*
    ** Get module handle.
    */
    hMod = ((PACKET *)LOWORD(lParam))->hMod;


    /*
    ** Delete 'Close' from system menu of dialog box.
    */
    if((hMenu = GetSystemMenu(hWndDialog, FALSE)) != NULL)
    {
        DeleteMenu(hMenu, 1, MF_BYPOSITION);
    }

    /*
    ** Determine module handle from hMod. If it's 0 it means
    ** that  the message (uType) is a standard error message
    ** which means it's held in the library's resources. Else
    ** the error is  not standard and must be pulled in from
    ** the callers resources it it's not dynamic.
    */
    if(hMod == 0)
    {
        hMod = hModuleFromhWnd(hWndDialog);
    }
    else
    {
        hMod = hModuleFromhWnd((HWND)hMod);
    }

    /*
    ** Failed to get module handle so quit.
    */
    if(hMod == NULL)
    {
        EndDialog(hWndDialog, -1);
    }

    /*
    ** Disable and hide all buttons in the dialog box.
```

```
        */
        for(uLoop = IDD_BUTTONSTART; uLoop <= IDD_BUTTONEND; uLoop++)
        {
            /*
            ** Window handle to each push button
            */
            auto HWND hWndControl;

            hWndControl = GetDlgItem(hWndDialog, uLoop);

            if(hWndControl != NULL)
            {
                EnableWindow(hWndControl, FALSE);
                ShowWindow(hWndControl, SW_HIDE);
            }
        }

        /*
        ** Now load in and parse the error description string. If
        ** we've already been passed a string (ID = 0) then
        ** bLoadAndParse doesn't try and load a string from the
        ** resources of the module hMod.
        */
        if(!bLoadAndParse(
                            hWndDialog
                           ,hMod
                           ,uType
                           ,pcStringBuffer
                           ,sizeof(pcStringBuffer)
                           )
          )
        {
            /*
            ** Parsing routine returned error.
            */
            MessageBox(
                        0
                       ,"Error loading or parsing error string in DLL!"
                       ,NULL
                       ,MB_OK | MB_TASKMODAL
                       );

            EndDialog(hWndDialog, -1);
        }
    }

    /*
    ** Have to return FALSE to retain the focus on the button
    ** specified in the string (1 by default).
    */
    return FALSE;

    /*
    ** When we get a WM_COMMAND we basically exit and return the
    ** ID of the button selected, this identifies the button to
    ** the caller.
    */
case WM_COMMAND:
```

```
            if(HIWORD(lParam) == BN_CLICKED)
            {
                /*
                ** End the dialog box - return selected button ID to caller.
                */
                EndDialog(hWndDialog, wParam);
            }
            break;

        default:
            return FALSE;
    }

    return TRUE;
}




/*
** Entry point. Called when error definition string lives in either
** library's or caller's string tables.
*/
WORD APIENTRY wTMS_ErrorBox(HWND hWndOwner, UINT uType)
{
    /*
    ** Function's result.
    */
    auto    int     nResult;

    /*
    ** Holds module handle.
    */
    static  HMODULE hModuleOfErrorString;

    /*
    ** Holds module handle, error type and pointer to definition string.
    */
    static  PACKET  tP;

    /*
    ** Examine type and set hModule to either 0 (library's) or derived
    ** module handle of caller.
    */
    if(uType >= TMSSTDERROR)
    {
        /*
        ** Standard error.
        */
        hModuleOfErrorString = 0;
    }
    else
    {
        /*
        ** Non-standard error.
        */
        hModuleOfErrorString = (HMODULE)hWndOwner;
    }
```

```
    /*
    ** Fill in PACKET structure with info required in call-back.
    */
    tP.hMod           = hModuleOfErrorString;
    tP.unType         = uType;

    /*
    ** Is set to NULL to signal that the error
    ** string comes from a resource somewhere.
    */
    tP.lpDefString   = NULL;

    /*
    ** Do the dialog.
    */
    nResult = DialogBoxParam(
                            hRetModInst(NULL)
                          , (LPCSTR)MAKEINTRESOURCE(MESSAGEBOX1)
                          , hWndOwner
                          , (DLGPROC)bTMSMessageBoxProc
                          , (LPARAM)(PACKET FAR *)&tP
                          );
    /*
    ** Check for dialog box manager error.
    */
    if(nResult == -1)
    {
        MessageBox(
                    hWndOwner
                  ,"Can't Produce TMS MessageBox"
                  ,NULL
                  ,MB_OK | MB_TASKMODAL
                  );

        nResult = 0;
    }
    /*
    ** Give result to caller.
    */
    return (WORD)nResult;
}



/*
** Other entry point. Used by those applications using dynamic
** definition strings.
*/
WORD APIENTRY wTMS_SimpleErrorBox(HWND hWndOwner, LPSTR lpDefinitionString)
{
    /*
    ** Function's result.
    */
    static   int      nResult;

    /*
    ** Holds module handle, error type and pointer to definition string.
```

```
   */
   static   PACKET   tP;

   /*
   ** Set module and uType to 0 (uType is the important one).
   */
   tP.hMod       = 0;
   tP.unType     = 0;

   /*
   ** Pointer to passed string.
   */
   tP.lpDefString = lpDefinitionString;

   /*
   ** Do the dialog.
   */
   nResult = DialogBoxParam(
                           hRetModInst(NULL)
                         , (LPCSTR)MAKEINTRESOURCE(MESSAGEBOX1)
                         , hWndOwner
                         , (DLGPROC)bTMSMessageBoxProc
                         , (LPARAM)(PACKET FAR *)&tP
                         );

   /*
   ** Check for dialog box manager error.
   */
   if(nResult == -1)
   {
      MessageBox(
                  hWndOwner
                , "Can't Produce TMS MessageBox"
                , NULL
                , MB_OK | MB_TASKMODAL
                );

      nResult = 0;
   }

   /*
   ** Give result back to caller.
   */
   return (WORD)nResult;
}


/*
** Function that parses definition string and determines the
** configuration  of  the  dialog  box  produced.  Called  in
** WM_INITDIALOG case of dialog callback.
**
** Passed -
**
** hWndDialog  - Window handle of the dialog box
**
** hModOwner   - Module, or instance,  handle which determines
```

```
**               the resource stringtable to use to access the
**               definition string (may be zero).
**
** uResourceID - String table ID which determines which string
**               in the string table to use (may be zero).
**
** lpBuffer    - Buffer to use to load string from resources.
**
** uBufferSize - The size of the buffer to which lpBuffer points.
**
** Returns -
**
** Result of caling DialogBoxParam.
**
**  -1 indicates dialog manager failed to produce dialog box.
*/
BOOL NEAR bLoadAndParse
(
   HWND    hWndDialog,
   HMODULE hModOwner,
   UINT    uResourceID,
   LPSTR   lpBuffer,
   UINT    uBufferSize
)
{

   /*
   ** If the resource ID is zero then we're handling a string passed as an
   ** argument in  which case lpBuffer points the argument string. Else we
   ** are dealing with a resource string so we'd better load it.
   */
   if(!uResourceID || LoadString(
                               hModOwner
                              ,uResourceID
                              ,lpBuffer
                              ,uBufferSize
                              )
     )
     {
       /*
       ** Definition string segments put in here.
       */
       static  RESOURCEFIELD   ResourceFields[MAXITEMS];

       /*
       ** Points to token delimiters (see below for what those are).
       */
       auto    LPSTR           lpTok;

       /*
       ** General counter variable.
       */
       auto    UINT            uCount;

       /*
       ** General loop counter variable.
       */
       auto    UINT            uLoop;
```

```
/*
** Holds ID of default control.
*/
auto    UINT           uDefControl;

/*
** Holds number of controls requested.
*/
auto    UINT           uCountrolCount;

/*
** General pointer to memory.
*/
auto    PBYTE          pMem;

/*
** Parsing token.
*/
lpTok   = "%";

/*
** Field counter.
*/
uCount = 0;

/*
** Parse input string (either load or passed) for tokens separated by
** '%'s. Make sure we don't over do it!
*/
while(uCount < MAXITEMS &&
      (
        (ResourceFields[uCount].lpResourceField =
        _fstrtok(lpBuffer,lpTok)
        ) != 0
      )
    )
{

    /*
    ** Needed to keep _fstrtok going.
    */
    lpBuffer = (LPSTR)NULL;

    /*
    ** Further, parse section of string for '+', replace if found
    ** with NULL.
    */
    vStripPlus(ResourceFields[uCount].lpResourceField);

    /*
    ** Increment field counter.
    */
    uCount++;
}


/*
```

```
    ** Now start to process individual fields from the definition string.
    */

    /*
    ** Number of controls required = . MANDATORY FIELD
    */
    if(ResourceFields[NUMCONTROLS].lpResourceField)
    {

        /*
        ** Need some NEAR memory for the atoi.
        */
        if(
            (pMem = npGetMem(lstrlen(ResourceFields[NUMCONTROLS]
                            .lpResourceField)
                            + 1)
                            )!= 0
          )
        {
            /*
            ** Copy field to buffer.
            */
            lstrcpy((LPSTR)pMem, ResourceFields[NUMCONTROLS]
            .lpResourceField);

            /*
            ** Get an integer from it. Set uCount.
            */
            uCount = atoi((NPSTR)pMem);

            /*
            ** Set control count.
            */
            uCountrolCount = uCount;

            /*
            ** Release local mem.
            */
            (void)bFreeMem(pMem);
        }
        else
        {
            /*
            ** Couldn't get local mem.
            */
            return FALSE;
        }
    }
    else
    {
        /*
        ** Button count field NULL.
        */
        return FALSE;
    }

    /*
```

```
** If count is less than 0 then reset to one.
*/
if(uCount <= 0)
{
    uCountrolCount = uCount = 1;
}


/*
** Now we know how many controls we need to enable and show those
** required.
*/
for(uLoop = 0; uCount; uCount--, uLoop++)
{
    /*
    ** Control's window handle.
    */
    auto HWND hWndControl;

    /*
    ** Get first control window.
    */
    hWndControl = GetDlgItem(hWndDialog, IDD_BUTTONSTART + uLoop);

    if(IsWindow(hWndControl))
    {
        /*
        ** This button required - enable it.
        */
        EnableWindow(hWndControl, TRUE);

        /*
        ** Position it.
        */
        vPositionControl(hWndControl, uLoop, uCountrolCount);

        /*
        ** Finally show it.
        */
        ShowWindow(hWndControl, SW_SHOWNORMAL);

        /*
        ** Subclass each and every button. Only subclass controls
        ** that can take keyboard input. Only like buttons can be
        ** subclassed, eg. buttons OK but not, say, buttons and a
        ** list box! This subclass adds F1 help key functionality.
        ** See lHelpSubProc for more information. Get subclass
        ** proc to remember the old procs address - all buttons
        ** use same old proc address so OK to do this more than
        ** once.
        */
        SendMessage(
                hWndControl
                ,UM_OLDPROCADDR
                ,0
                ,(LPARAM)(LONG)SetWindowLong(
                                        hWndControl
                                        ,GWL_WNDPROC
```

```
                                                    , (LONG) lHelpSubProc
                                                    )
                        );

        /*
        ** Each button has a caption.
        */
        if(ResourceFields[uLoop + BUTTONCAPTIONS].lpResourceField != NULL)
        {
            SetWindowText(
                        hWndControl
                        ,ResourceFields[uLoop + BUTTONCAPTIONS].
                        lpResourceField
                        );
        }
        else
        {
            /*
            ** No caption for button.
            */
            return FALSE;
        }
    }
}


/*
** Number of the default control = . Default IDD_BUTTONSTART.
*/
if(ResourceFields[DEFCONTROL].lpResourceField != NULL)
{
    /*
    ** Need some NEAR memory for the atoi.
    */
    if(
        (pMem = npGetMem(
                        lstrlen(ResourceFields[DEFCONTROL].
                        lpResourceField)
                            + 1)
                        ) != 0
    )
    {
        /*
        ** Copy it into buffer.
        */
        lstrcpy(
                (LPSTR)pMem
                ,ResourceFields[DEFCONTROL].lpResourceField
                );

        /*
        ** Get def control ID.
        */
        uDefControl = atoi((NPSTR)pMem);

        /*
        ** Release local mem.
        */
        (void)bFreeMem(pMem);
    }
```

```
        else
        {
            /*
            ** Couldn't get local mem.
            */
            return FALSE;
        }
    }
    else
    {
        /*
        ** No def ID so use first button.
        */
        uDefControl = IDD_BUTTONSTART;
    }


    /*
    ** Make sure that default is within range - reset if necessary.
    */
    if(uDefControl > uCountrolCount || uDefControl <= 0)
    {
        uDefControl = IDD_BUTTONSTART;
    }


    /*
    ** Tell dialog procedure which button needs to be the default.
    */
    SendMessage(hWndDialog, UM_SETDEFAULTPB, (WPARAM)uDefControl, 0);


    /*
    ** Get Dialog box caption and internal text.
    */
    if(ResourceFields[DIALOGTEXT]    .lpResourceField &&
       ResourceFields[DIALOGCAPTION].lpResourceField
      )
    {
        /*
        ** Find any \n in string (for VB callers) and replace with
        ** 'real' CRLF sequence.
        */

        /*
        ** What to look for.
        */
        auto LPCSTR  lpszSubString = "\\n";

        /*
        ** Points to found deliminator.
        */
        auto LPSTR   lpszCRLF;

        /*
        ** Used for getting module name of error box owner.
        */
        auto HWND    hWndOwner;

        /*
        ** Can't use strtok (multiple deliminator token) use strstr.
```

```
*/
while((lpszCRLF = _fstrstr(
                             ResourceFields[DIALOGTEXT]
                             .lpResourceField
                             ,lpszSubString
                             )
      ) != NULL
     )
{
    /*
    ** Found \n so replace.
    */
    *lpszCRLF          = 0x0D;
    *(lpszCRLF + 1)    = 0x0A;
}


/*
** This next piece of code adds the module name (of the
** caller) to  the caption  bar of the dialog produced.
*/
hWndOwner = GetParent(hWndDialog);

if(hWndOwner != NULL)
{
    /*
    ** Length of existing dialog box title.
    */
    auto UINT        uLenOldTitle;

    /*
    ** Buffer used in concatenating old/new title. Static
    ** coz we're on the caller's stack and  we don't want
    ** to trash their stack.
    */
    static char      carModuleName[MAX_MODULENAME];

    /*
    ** Used to get the module name of the caller (or owner).
    */
    auto HINSTANCE   hInstOfCaller;

    /*
    ** Length of the retrieved module name.
    */
    auto UINT        uLenModuleName;

    /*
    ** General pointer to memory.
    */
    auto PBYTE       pb;

    /*
    ** Get the caller's instance handle.
    */
    hInstOfCaller = (HINSTANCE)GetWindowWord(
                                             hWndOwner
                                             ,GWW_HINSTANCE
                                             );
```

```
        /*
        ** Get the caller's module name.
        */
        uLenModuleName = GetModuleFileName(
                                          hInstOfCaller
                                          ,&carModuleName[0]
                                          ,sizeof(carModuleName)
                                          );


    /*
    ** Get the length of the normal caption...
    */
    uLenOldTitle = lstrlen(ResourceFields[DIALOGCAPTION].lpResourceField);

    /*
    ** Add the two strings after scanning module name for last
    ** occurance of '/'.
    */
    if((pb = npGetMem(uLenOldTitle + uLenModuleName + 3)) != NULL)
    {
        /*
        ** Build composite caption.
        */
      lstrcpy((LPSTR)pb, ResourceFields[DIALOGCAPTION].lpResourceField);
      lstrcat((LPSTR)pb, " (");
      lstrcat((LPSTR)pb, _fstrrchr(&carModuleName[0],(int)'\\')+ 1);
      lstrcat((LPSTR)pb, ")");

        /*
        ** Set dialog's caption.
        */
        SetWindowText(hWndDialog,(LPSTR)pb);

        /*
        ** Release local mem.
        */
        (void)bFreeMem(pb);
    }

}
else
{
    /*
    ** hWndOwner no parent so can't get module name.
    */
    SetWindowText(
                hWndDialog
                ,ResourceFields[DIALOGCAPTION].lpResourceField
        );
}

/*
** Set contents of text control in dialog.
*/
SetDlgItemText(
            hWndDialog
            ,IDD_TEXT
            ,ResourceFields[DIALOGTEXT].lpResourceField
```

```
                );
}
else
{
    /*
    ** No dialog box caption AND internal text.
    */
    return FALSE;
}


/*
** Icon required.
*/
if(ResourceFields[ICONNAME].lpResourceField != NULL)
{
    /*
    ** Upper case icon name.
    */
    _fstrupr(ResourceFields[ICONNAME].lpResourceField);

    /*
    ** Tell dialog procedure the icon name.  It decides
    ** what icon to use given the name.
    */
    SendMessage(
                hWndDialog
                ,UM_ICONNAME
                ,0
                ,(LONG)ResourceFields[ICONNAME].lpResourceField
                );
}


/*
** Retrieve mode type required.
*/
if(ResourceFields[MODE].lpResourceField != NULL)
{
    /*
    ** Holds dialog box MODE.
    */
    auto LPARAM lMode;

    /*
    ** Upper case it.
    */
    _fstrupr(ResourceFields[MODE].lpResourceField);

    /*
    ** Check for systemmodal.
    */
    if(lstrcmp(ResourceFields[MODE].lpResourceField, "SYSTEMMODAL") == 0)
    {
        lMode = (LPARAM)SYSMODAL;
    }
    else
    {
        /*
        ** Not systemmodal - must be applmodal.
```

```
                            */
                            lMode = (LPARAM)MODAL;
                  }

                  /*
                  ** Tell dialog procedure about it. It sets its own mode.
                  */
                  SendMessage(hWndDialog, UM_USERMODE, 0, lMode);
            }

            /*
            ** All funky -
            */
            return TRUE;
      }
      else
      {
            /*
            ** Loadstring failed if id not 0.
            */
            MessageBox(0,"DLL couldn't load error message string!",NULL,MB_OK);

            return FALSE;
      }
}




/*
** Gets a module handle from a window handle by accessing
** the window words of the window.
*/
HMODULE NEAR hModuleFromhWnd(HWND hWnd)
{
    if(IsWindow(hWnd))
    {
        return (HMODULE)GetWindowWord(hWnd, GWW_HINSTANCE);
    }
    else
    {
        return NULL;
    }
}




/*
** Window procedure for 'ICON' in dialog box
*/
LRESULT APIENTRY lTMSStaticClassWndProc
(
    HWND      hWnd
  , UINT      uMessage
  , WPARAM    wParam
  , LPARAM    lParam
)
{
    /*
```

```
** Just interested in a WM_PAINT.
*/
if(uMessage == WM_PAINT)
{
    /*
    ** Points to selected icon name.
    */
    auto  LPCSTR          lpIcon;

    /*
    ** Holds icon window window text. Static coz we're on the caller's
    ** stack and we don't want to trash it.
    */
    static  char          carBuffer[ICONTITLE];

    /*
    ** Get our caption, decide as to what icon it specifies, load it
    ** and paint it in.
    */
    GetWindowText(hWnd, carBuffer, sizeof(carBuffer));

    /*
    ** Determine the icon type from its name.
    */
    if((lstrcmp(carBuffer, "HAND") == 0) ||
       (lstrcmp(carBuffer, "STOP")==0)
      )
    {
        lpIcon = IDI_HAND;
    }
    else
    if(lstrcmp(carBuffer, "QUESTION") == 0)
    {
        lpIcon = IDI_QUESTION;
    }
    else
    if(lstrcmp(carBuffer, "EXCLAMATION") == 0)
    {
        lpIcon = IDI_EXCLAMATION;
    }
    else
    if((lstrcmp(carBuffer, "ASTERISK" == 0) ||
       (lstrcmp(carBuffer, "INFORMATION")==0)
      )
    {
        lpIcon = IDI_ASTERISK;
    }
    else
    if(lstrcmp(carBuffer, "APPLICATION") == 0)
    {
        lpIcon = IDI_APPLICATION;
    }
    else
    {
        /*
        ** Unknown icon name  - set to NULL.
        */
        lpIcon = NULL;
```

```
}

/*
** If it's one we know...
*/
if(lpIcon != NULL)
{
    /*
    ** DC for icon window.
    */
    auto  HDC            hDC;

    /*
    ** Used in BeginPaint() EndPaint().
    */
    auto PAINTSTRUCT    ps;

    /*
    ** Handle to loaded standard icon.
    */
    auto  HICON          hIcon;

    /*
    ** Get a DC handle for the icon window.
    */
    hDC = BeginPaint(hWnd, &ps);

    if(hDC != NULL)
    {
        /*
        ** If we load standard icon...
        */
        if((hIcon = LoadIcon(NULL, lpIcon)) != NULL)
        {
            /*
            ** Paint it in.
            */
            DrawIcon(hDC, 0, 0, hIcon);
        }

        /*
        ** Finished painting - release DC.
        */
        EndPaint(hWnd, &ps);
    }
}
else
{
    /*
    ** Used in BeginPaint() EndPaint().
    */
    auto PAINTSTRUCT ps;

    /*
    ** No known icon so draw nothing but erase/repaint background.
    ** This'll happen if the definition string contains, say,
    ** 'nothing' for the icon name, this is allowed.
    */
```

```
                BeginPaint(hWnd, &ps);
                EndPaint(hWnd, &ps);
        }
    }
    else
    {
        /*
        ** Message NOT paint.
        */
        return DefWindowProc(hWnd, uMessage, wParam, lParam);
    }

}




/*
** Replaces the first '+'in a  string with a '0'.  This delimiter is used
** so that the caller can format tidy definition strings and signal where
** a piece of text finishes by including a '+' after the required text.
*/
VOID NEAR vStripPlus(LPSTR lpString)
{
    /*
    ** So simple just use straight pointers.
    */
    while(*lpString++)
    {
        if(*lpString == '+')
        {
            *lpString ='\0';
        }
    }

    return VOID_RETURN;
}




/*
** Allocate and lock memory in DLL's local heap.
*/
PBYTE NEAR npGetMem(UINT uSize)
{
    /*
    ** Handle to load heap space.
    */
    auto HLOCAL hLocMem;

    /*
    ** Pointer to local heap space.
    */
    auto PBYTE  pb = NULL;

    /*
    ** Allocate and lock memory.
```

```
    */
    if((hLocMem = LocalAlloc(LMEM_ZEROINIT, uSize)) != 0)
    {
        pb = LocalLock(hLocMem);
    }

    /*
    ** Return pointer to local mem or NULL on error.
    */
    return pb;
}




/*
** Free memory allocated with npGetMem. The local heap 'undo' functions
** return 0 for success, as we want to return 1 for success we 'NOT' the
** result in here.
*/

BOOL NEAR bFreeMem(PBYTE pbLocMem)
{
    /*
    ** Valid pointer value?
    */
    if(pbLocMem != NULL)
    {
        /*
        ** Holds local mem handle.
        */
        auto HLOCAL hMem;

        /*
        ** Get handle from pointer.
        */
        if((hMem = LocalHandle(pbLocMem)) != NULL)
        {
            /*
            ** Unlock mem.
            */
            if(LocalUnlock(hMem) == 0)
            {
                /*
                ** Free mem.
                */
                return (BOOL)LocalFree(hMem) == 0;
            }
        }
    }

    /*
    ** Pointer equals NULL.
    */
    return FALSE;
}
```

```
/*
** Centre the dialog's window.
*/
LONG NEAR lSetDlgPos(HWND hDlg)
{
    /*
    ** Dialog's device based position.
    */
    auto RECT rsWindow;

    /*
    ** Device width etc.
    */
    auto int nXOrg;

    /*
    ** Device height etc.
    */
    auto int nYOrg;

    /*
    ** Get dialog device relative position.
    */
    GetWindowRect(hDlg, &rsWindow);

    /*
    ** Work out centre position from dialog window's device position
    ** and the device's dimensions.
    */
    nXOrg=GetSystemMetrics(SM_CXSCREEN) / 2 - (rsWindow.right - rsWindow.left) / 2;
    nYOrg=GetSystemMetrics(SM_CYSCREEN) / 2 - (rsWindow.bottom - rsWindow.top) / 2;

    /*
    ** Move it.
    */
    MoveWindow(
              hDlg
             ,nXOrg
             ,nYOrg
             ,rsWindow.right  - rsWindow.left
             ,rsWindow.bottom - rsWindow.top
             ,FALSE
             );

    /*
    ** Return dialog's new position.
    */
    return MAKELONG(nXOrg, nYOrg);
}



/*
** Button sub class proc.
```

```
**
** Determine if control has received a WM_KEYDOWN message that corresponds
** to the F1 key being hit.
**
** Find the first child from the parent of all the childs.
**
** If child found, get its caption.
**
** If we have a child, and therefore its caption check to make sure that
** the control is a pushbutton.
**
** Then, check to see if the caption contains 'HELP'.
**
** If it contains help send a message to the dialog simulating a click on
** this button.
**
** Note that if more than one button contains 'HELP' that only the first
** button will be clicked - the 'sent' message  causes  the dialog, and its
** buttons to  be  destroyed  so  that  the  next  iteration (call  made  to
** GetNextWindow()) will fail  as  the  childs  have  been removed from the
** system.
**
** End of loop. Did we find a help button?  hWndThisControl will be non NULL
** if we did. If it's NULL, tell the  user that no help is available. Before
** we  bring  up  a  message box,  check to see if a system modal window is
** present, if there is, it must be our  parent  dialog window, we therefore
** need to create our message box as a system modal window.
*/



LRESULT CALLBACK __export lHelpSubProc
(
   HWND     hWndControl
  ,UINT     uMessage
  ,WPARAM   wParam
  ,LPARAM   lParam
)
{
   /*
   ** Old proc address of button(s).
   */
   static FARPROC fp = NULL;


   /*
   ** Button's parent window.
   */
   auto   HWND    hWndParent;

   switch(uMessage)
   {
      case WM_KEYDOWN:
           if(wParam == VK_F1)
           {
               /*
               ** This button's window handle.
```

```
*/
auto HWND hWndThisControl;


/*
** Caption on button.
*/
static char carControlCaption[BUTTONTITLE];


/*
** Find the dialog window. Used for walking
** its button windows.
*/
hWndParent = GetParent(hWndControl);


/*
** Walk like an ..
** Each walk - get the caption text of the child,
** compare caption text against 'Help'.
*/
for(
    hWndThisControl = GetTopWindow(hWndParent)
   ;hWndThisControl ? GetWindowText(
                                    hWndThisControl
                                   ,&carControlCaption[0]
                                   ,sizeof(carControlCaption)
                                   )
                    : 0
   ;hWndThisControl = GetNextWindow(
                                    hWndThisControl
                                   ,GW_HWNDNEXT
                                   )

    )
{
    auto NPSTR pszHelp = "HELP";

    {
        if(
            /*
            ** Make sure that  only pushbuttons are checked.
            ** Check  for  button text  equal to HELP.  Note
            ** that the presence of  an '&'  anywhere in the
            ** HELP  will screw this up. We rely on standard
            ** mnemonics for  help ie &Help, we will fail on
            ** &Help etc.  This routine will require a small
            ** mod to cope with the & being inside the text.
            */
            IsPush(hWndThisControl) &&
            _fstrstr(
                    _fstrupr(&carControlCaption[0])
                   , pszHelp
                   )
            )
        {
            /*
            ** Found help button to get here.
            */

            /*
```

```
                              ** Make   a   suitable   WM_COMMAND
                              ** message and send it to parent.
                              */
                              SendMessage(
                                          GetParent(hWndThisControl)
                                          ,WM_COMMAND
                                          ,GetWindowWord(hWndThisControl, GWW_ID)
                                          ,MAKELONG(hWndThisControl, BN_CLICKED)
                                          );

                              break;
                         }
                    }
               }

          /*
          ** All buttons walked - no help button found.
          */
          if(hWndThisControl == NULL)
          {
               /*
               ** Style for message box telling user that no
               ** help is available.
               */
               auto UINT uStyle;

               /*
               ** If dialog box is system modal this message box
               ** had better be else we're really f***ed!
               */
               uStyle = GetSysModalWindow(VOID_ARG) ?
                         MB_OK | MB_SYSTEMMODAL       :
                         MB_OK | MB_TASKMODAL;
               /*
               ** Tell 'em.
               */
               MessageBox(
                         hWndParent
                         ,"No Help Available!"
                         ,"Help!"
                         ,uStyle
                         );
          }

          /*
          ** Handled it.
          */
          return 0L;
     }
     /*
     ** Didn't handle it so send it to CallWindowProc() hole.
     */
     break;


case WM_DESTROY:
     /*
     ** Restore old proc address when buttons are destroyed
```

```
        ** not really necessary.
        */
        SetWindowLong(hWndControl, GWL_WNDPROC, (LPARAM)fp);
        break;

        /*
        ** Called to subclass ourselves - old proc address in
        ** lParam - store it  away, called four times - don't
        ** care as called for controls that all have the same
        ** default WndProc address..
        */
    case UM_OLDPROCADDR:
        {
            if(fp == NULL)
            {
                fp = (FARPROC)lParam;
            }
            break;
        }
    }

    /*
    ** Pass on messages to old proc.
    */
    return CallWindowProc((WNDPROC)fp, hWndControl, uMessage, wParam, lParam);
}



/*
** Decides whether or not hWnd is a push button or not. It gets the
** classname ofhWnd (not enough for check as hWnd could be a frame and
** still have this class name) and compares this against 'button' as well
** as checking the lower 4 bits of the control's style against 0 or 1. Push
** buttons should have a style of 0 if they're BS_PUSHBUTTON and 1 if
** they're BS_DEFPUSHBUTTONs according to the following extract from
** WINDOWS.H : NOTE  - We could also do this using
** WM_GETDLGCODE processing.
**
**  BS_PUSHBUTTON            0x00000000L
**  BS_DEFPUSHBUTTON         0x00000001L
**  BS_CHECKBOX              0x00000002L
**  BS_AUTOCHECKBOX          0x00000003L
**  BS_RADIOBUTTON           0x00000004L
**  BS_3STATE                0x00000005L
**  BS_AUTO3STATE            0x00000006L
**  BS_GROUPBOX              0x00000007L
**  BS_USERBUTTON            0x00000008L
**  BS_AUTORADIOBUTTON       0x00000009L
**  BS_OWNERDRAW             0x0000000BL
*/
BOOL NEAR IsPush(HWND hWnd)
{
    /*
    ** Holds hWnd's window style.
    */
    auto    DWORD dwStyle;
```

```
    /*
    ** Buffer for class name, static
    ** as on stack of caller.
    */
    static  char  carClassNameBuffer[MAX_CLASSNAME];

    /*
    ** If window handle passed is not a window handle return failure.
    */
    if(IsWindow(hWnd) == NULL)
    {
        return FALSE;
    }

    /*
    ** Window handle valid so this must work - get class name.
    */
    (void)GetClassName(hWnd, &carClassNameBuffer[0], MAX_CLASSNAME);

    /*
    ** Uppercase it.
    */
    _fstrupr(&carClassNameBuffer[0]);

    /*
    ** Get window's style and keep only the least most four bits.
    */
    dwStyle = GetWindowLong(hWnd, GWL_STYLE);

    /*
    ** Mask all but the lower bits.
    */
    dwStyle &= 0x0000000F;

    /*
    ** Return TRUE if name and style match push button.
    */
    return !lstrcmp("BUTTON", &carClassNameBuffer[0]) &&
           ((dwStyle == 0) || (dwStyle == 1));
}




/*
** Repositions push button controls so that they are 'MessageBox() like'.
** Called once for each pushbutton on the dialog for a given dialog.
**
** This function handles positioning buttons  a  little  differently than
** MessageBox() in that the relative positions of each button to the dialog
** size is a relative position. In other words as our dialog cannot grow in
** width (unlike messagebox's) we have no  need to group our buttons in the
** middle of the box  -  it looks a  little nicer this way and we make full
** use of the space provided!
**
** Passed -
**
** hWndControl    -   A handle to a pushbutton
```

```
**
** uLoop          -      The number of the pushbutton, as in this is the first
**                       button to place etc. uLoop is zero on entry.
**
** uControlCount -      The total number of pushbuttons to position, constant
**                      successive calls for a given dialog.
*/
VOID NEAR vPositionControl(HWND hWndControl, UINT uLoop, UINT uControlCount)
{
    /*
    ** The parent window of the
    ** control to be positioned.
    */
    auto HWND hWndParent;

    hWndParent = GetParent(hWndControl);

    /*
    ** Shouldn't really fail, but...
    */
    if(hWndParent != NULL)
    {
        /*
        ** Client rect of main dialog window.
        */
        auto RECT rsParent;

        /*
        ** Window rect of pushbutton ctrl window.
        */
        auto RECT rsControl;

        /*
        ** Main window width.
        */
        auto UINT uParentWidth;

        /*
        ** Section size.
        */
        auto UINT uSectionWidth;

        /*
        ** Width of current pushbutton.
        */
        auto UINT uControlWidth;

        /*
        ** Offset required to re-position control.
        */
        auto UINT uOffset;

        /*
        ** Get parent window's width; divide by number of controls
        ** plus one to get  a division  width.  Get control's rect
        ** and convert  to parent  relative co-ords. Get control's
        ** width.
        */
```

```
            GetClientRect(hWndParent, &rsParent);
            uParentWidth  = rsParent.right - rsParent.left;
            uSectionWidth = uParentWidth / (uControlCount + 1);
            GetWindowRect(hWndControl, &rsControl);
            ScreenToClient(hWndParent, (LPPOINT)&rsControl.left);
            ScreenToClient(hWndParent, (LPPOINT)&rsControl.right);
            uControlWidth = rsControl.right - rsControl.left;

            /*
            ** Work out required offset for this control number.
            */
            uOffset = (uLoop + 1) * uSectionWidth;

            /*
            ** Move it to its new location.
            */
            MoveWindow(
                     hWndControl
                    ,uOffset - (uControlWidth / 2)
                    ,rsControl.top
                    ,uControlWidth
                    ,rsControl.bottom - rsControl.top
                    ,FALSE
                    );
      }

   return VOID_RETURN;
}
```

The makefile :

```
CC = cl -G2 -W4 -WX -c -AMw -GsD -Od -Zpe -Zid -NT$* $*.c > $*.err

all: tmserror.dll

tmserror.obj: tmserror.c tmserror.h makefile tmserr.h
    $(CC)

wep.obj: wep.c makefile
    $(CC)

libentry.obj: libentry.asm
    \masm\binb\masm -Mx libentry,libentry;

tmserror.dll: wep.obj libentry.obj $*.obj $*.def $*.rc $*.dlg tmserr.h
    link /CO /NOD $*.obj libentry.obj wep.obj, $*.dll,, libw mdllcew, $*.def
    rc -r -v $*.rc
    rc -t -v $*.res tmserror.dll
    implib $*.lib $*.def
    copy $*.dll \win31\system
```

The .def file :

```
LIBRARY    TMSERROR
```

```
PROTMODE

EXETYPE   WINDOWS 3.1

CODE      PRELOAD FIXED
DATA      PRELOAD SINGLE MOVEABLE

SEGMENTS
          WEP        FIXED                      PRELOAD     ; WEP
          TMSERROR   DISCARDABLE MOVEABLE LOADONCALL   ; TMSERROR

          ; _TEXT contains 'C' library routines and start-up code.
          _TEXT      DISCARDABLE MOVEABLE LOADONCALL

HEAPSIZE  10000
STACKSIZE 0

EXPORTS
    WEP                    @1 RESIDENTNAME
    wTMS_ErrorBox          @2
    wTMS_SimpleErrorBox    @3
    bTMSMessageBoxProc     @4
    lTMSStaticClassWndProc @5
    lHelpSubProc           @6
```

rc file :

```
#include "windows.h"

/*
** For dialog box stuff.
*/
#include "tmserror.h"

/*
** For tms error codes - TMSSTDERROR1 etc.
*/
#include "tmserr.h"

/*
** Dialog box template.
*/
rcinclude tmserror.dlg

/*
** Standard error definiton strings defined below.
*/
STRINGTABLE
BEGIN

 TMSERR_FATALEXIT,
   "
  %Application Error+
  %An error has occurred in the application and the program will terminate+
```

```
    %2+
    %&OK+
    %&Help+ %+
    %+
    %stop+
    %1+
    %modal
    "


TMSERR_FATALNOMEM,
    "
    %Application Error+
    %A memory error has occurred and the application will terminate+

    %2+
    %&OK+
    %&Help+
    %+
    %+
    %stop+
    %1+
    %modal
    "


TMSERR_NONFATALNOMEM,
    "
    %Application Error+
    %A memory error has occurred!+

    %3+
    %&Abort+
    %&Retry+
    %&Help+
    %+
    %information+
    %1+
    %modal
    "


TMSERR_INVALIDUSERDATA,
    "
    %Invalid Data Entered+
    %The application has detected that some entered data is invalid+

    %2+
    %&Retry+
    %&Help+
    %+
    %+
    %exclamation+
    %1+
    %modal
    "


TMSERR_INVALIDDATA,
    "
    %Invalid Data+
    %The application has been supplied with invalid data!+
```

```
    %2+
    %&Retry+
    %&Help+
    %+
    %+
    %exclamation+
    %1+
    %modal
    "


TMSERR_LOGINFAIL,
    "
    %Login Failed+
    %The application failed to login using the supplied user details+

    %2+
    %&Retry+
    %&Abort+
    %+
    %+
    %exclamation+
    %1+
    %modal
    "


TMSERR_AREYOUSURE,
    "
    %+
    %Are You Sure?+

    %3+
    %&Yes+
    %&No+
    %&Help+%+
    %question+
    %2+
    %modal
    "


TMSERR_INCORRECTFILETYPE,
    "
    %Incorrect File Type+
    %The specified file is of an incorrect file type+

    %2+
    %&Abort+
    %&Help+
    %+
    %+
    %exclamation+
    %1+
    %modal
    "


TMSERR_UNRECOGNISEDFILETYPE,
    "
    %Unrecognised File Type+
```

```
        %The specified file is of an unrecognised file type+

    %3+
    %&Abort+
    %&Retry+
    %&Help+
    %+
    %exclamation+
    %1+
    %modal
    "


 TMSERR_GHOSTBUSTERSERROR,
    "
    %Serious System Error!+
    %The integrity of the system has been seriously damaged.
     Do NOT continue. Call Technical support!+
    %1+
    %&OK
    %+
    %+
    %+
    %stop+
    %1+
    %systemmodal
    "


END
```

Couple of include files (tmserror.h) :

```c
/*
**
** Typedefs for call-back and window functions.
**
*/
typedef LRESULT (CALLBACK __export GWNDPROC)(HWND, UINT, WPARAM, LPARAM);
typedef BOOL    (CALLBACK __export GDLGPROC)(HWND, UINT, WPARAM, LPARAM);

/*
** The resource field type
*/
typedef struct
{
   LPSTR lpResourceField;

}RESOURCEFIELD;

/*
** The packet type
*/
typedef struct
{
   HMODULE hMod;
   UINT    unType;
   LPSTR   lpDefString;
}PACKET;
```

```
/*
** Function predeclarations.
*/
#define APIENTRY WINAPI __export

WORD        APIENTRY  wTMS_ErrorBox        (HWND,   UINT);
WORD        APIENTRY  wTMS_SimpleErrorBox (HWND,    LPSTR);

GWNDPROC              lHelpSubProc;
GWNDPROC              lTMSStaticClassWndProc;
GDLGPROC              bTMSMessageBoxProc;

LPCSTR           FAR  lpszClassName(VOID);
HINSTANCE        FAR  hRetModInst(HINSTANCE);
HMODULE          NEAR hModuleFromhWnd      (HWND);
VOID             NEAR vStripPlus           (LPSTR);
BOOL             NEAR bFreeMem             (PBYTE);
PBYTE            NEAR npGetMem             (UINT);
LONG             NEAR lSetDlgPos           (HWND);
BOOL             NEAR IsPush               (HWND);
VOID             NEAR vPositionControl(HWND, UINT, UINT);
BOOL             NEAR bLoadAndParse  (
                                      HWND
                                     ,HMODULE
                                     ,UINT
                                     ,LPSTR
                                     ,UINT
                                     );

/*
**
** Defines
**
*/


/*
** Maximum items in string identifying dialog type etc.
*/
#define MAXITEMS 10

/*
** Maximum length of classname.
*/
#define MAX_CLASSNAME 255

/*
** Max length of a definition string.
*/
#define MAX_DEFSTRINGLEN 300

/*
** Makimum module name
*/
#define MAX_MODULENAME _MAX_PATH

/*
** Maximum icon title len.
*/
```

```
#define ICONTITLE    50

/*
** Maximum button caption text len.
*/
#define BUTTONTITLE 50

/*
** Field names.
*/
#define DIALOGCAPTION  0
#define DIALOGTEXT     1
#define NUMCONTROLS    2
#define BUTTONCAPTIONS 3
#define BUTTONCAPTION1 3
#define BUTTONCAPTION2 4
#define BUTTONCAPTION3 5
#define BUTTONCAPTION4 6
#define ICONNAME       7
#define DEFCONTROL     8
#define MODE           9

/*
** Message Box resource ID.
*/
#define MESSAGEBOX1 100

/*
** User messages.
*/
#define UM_ICONNAME        WM_USER + 10
#define UM_USERMODE        WM_USER + 11
#define UM_SETDEFAULTPB    WM_USER + 12
#define UM_OLDPROCADDR     WM_USER + 13
#define UM_HELPREQUEST     WM_USER + 14

/*
** Modal states
*/
#define SYSMODAL 1
#define MODAL 0

/*
** Control IDs for the dialog box.
*/
#define IDD_ICON       101
#define IDD_TEXT       200

/*
** Begining/Ending button IDs.
*/
#define IDD_BUTTONSTART 1
#define IDD_BUTTONEND   4

/*
** Actual button IDs.
*/
#define IDD_BUTTON1 IDD_BUTTONSTART
```

```
#define IDD_BUTTON2 IDD_BUTTON1 + 1
#define IDD_BUTTON3 IDD_BUTTON2 + 1
#define IDD_BUTTON4 IDD_BUTTON3 + 1

/*
** Coding standards stuff.
*/
#define VOID_ARG
#define VOID_RETURN
```

tmserr.h :

```
/*
**
** TMS error codes are defined in here.
**
** Standard Errors should be given 'real' names instead of ordinal names
** like TMSSTDERROR1. A better name would be TMS_FILEOPEN_ERROR.
**
*/

/*
** Error Box resource ID.
*/
#define MESSAGEBOX1 100

/*
** Error Box control IDs.
*/
#define IDD_ICON 101
#define IDD_TEXT 200

/*
** Standard errors begin at 500.
*/
#define TMSSTDERROR       0x500

#define TMSERR_FATALEXIT                TMSSTDERROR + 1
#define TMSERR_FATALNOMEM               TMSSTDERROR + 2
#define TMSERR_NONFATALNOMEM            TMSSTDERROR + 3
#define TMSERR_INVALIDUSERDATA          TMSSTDERROR + 4
#define TMSERR_INVALIDDATA              TMSSTDERROR + 5
#define TMSERR_LOGINFAIL                TMSSTDERROR + 6
#define TMSERR_AREYOUSURE               TMSSTDERROR + 7
#define TMSERR_INCORRECTFILETYPE        TMSSTDERROR + 8
#define TMSERR_UNRECOGNISEDFILETYPE     TMSSTDERROR + 9
#define TMSERR_GHOSTBUSTERSERROR        TMSSTDERROR + 10

/*
** Non-standard errors begin at 400.
*/
#define TMSNONSTDERROR 0x400

#define TMSNONSTDERROR1 TMSNONSTDERROR  + 1
#define TMSNONSTDERROR2 TMSNONSTDERROR1 + 1
#define TMSNONSTDERROR3 TMSNONSTDERROR2 + 1
#define TMSNONSTDERROR4 TMSNONSTDERROR3 + 1
```

```
/*
**
** TMS error functions return one of the following indictating which
** button in the TMSMessageBox was selected.
**
*/
#define BUTTON1 1
#define BUTTON2 2
#define BUTTON3 3
#define BUTTON4 4
```

pragma.h :

```
/*
**Just contains any useful #pragmas.
*/

#pragma warning(disable:4001)   /* Non-standard extension used    - OFF. */
#pragma warning(disable:4100)   /* Unreferenced formal parameter - OFF. */
```

dlg file :

```
/*
** This is our ErrorBox dialog.
*/

DLGINCLUDE RCDATA DISCARDABLE
BEGIN
    "TMSERR.H\0"
END

MESSAGEBOX1 DIALOG PRELOAD 24, 30, 216, 60
STYLE DS_MODALFRAME | WS_POPUP | WS_CAPTION | WS_SYSMENU
BEGIN
    CONTROL
            ""
            ,IDD_ICON
            ,"tmsstatic"
            ,0x0000
            ,3, 9, 22, 23

    CONTROL
            "This is the text control"
            ,IDD_TEXT
            ,"Static"
            ,SS_CENTER
            ,29, 7, 162, 27

    CONTROL
            "button1"
            ,BUTTON1
            ,"Button"
            ,WS_TABSTOP
            ,22, 40, 40, 14
```

```
    CONTROL
            "button2"
            ,BUTTON2
            ,"Button"
            ,WS_TABSTOP
            ,68, 40, 40, 14

    CONTROL
            "button3"
            ,BUTTON3
            ,"Button"
            ,WS_TABSTOP
            ,114, 40, 40, 14

    CONTROL
            "button4"
            ,BUTTON4
            ,"Button"
            ,WS_TABSTOP
            ,160, 40, 40, 14
END
```

Another (and lastly) 'C' file (The DLL's WEP) :

```c
#include "pragma.h"

#define STRICT

#include "windows.h"
#include "tmserror.h"




/*
** The WEP
**
*/
int FAR PASCAL WEP(int bSystemExit)
{
    _asm
    {
        /*
        ** Test to see if our DGROUP is still here before we
        ** explicitly unregister our class!
        */

        push    ds
        pop     cx
        lar     ax,     cx
        jnz     ExitWEP
        test    ax,     0x8000
        jnz     ExitWEP
    }

    /*
    ** If we get here our DGROUP is still with us so we can get at
```

```
    ** our static data.
    **
    */
    UnregisterClass(lpszClassName(VOID_ARG),hRetModInst(0));

ExitWEP:

    return 1 ;
}
```

OK, now for the modified generic application (modifications minimal - what's here is very close to the generic you all love or hate) :

generic.c :

```
/******************************************************************************
 *
 * modified GENERIC application  used to  test/create the TMSERROR DLL
 * Not much has been changed in here thus the inconsistent programming
 * style - sorry!
 */


#include "windows.h"       /* required for all Windows applications   */
#include "generic.h"       /* specific to this program                */

/*
** Standard Error Stuff.
*/
#include "tmserror.h"
#include "tmserr.h"


HANDLE hInst;


int PASCAL WinMain(HINSTANCE hInstance
                  ,HINSTANCE hPrevInstance,LPSTR lpCmdLine,int nCmdShow)
{
    MSG msg;

    if (!hPrevInstance)
      if (!InitApplication(hInstance))
          return (FALSE);


    if (!InitInstance(hInstance, nCmdShow))
        return (FALSE);

    while (GetMessage(&msg,NULL,NULL,NULL))
    {
      TranslateMessage(&msg);
```

```
        DispatchMessage(&msg);
    }
    return (msg.wParam);
}



BOOL InitApplication(HINSTANCE hInstance)
{
    WNDCLASS  wc;

    /* Fill in window class structure with parameters that describe the    */
    /* main window.
*/

    wc.style = NULL;
    wc.lpfnWndProc      = (WNDPROC)MainWndProc;
    wc.cbClsExtra       = 0;
    wc.cbWndExtra       = 0;
    wc.hInstance        = hInstance;
    wc.hIcon            = LoadIcon(NULL, IDI_APPLICATION);
    wc.hCursor          = LoadCursor(NULL, IDC_ARROW);
    wc.hbrBackground    = GetStockObject(WHITE_BRUSH);
    wc.lpszMenuName     = "TMSMENU";
    wc.lpszClassName    = "TMS_CLASS";

    return (RegisterClass(&wc));
}



BOOL InitInstance(HINSTANCE hInstance,int nCmdShow)
{
    HWND            hWnd;

    hInst = hInstance;

    hWnd = CreateWindow(
                    "TMS_CLASS"
                    ,"App to demonstrate TMS standard error box"
                    ,WS_OVERLAPPEDWINDOW
                    ,CW_USEDEFAULT
                    ,CW_USEDEFAULT
                    ,CW_USEDEFAULT
                    ,CW_USEDEFAULT
                    ,NULL
                    ,NULL
                    ,hInstance
                    ,NULL
                    );

    if (!hWnd)
        return (FALSE);

    ShowWindow(hWnd, nCmdShow);
    UpdateWindow(hWnd);
```

```
    return (TRUE);
}


LONG FAR PASCAL MainWndProc
(
   HWND    hWnd
  ,WORD    message
  ,WORD    wParam
  ,LONG    lParam
)
{
   auto    WORD            wResult;
   auto    PAINTSTRUCT     ps;
   auto    HDC             hDC;

   switch (message)
   {
     case WM_COMMAND:
          /*
          ** If menu selection requires a standard error...
          */
          if(wParam > TMSSTDERROR)
          {
              wResult = wTMS_ErrorBox(hWnd, wParam);
          }
          else
          /*
          ** Non-standard error...
          */
          switch(wParam)
          {
              case IDM_ONE:
                    wResult = wTMS_ErrorBox(hWnd,TMSNONSTDERROR1);
                    break;

              case IDM_TWO:
                    wResult = wTMS_ErrorBox(hWnd,TMSNONSTDERROR2);
                    break;

              case IDM_THREE:
                    wResult = wTMS_ErrorBox(hWnd,TMSNONSTDERROR3);
                    break;

              case IDM_FOUR:
                    wResult = wTMS_ErrorBox(hWnd,TMSNONSTDERROR4);
                    break;
          }

          /*
          ** Now pick up response.
          */
          switch(wResult)
          {
              case IDD_BUTTON1:
                    MessageBox(hWnd,"First button hit","Hit!",MB_OK);
                    break;
```

```
                case IDD_BUTTON2:
                    MessageBox(hWnd,"Second button hit","Hit!",MB_OK);
                    break;

                case IDD_BUTTON3:
                    MessageBox(hWnd,"Third button hit","Hit!",MB_OK);
                    break;

                case IDD_BUTTON4:
                    MessageBox(hWnd,"Fourth button hit","Hit!",MB_OK);
                    break;
            }
            break;

        case WM_DESTROY:
            PostQuitMessage(0);
            break;

        case WM_PAINT:
            hDC = BeginPaint(hWnd,&ps);
            EndPaint(hWnd,hDC);
            break;

        default:
            return (DefWindowProc(hWnd, message, wParam, lParam));
    }

    return (LRESULT)0;
}
```

generic.h :

```
#define IDM_ONE     100
#define IDM_TWO     200
#define IDM_THREE   300
#define IDM_FOUR    400
#define IDM_FIVE    500
#define IDM_SIX     600
#define IDM_SEVEN   700
#define IDM_EIGHT   800

int        PASCAL     WinMain         (HINSTANCE, HINSTANCE, LPSTR, int);
BOOL                  InitApplication (HANDLE);
BOOL                  InitInstance    (HANDLE, int);
LONG    FAR PASCAL    MainWndProc     (HWND, WORD, WORD, LONG);
BOOL    FAR PASCAL    About           (HWND, unsigned, WORD, LONG);
```

generic.def :

```
; module-definition file for generic -- used by LINK.EXE

NAME          Generic        ; application's module name

DESCRIPTION        'Sample Microsoft Windows Application'
```

```
PROTMODE

EXETYPE     WINDOWS  3.1   ; required for all Windows applications

STUB        'WINSTUB.EXE'     ; Generates error message if application
                             ; is run without Windows

;CODE can be moved in memory and discarded/reloaded
CODE  PRELOAD MOVEABLE DISCARDABLE

;DATA must be MULTIPLE if program can be invoked more than once
DATA  PRELOAD MOVEABLE MULTIPLE


HEAPSIZE      10000
STACKSIZE     10000               ; recommended minimum for Windows applications


; All functions that will be called by any Windows routine
; MUST be exported.

EXPORTS
  MainWndProc   @1   ; name of window processing function
```

generic.rc :

```
#include "windows.h"
#include "generic.h"
#include "tmserr.h"

TMSMENU MENU
BEGIN
    POPUP       "&Non-Standard"
    BEGIN
        MENUITEM "&Box With &One Button",         IDM_ONE
        MENUITEM "&Box With &Two Buttons",        IDM_TWO
        MENUITEM "&Box With &Three Buttons",      IDM_THREE
        MENUITEM "&Box With &Four Buttons",       IDM_FOUR
    END
    POPUP       "&Standard"
    BEGIN
        MENUITEM "Fatal Exit Standard Error",          TMSERR_FATALEXIT
        MENUITEM "No Memory Fatal Standard Error",      TMSERR_FATALNOMEM
        MENUITEM "No Memory Non-Fatal Standard Error",TMSERR_NONFATALNOMEM
        MENUITEM "Invalid User Data Standard Error",  TMSERR_INVALIDUSERDATA
    END
END

STRINGTABLE
BEGIN
        TMSNONSTDERROR1,
        "
        %One Button+
        %This is a TMS\nnon-standard error box\nwith  one button+
        %1+
        %&OK+
        %+
```

```
            %+
            %+
            %application+
            %2+
            %modal"

            TMSNONSTDERROR2,
            "
            %Caption+
            %Main Text+
            %2+
            %&OK+
            %&Cancel+
            %+
            %+
            %stop+
            %3+
            %systemmodal"

            TMSNONSTDERROR3,
            "
            %Three Buttons+
            %This TMS non-standard error box contains three buttons+
            %3+
            %&Abort+
            %&Retry+
            %Ignore+
            %+
            %asterisk+
            %2+
            %modal"

            TMSNONSTDERROR4,
            "
            %Four Buttons+
            %Help TMS non-standard error box contains four buttons+
            %4+
            %&Oops!...+
            %&Help+
            %Terminate+
            %Panic+ %nothing+
            %1+
            %modal"
END
```

Lastly, generic's makefile :

```
all: generic.exe

generic.obj: generic.c generic.h
    cl -c -AS -Gsw -Od -Zidpe -DSTRICT generic.c > generic.err

generic.exe: generic.obj generic.def generic.rc
    link /CO /M /NOD generic,,, libw slibcew tmserror, generic.def
    rc -r generic.rc
    rc generic.res
    mapsym generic
```

Well, having seen the code, and there's quite a lot of it, you're probably awaiting some sort of detailed discussion/dissection of it? Well, you're not getting it - Sorry (A brief explanation of each function in the DLL follows however)! If I were to break this down and talk it through at length we'd be here for another 40 pages or so and to be candid – we simply don't have the space!

The code above is, as normal, *comment heavy,* and is <u>really</u> very straight forward. If you follow it through you should perhaps start with the *generic* code. Take a look at how generic calls the DLL and what gets passed, then start in on the DLL. The entry point wTMS_SimpleErrorBox is not called by generic so you can ignore it; it is there to be called by applications that cannot, or will not pass a definition string to the DLL as a string resource ID.

In essence the *error box* code breaks down into the following sub-routines :

wTMS_ErrorBox
Exported entry point. The API called by *normal* applications or DLLs that require an error box built from an error definition string which is contained somewhere in the calling module's string table. The API can also be used to create error boxes which are constructed from the library's own string table, ie. *standard errors.* The *id* of the string determines whether or not the string is internal (standard) or external - if the id of the error string is above 0x400 then it *lives* in the calling module's resources, else, it's internal. All standard errors, which are obviously built into the DLL, have ids which are below 0x400; or to put it another way, there is provision for 1024 internal, or standard, errors!

wTMS_SimpleErrorBox
Exported entry point. Called by those apps or DLLs that cannot or will not pass error definition strings via a string table ordinal or that create truly dynamic error definition strings based upon some current predicament. Using this API the error definition string is passed to the DLL via an actual parameter, ie. as a pointer to a character string. Otherwise, this function's very similar to wTMS_ErrorBox.

bTMSMessageBoxProc
Exported entry point. This call-back function is that used by the error box dialog, ie. it is a normal modal dialog call-back function. The actual dialog box is created by either wTMS_SimpleErrorBox or wTMS_ErrorBox. The dialog box is built in to the DLL via the normal .dlg template file inclusion method, ie. the dialog box definition is static (see .rc file for definition of dialog box template). The call-back, at WM_INIT-DIALOG time, calls the internal function bLoadAndParse to customise the dialog according to the current error definition string id. bLoadAndParse always *causes* the customisation of the dialog, but it may use the call-back to do some of the work, ie. bLoadAndParse may send user defined messages to the dialog window in order to get it to do something – see bLoadAndParse below for more information.

lTMSStaticClassWndProc

Exported entry point. This is a class window procedure used to manage a *static type* control contained within the dialog template (*tmsstatic class*). This control is used, if required, to display a message box type icon in the error box.

lHelpSubPoc

Exported entry point. This is a sub-classing call-back function. Each push-button in the dialog is sub-classed via this function – the actual sub-classing is done in bLoadAndParse. It is primarily used to monitor the push-buttons for key presses. Should any button receive a WM_KEYDOWN whose wParam is VK_F1 (help request) the call-back scans the push-buttons to determine whether or not any button has the label *Help*. If it finds a button so labelled to *pushes* the button by passing a WM_COMMAND message to the error box call-back function. Thus help via the F1 hot key is supported.

vPositionControl

This function arranges the visible push-buttons in the error box. It is passed the number of required buttons by the bLoadAndParse routine. This is very similar to a real message box, ie. a real message box, just like this error box, <u>always</u> creates all of its possible buttons (for a message box that's three, for an error box it's four). Some buttons however are hidden according to the message box button *style* requested.

lsPush

This function determines whether a control is a push-button or not – it does it the hard way!

lSetDlgPos

This function centres the error box on the screen.

bFreeMem

This function de-allocates local heap objects used by the DLL.

npGetMem

This function allocates local heap objects as requested by the DLL.

vStripPlus

This function is used to remove the + sign from the error definition string; the plus sign is used to signal that the end of a particular field has been found. The first occurrence of a plus is replaced by a \0 by this function. The plus sign is used to allow the tidy formatting of multiple error definition strings in the module's string-table.

hModuleFromhWnd

This simple function turns a window handle into a module, or instance, handle. It is used to acquire the necessary instance handle (from the error box's *parent* window) in the case where a definition string has to be loaded from another module's string table.

bLoadAndParse

This function really configures the error box. It is called by the WM_INITDIALOG case of the error box call-back. It actually loads the error definition string and parses, or makes sense, of its contents ¬ the string may have to be loaded from another module's string-table. As it parses the string it configures the error box accordingly, eg. it *tells* the error box's tmsstatic class window what icon it should display, sets the default push-button (via a private user message), sets the required dialog mode state, sets the text used in all controls and for the dialog box window itself, and shows and labels the required button controls etc.

I have omitted to include the VB source as you should be able to work it out by reviewing the short wTMS_SimpleErrorBox function. The tmserror.c code remember is DLL code; we have yet to discuss these in detail so if you're unfamiliar with DLLs ignore the LibMain() and WEP functions from your review; also the main code creates and maintains a custom control and sub-classes the standard push-button controls used in the dialog box. Once again, we haven't yet talked about controls or sub-classing so you might want to check out the discussions on those topics before starting in on the code presented here.

☐ Dialog Miscellaneous

IsDialogMessage()

Have you ever wondered how the dialog box manager manages keyboard input to a control, for example, how does it *know* that a list box requires keyboard messages from direction keys (arrow keys) and that push buttons, say, do not? Well if you have wondered, here's how.

The IsDialogMessage() function can be used outside of dialog boxes altogether and is the key, when used with dialog boxes, to the keyboard control managed by the dialog box manager. This function takes two parameters, a window's handle (normally a modeless dialog box window handle) and a long pointer to a message structure. It's this function that manages the keyboard input (all other messages are ignored by it) to your dialog's controls.

When it's called it tests the window handle in the messages structure against the window handle passed as the function's first parameter - it's not a straight comparison, its a relationship test (no DNA analysis involved!). The code would look something like this :

```
BOOL WINAPI IsDialogMessage(HWND hWnd, LPMSG lpmsg)
{
if(IsWindow(hWnd) != NULL && lpmsg->message == 'a keyboard event')
{
      if(GetParent(lpmsg->hwnd) == hWnd)
      {
               ... Strut your stuff
      }
```

```
        else
        {
                return FALSE;
        }
    }
}
```

The code checks to see if the message retrieved from the task's message queue is for a window that is a child of the passed hWnd window AND that the actual message is a keyboard message. If that test is not TRUE than no further action is taken by the function and it returns FALSE. The message will then be translated and dispatched in the normal way (DispatchMessage() etc). If the message is for a child of hWnd then that child needs to be tested to see if it processes this particular keyboard event.

Consider what happens when you press the tab key in a dialog box. Let's say that a push-button currently has the focus. The event is posted to the control (WM_KEY-DOWN event), the event is pulled from the task's message queue and is passed to IsDialogMessage(). IsDialogMessage() determines that the push-button is a child of the main dialog window and has to determine what to do with the message in the message structure, ie. should it move the focus from the push-button to the next control with the WM_TABSTOP style bit set or should it pass it to the push-button? It doesn't know that the push-button doesn't somehow require the tab key! To determine exactly what's required the DM has to ask the control itself. The IsDialog-Message() function <u>sends</u> the control a WM_GETDLGCODE message; this is the dialog box manager's way of saying 'hey guy – what kinda key input do you want?'. The fate of the waiting message is now entirely dependant upon the control's response. If the control doesn't require the key then the dialog box manager shifts the focus to the next control with the WM_TABSTOP bit set. If you want to roll your own controls knowing how to respond to the WM_GETDLGCODE message is therefore critical!

Before we go a little deeper in to this, keep in mind what I said before about using this outside of dialogs. Any window that is a child of another can be used in this way – there's nothing special about controls other than they're child windows.

WM_GETDLGCODE has 12 straight replies, more if these replies are combined. Here's a list of the 11 possible replies listed in WINDOWS.H (the ones with a *X* against them are documented (kinda) in volume three of the programmer's reference (see note below) :

```
DLGC_WANTARROWS              0x0001  X
DLGC_WANTTAB                 0x0002  X
DLGC_WANTALLKEYS             0x0004  X
DLGC_WANTMESSAGE             0x0004  X
DLGC_HASSETSEL               0x0008  X
DLGC_DEFPUSHBUTTON           0x0010  X
DLGC_UNDEFPUSHBUTTON         0x0020
DLGC_RADIOBUTTON             0x0040  X
DLGC_WANTCHARS               0x0080  X
```

```
DLGC_STATIC                          0x0100
DLGC_BUTTON                          0x2000
```

Note that the Programmer's Reference says that 'this message has no parameters', ie. wParam and lParam are not used – not so, it's also very vague in its description of these codes! The standard control's responses to WM_GETDLGCODE are also not documented and indeed a push button, say, may have different responses from time to time (for example, it will respond differently if it's a default control). It makes great sense to have the control respond in this way (when you know what the responses mean) rather than to have the dialog box manager use some defaults, say, which are dependant upon the control's class name and window style bits, giving the control the responsibility to determine over time how it should react to keyboard input gives controls unlimited flexibility.

Getting back to the list above, some of you may have noticed that we're a response short, ie. only 11 are given. The 12th reply is that which is provided by DefWindow-Proc() - zero; this is translated by the dialog box manager as 'I'm a dumb SOB so you'd better give me some default handling please'! No control should really let DefWindowProc() speak for it – unless of course it's dumb!

If you were to drop one of each of the standard controls on to a dialog box using the 3.1 dialog editor allowing each control to adopt its standard state, and then could interrogate each control by sending it a WM_GETDLGCODE message, you'd find that they'd respond like so :

```
Control            Standard Response

Edit
                   DLGC_WANTCHARS
                   DLGC_HASSETSEL
                   DLGC_WANTARROWS

Group Box
                   DLGC_STATIC

Push Button
                   DLGC_BUTTON
                   DLGC_UNDEFPUSHBUTTON

Edit (of Combo)
                   (As Edit above)

Combo
                   DLGC_WANTCHARS
                   DLGC_WANTARROWS

Scroll
                   DLGC_WANTARROWS

Radio Button
                   DLGC_BUTTON
```

```
                    DLGC_RADIOBUTTON

Check Box
                    DLGC_BUTTON

Static Frame
                    DLGC_STATIC

Rectangle
                    DLGC_STATIC

Icon
                    DLGC_STATIC

List Box
                    (As Combo above)
```

Well what do these responses mean? Each response, or set of responses, (responses ORed together) signals that this control requires certain keyboard input. For example, if a control responds DLGC_WANTCHARS it will receive a WM_CHAR message for any WM_KEYDOWN message that maps to an ASCII value; if it doesn't ask for CHARS it won't get them.

A WM_GETDLGCODE message is sent to a control anytime IsDialogMessage() has a keyboard message for that control; the sequence is – control is focused and a key is pressed, message pulled from task queue and passed to IsDialogMessage(), IsDialog-Message() asks control what keyboard input is required, let's say that it responds DLGC_WANTCHARS. The WM_KEYDOWN message is sent to the control; IsDia-logMessage() calls TranslateMessage() for the WM_KEYDOWN message if the control responds DLGC_WANTCHARS – WM_CHAR message put into task's message queue. The control processes the WM_KEYDOWN message. WM_CHAR message pulled from queue and passed to IsDialogMessage(), WM_GETDLGCODE message sent to control to see what keyboard input it requires; there are only so many responses the control can now make – typically they don't change much if at all for standard controls. The control replies DLGC_WANTCHARS, we already have a char message so no TranslateMessage() call is done by IsDialogMessage() and the char is eventually passed to the control.

It is possible to modify the behaviour of standard controls by sub-classing (or super-classing them); if you do this you may add or subtract responses from the controls desired set of responses by using either the bitwise OR or AND operators. You might want to do this, say, to allow an edit control to accept keyboard input from the tab key; this would allow the standard edit control to insert a tab character into its text following the insertion point. The default behaviour is of course for the dialog box manager to shift the input focus away from the edit control to the next control with the WM_TABSTOP bit set (this default behaviour is default because the edit control doesn't normally ask for the tab key)! To override this default behaviour you would subclass the edit control and wait for a WM_GETDLGCODE message. When one arrives you would typically return whatever the *real* class window procedure returns PLUS DLGC_WANTTAB :

```
case WM_GETDLGCODE:
    {
    auto LRESULT lR;

    return lR = CallWindowProc(...) | DLGC_WANTTAB;
    }
```

This should ensure that the edit control gets at least the minimum required key input for its class.

DLGC_WANTALLKEYS will quite effectively do away with any dialog box manager default behaviour, if a control responds DLGC_WANTALLKEYS it gets everything, even the WM_KEYDOWN associated with hitting the enter key – use it carefully as it will probably freak the user out!

One of the most useful codes is DLGC_WANTMESSAGE. This code allows you to look ahead, so to speak, and make on the fly decisions as to which key input you decide to handle and which you want to throw away. If a control (child window) responds with DLGC_WANTMESSAGE the message held by the dialog box manager is forwarded to the control, no default dialog box manager handling for the message is carried out. This allows you to be truly dynamic when it comes to reading keyboard input, but how on earth do you look ahead, the WM_GETDLGCODE message simply states that there's a message waiting, it doesn't say anything about the message contents does it? Well according to the programmers reference no it doesn't, BUT – If the WM_GETDLGCODE message's lParam is non-zero it's actually a pointer to *the* message structure currently being investigated by the IsDialogMessage() function. You can inspect the message (and change it if you wish!) by using this lParam value; you may therefore inspect the message before it gets delivered and decide whether or not you want it. If you want to take it simply respond with DLGC_WANTMESSAGE, the next message to arrive will be the one you gave the nod to.

We'll revisit this message and function again when we look at writing our own controls, until then, on to something else.

☐ Default Push Buttons

When the dialog box manager creates dialog box controls it notes, as it creates them, the ID of the last button it creates that has the BS_DEFPUSHBUTTON style. It inserts the control's ID into the dialog window's window words (see earlier section). If you don't have a push button with this style set the dialog manager still reports that you have and that its ID is 1 or IDOK. When you press return the ID of the default push-button is wrapped up in a WM_COMMAND message and passed to the dialog box main window. However, if another push button has the input focus that control's ID is passed back instead – setting the focus to another control does not change the

ID of the stored default push-button. If any other type of control (including radio buttons and check boxes) has the focus and the enter key is pressed the ID of the default push button is passed back to the main dialog box window.

You can set the control that is the default push button by either giving it the style BS_DEFPUSHBUTTON or by sending the main dialog box window the message DM_SETDEFID. This also works for other controls and should be used with some caution, ie. whereas the dialog box manager (when it's creating your controls) only notes which push button has the style BS_DEFPUSHBUTTON and stores its ID – thus disallowing say a static control to be the default control; the DM_SETDEFID handler part of the dialog box manager isn't nearly so fussy. You can set the default ID to be that of a static text control if you like; now if no push button is focused pressing return will pass the ID of the static control to the parent window via the WM_COMMAND message – probably not what you want?! I guess the dialog box manager should really test the control to see if it's a button before allowing this (you can even use an invalid ID), it could very simply use WM_GETDLGCODE to do it of course or check that such a control exists using, say, GetDlgItem()..

The Esc key and the *Close* system menu item cause an ID of 2, or IDCANCEL, to be passed to the main dialog window. It's always a good idea to have a control with the ID of IDOK that accepts the dialog box settings, and one with the ID of IDCANCEL that ignores the dialog settings.

☐ GetNextDlgTabItem()

This function is used to find the window handle of a control that will be the next or previous control that may be tabbed to. The function is given a starting point (control handle) and asked to find the next or previous control with the WS_TABSTOP style. There is no *Set* equivalent of this function although SetWindowPos() may be used. It would be relatively easy to write a *Set* version as it would be to write a more generally useful function to find the next/previous control with a certain style bit set.

Oh, I just happen to have one here :

```
/*
** Searches for a child window  with a particular window style within a main
** window. When using this function be aware that some controls use the same
** constant value for differing class styles;  for example,  SS_LEFT  is the
** same as BS_DEFPUSHBUTTON.
*/
HWND hGetNextDlgStyleItem
(
    HWND     hDlg            /* The window that contains the child windows. */
  , HWND     hWndControl     /* The starting child window.                  */
  , BOOL     bDirection      /* The direction in which to search.           */
  , DWORD    dwStyle         /* The style to search for.                    */
)
{
```

```
// TRUE is previous, FALSE next.

/*
** Make sure that both the window handles passed are valid.
*/
if(IsWindow(hDlg) == FALSE || IsWindow(hWndControl) == FALSE)
{
    /*
    ** Invalid window handle - return NULL;
    */
    return NULL;
}
else
{
    /*
    ** Used in walking window list.
    */
    auto HWND hWndControlNext;

    /*
    ** Set it to the known child to start with.
    */
    hWndControlNext = hWndControl;

    /**********************************************************
    *
    * Initialisation.
    * Depending upon direction set hWndControlNext to next/
    * previous control.
    *
    * Conditional Test.
    * Loop enters compound statement only if hWndControlNext
    * is not NULL.
    *
    * Iteration.
    * Depending upon direction set hWndControlNext to next/
    * previous control.
    *
    */

    for(
        hWndControlNext = GetWindow(
                                    hWndControl
                                    ,bDirection ? GW_HWNDPREV
                                                : GW_HWNDNEXT
                                   )
        ;hWndControlNext
        ;hWndControlNext = GetWindow(
                                    hWndControlNext
                                    ,bDirection ? GW_HWNDPREV
                                                : GW_HWNDNEXT
                                   )
       )
    {
        /*
        ** On each iteration test to see if window has
        ** specified style.  If it has return with its
        ** window handle.
        */
        if(GetWindowLong(hWndControlNext, GWL_STYLE) & dwStyle)
        {
            return hWndControlNext;
```

```
        }
    }

    /*
    ** Reached end of list and didn't find  window with required
    ** style so now start  at the other end of the list and work
    ** back towards starting window checking for style (circular
    ** list walk).
    */


    /**************************************************************
    *
    * Initialisation.
    * Depending upon direction set hWndControlNext to last/
    * first control.
    *
    * Conditional Test.
    * Loop enters compound statement only if hWndControlNext
    * is not NULL.
    *
    * Iteration.
    * Depending upon direction set hWndControlNext to next/
    * previous control.
    *
    */

    for(
        hWndControlNext = GetWindow(
                                    hWndControl
                                    ,bDirection ? GW_HWNDLAST
                                                : GW_HWNDFIRST
                                    )
        ;hWndControlNext
        ;hWndControlNext = GetWindow(
                                    hWndControlNext
                                    ,bDirection ? GW_HWNDPREV
                                                : GW_HWNDNEXT
                                    )
        )
    {
        /*
        ** On each iteration test to see if window has
        ** specified style.  If it has return with its
        ** window handle.
        */
        if(GetWindowLong(hWndControlNext, GWL_STYLE) & dwStyle)
        {
            return hWndControlNext;
        }
    }

    /*
    ** Entire list walked and no control found with this style -
    ** therefore return NULL.
    */
    return NULL;

}
}
```

If you feel like modifying this function so that it checks only certain types of control simply add a call to SendMessage() to the style test (compare this with the function IsPush() used in the error box DLL) :

```
if(
   (GetWindowLong(hWndControlNext, GWL_STYLE) & dwStyle)) &&
   (SendMessage(hWndControl, WM_GETDLGCODE, 0, 0) & DLGC_STATIC)
   )
{
    ... static control with dwStyle found.
}
```

Another related function is GetNextDlgGroupItem(), this function searches for a control that is group related, ie. a control that forms part of the same control group according to a control's WS_GROUP bit. A control with the WS_GROUP style starts the group, the group continues extending through to the next control that has the WS_GROUP style – this last control is not included in the group but starts a new group.

☐ The Undocumented Dialog Box

There's one more dialog we ought to have a look at; actually this is *revisit* really as we talked about it (kinda) earlier. This dialog box can be quite handy as we'll see but does come with a warning – <u>This dialog box is undocumented so Microsoft are not obliged to continue supporting it!</u> The dialog in question is called a system error box. We've seen one of these already in the guise of a system modal message box.

The documented MessageBox() function actually calls an undocumented function called SysErrorBox() when the message box requested by you is to be system modal.

So why don't you just use MessageBox() to get to a SysErrorBox(), ie. why go into SysErrorBox() directly? The answer is that by accessing the SysErrorBox() function directly you can configure the resultant box more or less however you want. Note that a SysErrorBox() is the only true kind of System Modal dialog there is (see note earlier about the difference between DS_SYSMODAL, SetSysModalWindow() and MessageBox() with a MB_SYSTEMMODAL style) in Windows. SysErrorBox() was also undocumented in Windows 3.0 (where I first found and used it) so it may well stay around for a while, note however that the function was available using the LIBW.LIB import library in 3.0 and that it has been removed from LIBW.LIB in 3.1; possibly a sign that it is to go in the future?

The function can be prototyped like so :

```
UINT FAR PASCAL __export SysErrorBox(LPCSTR, LPCSTR, UINT, UINT, UINT);
```

The function's parameters are similar to those (unsurprisingly) of MessageBox(). The first two are pointers to strings that specify the contents of the title bar and *text* portion of the box, ie. the message that appears internally in the box. The next three parameters specify the button configuration. You may, unlike MessageBox() configure the box to contain one left aligned button labelled, say, *Abort* if you wish – you cannot configure the captions to be anything but those provided by default. Additionally you may *set* any button to be the default button by ORing it with SB_DEFAULT below (32768 or 0x8000). The function blocks until the error box is closed down – everything stops when the function's called, even timers in the calling application! The defines listed below can be used to configure the box accordingly.

```
/*
** SysErrorBox() button configuration codes.
*/
#define SB_NOTHING 0
#define SB_OK       1
#define SB_CANCEL   2
#define SB_YES      3
#define SB_NO       4
#define SB_RETRY    5
#define SB_ABORT    6
#define SB_IGNORE   7


/*
** SysErrorBox() reply codes.
*/
#define SB_FIRST    1
#define SB_SECOND   2
#define SB_THIRD    3

/*
** SysErrorBox() default button code. Bitwise OR with button ID.
*/
#define SB_DEFAULT 32768
```

The code fragment below can be used to create a SysErrorBox() with three buttons, they are labelled (left to right) *Ignore, Retry* (The default button), and *Abort*. The function returns either 1 2 or 3 (or SB_FIRST, SB_SECOND, SB_THIRD) depending upon which button was selected. Following the call to SysErrorBox() below Message-Box() is called using MB_SYSTMMODAL – the resultant box is created by MessageBox() directly calling SysErrorBox(). Note once again that everything stops when either or these two boxes is present. This means that I cannot include a *snap shot* of what such a box lots like as Alt + Print Scrn is disabled – you'll have to use your imagination, or better still try it yourself!

```
        auto UINT uRes;

        uRes = SysErrorBox(
                  "This is a system error – really panic!"
                 ,"PANIC BUTTON!"
                 ,SB_IGNORE
                 ,SB_RETRY  | SB_DEFAULT
                 ,SB_ABORT
                 );
    {
```

```
            auto char * pcMessage;
            auto char * pcHeader = "You Pressed";

            switch(uRes)
            {
                case SB_FIRST:
                    pcMessage = "Ignore";
                    break;

                case SB_SECOND:
                    pcMessage = "Retry";
                    break;

                case SB_THIRD:
                    pcMessage = "Abort";
                    break;
            }

            MessageBox(hWnd, pcMessage, pcHeader, MB_SYSTEMMODAL);

    }
```

One last point to note about using SysErrorBox(); as was mentioned above, this function is still currently exported from USER but does not appear in LIBW.LIB (the Windows' master import library); this means that you have to either import it directly using something like :

```
IMPORTS
    USER.SYSERRORBOX
```

or

```
IMPORTS
    SYSERRORBOX = USER.320
```

or

Use GetProcAddress() using either the ordinal or function name.

or

Build your own Windows' master import library using IMLIB.EXE.

I use the latter method, ie. I rebuild LIBW using GDI.EXE USER.EXE and either or KRNL286.EXE or KRNL386.EXE (I forgot real mode!) :

```
IMPLIB  GDI.LIB            GDI.EXE      // builds GDI.LIB
IMPLIB  USER.LIB           USER.EXE     // builds USER.LIB
IMPLIB  KERNEL.LIB         KRNL386.EXE  // builds KERNEL.LIB
```

You then either link with these (omit LIBW.LIB) or combine these into another LIBW.LIB :

```
LIBS=USER.LIB GDI.LIB KERNEL.LIB
```

Your link line will now look something like this :

```
link ....obj,....exe,, $(LIBS),....def
```

NOTE: The resulting libraries will include those functions omitted either deliberately on inadvertently by Microsoft; for example DebugOutput() and SysErrorBox().

☐ Auto Dismissing Dialogs

Sometimes it's nice to produce a window for a finite time that is dismissed independently of user interaction (see the Perf-Meter application in the Miscellaneous chapter for such a dialog). The dialog box class is an ideal choice for creating such a window. Here's a simple example of how such a dialog may be implemented (explanation follows the code).

Some necessary types and defines :

```
typedef struct
{
   UINT     uTimeOut;
   BOOL     bShowOK;
   LPCSTR   lpszMessageTitle;
   LPCSTR   lpszMessageText;
   UINT     uMode;
} PROMPTBOXINFO, FAR * LPPROMPTBOXINFO;


/*
** System modal ID.
*/
#define PB_SYSTEMMODAL MB_SYSTEMMODAL

/*
** Error defines.
*/
#define PBERR_NOTIMER 100
#define PBERR_PARAM   110
```

The PromptBox call-back :

```
/*
** Prompt box call-back function.
*/
BOOL __export CALLBACK Prompt
(
   HWND     hDlg
  ,UINT     uMessage
  ,WPARAM   wParam
```

```
    ,LPARAM    lParam
)
{
    /*
    ** Required number of seconds.
    */
    static UINT uTicks;

    /*
    ** Seconds that have passed.
    */
    static UINT uTickCount;

    switch(uMessage)
    {
        case WM_INITDIALOG:

            /*
            ** If we want a time out set it up.
            */
            if(((LPPROMPTBOXINFO)lParam)->uTimeOut > 0)
            {
                if(SetTimer(hDlg, 1, 1000, NULL) == NULL)
                {
                    EndDialog(hDlg, PBERR_NOTIMER);
                }

                /*
                ** Remember wanted seconds and re-set
                ** counter.
                */
                uTicks = ((LPPROMPTBOXINFO)lParam)->uTimeOut;
                uTickCount = 0;
            }

            /*
            ** Push button wanted?
            */
            if(((LPPROMPTBOXINFO)lParam)->bShowOK == FALSE)
            {
                /*
                ** No so hide it.
                */
                ShowWindow(
                            GetDlgItem(hDlg, IDOK)
                          ,SW_HIDE
                          );
            }

            /*
            ** Must have valid title and message text.
            */
            if(
                ((LPPROMPTBOXINFO)lParam)->lpszMessageTitle == NULL ||
                ((LPPROMPTBOXINFO)lParam)->lpszMessageText  == NULL
              )
            {
                EndDialog(hDlg, PBERR_PARAM);
```

```
        }
        else
        {
            /*
            ** Set dialog box's title.
            */
            SetWindowText(
                        hDlg
                        , ((LPPROMPTBOXINFO) lParam)->lpszMessageTitle
                        );

            /*
            ** Set dialog box's static control text.
            */
            SetWindowText(
                        GetDlgItem(hDlg, IDC_MESS)
                        , ((LPPROMPTBOXINFO) lParam)->lpszMessageText
                        );
        }

        /*
        ** Determine mode state and set it up.
        */
        if(
            ((LPPROMPTBOXINFO) lParam)->uMode == PB_SYSTEMMODAL
          )
        {
            SetSysModalWindow(hDlg);
        }

        return TRUE;


    case WM_TIMER:

        /*
        ** Inc tick count and check against ticks required.
        ** If tick count greater or equal dismiss dialog.
        */
        if(uTickCount++ >= uTicks)
        {
            /*
            ** Stop timer.
            */
            KillTimer(hDlg, 1);

            /*
            ** Hose dialog.
            */
            SendMessage(hDlg, WM_COMMAND, IDOK, 0);
        }
        return TRUE;
        break;

    case WM_COMMAND:

        /*
        ** Either 'really' clicked or else 'sent' by
```

```
                        ** WM_TIMER handler.
                        */
                        if(wParam == IDOK || wParam == IDCANCEL)
                        {
                            EndDialog(hDlg, TRUE);
                            return TRUE;
                        }
                        return TRUE;
                        break;
            }

        return FALSE;
}
```

The PromptBox function :

```
int PromptBox
(
    HWND      hWndParent
    ,UINT     uTimeOut
    ,BOOL     bShowOK
    ,LPCSTR   lpszMessageTitle
    ,LPCSTR   lpszMessageText
    ,UINT     uMode
)
{
    /*
    ** Result of DialogBoxParam() call.
    */
    auto int nResult;

    /*
    ** Make sure we're using a real window.
    */
    if(IsWindow(hWndParent) != NULL)
    {
        auto PROMPTBOXINFO tPBI;

        /*
        ** Fill in prompt box info struct with passed info.
        */
        tPBI.uTimeOut           = uTimeOut;
        tPBI.bShowOK            = bShowOK;
        tPBI.lpszMessageTitle   = lpszMessageTitle;
        tPBI.lpszMessageText    = lpszMessageText;
        tPBI.uMode              = uMode;

        /*
        ** Do dialog - pass prompt info in lParam.
        */
        nResult = DialogBoxParam(
                                (HINSTANCE)GetWindowWord(
                                                        hWndParent
                                                        ,GWW_HINSTANCE
                                                        )
                                ,"Prompt"
                                ,hWndParent
                                ,(DLGPROC)Prompt
```

```
                                        ,(LPARAM)(LPPROMPTBOXINFO)&tPBI
                                        );
    }

    /*
    ** Return whether or not it worked.
    */
    return nResult;
}
```

Main WndProc - Testing Function :

```
LRESULT __export CALLBACK MainWndProc
(
    HWND      hWnd
   ,UINT      uMessage
   ,WPARAM    wParam
   ,LPARAM    lParam
)
{
    switch(uMessage)
    {
    case WM_COMMAND:
        switch(wParam)
        {
            case IDM_PROMPT:
                PromptBox(
                        hWnd
                        ,3
                        ,TRUE
                        ,"Selected Prompt"
                        ,"3 second system modal prompt box"
                        ,PB_SYSTEMMODAL
                        );

                break;

            case IDM_LONGJOB:
                PromptBox(
                        hWnd
                        ,5
                        ,FALSE
                        ,"Selected Long Job"
                        ,"We're starting a long job now - this will take a while"
                        ,0
                        );

                // Call func to start long job...

                PromptBox(
                        hWnd
                        ,1
                        ,FALSE
                        ,"Selected Long Job"
                        ,"Long job completed - wait a second"
                        ,0
                        );
                break;
```

```
        }
        break;

    case WM_DESTROY:
        PostQuitMessage(0);
        break;

    default:
        return DefWindowProc(hWnd, uMessage, wParam, lParam);
    }

    return (LRESULT)0;
}
```

.h file defines :

```
#define IDM_PROMPT   100
#define IDM_LONGJOB 110
#define IDC_MESS     200
```

Dialog template :

```
PROMPT DIALOG 56, 31, 144, 61
STYLE DS_MODALFRAME | WS_CAPTION | WS_SYSMENU
BEGIN
    CONTROL          "", IDC_MESS, "Static", SS_CENTER | WS_GROUP, 22, 5, 98,
                     32
    CONTROL          "&OK", IDOK, "Button", BS_DEFPUSHBUTTON | WS_GROUP |
                     WS_TABSTOP, 53, 42, 32, 14
END
```

.rc File :

```
#include "windows.h"
#include "generic.h"

GenericMenu MENU
BEGIN
    POPUP       "&Help"
    BEGIN
        MENUITEM "&Prompt Box...", IDM_PROMPT
        MENUITEM "&Long Job...",   IDM_LONGJOB
    END
END


rcinclude generic.dlg
```

The prompt box code above allows the user to create dialog boxes that stay around for some finite time. Each prompt box may have the following features set for it :

- Time out in seconds.
- Option to show or hide the dialog's OK button.
- The caption and contents text.
- The mode of the dialog.

The user simply calls the function PromptBox passing a small set of parameters which specify the required settings. These parameters are wrapped up in a structure and passed to the prompt box call-back upon creation via the WM_INITDIALOG's lParam. The dialog call-back unwraps the structure and sets up the dialog as requested.

Also shown above is some MainWndProc code that is used to exercise the box, ie. test it.

The code could be greatly improved. For example the box could centre itself, it could use an owner draw control and DrawText() to draw in the static control text thus allowing text position and colour to be configurable, it could also provide a task modal mode state instead of just the two it currently provides, ie. system-modal and appl-modal etc etc.

From the MainWndProc code above here are some screen shots of the prompt box running :

The *Prompt* PromptBox() - System Modal WITH push-button (a 3 second box).

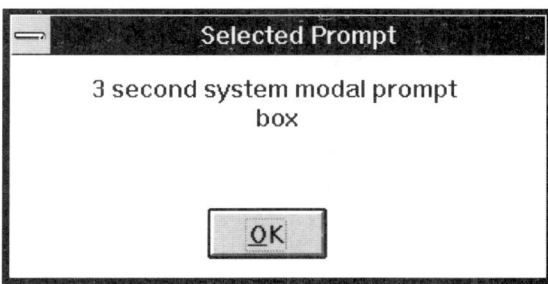

Starting a long job (a 5 second box).

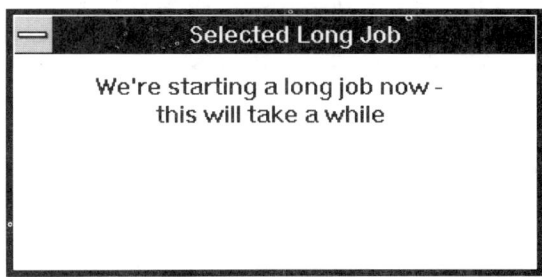

Completing a long job (a 1 second box).

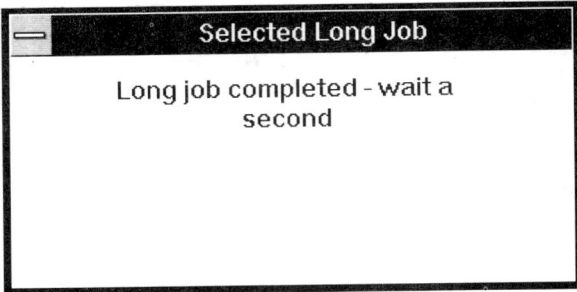

Menus in Dialogs

Dialogs and menus don't really go together, that is to say that dialogs do not normally have menus and further that some dialog styles are not compatible with the menu format at all. For example you cannot have a menu in a dialog that's got the DS_MODALFRAME style. Essentially the dialog should have the simple WS_BORDER or WS_THICKFRAME styles in order to *hold a menu*.

If your dialog does have a menu it receives menu input via the normal WM_COMMAND message – be careful when choosing menu-item IDs therefore, ie. a control also notifies its parent window via a WM_COMMAND message. Sometimes it will be desirable to give both a control and a menu-item the same ID, ie. selecting either causes some operation to be carried out – using this approach you may easily give both a menu and control interface to some operation.

Also note that the WM_COMMAND message may be interrogated to ascertain whether or not the message comes from a control etc. The WM_COMMAND message's lParam, or rather the lParam's hi-word should be tested here. The value of this word will be either a window handle – the message is from a control, 1 – the message was generated by using an accelerator or 0 – the message comes from a menu selection.

Hiding vs. Destroying Dialogs

Sometimes it is handy to keep a dialog around rather than destroy it. For example, often you'll produce a complex dialog to get some user input and when the user selects OK etc copy inputted information to some other place in your application before you call EndDialog(), ie. you'll have to retrieve the entered data as you're about to destroy the dialog, which of course would cause you to loose the entered data.

In such circumstances consider hiding the dialog instead of destroying it. Of course, if the dialog's modal you'll have to re-enable the parent window (as shown earlier in this chapter) in order for the main, or parent, window to gain control. If you keep the dialog around like this you can retrieve the entered data at your leisure.

Keeping the dialog around also allows you to show the dialog in its previous state very simply of course, ie. you'd show it and re-disable the parent window!

The one potential problem with keeping complex dialogs around like this is that they are obviously not destroyed, ie. by keeping them, any resources allocated to them remain allocated – keep an eye therefore on free system resources.

☐ Painting in Dialogs

A dialog box is simply a window (we've seen that the actual type of window used could be either a WS_CHILD, WS_POPUP or a WS_OVERLAPPED). It receives WM_PAINT messages etc therefore just like any normal window. To paint in the non-client area however requires a little more effort as detailed earlier when we talked about processing a message in our call-back after the DM had!

To paint in your dialog could be as easy as this :

```
case WM_CTLCOLOR:
    /*
    ** Draw controls in gray.
    */
    SetBkMode((HDC)wParam, TRANSPARENT);
    return (BOOL)GetStockObject(LTGRAY_BRUSH);
    break;

case WM_PAINT:
    {
        auto PAINTSTRUCT ps;
        auto HDC         hDC;
        auto RECT        rsClient;
        auto HBRUSH      hbr;

        /*
        ** Draw dialog client area in gray.
        */
        hDC = BeginPaint(hDlg, &ps);
        hbr = SelectObject(hDC, GetStockObject(LTGRAY_BRUSH));
        GetClientRect(hDlg, &rsClient);
        Rectangle(hDC, 0, 0, rsClient.right, rsClient.bottom);
        hbr = SelectObject(hDC, hbr);
        EndPaint(hDlg, &ps);
    }
    return TRUE;
    break;
```

We'll look at painting in the dialog control windows when we look at creating custom controls later.

Chapter 4

C l e a n i n g   W i n d o w s

Covers sub-classing/super classing also.

☐ **Windows**

This chapter examines windows, window procedures and the relationship each has with the other.

Everything in Windows really happens either through, or to, a window. A window is the instanciation of a Windows' class, and is really an essential part of practically all Windows' applications.

A class defines the behaviour of a window which is derived, or instanciated, from it; it's like a integer in 'C' – An integer doesn't exist until you have an instance of an integer object. All integer objects behave exactly the same, ie. each has a pre-defined set of rules which govern your interaction with it and the set of values that it may hold. In a 'C' declaration int x; x is the *handle* you have on an area of memory used to hold the integer's values. Of course each integer may hold a different value from any of the others in the system, ie. its value property holds a value that may be unique given a set of integer's values. Well, it is the same for a window. Of course a window is a rather more complex object, or data type, than an integer, but each window class does still define the behaviour of an instance of the class – a window. Just like an integer, a window instance must be referenced through a handle. A window's handle is returned from any Windows' API function that creates one. Unlike the integer x in the example above, the handle returned from CreateWindow() etc doesn't contain any particular property of our window.

Instanciating a window is extremely close to, say, using malloc to allocate some memory for a rather more complex data type like a struct, indeed, a window handle is currently implemented as a near pointer to a *window struct* held in USER's data segment.

All UI interaction in Windows takes place through a window whether it be a control or a main window – even a menu and the desktop are windows built from internal (belonging to, and registered by Windows) classes. In fact Windows has quite a few classes that it uses for special purposes. Most of these special classes have at least one window derived from them. Some of these windows are invisible (for some or all of the duration of the Windows' session) and are used for various system or UI things; here's a bit of a list of some of these Windows' classes/windows (all system classes are in the 0x8000 range) :

```
Desktop Class #32769          - The desktop window is created from this class.
```

Class Member	Setting	Meaning
Class Style	= 8	= CS_DBLCLKS
WndProc Address	= 39FAE3F	
Class Extra	= 0	
Window Extra	= 0	
Reg Instance	= 6DE	= USER
Icon	= 0	
Cursor	= 2EE	= IDC_ARROW
Background	= 2	= COLOR_BACKGROUND
Visible	= TRUE	

```
Menu Class #32768 - All menus are created from this class. The class is in-
stanciated on boot up and is multiply instanciated when cascaded menus are
visible (see example of how this class can be used to build 'Tear Off'
menus later in this chapter).
```

Class Member	Setting	Meaning
Class Style	= 800	= CS_SAVEBITS
WndProc Address	= 5C715ED	
Class Extra	= 0	
Window Extra	= 2	
Reg Instance	= 6DE	= USER
Icon	= 0	
Cursor	= 0	
Background	= 0	
Visible	= FALSE	

```
Task Switch Class #32771 - Used to create the window that appears when you
press Alt + Tab. Called the 'Switch Window' internally.
```

Class Member	Setting	Meaning
Class Style	= 803	= CS_SAVEBITS | CS_HREDRAW | CS_VREDRAW
WndProc Address	= 39F6A72	
Class Extra	= 0	
Window Extra	= 0	
Reg Instance	= 6DE	= USER
Icon	= 0	
Cursor	= 2EE	= IDC_ARROW
Background	= 2	= COLOR_BACKGROUND
Visible	= FALSE	

Dialog Class #32770 - The dialog box class (see separate chapter on dialogs for more on this class).

Class Member	Setting	Meaning
Class Style	= 2808	= CS_BYTEALIGNWINDOW |
		CS_SAVEBITS |
		CS_DBLCLKS
WndProc Address	= 63F2A13	= DefDlgProc
Class Extra	= 0	
Window Extra	= 30	= DLGWINDOWEXTRA
Reg Instance	= 6DE	= USER
Icon	= 0	
Cursor	= 2EE	= IDC_ARROW
Background	= 0	= 0
Visible	= TRUE	

Multi-Media Class #42 - Used when you running the MM version of Windows.

Class Member	Setting	Meaning
Class Style	= 4000	= CS_GLOBALCLASS
WndProc Address	= 140704EC	
Class Extra	= 0	
Window Extra	= 0	
Reg Instance	= 6DE	= USER
Icon	= 0	
Cursor	= 0	
Background	= 6	= COLOR_WINDOW
Visible	= FALSE	

Icon Caption Class #32772 - Multiply instanced - this window class is used
to create the small window used to label an icon. It displays the caption
text of the window to which it is attached.

Class Member	Setting	Meaning
Class Style	= 0	= 0
WndProc Address	= 39F7452	
Class Extra	= 0	
Window Extra	= 0	
Reg Instance	= 6DE	= USER
Icon	= 0	
Cursor	= 2EE	= IDC_ARROW
Background	= 0	
Visible	= TRUE	

You can change the way these classes work, and to some degree instances of them
already in existence (by this I mean windows) by changing the properties of the class
and/or window.

For example, say you wanted to stop one of the standard ways to access the task list.
One of the ways to access the list is to double click the desktop (window); the desktop
window, on receipt of a double click event, exec's the TASKMAN.EXE application.

To prevent it doing this all we need to do is prevent the double click event being generated :

```
hWnd = GetDesktopWindow(); // OR GetDesktopHWnd()

SetClassWord(
          hWnd
         ,GCW_STYLE
         ,GetClassWord(hWnd, GCW_STYLE) & ~CS_DBLCLKS
         );
```

> Just in case you didn't know; the TASKMAN list box displays the window captions of all windows that are siblings of the desktop window as long as they're visible and not owned by any other window (or that owner is zero ie. the desktop). See discussions on Parent vs. owned & child windows late in this chapter. (You can get Ctrl + Esc to exec anything you want by either adding the taskman.exe= entry in the [boot] section of system.ini or by renaming any existing Windows' application TASKMAN.EXE – ie. replace the old with a *new;* I have mine set to taskman.exe = winmine.exe!), by setting it to nothing you can effectively stop access to the task list.

The code fragment above will prevent the desktop window from picking up the mouse double click and therefore from firing off the TASKMAN.EXE application. It *negates* the class style CS_DBLCLKS from the class's style – these style bits are checked as certain events happen, like a double click, to determine what if any action should be taken. This isn't guaranteed by Windows however, ie. There's nothing to stop Windows from storing a class's style bits, say, elsewhere. The elsewhere style bits would be set as part of the RegisterClass() call and would be the bits that are checked when required. Changing those bits that are available through Set-ClassWord()/Long() now has no effect on any already instanciated class window! I wish Microsoft would specify just what bits are, or maybe, volatile in this way – perhaps they will one day?

As another example say you wanted to force the re-painting of any part of the screen which has been obscured by a menu :

```
hWnd = FindWindow("#32768", NULL);

SetClassWord(
          hWnd
         ,GCW_STYLE
         ,GetClassWord(hWnd, GCW_STYLE) & ~CS_SAVEBITS
         );
```

The code above does just that by turning off the menu class's CS_SAVEBITS style. This will work for any menu created from #32768 (which is all of 'em).

You can't change everything (and get away with it!) however – and all of this, even the examples above, might change (see note above). For example you can change the number of window words defined by the class by changing the class offset at

GCW_CBWNDEXTRA – BUT – the allocation only comes into affect when a new window is created from the class, any existing window will only have the old number of window words allocated for it (although using GetClassWord(hOldWnd, GCW_CBWNDEXTRA) will report the new value assigned to the class!). You also cannot change the amount of class words allocated as again the allocation would only come into affect when the new class was instanciated via another RegisterClass() call – of course you cannot duplicate another class (using the same name (and keep it a global class)) so the RegisterClass() call will fail! The result is that, if you interrogate the class, it will report that more class words are available than there really are! Again, I wish Microsoft would publish just what can and cannot be changed without breaking something.

You can do similar things by changing the style of a window rather than that window's class, again some things cannot be done, say, changing a window from a child window to a popup!

Here's a code snippet that can be used to change a window's style on the fly (NOTE: The bottom or low 16 bits of a window's style are processed by the class call-back function; the high 16 bits are interpreted by Windows as it creates a window. A class call-back doesn't therefore choose to create a child window (say) – it gets one automatically. A class call-back could however decide whether or not it was, say, a radio button as opposed to a push button). Note that the set of style bits attached to window's class are not modifiable, ie. these bits are interpreted by Windows and no provision has been made within their design to allocate any of them to the programmer.

Somewhere in a WndProc :

```
auto DWORD    dwStyle;

/*
** Get existing window style.
*/
dwStyle = GetWindowLong(hWnd, GWL_STYLE);


 *
 ** Some menu selection.
 */
    switch(uMessage)
    {
    case WM_COMMAND:

    /*
    ** Switch on menu IDs and toggle style bits on/off.
    */
        switch(wParam)
        {
          case IDM_CAPTION :
              dwStyle ^= WS_CAPTION;
              break;

          case IDM_MINBOX  :
```

```
            dwStyle ^= WS_MINIMIZEBOX;
            break;

    case IDM_MAXBOX  :
            dwStyle ^= WS_MAXIMIZEBOX;
            break;

    case IDM_THICK   :
            dwStyle ^= WS_THICKFRAME;
            break;

    case IDM_DLGFRAME:
            dwStyle ^= WS_DLGFRAME;
            break;

    case IDM_BORDER  :
            dwStyle ^= WS_BORDER;
            break;

    case IDM_SYSMENU :
            dwStyle ^= WS_SYSMENU;
            break;

    }

/*
** Set new style to window.
*/
SetWindowLong(hWnd, GWL_STYLE, dwStyle);

/*
** Cause a WM_PAINT message so that the new styles show up.
*/
DrawMenuBar(hWnd);

/* Done... */
    break;
```

In the code above the menu IDs are not important, each WM_COMMAND case handler toggles a style bit on or off (the list is not exhaustive). The current style is read outside of the main message switch and set again after the command switch. The window then has to be re drawn – I used DrawMenuBar() here (old habits die hard), you might like to check out RedrawWindow() if you're using 3.1 – I have however found that this new function is not as useful or as consistent as DrawMenuBar() – yet another way to re-draw the non-client part of the window is to use SetWindowPos() with the SWP_DRAWFRAME | SWP_NOMOVE | SWP_NOSIZE flags set.

Being able to decide at run-time just whether or not, say, a window is resizable can be real handy; or perhaps there comes a time when you no longer want the user to be able to iconise a window – by changing a window's style these things, and more, are possible.

☐ Basic Window Types
Overlapped Windows

Back in the bad old days, according to the SDK documentation, you were only supposed to have one, and only one, of these per task; no explanation given other than under Windows 1.0 it was seen as stylistically correct for each application to create a single tiled window to *fit* into the desktop area. Nowadays the documentation suggests that you can have as many as you like, in fact the default window style for a dialog box is now WS_OVERLAPPED! In fact you could always have as many as you liked and could even omit tiled/overlapped windows from you application entirely.

An overlapped window is a top level window, ie. its existence is not reliant upon another window as say a child window's would be. An overlapped window may be owned by another window but that other window is not this new window's parent – it's the new window's owner (see discussion below on parent/owner). Window ownership determines some UI characteristics of just how a window, or windows interact with each other. For example an owned window is always ordered (Z order) so that it is shown above its owner. If the owner is hidden or iconised then the owned window is not made iconic (a child window is but that is because it is a child and has a parent – it does not have an owner). Even if you use, say, SetWindowPos() or BringWindowToTop() you will not be able to disturb the Z order imposed by owner-ship.

Overlapped windows may have their initial window position and size decided upon by Windows. This is achieved by specifying the constant CW_USEDEFAULT as an initial X and width in any CreateWindow() type call. NOTE : CW_USEDEFAULT (or anything for that matter) is ignored in the initial Y and height parameters if CW_USEDEFAULT has been given for X and width; set Y and height to 0 therefore (this has not always been the case; at one time it was possible to use Y as an implicit show window value; the subsequent ShowWindow() was ignored). If an overlapped window uses CW_USEDEFAULT for initial X and Y the width and height of the window created is such that width = screen width – initial X and height = screen height – initial height. Another reason for using overlapped windows is that WS_OVERLAPPEDWINDOW can save some typing!

☐ Popup Windows

A popup window is more or less the same as an overlapped window, ie. it is a top level window. A dialog box built as a WS_POPUP window is indistinguishable from a dialog box built as a WS_OVERLAPPED window (unless you use SPY etc). This type of window was really there in the past to enforce a strategic desktop management system, ie. The desktop was tiled in Windows 1 – this was a *new* idea – other contemporary systems were using overlapping window arrangements and for whatever reason Microsoft decided to go for the tiled approach. It was further decided that dialog boxes should be free floating or overlapping windows, although owned, and thus the WS_POPUP style came into being. It was possible under Windows 1 to create your application using just popup windows but of course the system said that this should not be the case – that your main window should be WS_TILED (still defined in the 3.1 WINDOWS.H) and so no one bothered. Nowadays tiled, overlapped and popup really amount to the same thing and you can take your pick.

Nowadays they really amount to the same thing and you can take your pick (note that there are some small differences, for example, a WS_POPUP window shouldn't use CW_USEDEFAULT positioning defaults (Try setting an overlapped window's width to 0 when using CW_USEDEFAULT)).

Popups can be owned or free floating (a *magic cookie* as it is sometimes called). If they're owned they behave just like an owned overlapped window, ie. hiding the owner doesn't hide the owned window. We used to describe this relationship in terms of parental relationships, ie. we used to say a popup could have a parent or not; the API guide also used to encourage this to some degree, eg. specifying that a dialog box needed a parent window handle instead of a window handle of some owning window – this has now been corrected. We shouldn't use the term parent anymore as it describes a rather special relationship with regard to the third type of window – a child window. Unfortunately we still need to use parent when getting a handle to the owning window via GetWindowWord() (note that GetParent() will not work for any non-child window – see table coming up).

☐ Child Windows

Child Windows are always kinda owned windows and they also always have a parent. If you think of a parent window as an owner then a child is owned and has a parent – as a child is clipped to its parent the term owner seems more appropriate than parent (you have parents but exist entirely outside of them) – Oh well! From one of the early chapters of this book recall that a child window is not really the same kind of beast as either a popup or an overlapped window because it lives entirely within the client area of some donor window, ie. it is really a logical window that is no more than some piece of another window! Of course it is a real window in that it has a window handle and everything else that a fashionable window should have.

Child windows are typically materialised as controls in Windows programs although they can be used for other things (see dialog box chapter for a child window dialog box!) too of course; also controls don't have to be child windows, they could be overlapped windows! A Class doesn't/shouldn't place a requirement upon the window type chosen by you the programmer unless there's a really good reason for it. For example, should the push button class restrict the types of window that may be derived from it to be of type WS_CHILD window? After all, the push button has to have a parent/owner to inform whenever it gets clicked?? No of course it shouldn't – you can get a push button to tell just about anyone that it's been clicked (an example of just this, ie. a push button as a top level window is included in this chapter).

Child windows can usually overwrite any sibling window's client area, so can the parent of the child window(s). If you want to prevent one or the other (or both) check out the WS_CLIPSIBLINGS and WS_CLIPCHILDREN window styles in the programmer's reference.

OK, we've talked a little/about standard window's (types) and about changing them so let's get one with doing some wacky things with them like creating buttons that are WS_POPUP windows etc.

The first app we'll look at uses a POPUP window to replace the caption on another window!

Left aligned text - Weird Font!

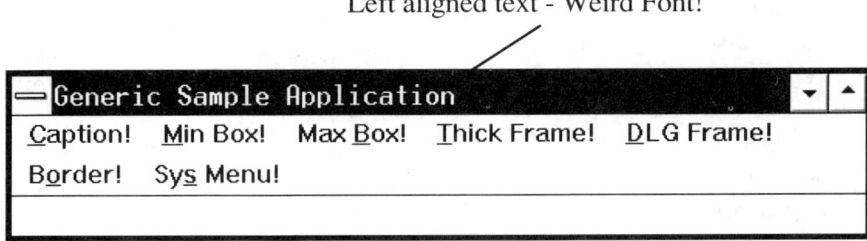

Caption window automatically re-sizing
as Sys menu etc are removed.

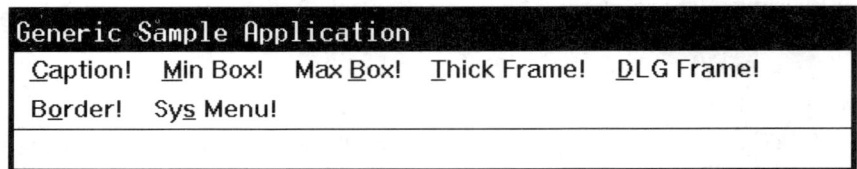

The two windows you see above are snapshots of the same application; the application is demonstrating two things. The first is the *style toggling* talked about earlier; the second is to do with the window's caption bar. Note that the caption text is firstly left justified and secondly that the actual font being used to draw the caption is a little different to normal. Here's another snapshot with a different font again :

Curious Font!

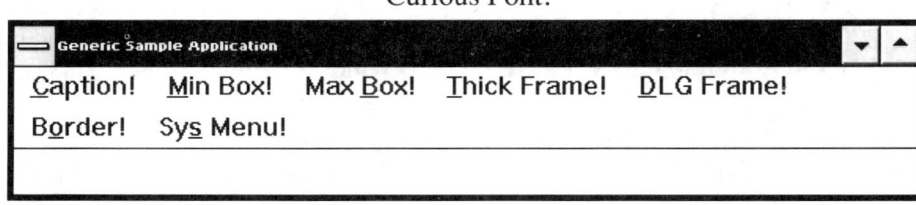

I call this the tiny caption font!

The caption is being modified in an interesting way. The caption – isn't! The caption of the generic application above has been replaced with a window; that window perfectly fits into the area occupied by the background window's caption and moves/resizes with it. I could have elected to change the background window's caption some other way – perhaps by processing its WM_NCPAINT message but I decided to do it the hard way instead (see the dialog box and miscellaneous chapters for code examples that demonstrates changing the non-client area on WM_NCPAINT handling. Also see the following note)! Doing it this way opens up some interesting areas for discussion and allows a much greater degree of object orientation to take place, ie. instead of having to change the background window(s) code all I have to do is to associate an instance of a *caption* window with an instance of a background window and presto, it's done. By doing it this way I've sort of PM-ised Windows a little; in Presentation Manager all the frame components of a window are in fact separate windows! This allows you to interact with them via the standard messaging system rather than, as in Windows, having to use a whole bunch of API calls.

There's quite a lot of code involved in producing this effect (relevant sections are shown just below); much more so than would have been needed to create a similar effect using WM_NCPAINT processing; as usual the actual app is a modified generic and is well documented; it should therefore require little further discussion :

> An aside :
> Note: To re-paint any window's non-client area using the **WM_NCPAINT** message should ideally be achieved as follows.
>
> - Handle the WM_NCPAINT message.
> - Get DefWindowProc() to paint in those areas that you don't want to paint.
> - Paint in those areas that you want to paint.
>
> Step 2 requires that you mask off those window style bits that describe those areas or components of a window that you want to paint. For example, say you wanted to paint in the system menu yourself. You could get DefWindowProc() to paint in everything apart from the system menu by removing the system menu temporarily from your window. You do this by toggling the window's WS_SYSMENU style bits (dwStyle ^= WS_SYS-MENU). You then call DefWindowProc(). When DefWindowProc() returns, you paint in the required component (find out the components size etc using GetSystemMetrics()) and switch back on the sysmenu style bits (dwStyle ^= WS_SYSMENU). See discussion later in this chapter about sub-classing windows for more on this kind of thing.

Taken from top of main source.

```
#define CAPTION_MAX          255
#define UM_DOCAPTION         WM_USER

LRESULT __export CALLBACK lCaptionProc
(
    HWND
  , UINT
  , WPARAM
  , LPARAM
);
```

Taken from the source code *Init* routines.

```
/*
** New Class for caption popup window.
*/
wc.style            = NULL;
wc.lpfnWndProc      = (WNDPROC)lCaptionProc;
wc.cbClsExtra       = 0;
wc.cbWndExtra       = 0;
wc.hInstance        = hInstance;
wc.hIcon            = NULL;
wc.hCursor          = LoadCursor(NULL, IDC_ARROW);
wc.hbrBackground    = NULL;
wc.lpszMenuName     = NULL;
wc.lpszClassName    = "GenericPopWClass";

return RegisterClass(&wc);
...
...


/*
** Create the popup caption window as an owned popup of the main window.
*/
hWnd = CreateWindow(
                    "GenericPopWClass"
                    ,""
                    ,WS_POPUP /* Just plain popup style required.    */
                    ,0        /* Created as any size - resized later. */
                    ,0
                    ,0
                    ,0
                    ,hWnd1    /* Owner (parent) window is the main window.*/
                    ,NULL
                    ,hInstance
                    ,NULL
                    );
if(!hWnd)
{
  return FALSE;
}
...
...
```

```
/*
** Show and update after main window's shown etc.
*/
ShowWindow(hWnd, nCmdShow);
UpdateWindow(hWnd);
```

Taken from main window's WndProc

```
/*
** These messages have an inmpact on the owned popup -
** signal the popup that it should do its stuff.
*/
case WM_NCPAINT:                            /* Fall Thru. */
case WM_ACTIVATE:                           /* Fall Thru. */
case WM_WINDOWPOSCHANGING:                  /* Fall Thru. */
case WM_SETTEXT:
    SendMessage(hWnd2, UM_DOCAPTION, 0, 0L);
    return DefWindowProc(hWnd, uMessage, wParam, lParam);
    break;
```

Complete code for CaptionProc – class call-back for caption window.

```
LRESULT __export CALLBACK lCaptionProc
(
  HWND     hWnd
 ,UINT     uMessage
 ,WPARAM   wParam
 ,LPARAM   lParam
)
{
  switch(uMessage)
  {
          /*
          ** If we get focused we should give it to our owner window.
          */
      case WM_SETFOCUS:
          SetFocus((HWND)GetWindowWord(hWnd, GWW_HWNDPARENT));
          break;

          /*
          ** Essentially being told to move our a*s to a new location
          ** as the owner window has been moved etc.
          */
      case UM_DOCAPTION:
          {
              /*
              ** Holds the device position of the owner window.
              */
              auto RECT         rsOwnerWindow;

              /*
              ** System sizes of - resizable/non-resizable borders
              ** Caption and window bitmaps.
              */
              auto int          nYCaptionHeight;
              auto int          nXBorder;
```

```
        auto int        nYBorder;
        auto int        nXFrame;
        auto int        nYFrame;
        auto int        nXIcon;

        /*
        ** Widths of Minimize Box, Maximize Box and System Menu
        ** icons based upon  owner window's  window style bits.
        */
        auto int        nMinWidth;
        auto int        nMaxWidth;
        auto int        nSysWidth;

        /*
        ** Owner, window handle and window style holders.
        */
        auto DWORD      dwOwnerStyle;
        auto HWND       hWndOwner;

/********** code start. **********/

        /*
        ** Get all the required system metrics stuff needed to
        ** calculate size and position of caption in owner.
        */
        nYCaptionHeight = GetSystemMetrics(SM_CYSIZE);
        nXIcon          = GetSystemMetrics(SM_CXSIZE);

        nXBorder        = GetSystemMetrics(SM_CXBORDER);
        nYBorder        = GetSystemMetrics(SM_CYBORDER);
        nXFrame         = GetSystemMetrics(SM_CXFRAME);
        nYFrame         = GetSystemMetrics(SM_CYFRAME);

        /*
        ** Get required owner window info - handle and
        ** window style bits.
        */
        hWndOwner    = (HWND)GetWindowWord(hWnd, GWW_HWNDPARENT);
        dwOwnerStyle = GetWindowLong(hWndOwner, GWL_STYLE);

        /*
        ** Get widths  of  Minimize  Box,  Maximize Box  and
        ** System Menu dependant upon whether or not they're
        ** attached (visible) to the owner window.
        */
        nMinWidth = dwOwnerStyle & WS_MINIMIZEBOX ? nXIcon : 0;
        nMaxWidth = dwOwnerStyle & WS_MAXIMIZEBOX ? nXIcon : 0;
        nSysWidth = dwOwnerStyle & WS_SYSMENU     ? nXIcon : 0;

        /*
        ** Find out where owner window is on the device.
        */
        GetWindowRect(hWndOwner, &rsOwnerWindow);

        /*
        ** Size and position popup so that it exactly fits
        ** into caption area of owner window.
```

```
                */
               SetWindowPos(
                          hWnd

                          ,NULL

                      /* Left */
                          ,rsOwnerWindow.left +
                          nXFrame              +
                          nSysWidth            +
                          nXBorder

                      /* Top */
                          ,rsOwnerWindow.top  +
                          nYFrame

                      /* Width */
                          ,rsOwnerWindow.right-
                          rsOwnerWindow.left  -
                          2 * nXFrame         +
                          nXBorder            -
                          nMinWidth           -
                          nMaxWidth           -
                          nSysWidth

                      /* Height */
                          ,nYCaptionHeight

                          ,SWP_NOZORDER |
                          SWP_NOACTIVATE
                          );
           /*
           ** Now let's paint it. Don't do an UpdateWindow() following
           ** the InvalidateRect() or we'll paint ourselves active!!
           */
           InvalidateRect(hWnd, NULL, TRUE);
       }
       break;

       /*
       ** Gotta paint ourselves - could  be coz we're changing
       ** the active state of the owner window and not because
       ** we're invalid in anyway.
       */
case WM_PAINT:
       {
           /*
           ** Stuff for BeginPaint().
           */
           auto HDC          hDC;
           auto PAINTSTRUCT  ps;

           /*
           ** Used in Rectangle() and DrawText() - hold client
           ** area size.
           */
           auto RECT         rsPopupClient;
```

```
            /*
            ** Pen and Brush for drawing.
            */
            auto HPEN        hP;
            auto HBRUSH      hB;

            /*
            ** Holds caption off owner window.
            */
            auto char        carBuff[CAPTION_MAX];

            /*
            ** Owner, window handle.
            */
            auto HWND        hWndOwner;

/********** Code Start **********/

            /*
            ** Get a DC.
            */
            hDC = BeginPaint(hWnd, &ps);

            /*
            ** Get owner window handle.
            */
            hWndOwner = (HWND)GetWindowWord(hWnd, GWW_HWNDPARENT);

            /*
            ** Get its caption and get our popup's client area
            ** dimensions.
            */
            GetWindowText(hWndOwner, &carBuff[0], sizeof(carBuff));
            GetClientRect(hWnd, &rsPopupClient);


            /*
            ** Create a pen and  a  brush suitable  for drawing into
            ** and on the caption; set the text color - do all  this
            ** depending upon the system colors selected.
            */
            hB = CreateSolidBrush(
                             GetActiveWindow() == hWndOwner    ?
                             GetSysColor(COLOR_ACTIVECAPTION)  :
                             GetSysColor(COLOR_INACTIVECAPTION)
                             );
            hP = CreatePen(
                     PS_SOLID
                    ,NULL
                    ,GetActiveWindow() == hWndOwner    ?
                     GetSysColor(COLOR_ACTIVECAPTION)  :
                     GetSysColor(COLOR_INACTIVECAPTION)
                     );
            SetTextColor(
                     hDC
                    ,GetActiveWindow() == hWndOwner  ?
```

```
                            GetSysColor(COLOR_CAPTIONTEXT)    :
                            GetSysColor(COLOR_INACTIVECAPTIONTEXT)
                       );

/*
** Show thru text selected.
*/
SetBkMode(hDC, TRANSPARENT);

/*
** Select new pen and brush - keep handles to old ones.
*/
hB = SelectObject(hDC, hB);
hP = SelectObject(hDC, hP);

/*
** Select a stock font - no need to keep handle of old
** font as new font  is a  stock  object  and does not
** require deletion after use.
*/
SelectObject(hDC, GetStockObject(ANSI_VAR_FONT));

/*
** Erase popup.
*/
Rectangle(
         hDC
        ,rsPopupClient.left
        ,rsPopupClient.top
        ,rsPopupClient.right
        ,rsPopupClient.bottom
        );

/*
** Draw in owner window's caption text.
*/
DrawText(
         hDC
        ,&carBuff[0]
        ,-1
        ,&rsPopupClient
        ,DT_LEFT          |
         DT_VCENTER       |
         DT_SINGLELINE
        );

/*
** Re-select old pen and brush; delete newly created ones.
*/
DeleteObject(SelectObject(hDC, hB));
DeleteObject(SelectObject(hDC, hP));

/*
** Release DC.
*/
EndPaint(hWnd, &ps);
```

```
        }
        break;

    case WM_NCHITTEST:
        return HTTRANSPARENT;

    default:
        return DefWindowProc(hWnd, uMessage, wParam, lParam);
    }
}
```

Explanation.

A new Windows' class is registered, it's called GenericPopWClass. This new class will be our caption class. A window created from this class should be a popup owned window. The owning window's caption will become obscured by a window of this class. A GenericPopWClass window tries to behave just like a caption bar but with two small differences; firstly, the text in the caption bar is left aligned (specified with a DrawText() flag and so easily modified), and secondly, the font used to draw the title bar text is changeable (see snapshots above). The class window procedure for windows of GenericPopWClass is lCaptionProc. This call-back function handles just four messages explicitly :

- **WM_NCHITTEST**
- **WM_PAINT**
- **WM_SETFOCUS**
- **UM_DOCAPTION**

The WM_SETFOCUS handler simply passes the focus on to the owner window so that whenever the popup is focused or activated it's the main window to which it is attached that eventually receives the focus.

The WM_NCHITTEST handler simply returns HTTRANSPARENT, this effectively makes the window appear as though it isn't there to mouse input (A similar effect could have been achieved using CreateWindowEx()). If the window procedure ignored this message you would not be able to move, or activate the main window by dragging or clicking on the caption window – not a good idea (or maybe it's just what you've been looking for?)! The caption, which is really a window, would swallow up all relevant input messages and they'd be lost to the main window. A WM_NCHITTEST message is passed to a window containing the cursor whenever the mouse pointer is moved (or if a click occurs), DefWindowProc() processes positional information contain in the message and from it generates the appropriate mouse message; for example, if we click in our caption window (which is all client area) DefWindowProc() would normally return HTCLIENT, ie. the click occurred in the client area; from this, Windows (the sender of the WM_NCHITTEST message) would send us a WM_LBUTTONDOWN message. By returning HTTRANSPARENT the actual click event is passed to any window that's beneath our caption window (that's our owner's *real* caption) and DefWindowProc() returns HTCAPTION, from there on in the mouse action is interpreted as though the caption on the owner window were being directly manipulated.

An Aside.

By using hit test results you may modify the standard windows' behaviour. For example, you could easily change the type of cursor displayed, say, when the mouse pointer's hot-spot position coincides with that of the caption. The WM_SETCURSOR message is sent to a window after a WM_NCHITEST message has been handled. The result of the hit test message is passed in the message's lParam (LOWORD) (the HIWORD contains a mouse message ID). If, say, the hit test code were HTCAPTION (cursor over caption) you could change the cursor to anything you like and return TRUE. By checking the mouse message ID also you could, say, change the cursor just when someone clicks in the caption area. See discussion of a standard window's behaviour later in this chapter. Talking about HTCAPTION – here's a question. How can the user move a window without a caption? Easy, use HTCAPTION. Let's say you've created a window without a caption and want the user to be able to click and drag the window to a new location. All you have to do is – return HTCAPTION when the user clicks (and holds down) the left mouse button in the window's client area! Have you seen all those nice small windows and captions that everyone's doing now (like the toolbox in Visual Basic), all done by drawing what looks like a caption and a system menu in a window's client area and then returning the correct HT code when the mouse is over it! See the Perf-Meter application in the Miscellaneous chapter for an example of how to do this.

The paint message handler paints the caption bar. The caption bar background should be coloured COLOR_ACTIVECAPTION or COLOR_INACTIVECAPTION according to whether or not the owning window is currently the active window. The colour used for the caption text should similarly be coloured COLOR_CAPTIONTEXT or COLOR_INACTIVECAPTIONTEXT. The actual colour values are set by the user typically by using the control panel. We obviously want to mimic their colour choice so we need to get those colour values whenever we re-paint the caption. The complete caption is drawn using Rectangle() and DrawText(); you could use PatBlt() to speed up the drawing of the caption bar then paint in the text using DrawText() – I've experimented with both ways and the speed difference is not noticeable to the human eye however. Of course you could paint the caption any colour you like – maybe NOT the normal caption and text colours, it would certainly make your windows stand out! You could decide to put a bit map in here, or some animation – anything is possible of course as long as you can do it in a window.

Real programmers do it behind an open window.

The *docaption* message is a private message passed from the owner window to the owned caption window, it essentially says— 'Hey, reposition yourself cos I've changed/moved'. The owner window sends this message to the caption bar window whenever it handles any of the following messages :

- **WM_NCPAINT**
- **WM_ACTIVATE**
- **WM_WINDOWPOSCHANGING**
- **WM_SETTEXT**

Any of these messages may signal a change in the location or state of the window – we therefore need to know about the change. For example if the main window's caption text gets set we (the caption) need to know about it. The docaption handler causes the caption to repaint – no big deal. Note that these messages also fall through to DefWindowProc() so that it can do some default processing (not all them need to go to DefWindowProc() but it was easier to code it this way!).

Note that there's no need, in the caption bar class proc, to handle a WM_SYSCOL-ORCHANGE. Windows causes any window that is affected by a change in the current system colours to re-paint itself automatically.

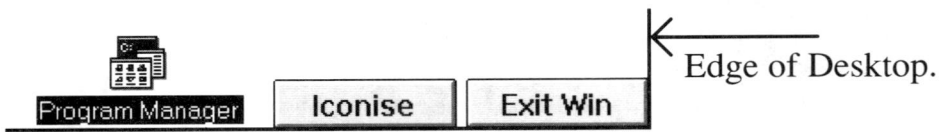

Edge of Desktop.

Controls attached to Desktop Window!

Top level window controls.

The snapshot above shows a very small section of my desktop (lower right corner of the desktop is shown). This is the next app following our windowing theme that we shall look at.

The application creates two push button controls as POPUP windows! These popup controls are owned by the desktop window and signal it – via the usual WM_COM-MAND mechanism whenever they are clicked. The application sub-classes the desktop window to pick up these button clicks and processes them. If you click on the Iconise button any overlapped window not already shown as an icon gets iconised. If you click the Exit Win button – guess what, you exit windows (no *are you sure* box is shown).

The application is very small, just a few lines of code in fact; the reason for this is that the real work is done by a DLL. Now you might not be familiar with DLLs yet so don't worry about the DLL itself and why it's done like this, ie. not in the main application. If you're one of those people that can't live with not knowing, you'd better skip on to the DLL section now!

Essentially the DLL is there so that we can sub-class the desktop; and that's something else we haven't talked about yet (I touched on this in the dialog chapter) so let's do a good job of it now.

☐ Sub-classing

Each class in Windows is maintained by a *class window procedure* (a class doesn't process messages, the class window procedure address is simply a place holder). An instance of the class (a window) is also, by default, looked after by that same class window procedure.

Each type of object, class and window, is materialised in Windows as a data structure. The programmer/class designer can allocate extra storage space for the class/window by allocating *extra* words via the cbWndExtra, cbClsExtra members of the WNDCLASS structure. By using the Window's APIs Get/Set – Window/Class – Long/Word the programmer may access these internal data structures which include, at this level, any extra class or window words allocated by him or her. When a class is registered the address of a window procedure must be given to the registration routine via a WNDCLASS structure member called lpfnWndProc. This member should be thought of as defining not just a window procedure but a class window procedure, ie. the window procedure that will maintain all instances of the class (windows created from the class). When an individual window is derived from the class, Windows copies the address of the class window procedure defined in the internal class structure to the window structure created for the window. The window procedure address for the window is, not surprisingly, now the same as the class window procedure address.

An application wishing to modify a window's behaviour can do so by substituting its own window procedure for a given window's default window procedure (any such sub-classing procedure should ideally be placed in a DLL). This, on a *per window basis*, is called *standard sub-classing*. As we've just heard, the mechanism by which this kind of thing is achieved is related to the window words of the window being sub-classed.

The window words of a window contain a lot of information about the window, its window style, its instance (the one given in its CreateWindow() call) and, most usefully, its window procedure address (a copy of the class window procedure address). It looks kinda like the diagram on the next page.

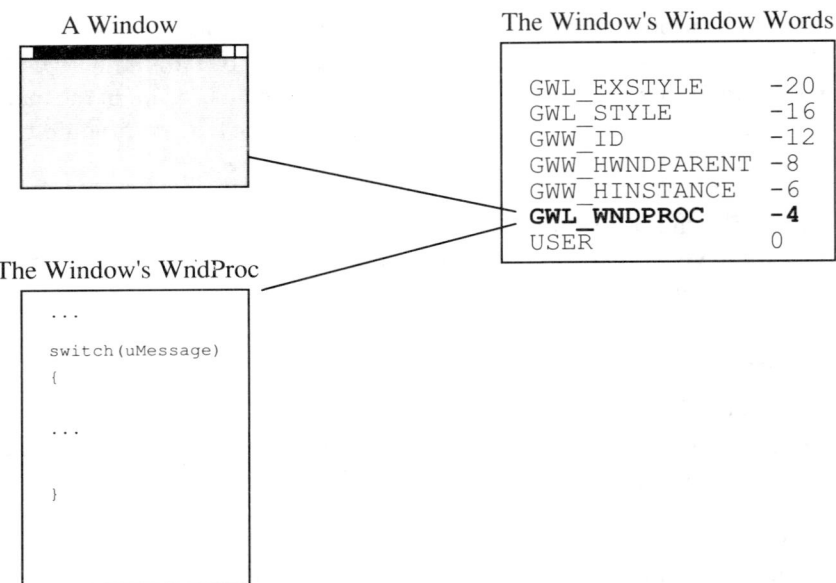

A Window

The Window's Window Words

The Window's WndProc

Every time a window's window procedure is required to handle a message, Windows gets the address of the relevant window procedure from the window's window words and calls the function to handle the message. Changing the address in the words (GWL_WNDPROC) so that it points to another window procedure means that we can change the way in which the window is managed.

Of course, unless you want to do <u>all</u> of the message processing and message management for this window you will have to keep the address of the original window procedure to hand -- you'll pass this *old* procedure any messages that you don't handle, or at least want some class specific handling for; this is very much like chaining an interrupt handler under DOS.

A sub-classing window procedure therefore works by changing the sub-classed window's words so that the window procedure address contained therein *points* to some other window procedure; in turn that new procedure maintains the address of the old window procedure so that it may pass on any messages for which it requires standard class processing to be carried out – the diagram above can now be re drawn to show this mechanism in place (message flow starts from the window and potentially ends at the DefWindowProc() black hole) :

Now, if the window below were a push button which was owned by the desktop it would pass any notification messages on to, naturally enough, the desktop window. The desktop window would of course ignore them and pass them on to DefWindowProc(). We want to *get in the way* of the desktop window's default handling (which is to ignore WM_COMMAND messages) and change it so that these buttons do something useful. By sub-classing the desktop window we get the push button's notification messages before the desktop window's standard window procedure can throw them away by passing them on to DefWindowProc().

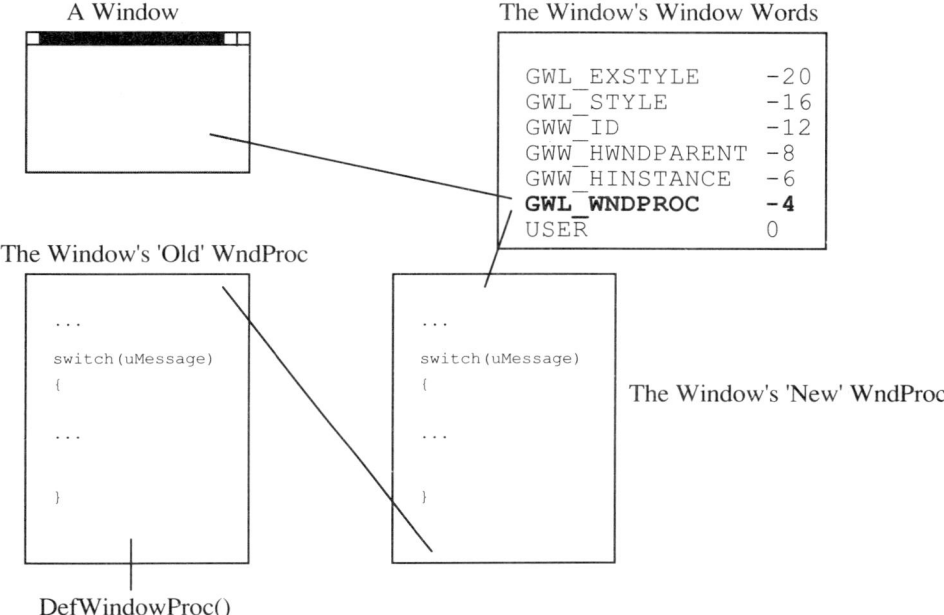

Sub-classing classes

It is possible, although a seldomly used technique, to sub-class an entire class of window (this shows up a little clearer when considering GetClassInfo() super-classing – see below), indeed, this can also be thought of as super-classing.

The class has a structure that is similar to that maintained for a window, ie. a class has a set of *class words* which are similar to those maintained by Windows as window words for any instance of a window which has been created. A class's words contain information such as the class style, the class icon used, the class menu used and the address of the class window procedure (this was discussed briefly towards the start of this chapter), in fact more or less anything specified in the WNDCLASS structure used when the class was registered.

When a class is instanciated (a class window is created) its window words receive a copy of some of this data, in particular the address of the window procedure associated with the class at the time the window was created. By changing the window procedure address given in the class's words any new window created from the class will be implicitly sub-classed (note that this *new* control could also be said to be super-classed as it is sub-classed in its type definition (class) and before it is even created) :

The Class's Class Words

```
GCW_STYLE            -26
GCL_WNDPROC          -24
GCW_CBCLSEXTRA       -20
GCW_CBWNDEXTRA       -18
GCW_HMODULE          -16
GCW_HICON            -14
GCW_CURSOR           -12
GCW_HBRBACKGROUND    -10


USER                   0
```

In the diagrams shown above *USER* shows the boundary between standard words and those allocated by changing the cbWndExtra and cbClsExtra members of a WNDCLASS structure – see note earlier about how changes in these affect new and existing windows/classes; also see dialog box manager stuff in dialog box chapter.

☐ Super-Classing & GetClassInfo().

The one problem with sub-classing (on the per-window level) is that it is impossible to intercept the window creation messages passed to a window as it is created because the window has to be in existence before it can be sub-class, ie. you access its words via its window handle. If it is in existence then it must have been created already. If it's been created already it's already handled its creation messages. This in essence is what super-classing is all about – changing the behaviour, or other basic properties, of an abstract entity prior to it being assembled.

Super-classing, like *class sub-classing* cures this problem by changing the class window procedure rather than the window instance window procedure, ie. the class's words rather than those of any particular window instance created from it and changed. In traditional super-classing you create a new class that replaces an old (existing class); this technique is talked about further in the dialog chapter when it is shown just how easy it is to add an icon to the existing dialog box class (for a task). Creating a new class may mean simply affecting the behaviour or properties of an existing class – isn't this process of change the same as defining a new data type?

The technique requires that you first discover all that is known about some existing class – Windows 3.0 & 3.1 has a function called GetClassInfo() which can be used for this purpose. The class information is then modified so that the class's name, window procedure and instance are changed (you cannot register a new class with the same name as an old class unless you want to override a global class locally – see dialog box chapter). You keep the old class window procedure pointer safe somewhere as it will be required later (a good place to keep it is in some extra class words). Any new window (within the task using this technique), which would have been created from the old class, is now changed so that it is created from the new class (change class-name used in CreateWindow() etc). The new class describes the same class styles etc as the old class but has a new class window procedure specified, ie. its behaviour is now defined by the message handling in two window procedures.

Windows gives each new window instance of this class a copy of this window procedure address. That new *class* window procedure will now be called as the window procedure for any window created from the class that has not since been sub-classed at the window instance level. The new class window procedure passes on any messages that it is not interested in (and maybe some that it is) to the old class window procedure.

These two (GetClassInfo() and Sub-classing a class) super-classing techniques are in fact slightly different and really before any explanations are offered we need another term. In the following discussion the term *hook* is a generic term meaning to change the window procedure address of a window or a class.

Sub-classing a class super-classing (!) will cause ALL <u>new</u> windows of an existing class to be hooked, ie. if you hook the *button* class, all new buttons created by ANY task will be implicitly sub-classed. This does provide you with enormous power over all new buttons but it also means that for day to day sub/super classing you've sub/super classed every button (not already created) in the system! On the other hand, in your application it means that any window built from the standard button class is hooked. The downside of this is that anyone maintaining your code will expect a window created from the button class to be handled by the real button class class-procedure. It also means that your hook function handles an awful lot of message traffic. Also, to sub-class the class requires that you create a window of the class to be hooked before you can hook it. Usually a button (or whatever) is created, SetClassLong() is used on the window handle of the newly created button to hook the class, and then the button is destroyed – having to instantiate an object in order to apply sub-classing class super-classing is a little messy.

Using the GetClassInfo() method of super-classing means that you cannot hook system classes (unlike the class sub-classing method). You cannot override a system class using RegisterClass() – if you re-register, say, *button*, RegisterClass() won't fail but you'll have registered a class called *button* that is valid only for button class objects created within your task (or if you registered the class in a DLL, whatever task/hInstance was using the DLL when the class got registered); all your new buttons (old ones left unhooked) will be hooked, but any new buttons in other tasks will not be. You don't have to handle the whole system's button traffic however as you've only hooked your task's buttons, nor do you have to create a button in the first place in order to hook the class – GetClassInfo() uses a class name, rather than a class instance (a window) to do its work. GetClassInfo() super-classing is typically used to modify the behaviour of an existing system class within a task. For example, you may wish to modify the edit class to, say, prevent the user pasting the clipboard contents into it using Shift + Insert.

In brief this is what each of the methods described above give you :

Sub-classing – the ability to change the behaviour of a single window created from any class (global or local). Requires a window be created so that it may be sub-classed.

Sub-classing a class super-classing – the ability to change the behaviour of any class (system or local) and therefore any window created from it. Requires that an object of the class be created as the technique uses SetClassLong() which in turn requires an existing window. Only objects created after the class is hooked are affected.

GetClassInfo() super-classing – the ability to change the behaviour of a system or global class within a single task only. Does not require a window on which to work. A new or existing class name may be given for the class. If the name is new than a new class is created (possibly global) that inherits its behaviour from the old class. If an existing class name is given (existing class must therefore be global) then a new local class is created. Any window created from the class within the task is hooked; existing class windows are not hooked.

Given all this I still prefer the Windows sub-classing class super-classing technique to the GetClassInfo() super-classing technique if I need to modify a global class – just a matter of personal choice.

Of course, if you are using the GetClassInfo() technique to change the behaviour of a standard Windows' class this is fine as a local class can have the same name as a global class. However, only windows created from this standard class and from within this Windows' task will use the *new* class, any standard class window created in any other tasks will continue to use the original class/window window procedure for its handling. By changing the class words (of a standard class say) you can modify the behaviour of any yet to be instanciated window (existing standard class windows remain unaffected as they're using a copy of the original class window procedure address given to them when they were created.

Another way to super-class, or is that sub-class, is to use a *Windows' hook*; these are discussed later in this chapter.

☐ A final word on sub-classing, *You Sub-class all the time*

Whenever we build a Windows' application we employ sub-classing.

Windows describes the behaviour of a standard window object by providing DefWindowProc() – if you like this is the default class WndProc. Likewise a dialog box has DefDlgProc() to define its standard behaviour. DefDlgProc() is a sub-classing procedure as it, in turn, uses DefWindowProc() to handle messages that it itself doesn't handle. Some of these standard behaviours are certainly interesting (some are useless and positively need to be modified). Take for instance DefDlgProc(). A dialog box created without a call-back, or with one that does nothing except return FALSE, essentially creates a useless dialog box. If such a dialog box had a button in it, pressing the button would have no effect, ie. the standard behaviour for a dialog box window is to ignore WM_COMMAND input – neither DefDlgProc() nor DefWindowProc() process it in any default way! DefWindowProc() on the other hand can be used to create a perfectly good and useful window all by itself. If you've never tried this, just return DefWindowProc() from any WS_OVERLAPPED window call-back function – you'll find that the window can be closed down, resized, gets painted, iconises etc all by itself – you can even use DefWindowProc() as your class's lpfnWndProc directly if you like!

So when we program for Windows we essentially program by describing the differences between some standard behaviour and the required behaviour, ie. we decide to handle some messages in our window procedure rather than pass them on to DefWindowProc(). The window-procedure/sub-classing mechanisms for changing a window's behaviour becomes very similar to the methods employed to do exactly the same thing in object oriented languages like C++. I think this is one of the main reasons that Windows' programmers take to OOT like the proverbial duck to water – it's natural for them to do so.

It is also possible to *get in back of* the standard behaviour in order to modify it, ie. sub-class (modify) it after it's done! Take for example (again!) the handling of a WM_NCPAINT message. You might want to handle one of these to, say, change the look of the system menu in your application. If you handle the WM_NCPAINT message, instead of DefWindowProc(), you have to re-paint ALL of the non-client area; no small job. What you do instead is pass the WM_NCPAINT message to DefWindowProc(), letting it do all the re-painting, and on its return (DefWindow-Proc's) you over-paint the system menu area (see earlier note that explains this process in a little more detail)! In this way you're still modifying the standard look', and to some degree the standard behaviour', but you're letting the standard handler do most of the work. You can do this with any super/sub classing hook, ie. let the original have a crack at handling the message before you do (of course it doesn't make sense to <u>always</u> allow the old proc handle the message first – but you could).

By applying all of these techniques things can become a little confusing; you could for example have a GetClassInfo() super-classed class that is globally sub-class via its class words – a window created from the super class can also be sub-classed at the window level by changes made to its window words – its behaviour could further be changed by *in-windowproc* code that allows the code that follows the window procedure to handle an event before it does. you now start finding yourself saying 'Who's handling the paint message Man'!

OK, so now we know what sub-classing does for our buttons which were introduced above : let's take a look at the code involved in making this small application/DLL – first the modified generic 'C' code :

```
#define STRICT

#include <windows.h>

/*
** Turn off silly warnings.
*/
#pragma warning(disable:4100)
#pragma warning(disable:4001)

/*
** Private message ID.
*/
#define UM_UNSETPROC   WM_USER + 1

#define VOID_ARG
#define VOID_RETURN

extern BOOL __export FAR PASCAL bInitControls
(
   VOID
);

/*********** Code Start *************/

int PASCAL WinMain
(
   HINSTANCE     hInstance
  ,HINSTANCE     hPrevInstance
  ,LPSTR         lpszCmdLine
  ,int           nCmdShow
)
{
    auto MSG msg;

    if(hPrevInstance != NULL)
    {
       return 0;

    }
    else

    /*
    ** Create control windows and sub-class the desktop.
    */
    if(bInitControls(VOID_ARG) == FALSE)
    {
       return 0;
    }

    /*
    ** Wait for WM_QUIT message.
    */
    while(GetMessage(&msg, NULL, 0, 0))
    {
       TranslateMessage(&msg);
```

```
        DispatchMessage(&msg);
    }

    /*
    ** Got WM_QUIT message - now un-subclass the desktop.
    */
    SendMessage(GetDesktopWindow(), UM_UNSETPROC, 0, 0);

    return msg.wParam;
}
```

Essentially, this application calls just one exported DLL function – bInitControls. It then waits for a message – the only one it's likely to receive (for itself) is the WM_QUIT message as it does not explicitly create any windows; however the DLL code does and the application's queue will contain messages for those control windows (in the same way as a dialog box or message box does).

When the application is terminated it sends a message to the desktop window. This user defined message tells the desktop that it should be un-sub-classed; we'll see in a moment that it is our code (in the DLL) that processes this message. Of course the application has a def file, make file etc but these are quite standard so to avoid wasting space I've omitted them. Let's look at the DLL code now :

The DLL main code module :

```
#define STRICT

#include <windows.h>

/*
** Turn off silly warnings.
*/
#pragma warning(disable:4100)
#pragma warning(disable:4001)

/*
** Control and message IDs.
*/
#define ID_ICON        20001
#define ID_EXIT        20002
#define UM_SETPROC     WM_USER
#define UM_UNSETPROC   WM_USER + 1

#define VOID_ARG
#define VOID_RETURN

#define APIENTRY CALLBACK

/*
** The width of the buttons.
*/
#define CONTROL_WIDTH 100

BOOL __export APIENTRY bInitControls
(
```

```
   VOID
);

HINSTANCE NEAR PASCAL hGetSetInstance(HINSTANCE);

LRESULT __export CALLBACK fpNewDeskProc
(
   HWND
  ,UINT
  ,WPARAM
  ,LPARAM
);

VOID NEAR PASCAL vDoIconise(VOID);

VOID NEAR PASCAL vDoExit(VOID);

BOOL __export CALLBACK bEnumProc
(
   HWND      hWnd
  ,LPARAM   lParam
);

/********** Code Start ************/

/*
** Saves DLL's instance/module handle.
*/
HINSTANCE NEAR PASCAL hGetSetInstance(HINSTANCE hInst)
{
   static HINSTANCE hInstance;

   if(hInst != NULL)
   {
       hInstance = hInst;
   }

   return hInstance;
}


/*
** Minimal LibMain() DLL entry point - see other
** section on DLLs for explanation.
*/
BOOL FAR PASCAL LibMain
(
   HINSTANCE   hInstance
  ,WORD        wDataSeg
  ,WORD        wHeapSize
  ,LPCSTR      lpszCmdLine
)
{
   if(wHeapSize != 0)
   {
      UnlockData(0);
   }
```

```
    hGetSetInstance(hInstance);

    return TRUE;
}


/*
** Called by app. Creates controls on desktop
** then sub-classes the desktop.
*/
BOOL __export APIENTRY bInitControls(VOID)
{
    /*
    ** Handles to  desktop and any newly
    ** created control (used twice here).
    */
    auto HWND hWndDesktop;
    auto HWND hWndControl;

    /*
    ** Get desktop handle, used in setting control's owner.
    ** Note that the HWND_DESKTOP constant would work just
    ** as well.
    */
    hWndDesktop = GetDesktopWindow();

    /*************************************************************
    *
    * Control creation follows  - create controls so that they
    * are positioned bottom  right  hand corner of the screen.
    * NOTE: As these controls are POPUP windows we cannot give
    * them an ID in the create window call.
    *
    */


    /*
    ** Now create first POPUP push button  - use CreateWindowEx()
    ** so that we can keep the control on top of everything else.
    */
    hWndControl = CreateWindowEx(
                                 WS_EX_TOPMOST
                                 ,"BUTTON"
                                 ,"Iconise"
                                 ,WS_POPUP | BS_PUSHBUTTON
                                 ,GetSystemMetrics(SM_CXSCREEN) -
                                 2 * CONTROL_WIDTH             -
                                 5
                                 ,GetSystemMetrics(SM_CYSCREEN) -
                                 GetSystemMetrics(SM_CYCAPTION)
                                 ,CONTROL_WIDTH
                                 ,GetSystemMetrics(SM_CYCAPTION)
                                 ,hWndDesktop
                                 ,NULL
                                 ,hGetSetInstance(NULL)
                                 ,NULL
                                 );
```

```
if(hWndControl == NULL)
{
    return FALSE;
}

/*
** Give the window an ID.
*/
SetWindowWord(hWndControl, GWW_ID, ID_ICON);

/*
** Show and update it.
*/
ShowWindow(hWndControl, SW_SHOWNORMAL);
UpdateWindow(hWndControl);

/*
** Now create second POPUP push button  - use CreateWindowEx()
** so that we can keep the  control on top of everything else.
*/
hWndControl = CreateWindowEx(
                        WS_EX_TOPMOST
                        ,"BUTTON"
                        ,"Exit Win"
                        ,WS_POPUP | BS_PUSHBUTTON
                        ,GetSystemMetrics(SM_CXSCREEN) -
                        1 * CONTROL_WIDTH
                        ,GetSystemMetrics(SM_CYSCREEN) -
                         GetSystemMetrics(SM_CYCAPTION)
                        ,CONTROL_WIDTH
                        ,GetSystemMetrics(SM_CYCAPTION)
                        ,hWndDesktop
                        ,NULL
                        ,hGetSetInstance(NULL)
                        ,NULL
                        );

if(hWndControl == NULL)
{
    return FALSE;
}

/*
** Give the window an ID.
*/
SetWindowWord(hWndControl, GWW_ID, ID_EXIT);

/*
** Show and update it.
*/
ShowWindow(hWndControl, SW_SHOWNORMAL);
UpdateWindow(hWndControl);

/*
** Now sub-class the desktop. Send the desktop window
** a message telling it we've subclassed it - our new
```

```
        ** proc picks up  this message.  The message contains
        ** the old proc address that the new proc stores.
        */
        SendMessage(
                    hWndDesktop
                    ,UM_SETPROC
                    ,0
                    ,(LPARAM)SetWindowLong(
                                        hWndDesktop
                                        ,GWL_WNDPROC
                                        ,(LONG)fpNewDeskProc
                                        )
                    );

        return TRUE;
}




/*
** Sub-class procedure for desktop window.
*/
LRESULT __export CALLBACK fpNewDeskProc
(
   HWND     hWnd
  ,UINT     uMessage
  ,WPARAM   wParam
  ,LPARAM   lParam
)
{
    /*
    ** Old proc address - keep in case we need to restore it later.
    */
    static WNDPROC fpOldDeskProc;

    switch(uMessage)
    {
        case UM_SETPROC:
            /*
            ** First message this sub proc receives - sent as
            ** the desktop is subclassed. Old proc address is
            ** passed in lParam. Keep it safe in static.
            */
            fpOldDeskProc = (WNDPROC)lParam;
            break;

        case UM_UNSETPROC:
            /*
            ** Being closed so un-hook the desktop, ie. restore
            ** the old proc address kept safe in static.
            */
            SetWindowLong(hWnd, GWL_WNDPROC, (LONG)fpOldDeskProc);
            break;

        case WM_COMMAND:
```

```
                /*
                ** Desktop receives click - sent by popup buttons.
                */
                if(HIWORD(lParam) == BN_CLICKED)
                {
                    switch(wParam)
                    {
                        case ID_ICON:
                            /*
                            ** Iconise button clicked.
                            */
                            vDoIconise(VOID_ARG);
                            break;

                        case ID_EXIT:
                            /*
                            ** Exit button clicked.
                            */
                            vDoExit(VOID_ARG);
                            break;
                    }
                }
                break;

                /*
                ** Pass any un-processed messages on to the real
                ** desktop proc.
                */
        default:
                return CallWindowProc(
                                        fpOldDeskProc
                                      ,hWnd
                                      ,uMessage
                                      ,wParam
                                      ,lParam
                                      );
                break;
    }

    return (LRESULT)0;
}


/*
** Iconises all overlapped windows.
*/
VOID NEAR PASCAL vDoIconise(VOID)
{
    /*
    ** Enumerate all windows to bEnumProc.
    */
    EnumWindows((WNDENUMPROC)bEnumProc, MAKELPARAM(0,0));

    /*
    ** After windows have been iconised make sure that
    ** the desktop icons are nicely arranged.
    */
    ArrangeIconicWindows(GetDesktopWindow());
```

```
   return VOID_RETURN;
}



/*
** Exits Windows without the 'Are You Sure' box showing up.
*/
VOID NEAR PASCAL vDoExit(VOID)
{
   ExitWindows(0L, 0);

   return VOID_RETURN;
}



/*
** This enum proc will iconise any overlapped window.
*/
BOOL __export CALLBACK bEnumProc
(
   HWND    hWnd
  ,LPARAM  lParam
)
{
   /*
   ** The style of the enumerated window.
   */
   auto DWORD dwWindowStyle;

   /*
   ** Flag set to TRUE if window (hWnd) is not a child or a
   ** popup window.
   */
   auto BOOL  bOkToMin;

   /********* Code Start *********/

   /*
   ** Get window style from incoming window.
   */
   dwWindowStyle = GetWindowLong(hWnd, GWL_STYLE);

   /*
   ** Check  window  style  so that only OVERLAPPED windows' handles
   ** are passed on to CloseWindow() - Although the SDK programmer's
   ** reference says 'This function  has  no  effect  if  the  hWnd
   ** parameter identifies a popup or child window' it's wrong!
   **
   ** EnumWindows() doesn't  enumerate child  windows so the check's
   ** just for popup windows.
   */
   bOkToMin = (dwWindowStyle & WS_POPUP) == 0;

   /*
   ** If the window's an overlapped window, is visible and is not
   ** already iconic make it an icon.
   */
```

```
   if(bOkToMin && IsWindowVisible(hWnd) && (IsIconic(hWnd) == FALSE))
   {
       CloseWindow(hWnd);
   }

   /*
   ** Keep the enumeration going.
   */
   return TRUE;
}
```

The DLL WEP source code :

```
#include <windows.h>

/*
** Minimal WEP() DLL exit point - see other
** section on DLLs for explanation.
*/
BOOL FAR PASCAL WEP (int nSystemExit)
{
    switch(nSystemExit)
    {
       case WEP_SYSTEM_EXIT:
           break;

       case WEP_FREE_DLL:
           break;
    }

    return TRUE;
}
```

The makefile :

```
# Decide whether or not to include debug information
!IFDEF DEBUG
CCDEB    =        -Zi
LKDEBUG =         /CO
!ELSE
CCDEB    =
!ENDIF


# Macro defines
RC              =        -r -v
CC              =        cl -G2 -c -W4 -WX -AMw -GDs -Od -Zpe $(CCDEB)
LINK            =        link /NOD $(LKDEBUG) $(OBJ)
OBJ             =        libentry.obj deskbutt.obj wep.obj
WEPDEPEND       =        $*.c makefile
DESKBUTTDEPEND  =        $*.c makefile
LIBENTRYDEPEND  =        $*.asm
RESDEPEND       =        $*.rc
LINKDEPEND      =        $(OBJ) $*.def $*.res


all: deskbutt.dll
```

```
# Build deskbutt.OBJ
deskbutt.obj: $(DESKBUTTDEPEND)
    $(CC) $*.c

# Build WEP.OBJ
wep.obj: $(WEPDEPEND)
    $(CC) $*.c

# Build LIBENTRY.OBJ
libentry.obj: $(LIBENTRYDEPEND)
    masm -Mx $*,$*;

# Build deskbutt.RES
deskbutt.res : $(RESDEPEND)
    rc $(RC) $*.rc

# Build deskbutt.DLL
deskbutt.dll: $(LINKDEPEND)
    $(LINK) , $@,$*.map, libw mdllcew, $*.def

# Attach resources to dll
    rc -v $*.res $@

# Build dll import lib
    implib $*.lib $*.def
```

The DLL .def file :

```
LIBRARY        DESKBUTT

EXETYPE        WINDOWS 3.1

PROTMODE

DESCRIPTION    'Button Controls DLL.'

STUB           'WINSTUB.EXE'


CODE           LOADONCALL    DISCARDABLE MOVEABLE
DATA           PRELOAD       SINGLE

SEGMENTS       WEP_TEXT      FIXED         NONDISCARDABLE PRELOAD
               DLLSHELL_TEXT       MOVEABLE DISCARDABLE   LOADONCALL
               _TEXT               MOVEABLE DISCARDABLE   LOADONCALL
               INIT_TEXT           MOVEABLE DISCARDABLE   LOADONCALL

HEAPSIZE  0

EXPORTS
    WEP               @1 RESIDENTNAME
    fpNewDeskProc     @2
    bInitControls     @3
    bEnumProc         @4
```

Explanation:

The main section of 'C' code is called via the bInitControls function – this is called by the application. The DLL code creates two windows in this function. They're built from a standard class – *BUTTON* but they're interestingly WS_POPUP windows. There's nothing to stop you doing this, ie. there's nothing within the standard button class that is dependant upon a window created from the button class being a child window (see following point however). In the two CreateWindow() calls I couldn't give the controls a child ID as you would normally do with buttons; as when any non-child window is created the value given for this parameter is interpreted as a handle to a menu – we don't want to have menus on your buttons (!) so this is set to NULL. We still need the controls to carry meaningful IDs however so these are poked into the control window's words using SetWindowWord(). I could have created the controls as child windows but they would have been obscured by any window whose position conflicted with that of the buttons (everything is higher than the desktop (and any child windows of the desktop) in the Z order list). I wanted to have these buttons always show through so that you could tidy the desktop (by clicking Iconise) or whatever without having to dig down for these controls through numerous windows that were simply stacked in the way!

The controls are created as owned popups – the owner window handle is obtained from GetDesktopWindow() – note that using HWDN_DESKTOP (or 0) would have produced exactly the same effect. I used CreateWindowEx() which allows us to specify some extra stylistic features. Here I have chosen to create the controls so that they stay on top of every other window that isn't also a *top most* window (if any other top most window's position clashed with the control's positions, which ever window is activated will come to the top). Of course this required the absence of a control ID at creation time (as they're popups).

After the two controls are successfully created, and given IDs, the desktop window is sub-classed so that another DLL function can pick up any notification messages from the buttons.

```
SendMessage(
        hWndDesktop
        ,UM_SETPROC
        ,0
        ,(LPARAM)SetWindowLong(
                        hWndDesktop
                        ,GWL_WNDPROC
                        ,(LONG)fpNewDeskProc
                        )
        );
```

This piece of code sub-classes the desktop and at the same time (immediately after it is sub-classed) sends the desktop window a message telling it that it has been sub-classed – that message will be picked up by our new desktop proc as we've already sub-classed it (as part of the evaluation of the expression used as the lParam value in the message)! The message (UM_SETPROC) contains the address of the old desktop window procedure in its lParam (returned by SetWindowLong()); this is stored in the sub-classing proc. Note that HWND_DESKTOP would not produce the same effect here! :

```
case UM_SETPROC:
    /*
    ** First message this sub proc receives - sent as
    ** the desktop is subclassed. Old proc address is
    ** passed in lParam. Keep it safe in static.
    */
    fpOldDeskProc = (WNDPROC)lParam;
    break;
```

fpOldDeskProc is a static variable. This is quite a nice way to subclass as it saves on global data and puts the responsibility/handling of the sub-classing details with the object (whose behaviour is determined by its window procedure chain), ie. the object, via our new window procedure, knows how to maintain the address of the old window procedure, and it surely should be that way, – we simply let it get on with it!

The other user message sent to the desktop is sent from the main application – this tells the new desktop window procedure to un-subclass itself by resetting its window words. This kinda breaks what I just said above but as the desktop window is always the last one to be destroyed (and our app may go before it does) there's very little that can be done about it.

The buttons now appear on the newly sub-classed desktop. When the either button is clicked we pick that up in the new desktop window procedure, ie. the button's messages come through our task's message queue :

```
case WM_COMMAND:
    /*
    ** Desktop receives click - sent by popup buttons.
    */
    if(HIWORD(lParam) == BN_CLICKED)
    {
        switch(wParam)
        {
            case ID_ICON:
                /*
                ** Iconise button clicked.
                */
                vDoIconise(hWnd);
                break;

            case ID_EXIT:
                /*
                ** Exit button clicked.
                */
                vDoExit(VOID_ARG);
                break;
        }
    }
    break;
```

Any non-relevant message is passed on to the old desktop window procedure pointed to now by fpOldDeskProc:

```
default:
      return CallWindowProc(
                            fpOldDeskProc
                          ,hWnd
                          ,uMessage
                          ,wParam
                          ,lParam
                          );
```

The support functions vDoExit and vDoIconise actually *do* very little :

```
VOID NEAR PASCAL vDoIconise(VOID_ARG)
{
   /*
   ** Enumerate all windows to bEnumProc.
   */
   EnumWindows((WNDENUMPROC)bEnumProc, MAKELPARAM(0,0));

   /*
   ** After windows have been iconised make sure that
   ** the desktop icons are nicely arranged.
   */
   ArrangeIconicWindows(GetDesktopWindow());

   return VOID_RETURN;
}
```

This function essentially has to start a window enumeration off. The enum function does most of the work :

```
BOOL __export CALLBACK bEnumProc
(
   HWND     hWnd
  ,LPARAM   lParam
)
{
   /*
   ** The style of the enumerated window.
   */
   auto DWORD dwWindowStyle;

   /*
   ** Flag set to TRUE if window (hWnd) is not a child or an
   ** overlapped window.
   */
   auto BOOL  bOkToMin;

   /********* Code Start **********/

   /*
   ** Get window style from incoming window.
   */
```

```
    dwWindowStyle = GetWindowLong(hWnd, GWL_STYLE);

    /*
    ** Check  window  style  so that only OVERLAPPED windows' handles
    ** are passed on to CloseWindow() - Although the SDK programmer's
    ** reference says 'This function  has  no  effect  if  the  hWnd
    ** parameter identifies a popup or child window' it's wrong!
    */
    bOkToMin = BOOL(((dwWindowStyle & WS_POPUP) == 0) &&
                    ((dwWindowStyle & WS_CHILD) == 0)
              )
                      ;

    /*
    ** If the window's an overlapped window, is visible and is not
    ** already iconic make it an icon.
    */
    if(bOkToMin && IsWindowVisible(hWnd) && (IsIconic(hWnd) == FALSE))
    {
        CloseWindow(hWnd);
    }

    /*
    ** Keep the enumeration going.
    */
    return TRUE;
}
```

EnumWindows() enumerates all top level windows, we're only interested in over-lapped windows, ie. we should only call CloseWindow() (Iconises a window) with window handles of WS_OVERLAPPED styled windows. CloseWindow()'s documen-tation says that if it is passed a child/popup window handle it ignores it – Ignore it!!

The other support function is really tiny :

```
VOID NEAR PASCAL vDoExit(VOID)
{
   ExitWindows(0L, 0);

   return VOID_RETURN;
}
```

ExitWindows() does the whole thing!

OK, we saw earlier that Windows registers and maintains several *private* classes for various things such as building menus and creating dialogs etc; these beg the following question to be asked – 'can these be used to do something useful?'. The answer is a resounding 'yes they can'! Let's look at an example of using a built in Windows' class to add functionality to your applications.

There's also an application called *Stacks* elsewhere in this book that shows you how to sub-class a window.

☐ Super-Sub-classing.

Windows allows you to intercept events such as keyboard and mouse messages that would otherwise be passed to an application; the intercepting application gets them first and decides whether or not to pass them on (modified or not). Such an interception facility is called a Windows' hook. A task that sets a hook is said to be installing a filter, indeed, the function within the intercepting application is called a filter function. Filter/Hook types are detailed below and more fully in volume 2 of the programmer's reference.

Filter functions are installed in a chain of installed filter functions, the last one installed is placed at the beginning of the chain and is the first to be called, ie. it is the first to intercept events. Each filter function decides whether or not to pass intercepted events on to other filter functions further on down the chain; if they decide not to pass the event on they must handle the event themselves. If you've ever installed an interrupt handler under DOS you've used the DOS equivalent of a filter function. The most recently installed interrupt handler gets called and decides whether or not to pass on the interrupt to *old* handlers further on down the chain. Some filters may also be set so that they are task, rather than system based, ie. they intercept events only for a particular task rather than for the system as a whole, this facility, by and large, is a new 3.1 feature.

Hooks are extremely powerful, by using them it is possible to change the meaning of a message and therefore cause deliberate misinterpretation of the message in the receiving task etc, indeed they are sometimes considered too powerful in that they can be used to malevolently conspire against the system and other resident tasks. It is unclear as to whether or not Windows NT (or even future versions of 16 bit Windows) will continue to allow such powerful hooks due to security restrictions. For example, in all current versions of Windows, it is possible to intercept keystrokes, even if those keystrokes represent somebody's password as entered in, say, an edit field (even one with the ES_PASSWORD style); this will obviously not be permitted in more secure versions of Windows!

Windows' hooks have changed between Windows 3.0 and 3.1 – they've become easier to use, more powerful and more plentiful. Here's a list of the types of hook you can set in 3.1:

WH_CALLWNDPROC

Installs a window-procedure filter. A hook of this type is called whenever the SendMessage() API is called. The hook function gets the message, and may process it, before the intended recipient does. Note that the interception takes place before any task switch occurs. The filter function is informed, via a parameter, whether or not it is the current task that is calling SendMessage(). The hook may be set so that it has task or system scope. See WH_GETMESSAGE for a way to pick up *posted* messages.

WH_CBT

Installs a computer-based training (CBT) filter. One of the most powerful hooks. Such a hook function is called before completing a system command, removing a mouse or keyboard event from the system message queue, setting the input focus, synchronising with the system message queue, and before activating, creating, destroying, minimising, maximising, moving, or sizing a window; . The hook may be set so that it has task or system scope. An example of setting a hook below shows a CBT hook in use.

WH_DEBUG

Installs a debugging filter. The debug filter function is called before Windows calls any type of installed filter function, ie. this filter is a kind of hook hook! It's intended to be used only in debuggers. The hook may be set so that it has task or system scope.

WH_GETMESSAGE

Installs a message filter. The message filter function is called whenever an application has called either GetMessage() OR PeekMessage() and will retrieve a message, ie. the calling task's task message queue contains a message. A GetMessage() hook is similar to a WH_CALLWNDPROC hook, the former is used to intercept *posted* messages while the latter is used to intercept sent messages. The hook may be set so that it has task or system scope.

WH_HARDWARE

Installs a non-standard hardware-message filter. This is similar to WH_GETMESSAGE in that it hooks into the API GetMessage() and PeekMessage() functions. This type of hook however only filters so called hardware events. A hardware event is initiated usually by an input type device driver for any non-standard hardware devices, eg. a pen used in pen computing. The hook may be set so that it has task or system scope.

WH_JOURNALRECORD

Installs a journaling record filter. This type of filter is used in applications that need to record events such that when they are played back some process may be automated, an example of an application that uses such a hook is the macro recorder that comes with 3.1. The filter function is called whenever Windows removes an event from the system queue; this means they are called for all mouse and keyboard events. The hook may be set so that it has system scope only.

WH_JOURNALPLAYBACK

Installs a journaling playback filter. The counterpart of WH_JOURNALRECORD, ie. it is this filter's responsibility to play back those events that have been recorded previously with a record hook. The hook may be set so that it has system scope only.

WH_KEYBOARD

Installs a keyboard filter. This filter is called whenever the GetMessage() or PeekMessage() functions are about to return a message that contains a keyboard event

(WM_KEYUP, WM_KEYDOWN, WM_SYSKEYUP, WM_SYSKEYDOWN, WM_CHAR). It is used primarily in *hot key* type applications that must react whenever a certain combination of keyboard keys are pressed. The hook may be set so that it has task or system scope.

WH_MOUSE

Installs a mouse-message filter. This filter is called whenever the GetMessage() or PeekMessage() functions is about to return a message that contains a mouse event such as WM_MOUSEMOVE, WM_LBUTTONDOWN etc.

WH_MSGFILTER

Installs a message filter. This filter is called whenever a message is retrieved for a menu, dialog box, scrollbar or message box. The filter only works for items created in the hooking task. The hook may be set so that it has task scope only.

WH_SYSMSGFILTER

Installs a system-wide message filter. Same as WH_MSGFILTER above except that the hook has system scope. The hook may be set so that it has task or system scope.

The filter function chain in 3.1 is maintained by Windows itself and not by installing/installed filter functions as was the case in 3.0 and earlier versions of Windows. This prevents disruption of the chain by errant applications and filter functions ('you should never break the chain – sounds like a song!). It also allows for greater performance, as control of the chain is in Windows, and easier chain management from the point of view of the filter function. Some hooks in 3.1 may also be installed on a per task basis, again reducing system overhead, ie. an application wishing to filter, say, keyboard events no longer has to filter them for the entire system when all it's interested in is filtering them for a given task. Task filters also allow applications to place the filter function within the task's code rather than within a DLL, again a saving on complexity. Lastly, task hooks will continue to work in future versions of Windows that would otherwise preclude their use as a system hook for security reasons.

In 3.1 Windows maintains a table of table pointers. Each entry in the first table, called the internal hook table, is a pointer to a table of pointers to filter functions of a given type. For example in the diagram below we can see that the first entry in the internal hook table points to another table, the table pointed to details filter functions of type WH_DEBUG. That second table is also a table of pointers but instead of pointing to other tables these pointers point to installed filter functions. The table is time-ordered, ie. the first entry is a pointer to the most recently installed filter function that was set using :

SetWindowsHookEx(WH_DEBUG, ...).

That's what this looks like in 3.1 .

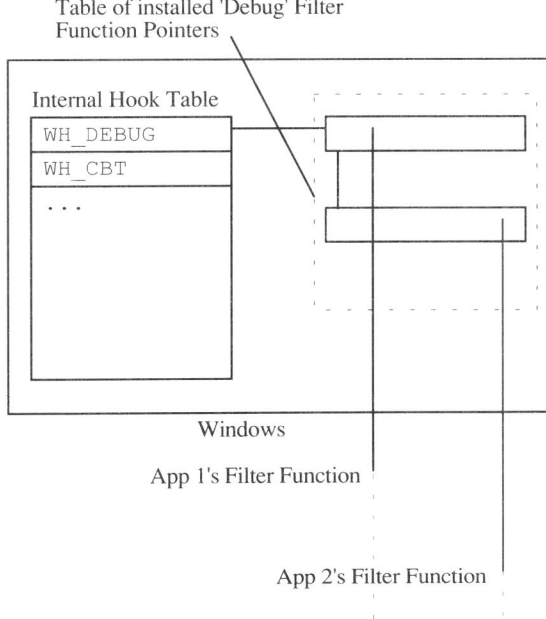

Table of installed 'Debug' Filter
Function Pointers

Internal Hook Table

WH_DEBUG

WH_CBT

. . .

Windows

App 1's Filter Function

App 2's Filter Function

Previously (3.0) app1
would pass events to app2

When Windows needs to call the installed filter functions it starts with the one that is at the top of the table and works through the list (note that you cannot tell where in the table you are, ie. you cannot say that your filter function will always be called first unless it has just been installed. This is one reason why many programmers remove and re-install hooks throughout their programs, ie. it is to ensure that they are at the head of the filter function list and to, in the case of a system wide hook, improve global performance).

A filter function has to tell Windows to call the next hook in the chain by calling CallNextHookEx(); it passes to this function its own hook handle plus those parameters which it was passed. Windows checks the hook handle against the table to determine the address of the next filter function in the chain and calls it. There is another way to stop Windows calling other filter functions which are further down the chain than you – return 1!

When a filter function returns 1 it's usually interpreted by Windows as *don't pass this event on or allow it to happen*. For example, a computer based training hook is informed when a window is about to be created. It can prevent this from happening by returning 1. If it returns 1 there is no point in Windows calling functions further along in the filter chain – It will only confuse them as their return value is now not significant (another way of wording this is to say, 'who's return value is significant'? – it's ambiguous!); also the overall state of the system hasn't changed, ie. no new Window has been created so again the later filters do not need to know about the event.

Consider what may happen however if the first filter wants the window to be created but allows other filter functions to be called, ie. it is passed HCBT_CREATEWND and doesn't return 0 but instead does a – return CallNextHookEx(...).

This could be dangerous, here's an example of why! Your filter function may be maintaining, say, a table which contains the window handles of all current windows. It would initially populate this table by using, say, EnumWindows(). Thereafter it would *watch* for HCBT_CREATEWND and HCBT_DESTROYWND notification codes. Each notification can be interrogated to determine the window handle of the window which is being created or destroyed so you can effectively maintain your table of current windows. However, if you pass the code on (as you should if you don't mind the event taking place) then a later CBT filter function may return 1 signalling that the creation/destruction has been denied. If you've returned CallNextHookEx() without testing its value you'll be unaware of this and your table will now contain an invalid window handle!

The earlier diagram shows how in 3.1 Windows itself maintains a table of filter function pointers. You'll remember that the first filter function pointer points to the most recently installed function. 3.0 hooks worked in very much the same way except that the filter function pointer table was distributed amongst filter functions themselves. As in 3.1, a 3.0 app in the chain was responsible for passing events on down the chain. Additionally it was also responsible for maintaining that next filter's address, ie. each filter function maintained the address of the next filter in a static variable. If an app half way down the chain wanted to get out Windows passed negative nCode values down the chain in order to *fix up* the previous filter function's pointer to the next function in the chain! Any negative value passed to you as a filter signalled to you that you should pass it straight back to Windows via a call to DefHookProc().

Note that even when using SetWindowsHook() in 3.1 that the filter function chain is kept internally. Although DefHookProc() appears to be the same old function as it was in 3.0 there is a subtle difference with it. Apparently, I haven't checked this out BTW, the last parameter to DefHookProc() is ignored, ie. the address of the next filter function stored in your program's DS is ignored! In 3.1 Windows knows who called DefHookProc() – it was the filter function that Windows has just called. When a filter calls DefHookProc() Windows knows that the next filter function in the chain must now be called – if it knew who it had just called, it can work out who to call now! The bottom line of this is that the address of the next filter function, which has been stored in a static variable, can become out of date at any time and must not be relied upon to have any special significance! The golden rule then is to return either 0 or 1 (or whatever's required to show that you've handled the event) to handle the event and cause it not to be passed on to later filter functions OR return CallNextHookEx() if you don't intend to handle the event. If you keep track of things in your code but don't handle an event watch the return value of CallNextHookEx() to see how any later filter handled it. Lastly, never call CallNextHookEx() and then return some other value to Windows.

In 3.1 the following functions are used to perform event filtering, ie. hooking :

SetWindowsHookEx()

Replaces SetWindowsHook() which although still available should no longer be used for pure 3.1 applications. SetWindowsHookEx() is the function that installs the filter function. It takes four parameters. The first is the hook ID, this is a code (see earlier) that specifies the type of hook being installed. The second parameter is the address of the filter function which may, depending upon whether or not the hook has task or system scope, reside in either a task or DLL. The third parameter is the instance handle of the module which contains the filter function; for DLLs this is the DLL's module handle. The last parameter is a task ID; if this is set to NULL the hook has system scope. The only other value that can be passed is a task handle – use GetCurrentTask() etc. The function returns a 32 bit value of type HHOOK, ie. a handle to a hook. If this value is zero (NULL) the hook couldn't be installed. This handle identifies your hook filter and is used in both UnhookWindowsHookEx() and CallNextHookProc().

UnhookWindowsHookEx()

Replaces UnhookWindowsHook() which although still available should no longer be used for pure 3.1 applications. UnhookWindowsHookEx() takes just one parameter, the hook handle returned by SetWindowsHookEx(). The function returns a BOOL which is FALSE if the hook couldn't be uninstalled.

CallNextHookEx()

Replaces DefHookProc() which although still available should no longer be used for pure 3.1 applications. This function is used to call the next filter function, for a given type of hook, in the internally maintained chain of filter functions. The function takes four parameters. The first is the hook handle returned by SetWindowsHookEx(); this identifies the current hook in the chain; Windows calls the next filter function in the chain if one exists. The second third and fourth parameters are those that were passed into the filter function, ie. nCode, wParam and lParam.

HookProc

This is your newly installed filter function which was set by calling SetWindowsHookEx(); HookProc is just a place holder – you can call your call-back functions anything you want to of course. It is called by Windows and unlike in 3.0 it is not responsible for maintaining, and calling directly, the address of the next filter function in the chain. All filter functions receive three parameters, the first is the hook code. The hook code specifies whether or not the filter function should process the event (being passed in another parameter) or simply pass it on by calling CallNextHookEx(). The second and third parameters contains information specific to the type of hook maintained by the filter function.

In 3.0 the filter function's first parameter could have a value that was less than zero, in that case it was required to immediately call the next filter function in the chain by calling DefHookProc(). In 3.1 filter functions <u>never</u> receive hook codes that are negative, indeed, if an app running under 3.1 but written so that it hooked using SetWindowsHook() passes a negative value to DefHookProc() Windows will fatal exit! These negative values were used in 3.0 to maintain the hook chain, ie. they were used when, say for example, a filter function was being removed from the centre of the chain.

The hook codes are hook specific – here's a list of them – Extract from WINDOWS.H:

```
/* Journalling hook codes */
#define HC_GETNEXT            1
#define HC_SKIP               2
#define HC_NOREMOVE           3
#define HC_NOREM              HC_NOREMOVE
#define HC_SYSMODALON         4
#define HC_SYSMODALOFF        5

/* Standard hook code */
#define HC_ACTION             0

/* Obsolete hook codes (NO LONGER SUPPORTED) */
#define HC_GETLPLPFN          (-3)
#define HC_LPLPFNNEXT         (-2)
#define HC_LPFNNEXT           (-1)
```

The best way to understand a hook is to see a simple one :

Hooker.c :

```
#define STRICT
#include <windows.h>

/*
** Turn off silly warnings.
*/
#pragma warning(disable:4100)
#pragma warning(disable:4001)

/*
** For accessing the HCBT_ACTIVATE's CBTACTIVATESTRUCT structure.
*/
typedef CBTACTIVATESTRUCT FAR* LPCBTACTIVATE;

/*
** Debug terminal output - must be enabled in DBWIN.EXE.
*/
#define DO(x) DebugOutput(DBF_TRACE | DBF_APPLICATION, x);




/*
** Stores module's instance handle.
*/
```

```
HINSTANCE NEAR PASCAL hAccesshInstance(HINSTANCE hInstance)
{
    static HINSTANCE hInst;

    if(hInstance != NULL)
    {
        hInst = hInstance;
    }

    return hInst;
}




/*
** Stores hook handle.
*/
HHOOK NEAR PASCAL hAccesshHook(HHOOK hHk)
{
    static HHOOK hHook;

    if(hHk != NULL)
    {
        hHook = hHk;
    }

    return hHook;
}




/*
** Filter function - installed as a CBT hook.
*/
LRESULT __export CALLBACK CBTProc
(
    int      nCode
  ,WPARAM   wParam
  ,LPARAM   lParam
)
{
    /*
    ** Because the programmer's reference says we should!
    */
    if(nCode < 0)
    {
        return CallNextHookEx(hAccesshHook(NULL), nCode, wParam, lParam);
    }

    /*
    ** nCode specific to hook type - why we're being called.
    */
    switch(nCode)
    {
        case HCBT_ACTIVATE:
```

```
            DO("Window about to become active");

            /*
            ** Use lParam as FAR pointer to structure detailed
            ** in WINDOWS.H.
            */
            if(((LPCBTACTIVATE)lParam)->fMouse)
            {
                DO("By a mouse action");
            }
            break;

    case HCBT_CLICKSKIPPED:
            DO("Mouse message removed from sys queue");
            break;

    case HCBT_CREATEWND:
            DO("Window about to be created");
            break;

    case HCBT_DESTROYWND:
            DO("Window about to be destroyed");
            break;

    case HCBT_KEYSKIPPED:
            DO("Keyboard message removed from sys queue");
            break;

    case HCT_MINMAX:
            DO("Window about to be zoomed or iconised");
            break;

    case HCBT_MOVESIZE:
            DO("Window about to be moved or sized");
            break;

    case HCBT_QS:
            DO("System handling a WM_QUEUESYNC message");
            break;

    case HCBT_SETFOCUS:
            DO("Window about to get focused");
            break;

    case HCBT_SYSCOMMAND:
            DO("System command about to be carried out");
            break;

    default:
            DO("Unknown nCode in hook proc");
            break;
    }

/*
** Ignore all nCodes, ie. allow - pass it on.
**
** HCBT_ACTIVATE
```

```
   ** HCBT_CREATEWND
   ** HCBT_DESTRYWND
   ** HCBT_MINMAX
   ** HCBT_MOVESIZE
   ** HCBT_SYSCOMMAND
   */
   return CallNextHookEx(hAccesshHook, nCode, wParam, lParam);
}




/*
** Standard libmain.
*/
BOOL FAR PASCAL LibMain
(
   HINSTANCE    hInstance
  ,WORD         wDataSeg
  ,WORD         cbHeapSize
  ,LPSTR        lpszCmdLine
)
{
   if(cbHeapSize > 0)
   {
       UnlockData(0);
   }

   return !!hAccesshInstance(hInstance);
}




BOOL __export FAR PASCAL StartHooker(void)
{
   /*
   ** Start hooking - install hook proc.
   */
   return hAccesshHook(SetWindowsHookEx(

                                        WH_CBT
                                       ,(HOOKPROC)CBTProc
                                       ,hAccesshInstance(NULL)
                                       ,NULL
                                       )
                   ) != NULL ? TRUE : FALSE;
}




BOOL __export FAR PASCAL StopHooker(void)
{
   /*
   ** Unhook hook proc.
   */
   return UnhookWindowsHookEx(hAccesshHook(NULL));
}
```

```
}




BOOL __export FAR PASCAL WEP(int bSystemExit)
{
    return TRUE;
}
```

Hooker.def :

```
LIBRARY    HOOKER

EXETYPE    WINDOWS 3.1

WINDOWSAPI

PROTMODE

CODE       PRELOAD MOVEABLE DISCARDABLE
DATA       PRELOAD SINGLE

HEAPSIZE  1024
STACKSIZE 0

EXPORTS
    WEP                @1 RESIDENTNAME
    CBTProc            @2 RESIDENTNAME
    STARTHOOKER        @3
    STOPHOOKER         @4

IMPORTS
    KERNEL._DebugOutput
```

Hooker.rc :

```
/* Nothing. */
```

The code above is used to create a small DLL. It demonstrates installing, using and removing a computer based training hook (CBTHook). The hook filter function, as it's a system hook, has been put into a DLL rather than an application. The DLL above exports CBTProc, which is the filter function, and two other functions (ignoring the WEP) called StartHooker and StopHooker; these install and remove the hook as required. Note that although the programmer's reference says that you should pass the address of the filter function through a call to GetProcAddress() that this is only required for libraries loaded explicitly with LoadLibrary(); there is a proviso even here however in that if the library installs its filter function a result of you calling another of its functions then GetProcAddress() is not required. So for example you could install the filter function when the DLL's LibMain() function is called. Please note that if you do this don't release the hook in the WEP. Despite what its says elsewhere in this book I have found that the DLL's DGROUP has been removed when a WEP has been called – funnily enough I have only noticed this in DLLs where filter functions are installed – there may be a connection!?

Any application may request that the DLL install/remove its filter function by calling either StartHooker or StopHooker – there's no checking in the code as to what order these functions are called in so please don't take it as a good robust example! StartHooker would be called, say, like this :

```
case WM_CREATE:
     if(StartHooker() == FALSE)
     {
       return (LRESULT)-1;
     }
     break;
```

StopHooker like this :

```
case WM_DESTROY:
     if(StopHooker == FALSE)
     {
     // Whatever...
     }
```

The DLL is used to display CBT *actions* on the debugging terminal (or DBWIN if you have it), a typical display looks like this :

```
t GENERIC     Window about to become active
t GENERIC     Window about to get focused
t GENERIC     System command about to be carried out
t GENERIC     Window about to be moved or sized
t GENERIC     System command about to be carried out
t GENERIC     System command about to be carried out
t GENERIC     Window about to be destroyed
t GENERIC     Window about to become active
t WINOLDAP    Windows about to get focused
t GENERIC     Window about to become active
t GENERIC     Window about to get focused
t GENERIC     System command about to be carried out
t GENERIC     System command about to be carried out
t GENERIC     Window about to be destroyed
t GENERIC     Window about to become active
t WINOLDAP    Window about to get focused
t GENERIC     Window about to become active
t GENERIC     Window about to get focused
t GENERIC     System command about to be carried out
t GENERIC     System command about to be carried out
t GENERIC     Window about to be destroyed
t GENERIC     Window about to become active
t WINOLDAP    Window about to get focused
```

The filter function returns either whatever CallNextHookEx() returns (nCode 0) or CallNextHookEx() meaning that the decision as to whether or not the action takes place is handed off to later filters (or the system if there are not other filters installed).

If necessary, the filter function may return 1 to cancel certain actions :

- **HCBT_ACTIVATE**
- **HCBT_CREATEWND**
- **HCBT_DESTROYWND**
- **HCBT_MINMAX**
- **HCBT_MOVESIZE**
- **HCBT_SYSCOMMAND**

Please note that some of these hooks seem a little buggy and you should therefore thoroughly test your code in order to ascertain that it does what you think it does – in a robust way. You should also test your code under the debugging environment as some *bugs* will only show up there in 3.1. Note that it is easy to say therefore, 'if they only show up in the debug build – why bother worrying about them?' The reason is that the next build (either 16 or 32 bit) might not be as happy to allow your program to run as the current release of 3.1 is! An example of where such things are not quite what they seem is in a CBTProc hook like the one shown above.

Whilst developing the example app I decided to *expand* upon some nCode processing to show how the code's parameters are used (I decided later to simplify this and took some handling back out! – after all, if you want a detailed example you could look in the \WINDEV\SAMPLES stuff!). A good nCode to expand would be HCBT_CREATEWND. The documentation says that when handling that code that lParam points to a CBT_CREATEWND structure. This structure looks like this :

```
/* HCBT_CREATEWND parameters pointed to by lParam */
typedef struct tagCBT_CREATEWND
{
    CREATESTRUCT FAR* lpcs;
    HWND       hwndInsertAfter;
} CBT_CREATEWND;

typedef CBT_CREATEWND FAR* LPCBT_CREATEWND;
```

As you can see, the lpcs member of this structure is a long pointer to a CREATESTRUCT structure that looks like this :

```
typedef struct tagCREATESTRUCT
{
    void FAR* lpCreateParams;
    HINSTANCE hInstance;
    HMENU     hMenu;
    HWND      hwndParent;
    int       cy;
```

```
    int      cx;
    int      y;
    int      x;
    LONG     style;
    LPCSTR   lpszName;
    LPCSTR   lpszClass;
    DWORD    dwExStyle;
} CREATESTRUCT;
```

So, if we wanted to, say, retrieve the class-name and caption text for a window that is about to be created we could access it via lParam. You might actually want to do this in a *real* CBT hook to, say, selectively allow the creation of certain types of window. The code above was expanded to display exactly that information, ie. the caption text and class-name of a window that was about to be created; guess what – it didn't work correctly. Occasionally I would see fatal exits on my debugging terminal, something to do with WVSPRINTF calling LSTRLEN with an invalid pointer! The pointer values were actually really bad! They weren't just slightly wrong, like they were really wrong. Most of the time they were 0x0000:0x0000!! Other times they were 0x0000:0x0032 etc. The common denominator was that the selector part of the long pointer was always zero – OOPS! Upon further investigation it turned out that the lpcs member of the CBT_CREATEWND pointed, sometimes, to an incomplete CREATESTRUCT, ie. sometimes lpszClass etc were not being filled in correctly! I had to modify the code to cope with this :

```
case HCBT_CREATEWND:
        DO("Window about to be created");
        {
            auto LPCBT_CREATEWND          CreateWndParam;
            auto LPCSTR                   lpszClass;
            auto LPCSTR                   lpszCaption;

            CreateWndParam = (LPCBT_CREATEWND)lParam;

            lpszClass   = CreateWndParam->lpcs->lpszClass;
            lpszCaption = CreateWndParam->lpcs->lpszName;

            /*
            ** Check for invalid selectors!
            */
            if(SELECTOROF(lpszCaption) == NULL)
            {
                lpszCaption = "Invalid Caption Name pointer!";
            }
            if(SELECTOROF(lpszClass) == NULL)
            {
                lpszClass = "Invalid Class Name pointer!";
            }

            DebugOutput(
                    DBF_TRACE | DBF_APPLICATION
                    ,"ClassName is -> %s"
                    ,lpszClass
                    );
```

```
            DebugOutput(
                        DBF_TRACE | DBF_APPLICATION
                        ,"Caption is -> %s\n"
                        ,lpszCaption
                        );

        }
        break;
```

Here we see that before using a pointer that we check its selector part to see if it's zero. If it is (its invalid) and we set the pointer to point to an error string. By using this modified code I produced the following output on the debugging terminal when running up a few of the SDK apps :

```
t SPY ClassName is -> Spy
t SPY Caption is -> Spy

t SPY ClassName is -> WPRINTF_10D6
t SPY Caption is ->
SPY = All OK


t DDESPY ClassName is -> DdeSpyWClass
t DDESPY Caption is -> DDESpy

t DDESPY ClassName is -> StringWindow
t DDESPY Caption is ->

t DDESPY ClassName is -> DMGClass
t DDESPY Caption is ->

t DDESPY ClassName is -> DMGMonitorClass
t DDESPY Caption is ->
DDE SPY = All OK


t HEAPWALK ClassName is -> HeapWalk
t HEAPWALK Caption is -> HeapWalker

t HEAPWALK ClassName is -> listbox
t HEAPWALK Caption is -> Invalid Caption Name pointer!
HEAPWALKER = ERRORS!


t DLGEDIT ClassName is -> DlgEdit
t DLGEDIT Caption is -> Invalid Caption Name pointer!

t DLGEDIT ClassName is -> Invalid Class Name pointer!
t DLGEDIT Caption is ->
.... lots more!!
DLGEDIT = ERRORS!
```

We can see from the output above that it is possible to access invalid CREATESTRUCT members, sometimes the class-name member is bad, sometimes the caption, and sometimes both are invalid. At the time of writing it is unclear as to what's going on here; Microsoft have confirmed this to be a *feature'*.

After further testing it seems as though the class-name problem can be tidied up a little. The icon title class, like all the other standard classes, hasn't got a name (in the traditional sense), ie. it's a system class so its class name is not a string but an atom! The icon title window is a window created from class #32772 (0x8004) and it looks as though what you get back in the CREATESTRUCT is an atom ID, which is 16 bits, squeezed into a 32 bit slot – result, one WORD of it is set to 0!!! When we do a SELECTOROF(lpszClass) we pick up the NULL word and BANG.

MAKEINTATOM is defined as :

```
#define  MAKEINTATOM(i)          ((LPCSTR)MAKELP(0, (i)))
```

and MAKELP is defined as :

```
#define MAKELP(sel, off)     ((void FAR*)MAKELONG((off), (sel)))
```

Note that in the case of using an atom ID for a class-name that the SELECTOR will be 0 therefore.

The solution is to *get* the offset part of the class-name pointer if the selector part is 0 and then to treat the offset part as an atom :

```
static carBuffer[BUFFER];

...

if(SELECTOROF(lpszClass) == NULL)
{
    GetAtomName(OFFSETOF(lpszClass), &carBuffer[0], sizeof(BUFFER));
    lpszClass = &carBuffer[0];
}
```

This works for the icon window class because the name of it is held in the global atom table. The control class (short versions / numbers – see dialog box chapter and dynamic dialogs for more on this) are kept in USER's local heap, ie. they don't seem to be atoms at all!! If the dialog box controls are created using these short names again the class name refers to an atom and once again BANG. The answer to this is to use the GetClassName() on the window handle passed in the wParam!

As this book goes to press it's still a mystery as to why window captions should sometimes be illegal.

◻ **Filter Functions and DLLs.**

Filter functions (except for those attached to application-specific hooks) should reside in a DLL for three reasons:

1. To support 3.0 real mode.

2. For compatibility with future versions of Windows.

3. Because SS is not equal to DS in a DLL.

In 3.0 real mode, Windows may swap entire inactive tasks (code and/or data) to expanded memory (EMS). Because filters are usually installed as system wide filters they must be available at all times. Windows will crash if an attempt is made to call a filter function that has been swapped to expanded memory! In 3.0 the only friendly way to ensure that the filter function was always available was to place the actual filter function inside a DLL. DLLs were <u>never</u> swapped to expanded memory. In 3.1, where real mode does not exist, filters may reside in an task's code instead of in a DLL's. However Microsoft recommends that you continue to site filter functions in DLLs to be compatible with future versions of Windows. The old EMS problem will not exist in future versions but protection of a task's code will, ie. its address space will be separated from that of any other task – this will create similar problems for task-based system filters. The bottom line is that filter functions will work correctly in future versions of Windows as long as they are situated in DLLs.

One other good reason for siting filters in a DLL is that when your filter's called it's called in the context of another task, ie. its stack will most likely not be that the hooking task, or more simply SS will not be equal to DS (also functions like GetCurrentTask() will not return a handle to the installing task – they return a handle to the task that has caused your filter function to be called). This of course is always the case in a DLL and so it is more natural to code filter functions as DLL functions; additionally the -A?w switch may be used to watch for silly programming errors when SS is not equal to DS.

◻ **All types of Menus – menus are windows.**

Windows 3.0 added an extra type of menu to the Windows' scene – trackable popup menus. These menus are *real* popups (as described by the term popup as it is used in nearly every GUI except Windows), ie. they popup rather than drop down – try and get used to calling menus attached to the menu bar drop downs and trackable menus popups – it will save a lot of time if we all use the same vocabulary! Windows now has – drop downs, popups, system menu drop downs, cascaded drop downs/popups, the task list (TASKMAN.EXE), single selection list/combo boxes and radio buttons to show mutually exclusive lists of things – unfortunately it still doesn't have scrollable menus (a list box is a kind of scrollable menu) and so we're left with menus on which only so much information can fit (this is why More Windows... is implemented as a list box) – and no, we're not going to create scrollable menus – yet.

It also lacks a type of menu found on most *X* (X Windows) machines and one variant of a standard menu that is to be found in IBM's Presentation Manager.

X systems usually implement what is called a *tear off* menu. A tear off allows you to literally tear a menu off, say, the menu bar and drag it to somewhere else on the desktop. This menu is then available without you having to go back to the menu bar – these are very useful especially if you can tear of a cascaded sub menu as it saves you having to navigate the cascaded sub menu every time you want something off a particularly important sub-menu. It might also be very useful to be able to tear off a window's system menu in this way.

Presentation Mangler also has a type of drop down menu that cannot be dismissed; menu items in a menu of this type are given a NODISMISS attribute when they are defined. When you select a no-dismiss item the window receives a WM_COMMAND message in the normal way but the menu is left hanging from the action rail (menu bar in PM).

> An Aside :
> You can implement crude non-dismissable menus in Windows by disabling (left un-greyed) all the items on a menu! Sounds odd I know but it works; of course the items no longer generate WM_COMMAND messages but they do still generate WM_MENUSELECT messages which are almost as good. To implement such menus in Windows doesn't just involve you processing WM_MENUSELECT messages however, no there's more to it than that, but the biggest thing that makes doing it this way undesirable or difficult to the point where you probably won't give it a try is that a disabled menu item cannot be a highlighted menu item. In other words to perfectly mimic such menus in PM the selected item should stay highlighted once selected. In Windows when you select a disabled menu item the highlight springs back from the current item to the top of the menu – called a park position. Now maybe you can live with this or maybe you feel that the last item shouldn't be left highlighted and that perhaps no highlight is shown at all. We might as well just have a look at how this might be done (there's no chapter on menus in this book so this'll have to do) before we get back to tear off menus!

Here's such a non-dismissable menu :

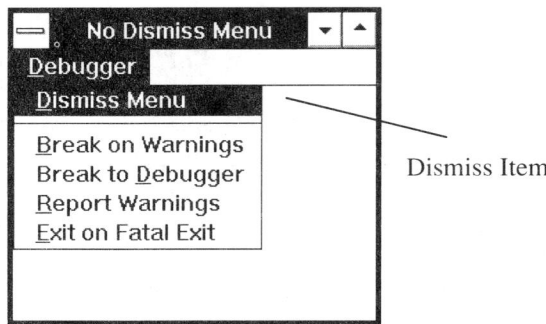

Dismiss Item

The item *Dismiss Menu* is a normal menu item. Selecting it makes the menu go away. Clicking on, or dragging over the items below the separator line will not make the menu go away. The very small piece of code behind this menu toggles a check mark either on or off against a selected menu item (apart from Dismiss Menu) :

Unfortunately you won't get a feel for this from the two static pictures above but the code is truly tiny so you could easily try this yourself; here's what's needed :

The menu resource.
Note that all the menu items, apart from the first is disabled (Inactive).

```
NODISMISS MENU
BEGIN

   POPUP         "&Debugger"
     BEGIN
       MENUITEM   "&Dismiss Menu",          IDM_DISMISS
       MENUITEM   SEPARATOR
       MENUITEM   "&Break on Warnings",     IDM_ONE,      INACTIVE
       MENUITEM   "&Break to Debugger",     IDM_TWO,      INACTIVE
       MENUITEM   "&Report Warnings",       IDM_THREE,    INACTIVE
       MENUITEM   "&Exit on Fatal Exit",    IDM_FOUR,     INACTIVE
     END

   END
```

Small section from main window's window procedure.

The WM_COMMAND handler handles just one message in this application, ie. the menu item with the ID of IDM_DISMISS – no other command message is received. All the other menu items are serviced by the WM_MENUSELECT handler. vProcessSelect is passed the handle of the menu being actioned and the ID of the item being selected. NOTE : it would be possible to have the WM_MENUSELECT handler also post the window a WM_COMMAND message – this would allow you to have all your menu handling in effectively one message handler.

```
case WM_MENUSELECT:
    if(wParam != IDM_DISMISS)
    {
        vProcessSelect((HMENU)HIWORD(lParam), wParam);
    }
    break;

case WM_COMMAND:
    switch (wParam)
    {
        case IDM_DISMISS:
            /*
            ** Nothing to do - menu is already dismissed.
            */
            break;

        /*
        ** The rest of your handlers in here.
        */

        default:
            break;

    }
    break;
```

Support function.
This Small function simply toggles the check status of the item whose ID is passed in wParam.

```
VOID vProcessSelect(HMENU hMenu, WPARAM wParam)
{
    if(hMenu != NULL)
    {
        auto BOOL bChecked;

/*
** Dragging across items causes selection! Need to really see if
** the mouse is down from one item to the next.
*/
        bChecked = GetMenuState(hMenu, wParam, MF_BYCOMMAND) & MF_CHECKED;

        CheckMenuItem(
                    hMenu
                    ,wParam
                    ,MF_BYCOMMAND | bChecked ? MF_UNCHECKED : MF_CHECKED
```

```
                              ) ;
          }
      }
```

This piece of code does a pretty poor job of creating a no dismiss menu and has some embarrassing short falls as it stands. For example, use the keyboard arrow keys to navigate your way through it and see what happens. Can you fix it – practical session time! Also, what happens if you click on the first no-dismiss item and then drag the cursor over the other items? P.S. These shortfalls could easily be fixed with some additional code and a half decent NODISMISS menu would result. You can do quite a nice implementation using a Window's hook – WH_MSGFILTER (see MessageProc() in 3.1 functions reference). See section on Windows' hooks above.

Getting back to the point. Wouldn't it be nice if we could have proper tear off and no-dismiss menus in Windows? Oh —go on, say it would!

Here's an application the implements *tear off* menus at work (a no-dismiss is just a slight variation on this):

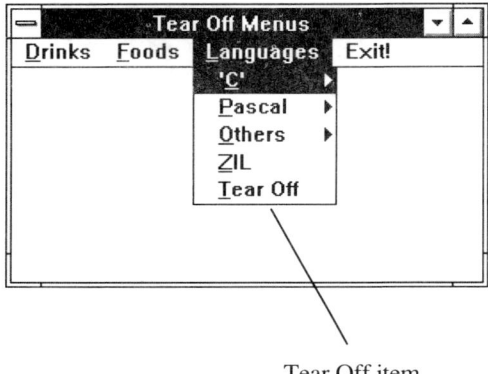

Tear Off item

Each drop down menu has an item labelled *Tear Off* at the bottom, this includes the system menu :

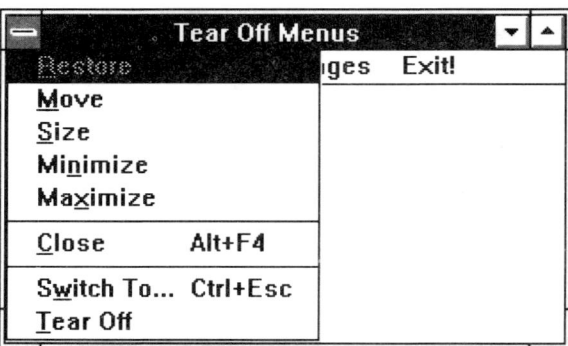

And all the cascaded menus :

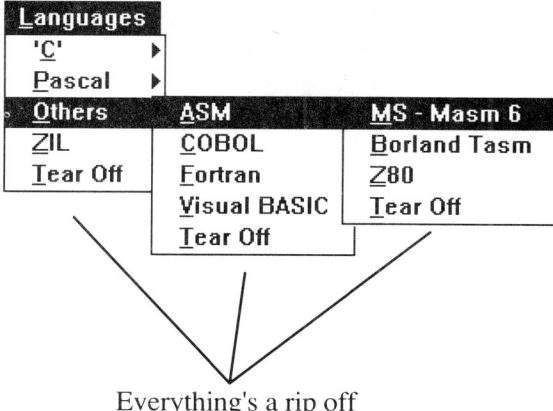

Everything's a rip off

If any *tear off* item is selected the menu is dismissed and immediately replaced with a floating tear off menu – the tear off appears such that its caption bar is positioned centred over the cursor's current position :

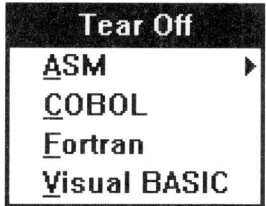

The tear off can be placed anywhere on the desktop – it also always stays on top of every other window and is always visible, even when the main window is iconised

Nested, or cascaded menus still work of course!

Here's just another couple of snapshots to show you how these look in use.

Prior to tearing off the menu :

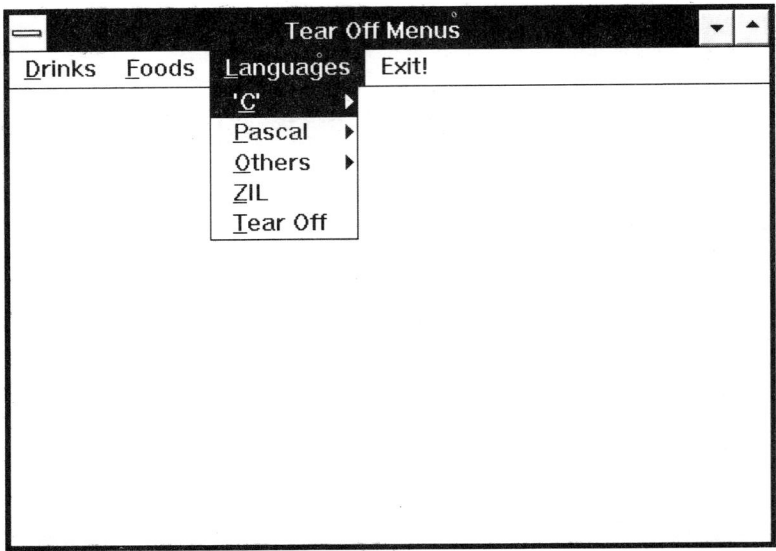

And once it's been torn off (Tear-off system menu shown also) :

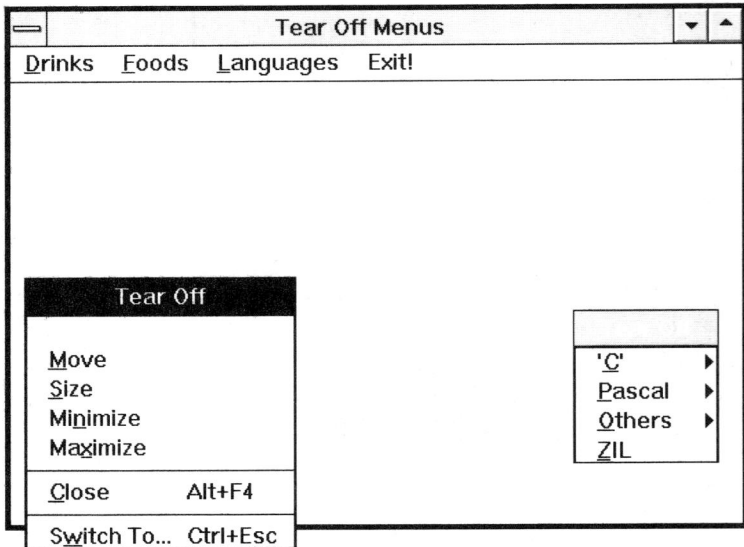

The way this application works is relatively trivial once you know that a menu is a window(s) of class #32768. When the menu is visible there are one or more (in the case of a cascaded menu) of these windows visible.

On start-up, the application creates a *top most* popup window that is 0 pixels wide and high and invisible. When you select Tear Off (WM_MENUSELECT) from any menu the application finds the menu window and takes a snap shot of it. The snap shot is stored in a bitmap and may or may not be used later (dependent upon whether or not tear off is actually selected). If the user releases the mouse on the Tear Off item the menu is dismissed and the application receives a WM_COMMAND message. In response to this WM_COMMAND message the popup window is shown resized to the size of the snap shot of the menu (minus the tear off menu item). The window's client area is filled using the bitmap saved before when a WM_MENUSELECT message was handled. Due to the way the menu windows are inserted into the window manager's list of windows the top most menu window is always the first one in the list; this makes finding it very easy – just use one FindWindow() call!

So, the floating/tear-off menu is nothing more than a picture of the menu. When the user clicks on what looks like a menu item in the picture TrackPopupMenu() is used to display the actual menu over the top of the popup – the popup menu exactly fits the popup window of course. The popup window *knows* which menu's image it's holding as its window words have been initialised with the menu's handle ready for when the menu needs displaying.

There is one problem with doing it this way however. The menu displayed in the popup is just a picture of the original menu: if that menu changes whilst the popup window is visible, the *picture* held in the popup window will not change, ie. change-able menu items (owner draw etc) are a no no if they might change whilst the real menu isn't visible!

This type of menu is fairly rare but I reckon could be used quite a lot; in particular I find that having the application's system menu, or font menu, around all the time is pretty handy! Oh yea; the mnemonic keys don't work either – they can't of course coz, it's just a picture!

As it stands the following code allows only one tear off to be created at a time. It would be trivial to change the code below to allow any number of them to co-exist. I wrote it this way so that the little code there is would stay clear. Having the code handle multiple instances of the tear off window would have made the code a little bigger but much harder to follow.

OK, here's the code :

The C source :

```
/*
** All the type checking we can get bud.
*/
#define STRICT

/*
```

```
** Turn off silly warnings.
*/
#pragma warning(disable:4100)
#pragma warning(disable:4001)

/*
** Necessary includes
*/
#include <windows.h>
#include <string.h>      /* For memset. */

/*
** Only two menu item IDs used!
*/
#define IDM_EXIT          100
#define IDM_TEAROFF       2001

/*
** Intra task messages (main window -> popup tear off window).
*/
#define UM_MAINMENUSELECT   WM_USER + 1
#define UM_MAKEVISIBLE      WM_USER + 2

/*
** Window word offsets to menu handles.
*/
#define GWW_MENUHANDLE1 0
#define GWW_MENUHANDLE2 2

/*
** Coding standards stuff.
*/
#define VOID_ARG
#define VOID_RETURN
/*
** Menu Class.
*/
#define WC_MENU (MAKEINTATOM(0x8000))

/*
** Function prototypes ********************************
*/
BOOL NEAR PASCAL MenuInit
(
   HINSTANCE
);

LRESULT __export CALLBACK fpMenuWndProc
(
   HWND
  ,UINT
  ,WPARAM
  ,LPARAM
);

LRESULT __export CALLBACK fpTearOffWndProc
(
```

```
      HWND
     ,UINT
     ,WPARAM
     ,LPARAM
);

LRESULT NEAR PASCAL SendTOMessage
(
     UINT
    ,WPARAM
    ,LPARAM
);


/*********** Code Starts ************/


int PASCAL WinMain
(
     HINSTANCE      hInstance
    ,HINSTANCE      hPrevInstance
    ,LPSTR          lpCmdLine
    ,int            nCmdShow
)
{
     auto HWND   hWnd;
     auto MSG    msg;

     /*
     ** Register application classes if this is the first instance.
     */
     if(hPrevInstance == NULL)
     {
         if(MenuInit(hInstance) == NULL)
         {
             return 0;
         }
     }

     /*
     ** Create floating popup window that will hold the torn off menu.
     ** Note   that   the   window   is  a 'top most' window and that it's
     ** parent id HWND_DESKTOP (or 0).
     */
     if(CreateWindowEx(
                      WS_EX_TOPMOST
                      ,MAKEINTATOM(2001)
                      ,"Tear Off"
                      ,WS_POPUP | WS_CAPTION
                      ,0
                      ,0
                      ,0
                      ,0
                      ,HWND_DESKTOP
                      ,NULL
                      ,hInstance
                      ,NULL
```

```
                         ) == NULL
        )
    {
        MessageBox(HWND_DESKTOP, "Couldn't create tear off menu window", NULL, MB_OK);

        return 0;
    }

    /*
    ** Main window creation
    */
    hWnd = CreateWindow(
                        "MenuWindow"
                        ,"Tear Off Menus"
                        ,WS_OVERLAPPEDWINDOW
                        ,CW_USEDEFAULT
                        ,0
                        ,CW_USEDEFAULT
                        ,0
                        ,HWND_DESKTOP
                        ,NULL
                        ,hInstance
                        ,(LPSTR) NULL
                        );

    if(hWnd == NULL)
    {
        MessageBox(HWND_DESKTOP, "Couldn't create main window", NULL, MB_OK);

        return 0;
    }

    /*
    ** Show main window - forget about showing the popup window.
    */
    ShowWindow(hWnd, nCmdShow);
    UpdateWindow(hWnd);

    while(GetMessage(&msg, NULL, NULL, NULL))
    {
        TranslateMessage(&msg);
        DispatchMessage(&msg);
    }

    return msg.wParam;
}



/*
** Registers classes used in this application.
*/
BOOL NEAR PASCAL MenuInit(HINSTANCE hInstance)
{
    /*
    ** Class structure.
```

```
 */
auto WNDCLASS   wc;

/*
** Registration success flag.
*/
auto BOOL       bSuccess;

memset(&wc, 0x0, sizeof(WNDCLASS));

wc.style            = 0;
wc.lpfnWndProc      = (WNDPROC)fpMenuWndProc;
wc.hInstance        = hInstance;
wc.hIcon            = LoadIcon(hInstance, "Menu");
wc.hCursor          = LoadCursor(NULL, IDC_ARROW);
wc.hbrBackground    = (HBRUSH)(COLOR_WINDOW + 1);
wc.lpszMenuName     = "TEAROFF",
wc.lpszClassName    = "MenuWindow";

bSuccess = RegisterClass(&wc);

if(bSuccess == 0)
{
   MessageBox(HWND_DESKTOP, "Couldn't register main class", NULL, MB_OK);

   return FALSE;
}

memset(&wc, 0x0, sizeof(WNDCLASS));

/*
** Tear Off class - Note that enough window words for
** HMENUs has been reserved.
*/
wc.style            = 0;
wc.lpfnWndProc      = (WNDPROC)fpTearOffWndProc;
wc.hInstance        = hInstance;
wc.cbWndExtra       = sizeof(HMENU) * 2;
wc.hIcon            = NULL;
wc.hCursor          = NULL;
wc.hbrBackground    = (HBRUSH)(COLOR_WINDOW + 1);
wc.lpszMenuName     = NULL,
wc.lpszClassName    = MAKEINTATOM(2001);

bSuccess = RegisterClass(&wc);

if(bSuccess == 0)
{
   MessageBox(HWND_DESKTOP, "Couldn't register tearoff class", NULL, MB_OK);

   return FALSE;
}

return bSuccess;
}
```

```
/*
** Used to 'send' the popup (tear off) window messages.
*/
LRESULT NEAR PASCAL SendTOMessage
(
   UINT    uMessage
  ,WPARAM  wParam
  ,LPARAM  lParam
)
{
   /*
   ** Window handle of 'tear off' window. Init once only.
   */
   static HWND hWndTearOff = NULL;

   /*
   ** If not already found - find i!
   */
   if(hWndTearOff == NULL)
   {
       hWndTearOff = FindWindow("#2001", NULL);
   }

   /*
   ** Send message to tear off  -  return 0 if tear off
   ** window not found, else result of sending message.
   */
   return hWndTearOff != NULL ? SendMessage(
                                            hWndTearOff
                                           ,uMessage
                                           ,wParam
                                           ,lParam
                                           )
                              : (LRESULT)0;
}




/*
** Class call-back for tear off menu window(s).
*/
LRESULT __export CALLBACK fpMenuWndProc
(
   HWND    hWnd
  ,UINT    uMessage
  ,WPARAM  wParam
  ,LPARAM  lParam
)
{
   /*
   ** Flags that a IDM_TEAROFF message has come from the system menu.
   */
   static BOOL bSysCommand;

   switch(uMessage)
```

```
{
        /*
        ** Add 'Tear Off' item to system menu.
        */
    case WM_CREATE:
        AppendMenu(
                    GetSystemMenu(hWnd, FALSE)
                  ,MF_STRING
                  ,IDM_TEAROFF
                  ,"&Tear Off"
                  );
        break;

        /*
        ** When menu item is selected  (by running the mouse over  it)
        ** tell the tear off about it - it will  copy the menu in case
        ** the user actually selects the item. HIWORD(lParam) contains
        ** a handle to the menu.
        */
    case WM_MENUSELECT:
        if(wParam == IDM_TEAROFF)
        {
            SendTOMessage(UM_MAINMENUSELECT, wParam, lParam);
        }
        break;

        /*
        ** Menu item selection.
        */
    case WM_SYSCOMMAND:
        if(wParam != IDM_TEAROFF)
        {
            return DefWindowProc(hWnd, uMessage, wParam, lParam);
        }

            /*
            ** Fall Thru.
            */


    case WM_COMMAND:
        switch(wParam)
        {
                /*
                ** 'Tear Off' selected - tell tear off window.
                */
            case IDM_TEAROFF:
                /*
                ** If message from system menu set flag.
                */
                bSysCommand = uMessage == WM_SYSCOMMAND ? TRUE : FALSE;

                /*
                ** Tell popup.
                */
                SendTOMessage(UM_MAKEVISIBLE, 0, 0);
```

```
                        break;

                        /*
                        ** Exit chosen so make it loo like syscommand
                        ** 'Close' selected.
                        */
                case IDM_EXIT:
                        PostMessage(hWnd, WM_SYSCOMMAND, SC_CLOSE, 0);
                        break;

                        /*
                        ** Anything else simply display message box
                        ** noting that a menu item was selected.
                        */
                default:
                        /*
                        ** Check to  see  if command  message is actually
                        ** due to a system  menu  item  selection;  if it
                        ** is then post ourselves a WM_SYSCOMMAND message.
                        */
                        if(bSysCommand == TRUE)
                        {
                             PostMessage(hWnd, WM_SYSCOMMAND, wParam, lParam);
                        }
                        else
                        {
                             MessageBox(
                                        hWnd
                                        ,"Main item was selected"
                                        ,"Way to go Wayne!"
                                        ,MB_OK
                                        );
                        }
                        break;
                }
                break;

                /*
                ** Main window being destroyed - tell tear off window
                ** so that it can destroy itself.
                */
        case WM_DESTROY:
                SendTOMessage(WM_CLOSE, 0, 0);
                PostQuitMessage(0);
                break;

        default:
                return DefWindowProc(hWnd, uMessage, wParam, lParam);
        }

   return (LRESULT)0;
}




LRESULT __export CALLBACK fpTearOffWndProc
```

```
(
  HWND    hWnd
 ,UINT    uMessage
 ,WPARAM  wParam
 ,LPARAM  lParam
)
{

  /*
  ** Handle to possible menu bitmap - set when menuselected.
  */
  static HBITMAP hBM1Global;

  /*
  ** Handle to bitmap showing currently selected tearoff menu.
  */
  static HBITMAP hBM2Global;


  switch(uMessage)
  {
    case UM_MAINMENUSELECT:
        {
          /*
          ** Handle to menu window.
          */
          auto HWND      hWndMenu;

          /*
          ** Stuff handle of possible menu into window words.
          */
          SetWindowWord(hWnd, GWW_MENUHANDLE1, HIWORD(lParam));

          /*
          ** Make copy of menu in readiness for a selection.
          */

          /*
          ** Find menu window.
          */
          if((hWndMenu = FindWindow(WC_MENU, NULL)) != NULL)
          {
            /*
            ** DC for menu and compat DC - used to copy
            ** menu window's contents.
            */
            auto HDC hDCMenu;
            auto HDC hDCCompatible;

            /*
            ** Get menu DC and create a compatible DC.
            */
            if(
                (hDCMenu      = GetDC(hWndMenu)) != NULL &&
                (hDCCompatible = CreateCompatibleDC(hDCMenu)) != NULL
              )
              {
```

```
/*
** For getting menu size.
*/
auto RECT          rsMClient;

/*
** Temp bitmap holder.
*/
auto HBITMAP      hBM;

/*
** Delete any old (previous) bitmap held in static.
*/
if(hBM1Global != NULL)
{
    DeleteObject(hBM1Global);
    hBM1Global = NULL;
}

/*
** Get size of menu window for CreateCompatBitmap()
** call.
*/
GetClientRect(hWndMenu, &rsMClient);

/*
** Get a new bitmap as big as the menu window.
*/
hBM = CreateCompatibleBitmap(
                            hDCMenu
                            ,rsMClient.right
                            ,rsMClient.bottom
                            );

/*
** Select it in to the compatDC...
*/
hBM = SelectObject(hDCCompatible, hBM);

/*
** Now 'snap shot' the visible menu to the
** compatBM...
*/
BitBlt(
        hDCCompatible
        ,0
        ,0
        ,rsMClient.right
        ,rsMClient.bottom
        ,hDCMenu
        ,0
        ,0
        ,SRCCOPY
        );

/*
** Get the snap shot out of the DC...
*/
```

```
                        */
                        hBM = SelectObject(hDCCompatible, hBM);

                        /*
                        ** And save it away 'til needed.
                        */
                        hBM1Global = hBM;

                        /*
                        ** Finish with compat and menu's DCs.
                        */
                        DeleteDC(hDCCompatible);

                        if(hDCMenu != NULL)
                        {
                            ReleaseDC(hWndMenu, hDCMenu);
                        }

                    } /* Got required DCs. */

                } /* Found menu window. */

            }
            break;

            /*
            ** Being blown up - probably getting this as a result of
            ** main window sending us a SYSCOMMAND message.
            */
    case WM_DESTROY:

            /*
            ** Delete any bitmaps we may have left around.
            */
            if(hBM1Global != NULL)
            {
                DeleteObject(hBM1Global);
            }

            if(hBM2Global != NULL && hBM2Global != hBM1Global)
            {
                DeleteObject(hBM2Global);
            }
            break;

    case WM_PAINT:
            {
                /*
                ** Holds width and height of window - these are set in
                ** UM_MAKEVISIBLE.
                */
                auto RECT           rsClient;

                /*
                ** For begin paint.
                */
                auto PAINTSTRUCT    ps;
```

```
/*
** For BitBlts.
*/
auto HDC hDC;
auto HDC hDCCompatible;

/*
** Get window width and height - should have been set
** to bitmap dimensions in UM_MAKEVISIBLE.
*/
GetClientRect(hWnd, &rsClient);

/*
** Get a DC for the window and a compatible DC for the
** the BitBlt().
*/
if(
    (hDC = BeginPaint(hWnd, &ps)) != NULL &&
    (hDCCompatible = CreateCompatibleDC(hDC)) != NULL
  )
{
    /*
    ** Hold s 'old' DC bitmap.
    */
    auto HBITMAP hBM;

    /*
    ** Get snap shot of menu to use
    */
    hBM = SelectObject(hDCCompatible, hBM2Global);

    /*
    ** And smack it in the window.
    */
    BitBlt(
            hDC
          ,0
          ,0
          ,rsClient.right
          ,rsClient.bottom
          ,hDCCompatible
          ,0
          ,0
          ,SRCCOPY
          );


    /*
    ** Tidy up - don't delete bitmap!
    */
    SelectObject(hDCCompatible, hBM);
    DeleteDC(hDCCompatible);
    if(hDC != NULL)
    {
        EndPaint(hWnd, &ps);
    }
```

```
                }
            else
                {
                MessageBox(HWND_DESKTOP, "Couldn't get a DC!", "", MB_OK);
                }
            }
        break;

        /*
        ** Punter selected 'Tear Off' so we need to get 'possible'
        ** menu into 'current' and move/show window.
        */
case UM_MAKEVISIBLE:
        {
            /*
            ** Used for sizing/positioning tear off window.
            */
            auto BITMAP thBMStruct;
            auto POINT  tpCurPos;

            /*
            ** Copy selected menu handle in window words.
            */
            SetWindowWord(
                        hWnd
                       ,GWW_MENUHANDLE2
                       ,GetWindowWord(
                                    hWnd
                                   ,GWW_MENUHANDLE1
                                   )
                        );

            /*
            ** Selected 'Tear Off' so use 'possible' menu snapshot.
            */
            hBM2Global = hBM1Global;

            /*
            ** Temporarily make window invisible.
            */
            if(IsWindowVisible(hWnd))
                {
                ShowWindow(hWnd, SW_HIDE);
                }

            /*
            ** Size and  position  tear  off window according
            ** to bitmap size (snap shot) and  current cursor
            ** position. The tear off window's caption should
            ** be centered over current cursor position.
            */
            GetObject(hBM2Global, sizeof(BITMAP), &thBMStruct);
            GetCursorPos(&tpCurPos);

            /*
            ** Reposition.
            */
            MoveWindow(
```

```
                            hWnd
                            ,tpCurPos.x                         -
                            thBMStruct.bmWidth                  /
                            2
                            ,tpCurPos.y                         -
                            GetSystemMetrics(SM_CYCAPTION)      /
                            2
                            ,thBMStruct.bmWidth                 +
                            GetSystemMetrics(SM_CXBORDER)
                            ,thBMStruct.bmHeight                +
                            GetSystemMetrics(SM_CYCAPTION)      -
                            GetSystemMetrics(SM_CYMENU)
                            ,FALSE
                            );

        /*
        ** Now show it and cause it to paint itself.
        */
        ShowWindow(hWnd, SW_SHOWNORMAL);
        InvalidateRect(hWnd, NULL, TRUE);
        UpdateWindow(hWnd);
    }
    break;

    /*
    ** Clicked in tear off window, need to cause
    ** required menu to appear.
    */
case WM_LBUTTONDOWN:
    {
        /*
        ** For changing/showing menu.
        */
        auto HMENU  hMenu;
        auto RECT   rsClient;

        /*
        ** Get client area...
        */
        GetClientRect(hWnd,&rsClient);

        /*
        ** Turn it into screen co-ords (using GetWindowRect() would
        ** have meant adding  GetSystemMetrics() stuff in the Track
        ** PopupMenu() below.
        */
        ClientToScreen(hWnd, (LPPOINT)&rsClient.left);
        ClientToScreen(hWnd, (LPPOINT)&rsClient.right);

        /*
        ** Get the required menu handle from window words.
        */
        hMenu = (HMENU)GetWindowWord(hWnd, GWW_MENUHANDLE2);

        /*
        ** Remove the 'Tear Off' menu item off the bottom
        ** of the menu  - it must have one and we want to
```

```
                         ** prevent it being shown.
                         */
                         DeleteMenu(hMenu, IDM_TEAROFF, MF_BYCOMMAND);

                         /*
                         ** Produce the menu so that it fits into the
                         ** 'tear off' window.
                         */
                         TrackPopupMenu(
                                         hMenu
                                        ,TPM_LEFTALIGN | TPM_LEFTBUTTON
                                        ,rsClient.left
                                        ,rsClient.top
                                        ,0
                                        ,FindWindow("MenuWindow",NULL)
                                        ,NULL
                                        );

                         /*
                         ** Put 'Tear Off' back on menu so that it appears when
                         ** selected off the 'real' menu bar.
                         */
                         AppendMenu(
                                 hMenu
                                ,MF_ENABLED | MF_STRING
                                ,IDM_TEAROFF
                                ,"Tear Off"
                                );
                 }
                 break;

         default:
                 return DefWindowProc(hWnd, uMessage, wParam, lParam);
    }

    return (LRESULT)0;
}
```

The .def file :

```
NAME                TEAROFF

DESCRIPTION         'Tear Off Menus'

EXETYPE             WINDOWS 3.1

PROTMODE

STUB                'WINSTUB.EXE'

CODE                PRELOAD MOVEABLE
DATA                PRELOAD MOVEABLE MULTIPLE

HEAPSIZE            1024
STACKSIZE           4096
```

```
EXPORTS
        fpMenuWndProc           @1
        fpTearOffWndProc        @2
@code sm =
```

The .rc file :

```
#include <windows.h>

#define IDM_EXIT    100
#define IDM_TEAROFF 2001


Menu    ICON            MENU.ICO

TEAROFF MENU
BEGIN
  POPUP    "&Drinks"
    BEGIN
      MENUITEM    "&Theakston's OP"       ,1
      MENUITEM    SEPARATOR
      MENUITEM    "&Bud"                  ,1
      MENUITEM    "&Caliber"              ,1
      MENUITEM    "B&lack Coffee"         ,1
      MENUITEM    "&Real Tea"             ,1
      MENUITEM    "&Tear Off"             ,IDM_TEAROFF
    END

  POPUP    "&Foods"
    BEGIN
      MENUITEM    "&Mc Donalds"           ,1
      MENUITEM    SEPARATOR
      MENUITEM    "&Chinese"              ,1
      MENUITEM    "C&hocolate Cookies"    ,1
      MENUITEM    "&Pop Corn"             ,1
      MENUITEM    "C&andy Bars"           ,1
      MENUITEM    "&Tear Off",            ,IDM_TEAROFF
    END

  POPUP    "&Languages"
    BEGIN
      POPUP       "'&C'"
        BEGIN
          MENUITEM    "&MSC"              ,1
          MENUITEM    "&Borland"          ,1
          MENUITEM    "&Zortech"          ,1
          MENUITEM    "&Watcom"           ,1
          MENUITEM    "&Light Speed"      ,1
          MENUITEM    "&Small"            ,1
          MENUITEM    "&K && R"           ,1
          MENUITEM    "&Tear Off"         ,IDM_TEAROFF
        END

      POPUP    "&Pascal"
        BEGIN
          MENUITEM    "&MSP"              ,1
          MENUITEM    "Turbo Pascal &Win" ,1
```

```
            MENUITEM    "&UCSD",                  ,1
            MENUITEM    "&Tear Off"               ,IDM_TEAROFF
        END
    POPUP   "&Others"
        BEGIN
        POPUP   "&ASM"
        BEGIN
            MENUITEM    "&MS - Masm 6"            ,1
            MENUITEM    "&Borland Tasm"           ,1
            MENUITEM    "&Z80"                    ,1
            MENUITEM    "&Tear Off"               ,IDM_TEAROFF
        END
        MENUITEM    "&COBOL"                      ,1
        MENUITEM    "&Fortran"                    ,1
        MENUITEM    "&Visual BASIC"               ,1
        MENUITEM    "&Tear Off"                   ,IDM_TEAROFF
    END

    MENUITEM "&ZIL"                               ,1
    MENUITEM "&Tear Off"                          ,IDM_TEAROFF
    END
  MENUITEM          "Exit!",                      ,IDM_EXIT
END
```

Once again, the code's pretty well documented and needs little in the way of additional explanation by me here (P.S. The menu's contain my favourite things – feel free to send any of them to me!).

The popup window is created along with the main window at the top of the code :

```
   if(CreateWindowEx(
                   WS_EX_TOPMOST
                   ,MAKEINTATOM(2001)
                   ,"Tear Off"
                   ,WS_POPUP | WS_CAPTION
                   ,0
                   ,0
                   ,0
                   ,0
                   ,HWND_DESKTOP
                   ,NULL
                   ,hInstance
                   ,NULL
                   ) == NULL
      )
   {
      MessageBox(
                HWND_DESKTOP
                ,"Couldn't create tear off menu window"
                ,NULL
                ,MB_OK
                );

      return 0;
   }
```

The window is created size *0* as it is resized when it is required later in the code. I've used MAKEINTATOM for the class-name in here and in the WNDCLASS structure – this saves a little space. MAKEINTATOM is also used to register the system classes BTW.

When a menu item is selected (that is to say is moved to or highlighted), the main window procedure receives a WM_MENUSELECT message. A check is done to see if the item being selected has the ID IDM_TEAROFF (that's a tear off item believe it or not!). When it does the popup window is passed a user message :

```
case WM_MENUSELECT:
        if(wParam == IDM_TEAROFF)
        {
            SendTOMessage(UM_MAINMENUSELECT, wParam, lParam);
        }
        break;
```

Essentially this says to the popup, 'Hey fella, get ready – the user might be selecting this menu item proper'. The popup window receives the message and in response takes a snap shot of the menu; this is held, as a bitmap in a window procedure static variable hBM1Global. A handle to the menu that contains the selected item is passed in the lParam of the WM_MENUSELECT message, this is passed on in the private message so that the menu window can set the menu's handle into its window words:

```
case UM_MAINMENUSELECT:
    {
        /*
        ** Handle to menu window.
        */
        auto HWND        hWndMenu;

        /*
        ** Stuff handle of possible menu into window words.
        */
        SetWindowWord(hWnd, GWW_MENUHANDLE1, HIWORD(lParam));

        /*
        ** Make copy of menu in readiness for a selection.
        */

        /*
        ** Find menu window.
        */
        if((hWndMenu = FindWindow(WC_MENU, NULL)) != NULL)
        {
            /*
            ** DC for menu and compat DC - used to copy
            ** menu window's contents.
            */
            auto HDC hDCMenu;
            auto HDC hDCCompatible;
```

```
/*
** Get menu DC and create a compatible DC.
*/
if(
    (hDCMenu       = GetDC(hWndMenu))  != NULL &&
    (hDCCompatible = CreateCompatibleDC(hDCMenu))
    != NULL
  )
{
    /*
    ** For getting menu size.
    */
    auto RECT       rsMClient;

    /*
    ** Temp bitmap holder.
    */
    auto HBITMAP    hBM;

    /*
    ** Delete any old (previous) bitmap held in static.
    */
    if(hBM1Global != NULL)
    {
        DeleteObject(hBM1Global);
        hBM1Global = NULL;
    }

    /*
    ** Get size of menu window for CreateCompatBitmap()
    ** call.
    */
    GetClientRect(hWndMenu, &rsMClient);

    /*
    ** Get a new bitmap as big as the menu window.
    */
    hBM = CreateCompatibleBitmap(
                                  hDCMenu
                                 ,rsMClient.right
                                 ,rsMClient.bottom
                                 );

    /*
    ** Select it in to the compatDC...
    */
    hBM = SelectObject(hDCCompatible, hBM);

    /*
    ** Now 'snap shot' the visible menu to the
    ** compatBM...
    */
    BitBlt(
            hDCCompatible
          ,0
          ,0
```

```
                          ,rsMClient.right
                          ,rsMClient.bottom
                          ,hDCMenu
                          ,0
                          ,0
                          ,SRCCOPY
                          );

            /*
            ** Get the snap shot out of the DC...
            */
            hBM = SelectObject(hDCCompatible, hBM);

            /*
            ** And save it away 'til needed.
            */
            hBM1Global = hBM;

            /*
            ** Finish with compat and menu's DCs.
            */
            DeleteDC(hDCCompatible);

            if(hDCMenu != NULL)
            {
                 ReleaseDC(hWndMenu, hDCMenu);
            }

         } /* Got required DCs. */

       } /* Found menu window. */

    }
   break;
```

If the popup gets painted it is because the user initially selects a *tear off* item. After this it may get painted if it is obscured by another top most window or by, say, a full screen DOS box. Initially however the popup only gets shown and painted if the user selects a tear off item; the main window once again signals the popup of this action using a private message :

```
//NOTE: Possible Fall Thru from WM_SYSCOMMAND here.

case WM_COMMAND:
     switch(wParam)
     {
            /*
            ** 'Tear Off' selected - tell tear off window.
            */
        case IDM_TEAROFF:
            /*
            ** If message from system menu set flag.
            */
            bSysCommand = uMessage == WM_SYSCOMMAND ? TRUE : FALSE;

            /*
```

```
                         ** Tell popup.
                         */
                         SendTOMessage(UM_MAKEVISIBLE, 0, 0);
                         break;
```

The popup has to now show and paint itself :

```
        case UM_MAKEVISIBLE:
            {
                 /*
                 ** Used for sizing/positioning tear off window.
                 */
                 auto BITMAP thBMStruct;
                 auto POINT  tpCurPos;

                 /*
                 ** Copy selected menu handle in window words.
                 */
                 SetWindowWord(
                             hWnd
                             ,GWW_MENUHANDLE2
                             ,GetWindowWord(
                                          hWnd
                                          ,GWW_MENUHANDLE1
                                          )
                             );

                 /*
                 ** Selected 'Tear Off' so use 'possible' menu snapshot.
                 */
                 hBM2Global = hBM1Global;

                 /*
                 ** Temporarily make window invisible.
                 */
                 if(IsWindowVisible(hWnd))
                 {
                     ShowWindow(hWnd, SW_HIDE);
                 }

                 /*
                 ** Size and  position  tear  off window according
                 ** to bitmap size (snap shot) and  current cursor
                 ** position. The tear off window's caption should
                 ** be centered over current cursor position.
                 */
                 GetObject(hBM2Global, sizeof(BITMAP), &thBMStruct);
                 GetCursorPos(&tpCurPos);

                 /*
                 ** Reposition.
                 */
                 MoveWindow(
                             hWnd
                             ,tpCurPos.x                        -
                             thBMStruct.bmWidth                 /
                             2
                             ,tpCurPos.y                        -
                             GetSystemMetrics(SM_CYCAPTION)     /
```

```
                2
               ,thBMStruct.bmWidth                    +
                GetSystemMetrics(SM_CXBORDER)
               ,thBMStruct.bmHeight                   +
                GetSystemMetrics(SM_CYCAPTION)    -
                GetSystemMetrics(SM_CYMENU)
               ,FALSE
               );

            /*
            ** Now show it and cause it to paint itself.
            */
            ShowWindow(hWnd, SW_SHOWNORMAL);
            InvalidateRect(hWnd, NULL, TRUE);
            UpdateWindow(hWnd);
        }
        break;
```

The possible menu (hBM1Global) is now *the* definite menu (hBM2Global). The window is resized so that the menu, minus the tear off item, can be accommodated in it client area.

```
        MoveWindow(
                hWnd
               ,tpCurPos.x                            -
                thBMStruct.bmWidth                    /
                2
               ,tpCurPos.y                            -
                GetSystemMetrics(SM_CYCAPTION)    /
                2
               ,thBMStruct.bmWidth                    +
                GetSystemMetrics(SM_CXBORDER)
               ,thBMStruct.bmHeight                   +
                GetSystemMetrics(SM_CYCAPTION)    -
                GetSystemMetrics(SM_CYMENU)
               ,FALSE
               );
```

It is also positioned so that when it becomes visible its caption bar is centrally placed beneath the cursor allowing the tear off to be moved with a simply click and drag.

Lastly the window is shown and told to paint itself :

```
            /*
            ** Now show it and cause it to paint itself.
            */
            ShowWindow(hWnd, SW_SHOWNORMAL);
            InvalidateRect(hWnd, NULL, TRUE);
            UpdateWindow(hWnd);
```

This causes the popup's WM_PAINT handler to get hit :

```
        case WM_PAINT:
            {
                /*
```

```
** Holds width and height of window - these are set in
** UM_MAKEVISIBLE.
*/
auto RECT           rsClient;


/*
** For begin paint.
*/
auto PAINTSTRUCT    ps;


/*
** For BitBlts.
*/
auto HDC hDC;
auto HDC hDCCompatible;


/*
** Get window width and height - should have been set
** to bitmap dimensions in UM_MAKEVISIBLE.
*/
GetClientRect(hWnd, &rsClient);


/*
** Get a DC for the window and a compatible DC for the
** the BitBlt().
*/
if(
    (hDC = BeginPaint(hWnd, &ps)) != NULL &&
    (hDCCompatible = CreateCompatibleDC(hDC)) != NULL
  )
{
    /*
    ** Hold s 'old' DC bitmap.
    */
    auto HBITMAP hBM;


    /*
    ** Get snap shot of menu to use
    */
    hBM = SelectObject(hDCCompatible, hBM2Global);


    /*
    ** And smack it in the window.
    */
    BitBlt(
           hDC
          ,0
          ,0
          ,rsClient.right
          ,rsClient.bottom
          ,hDCCompatible
          ,0
          ,0
          ,SRCCOPY
          );



    /*
    ** Tidy up - don't delete bitmap!
```

```
                */
                SelectObject(hDCCompatible, hBM);
                DeleteDC(hDCCompatible);
                if(hDC != NULL)
                {
                    EndPaint(hWnd, &ps);
                }
            }
        }
    break;
```

The paint handler simply uses hBM2Global to paint its client area using a BitBlt().

The window is now visible and we have to wait... (time passes)....

If the user clicks in the popup's window (on what they think is a menu item) we have to produce the menu. The menu's handle has been stored away in the window words of the popup :

```
case WM_LBUTTONDOWN:
    {
        /*
        ** For changing/showing menu.
        */
        auto HMENU  hMenu;
        auto RECT   rsClient;

        /*
        ** Get client area...
        */
        GetClientRect(hWnd,&rsClient);

        /*
        ** Turn it into screen co-ords (using GetWindowRect() would
        ** have meant adding  GetSystemMetrics() stuff in the Track
        ** PopupMenu() below.
        */
        ClientToScreen(hWnd,(LPPOINT)&rsClient.left);
        ClientToScreen(hWnd,(LPPOINT)&rsClient.right);

        /*
        ** Get the required menu handle from window words.
        */
        hMenu = (HMENU)GetWindowWord(hWnd, GWW_MENUHANDLE2);

        /*
        ** Remove the 'Tear Off' menu item off the bottom
        ** of the menu  - it must have one and we want to
        ** prevent it being shown.
        */
        DeleteMenu(hMenu, IDM_TEAROFF, MF_BYCOMMAND);

        /*
        ** Produce the menu so that it fits into the
        ** 'tear off' window.
        */
        TrackPopupMenu(
```

```
                          hMenu
                         ,TPM_LEFTALIGN | TPM_LEFTBUTTON
                         ,rsClient.left
                         ,rsClient.top
                         ,0
                         ,FindWindow("MenuWindow",NULL)
                         ,NULL
                         );
            /*
            ** Here only when menu's gone away.
            */

            /*
            ** Put 'Tear Off' back on menu so that it appears when
            ** selected off 'real' menu bar.
            */
            AppendMenu(
                      hMenu
                     ,MF_ENABLED | MF_STRING
                     ,IDM_TEAROFF
                     ,"Tear Off"
                     );
         }
         break;
```

The menu is positioned so that it is aligned correctly with the client area. Note also that the tear off menu item is removed prior to calling TrackPopupMenu() and reinstated after the trackable popup is removed :

```
            DeleteMenu(hMenu, IDM_TEAROFF, MF_BYCOMMAND);

   ... TrackPopupMenu(...)

            AppendMenu(
                      hMenu
                     ,MF_ENABLED | MF_STRING
                     ,IDM_TEAROFF
                     ,"Tear Off"
                     );
```

This is so that the *tear off* doesn't appear – it would spill out of the popup's window if we allowed it to remain as we resized the popup so that this item would be clipped. There's no point in showing this item as it would just produce another popup menu exactly the same as the one that's currently visible!

Communication between the main window and the popup is essentially one way. The function SendTOMessge (TO = Tear Off) is used for this purpose :

```
LRESULT NEAR PASCAL SendTOMessage
(
   UINT    uMessage
  ,WPARAM  wParam
  ,LPARAM  lParam
)
{
   /*
```

```
** Window handle of 'tear off' window. Init once only.
*/
static HWND hWndTearOff = NULL;

/*
** If not already found - find i!
*/
if(hWndTearOff == NULL)
{
    hWndTearOff = FindWindow("#2001", NULL);
}

/*
** Send message to tear off  -  return 0 if tear off
** window not found, else result of sending message.
*/
return hWndTearOff != NULL ? SendMessage(
                                        hWndTearOff
                                       ,uMessage
                                       ,wParam
                                       ,lParam
                                       )
                           : (LRESULT)0;
}
```

Of course tear offs should contain frequently used menus, character formatting menus and font selection etc like that shown on the previous page. Large tear offs can be more of a hindrance that a help – perhaps the menu should be scrollable? See Chapter 8 for more on scrollable menus.

Tear Off

Optima-Bold
Palatino
Palatino-Roman
Parisian
ParkAvenue
Peignot-Demi
Peignot-Light
Ponderosa
PostAntiqua-Roman
PostCrypt
Present
Revue
Roman
SaintFrancis
Script
Sonata
Souvenir-Light
Stencil
Symbol
Tekton
Tiffany
Tiffany-HeavyItalic
TimesNewRomanPS
Tms Rmn
Umbra
ZapfChancery
ZapfDingbats

Fonts O - Z.
Tear off font menu showing just a 'small' selection of fonts! What's needed is a scrollable menu!

☐ The difference between owner and parent.

Being an *owner* window, as opposed to being a parent may often appear to be the same thing; as does, from an observer's point of view, being a WS_POPUP window as opposed to being a WS_OVERLAPPED. Before now, as was stated earlier, owned POPUPs were usually called child windows. Of course this was <u>always</u> wrong as a WS_CHILD is a child window and a WS_CHILD is most certainly NOT a WS_POPUP window. This lead some to call owned popups *childs* – it made you feel kinda odd talking with someone who spoke like this— 'Yea, I built several childs and...', see what I mean?! Of course the term that should be applied to an owned popup is owned popup! Well what does owner mean and is it more or less the same as parent?

The answer is a little grey unfortunately due to some interesting wording in WINDOWS.H and behaviour in Windows.

Windows exports three functions for enquiring after a window's parent and/or owner; they are :

- GetWindow()   Using GW_OWNER
- GetWindowWord()   Using GWW_HWNDPARENT
- GetParent()

Which is your favourite?

These functions however are not all front-ends to the same thing. If we were to create several combinations of window such as :

- Main Window   Secondary Window
- Main Overlapped   Owned Overlapped
- Main Overlapped   Owned Popup
- Main Overlapped   Child

and use these functions to establish, from the secondary window's point of view, just who our main window is (and their relationship to us) we would find the following:

	1	2	3
`Main Window`	Overlapped	Overlapped	Overlapped
`Secondary Window`	Overlapped	Popup	Child
`Relationship, Main -> Secondary`	Owner	Owner	Parent
`GetWindow`	O	O	X
`GetWindowWord`	O	O	O
`GetParent`	X	O	O

Key O   Valid Return (worked)
**   X   Zero Returned (didn't work)**

We can see from this table that according to GetWindow() a child does not have an owner; however, for a child, both *get parent* functions work as expected. An owned popup can retrieve its parent/owner using any of the functions – so is it a childs [sic], a child, or an owned popup?. An owned overlapped also seems to be a bit confused (or is it us?) as GetParent() doesn't work but GetWindowWord(..., HWND_PARENT) does! The MS SDK tool SPY must use GetParent() to test this relationship thing coz it gets it wrong when you test an owner overlapped, ie. it reports that the window has *no parent* (although given the wording No Parent – it's right, isn't it?!). Also, saying that a parent is always an owner (to try and clear this up) doesn't work else GetWindow(..., GW_OWNER) should work for a child window!

Another area where this can become confusing, although it's probably due to a wording problem, is that a top level window can have siblings that are also top level windows. In a way you'd expect this not to happen as to be a sibling you've got to be a child right? Wrong. Also, all top level windows can also be considered to be child windows created from the desktop! If you were to get the desktop window's window handle (GetDesktopWindow()) and then use that to get *the handle of the top-level child window that belongs to the given parent* you'd find that you get back a handle to a top-level window, ie. NOT a handle to a window that has the style WS_CHILD. Using GetTopWindow() or GetWindow(GW_CHILD) on the desktop window produces this effect – ergo, a top-level window is a child (now this doesn't mean that it has the style WS_CHILD but that it is descended from the desktop!). In fact all windows are descended from the desktop window ultimately and all top-level windows are first generation descendants of it. Note that once again HWND_DESKTOP cannot be used in replace of the real window handle for the desktop.

Now we have *child* meaning descendant, child meaning WS_CHILD and owned meaning special behaviour. In fact it's probably best to think of windows that are WS_CHILD windows and those that are owned as simply designating special behaviour. What's most frustrating about this is you can't use HWND_DESKTOP (defined in WINDOWS.H) in the same way as you can use the result of GetDesktopWindow(); it is best to think of HWND_DESKTOP not as specifying the desktop's window handle value but specifying a window relationship. The only problem now is that we have one parameter that means two different things, ie. the hWnd Parent parameter of CreateWindow() now means either a window handle to a parent/owner window OR a relationship specifier taken from the set (of one) HWND_DESKTOP. Of course, you're probably used to the meaning of parameters changing in context; consider the HMENU parameter of the same function call with regard to the window types WS_CHILD and WS_POPUP! Get the impression that this requires sorting out? NOTE : That given any window handle that the GetWindow() function alone can be used to walk the entire window tree of windows. Programmers using environments in which call-backs are either impossible or difficult to define should remember this especially.

There are also some behavioural ambiguities within these relationships – most of which are documented – some are not (and some change between versions).

Here are some of the behavioural observations made on the windows above :

case 1.

- Secondary window always stays on top of main window.
- Activating secondary window also brings main window to TOP – 1 Z position (secondary always at top Z position).
- Iconising main window causes secondary window to be hidden.
- Hiding main window using, say, ShowWindow() does not cause secondary window to be hidden.
- If secondary window is iconised and then the main window is iconised, the secondary window's icon is removed from the desktop. When the main window is restored the secondary window is also restored automatically, ie. it is not left in its previous iconic state.
- Destroying the main window causes the secondary window to be destroyed also. The main window is sent a WM_DESTROY message after the secondary window has been sent a WM_DESTROY message.
- CW_USEDEFAULT positioning works for both windows.
- Secondary window does not pass the main window any notification messages.
- Main or secondary windows can be activated.
- Only the main window's title appears in task list.

case 2.

- As 1 but CW_USEDEFAULT doesn't work for secondary POPUP window.

case 3.

- Secondary window always stays on top of main window.
- Activating secondary window also brings main window to TOP – 1 Z position (secondary always at top Z position).
- Iconising main window causes secondary window to be hidden.
- Hiding main window using, say, ShowWindow() does cause secondary window to be hidden.
- If secondary window is iconised and then the main window is iconised, the secondary window's icon is removed from the screen (as it was shown in the client area of the main window – and that has now been removed from the desktop). When the main window is restored the secondary window is not restored automatically, ie. it is left in its previous iconic state.

- Destroying the main window causes the secondary window to be destroyed also. The main window is sent a WM_DESTROY message before the secondary window has been sent a WM_DESTROY message (although during the childs handling of the WM_DESTROY message the main window is still a window).

- CW_USEDEFAULT positioning doesn't work for child.

- Secondary window passes the main window notification messages such as WM_SETCURSOR.

- Only Main window can be activated – either can be focused (active window and focused window are NOT the same thing).

- Only the main window's title appears in task list.

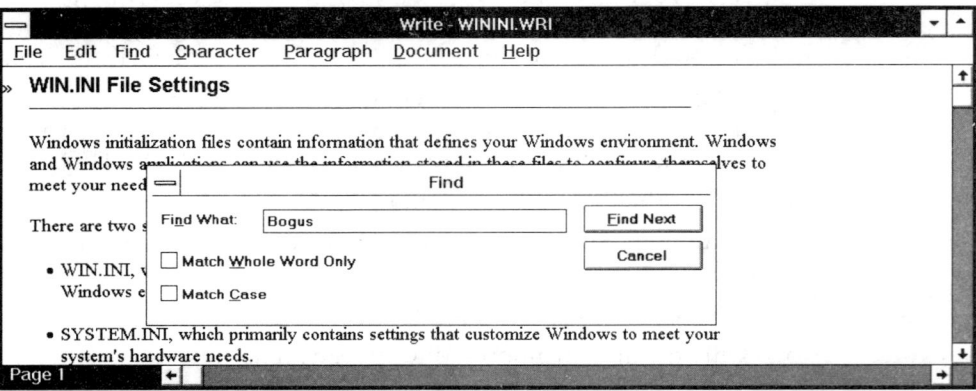

Most of this is documented but not many programmers have sat down and tried this out. The most surprising thing above to some programmers is the apparent reversal of the handling of a WM_DESTROY message between the windows in 1 & 3 above. Just because a WS_CHILD is always created after its parent, doesn't mean that the child gets a WM_DESTROY first – as can be seen (and read on page 120 of Volume 3 of the Programmer's Reference) it aint so!

The confusion between owner vs. parent has caused problems also when an attempt is made to *set* a secondary window to a new main window. The function SetParent() can be used to change the parent of a child window; it cannot be used to change the owner of a popup window (using this function can be quite amusing as you watch, say, a push button fly back and forth between two dialog boxes!). You can change the owner by using SetWindowWord() however. This can be very useful in environments such as Visual Basic where all windows (or forms as it calls them) are actually owner-less overlapped windows. This means that trying to emulate an owned modeless dialog box is impossible.

Here you can see Microsoft Write's *Find* owned modeless dialog box. It always stays on top of the main window because the main window is the Find window's owner. In Visual Basic this would be impossible to do as each window is an owner-less overlapped window, ie. if Write were a VB application then activating the main window would cause the Find window to fall through or go beneath the main window. You can fix this flaw in VB by using SetWindowWord() to attach ownership of it to another window. The owned overlapped will always appear on top of its owner. Note that the SetWindowWord() documentation doesn't document the GWW_HWNDPARENT offset and it is unclear as to whether or not this offset (and the others left undocumented) are endorsed by Microsoft.

Res.

The last code example we'll look in this chapter is called *Res*. Res displays percent free figures for USER's and GDI's heaps. It doesn't use GetFreeSystemResources() to obtain these figures but instead uses a function that eventually calls GetFreeSystem-Resources() – SystemHeapInfo(). SystemHeapInfo() is a TOOLHELP function.

TOOLHELP provides many functions and structures for doing most of those naughty things we used to do using so called *back door* or undocumented functions!

Res loads (and remains) iconic – almost catatonic! The icon is however animated and not static as normal.

When you register a Window's class and specify that the class icon is NULL (hIcon = NULL) something a bit special happens when any window created from the said class is made iconic. Windows, instead of displaying an icon for your window allows your application to use its actual window as an icon. Essentially the difference is that instead of removing the window's normal-state attributes (resizable frame, caption etc), making what remains of your window *icon sized* and then filling it with your class icon, Windows simply omits the last step, ie. as you have no class icon, no icon is displayed and your icon is simply a small icon sized version of your main window's client area.

Drawing in an icon can be very handy, especially for applications such as Res that require very little space in which to strut their stuff. Res, as I've said displays the amount of free, and of course used system resources :

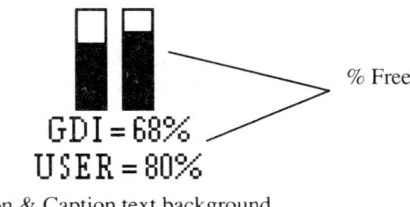

Icon & Caption text background
colors the same as the desktop.

Res also tries to make its display look as weird as possible in that it tries to make the bars look as though they're maybe two small windows on the desktop. It does this by painting the background of its window the same colour as your desktop – the bars then appear to be two something's instead of one something!

Applications like Res cannot be restored (well they could – you have to stop them) and so if they need some user input they have to use either the application's system menu, a trackable popup menu, or some direct means of giving input through the app's client area. Res uses the most common method – the system menu :

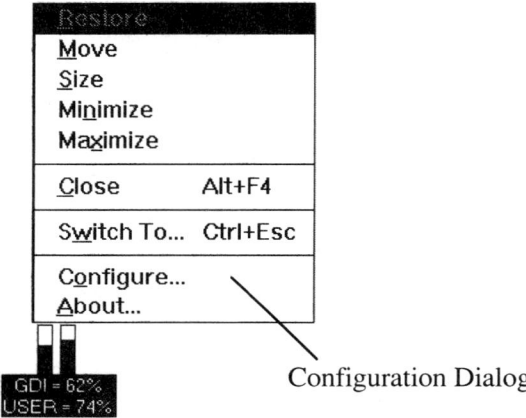

Configuration Dialog

How to get user input
when you're iconic

The actual configuration dialog is quite simple. It allows the user to set a limit or threshold such that when/if the available system resources (for either GDI or USER) becomes less than the limit an alarm sounds :

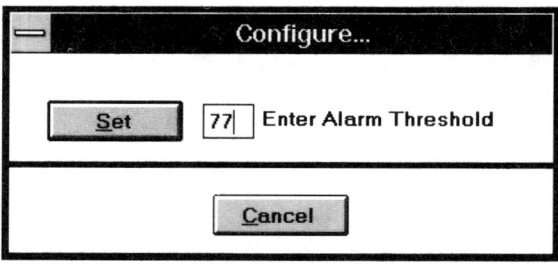

The *alarm* is a couple of message beeps and a flashing icon!

OK. Here's the code :

The .c source file :

```c
#define STRICT

#include <windows.h>
#include <toolhelp.h>
#include "res.h"




/*
** EnumWindows() call-back used for locating icon-caption window
** of minimized main window.
*/
BOOL __export CALLBACK bEnumProc(HWND hWnd, LPARAM lParam)
{
    /*
    ** Look for icon-caption window. Main window handle
    ** passed in lParam.  Icon-caption window should be
    ** 'owned' by the main window.
    */
    if(GetWindowWord(hWnd, GWW_HWNDPARENT) == LOWORD(lParam))
    {
        /*
        ** Found it so invalidate it and cause it to re-paint.
        */
        InvalidateRect(hWnd, NULL, TRUE);
        UpdateWindow(hWnd);

        /*
        ** Enough enumeration - cancel further enumeration.
        */
        return FALSE;
    }

    return TRUE;
}




/*
** Causes, using function above, the re-painting of the caption
** window seen under an icon main window.
*/
VOID vRepaintTitle(HWND hWnd)
{
    /*
    ** Look through window manager's list of windows to find
    ** icon-caption window. Pass bEnumProc the 'main' window
    ** handle.
    */
    EnumWindows((WNDENUMPROC)bEnumProc, MAKELPARAM(hWnd, 0));

    return VOID_RETURN;
}
```

```
/*
** Normal 'generic type' WinMain().
*/
int PASCAL WINMAIN
(
   HINSTANCE    hInstance
  ,HINSTANCE    hPrevInstance
  ,LPSTR        lpCmdLine
  ,int          nCmdShow
)
{
   auto MSG msg;

   if(hPrevInstance == NULL)
   {
      if(bInitApplication(hInstance) == FALSE)
      {
         return FALSE;
      }
   }

   if(bInitInstance(hInstance, nCmdShow) == FALSE)
   {
      return FALSE;
   }

   while(GetMessage(&msg, NULL, 0, 0))
   {
      TranslateMessage(&msg);
      DispatchMessage(&msg);
   }

   return msg.wParam;
}




/*
** Normal 'generic type' InitApp.
*/
BOOL bInitApplication(HINSTANCE hInstance)
{
   auto WNDCLASS  wc;

   /*
   ** WNDCLASS for main iconic window. NOTE that both the
   ** ICON and background brush are set to NULL.
   */
   wc.style          = 0;
   wc.lpfnWndProc    = (WNDPROC)lMainWndProc;
   wc.cbClsExtra     = 0;
   wc.cbWndExtra     = 0;
```

```
    wc.hInstance        = hInstance;
    wc.hIcon            = NULL;
    wc.hCursor          = LoadCursor(NULL, IDC_ARROW);
    wc.hbrBackground    = NULL;
    wc.lpszMenuName     = NULL;
    wc.lpszClassName    = "ResClass";


    return RegisterClass(&wc);
}




/*
** Normal 'generic type' InitInst.
*/
BOOL bInitInstance(HINSTANCE hInstance, int nCmdShow)
{
    /*
    ** Window handle of main window.
    */
    auto HWND hWnd;

    /*
    ** Create main  window so that it's topmost. Width
    ** and height and  origin  set  to  zeros  as we're
    ** gonna only run iconic. Also, window caption set
    ** to NULL - it doesn't say that you can do this
    ** in the function ref but you can!
    */
    hWnd = CreateWindowEx(
                        WS_EX_TOPMOST           // TOPMOST.
                        ,"ResClass"
                        ,NULL                   // Caption set later.
                        ,WS_OVERLAPPEDWINDOW
                        ,0
                        ,0
                        ,0
                        ,0
                        ,HWND_DESKTOP           // Owned by desktop.
                        ,NULL                   // No menu on window.
                        ,hInstance
                        ,NULL
                        );

    if(hWnd == NULL)
    {
        return FALSE;
    }

    /*
    ** Show window hidden (don't really need this as it's
    ** hidden by default) - we show it later.
    */
    ShowWindow(hWnd, SW_HIDE);
    UpdateWindow(hWnd);
```

```
   return TRUE;
}




/*
** Main window's window procedure.
*/
LRESULT __export CALLBACK lMainWndProc
(
   HWND     hWnd
  ,UINT     uMessage
  ,WPARAM   wParam
  ,LPARAM   lParam
)
{
   /*
   ** Timer ID. Set in WM_CREATE case and used in WM_DESTROY
   ** to kill off the timer create in WM_CREATE.
   */
   static UINT uTimer;

   /*
   ** Percentage of USER/GDI heaps free. Set
   ** in timer handler.
   */
   static WORD wPctUSRFree;
   static WORD wPctGDIFree;

   /*
   ** Minimum  percentage free  of either  heap required
   ** to start alarm bell (well beeps really) ringing.
   */
   static UINT uMin;

   switch(uMessage)
   {
        /*
        ** Init all the stuff we need. A timer and a modified
        ** system menu.
        */
      case WM_CREATE:
           {
                /*
                ** Handle to system menu.
                */
                auto HMENU hSysMenu;

                /*
                ** Set min to 0 = no alarm.
                */
                uMin = 0;

                /*
                ** Hook a timer for once per second so we can check
                ** resources.
```

```
*/
if((uTimer = SetTimer(hWnd, 0, 1000, NULL)) == 0)
{
    /*
    ** No timers free so tell user and exit.
    */
    MessageBox(
                HWND_DESKTOP
                ,"No Timers Free! - Closing."
                ,NULL
                ,MB_OK
                );

    return -1;
}

/*
** Get and modify system menu - add three menu items.
** A separator and two real items for getting to the
** dialog boxes - 'Configure...' and 'About...'.
*/
if((hSysMenu = GetSystemMenu(hWnd, FALSE)) == NULL)
{
    /*
    ** Couldn't get sys menu so exit.
    */
    return -1;
}
else
{
    InsertMenu(
                hSysMenu
                ,(UINT) -1
                ,MF_SEPARATOR
                ,0
                ,0
                );

    InsertMenu(
                hSysMenu
                ,(UINT) -1
                ,MF_BYPOSITION | MF_STRING
                ,IDM_CONFIGURE
                ,"C&onfigure..."
                );

    InsertMenu(
                hSysMenu
                ,(UINT) -1
                ,MF_BYPOSITION | MF_STRING
                ,IDM_ABOUT
                ,"&About..."
                );
}

/*
** Get 'last saved' threshold limit into uMin.
```

```
         ** This is '0' by default.
         */
         uMin = GetPrivateProfileInt("Res", "Threshold", 0, "RES.INI");
    }
    break;

    /*
    ** On a timer event check to see if resources free
    ** figure has changed - it it has cause a re-paint.
    */
case WM_TIMER:
    {
         /*
         ** Defined in TOOLHELP.H - two fields used
         ** for checking USER/GDI local heaps. Could
         ** have  used  GetFreeSystemResources()   -
         ** toolhelp calls that same function!
         */
         auto SYSHEAPINFO shi;

         /*
         ** Required by TOOLHELP.
         */
         shi.dwSize = sizeof shi;

         /*
         ** Get heap info.
         */
         SystemHeapInfo(&shi);

         /*
         ** If USR OR GDI free has changed since last
         ** check update statics and
         ** cause a re-paint.
         */
         if(wPctUSRFree != shi.wUserFreePercent ||
            wPctGDIFree != shi.wGDIFreePercent
           )
         {
            /*
            ** Update both, even if only one has changed.
            */
            wPctUSRFree = shi.wUserFreePercent;
            wPctGDIFree = shi.wGDIFreePercent;

            InvalidateRect(hWnd, NULL, TRUE);
            UpdateWindow(hWnd);
         }

         /*
         ** See if either GDI/USER heap is below min,
         ** if so beep, beep!!
         */
         if(min(wPctGDIFree, wPctUSRFree) < uMin)
         {
            /*
            ** Alarm.
```

```
                */
                FlashWindow(hWnd, TRUE);
                MessageBeep(0);

                FlashWindow(hWnd, FALSE);
                MessageBeep(0);
            }

            /*
            ** Check to see if we're visible. Already
            ** done a paint.  If we're invisible make
            ** us  visible - this  shows  the icon as
            ** 'already painted'.
            */
            if(IsWindowVisible(hWnd) == FALSE)
            {
                ShowWindow(hWnd, SW_SHOWMINNOACTIVE);
            }
        }
        break;

        /*
        ** Turn relevant system menu selections into
        ** WM_COMMAND messages for handling later.
        */
case WM_SYSCOMMAND:
        switch(wParam)
        {
          case IDM_CONFIGURE:
          case IDM_ABOUT:
              PostMessage(hWnd, WM_COMMAND, wParam, 0);
              break;

          default:
              return DefWindowProc(hWnd, uMessage, wParam, lParam);
        }
        break;

        /*
        ** System menu item selected (see above).
        */
case WM_COMMAND:

        /*
        ** Bring up appropriate dialog box. Use the same
        ** call-back handler.
        */
        switch(wParam)
        {
          case IDM_ABOUT:
              DialogBox(
                      (HINSTANCE)GetWindowWord(hWnd, GWW_HINSTANCE)
                      ,(LPCSTR)MAKEINTRESOURCE(ABOUTBOX)
                      ,hWnd
                      ,(DLGPROC)bDialogs
                      );
              break;
```

```
            case IDM_CONFIGURE:
                DialogBox(
                        (HINSTANCE)GetWindowWord(hWnd, GWW_HINSTANCE)
                        ,(LPCSTR)MAKEINTRESOURCE(CONFIGURE)
                        ,hWnd
                        ,(DLGPROC)bDialogs
                        );
                break;
        }
        break;

    /*
    ** Being blown away. Release timer.
    */
case WM_DESTROY:
    KillTimer(hWnd, uTimer);
    PostQuitMessage(0);
    break;

    /*
    ** Someone's trying to open our ICON - tell 'em to &*%*& off.
    */
case WM_QUERYOPEN:
    break; ·

    /*
    ** Class NULL brush so we need to repaint our own window
    ** background when needed.  We paint it with the desktop
    ** color to make it appear transparent.
    */
case WM_ERASEBKGND:
    {
        /*
        ** Our client rectangle.
        */
        auto RECT    rsClient;

        /*
        ** Pen and a brush used for painting the whole of the
        ** window one color.
        */
        auto HBRUSH hbr;
        auto HPEN   hpe;

        /*
        ** Create brush and pen of background color.
        */
        hbr = CreateSolidBrush(GetSysColor(COLOR_BACKGROUND));
        hpe = CreatePen(PS_SOLID, 1, GetSysColor(COLOR_BACKGROUND));

        /*
        ** Get 'em into DC.
        */
        hbr = SelectObject((HDC)wParam, hbr);
        hpe = SelectObject((HDC)wParam, hpe);
```

```
            /*
            ** See how big we are (could have used GetSystemMetrics() as
            ** we're an ICON (I'm a little ICON short and stout...).
            */
            GetClientRect(hWnd, &rsClient);

            /*
            ** Wipe it...
            ** Could just use rsClient.right  for width and
            ** rsClient.bottom for  height as left  and top
            ** are always 0 for GetClientRect() - left this
            ** way a change to GetWindowRect() requires  no
            ** work.
            */
            Rectangle(
                    (HDC)wParam
                  ,0
                  ,0
                  ,rsClient.right  - rsClient.left
                  ,rsClient.bottom - rsClient.top
                  );

            /*
            ** Tidy up brush and pen.
            */
            DeleteObject(SelectObject((HDC)wParam, hbr));
            DeleteObject(SelectObject((HDC)wParam, hpe));
        }
        break;

        /*
        ** Need to paint in bars and set the window's caption.
        */
case WM_PAINT:
        {
            /*
            ** Used for wsprintf.
            */
            static char        carPctBuff[PAINTBUFF];

            /*
            ** All the rest used in painting graph.
            */
            auto HDC           hDC;
            auto PAINTSTRUCT   ps;

            auto RECT          rsClient;
            auto UINT          uGDIHeight;
            auto UINT          uUSRHeight;
            auto UINT          uWindowHeight;
            auto UINT          uWindowWidth;

            auto HBRUSH        hbr;

            auto int           nInflateAndOffset;

            /*
```

```
        ** Kinda magic number used as a scaling factor  -  alter this to
        ** increase/decrease the width of the displayed bars. The bigger
        ** the number, the bigger the bars.
        */
        nInflateAndOffset = 10;

        /*
        ** NOTE: newline processed by small icon window!
        */
        wsprintf(
                &carPctBuff[0]
                ,"GDI/USER Free\nGDI = %d%%\nUSER = %d%%"
                ,wPctGDIFree
                ,wPctUSRFree
                );
        /*
        ** Set the window's caption (this is for the iconic
           caption-window.
        */
        SetWindowText(hWnd, &carPctBuff[0]);

        /*
        ** Force the icon-window to update.
        */
        vRepaintTitle(hWnd);

        /*
        ** Now paint in the bars on the icon.
        */
        hDC = BeginPaint(hWnd, &ps);

        /*
        ** Get our size.
        */
        GetClientRect(hWnd, &rsClient);

        /*
        ** Change percieved window size to adjust for required bar width.
        ** Do not affect a height change.
        */
        InflateRect(
                &rsClient
                ,- (rsClient.right - rsClient.left) / nInflateAndOff-
set
                ,0
                );

        /*
        ** Work out height and width (could have used  GetSystemMetrics()
        ** as we're an icon, also as we're using GetClientRect() we could
        ** have simply used right and bottom as left and top are 0.
        */
        uWindowHeight = rsClient.bottom - rsClient.top;
        uWindowWidth  = rsClient.right  - rsClient.left;

        /*
        ** Work out size of 'free' bars. Need floating point to get
```

```
** precision.
*/
uGDIHeight = (UINT)(((float)uWindowHeight / 100) * wPctGDIFree);
uUSRHeight = (UINT)(((float)uWindowHeight / 100) * wPctUSRFree);


/*
** Paint 100% bars white.
*/
SelectObject(hDC, GetStockObject(WHITE_BRUSH));

Rectangle(
         hDC
         ,rsClient.left
         ,0
         ,uWindowWidth / 2 - 1
         ,uWindowHeight
         );

Rectangle(
         hDC
         ,rsClient.left + uWindowWidth / 2 + 1
         ,0
         ,uWindowWidth
         ,uWindowHeight
         );

/*
** 'Free' bars in red.
*/
hbr = CreateSolidBrush(RGB(255, 0, 0));

/*
** Paint 'Free' bars.
*/
hbr = SelectObject(hDC, hbr);

Rectangle(
         hDC
         ,rsClient.left
         ,uWindowHeight - uGDIHeight
         ,uWindowWidth / 2 - 1
         ,uWindowHeight
         );

Rectangle(
         hDC
         ,rsClient.left + uWindowWidth / 2 + 1
         ,uWindowHeight - uUSRHeight
         ,uWindowWidth
         ,uWindowHeight
         );

/*
** Get rid of old red brush.
*/
DeleteObject(SelectObject(hDC, hbr));
```

```
            EndPaint(hWnd, &ps);
         }
      break;

      /*
      ** Memory low - tell user using SysErrorBox().
      */
   case WM_COMPACTING:
      MessageBox(
               hWnd
              ,"Windows Compacting - Resources/System Memory Low!"
              ,"Resource Gauge"
              ,MB_OK | MB_SYSTEMMODAL
              );
      break;

      /*
      ** Sent from configure dialog window. Sets min limit.
      */
   case UM_SETALARM:
      uMin = LOWORD(lParam);
      break;

   default:
      return DefWindowProc(hWnd, uMessage, wParam, lParam);
   }

   return (LRESULT)0;
}




/*
** Handles BOTH dialog boxes, ie. About... and Configure...
*/
BOOL __export CALLBACK bDialogs
(
   HWND     hDlg
  ,UINT     uMessage
  ,WPARAM   wParam
  ,LPARAM   lParam
)
{
   switch(uMessage)
   {
      case WM_INITDIALOG:
         {
            /*
            ** Used to center the dialog windows.
            */
            auto RECT rsWindow;

            /*
            ** Window handle to configure dialog's edit control.
            */
            auto HWND hWndEdit;
```

```
/*
** Center dialog window.
*/
GetWindowRect(hDlg, &rsWindow);

MoveWindow(
          hDlg
          ,(GetSystemMetrics(SM_CXSCREEN) -
          (rsWindow.right - rsWindow.left)) /
          2
          ,(GetSystemMetrics(SM_CYSCREEN) -
          (rsWindow.bottom - rsWindow.top)) /
          2
          ,rsWindow.right - rsWindow.left
          ,rsWindow.bottom - rsWindow.top
          ,TRUE
          );

/*
** If configure dialog set up edit field and set focus
** to  it,  else  let  focus rest on About... dialog's
** OK button.
*/
if((hWndEdit = GetDlgItem(hDlg, IDC_THRESH)) != NULL)
{
    /*
    ** For reading threshold limit from private
    ** ini file.
    */
    auto char carThresholdBuffer[THRESHBUFF];

    /*
    ** Only  two  chars allowed, ie. 0  -  99.  If we'd
    ** allowed 3 figures we  would  have  to check that
    ** the user didn't enter something like 500! Anyway
    ** the  only legal  figure we're stopping them from
    ** entering  is 100 and  that would always cause an
    ** alarm to sound so 2 digits sounds good!
    */
    SendMessage(hWndEdit, EM_LIMITTEXT, 2, 0);

    /*
    ** Get current setting from private ini file. 0
    ** is the default.
    */
    GetPrivateProfileString(
                           "Res"
                           ,"Threshold"
                           ,"0"
                           ,&carThresholdBuffer[0]
                           ,sizeof(carThresholdBuffer)
                           ,"RES.INI"
                           );

    /*
    ** And set it.
```

```
                            */
                            SetWindowText(hWndEdit, &carThresholdBuffer[0]);

                            /*
                            ** Stay with the edit.
                            */
                            SetFocus(hWndEdit);

                            return FALSE;
                        }

                    /*
                    ** Let dialog manager figure out focus if About... box.
                    */
                    return TRUE;
                }
            break;

        case WM_COMMAND:
            switch(wParam)
            {
                /*
                ** Sys menu close or OK button on About... box,
                ** Cancel button (IDOK) on Configure... box.
                */
                case IDCANCEL:                              // FALL THRU.
                case IDOK:
                    EndDialog(hDlg, TRUE);
                    break;

                /*
                ** Configure box 'Set' button selected. Get number
                ** entered in edit field and tell owner window.
                */
                case IDC_SET:
                    {
                        /*
                        ** For GetDlgItemInt().
                        */
                        auto BOOL bTranslated;

                        /*
                        ** The current threshold integer value.
                        */
                        auto UINT uThreshold;

                        /*
                        ** Used to hold threshold value which is set into
                        ** private ini file.
                        */
                        auto char carThresholdBuffer[THRESHBUFF];

                        /*
                        ** Get required 'new' threshold.
                        */
                        uThreshold = GetDlgItemInt(
                                                    hDlg
```

```
                                              ,IDC_THRESH
                                              ,&bTranslated
                                              ,TRUE
                                              );

                    /*
                    ** Tell parent about it so that it can use it
                    ** to trigger an alarm signal.
                    */
                    SendMessage(
                                (HWND)GetWindowWord(
                                                    hDlg
                                                    ,GWW_HWNDPARENT
                                                    )
                                ,UM_SETALARM
                                ,0
                                ,MAKELPARAM(uThreshold, 0)
                                );

                    /*
                    ** Convert threshold to string ready for writing
                    ** out.
                    */
                    wsprintf(&carThresholdBuffer[0], "%d", uThreshold);

                    /*
                    ** Write out threshold value to private INI file.
                    */
                    WritePrivateProfileString(
                                              "Res"
                                              ,"Threshold"
                                              ,&carThresholdBuffer[0]
                                              ,"RES.INI"
                                              );

                    EndDialog(hDlg, TRUE);
                }
                break;
        }

    default:
        return FALSE;
    }

    return TRUE;
}
```

The .rc file :

```
#include <windows.h>
#include "res.h"

DLGINCLUDE RCDATA DISCARDABLE
BEGIN
    "RES.H\0"
END
```

```
/*
** Used in About... box.
*/
Resicon ICON ABOUT.ICO

/*
** Configure dialog.
*/
CONFIGURE DIALOG 0, 0, 160, 68
STYLE DS_MODALFRAME | WS_POPUP | WS_VISIBLE | WS_CAPTION | WS_SYSMENU
CAPTION "Configure..."
FONT 8, "MS Sans Serif"
BEGIN
    CONTROL
                    "&Set"
                    ,IDC_SET
                    ,"Button"
                    ,WS_TABSTOP | BS_DEFPUSHBUTTON
                    ,11
                    ,16
                    ,40
                    ,14

    CONTROL
                    ""
                    ,IDC_THRESH
                    ,"Edit"
                    ,WS_BORDER | WS_TABSTOP
                    ,57
                    ,17
                    ,15
                    ,12

    CONTROL
                    "Enter Alarm Threshold"
                    ,-1
                    ,"Static"
                    ,WS_GROUP
                    ,74
                    ,18
                    ,86
                    ,8

    CONTROL
                    "&Cancel"
                    ,IDOK
                    ,"Button"
                    ,WS_TABSTOP
                    ,60
                    ,48
                    ,40
                    ,14

    CONTROL
                    ""
                    ,-1
```

```
                    ,"Static"
                    ,SS_BLACKRECT
                    ,0
                    ,37
                    ,160
                    ,2

END


ABOUTBOX DIALOG 0, 0, 223, 67
STYLE DS_MODALFRAME | WS_CAPTION | WS_SYSMENU
CAPTION "About Resources..."
FONT 8, "MS Sans Serif"
BEGIN
    CONTROL
                    """Resources"" was written by :"
                    ,-1
                    ,"Static"
                    ,SS_CENTER | WS_GROUP
                    ,0
                    ,5
                    ,223
                    ,8

    CONTROL         "Peter J. Morris"
                    ,-1
                    ,"Static"
                    ,SS_CENTER | WS_GROUP
                    ,0
                    ,14
                    ,223
                    ,8

    CONTROL         "Version 1.0"
                    ,-1
                    ,"Static"
                    ,SS_CENTER | WS_GROUP
                    ,0
                    ,27
                    ,223
                    ,8

    CONTROL         "OK"
                    ,IDOK
                    ,"Button"
                    ,BS_DEFPUSHBUTTON | WS_GROUP | WS_TABSTOP
                    ,84
                    ,50
                    ,54
                    ,11

    CONTROL
                    "Resicon"
                    ,-1
                    ,"Static"
```

```
                        ,SS_ICON
                        ,15
                        ,8
                        ,14
                        ,13

END
```

The res.h file :

```c
/*
** Menu IDs.
*/
#define IDM_ABOUT              -    100
#define IDM_CONFIGURE               200


/*
** Dialog control IDs.
*/
#define IDC_ALARM                   301
#define IDC_SET                     302
#define IDC_THRESH                  303


/*
** Resource IDs.
*/
#define CONFIGURE                   100
#define ABOUTBOX                    200


/*
** If we're not being used by the resource compiler...
*/
#if !defined RC_INVOKED


/*
** Turn off silly warnings.
*/
#pragma warning(disable:4100)
#pragma warning(disable:4001)


/*
** Function prototypes.
*/
int  PASCAL WinMain           (HINSTANCE, HINSTANCE, LPSTR, int);

BOOL        bInitApplication (HINSTANCE);

BOOL        bInitInstance    (HINSTANCE, int);
```

```
VOID           vRepaintTitle      (HWND);

BOOL      __export CALLBACK bEnumProc
(
    HWND
  ,LPARAM
);

LRESULT __export CALLBACK lMainWndProc
(
    HWND
  ,UINT
  ,WPARAM
  ,LPARAM
);

BOOL      __export CALLBACK bDialogs
(
    HWND
  ,UINT
  ,WPARAM
  ,LPARAM
);


/*
** Coding standard stuff.
*/
#define VOID_ARG
#define VOID_RETURN


/*
** Private message.
*/
#define UM_SETALARM              WM_USER


/*
** Buffer size for reading entry from RES.INI.
*/
#define THRESHBUFF               3


/*
** Buffer size for wsprintf in paint routine.
*/
#define PAINTBUFF                100

/*
** RC_DEFINED.
*/
#endif
```

Brief Description.

Res creates a hidden *top-most* window using CreateWindowEx(). The window is created hidden because it makes sense to only show the window once you've got something to show in it! At this stage we haven't yet worked out the free system resources figure so we want to keep it hidden. It's also a top-most window, so when it does get shown it will always remain on top of every other window that is not a top-most window itself.

When the window's created its WM_CREATE handler is used to create a one second Windows' timer and alter the window's system menu, ie. the *Configure* and About items are added to the menu at this time. Additionally the create handler reads something called Threshold from RES.INI if it exists. The Threshold value is used as an alarm state indicator, ie. should the free system resources go below the value read from the INI file then an alarm will sound. Initially, until you've explicitly set a threshold value, this value will be zero – no alarm.

The WM_TIMER handler is used primarily to calculate available system resources using a TOOLHELP API called SystemHeapInfo(). The WM_TIMER handler checks the available heap information against two statics (wPctUSRFree, wPctGDIFree). These statics keep track of the state of the heaps and are used to prevent multiple re-paints when no re-paint is actually necessary, ie. the *free space* values are held in the statics and tested against the information returned by SystemHeapInfo() – if the test results are equal, ie. no change, then no re-paint is performed. If the values are different, the statics are updated, and a re-paint is initiated. The WM_TIMER handler is also responsible for checking for an alarm condition and sounding the alarm should it be required. The alarm itself is also part of the timer handler; currently it consists of calls to MessageBeep() and FlashWindow().

The *Res* class doesn't have a brush, ie. a NULL brush is given in the WNDCLASS used to register the class. This means that the app must erase the window when required to do so by processing the WM_ERASEBKGRND message. The app paints the background of the icon the same colour as the desktop in an attempt to create the illusion that the iconic window essentially isn't there at all – note that this could have been achieved automatically by giving GetStockObject(COLOR_BACKGROUND) as the background brush but by doing it this way we get to see WM_ERASEBKGRND processing for real!

The WM_PAINT handler uses the statics (talked about above) to draw the *thermometer* type bars shown in the earlier snap-shots of Res. It also causes the caption window, which is shown beneath the iconised main window, to get re-painted by calling an internal function called vRepaintTitle. The caption window carries, or displays, the caption text off the main window – this is changed to reflect the state of the available system resources in the

WM_PAINT handler (the WM_PAINT handler calls SetWindowText() to set its caption) -- unfortunately, the caption window has to re-painted to show any change made in the main window's caption and thus the requirement for vRepaintTitle.

That's really all we've got time for on windows at the moment; now for something completely different!

Chapter 5

C o n t r o l s

In this chapter we'll look at a small custom control example, but first....there any many sources of information on how to write custom controls; many other books on Windows' programming have sections that deal entirely with custom controls, and indeed, the SDK examples even include a custom control example called *rotary* which was written by my old work mate Nigel Thompson. Then why include a chapter on this myself?

Well in my opinion many of the existing samples are either technically a little thin (from a pure Windows' control viewpoint) or physically a little too fat in other Windows' areas and thus can cloud the main point – which is how to write robust, reusable controls in Windows. For example, I, and others, have observed that many control examples really ought to belong in a chapter on advanced GDI programming as they present an overly complex graphical interface to the user (and the coder trying to understand control essentials); all that GDI code can make it difficult to see what is required to write a control – period.

Often, also, the control is not *standard,* ie. it doesn't for example pass it's parent/owner a WM_CTLCOLOR message when it is about to paint itself like all of the standard controls do; you can't set the control's font by sending it a WM_SETFONT message etc.

The last thing about *my* control is that like the standard controls there's nothing in it that prevents an instance of it being created as, say, an overlapped window – as there is in many other *popular* examples.

In this <u>very short</u> chapter I present an extremely simple control that is more or less complete in that it supports all of the things that a standard control does, the control is not implemented in a DLL but is nonetheless still shareable. The effort required to move this control into a DLL and make it globally available is trivial and is outlined in brief later in the chapter (see also the DLL chapter) .

I decided to leave the control *in* an application so that you may see more clearly what is required in the actual control rather than what is required from a system's point of view in getting it going.   Also, the control is verbose to an extreme, by this I mean <u>I have chosen to place all code *in-line* even if that code were an ideal candidate to make</u>

into a stand-alone subroutine; or to put it another way, I have resisted writing many external support routines and opted for duplicating some of the code *in-line* rather than making calls to some external routine. This makes the code longer (as code is sometimes duplicated) but allows you to easily follow message processing, ie. each message handler is self contained. The code is therefore bigger than it would be if I or you were doing this for real. A good example of where this occurs is for example in the code for the keyboard/mouse handling message-handlers that inverts the control window to show that the control's been clicked etc – this code seems to appear all over the place and is of course an ideal candidate to be placed in a separate routine.

The control I've written, to some extent, mimics the push-button controls included with versions of Windows up to, but not including, version 3.0 of Windows. These push-buttons were fairly simple 2D affairs (if you remember?). My *button* class does not encapsulate the button variants seen in Windows 1.X & 2.X however, ie. you cannot create, say, radio buttons, or group boxes from it. You can however create several sorts of push-button. The class allows the user to create elliptical, rectangular or rounded-rectangular push-buttons only.

☐ Control Basics

A control is a window. All windows are created from a class. A control window is a window created from a control class therefore. A control class is typically generally useful, ie. it is one of those objects in Windows that is typically written such that any application can make use of the services that it provides – ergo, it's usually placed in a DLL to make it shareable.

Windows has many such classes named loosely (explained in an moment) after the type of object produced by the class. Standard Windows' control classes are :

- BUTTON
- COMBOBOX
- EDIT
- LISTBOX
- MDICLIENT
- SCROLLBAR
- STATIC

All of these standard classes, except MDICLIENT, are control classes. I said just above that these control classes create objects that are loosely defined by their respective names, this warrants an explanation which is best shown using a standard class – BUTTON. The BUTTON class creates windows that, not surprisingly, can be called *button-type* controls, eg. check-boxes, radio buttons and push-buttons; it can also be used however to create group boxes! A group box is one of those control frames that includes a textual component. In the snap-shot below all the controls, including the frame control, are window instances created or derived from the standard Windows' button class :

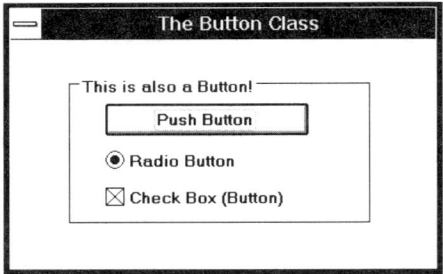

The button class made flesh

If you were to run up SPY and check out these control windows you'd find that only one of them shows up – the group box. The group box window, like all the other controls shown above, is created from the BUTTON class, it is however positioned (in the Z order) above those other controls and so SPY only reports that it can find the group box control even when the pointer is positioned above, say, the radio button :

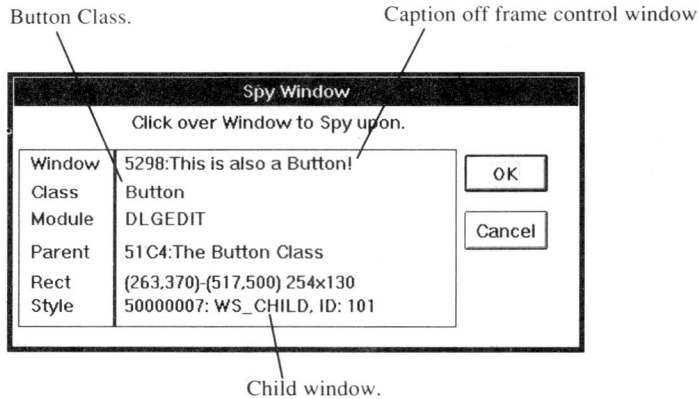

This is because the group box window really does cover all those other controls, and SPY queries the system to find out which window the pointer is currently positioned over – the answer therefore is the group box window. So how does the use interact with the windows that are located beneath the, obviously transparent, group box?

When you click on the radio button you are actually clicking on the group box window, the radio button receives the click however due to the group box replying -1 to a WM_NCHITTEST message. A WM_NCHITTEST message is sent to the window beneath the cursor whenever the cursor moves – it Windows' way of determining just where the cursor is over a window's real estate. -1 is defined as HTTRANSPARENT, ie. the window replies, 'I'm not really here as far as mouse input is concerned'. Windows therefore passes the click on to the window located beneath the group box which, in this example, would be the radio button (see Cleaning Windows and the Miscellaneous chapters for more on hit test processing). Of course a radio button doesn't respond in a like way otherwise you wouldn't be able to click on it (you can do this however in order to conveniently *disable* one of your controls!)! The point to all of this is that all the control windows discussed so far are actually created from the same window class – BUTTON. each is, therefore, handled by the same window procedure but each presents a different visual interface and handles (some) messages differently – **Wow!**

> SPY, I suspect, like most *spying* programs uses WindowFromPoint() to *find* a window; my own *spying* program uses the windows' co-ordinates to *find* a window given a screen relative position and additionally performs hit-testing on a window to see if it's transparent, so it does actually *find* the logical control over which the cursor is positioned – you ought to consider doing this if you are going to write your own *spy* type program.

The lesson that should be learned from this is that a Windows' class can be used to describe different objects, ideally, those objects should of course be related, ie. they should all be types of button etc. The group box is an oddball and, in my opinion, should be a variant of the static class. It does however quite nicely show just how different instances of a class (an instance of a class is a window) can be made to act and look quite differently from one another.

Taking this argument further, it would have been possible for Microsoft to have created all of the standard controls from a single Windows' class called, say, CONTROL, and indeed, rumour has it that this has been considered in the past but was dropped due to the lack of bits available in a long integer (window style bits)!

We're once again seeing a kind of sub-classing mechanism, ie. objects with a common root behaving differently according to their window style bits – the bits are defining a sub-type therefore. Additionally we could also say that we're seeing a sort of late binding in operation, ie. the shared class window procedure reacts differently to certain messages and has to dynamically adapt its responses according to the object type.

Each instance of a BUTTON above *knows* what sub-type of button it is (radio, push, check group) by examining its window style bits (all the *standard* window styles occupy the top 16 bits of the style DWORD whilst the *user defined* ones live in the lower 16):

```
BS_PUSHBUTTON              0x00000000L

BS_DEFPUSHBUTTON           0x00000001L

BS_CHECKBOX                0x00000002L

BS_AUTOCHECKBOX            0x00000003L
```

BS_RADIOBUTTON	0x00000004L
BS_3STATE	0x00000005L
BS_AUTO3STATE	0x00000006L
BS_GROUPBOX	0x00000007L
BS_USERBUTTON	0x00000008L
BS_AUTORADIOBUTTON	0x00000009L
BS_OWNERDRAW	0x0000000BL
BS_LEFTTEXT	0x00000020L

These style bits define the look and feel of the individual control window as presented by the class window procedure. Whenever a control is for example re-painted it paints itself according to certain style bits, ie. the class window procedure tests the window style bits of the current window in order to determine just how it should look. Some style bits are used to refine this look, BS_LEFTTEXT for example, or the control's behaviour, BS_3STATE for example. Certain window style bits may be also truly dynamic, ie. they are not defined statically; a good example is the WS_VISIBLE window style bit – this gets set/re-set when the window is toggled from being made invisible to visible and back again; indeed, even the *type* style bits may be altered dynamically thus allowing us to change the button sub-type on the fly.

The low 16 bits of a window's style is class specific, ie. it is up to you, the class designer to determine what these style bits mean. The high 16 bits are used by windows internally to determine, for example, the *type* of window (child popup etc) and visible state etc as explained above.

Control windows, like most other windows, have no pre-requisites in terms of their class style (although you'll often find them using CS_PARENTDC etc). As a general rule, windows do not test their class style bits. All Windows class style bits create/determine behaviour which is maintained by Windows itself. I would have preferred Microsoft to have added *class designer style bits* so that class specific *things* might have been defined as class attributes rather than window attributes (see Miscellaneous chapter for more on some of these CS_????? styles). One way around this deficiency is to use class words, ie. use, say, two class words to store your class specific styles?

The control I present in this chapter, like Windows' own controls, tests its window style bits in order to determine just how it should look. I have kept this to a minimum as I want to keep the code as readable and as straight forward as possible. Any instance of the control can appear like an elliptical, rectangular or rounded-rectangular push-button – as I've just said this *look* is dependent upon a window's style (default is rectangular). It would be very easy to extend this to include, say, a text alignment bit which would specify the alignment of the text (caption) within the control's client area.

Getting back to a window's style bits – here's an example of changing a control sub-type dynamically via indirect manipulation of its style bits :

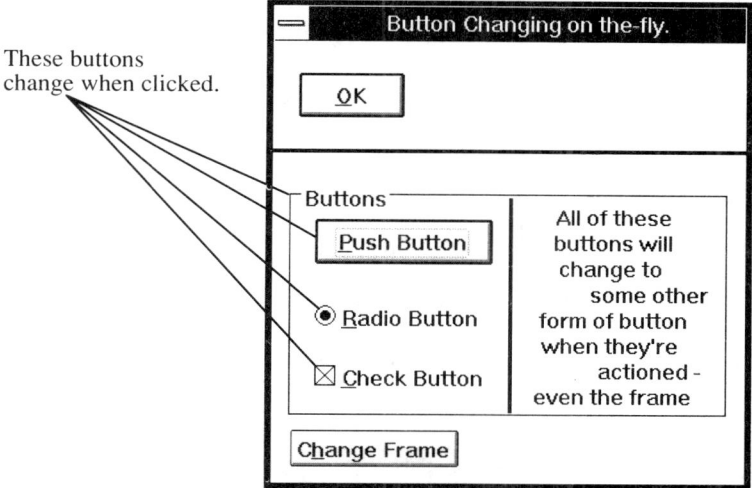

In the diagram above each of the buttons in the group box, and the group box itself, will change if they are clicked. Well actually the group box won't because the button class doesn't pass the parent/owner window a WM_COMMAND message when a group box is clicked etc, ie. it *really* is like a static class thing. To change the group box we use the dedicated button labelled *Change Frame*. When this button is clicked the group box changes to a button of another style. Following this the group box button may be actioned directly, ie. if we change the group box to, say, a push button by clicking on the Change Frame button, we no longer need the Change Frame button because the button that the frame has *become* will now respond to button clicks!

The changes made are random – each button will become either a default push-button, a radio button, a check box or a group box. Here's what it may look like when each control within the frame is clicked once :

If we click on the Change Frame button we may get what is shown in the first digram on the next page

Note that the group box's caption is now drawn centred as you'd expect when the control's a push button.

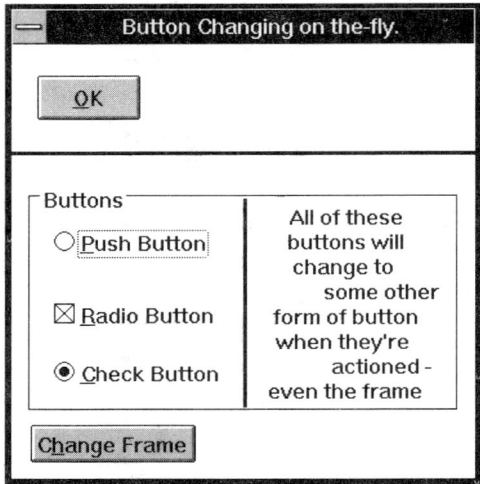

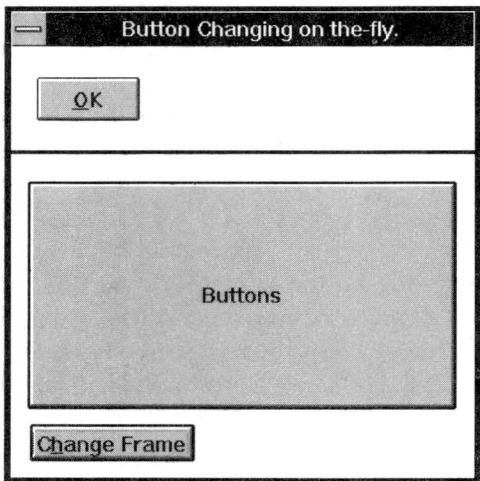

The code required to do this is all contained within the dialog's call-back, it looks like this :

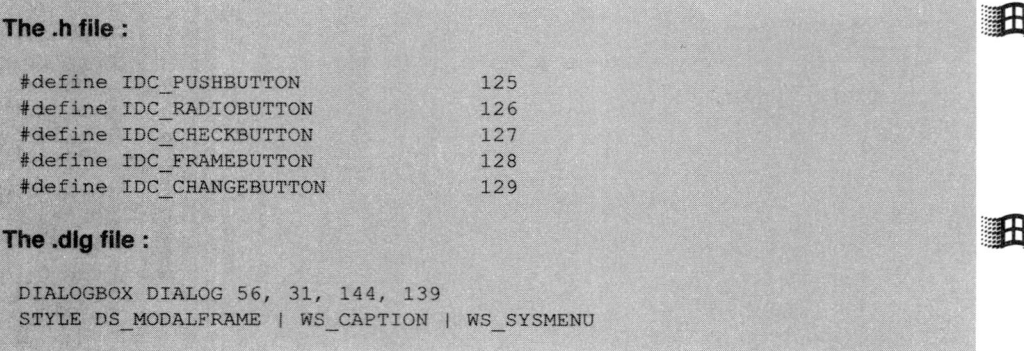

The .h file :

```
#define IDC_PUSHBUTTON          125
#define IDC_RADIOBUTTON         126
#define IDC_CHECKBUTTON         127
#define IDC_FRAMEBUTTON         128
#define IDC_CHANGEBUTTON        129
```

The .dlg file :

```
DIALOGBOX DIALOG 56, 31, 144, 139
STYLE DS_MODALFRAME | WS_CAPTION | WS_SYSMENU
```

```
CAPTION "Button Changing on the-fly."
BEGIN
    CONTROL
            "&OK"
            ,IDOK
            ,"Button"
            ,BS_DEFPUSHBUTTON
            ,8, 10, 32, 14

    CONTROL
            "Buttons"
            ,IDC_FRAMEBUTTON
            ,"Button"
            ,BS_GROUPBOX
            ,5, 44, 133, 73

    CONTROL
            "&Push Button"
            ,IDC_PUSHBUTTON
            ,"Button"
            ,WS_TABSTOP
            ,13, 56, 54, 14

    CONTROL
            "&Radio Button"
            ,IDC_RADIOBUTTON
            ,"Button"
            ,BS_RADIOBUTTON
            ,13, 79, 54, 14

    CONTROL
            "&Check Button"
            ,IDC_CHECKBUTTON
            ,"Button"
            ,BS_CHECKBOX | WS_TABSTOP
            ,13, 98, 54, 14

    CONTROL
            "All of these buttons will change to
             some other form of button when they're
             actioned - even the frame button!"
            ,-1
            ,"Static"
            ,SS_CENTER | WS_GROUP
            ,74, 51, 61, 63

    CONTROL
            ""
            ,-1
            ,"Static"
            ,SS_BLACKRECT
            ,0, 34, 144, 1

    CONTROL
            ""
            ,-1
            ,"Static"
```

```
                ,SS_BLACKRECT
                ,72, 49, 1, 67

        CONTROL
                "C&hange Frame"
                ,IDC_CHANGEBUTTON
                ,"Button"
                ,WS_TABSTOP
                ,6, 122, 51, 12
    END
```

The dialog call-back :

```
BOOL __export CALLBACK Dialog
(
    HWND    hDlg
   ,UINT    uMessage
   ,WPARAM  wParam
   ,LPARAM  lParam
)
{
    static HWND hWndFrame;

    switch(uMessage)
    {
        case WM_INITDIALOG:
                {
                    auto HWND hWndRadio;
                    auto HWND hWndCheck;

                    /*
                    ** Get required control's window handles. Note
                    ** that frame's is held in a static.
                    */
                    hWndRadio = GetDlgItem(hDlg, IDC_RADIOBUTTON);
                    hWndCheck = GetDlgItem(hDlg, IDC_CHECKBUTTON);
                    hWndFrame = GetDlgItem(hDlg, IDC_FRAMEBUTTON);

                    /*
                    ** Turn radio button and check box on.
                    */
                    SendMessage(hWndRadio, BM_SETCHECK, 1, 0);
                    SendMessage(hWndCheck, BM_SETCHECK, 1, 0);
                }
                return TRUE;

        case WM_COMMAND:
                switch(wParam)
                {
                    /*
                    ** Holds a random style.
                    */
                    auto WORD wStyle;

                    /*
                    ** Holds a control's style.
```

```
*/
auto LONG lStyle;

      /*
      ** End dialog on OK.
      */
case IDOK:                // FALL THRU.
case IDCANCEL:
      EndDialog(hDlg, TRUE);
      break;

      /*
      ** Either radio button, check box or
      ** push button control clicked.
      */
case IDC_RADIOBUTTON: // FALL THRU.
case IDC_CHECKBUTTON:
case IDC_PUSHBUTTON:
case IDC_FRAMEBUTTON:

      tryagain:

      /*
      ** Get a random style for setting the actioned
      ** control to another type of button.
      */
      do
      {
         wStyle = (WORD)rand();
         wStyle = (WORD)(wStyle / 1000);
      }
      while(
            wStyle != BS_GROUPBOX        &&
            wStyle != BS_DEFPUSHBUTTON   &&
            wStyle != BS_CHECKBOX        &&
            wStyle != BS_RADIOBUTTON
           );

      /*
      ** Check that randomised style is NOT the
      ** same as control's current style, retry
      ** if they are.
      */
      lStyle = GetWindowLong(
                             (HWND)LOWORD(lParam)
                             ,GWL_STYLE
                             );

      if((lStyle & 0xF) == (LONG)wStyle)
      {
         goto tryagain;
      }

      /*
      ** If randomised  style is a group, box cause
      ** the dialog window, and all control windows
      ** to  re-paint  as  the  button  class won't
      ** draw a frame correctly otherwise.
```

```
                              */
                              if(wStyle == BS_GROUPBOX)
                              {
                                   InvalidateRect(hDlg, NULL, TRUE);
                              }


                              /*
                              ** Set control's style. SendMessage() is used
                              ** so that if the  control's  now a frame its
                              ** style will be  changed before the WM_PAINT
                              ** message (see above) is delivered.
                              */
                              SendMessage(
                                           (HWND)LOWORD(lParam)
                                          ,BM_SETSTYLE
                                          ,wStyle
                                          ,TRUE
                                          );
                              break;


                              /*
                              ** Change group box surrounding other controls.
                              */
                         case IDC_CHANGEBUTTON:

                              /*
                              ** Use a user sent WM_COMMAND message to instigate
                              ** this.
                              */
                              wParam   = IDC_FRAMEBUTTON;
                              lParam   = MAKELPARAM(hWndFrame, 0);
                              uMessage = WM_COMMAND;

                              PostMessage(hDlg, uMessage, wParam, lParam);
                              break;


                    }
                    return TRUE;
          }

     return FALSE;
}
```

The WM_INITDIALOG simply *turns on* the radio button and the check box prior to
the dialog being shown. Note that SendMessage() is used instead of CheckRa-
dioButton() etc as it's faster. Additionally the group box's window handle is retrieved
at this time and stored in a static variable.

When either of the *normal* buttons within the group box are selected a new style is
selected for the control at random :

```
tryagain:

/*
** Get a random style for setting the actioned
** control to another type of button.
```

```
*/
do
{
   wStyle = (WORD)rand();
   wStyle = (WORD)(wStyle / 1000);
}
while(
      wStyle != BS_GROUPBOX       &&
      wStyle != BS_DEFPUSHBUTTON  &&
      wStyle != BS_CHECKBOX       &&
      wStyle != BS_RADIOBUTTON
     );

/*
** Check that randomised style is NOT the
** same as control's current style, retry
** if they are.
*/
lStyle = GetWindowLong(
                       (HWND)LOWORD(lParam)
                       ,GWL_STYLE
                       );

if((lStyle & 0xF) == (LONG)wStyle)
{
   goto tryagain;
}
```

If the control style chosen is not the same as that awarded to the control currently the control's style is changed to the randomly selected style by sending it a BM_SETSTYLE message – Note that if the style set is BS_GROUPBOX that the control will no longer be selectable, ie. it is effectively killed! Note also that if the style selected is BS_GROUPBOX that the dialog box, and its contents, are forced to re-paint. This is done because the BUTTON class doesn't seem to draw itself properly if the style selected is BS_GROUPBOX (a part of the old button's image is left visible within the new group box button).

If the group box surrounding the other buttons requires changing then the *Change Frame* button must be used as BS_GROUPBOXs do not respond to user input (as was noted earlier). The *Change Frame* button causes the group box to be changed by passing the dialog a WM_COMMAND message, ie. it makes it look as though the group box has responded to user input.

Note that the same effect, ie. changing a control's sub-type could have been achieved using SetWindowLong() but it's usually better, and certainly more polite, to use an object's *change type* service, ie. in this case the BM_SETSTYLE method of the BUTTON object – it's only this technique that the BUTTON based object expressly supports.

☐ The 2D button control

OK, back to my custom control. Here's what the control looks like when created by my application :

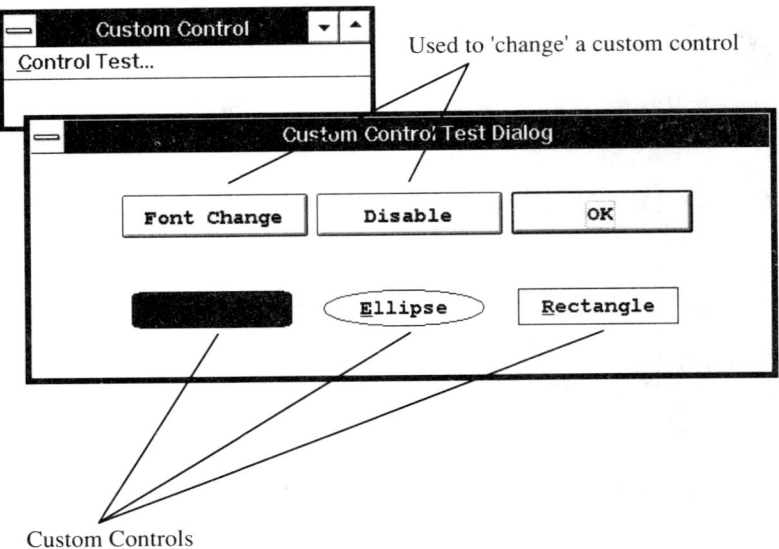

Custom Controls

Dialog box showing three custom controls

Here we can see all the variants of this *new* control type (ControlWClass). Note that the controls are shown as part of a dialog box and that they can therefore be (easily) included in the dialog definition (see dialog box chapter for more on this).

Two of the controls above have significant class based window styles. The elliptical and rounded-rectangle buttons are created with the following style bits :

```
CONTROL          "&RoundRect"
                ,NEWBUTTON
                ,"ControlWClass"
                ,WS_GROUP        |
                 WS_TABSTOP      |
                 NB_RRECTANGLE   |
                 BS_DEFPUSHBUTTON
                ,32
                ,46
                ,51
                ,12

CONTROL          "&Ellipse"
                ,203
                ,"ControlWClass"
                ,NB_ELLIPSE
                ,93
                ,46
                ,51
                ,12
```

NB_RRECTANGLE and NB_ELLIPSE are the significant ones here. As you can see I have also *used* a BUTTON class style – BS_DEFPUSHBUTTON for the rounded rectangle button; we'll see how this is used later. Note that WS_GROUP and WS_TAB-

STOP are not tested or processed within the control class code – they are used by Windows (the dialog box manager (DM)) directly.

As each control is moved to (using the keyboard or mouse) that control gets focus and should, as it is a button, show that it can be selected by pressing the enter key, ie. it becomes a default push-button of sorts. In the diagram below the *Rectangle* button is shown focused :

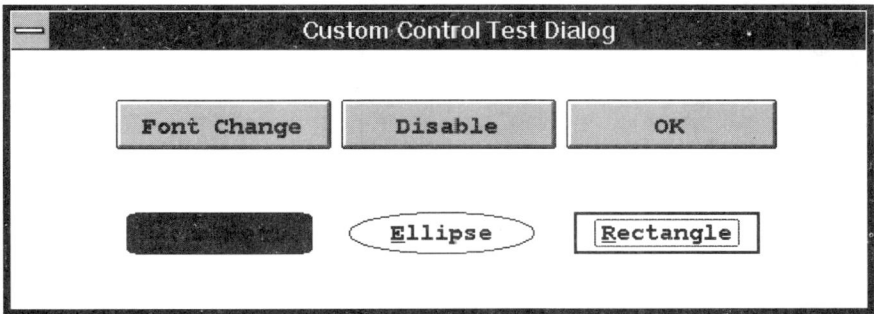

Note that the control that is focused above has a thick border and that its caption text is shown framed denoting that it may be selected by pressing the enter key.

The *extra* buttons in the dialog *exercise* the control class. The disable button disables a control so that the control's notification codes may be checked. The font change button makes a control change the font it is using to display its caption text.

OK, let's have a look at the code for this application and control class :

```
/*
** Note that this code has minimal error handling/checking.
*/

#define STRICT

#include <windows.h>
#include "generic.h"

/*
** Turn off silly warnings.
*/
#pragma warning(disable:4100)
#pragma warning(disable:4001)

int PASCAL WinMain
  (
    HINSTANCE    hInstance
  , HINSTANCE    hPrevInstance
  , LPSTR        lpszCmdLine
```

```
  ,int         nCmdShow
)
{
   auto MSG msg;

   if(hPrevInstance == NULL)
   {
      if(bInitApplication(hInstance) == FALSE)
      {
         return FALSE;
      }
   }


   if(bInitInstance(hInstance, nCmdShow) == FALSE)
   {
      return FALSE;
   }


   while(GetMessage(&msg, NULL, 0, 0))
   {
      TranslateMessage(&msg);
      DispatchMessage(&msg);
   }

   return msg.wParam;
}



BOOL bInitApplication(HINSTANCE hInstance)
{
   auto WNDCLASS  wc;

   wc.style          = NULL;
   wc.lpfnWndProc    = (WNDPROC)MainWndProc;
   wc.cbClsExtra     = 0;
   wc.cbWndExtra     = 0;
   wc.hInstance      = hInstance;
   wc.hIcon          = LoadIcon(NULL, IDI_APPLICATION);
   wc.hCursor        = LoadCursor(NULL, IDC_ARROW);
   wc.hbrBackground  = (HBRUSH)(COLOR_WINDOW + 1);
   wc.lpszMenuName   = "ControlMenu";
   wc.lpszClassName  = "MainWClass";

   if(RegisterClass(&wc) == NULL)
   {
      return FALSE;
   }

   /*
   ** Register new control class. Note that no control 'class' bits
   ** are set.
   */
   wc.style          = NULL;
   wc.lpfnWndProc    = (WNDPROC)ControlWndProc;
```

```
   wc.cbClsExtra       = 0;
   wc.cbWndExtra       = CONTROLEXTRA; /* Should be 40 or less. */
   wc.hInstance        = hInstance;
   wc.hIcon            = LoadIcon(NULL, IDI_APPLICATION);
   wc.hCursor          = LoadCursor(NULL, IDC_ARROW);
   wc.hbrBackground    = (HBRUSH)(COLOR_WINDOW + 1);
   wc.lpszMenuName     = NULL;
   wc.lpszClassName    = "ControlWClass";

   /*
   ** Return TRUE or FALSE only.
   */
   return !!RegisterClass(&wc) ;
}




BOOL bInitInstance(HINSTANCE hInstance, int nCmdShow)
{
   auto HWND hWnd;

   hWnd = CreateWindow(
                       "MainWClass"
                       ,"Custom Control"
                       ,WS_OVERLAPPEDWINDOW
                       ,200
                       ,200
                       ,300
                       ,100
                       ,NULL
                       ,NULL
                       ,hInstance
                       ,NULL
                       );

   if(hWnd == NULL)
   {
       return FALSE;
   }

   ShowWindow(hWnd, nCmdShow);
   UpdateWindow(hWnd);

   return TRUE;
}




LRESULT __export CALLBACK MainWndProc
(
  HWND     hWnd
 ,UINT     uMessage
 ,WPARAM   wParam
 ,LPARAM   lParam
)
{
  /*
```

```
** The only things to do here are to create the dialog and
** handle the destroy message.
*/

switch(uMessage)
{
    case WM_COMMAND:
        switch(wParam)
        {
            case IDM_TEST:
                {
                    DialogBox(
                              (HINSTANCE)GetWindowWord(
                                                        hWnd
                                                       ,GWW_HINSTANCE
                                                       )
                             ,"AboutBox"
                             ,hWnd
                             ,(DLGPROC)About
                             );
                }
                break;

        }
        break;

    case WM_DESTROY:
        PostQuitMessage(0);
        break;

    default:
        return DefWindowProc(hWnd, uMessage, wParam, lParam);
}

return (LRESULT)0;
}



BOOL __export CALLBACK About
(
  HWND     hDlg
 ,UINT     uMessage
 ,WPARAM   wParam
 ,LPARAM   lParam
)
{
    /*
    ** Holds RED brush for life of dialog box, used in
    ** processing WM_CTLCOLOR messages.
    */
    static HBRUSH hbr;

    switch(uMessage)
    {
        case WM_COMMAND:
            switch(wParam)
```

```
{
    case IDOK:                        // FALL THRU.
    case IDCANCEL:

        /*
        ** Tidy up and go to bed.
        */
        if(hbr != NULL)
        {
            DeleteObject(hbr);
        }

        hbr = NULL;

        EndDialog(hDlg, TRUE);

        return TRUE;

        break;

        /*
        ** Font change button pressed. Change the font
        ** in a custom control.
        */
    case IDM_FONTCHANGE:
        SendMessage(
                    (HWND)GetDlgItem(hDlg, NEWBUTTON)
                    ,WM_SETFONT
                    ,(WPARAM)GetStockObject(ANSI_VAR_FONT)
                    ,MAKELPARAM(TRUE, 0)
                    );

        break;

        /*
        ** Disable button pressed, disable a custom
        ** control to test notification message.
        */
    case IDM_DISABLE:
        EnableWindow((HWND)GetDlgItem(hDlg, NEWBUTTON), FALSE);

        break;

        /*
        ** If we get a notification code from
        ** one of the custom controls...
        */

    case NEWBUTTON:
        switch(HIWORD(lParam))
        {

            case BN_CLICKED:
                MessageBox(
                            hDlg
                            ,"Clicked"
                            ,"Notification"
```

```
                                ,MB_OK
                                );
                        break;

                case BN_DISABLE:
                    /*
                    ** Change caption in custom control.
                    */
                    SetWindowText(
                                GetDlgItem(
                                            hDlg
                                            ,NEWBUTTON
                                            )
                                ,"Disabled"
                                );

                    MessageBox(
                            hDlg
                            ,"Disabled"
                            ,"Notification"
                            ,MB_OK
                            );
                        break;
                }
            break;
    }
    break;

case WM_CTLCOLOR:
    {
        switch(HIWORD(lParam))
        {
            case CTLCOLOR_BTN:
                {
                    /*
                    ** Handle & ID of custom control.
                    */
                    auto HWND hWndControl;
                    auto WORD wCntlID;

                    /*
                    ** Get ID of sending child control.
                    */
                    hWndControl = (HWND)LOWORD(lParam);
                    wCntlID = GetWindowWord(hWndControl, GWW_ID);

                    /*
                    ** See if it was NEWBUTTON.
                    */
                    switch(wCntlID)
                    {
                        /*
                        ** If it's the NEWBUTTON control paint
                        ** it red.
                        */
                        case NEWBUTTON:
                            return (BOOL)hbr;
                            break;
```

```
                                        default:
                                                break;
                                }
                                break;
                        }
                        break;

                default:
                        break;
                }
            break;
        }
        break;

    case WM_INITDIALOG:
        /*
        ** Create a nice red brush for painting the NEWBUTTON control.
        */
        hbr = CreateSolidBrush(RGB(255, 0, 0));

        return TRUE;
    }

    return FALSE;
}



LRESULT __export CALLBACK ControlWndProc
(
    HWND     hWnd
  , UINT     uMessage
  , WPARAM   wParam
  , LPARAM   lParam
)
{

    switch(uMessage)
    {
        /*
        ** Treat WM_CREATE as a constructor.
        */
    case WM_CREATE:

        /*
        ** Although not strictly necessary, clean the control
        ** window's extra bytes prior to them being used.
        */
        SetWindowWord(hWnd, GWW_OWNER,     NULL);
        SetWindowWord(hWnd, GWW_INVERTED,  NULL);
        SetWindowWord(hWnd, GWW_FONT,      NULL);
        SetWindowWord(hWnd, GWW_USERBRUSH, NULL);
        SetWindowLong(hWnd, GWL_DLGCODE,   NULL);

        /*
        ** Now play find the owner/parent.
        */
```

```
{
    /*
    ** Holds the window handle of the parent/owner window
    ** as it's found.
    */
    auto HWND hWndOwner;

    /*
    ** Who do we communicate with for notification messages?
    **
    ** First test to see if we're a child window. All child
    ** windows MUST have a parent in order to be successfully
    ** created - no need to check return of GetParent()
    ** therefore.
    */
    if((GetWindowLong(hWnd, GWL_STYLE) & WS_CHILD) == WS_CHILD)
    {
        /*
        ** Remember owner/parent.
        */
        SetWindowWord(
                    hWnd
                    ,GWW_OWNER
                    ,(WORD)GetParent(hWnd)
                    );
    }
    else
    {
        /*
        ** Not a child window so use GWW_HWNDPARENT to get the
        ** handle of the owner (if any). See section on Parent/
        ** Owner in 'Cleaning Windows' chapter for more on why
        ** we use GWW_HWNDPARENT when apparently a test for
        ** a parent just failed!
        */

        /*
        ** If owner is NULL use the desktop else use the owner.
        */
        if(
            (hWndOwner = (HWND)GetWindowWord(
                                            hWnd
                                            ,GWW_HWNDPARENT
                                            )
            ) != NULL
          )
        {
            /*
            ** Remember parent/owner.
            */
            SetWindowWord(
                        hWnd
                        ,GWW_OWNER
                        ,(WORD)hWndOwner
                        );
        }
    }
```

```
                    else
                    {
                        /*
                        ** Remember parent/owner.
                        */
                        SetWindowWord(
                                        hWnd
                                      ,GWW_OWNER
                                      ,(WORD)GetDesktopWindow(VOID_ARG)
                                      );
                    }


            }
        }
        break;

        /*
        ** Treat WM_DESTROY as a destructor.
        */
case WM_DESTROY:
        /*
        ** If we needed to clean up anything we'd do it in here.
        ** NOTE that a child window is not necessarily destroyed
        ** before its parent is.
        */
        break;

        /*
        ** Example notification message - tell our owner/parent
        ** when we've become disabled.
        */
case WM_ENABLE:
        if(wParam == FALSE)
        {
            SendMessage(
                        (HWND)GetWindowWord(hWnd, GWW_OWNER)
                      ,WM_COMMAND
                      ,GetWindowWord(hWnd, GWW_ID)
                      ,MAKELPARAM(hWnd, BN_DISABLE)
                      );
        }

        /*
        ** Cause a re-paint so that the control can change its
        ** look  (Text Color used  etc)  whenever  it  becomes
        ** enabled/disabled.
        */
        InvalidateRect(hWnd, NULL, TRUE);
        UpdateWindow(hWnd);

        break;

        /*
        ** Got to tell the DM what we are and what we want.
        ** Check our window words for the answer.
        */
case WM_GETDLGCODE:
```

```
        /*
        ** Return whatever's in the words.
        */
        return GetWindowLong(hWnd, GWL_DLGCODE);

        break;

        /*
        ** User wants our font so we return whatever that currently
        ** is. It may of course be NULL - no font. This is OK, ie. a
        ** control should return NULL to indicate that it's using the
        ** default.
        */
case WM_GETFONT:

        /*
        ** Return whatever's in the words.
        */
        return GetWindowWord(hWnd, GWW_FONT);

        break;

case WM_KEYDOWN:
        if(wParam == VK_SPACE)
        {
            /*
            ** Used in inverting the control window.
            */
            auto HDC    hDC;
            auto RECT   rsClient;

            /*
            ** May be holding down the space bar - check it.
            */
            if(GetWindowWord(hWnd, GWW_INVERTED) == TRUE)
            {
                break;
            }

            /*
            ** Get the client rect and invert it to show that the
            ** button's been clicked.
            */

            hDC = GetDC(hWnd);

            GetClientRect(hWnd, &rsClient);

            InvertRect(hDC, &rsClient);

            SetWindowWord(hWnd, GWW_INVERTED, TRUE);

            ReleaseDC(hWnd, hDC);
        }
        break;

case WM_KEYUP:
        /*
```

```
          ** Check to see if key is the space bar  - same as lbutton click
          ** if it is the space bar. Get the control to send a WM_CTLCOLOR
         ** message if it is.
         */
         if(wParam == VK_SPACE)
         {
             /*
             ** Used in inverting the control window.
             */
             auto HDC     hDC;
             auto RECT    rsClient;

             /*
             ** Get the client rect and invert it to show that the
             ** button's been un-clicked.
             */

             hDC = GetDC(hWnd);

             GetClientRect(hWnd, &rsClient);

             InvertRect(hDC, &rsClient);

             SetWindowWord(hWnd, GWW_INVERTED, FALSE);

             ReleaseDC(hWnd, hDC);

             /*
             ** Force WM_CTLCOLOR.
             */
             InvalidateRect(hWnd, NULL, TRUE);
             UpdateWindow(hWnd);

             /*
             ** Pass click to parent/owner.
             */
             SendMessage(
                     (HWND)GetWindowWord(hWnd, GWW_OWNER)
                     ,WM_COMMAND
                     ,GetWindowWord(hWnd, GWW_ID)
                     ,MAKELPARAM(hWnd, BN_CLICKED)
                     );
         }
         break;

case WM_KILLFOCUS:
     /*
     ** Cause repaint, this will remove/show the focus rect.
     ** Same thing is done for WM_SETFOCUS.
     */
     InvalidateRect(hWnd, NULL, TRUE);
     UpdateWindow(hWnd);

     /*
     ** Set up WM_GETDLGCODE return.
     */
     SetWindowLong(
             hWnd
```

```
                            ,GWL_DLGCODE
                            ,DLGC_UNDEFPUSHBUTTON | DLGC_BUTTON
                            );

        break;

    case WM_LBUTTONDOWN:

        /*
        ** Clicked in so focus control.
        */
        SetFocus(hWnd);

        /*
        ** Capture mouse so that we can track it outside of our
        ** control's window area.
        */
        SetCapture(hWnd);
        {
            /*
            ** Used in inverting the control window.
            */
            auto HDC    hDC;
            auto RECT   rsClient;

            /*
            ** Get the client rect and invert it to show that the
            ** button's been clicked.
            */

            hDC = GetDC(hWnd);

            GetClientRect(hWnd, &rsClient);

            InvertRect(hDC, &rsClient);

            SetWindowWord(hWnd, GWW_INVERTED, TRUE);

            ReleaseDC(hWnd, hDC);
        }
        break;

    case WM_LBUTTONUP:

        /*
        ** First check to see if lbuttondown has been generated
        ** outside of our control's window. If it wasn't we will
        ** have captured all pointer input.
        */
        if(hWnd == GetCapture(VOID_ARG))
        {
            /*
            ** In here - button up DOES follow an lbuttondown that
            ** occurred in our client area.  Finished with capture.
            */
            ReleaseCapture(VOID_ARG);

            /*
```

```
        ** This bit not required if we could always count on
        ** getting a mouse move before an lbuttonup; if we
        ** could we could just invert the rect without checking
        ** whether or not it is currently inverted as it will
        ** have been in the mousemove handler.
        */
        if(GetWindowWord(hWnd, GWW_INVERTED) == TRUE)
        {
            /*
            ** Used in inverting the control window.
            */
            auto HDC    hDC;
            auto RECT   rsClient;

            /*
            ** Get the client rect and invert it to show that the
            ** button's been un-clicked.
            */

            hDC = GetDC(hWnd);

            GetClientRect(hWnd, &rsClient);

            InvertRect(hDC, &rsClient);

            SetWindowWord(hWnd, GWW_INVERTED, FALSE);

            ReleaseDC(hWnd, hDC);
        }

        /*
        ** As we're getting the lbuttonup after we've processed
        ** an lbuttondown we've been clicked - tell the parent/
        ** owner about it. Check that the 'up' happens within the
        ** control's window area first.
        */
        ClientToScreen(hWnd, (LPPOINT)&lParam);

        if(WindowFromPoint(MAKEPOINT(lParam)) == hWnd)
        {
            SendMessage(
                        (HWND)GetWindowWord(hWnd, GWW_OWNER)
                        ,WM_COMMAND
                        ,GetWindowWord(hWnd, GWW_ID)
                        ,MAKELPARAM(hWnd, BN_CLICKED)
                        );
        }
    }
    else
    {
        /*
        ** Got an lbuttonup without first getting an lbuttondown,
        ** ignore it, in other words someone clicked down outside
        ** of our window, moved into it, then released the mouse
        ** button - sneaky!
        */
        break;
```

```
            }
        break;

    case WM_MOUSEMOVE:

        /*
        ** If the mouse is moving as a result of an lbuttondown...
        */
        if(hWnd == GetCapture(VOID_ARG))
        {
            /*
            ** Determine whether  or not the pointer  is within our
            ** window's client  area, and  do  the  necessary  rect
            ** inversion. NOTE : PtInRect() would probably a faster
            ** way to determine this.
            */

            /*
            ** If it's gone outside of the window's client area AND
            ** we're currently  inverted  we should invert again to
            ** restore the image (no longer armed).
            */
            ClientToScreen(hWnd, (LPPOINT)&lParam);

            if(
                WindowFromPoint(MAKEPOINT(lParam)) != hWnd &&
                GetWindowWord(hWnd, GWW_INVERTED)  == TRUE
              )
            {
                /*
                ** Used in inverting the control window.
                */
                auto HDC      hDC;
                auto RECT     rsClient;

                /*
                ** Get the client rect and invert it to show that the
                ** button's been un-armed.
                */
                hDC = GetDC(hWnd);

                GetClientRect(hWnd, &rsClient);

                InvertRect(hDC, &rsClient);

                SetWindowWord(hWnd, GWW_INVERTED, FALSE);

                ReleaseDC(hWnd, hDC);
            }
            /*
            ** If it's gone outside of  the window's client area we
            ** will have restored  the window's image.  If it comes
            ** back  into  the control window's client area we need
            ** to invert it  again to  show that the button's armed
            ** once  more. NOTE : PtInRect() would  probably  be  a
            ** faster way to determine this.
            */
            else
```

```
            if(
               WindowFromPoint(MAKEPOINT(lParam))  == hWnd &&
               GetWindowWord(hWnd, GWW_INVERTED)   != TRUE
               )
            {
               /*
               ** Used in inverting the control window.
               */
               auto HDC hDC;
               auto RECT rsClient;

               /*
               ** Get the client rect and invert it to show that the
               ** button's been armed.
               */
               hDC = GetDC(hWnd);

               GetClientRect(hWnd, &rsClient);

               InvertRect(hDC, &rsClient);

               SetWindowWord(hWnd, GWW_INVERTED, TRUE);

               ReleaseDC(hWnd, hDC);
            }
         }
         break;

         /*
         ** Most everything is done in here!
         */
      case WM_PAINT:
         {
            /*
            ** Begin/End-Paint stuff.
            */
            auto HDC            hDC;
            auto PAINTSTRUCT    ps;

            /*
            ** Used for drawing and filling the control window.
            */
            auto HBRUSH         hbr;
            auto RECT           rsClient;
            auto HPEN           hpn;
            auto LOGPEN         lpn;

            /*
            ** Used for rendering the control's caption.
            */
            auto char           carCaptionBuff[MAX_CAPTION];
            auto DWORD          dwText;
            auto HFONT          hFont;

            /*
            ** Control style.
            */
            auto LONG           lStyle;
```

```
/*
** Get ready, (they come!)...
*/
hDC = BeginPaint(hWnd, &ps);
/*
** Give parent/owner a chance to change control's DC and
** see  if  it wants us to use a different brush for the
** control's background color.
*/

if((hbr = (HBRUSH)LOWORD(SendMessage(
                        (HWND)GetWindowWord(hWnd, GWW_OWNER)
                        ,WM_CTLCOLOR
                        ,(WPARAM)hDC
                        ,MAKELPARAM(hWnd, CTLCOLOR_BTN)
                        ))) != NULL
)
{
    /*
    ** YES.  The user's wanting us  to  use a different
       ** brush  so select it  and set window word to TRUE,
       ** this is tested later to see if the selected brush
       ** should  be de-selected. If  we  were to use, say,
       ** a white  brush  to  always  paint  the backgrund,
       ** given  that  the  user doesn't  want  to use some
       ** weird color  AND  that  we  would  always want to
       ** even de-select  a  stock  object  this test, and
       ** window word could be removed/freed.
       **
       ** If you want to prevent any changes being made to
       ** the DC use  SaveDC()  to 'push' before the Send-
       ** Message() call  and  RestoreDC() to pop it after
       ** it's returned.
       */
    hbr = SelectObject(hDC, hbr);

    SetWindowWord(hWnd, GWW_USERBRUSH, TRUE);
}

/*
** It always pays to  remember  that  the  user has had the
** opportunity  to change  the  DC  in  whatever  way - you
** should tidy it up in whatever way you feel is justified,
** remember  however  that the  whole point of giving it to
** them is so  that  they can change it, ie. don't undo all
** their work! We  change  a few things : the  map  mode as
** MM_TEXT is  the  quickest  to  use  in drawing, the text
** color, the DrawMode to TRANSPARENT and the pen.
*/
SetMapMode(hDC, MM_ANISOTROPIC);

/*
** Get ready to draw in the button's shape within the
** control's client area.
*/
```

```
GetClientRect(hWnd, &rsClient);

/*
** Fill in pen struct with appropriate pen details.
*/

/*
** Change the pen width if  the control's focused. NOTE :
** could have used something like FrameRect() to do this.
*/

lpn.lopnWidth.x = GetFocus(VOID_ARG) == hWnd ? 2 : 1;

lpn.lopnStyle    = PS_SOLID | PS_INSIDEFRAME;
lpn.lopnColor    = RGB(0, 0, 0);

/*
** Get a new pen.
*/
hpn = CreatePenIndirect(&lpn);

/*
** And select it.
*/
hpn = SelectObject(hDC, hpn);

/*
** Now test the control's style bits to see what type
** of  button  it wants to be - an ellipse, a rounded
** rectangle or a rectangle (default).  Draw  in  the
** required shape.
*/

lStyle = GetWindowLong(hWnd, GWL_STYLE);

if((lStyle & NB_RRECTANGLE) == NB_RRECTANGLE)
{
    RoundRect(
            hDC
          , 0
          , 0
          , rsClient.right    - rsClient.left
          , rsClient.bottom   - rsClient.top
          , (rsClient.right   - rsClient.left) / 5
          , (rsClient.bottom  - rsClient.top)  / 5
          );

}
else
if((lStyle & NB_ELLIPSE) == NB_ELLIPSE)
{
    Ellipse(
            hDC
          , 0
          , 0
          , rsClient.right  - rsClient.left
          , rsClient.bottom - rsClient.top
          );
```

```
        }
        else
        {
            Rectangle(
                      hDC
                     ,0
                     ,0
                     ,rsClient.right  - rsClient.left
                     ,rsClient.bottom - rsClient.top
                     );

        }

        /*
        ** Now  draw in the control's caption; use the DC's stock
        ** font if  the  user  hasn't  set a different one in the
        ** setfont handler. If they sent us a different font then
        ** it will be held in our window's words.
        */
        if((hFont = (HFONT)GetWindowWord(hWnd, GWW_FONT)) != NULL)
        {
            SelectObject(hDC, hFont);
        }

        /*
        ** Get the window's caption text, only
        ** the first 100 bytes retrieved.
        **
        ** If you want to handle captions of any
        ** length you'd better process WM_SETEXT
        ** messages.
        */
        GetWindowText(
                      hWnd
                     ,&carCaptionBuff[0]
                     ,sizeof carCaptionBuff
                     );

        /*
        ** Select a  suitable text  color  depending upon
        ** whether or not the control's actually enabled.
        */
        SetTextColor(
                     hDC,
                     IsWindowEnabled(hWnd)          ?
                     GetSysColor(COLOR_BTNTEXT) :
                     GetSysColor(COLOR_GRAYTEXT)
                     );

        /*
        ** Enable the background color to show thru the text.
        */
        SetBkMode(hDC, TRANSPARENT);

        /*
        ** And draw it in using DrawText() in this example so that
        ** we may easily get it centered etc - if our control were
        ** to offer alignment styles (like a static) we would have
```

```
** to check our control's window style and ammend any
** DrawText() flags accordingly. By default we center all.
*/
DrawText(
        hDC
       ,&carCaptionBuff[0]
       ,-1
       ,&rsClient
       ,DT_SINGLELINE | DT_CENTER | DT_VCENTER
       );

/*
** Whenever we re-paint we MAY have to give the user some
** indication as to whether or not we have the input focus.
** Note that if we aren't focused that we don't have to
** 'rub-out' any previous focus rect; as we always re-paint
** the whole of the control window the paint handler will
** take care of it all.
*/


/*
** Test to see if we're the focused window.
*/
if(GetFocus(VOID_ARG) == hWnd)
{
    /*
    ** If we are we need to draw a focus rect around our
    ** control's caption text. We therefore need to know
    ** the width and height of the caption text.
    */
    dwText = GetTextExtent(
                        hDC
                       ,&carCaptionBuff[0]
                       ,lstrlen(&carCaptionBuff[0])
                       );

    /*
    ** We now adjust the rect that was used to hold the
    ** client area width/height so that it describes a
    ** a rectangle that neatly fits the text.
    */
    InflateRect(
                &rsClient
               ,- (int)(((rsClient.right - rsClient.left)

                 LOWORD(dwText)) / 2)
               ,- (int)(((rsClient.bottom - rsClient.top) -

                 HIWORD(dwText)) / 2)
               );

    /*
    ** Now draw in the dots.
    */
    DrawFocusRect(hDC, &rsClient);

}
```

```
                  /*
                  ** Did we select a user's brush? If we did we should
                  ** de-select it prior to releasing the DC.
                  */
                  if(GetWindowWord(hWnd, GWW_USERBRUSH) == TRUE)
                  {
                       hbr = SelectObject(hDC, hbr);
                  }

                  /*
                  ** Scrap pen.
                  */
                  DeleteObject(SelectObject(hDC, hpn));

                  /*
                  ** Done.
                  */
                  EndPaint(hWnd, &ps);
             }
             break;

        case WM_SETFOCUS:
             /*
             ** Cause repaint, this will remove/show the focus rect.
             ** Same thing is done for WM_KILLFOCUS.
             */
             InvalidateRect(hWnd, NULL, TRUE);
             UpdateWindow(hWnd);

             /*
             ** Set up WM_GETDLGCODE return so that the return key will
             ** work and select our button.
             */
             SetWindowLong(
                        hWnd
                       ,GWL_DLGCODE
                       ,DLGC_DEFPUSHBUTTON | DLGC_BUTTON
                       );
             break;

        case WM_SETFONT:
             /*
             ** The user has requested that we use a special font so store
             ** it away in the control's window words. Cause a re-paint so
             ** that the new font is used to paint the control right away.
             **
             ** The caller should first use WM_GETFONT to retrieve any
             ** previous font they may have 'poked' into our control. They
             ** know whether or not to destroy the old font using
             ** DeleteObject() - we don't.
             */
             SetWindowWord(hWnd, GWW_FONT, (WORD)wParam);

             if(LOWORD(lParam) == TRUE)
             {
                InvalidateRect(hWnd, NULL, TRUE);
                UpdateWindow(hWnd);
             }
```

```
        break;


        /*
        ** NOTE : Windows takes care  of  some messages that you
        ** might  imagine  you'd  have  to  handle, for example,
        ** WM_SETTEXT.
        */
    default:
        return DefWindowProc(hWnd, uMessage, wParam, lParam);

  }


  return (LRESULT)0;
}
```

Note that in the application there is minimal error handling or checking for that matter; some of this is deliberate (to keep the code as short as possible) whilst some is omitted because it cannot really be included. For example; the control class allows the user of a class object to change the font used by that object in painting its caption. It would have been nice to have included some code that checked just whether or not the font passed to the control is a font, ie. the font passed to the control is just a handle (or a number) and we have no way of knowing whether or not that number is in error! Windows does have some support (now) for checking this kind of thing but it does not go far enough (**see note just below**).

Windows 3.1 includes an API called IsGDIObject() – this however cannot be used (officially) to determine that the font handle passed to the control is a handle to a font – it could be a handle to, say, a brush! It's not even easy to test the validity of an object by using it, ie. if we were to say, 'OK I'll see if this is a valid font handle by selecting it into my DC', this too might give erroneous result as selecting a a *real* brush into a DC using SelectObject() is of course legal! In fact it turns out that there is no documented way to actually test the validity of such an object absolutely – Microsoft, please give us the necessary information to allow us to do this; only by providing us with the required information may we build genuinely robust applications (if you know of a pucker (proper/documented) way to do this – please let me know it).

NOTE:
Actually you **CAN** use IsGDIObject() to precisely test for *object types* although the following is undocumented! IsGDIObject() doesn't really return a BOOL – it returns a WORD. The value of the word is 0 (maybe – see the docs) if the object is not a GDI object and one of the following values if it is :

Object Type	IsGDIObject() returns
• PEN	1
• BRUSH	2

- FONT   3
- PALETTE   4
- BITMAP   5
- RGN   6
- DC   7

I didn't build in object-type checking using this *feature* as it's undocumented – maybe Microsoft will document this now (please)?

Here are the other *unique* required files :

The .dlg file :

```
DLGINCLUDE  RCDATA  DISCARDABLE
LGINCLUDE  RCDATA  DISCARDABLE
BEGIN
    "GENERIC.H\0"
END

ABOUTBOX DIALOG 56, 31, 236, 74
STYLE DS_MODALFRAME | WS_CAPTION | WS_SYSMENU
CAPTION "Custom Control Test Dialog"
FONT 10, "Courier New"
BEGIN
    CONTROL          "OK"
                     , IDOK
                     , "Button"
                     , WS_GROUP | WS_TABSTOP
                     , 153
                     , 14
                     , 58
                     , 14

    CONTROL          "Font Change"
                     , IDM_FONTCHANGE
                     , "Button"
                     , 0
                     , 29
                     , 14
                     , 59
                     , 14

    CONTROL          "Disable"
                     , IDM_DISABLE
                     , "Button"
                     , 0
                     , 91
                     , 14
                     , 59
                     , 14

    CONTROL          "&RoundRect"
                     , NEWBUTTON
                     , "ControlWClass"
                     , WS_GROUP               |
```

```
                        WS_TABSTOP          |
                        NB_RRECTANGLE       |
                        BS_DEFPUSHBUTTON
                        ,32
                        ,46
                        ,51
                        ,12

    CONTROL             "&Ellipse"
                        ,203
                        ,"ControlWClass"
                        ,NB_ELLIPSE
                        ,93
                        ,46
                        ,51
                        ,12

    CONTROL             "&Rectangle"
                        ,204
                        ,"ControlWClass"
                        ,0
                        ,155
                        ,46
                        ,51
                        ,12

END
```

The .rc file :

```
#include <windows.h>
#include "generic.h"

ControlMenu MENU
BEGIN
    MENUITEM "&Control Test...", IDM_TEST
END


rcinclude generic.dlg
```

The .h file :

```
/*
** Prototypes.
*/
int     PASCAL              WinMain(HINSTANCE, HINSTANCE, LPSTR, int);
BOOL                       bInitApplication(HINSTANCE);
BOOL                       bInitInstance(HINSTANCE, int);

LRESULT __export CALLBACK  MainWndProc
(
   HWND
  ,UINT
  ,WPARAM
  ,LPARAM
);
```

```
BOOL    __export CALLBACK  About
(
   HWND
  ,UINT
  ,WPARAM
  ,LPARAM
);


LRESULT __export CALLBACK ControlWndProc
(
   HWND
  ,UINT
  ,WPARAM
  ,LPARAM
);


/*
** Max space catered for in custom control caption.
*/
#define MAX_CAPTION     100


/*
** Menu item ID.
*/

#define IDM_TEST        50


/*
** Relevant control IDs.
*/
#define NEWBUTTON       100 /* Only Custom Control with ID. */
#define IDM_FONTCHANGE  700
#define IDM_DISABLE     800


/*
** Explicit control window styles.
*/
#define NB_ELLIPSE      0x00000022L /* Makes control ellipse.    */
#define NB_RRECTANGLE   0x00000024L /* Makes control round rect. */


/*
** Number  of  extra  bytes to give
** custom control (see list below).
*/
#define CONTROLEXTRA    16


/*
** 'Extra' bytes access offsets  for custom controls. NOTE : that
** offsets start at '2' - often the first word can be overwritten
** by the DM.
*/

#define GWW_OWNER       2    /* Window handle of parent/owner.   */
#define GWW_INVERTED    4    /* Flag used in highlighting.       */
#define GWW_FONT        6    /* Handle to user supplied font.    */
#define GWW_USERBRUSH   8    /* Flag indicating user brush used. */
#define GWL_DLGCODE     12   /* Reply code to WM_GETDLGCODE.     */
```

```
/*
** Coding standards stuff.
*/
#define VOID_ARG
#define VOID_RETURN
```

Most of the *real* work in this control is done in the control's WM_PAINT handler – in fact this handler is probably relied on a little too much. For example whenever the control gains or loses focus it causes the control to be re-painted so that the control's caption and border may be painted showing that the control's gained or lost the focus. It would have been better to have NOT re-drawn the control in response to a focus shift like this. The paint handler is simply convenient and so I used it. For a button it's not really too bad but if the control had a more ambitious *look* this may have been a little too costly and some alternative would have to be found – bear this in mind when and if you do your own controls.

The control makes great use of window words to store information. The information stored by this control is:

- GWW_OWNER   The handle of the owning window.
- GWW_INVERTED   The inverted state of the control window.
- GWW_FONT   The handle (or NULL) of a user supplied font.
- GWW_USERBRUSH   A flag indicating CTLCOLOR processing state.
- GWW_DLGCODE   The answer to a WM_GETDLGCODE message.

Using window words is a convenient way of storing *per instance* data for each instance of a control. This is required as there may be many instances of a control window created and as each instance is *handled* by the class call-back we need some *per instance* way of storing state information with the control. Static variables declared within the class call-back are no good as each instance of the control would share the one *set* of variables – any change made by one control would affect all instances of the control. Automatic variables, whilst allowing each control access to *unique* data space are of limited use as they *die* as they go out of scope, ie. they are not persistent. What we need is persistent-per instance data items that each control instance can access and use as it sees fit. Using window words facilitates this need. I could have used window properties but these are normally slower to read/write to than window words, they also require a certain amount of string handling (to identify the property) and this requires more time and space – both of which you should normally keep to a minimum (see Miscellaneous chapter). You should try and keep your window word requirements down to, say, 40 bytes or less – Microsoft have, in the past, suggested that the allocation should be kept to below 8 bytes, ie. enough to store a long pointer but no more. The debugging libraries supplied with the SDK give you a warning if you should ever use more than 40 (decimal) so we must now assume that 40 or below is OK? The window's extra bytes are stored in USER's DS and as this space is a shared system resource you can see why these figures are keep so small. If you require more than 40 bytes consider allocating sizeof(HGLOBAL) bytes. This would allow you to store your instance data in a global memory object – you store the handle of the object in the window's extra words. The access overhead of doing this is so minimal it's just not worth taking into account! One last point here – always use GetClassInfo() if you intend to super class a control; by using GetClassInfo() you will be sure of allocating enough window and class words for the control. Windows 3.1 debug doesn't allow you to overwrite an unallocated window/class word and so you may observe that you haven't allocated enough window/class words by keeping an eye on your debug monitor – also the control is bound to behave strangely as it cannot maintain correct state information; a truly first class control would also probably inform you of this fact by employing *state of the art* error checking/handling!

☐ WM_CTLCOLOR handling

The control gives its user (a program) the opportunity to specify a brush to be used in painting the interior of the control. During WM_PAINT processing the control asks its parent/owner the question, 'do you want to use a non-default brush to paint me?'. The mechanics of this are that the control **sends** its parent/owner a WM_CTLCOLOR message; the wParam of this message contains an HDC that will be used by the control in its painting. The receiving application code may use the HDC to change any or all of the DC's settings (note that some of these are set/reset by the control painting code!). The control passes the window handle of the control and a *CTL* code in the lParam of the WM_CTLCOLOR message to give the receiving application enough information so that it (the receiving application) can identify the control asking the question.

```
if((hbr = (HBRUSH) LOWORD (SendMessage (
                          (HWND) GetWindowWord (hWnd, GWW_OWNER)
                         , WM_CTLCOLOR
                         , (WPARAM) hDC
                         , MAKELPARAM (hWnd, CTLCOLOR_BTN)
                         ))) != NULL
    )
    {
            ... Yes, use a non-standard brush.
    }
```

In my control we find the parent window handle by using GetWindowWord(hWnd, GWW_OWNER), this is set when the control is created. If the using application responds to the WM_CTLCOLOR message with a non-NULL answer then the answer is a handle to a valid GDI brush. This brush, in my code, is then selected into the DC ready for use; also a flag is set in the control's window words that indicate that a *user supplied* brush is in place. Any brush passed to the control by the application is owned by the application, ie. the control must not destroy the supplied brush when it is through painting the control – it simply de-selects it so that the creating application can destroy it later. Note that the way in which the *using* application usually creates and uses brushes is that it creates brushes once (handles usually held in static variables), uses them (passes them back to the control in response to WM_CTLCOLOR messages), then destroys them when they are no longer needed. For example in my code, where I'm using my button controls in a dialog box, any required brushes are created in the WM_INITDIALOG handler, used in the WM_CTLCOLOR handler and finally destroyed in the WM_COMMAND handler when the dialog is closed down. Note also that the dialog window itself passes a WM_CTLCOLOR message to the dialog call-back function so that even the background of the dialog may be painted with a different colour brush.

The WM_CTLCOLOR message applies to the following standard classes :

- **BUTTONS** – Push-buttons, Radio Boxes, Check Boxes, Group Boxes – paints the background of the control with the selected brush (note push-buttons although technically still painted are unaffected – user owner draw push-buttons to change them). Group Box – paints the area behind the text which labels the group.
- **EDIT** – Paints the text editing area of the control.
- **SCROLLBAR** – Paints the area around the thumb (lift/elevator), ie. everything but the arrows and the thumb are painted. Only real control scrollbars are affected, ie. windows' scrollbars and those that form part of another control (like those on a list box) are unaffected (they do not generate WM_CTLCOLOR messages).
- **LISTBOX** – Paints the area in which the list text appears.
- **COMBOBOX** – Paints the part of the control that falls between the drop down arrow and the edit control.
- **STATIC** – Static text fields – Paints the area beneath the text. Frames and rectangles are unaffected.

☐ WM_CREATE handling

Essentially the WM_CREATE message is used to construct the button control. Construction here is not window creation (a WM_CREATE message is sent to the window once it is created) but window word initialisation. As was stated earlier, my control uses window words to store state/property information; in the create handler I first set all the window words which we may or may not use to zero (this is not strictly needed by shows that you care!), and then set GWW_OWNER to be the window handle of the parent/owner window – some investigation is required to find the window's owner/parent (see chapter on cleaning Windows for more on this subject).

```
case WM_CREATE:

    /*
    ** Although not strictly necessary, clean the control
    ** window's extra bytes prior to them being used.
    */
    SetWindowWord(hWnd, GWW_OWNER,      NULL);
```

```
        SetWindowWord(hWnd, GWW_INVERTED,   NULL);
        SetWindowWord(hWnd, GWW_FONT,       NULL);
        SetWindowWord(hWnd, GWW_USERBRUSH,  NULL);
        SetWindowLong(hWnd, GWL_DLGCODE,    NULL);


    /*
    ** Now play find the owner/parent.
    */
    {
        /*
        ** Holds the window handle of the parent/owner window
        ** as it's found.
        */
        auto HWND hWndOwner;


        /*
        ** Who do we communicate with for notification messages?
        **
        ** First test to see if we're a child window. All child
        ** windows MUST have a parent in order to be successfully
        ** created - no need to check return of GetParent()
        ** therefore.
        */
        if((GetWindowLong(hWnd, GWL_STYLE) & WS_CHILD) == WS_CHILD)
        {
            /*
            ** Remember owner/parent.
            */
            SetWindowWord(
                        hWnd
                        ,GWW_OWNER
                        ,(WORD)GetParent(hWnd)
                        );
        }
        else
        {
            /*
            ** Not a child  window so use GWW_HWNDPARENT to get the
            ** handle of the owner (if any). See section on Parent/
            ** Owner in 'Cleaning Windows' chapter  for more on why
            ** we  use  GWW_HWNDPARENT  when  apparently a test for
            ** a parent just failed!
            */

            /*
            ** If owner is NULL use the desktop else use the owner.
            */
            if(
                (hWndOwner = (HWND)GetWindowWord(
                                                hWnd
                                                ,GWW_HWNDPARENT
                                                )
                ) != NULL
              )
            {
                /*
                ** Remember parent/owner.
                */
```

```
                        SetWindowWord(
                                    hWnd
                                    , GWW_OWNER
                                    , (WORD)hWndOwner
                                    );
                }
                else
                {
                        /*
                        ** Remember parent/owner.
                        */
                        SetWindowWord(
                                    hWnd
                                    , GWW_OWNER
                                    , (WORD)GetDesktopWindow(VOID_ARG)
                                    );
                }

        }
    }
    break;
```

Once the WM_CREATE handler is through we should have initialised all the window
words correctly, ie. they're all set to zero except GWW_OWNER which is set to be the
window handle of the owner/parent window.

WM_SETFONT handling

Controls usually paint out their caption text in some way. For a push-button that
caption text is used to label the control. The font used to paint the text may be set by
the application using the control via the WM_SETFONT message.

In my dialog I have a button that is used to change the font in one of the *new* button
controls. Its ID is IDM_FONTCHANGE.

```
            case IDM_FONTCHANGE:
                SendMessage(
                            (HWND)GetDlgItem(hDlg, NEWBUTTON)
                            , WM_SETFONT
                            , (WPARAM)GetStockObject(ANSI_VAR_FONT)
                            , MAKELPARAM(TRUE, 0)
                            );
```

As you can see it sends a WM_SETFONT message to the NEWBUTTON control. The
wParam of the message is a handle to the font that should be used in any subsequent
painting operations by the control. The WM_SETFONT handler in the control code
looks like this :

```
        case WM_SETFONT:
            /*
            ** The user has requested that we use a special font so store
            ** it away in the control's window words. Cause a re-paint so
            ** that the new font is used to paint the control right away.
```

```
**
** The caller should first use WM_GETFONT to retrieve any
** previous font they may have 'poked' into our control. They
** know whether or not to destroy the old font using
** DeleteObject() - we don't.
*/
SetWindowWord(hWnd, GWW_FONT, (WORD)wParam);

if(LOWORD(lParam) == TRUE)
{
    InvalidateRect(hWnd, NULL, TRUE);
    UpdateWindow(hWnd);
}
break;
```

The *incoming* font's handle is stored in the control's window words and the control is forced to repaint. The paint handler checks the words to see if a font has been selected by the user. If it has it uses it to paint the control's caption, else it uses a *standard* font. The relevant bits of the paint routine are shown below :

```
/*
** Now  draw in the control's caption; use the DC's stock
** font if  the  user  hasn't  set a different one in the
** setfont handler. If they sent us a different font then
** it will be held in our window's words.
*/
if((hFont = (HFONT)GetWindowWord(hWnd, GWW_FONT)) != NULL)
{
    SelectObject(hDC, hFont);
}

/*
** Get the window's caption text, only
** the first 100 bytes retrieved.
*/
GetWindowText(
            hWnd
            ,&carCaptionBuff[0]
            ,sizeof carCaptionBuff
            );

/*
** Select a  suitable text  color  depending upon
** whether or not the control's actually enabled.
*/
SetTextColor(
            hDC,
            IsWindowEnabled(hWnd)        ?
            GetSysColor(COLOR_BTNTEXT) :
            GetSysColor(COLOR_GRAYTEXT)
            );

/*
** Enable the background color to show thru the text.
*/
SetBkMode(hDC, TRANSPARENT);
```

```
/*
** And draw it in using DrawText() in this example so that
** we may easily get it centered etc - if our control were
** to offer alignment styles (like a static) we would have
** to check our  control's  window  style  and  ammend any
** DrawText() flags accordingly. By default we center all.
*/
DrawText(
        hDC
        ,&carCaptionBuff[0]
        ,-1
        ,&rsClient
        ,DT_SINGLELINE | DT_CENTER | DT_VCENTER
        );


/*
** Whenever  we re-paint we MAY  have to give the user some
** indication as to whether or not we have the input focus.
** Note that  if  we  aren't  focused that we don't have to
** 'rub-out' any previous focus rect; as we always re-paint
** the  whole  of the control window the paint handler will
** take care of it all.
*/


/*
** Test to see if we're the focused window.
*/
if(GetFocus(VOID_ARG) == hWnd)
{
    /*
    ** If we are we need to draw a focus rect around our
    ** control's caption text. We therefore need to know
    ** the width and height of the caption text.
    */
    dwText = GetTextExtent(
                         hDC
                         ,&carCaptionBuff[0]
                         ,lstrlen(&carCaptionBuff[0])
                         );


    /*
    ** We now adjust the rect that was used to hold the
    ** client area width/height  so that it describes a
    ** a rectangle that neatly fits the text.
    */
    InflateRect(
            &rsClient
            ,- (int)(((rsClient.right - rsClient.left) -
              LOWORD(dwText)) / 2)
            ,- (int)(((rsClient.bottom - rsClient.top) -
              HIWORD(dwText)) / 2)
            );


    /*
    ** Now draw in the dots.
    */
    DrawFocusRect(hDC, &rsClient);
```

Some other stuff to notice in here is that the text is drawn using a transparent background so that the colour of the push-button shows through the text. Also the focus rect size is calculated so that it always fits snugly around the text – the calculation is based on the selected font – don't base yours on, say, the standard font as it will get all messed up if the font is changed.

NOTE that our WM_SETFONT handler doesn't return anything apart from the result of calling DefWindowProc() – which returns 0. Some controls might want to return a handle to any old font instead of returning DefWindowProc().

Our control could return NULL or a valid font handle therefore. The WM_SETFONT handler would now look like this :

```
case WM_SETFONT:
    {
        auto WORD hOldFont;

        hOldFont = SetWindowWord(hWnd, GWW_FONT, (WORD)wParam);

        if(LOWORD(lParam) == TRUE)
        {
            InvalidateRect(hWnd, NULL, TRUE);
            UpdateWindow(hWnd);
        }

        return hOldFont;

        break;
    }
```

Why do this? Well in some respects it's very handy in the case where you're simply exchanging fonts in a control – remember that you're responsible for deleting any old font, ie. having set a font once, using a newly created font, you could do this to exchange the font to another newly created font :

```
/*
** Replace the control's font & delete the old font.
*/
DeleteObject(
        SendMessage(
                    hWndControl
                    ,WM_SETFONT
                    ,(WPARAM)GetStockObject(ANSI_VAR_FONT)
                    ,MAKELPARAM(TRUE, 0)
                    )
            );
```

Some Windows' controls already do this, ie. they return the old font (despite what the WM_SETFONT docs say), for example an edit control does this, but a button control does not.

WM_GETFONT is *the other case* of WM_SETFONT, ie. the user wants to retrieve a handle to the font currently used by the control window. The SDK notes say that the control wndproc should return the handle of the font used OR NULL if the font is the default font. We return whatever's in our window words; this will be NULL if no font has been selected so we're standard.

☐ WM_GETDLGCODE handling

Whenever the control receives a WM_GETDLGCODE message it responds to it by passing back the value held in GWL_DLGCODE :

```
case WM_GETDLGCODE:

    /*
    ** Return whatever's in the words.
    */
    return GetWindowLong(hWnd, GWL_DLGCODE);

    break;
```

This in turn is set in the control code to reflect the *type* of control at various times in the control's life. For example, when the control window loses focus it sets the long at GWL_DLGCODE thus :

```
SetWindowLong(
            hWnd
            ,GWL_DLGCODE
            ,DLGC_UNDEFPUSHBUTTON | DLGC_BUTTON
            );
```

This disables the *enter* key interface to the control, ie. when the button is focused it becomes the *default push-button* and when it loses the focus it becomes the non-default push-button (UNDEFPUSHBUTTON). When it is focused therefore it is the default push-button, now when the enter key is pressed the DM asks the control what type of control it is in order to ascertain what keyboard input it requires. The DM asks the control by sending it a WM_GETDLGCODE message. the control responds by returning the long value in GWL_DLGCODE which is DLGC_DEFPUSHBUTTON, upon receipt of this reply the DM forwards the WM_CHAR message (for the enter key) to the control. This causes the control to be actioned.

☐ Designer Messages

Note that we (the class) don't define any *special* class specific messages in the class definition. For example, the control cannot have its sub-type changed once it's created by, say, using a BM_SETSTYLE message. However, it does respond to standard control type messages of course (WM_SETFONT etc). We could add *special* messages as we saw fit – apparently we can't change the sub-type of a ControlWClass control without currently resorting to using SetWindowLong(), ie. we could change the control type by changing a control's window style directly. This shouldn't really be done from outside of the control as we can't say, without having access to the source, what effect this would have on the control. Potentially it will have no effect. We can't tell, from the outside looking in, whether or not the control refers to the *type* part of its window style once it's created – of course we could experiment and find out but we still can't be too sure that juggling its style bits is good for the control's health and well-being. What we need to provide, as the class designer, is some sure way for some outside force to influence our control objects by defining a method, or message, based interface to it. For example we could provide for dynamically changing the control's sub-type by implementing a BM_SETSTYLE message handler directly; it would look something like this :

```
case BM_SETSTYLE:
        SetWindowLong(hWnd, GWL_STYLE, wParam);
        InvalidateRect(hWnd, NULL);
        UpdateWindow(hWnd);
```

Here the control is being told what type of ControlWClass object it is. The control class procedure sets its style, in this case the implementation uses SetWindowLong(), and causes itself to be re-painted. The WM_PAINT handler paints the control according to its window style bits – result, we have changed the sub-type of the control. Wherever possible define a class specific message to interact with your control – believe me, one day you'll appreciate the abstraction you've provided.

☐ Control States

Most controls, and my button is no exception, are always in one of three states (while they exist). No formal names exist for these states so here's my own attempt at naming them – the definitions I've used are those that are more or less excepted in the industry:

Inert   Focused or non-focused (this may be split to deal with the focused vs. non-focused state).

Armed   The state that a control enters when it is selected, ie. for a button this may be that the user has *clicked* down on the button. Selected is another popular term although I feel it might best be used to describe a focused, or even actioned state described below.

Actioned   The control has been utilised, ie. in the case of a button the mouse button used to arm it has been released causing the control to operate – the mouse button is release whilst the cursor is still positioned over the control's client area.

Typically a control such as a button works thus. The button is first created and displayed in an inert state. The user then moves the mouse cursor to the button and clicks the left mouse button down in the control's client area. This puts the control into the armed state, ie. it is *ready*. At this time the user may still elect not to action the button; if they wish to *cancel* at this time they move the mouse cursor away from the control's client area and release the mouse button. If they wish to action the button they release the mouse button in the control's client area. Note that it is the releasing of the mouse button that actions the control. During all of these phases the control usually provides visual or auditory feedback as to its current state. For example, a button usually inverts its client area to show that it is armed; also, and typically, the visual clue indicating that the button has been actioned is, in Windows, signalled by the same visual clue used in the inert state (the inert state is also usually used to show that the mouse cursor has been moved from the control's client area following the control becoming armed – ie. that the control is no longer armed). Some GUIs have a separate state (although usually it is a fleeting thing) to show that the button has been actioned, for example the Macintosh momentarily flashes the control (inverts – re-inverts it) a couple of times to show that the control has been utilised.

The states and visual clues talked about briefly above have been subject to much discussion, particularly in the standards area (IEEE P1201.2 group etc); it is important, if GUIs are to exhibit a *common* look and feel that all these states (the visual feedback is not as important) function identically across all popular GUIs – this poses an important question for the GUI designers – should they (controls) faithfully mimic their real world counterparts in the process or do we *add* functionality through our ability to alter the world of the GUI button through software innovation? Consider again the humble button. The button control mimics, apparently a *real* button but how many buttons do you know of that cause something to happen when they are released as opposed to when they are pushed, ie. is an elevator summoned on the pressing or releasing of a *call* button? Also, if you've decided to summon an elevator (let's say that it is the releasing of the *call* button that does this) by pressing the call button but then change your mind and decide to cancel the operation how do you do it – ie. how can you mimic the Windows' *disarming* control feature discussed above? There is no way that you cannot complete the operation in the real world (if you know of an elevator that provides this function please let me know!). So does a Windows' button really mimic a button? The answer might be *who cares* – an arrogant answer! Ideally controls should of course mimic their real world counterparts but of course once a standard has been created it's hard to change and I suggest that such a change now to the way in which these controls function would generally be a bad thing? Moral – If you're mimicking a real world object, ensure that your impersonation is complete, or at the very least logical.

☐ The DLL Control

This control may be made into a DLL based control by simply adding the class registration into, say, the DLL's LibMain() function. The control class would also need to have the class style CS_GLOBALCLASS added to it – and that's essentially it! Here's a *dummy* control contained within a DLL to give you some sort of foundation to work with, first the code then some explanation :

The squarec.c file :

```
#define STRICT

#include <windows.h>
```

```c
#pragma warning(disable:4100)
#pragma warning(disable:4001)

static char carClassName[] = "SQUARECLASS";

HINSTANCE FAR PASCAL hGetSetInstance(HINSTANCE);
LRESULT __export CALLBACK SquareWndProc
(
   HWND
  ,UINT
  ,WPARAM
  ,LPARAM
);



/*
** Saves DLL's instance/module handle.
*/
HINSTANCE FAR PASCAL hGetSetInstance(HINSTANCE hInst)
{
   static HINSTANCE hInstance;

   if(hInst != NULL)
   {
       hInstance = hInst;
   }

   return hInstance;
}



/*
** Custom control class call-back function.
*/
LRESULT __export CALLBACK SquareWndProc
(
   HWND     hWnd
  ,UINT     uMessage
  ,WPARAM   wParam
  ,LPARAM   lParam
)
{
   return DefWindowProc(hWnd, uMessage, wParam, lParam);
}



/*
** Minimal LibMain() DLL entry point - see other
** section on DLLs for explanation.
*/
BOOL FAR PASCAL LibMain
(
   HINSTANCE  hInstance
  ,WORD       wDataSeg
  ,WORD       wHeapSize
```

```
    ,LPCSTR        lpszCmdLine
)
{
    if(wHeapSize != 0)
    {
        UnlockData(0);
    }

    hGetSetInstance(hInstance);

    return TRUE;
}



/*
** Registers global control class.
*/
BOOL __export FAR PASCAL bInitDLL(VOID)
{
    auto   WNDCLASS  wc;
    static BOOL      bDone;

    if(bDone == TRUE)
    {
        return TRUE;
    }

    wc.style          = CS_GLOBALCLASS;
    wc.lpfnWndProc    = (WNDPROC)SquareWndProc;
    wc.cbClsExtra     = 0;
    wc.cbWndExtra     = 0;
    wc.hInstance      = hGetSetInstance(NULL);;
    wc.hIcon          = NULL;
    wc.hCursor        = LoadCursor(NULL, IDC_ARROW);
    wc.hbrBackground  = (HBRUSH)(COLOR_BACKGROUND + 1);
    wc.lpszMenuName   = NULL;
    wc.lpszClassName  = &carClassName[0];

    return bDone = !!RegisterClass(&wc);
}



/*
** Un-registers global control class.
*/
BOOL __export FAR PASCAL bDeInitDLL(VOID)
{
    static BOOL bDone;

    if(bDone == TRUE)
    {
        return TRUE;
    }

    return bDone = !!UnregisterClass(
                             &carClassName[0]
```

```
                                          ,hGetSetInstance(NULL)
                                          );
}
```

The wep.c file :

```c
#include <windows.h>

/*
** Minimal WEP() DLL exit point - see other
** section on DLLs for explanation.
*/
BOOL FAR PASCAL WEP (int nSystemExit)
{
    switch(nSystemExit)
    {
      case WEP_SYSTEM_EXIT:
            break;

      case WEP_FREE_DLL:
            break;
    }

    return TRUE;
}
```

The .def file :

```
LIBRARY          SQUAREC

EXETYPE          WINDOWS 3.1

PROTMODE

DESCRIPTION      'SQUARE for WINDOWS.'

STUB             'WINSTUB.EXE'

CODE             LOADONCALL     DISCARDABLE MOVEABLE
DATA             PRELOAD        SINGLE

SEGMENTS         WEP_TEXT       FIXED            NONDISCARDABLE PRELOAD
                 DLLSHELL_TEXT        MOVEABLE DISCARDABLE      LOADONCALL
                 _TEXT                MOVEABLE DISCARDABLE      LOADONCALL
                 INIT_TEXT            MOVEABLE DISCARDABLE      PRELOAD

HEAPSIZE  0

EXPORTS
    WEP                   @1 RESIDENTNAME
    SquareWndProc         @2
    bInitDLL              @3
    bDeInitDLL            @4
```

The makefile :

```
# Decide whether or not to include debug information
!IFDEF DEBUG
CCDEB    =        -Zi
LKDEBUG  =        /CO
!ELSE
CCDEB    =
!ENDIF


# Macro defines
RC              =        -r -v
CC              =        cl -G2 -c -W4 -WX -AMw -GDs -Od -Zpe $(CCDEB)
LINK            =        link /NOD $(LKDEBUG) $(OBJ)
OBJ             =        libentry.obj squarec.obj wep.obj
WEPDEPEND       =        $*.c makefile
SQUARECDEPEND   =        $*.c master.h makefile
LIBENTRYDEPEND  =        $*.asm
RESDEPEND       =        $*.rc
LINKDEPEND      =        $(OBJ) $*.def $*.res


all: squarec.dll

# Build squarec.OBJ
squarec.obj: $(SQUARECDEPEND)
    $(CC) $*.c

# Build WEP.OBJ
wep.obj: $(WEPDEPEND)
    $(CC) $*.c

# Build LIBENTRY.OBJ
libentry.obj: $(LIBENTRYDEPEND)
    masm -Mx $*,$*;

# Build SQUAREC.RES
squarec.res : $(RESDEPEND)
    rc $(RC) $*.rc

# Build SQUAREC.DLL
squarec.dll: $(LINKDEPEND)
    $(LINK) , $@,$*.map, libw mdllcew, $*.def

# Attach resources to dll
    rc -v $*.res $@

# Build dll import lib
    implib $*.lib $*.def
```

The control contained within this DLL, Square, creates – Yes, Square(ish) controls, ie. a control that's an empty window. The call-back function for the class, SquareWnd-Proc() doesn't even explicitly process any Windows' messages – it simply passes them all through to DefWindowProc().

The DLL has two functions that are used to initialise and decommission the class. bInitClass registers the class if it has not been registered already. bDeInitDLL un-registers the class, again only if it hasn't been done already. It would be possible to build the class registration into the LibMain() function processing (if you're not familiar with DLLs ignore this brief discussion and return to it once you've read the DLL chapter) and have Windows clear up the class automatically when the DLL was eventually unloaded but what the heck!

The class may be easily tested using the dialog editor and the generic application. If we modify the generic app's dialog template to include a control created from SquareC we're almost ready to go :

```
ABOUTBOX DIALOG 56, 31, 144, 75
STYLE DS_MODALFRAME | WS_CAPTION | WS_SYSMENU
CAPTION "About Generic"
BEGIN
 CONTROL
        "Microsoft Windows"
        ,-1
        ,"Static"
        ,SS_CENTER | WS_GROUP
        ,0, 5, 144, 8
 CONTROL
        "Generic Application"
        ,-1
        ,"SQUARECLASS"
        ,SS_CENTER | WS_GROUP
        ,0, 14, 144, 8

 CONTROL
        "Version 3.0"
        ,-1
        ,"Static"
        ,SS_CENTER | WS_GROUP
        ,0, 34, 144, 8

 CONTROL
        "OK"
        ,IDOK
        ,"Button"
        ,BS_DEFPUSHBUTTON | WS_GROUP | WS_TABSTOP
        ,53, 59, 32, 14
 END
```

Now all we have to do is change generic's message polling loop like this :

```
    if(bInitDLL())
    {

        while(GetMessage(&msg, NULL, 0, 0))
        {
            TranslateMessage(&msg);
            DispatchMessage(&msg);
        }
```

```
        bDeInitDLL();
    }
    return msg.wParam;
```

This code ensures that the SQUARECLASS is registered. Note that any number of applications can call this function – the class is only registered once. If the class has already been registered the function bInitDLL returns TRUE.

Note that if the DLL hadn't given the class style attribute CS_GLOBALCLASS that no application would have been able to create a window of this class. Only the DLL could have, ie. the class would have entirely belonged, if you like, to the module registering the class – the DLL.

The only thing the control does to make itself conspicuous is to draw itself the same colour as the desktop – here's what generic's about box looks like now :

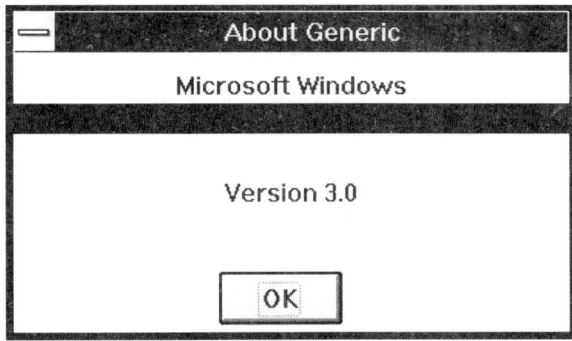

☐ Controls in essencece

In essence, a control is an object oriented *thing* in that it should provide something that is genuinely useful and is not overly complex requiring the user to super/sub-class it in order to remove undesirable properties. It should provide a consistent set of services that *match* or mimic those provided by other *related* objects, ie. it is easy to use and understand. Ideally it should be encapsulated in a DLL – this increases its general usability. It should conform to your chosen user interface guidelines.

☐ Rappin' with controls

When you *talk* to controls you'll typically need to use SendMessage() instead of PostMessage() as you'll either want :

- To synchronise some action with some processing in the control window procedure.
- To use a control (window) message that has some reply.

If you use PostMessage() any reply to the message is lost, ie. when the control window procedure is called it will be called by Windows. The result, or reply, therefore will be returned to Windows and not to you. When you use SendMessage() you are of course the caller – the returned, or reply value is now returned to you.

You'll also want to decide whether or not to use Windows' messages or *USER* messages. A Windows' message is a message created by registering a message string with Windows via RegisterWindowMessage() whereas a *USER* message is a message chosen, arbitrarily, from the message range WM_USER thru 0x7FFF. The obvious advantage to using private messages is that they're unique, ie. no other app or task should be using your message ID unless it knows you intimately!

Windows uses a mixture of the two strategies above. Normal controls use *private* message which are defined relative to WM_USER :

```
/* Button Control Messages */
#define BM_GETCHECK      (WM_USER+0)
#define BM_SETCHECK      (WM_USER+1)
#define BM_GETSTATE      (WM_USER+2)
#define BM_SETSTATE      (WM_USER+3)
#define BM_SETSTYLE      (WM_USER+4)
```

Whereas the common dialogs use RegisterWindowMessage() messages for many things (see dialog box chapter). If you use WM_USER type messages the convention is to define your messages from WM_USER+0 as shown above.

☐ UnRegisterClass()

You, strictly speaking, un-register any control class, when the class is no longer required. For a global class the best place to do this is within the DLL's exit procedure, ie. a global class should only be un-registered when all its clients or users have been terminated. The control class used in the example app was private to the task and so I let Windows un-register the class when the app terminated – it will un-register the class if you don't. Using, or pairing calls like this is generally a good programming practice to get into.

☐ Bold fonts in controls

If you use the *FONT* dialog statement to set a font into all your dialog's controls Windows will attempt to use a bold version of that font – this may or may not be desirable. Using FONT can be convenient because it sets the same font in all the dialog controls. If you want a different font in any given control set it at WM_INITDIALOG time. The result will be that all the dialog's controls except one use the same font – very handy. You can also change font attributes at WM_INITDIALOG time, ie. the Dialog Manager or DM will already have set the control's font by sending it a WM_SETFONT message by the time the dialog call-back receives the WM_INITDIALOG message. By processing this message you can even change the font awarded to the controls back to a non-bold font :

```
case WM_INITDIALOG:
    {
        auto   HWND    hDlg;
        static HFONT   hDlgFont;
        auto   LOGFONT tLF;

        /*
        ** Retrieve dialog box's font and build non-bold version of it.
        */
        if(
            (
            /*
            ** Dialog has 'given' font?
            */
            hDlgFont = (HFONT)SendMessage(
                                          hDlg
                                          ,WM_GETFONT
                                          ,0
                                          ,0
                                          )
            ) != NULL
        )
        {
            /*
            ** Get font info from font handle.
            */
            if(GetObject(hDlgFont, sizeof(LOGFONT), (LPSTR)&tLF) != NULL)
            {
                /*
                ** Set font weight to normal.
                */
                tLF.lfWeight = FW_NORMAL;

                /*
                ** Build normal versioni of font.
                */
                if((hDlgFont = CreateFontIndirect(&tLF)) != NULL)
                {
                    /*
                    ** Set normal font into required controls...
                    */
                    SendMessage(hWndCtrl1, WM_SETFONT, hDlgFont, 0);

                    /*
                    ** Etc. Or use EnumChildWindows() to get the lot!
                    */
                    SendMessage(???, WM_SETFONT, hDlgFont, 0);
                }
            }
        }

        return TRUE;
        break;

    case WM_COMMAND:
        switch(wParam)
        {
```

```
...
...
case IDOK:
        if(hDlgFont != NULL)
        {
            DeleteObject(hDlgFont);
        }
        ...
        ...
    ...
    ...
}
break;
```

Note that hDlgFont is a static – remember that you're supposed to delete objects used by controls, ie. they don't do it!

Notice in the code above that SendMessage() rather than SendDlgItemMessage() was used. Why – SendMessage()? It's quicker? SendDlgItemMessage() calls GetDlgItem() to get the window handle of the control specified. The GetDlgItem() function searches through all controls in a given dialog box to find one that matches the passed ID. If there are many controls in a dialog box, the GetDlgItem() function can be quite slow. Therefore, if you're going to send a lot of messages to a control; or if you're going to occasionally send a number of messages, use SendMessage() and keep the control's window handle in a static, ie. get the control's window handle at, say, WM_INITDIA-LOG time and keep it in a static. Now whenever you need to send the control a message you can use SendMessage(). Of course, if the control's response to a message takes some considerable time then the overhead in using SendDlgItemMessage() is insignificant and should be disregarded.

Chapter 6

D L L s

The definition of a DLL is :- <u>A DLL is (usually) a module that contains executable</u> <u>non-taskable code, ie. it contains code that *runs*</u> in the context of the task that's using it – in other words; it's a library of code!

Before we actually take a look at building a DLL let's first discuss *things* DLLish – later we'll see two full DLL examples.

If DLLs had the normal file extension of .LIB there'd be little confusion as to what they were or how they (to a point) worked. DLLs can have any file name extension as the Windows' loader examines the file, and not its extension, in order to *find out* just what kind of file it is, you could even call one .TXT if you wanted to!

DLL's magic is primarily in their ability to share their contents at run-time, ie. multiple tasks use the same code; this is a different situation from the *static link* norm whereby a library's code is copied into an executable; here it remains in the library and is shareable. Applications wishing to use the library's code dynamically link (on the fly) to it at run-time. The main advantage of this is that the code in the library is NOT in the application (the code is in the application – NOT!). This is very important in a multi-tasking OS where several applications may be running (and using the library) at the same time – it saves space. In fact some application code is *DLL like*. For example an exported function in an application is shareable in that any outside agent may call it (to a degree); also application code, like DLL code, is used by multiple tasks, ie. instances of the app – so just like a DLL an app's code is sharable – many tasks use code that is in memory just once.

A DLL usually consists of a set of sub-routines that may be called by other DLL routines or code contained in an application that is the currently executing task (some DLLs operate differently in that they contain code that may be called by a non-Windows' task – such DLLs are called device drivers – these too are a kinda DLL). If a DLL routine is called by another DLL routine (one DLL calling another) then each call to a DLL routine is made in the *task context* of some originating task – no DLL code executes without impetus coming from a calling task. For example if you call the Windows' routine MessageBox() it may, if you've requested a system modal message box, call SysErrorBox() (this happens to be an undocumented call but what the heck);

each piece of code, that is each DLL routine, operates in the context of the task that originally called MessageBox(). Some DLLs do not contain much, if anything, in the way of code, such libraries usually contain resources or fonts – yes a .FON file is also a DLL (Note a .FON file is also a DATA NONE DLL – See later notes on DATA NONE)!

A task context is many things, firstly it means that the DLL routine operates on the stack of the originating task, only tasks get stacks. It also means that while the DLL code is being executed that a call to GetCurrentTask() (for example) will return the handle of the task that initiated the call into the DLL, ie. the originating task, we'll come back to this soon. A task is closely related to a task database, in fact every task requires a task database (in point of fact a task handle is a global memory handle to the task database). The task database contains all the stuff required for a task that a library doesn't, ie. a TDB is one of the main differences between a task and a library – a task has one, a library does not. A TDB contains things such as a task's message queue, a DOS path name (identifying the task file), a file handle table and an environment block (like a PSP). Of course, having a DLL use your stack is convenient for parameter passing etc and nowadays can even help debugger writers write better debuggers!

☐ Back to the stack

The biggest difference is that a DLL does not have its own stack but has to borrow the stack of the current task, this one feature – that when DLL code is executing DS is (usually) not equal to SS, has historically caused developers more tears than any other Windows' feature.

This <u>default</u> behaviour precludes the use of some of the standard Windows application programming practices and C run-time functions in a DLL. The DS not equal to SS (I hate it when you see DS != SS) thing used to cause many problems mainly because the 'C' run-time library code that got linked into DLLs assumed that DS was equal to SS, ie. the library would simply use DS as the segment part of any internal near pointer addressing.

Consider passing to the runtime library function strlen() a near pointer to some string (maybe a parameter) which was allocated on the stack; internally the strlen function would assume that the string was in your default data segment and use DS as a segment register to find its length, the result was often – BANG! This has little to do with Windows but more to with the segmented addressing of the Intel chip (#if defined IBDA !!!). Most DLLs, and apps, are written using either small or medium memory models, the definition of each of these models states that each shall have just one data segment – ie. the unit's data space (including stack) is in D#GROUP. If you now call a static link library routine from the standard library (for each of these models – SLIBCE.LIB, MLIBCE.LIB) the routine expects to address all data, whether stack based or not, through the use of DS – which points to the base of DGROUP! You can see the problem? Of course, you can consider your code, ie. code in your application that calls a DLL function, as simply another type of library code, ie. you have routines that *do* something just like a library. Now, when you need to use either a static link library, or a DLL you have to think, 'where is my data?' AND 'can the called routine *know* where it is?' AND 'where does the called routine assume my data is!'

One solution is to forget all about near and far etc and write in large model where the standard library functions don't care where a data item is located; in this model you have to pass a long pointer (far) to your data item so that the library function can locate it. The problem with this is that for applications, that create more than one data segment, Windows (still) won't allow more than a single instance of the application to run (as it does not have an instance thunk type mechanism for data items). Also that single instance's data segments are locked in memory and cannot be efficiently *managed* by Windows' memory manager. For DLLs this is less of a problem as they are not taskable so there can only ever be one instance of them in memory (scratch one restriction), however, that DLL's data segments are still locked up and could potentially cause the memory manager some problems (it is unlikely however, esp. in 386 Enhanced Mode). You could also continue to use small and medium models for development and use the model independent functions provided within the library. These functions, just like all large model functions, *take* far pointers to data items. The model independent functions all begin with _f – they are available in all versions of the standard libraries, here's a list of some of the most useful of these :

```
File MALLOC.H:
VOID    FAR *       CDECL _fcalloc  (size_t, size_t);
VOID    FAR *       CDECL _fexpand  (VOID FAR *, size_t);
VOID                CDECL _ffree    (VOID FAR *);
VOID    FAR *       CDECL _fmalloc  (size_t);
size_t              CDECL _fmsize   (VOID FAR *);
VOID    FAR *       CDECL _frealloc (VOID FAR *, size_t);

File STRING.H:
VOID    FAR * FAR CDECL _fmemccpy (VOID FAR *, const VOID FAR *,
VOID    FAR * FAR CDECL _fmemchr  (const VOID FAR *, int, size_t);
int     FAR       CDECL _fmemcmp  (const VOID FAR *, const VOID FAR *,
VOID    FAR * FAR CDECL _fmemcpy  (VOID FAR *, const VOID FAR *,
int     FAR       CDECL _fmemicmp (const VOID FAR *, const VOID FAR *,
VOID    FAR * FAR CDECL _fmemmove (VOID FAR *, const VOID FAR *,
VOID    FAR * FAR CDECL _fmemset  (VOID FAR *, int, size_t);
char    FAR * FAR CDECL _fstrcat  (char FAR *, const char FAR *);
char    FAR * FAR CDECL _fstrchr  (const char FAR *, int);
int     FAR       CDECL _fstrcmp  (const char FAR *, const char FAR *);
int     FAR       CDECL _fstricmp (const char FAR *, const char FAR *);
char    FAR * FAR CDECL _fstrcpy  (char FAR *, const char FAR *);
size_t  FAR       CDECL _fstrcspn (const char FAR *, const char FAR *);
char    FAR * FAR CDECL _fstrdup  (const char FAR *);
size_t  FAR       CDECL _fstrlen  (const char FAR *);
char    FAR * FAR CDECL _fstrlwr  (char FAR *);
char    FAR * FAR CDECL _fstrncat (char FAR *, const char FAR *,
int     FAR       CDECL _fstrncmp (const char FAR *, const char FAR *,
int     FAR       CDECL _fstrnicmp (const char FAR *, const char FAR *,
char    FAR * FAR CDECL _fstrncpy (char FAR *, const char FAR *,
char    FAR * FAR CDECL _fstrnset (char FAR *, int, size_t);
char    FAR * FAR CDECL _fstrpbrk (const char FAR *,
char    FAR * FAR CDECL _fstrrchr (const char FAR *, int);
```

```
char    FAR * FAR CDECL _fstrrev    (char FAR *);
char    FAR * FAR CDECL _fstrset    (char FAR *, int);
size_t  FAR       CDECL _fstrspn    (const char FAR *, const char FAR *);
char    FAR * FAR CDECL _fstrstr    (const char FAR *,
char    FAR * FAR CDECL _fstrtok    (char FAR *, const char FAR *);
char    FAR * FAR CDECL _fstrupr    (char FAR *);
```

If you're developing in 'C' or C++ AND using *standard* library functions AND using small or medium model – always check the documentation to see if the function you want could cause problems – and use _WINDLL/_WINDOWS.

Another way around the DS not equal to SS thing is to ensure that DS actually is equal to SS! How can this be done? Well, it's quite simple to do this in various ways although the simplest requires just that you declare the DLL as containing no data segment of its own! You do this by using the DATA NONE statement in the DLL's .def file (if you're using 3.0 see the note below about a bug in using DATA NONE). When you do this the DLL will use the data segment (DS) and stack (SS) of the calling task – DS is now equal to SS and all those functions that you couldn't use before are now available. In fact the .def file allows some extra refinement on this. Note that this is the normal case for a font file, ie. that it does not have a data segment of its own. An example of a DLL that does this is the PTrace DLL supplied with Windows called WINDEBUG.DLL. Note that you cannot use static data in your DLL and then declare it DATA NONE, ie. to qualify your DLL must use no static or literal data at all.

You can actually specify that certain functions use the DS of the caller and others use the DS of the DLL – you do this by *marking* each function that uses the DS of the caller in the EXPORTS section of the .def file. When the linker fixes up a DLL entry point, it can be told to omit the code that changes DS on DLL entry. This can be done on a per export (per function) basis, this allows for much greater flexibility because a data segment for the DLL can still exist, although it is only set for certain entry points; those entry points that use the DS of the caller (NODATA) can assume that DS is equal to SS when they are called. Here's an example of the required NODATA declaration in a .def file :

```
ORTS
    WEP                @1 RESIDENTNAME
    vTotTable          @2
    vTstTable          @3 NODATA
```

The function marked NODATA above will use the DS of the caller, the others will use the DS of the DLL; obviously if you use this *per function* technique you should NOT use DATA NODATA. Note. The linker normally warns you that an application doesn't contain a data segment – L4036 *no automatic data segment*, this warning is omitted if the application's .def file specifies DATA NONE or if the module being linked is a DLL.

As was previously mentioned, a DLL without a data segment will use both the data segment and the stack segment of the calling task; therefore, DS does equal SS. This statement is complicated by the fact that some items within a DLL will (may implicitly or explicitly) declare their own data segment! These offending *extra*data segments are created by the 'C' Compiler to store global (static storage class), static variables (using *static)* and literal data (such as the string *ABC*). The DATA statement in the .def file is the mechanism that Windows uses to determine if the DLL has a data segment. If the .DEF file declares DATA NONE, then Windows assumes that no data segment exists for this DLL – after all that's what DATA NONE *says.* Since Windows assumes that a *no data* DLL does not have a data segment, a data segment that is created implicitly by the DLL code itself is not loaded into memory and will not be visible by Heap Walker or any other heap management utilities – the segment's not been loaded! When a *no data* DLL does in fact have a data segment (that's not loaded), the DLL will use the application's DS as it was directed to do by using the NODATA keyword; however, the offset into the data segment is then calculated as being relative to the DLL's non-loaded data segment (when accessing an item of data that <u>was</u> actually defined in the DLL). Assigning any value to a variable declared in the DLL will therefore overwrite an arbitrary area of data in the calling task's data segment – OOPS! This type of abnormality will be extremely difficult to track down and debug. When the data segment is built for the DLL, data items are positioned in the data segment starting from the bottom of the heap and progress upwards towards the top, eg. a WORD sized variable requires two bytes on the bottom of the DLL's data segment, a following DWORD sized item would occupy the four bytes above (towards the top of the heap) the WORD that had been previously allocated. Writing to this DWORD variable will overwrite 4 bytes on the bottom of the calling application's data segment – 2 bytes in to be exact as the WORD sized item was allocated on the heap in front of us (below us). The result is that four bytes of the calling task's heap have now been trashed! Since the size of a calling task's data segment is often many thousands of bytes, this type of error may go unnoticed for weeks and will most likely not cause a trap (GPF). OK, so how do you know there may be problems with *hidden*data segments in your DATA NONE DLL?

One symptom of an unexpected data segment is that the Resource Compiler may provide you with the following warning :

```
Warning   Segment Number set to PRELOAD
```

This warning is produced by the resource compiler (see *Programming Tools* Page 228 for more information) when a data segment that has been created by the 'C' Compiler is missing its *behavioural flags* (MULTIPLE DISCARDABLE etc), ie. the flags have not been defined for the segment. In such cases the default setting for these segments is PRELOAD SINGLE. The warning above is issued when the resource compiler copies a segment that must be pre-loaded but that segment is not marked as PRELOAD etc in the .def file. Should a data segment exist for which their are no flags this warning is issued, if you see it – think about it!

If you use the 'C' run time libraries (CRT) in the DLL you will automatically *get*an *extra*data segment. A DLL that uses the CRT code references a global internal variable called __acrtused, this is declared in the file LIBENTRY.ASM (the code that ultimately calls LibMain() – see later section on *what's required* for the LibEntry() code):

```
externA <_acrtused>

OR

extrn    __acrtused:abs
  [
```

Referencing this variable informs the linker that the DLL will use the CRT library code. If the CRT library is not required by the DLL, this line should be removed to allow a true *no data* DLL to be created. If the CRT code is really used in the DLL, __acrtused <u>must</u> be declared. This will cause a data segment to be created; however, the warnings concerning that data segment may be ignored if all the tasks using the DLL also use the CRT library. If the DLL doesn't use the CRT library code it should be linked with the xNOCRTD (x = model) libraries instead of the normal DLL/Windows libraries xDLLCyW (x = model, y = e or a).

If you're using Windows 3.0 you may find that a *no data* DLL does not use the DS of the calling task, ie. a DLL created without a data segment (__acrtused removed, DATA NONE and HEAPSIZE 0) under 3.0 still uses a *different* DS to that used by the calling task, or to put it another way, the value of DS changes over the call! This was a known bug in Windows 3.0 and was fixed in 3.1. To remedy the problem when using 3.0, declare each function of the DLL in the EXPORTS section as *NODATA*, eg.

```
EXPORTS
      vFunction @10   NODATA
```

One last point about this. The standard library macros for processing variable function arguments (variable number and type – or variadic functions) rely on DS being equal to SS – be careful.

☐ WINDLL & Windows

The headers (.h) provided with the Microsoft 'C' compiler include some conditional compilation directives based upon whether or not the pre-processor symbols _WINDLL and _WINDOWS are currently defined, ie. defined whilst a translation unit is being compiled. _WINDOWS is defined automatically if you include the -GA? compiler switch whilst compiling an application and _WINDLL is automatically defined (as well as _WINDOWS) if you use -GD? whilst compiling a DLL (if you're not using either of those switches either use #define in your code or the -D compiler switch).

The standard headers typically define standard types, prototypes (for standard functions) and manifest constants to use with those functions. When you're writing code for Windows you may not use some of the standard functions (the actual set of functions that are unavailable depends upon whether or not you're building a DLL or an application). Some of these rules for DLLs don't hold if you're building a *no data*

DLL, ie. if DS and SS are equal (see above). The headers may, or may not, prototype some of the standard library functions based upon the value of the symbols _WINDOWS and _WINDLL. Typical header file source looks like this :

Taken from STDIO.H

```
#ifndef _WINDLL
int __cdecl getchar(void);
char * __cdecl gets(char *);
#endif
```

Here we can see that as long as _WINDLL is NOT defined that getchar() and gets() are prototyped and therefore available (why I don't know, but they are available!). If _WINDLL is defined they are not prototyped. Should you use a function for which the compiler has not seen a prototype (and if your warning level is high enough – level 3 min using MSC 7) you'll get a C4013 warning, ie. undefined function. Of course in order to spot the fact that you've used an unsupported function in your code you'll have to spot the warning message! I recommend that you compile using -W4 -WX if you're using the Microsoft compiler and always #define STRICT. W4 is the highest warning level and will spot just about anything worth mentioning in your code that might cause a problem. WX tells the compiler to treat any, repeat any, warning as an error – no object file is built. This ensures that you code MUST compile without any warnings (and of course errors). Of course, your code may still contain bugs but it's clean as far as the compiler can tell! Just one other word of caution about using _WINDOWS etc. Be careful to check that the headers you're using actually contain the #ifndef _WINDOWS stuff! Older versions of the headers may exist in your system that do not contain the conditional compilation directives so check to make sure that you pick up the correct version of STDIO.H etc. Check your INCLUDE= environment variable and follow it bit by bit until you find your standard headers – you'll be picking up the first occurrence you find of them in the include path.

The *modern* Windows' run-time library (and those issued with *modern* compilers like C7) are more or less (75% ish) safe to use in Windows' DLLs and applications; the C7 documentation now flags routines as Windows and Windows DLL compatible/incompatible so remember to consult the documentation. In fact you might want to check out other more convenient ways of writing your DLLs. By more convenient I mean ways that are model independent and whose libraries never assume anything about the *nearness* of any passed parameters. Such an environment is Borland's Pascal for Windows (I use version 7 – *Borland Pascal With Objects*). It's a piece of pie (I wanted to say something else but it would have been edited out!) and as easy as cake (2010 fan) to write DLLs using this product – if you haven't considered it before consider it now – even if you just write DLL code using it (see end of this chapter for a small example DLL and application written in Borland's Pascal version 7). I think that using Visual Basic as a front ending tool with Borland's Pascal for writing DLL code (back end) is an almost *dream team* when it comes to writing 95% of Windows' applications quickly.

☐ The DLL promise

DLLs provide for the following :

Sharing of code

Unlike a conventional application that uses code from a static link library an application that uses sub-routines in a DLL does not include those used routines. In other words by using, say, MessageBox() the application does not contain the code for MessageBox() – that code is kept in the library. This is the reverse of what happens when a conventional 'C' application for example uses, say, printf – the application *gets* a copy of the printf code inserted into it by the linker. If DOS were a multi-tasking OS this would mean that if there were three applications running and each used printf that there would be three copies of printf in memory (somewhere!). This is wasteful as each copy of the printf code is identical – wouldn't it be better if those apps could share one copy of printf instead? A side-effect of this is that code (in a library or application) should not be modified by a task; if a task alters its own application code it does so for all instances of the application as each shares the same code. If a task alters a DLL's code it alters it for all clients of that library. It would also mean, if we had pre-emptive multi-tasking, that libraries either ought to be re-entrant or at the very least protect against re-entrancy via some semaphore mechanism – as Windows isn't pre-emptive we don't have to worry (not that re-entrancy isn't possible – just that it's harder to do it accidentally!).

Easy upgrade of code

Given the example above consider what would happen if your compiler vendor suddenly found a serious bug in printf()? They would (hopefully) issue some sort of patch disk that fixed the problem, but hold on. You've been shipping your application now for 6 months, sold maybe 10,000 copies and have now been informed that each application may have a serious bug in it. OK, so you patch the compiler and re-compile your application code; you now have a bug free version that you have to ship to all your existing 10,000 customers! P.S. Don't ask the compiler vendor for financial assistance in upgrading your customers – typically they don't want to know as you buy the product always *as is* according to many a licence! Now consider what would happen if Microsoft found a serious bug in, say, TextOut(). They would upgrade each registered user of Windows (hopefully!) with a Windows' patch disk to fix the problem. Your application doesn't have to be altered whatsoever and Microsoft pays the bill for fixing buggy code (they can afford to do so I think)!

The best example of this *free upgrade* mechanism happens when Microsoft releases a new version of Windows which of course is faster, smaller, better etc in every way – your application instantly benefits from the new version because it uses new, faster, smaller etc sub-routines contained within the new version of Windows. BTW, If you think about it, a Windows application usually consists primarily of code that bolts together API calls.

Abstraction

An example of abstraction, which partly falls into the category of *Sharing of code* is controls. Abstraction is the process of confining some functionality and/or data in some identifiable way. A control is a good example. DLLs allow you to *objectise*your application by providing a natural and straight forward object oriented packaging mechanism. The DLL *object* offers services via its API interface, the actual mechanics of how the APIs work is of course hidden within the DLL.

This is nothing new as static libraries have always provided for a level of abstraction, ie. printf() is ultimately coded differently in Microsoft's standard library to how it is coded in, say, Cray's standard library; your 'C' code, which is ANSI compliant (isn't it?!) works equally well on a PC and a CRAY II (OK – so it's a little faster on a CRAY II!) due to the fact that you use the *printf service* and don't get involved in OS or system internals to display a message (like writing to screen mapped memory) on the screen.

Control of code segments

Again nothing *really* new here as you can do this in an application. Each routine (if necessary) in a DLL can be coded, compiled and linked so that it is contained in its own code segment. Each code segment may be awarded a distinct set of handling characteristics so that the Windows memory manager may handle memory allocation etc in an efficient way.

Increased privilege

This is only *really* true for DLLs that are device drivers. Processes, ie. applications in Windows always run at ring 3 (in 3.1, in 3.0 they run at ring 1) whilst device drivers may run at any ring level including the so called kernel privilege of ring 0 (VxDs typically always run at ring 0). Rings, or more fully, Privilege Rings are levels or CPU system privilege supported by the Intel 80386/486 CPUs. These *levels* of privilege are called rings since the more privileged levels or rings protect operating system *objects* from outer rings which have a lower, and therefore more restricted, privilege. The highest privilege is 0, the lowest 3.

☐ Sugar and Spice

Windows itself is made up of (almost entirely – there is an app or two as well) a collection of DLLs (device drivers and *normal* DLLs), ie. libraries of sub-routines that are *generally useful*. The three most important DLLs in Windows are called KERNEL, GDI and USER (Note that these are module names – not file names). Each of these DLLs makes available (through exports) numerous sub-routines that are used by you, the Windows' developer, to perform some function of your application.

Often you'll see texts that say Windows is made up of just GDI, KERNEL and USER – don't believe them! For example the common dialog functions live in COMMDLG, the sound functions in SOUND.DRV etc. Depending upon your Windows' system you'll find that Windows' is actually made up of around 20 modules (DLLs and applications (like The Print Manager and The Program Manager)).

☐ DLL/Module makeup

Two of the most useful tools provided by Microsoft for looking more closely at modules are HEAPWALK.EXE (HEAPSPY.EXE is the Borland equivalent (complete with source) of HEAPWALK) and EXEHDR.EXE (TDUMP is the Borland equivalent of EXEHDR). Heap Walker is a Windows application, exehdr is a DOS application – each application can be used to view a module from a different angle. Heap Walker is actually used for examining Windows' global heap (from which all segments come – it's as omniscient as it sounds!); if you run it up you'll be able to ascertain just what DLLs, drivers and applications are currently loaded (modules allocating segments from the global heap). Here's a view of Heap Walker running on my machine:

```
┌─────────────────────────────────────────────────────────────────┐
│ ─              HeapWalker- [Main Heap]                   ▼ ▲      │
│ File  Walk  Sort  Object  Alloc  Add!                            │
│ ADDRESS   HANDLE   SIZE LOCK      FLG HEAP OWNER    TYPE          │
│ 8058A000      0                                     Sentinel    ▲ │
│ 0006C8C0 02EE    256                    ARIALB   Module Database  │
│ 00095EE0 041E    224                    CGA40WOA Module Database  │
│ 80741160 12E6    224                    CGA80WOA Module Database  │
│ 8055E500 044E    320        D           COMM     Code 1          │
│ 8055D260 0456   4768        D           COMM     Code 2          │
│ 0003F6C0 045F   1440 P1     F           COMM     Code 3          │
│ 0003FC60 0467   1248 P1     F           COMM     DGroup          │
│ 80757BA0 0236    384                    COMM     Module Database  │
│ 00089560 1226   4448              Y     COMMDLG  DGroup          │
│ 0006B3E0 1276   1184                    COMMDLG  Module Database  │
│ 0006CDE0 02DE    224                    COURB    Module Database  │
│ 000948C0 030E    224                    COURE    Module Database  │
│ 80735EE0 23BE   4448        D           COURE    Private         │
│ 0008C5E0 1216   3808                    DBWIN    Code 1          │
│ 0008D4C0 120E  10144                    DBWIN    DGroup          │
│ 0006B880 126E    448                    DBWIN    Module Database  │
│ 0008A6C0 1286   7968                    DBWINEXE Code 1          │
│ 00087320 127E   8768              Y     DBWINEXE DGroup          │
│ 80746200 12B6    608                    DBWINEXE Module Database ▼ │
│ 0025CDC0 11EE    672        D           DBWINEXE Resource  Lang   │
│ ◄ │                                                          ► │
└─────────────────────────────────────────────────────────────────┘
```

A typical Heap Walker view of the global heap.

The Heap Walker display above shows the global heap requirements for the modules whose names appear under *Heap Owner* – each Windows' module requires at least one segment allocated from the global heap and so Heap Walker effectively lists the entire set of loaded modules. A module can be anything from an application, a dynamic link library to a device driver (only application modules can become tasks); in fact the only requirement to be a module is that you're a *new executable* (NE file). A module's name is a string of text embedded into the NE file (resident name table entry 0 to be exact) and has nothing to do with the name given to the disk file which physically contains the module's binary image on disk. This means that several different disk files may have the same module name (attempting to run them all concurrently will however fail (sometimes this is what you want!))! When you try and run an application Windows uses the application's *module name* to ascertain whether or not it currently has an instance of module X running, if it thinks that it has it creates another instance of the existing running application; in other words if you've got, say, two executables with the same module name but different executable names you won't be able to run any combination of them simultaneously – as soon as you try and run application B, having already run application A, you'll simply get another A! Moral – always use carefully thought out module names (there's a similar situation with Windows' classes – see other area of this book for more on the conflicts that can occur there).

Consider the module KERNEL. This *core* Windows' module provides all those low level things that any fashion conscious operating system's kernel should, eg. functions for allocating memory and scheduling tasks etc. Of course depending upon whether or not the processor is running in protect mode or not, and maybe if it (the OS) provides virtual memory allocation, functions like GlobalAlloc() will ultimately be coded differently, ie. the actual mechanics of how it *does* something will typically differ. So how does Windows' KERNEL module cope – does it have *clever code* that detects the processor mode etc before allocating heap space or what? In fact it doesn't – there are several different KERNEL modules (3 in 3.0, 2 in 3.1) that perform all the kernel's functions. When Windows starts it determines (unless you force it) automatically which mode ([real]/standard/enhanced) it should start in, it then loads the necessary KERNEL module. The KERNEL module as a disk file might be called KRNL386.EXE (enhanced mode), KRNL286.EXE (standard mode) or, if you're using 3.0 KERNEL.EXE (for real mode). Once the module is loaded it presents itself to the rest of the system as *KERNEL*(the name used in its LIBRARY statement); now whenever your application requires memory from the global heap you call a function in KERNEL that does the job.

Each module has a module database associated with it. The module database contains information held in the NE disk file header (and some other stuff). Whilst on the subject of module vs. filename, one very useful bit of information is the disk file name that *is*the module *on disk*. For example, say you wanted to know the disk file name (and location) of the COMM driver. If you double click (in Heap Walker) the COMM driver's module database segment and look towards the end of it you'll find something like this :

```
    Global Object - 00097EE0 0236   384        COMM   Module Data
00C0 FF 03 02 B2 00 FF 03 02 CE 00 FF 03 02 E7 00 FF  ÿ..².ÿ..Î.ÿ..ç.ÿ
00D0 03 02 07 01 FF 03 02 23 01 FF 03 02 43 01 FF 03  ....ÿ..#.ÿ..C.ÿ.
00E0 02 5F 01 FF 03 02 7B 01 FF 03 02 98 01 FF 03 02  ._.ÿ..{.ÿ....ÿ..
00F0 B5 01 FF 03 02 1F 02 FF 03 02 46 0A FF 03 02 47  µ.ÿ....ÿ..F.ÿ..G
0100 0A FF 03 02 D2 01 FF 03 02 73 00 63 00 65 00 00  .ÿ..Ò.ÿ..s.c.e..
0110 00 FF 03 02 F9 01 FF 00 02 26 02 20 01 00 00 6A  .ÿ..ù.ÿ..&. ...j
0120 18 40 19 43 3A 5C 57 49 4E 33 31 5C 53 59 53 54  .@.C:\WIN31\SYST
0130 45 4D 5C 43 4F 4D 4D 2E 44 52 56 00 02 26 02 00  EM\COMM.DRV..&..
```

Here we can see that the *module*called COMM on disk is called COMM.DRV, as another example (which was talked about above) let's look at KERNEL.

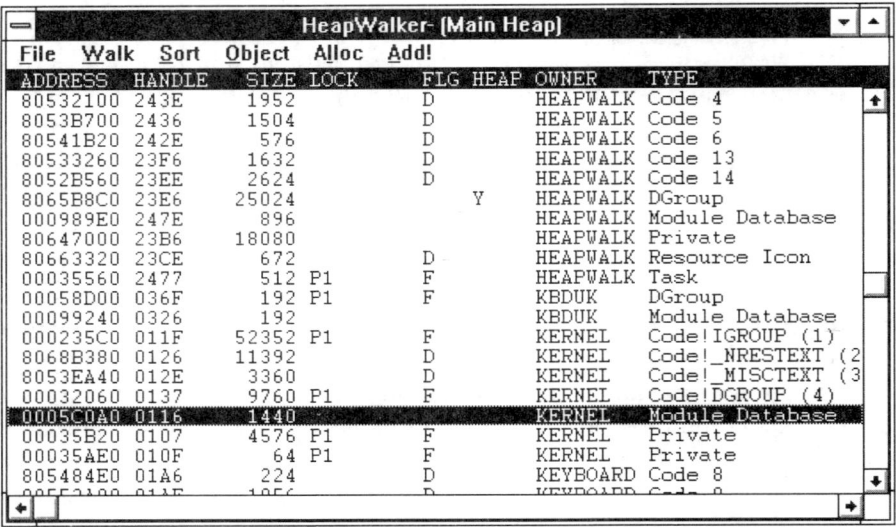

By double clicking the module database entry we can see what KERNEL is called on disk – we can also as a side effect determine the operating mode of Windows :

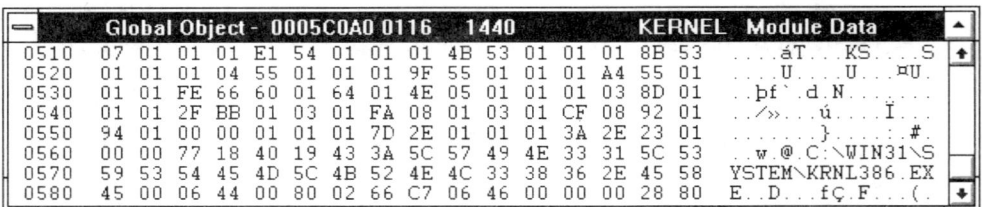

Here we can see that we are *in* 386 enhanced mode (as the KERNEL module disk file is called KRNL386.EXE). You can do the same thing *from code* by using GetModule-FileName() (it accesses the module's database to get it!).

I'm sure you're all familiar with the *normal* Heap Walker functionality so I won't go over it here – we will re-visit it however in the chapter on debugging.

The other useful application I mentioned earlier was called EXEHDR.EXE (exe header). It is used for examining various types of files. The Microsoft exe file header utility displays file headers for DOS programs and segmented executable files. You can even use EXEHDR to alter some fields in the header so as to make fresh (or anyway different) demands upon the system. segmented executable files include all New Executable files, ie. Windows device drivers, DLLs, Windows applications and even OS/2 applications. Exehdr's output is straight forward and by and large should be useful to anyone with a knowledge of the NE executable file format. Exehdr is very useful for establishing what functions are exported (made available by) and imported (used by) by a module. For example if we were to run exehdr on the communications driver COMM.DRV we would get something like this :

```
Microsoft (R) EXE File Header Utility  Version 3.00
Copyright (C) Microsoft Corp 1985-1992.  All rights reserved.

.EXE size (bytes)          2440
Magic number:              5a4d              , 5A = Z, 4D = M, ie MZ magic.
Bytes on last page:        009cZ
Pages in file:             0002
Relocations:               0000
Paragraphs in header:      0004
Extra paragraphs needed:   0005
Extra paragraphs wanted:   ffff
Initial stack location:    0000:00b8
Word checksum:             0000
Entry point:               0000:0000
Relocation table address:  0040
Reserved words:
 0000 0000 0000 0000 0000 0000 0000 0000
 0000 0000 0000 0000 0000
New .EXE header address:   00000080
Memory needed:             1K

Library:                   COMM            , This is a library.
Description:               Windows Communications Driver
Operating system:          Microsoft Windows - version 3.10
Data:                      SHARED
Initialization:            Global
Initial CS:IP:             seg   1 offset 002a
Initial SS:SP:             seg   0 offset 0000
DGROUP:                    seg   4 , DGROUP is in the 4th segment in the
                                   , segment table listed below.
Linker version:            5.20
32-bit Checksum:           9dc0ec4e
Segment Table:             000000c0 length 0020 (32)
Resource Table:            000000e0 length 0018 (24)
Resident Names Table:      000000f8 length 000e (14)
Module Reference Table:    00000106 length 0004 (4)
Imported Names Table:      0000010a length 000f (15)
Entry Table:               00000119 length 008b (139)
Non-resident Names Table:  000001a4 length 0110 (272)
Movable entry points:      22
Segment sector size:       16
Application type:          WINDOWAPI
Other module flags:

' Medium memory module driver, ie. multiple code segments and one data seg.
no. type address  file  mem   flags
  1 CODE 00000300 00134 00134 EXECUTEREAD, PRELOAD, NONCONFORMING, NOIOPL,
                             relocs, (movable), (discardable), (shared)
  2 CODE 00000f80 01287 01288 EXECUTEREAD, LOADONCALL, NONCONFORMING, NOIOPL,
                             relocs, (movable), (discardable), (shared)
```

```
' Fixed. This segment probably contains an interrupt handler.
3 CODE 000004a0 00592 00592 EXECUTEREAD, PRELOAD, NONCONFORMING, NOIOPL,
                            relocs, (fixed), (nondiscardable), (shared)


' This segment contains the DGROUP or default data segment of the DLL.
 4 DATA 00000a60 004d8 004d8 READWRITE, SHARED, PRELOAD, NOEXPANDDOWN,
NOIOPL,
                            relocs, (fixed), (nondiscardable)



' Functions made available by this DLL are :-
Exports:
ord seg offset name
 16   2  021f  WEP exported, shared data
 14   2  0198  CCLRBRK exported, shared data
  3   2  0032  SETQUE exported, shared data
  7   2  00ce  TRMCOM exported, shared data
  2   2  0019  SETCOM exported, shared data
 13   2  017b  CSETBRK exported, shared data
 19   2  01d2  COMMWRITESTRING exported, shared data
 17   2  0a46  SUSPENDOPENCOMMPORTS exported, shared data
100   2  01f9  ENABLENOTIFICATION exported, shared data
  6   2  00b2  CTX exported, shared data
  9   2  0107  CEXTFCN exported, shared data
 20   2  0073  READCOMMSTRING exported, shared data
 11   2  0143  CEVT exported, shared data
 12   2  015f  CEVTGET exported, shared data
  4   2  004e  RECCOM exported, shared data
  8   2  00e7  STACOM exported, shared data
  5   2  0096  SNDCOM exported, shared data
 15   2  01b5  GETDCB exported, shared data
 10   2  0123  CFLUSH exported, shared data
 18   2  0a47  REACTIVATEOPENCOMMPORTS exported, shared data
  1   2  0000  INICOM exported, shared data


' Functions used by the DLL (by segment) are (imp) :-
 1 type    offset target
   OFFSET  00f2   imp KERNEL.193
   OFFSET  0033   imp KERNEL.194
   PTR     0127   imp SYSTEM.2
   BASE    011f   seg  3 offset 0000
   PTR     00b7   imp KERNEL.170
   PTR     00ed   imp KERNEL.176
   PTR     00a5   imp KERNEL.186
   OFFSET  008a   imp KERNEL.178
  8 relocations


 2 type    offset target
   OFFSET  1227   imp KERNEL.193
   BASE    0aa1   seg  3 offset 0000
   PTR     117d   imp SYSTEM.6
   PTR     0bc3   imp KERNEL.127
   PTR     0b37   imp KERNEL.128
   PTR     079b   imp KERNEL.47
   PTR     07a7   imp KERNEL.50
   PTR     0229   imp KERNEL.186
   PTR     0582   seg  2 offset 0226
   OFFSET  0703   imp KERNEL.178
   PTR     08ef   imp KERNEL.354
```

```
  11 relocations

  3 type    offset target
    BASE      0511  seg    3 offset 0000
    BASE      054d  seg    4 offset 0000
   2 relocations

  4 type    offset target
    BASE      0282  seg    3 offset 0000
    BASE      0284  seg    4 offset 0000
   2 relocations
```

By the way MZ is the initials of Mark Zbikowski. Mark was the guy that came up with the format of a DOS executable's header.

An MZ file is a DOS executable file or as it is called now, *an old app*. The reason that exehdr apparently thinks of this Windows' DLL as a DOS application (in that the *Magic* is MZ) is due to the *old app* DOS stub attached to the beginning of the Windows' DLL – the stub allows you to execute a Windows (or whatever) program from DOS; at which point you typically see the stub produce some message about you being a dummy. The NE file is attached to the end of the stub code. If you have a HEX dumping tool handy (such as XTree) you can see the MZ and NE file signatures a *stub's width* apart in the NE's header.

Note that each function is exported from the driver by name and by ordinal reference. Note also that each imported function is imported by ordinal only, eg. KERNEL.50 means that the comm's driver uses the function in the kernel module whose export ordinal is 50 (which is GetProcAddress() by the way). Programmers often use exehdr and tools like it to find functions that are *available* but undocumented, indeed by cross referencing from one library to another (or an application to a library) it is possible to determine what if any undocumented functions are being utilised (see note on __export below for more on this). It's often handy to keep exehdr listings around (hard copy), in particular it's useful to know a function's ordinal reference when using a function like GetProcAddress() (importing using a function's name vs. importing using a function's ordinal is not only more costly in data space in the calling application but is slower (to perform the dynamic link)). I usually keep two listings of each library etc, one is sorted by (using DOS sort with the /+ switch) ordinal value (export) whilst the other is sorted by function name. Here's an brief extract of USER sorted both ways to give you an idea:

USER sorted on ordinal number :

```
  ord seg offset  name

       1    1  bcc0  MESSAGEBOX exported, shared data
     2    3  0059  OLDEXITWINDOWS exported, shared data
     3    5  0165  ENABLEOEMLAYER exported, shared data
     4    5  01a2  DISABLEOEMLAYER exported, shared data
     5    5  03a2  INITAPP exported, shared data
     6    1  8c3a  POSTQUITMESSAGE exported, shared data
```

```
 7    5   0303   EXITWINDOWS exported, shared data
 8    3   0232   WEP exported, shared data
10    1   b9ce   SETTIMER exported, shared data
11    1   7c00   BEAR11 exported, shared data
12    1   b9eb   KILLTIMER exported, shared data
13    1   7a53   GETTICKCOUNT exported, shared data
14    1   7bed   GETTIMERRESOLUTION exported
15    1   7a53   GETCURRENTTIME exported, shared data
16    1   bd28   CLIPCURSOR exported, shared data
17    1   bd0e   GETCURSORPOS exported, shared data
18    1   b99e   SETCAPTURE exported, shared data
19    1   2c91   RELEASECAPTURE exported, shared data
20    1   8bc7   SETDOUBLECLICKTIME exported, shared data
21    1   8bd7   GETDOUBLECLICKTIME exported, shared data
22    1   b93f   SETFOCUS exported, shared data
23    1   8be9   GETFOCUS exported, shared data
24   13   257e   REMOVEPROP exported, shared data
25    1   bbff   GETPROP exported, shared data
26   13   2561   SETPROP exported, shared data
27   13   259b   ENUMPROPS exported, shared data
28    1   bd5c   CLIENTTOSCREEN exported, shared data
29    1   bd7c   SCREENTOCLIENT exported, shared data
30    1   78f0   WINDOWFROMPOINT exported, shared data
31    1   b8fd   ISICONIC exported, shared data
32    1   bca0   GETWINDOWRECT exported, shared data
33    1   bc80   GETCLIENTRECT exported, shared data
34    1   b9ff   ENABLEWINDOW exported, shared data
35    1   ba13   ISWINDOWENABLED exported, shared data
36    1   bc3c   GETWINDOWTEXT exported, shared data
37    1   bc1c   SETWINDOWTEXT exported, shared data
38    1   bc6c   GETWINDOWTEXTLENGTH exported, shared data
39    1   ba6b   BEGINPAINT exported, shared data
40    1   ba8b   ENDPAINT exported, shared data
41    8   148e   CREATEWINDOW exported, shared data
42   14   1117   SHOWWINDOW exported, shared data
43   14   1161   CLOSEWINDOW exported, shared data
44   14   114d   OPENICON exported, shared data
45    7   1a57   BRINGWINDOWTOTOP exported, shared data
46    2   1008   GETPARENT exported, shared data
47    1   1a4f   ISWINDOW exported, shared data
48    1   b8cf   ISCHILD exported, shared data
49    1   b8e9   ISWINDOWVISIBLE exported, shared data
50    6   1fb0   FINDWINDOW exported, shared data
51    1   1d11   BEAR51 exported, shared data
52   14   03f0   ANYPOPUP exported, shared data
53    8   151d   DESTROYWINDOW exported, shared data
54    1   c083   ENUMWINDOWS exported, shared data
55    1   c066   ENUMCHILDWINDOWS exported, shared data
56    7   19c7   MOVEWINDOW exported, shared data
57    8   13ef   REGISTERCLASS exported, shared data
58    8   145e   GETCLASSNAME exported, shared data
59    1   ba43   SETACTIVEWINDOW exported, shared data
60    1   8bf3   GETACTIVEWINDOW exported, shared data
61   13   2474   SCROLLWINDOW exported, shared data
62   18   1a00   SETSCROLLPOS exported, shared data
63   18   1a22   GETSCROLLPOS exported, shared data
```

```
64   18   1a44   SETSCROLLRANGE exported, shared data
65   18   1a66   GETSCROLLRANGE exported, shared data
66    1   b6c9   GETDC exported, shared data
67    1   b6b5   GETWINDOWDC exported, shared data
68    1   b6dd   RELEASEDC exported, shared data
```

USER sorted on function name :

```
ord  seg  offset   name
102    2   0efc   ADJUSTWINDOWRECT exported, shared data
454    2   0f16   ADJUSTWINDOWRECTEX exported, shared data
432   11   03c1   ANSILOWER exported, shared data
438   11   03f7   ANSILOWERBUFF exported, shared data
472   11   0411   ANSINEXT exported, shared data
473   11   042b   ANSIPREV exported, shared data
431   11   03a5   ANSIUPPER exported, shared data
437   11   03dd   ANSIUPPERBUFF exported, shared data
 52   14   03f0   ANYPOPUP exported, shared data
411    9   132a   APPENDMENU exported, shared data
170    4   04c0   ARRANGEICONICWINDOWS exported, shared data
 11    1   7c00   BEAR11 exported, shared data
182    1   7ca8   BEAR182 exported, shared data
285   41   18b9   BEAR285 exported, shared data
306   10   15ed   BEAR306 exported, shared data
 51    1   1d11   BEAR51 exported, shared data
 86   13   0229   BEAR86 exported, shared data
259    7   00b8   BEGINDEFERWINDOWPOS exported, shared data
 39    1   ba6b   BEGINPAINT exported, shared data
301   26   0000   BOZOSLIVEHERE exported, shared data
 45    7   1a57   BRINGWINDOWTOTOP exported, shared data
213   40   0af4   BUILDCOMMDCB exported, shared data
462   15   027d   CALCCHILDSCROLL exported, shared data
123    1   b925   CALLMSGFILTER exported, shared data
293    1   c198   CALLNEXTHOOKEX exported, shared data
122    1   b89b   CALLWINDOWPROC exported, shared data
198   15   087c   CASCADECHILDWINDOWS exported, shared data
149   39   07bc   CHANGECLIPBOARDCHAIN exported, shared data
153    9   11b5   CHANGEMENU exported, shared data
 97   25   29af   CHECKDLGBUTTON exported, shared data
154    9   127c   CHECKMENUITEM exported, shared data
 96   25   29c3   CHECKRADIOBUTTON exported, shared data
191    1   bdc2   CHILDWINDOWFROMPOINT exported, shared data
211   40   0bab   CLEARCOMMBREAK exported, shared data
 28    1   bd5c   CLIENTTOSCREEN exported, shared data
 16    1   bd28   CLIPCURSOR exported, shared data
138   39   06c7   CLOSECLIPBOARD exported, shared data
207   40   0aaf   CLOSECOMM exported, shared data
253   41   1ab7   CLOSEDRIVER exported, shared data
 43   14   1161   CLOSEWINDOW exported, shared data
273   41   1857   CONTROLPANELINFO exported, shared data
369   12   176c   COPYCURSOR exported, shared data
368   12   17e3   COPYICON exported, shared data
 74    1   bf1c   COPYRECT exported, shared data
143   39   0075   COUNTCLIPBOARDFORMATS exported, shared data
163   13   25b8   CREATECARET exported, shared data
```

```
 406  12  172c   CREATECURSOR exported, shared data
 408  12  0000   CREATECURSORICONINDIRECT exported, shared data
  89  24  0a98   CREATEDIALOG exported, shared data
 219  24  0ac4   CREATEDIALOGINDIRECT exported, shared data
 242  24  0b1f   CREATEDIALOGINDIRECTPARAM exported, shared data
 241  24  0af3   CREATEDIALOGPARAM exported, shared data
 407  12  17a3   CREATEICON exported, shared data
 151   9  089b   CREATEMENU exported, shared data
 415   9  08a8   CREATEPOPUPMENU exported, shared data
  41   8  148e   CREATEWINDOW exported, shared data
 452   8  14ca   CREATEWINDOWEX exported, shared data
 362   1  970a   DCHOOK exported, shared data
 308  25  2a13   DEFDLGPROC exported, shared data
 255   2  109a   DEFDRIVERPROC exported, shared data
 260   7  1a0c   DEFERWINDOWPOS exported, shared data
 445  15  1ba0   DEFFRAMEPROC exported, shared data
 235   1  c127   DEFHOOKPROC exported, shared data
 447  15  1bb4   DEFMDICHILDPROC exported, shared data
 107   1  b870   DEFWINDOWPROC exported, shared data
 413   9  1390   DELETEMENU exported, shared data
 164  13  0bfa   DESTROYCARET exported, shared data
 458  12  1758   DESTROYCURSOR exported, shared data
 457  12  17cf   DESTROYICON exported, shared data
 152   9  1268   DESTROYMENU exported, shared data
  53   8  151d   DESTROYWINDOW exported, shared data
```

The functions shown in bold face in the listing above are undocumented. If you have 3.0 (still) use EXEHDR on USER to get a 3.0 listing; sort that listing by ordinal and look up some of the *bear???* functions – you'll find have more sensible names! Some of the names are very helpful – others are not helpful at all in trying to determine just what a function does! Take for example CreateCursorIconIndirect() and contrast this with BozosLiveHere()!!

Here's another look at USER.EXE. This listing shows all the functions (name + ordinal) exported by USER.EXE that are not prototyped in WINDOWS.H (some of these are documented in various headers that come with the DDK). The program exeutil comes from the book Undocumented Windows (Andrew Schulman, David Maxey, Matt Pietrek) which is published by Addison Wesley – ISBN 0-201-60834-0, it's good, you should get a copy (The normal output from this program shows the entry points sorted on ordinal, I've sorted them by name so that you can easily confirm the comments above)!

```
>exeutil -findundoc \win31\system\user.exe \windev\include\windows.h
Windows New-Executable (NE) Header Utilities version 1.0
from "Undocumented Windows" by Schulman et al. (Addison-Wesley, 1992)
Copyright (c) 1992 Andrew Schulman. All rights reserved.
5800 \windev\include\windows.h
;
;
; Functions in \win31\system\user.exe but not in \windev\include\windows.h:
USER . 11     BEAR11
USER . 182    BEAR182
```

USER	.	285	BEAR285
USER	.	306	BEAR306
USER	.	51	BEAR51
USER	.	86	BEAR86
USER	**.**	**301**	**BOZOSLIVEHERE**
USER	.	462	CALCCHILDSCROLL
USER	.	198	CASCADECHILDWINDOWS
USER	.	273	CONTROLPANELINFO
USER	.	408	CREATECURSORICONINDIRECT
USER	.	362	DCHOOK
USER	.	4	DISABLEOEMLAYER
USER	.	465	DRAGDETECT
USER	.	464	DRAGOBJECT
USER	.	459	DUMPICON
USER	.	3	ENABLEOEMLAYER
USER	.	187	ENDMENU
USER	.	324	FILLWINDOW
USER	.	400	FINALUSERINIT
USER	.	326	GETCONTROLBRUSH
USER	.	278	GETDESKTOPHWND
USER	.	343	GETFILEPORTNAME
USER	.	455	GETICONID
USER	.	372	GETINTERNALICONHEADER
USER	.	460	GETINTERNALWINDOWPOS
USER	.	323	GETMESSAGE2
USER	.	337	GETMOUSEEVENTPROC
USER	.	274	GETNEXTQUEUEWINDOW
USER	.	480	GETUSERLOCALOBJTYPE
USER	.	481	HARDWARE_EVENT
USER	.	5	INITAPP
USER	.	333	ISUSERIDLE
USER	.	289	KEYBD_EVENT
USER	.	336	LOADCURSORICONHANDLER
USER	.	356	LOADDIBCURSORHANDLER
USER	.	357	LOADDIBICONHANDLER
USER	.	456	LOADICONHANDLER
USER	.	276	LOCKMYTASK
USER	.	217	LOOKUPMENUHANDLE
USER	.	299	MOUSE_EVENT
USER	.	2	OLDEXITWINDOWS
USER	.	279	OLDSETDESKPATTERN
USER	.	325	PAINTRECT
USER	.	275	REPAINTSCREEN
USER	.	463	SCROLLCHILDREN
USER	.	321	SETEVENTHOOK
USER	.	461	SETINTERNALWINDOWPOS
USER	.	280	SETSYSTEMMENU
USER	.	314	SIGNALPROC
USER	.	470	STRINGFUNC
USER	.	172	SWITCHTOTHISWINDOW
USER	.	320	SYSERRORBOX
USER	.	199	TILECHILDWINDOWS
USER	**.**	**216**	**USERSEEUSERDO**
USER	.	332	USERYIELD
USER	.	8	WEP
USER	**.**	**322**	**WINOLDAPPHACKOMATIC**
USER	*.*	*503*	*WNETABORTJOB*
USER	*.*	*515*	*WNETBROWSEDIALOG*
USER	*.*	*506*	*WNETCANCELJOB*

See DDK documentation.
|
|

```
USER . 502    WNETCLOSEJOB                              /
USER . 525    WNETCONNECTDIALOG                        /
USER . 527    WNETCONNECTIONDIALOG                     /
USER . 514    WNETDEVICEMODE                           /
USER . 531    WNETDIRECTORYNOTIFY                      /
USER . 522    WNETDISABLE                              /
USER . 526    WNETDISCONNECTDIALOG                     /
USER . 521    WNETENABLE                               /
USER . 499    WNETERRORTEXT                            /
USER . 513    WNETGETCAPS                              /
USER . 530    WNETGETDIRECTORYTYPE                     /
USER . 519    WNETGETERROR                             /
USER . 520    WNETGETERRORTEXT                         /
USER . 532    WNETGETPROPERTYTEXT                      /
USER . 516    WNETGETUSER                              /
USER . 504    WNETHOLDJOB                              /
USER . 510    WNETLOCKQUEUEDATA                        /
USER . 501    WNETOPENJOB                              /
USER . 529    WNETPROPERTYDIALOG                       /
USER . 505    WNETRELEASEJOB                           /
USER . 523    WNETRESTORECONNECTION                    /
USER . 507    WNETSETJOBCOPIES                         /
USER . 511    WNETUNLOCKQUEUEDATA                      /
USER . 509    WNETUNWATCHQUEUE                         /
USER . 528    WNETVIEWQUEUEDIALOG                      /
USER . 508    WNETWATCHQUEUE                           /
USER . 524    WNETWRITEJOB                             /
USER . 341    _FFFE_FARFRAME
USER . 420    _WSPRINTF
USER . 484    __GP
```

Just as a point of interest, note also that the name of wsprintf in USER – it is actually _WSPRINTF, ie. it has a leading underscore (which CDECL functions typically do) but that it's in uppercase unlike its WINDOWS.H declaration (remember the 'C' is case sensitive) :

```
int     FAR CDECL wsprintf(LPSTR lpszOut, LPCSTR lpszFmt, ...);
```

In other words (and as 'C' maintains case) the function has ended up being defined with its name in uppercase just as though it were written like this –

```
int     FAR CDECL WSPRINTF(LPSTR lpszOut, LPCSTR lpszFmt, ...);
```

The case conversion is done by the linker, any import library built using the DLL will have the name in uppercase, an import library built using the .def file however will contain symbols of the correct case (as used in the .def file). The bottom line – watch out for linker problems and case sensitivity if using the NOI linker switch!

Back to DLLs and exported names. When you export a function from a DLL it will get an ordinal number assigned to it whether or not you actually assign it one or not – it's a good idea to assign ordinals, ie. take control over what a function's ordinal number will be as in so doing you create a quicker way to build true dynamic links to your library code at run-time. When you use GetProcAddress() to find an exported function's entry point in a DLL Windows may have to load the module's (DLL's) non-resident name table in order to *find* the requested function. This obviously takes some time. If you use a function's ordinal number Windows can create the link without resorting to having to reference the module's name table. Of course, if you've hard-coded the function's name into your application (instead of using a string table resource) you've also used up precious DS space, ie. using the string constant *SendMessage* in your code results in that string being placed in your application's (or DLL's) DGROUP; the name will never be discarded from memory because it *lives* in your data segment (if you must do this put the string in a string table resource)! By using an ordinal the function's reference (its ordinal) will be either placed directly into your code (load direct via immediate data) or at the very least take up less precious DGROUP space. Remember also that any data space you save could mean a saving in the amount of global heap available to other tasks.

There's been a lot of controversy recently about finding, and using, *hidden* APIs in various libraries, including of course those found in THE API – Windows. The discourse has been along the lines of a discussion on how someone might protect their investment in designing/developing their DLL from the world, or to put it another way – *How can I stop someone from easily using my DLL!* The reason that this kind of question is being asked is due directly to the names of functions appearing in the exehdr view of the DLL, ie. it is easy to find the function names given a DLL – run exehdr or tdump on it. Once you've got those names how difficult is it to use the functions? Not terribly is the answer unless a function's name is non-helpful or deliberately misleading (one way to make it harder (just a little) is to exclude it from the DLL's import library – see section on __export to see how this is done). As an example let's go back to Windows 3.0. I was involved on a project where we had to take a snapshot of the currently active window and put it into the clipboard. The standard Alt+Print Screen key combination was just what we wanted and we were faced with either mimicking its behaviour or causing it to happen by pretending someone had pressed the relevant keys. However, we were saved from pursuing these interesting alternatives (phew) when we spotted the function SnapWindow() which was exported from the USER module. We guessed that this was the function that *snapped* a window into the clipboard now all we had to do was figure out how it should be called. On the first attempt (and before we tried stepping through the SnapWindow() code with a decent debugger) we succeeded – all it took as its single parameter was a window handle! So this was all that was needed:

```
SnapWindow(GetActiveWindow());
```

A typical side effect of this (well maybe not so typical) was that SnapWindow() was taken out (not exported) by USER in 3.1 – OOPS!! We've had to implement an alternative strategy in 3.1 but that's another matter and might give too much away! That's the rub, ie. use today but don't bitch if it's gone tomorrow!

The easiest way to protect your DLL is to change the names of the functions that appear in it or remove them completely. For example it's possible to change the names to some sort of meaningless trash by selective use of the 'C' pre-processor, ie. you can *define* (do text substitution) on your names for other names like changing the function TurnWindowUpsideDown() into MODAFUNC1()! Another way would be to use weird names in the first place but that hinders the team building and using the DLL, yet another way you can do this is by processing further your built DLL so that the names it exports are meaningless – for example the function names below (except the WEP) are all question marks when viewed by exehdr :

```
Exports:
ord seg offset name
  5   1  0674   ????????????? exported, shared data
  3   1  04d3   ?????????????? exported, shared data
  8   1  063d   ????????????? exported, shared data
 10   1  0491   ????????? exported, shared data
 14   1  06e5   ?????????????? exported, shared data
  4   1  054b   ??????????? exported, shared data
  7   1  07ae   ????????????? exported
  9   1  0473   ?????????? exported, shared data
 16   1  0717   ?????????????? exported, shared data
  2   1  04a7   ?????????????? exported, shared data
 17   1  000a   ?????? exported, shared data
 13   1  0786   ?????????????? exported, shared data
  6   1  07b3   ?????????????? exported
  1   1  03f0   WEP exported, shared data
 12   1  07ab   ????????????? exported
 15   1  06ff   ?????????????? exported, shared data
```

At one time such a processing utility was difficult to write (before Microsoft documented the format of a NE executable's header), now it's a piece of cake (see example below); If you do this remember that an application that uses your library's functions can't get a hold of it by using its name (true dynamic link) – you'll have to use GetProcAddress() with an ordinal reference (which is typically good – see note earlier on); of course applications you build will be unaffected as presumably they're linked with .LIB file that was either built from the .DEF file or a pre-screwed-up DLL file?! If you want to do this with your DLL files (don't do it for DLLs that aren't yours as you don't know if some application, or function, requires a function's name in order to link with it) look in the C7 docs for the format of the *new executable's* header; what you're looking for is the non-resident name table.

You can remove the names completely by specifying that a function is NONAME in the EXPORTS section of the .def file :

```
EXPORTS
     MyFunc    @1 NONAME
```

This causes the function's name to be removed from the built DLL. This does mean however that the function must be linked to using its ordinal using either GetProcAddress() or an explicit IMPORTS clause in the importing application or DLL.

The names of those functions that a DLL exports are kept in one of two places, the resident name table or the non-resident name table (each entry in each table is used to *index* a particular function, one by name (resident) the other by ordinal (non-resident)). Most names (if you don't specify RESIDENTNAME in the .def file) *live* in the latter, ie. the non-resident name table. These names (both tables) are the names that are dumped by exehdr (if you want to see what's in each table use Borland's tdump instead of exehdr). The names in the resident name table are typically names of functions that are always called by name (GetProcAddress() using the function's name); such a function is the library's WEP (Windows' Exit Procedure) another is, as mentioned earlier, the module name (entry 0). These names, because the functions to which they refer, are called by name, must be kept in memory. If they were discardable (and discarded) and another DLL wanted to call any of them they'd need reloading; if there's not enough memory to reload the non-resident name table Windows will fatal exit on you – and we don't want that! By the way, be careful when using multiple RESIDENTNAME specifiers with 3.0 .def files, there was a problem that could cause a 0x0403 (invalid ordinal reference)fatal exit.

Just for interest sake these are the *names* in the *core* modules that are always resident:

```
Module              Names in Resident Name Table
GDI         –          __GP and WEP
KERNEL      –          __GP
USER        –          __GP and WEP
```

You'll notice that a WEP is not in the resident name table for the KERNEL module – it hasn't got a WEP – period! __GP is not actually a function, rather it is a pointer that is used to determine whether a protection fault occurring within the module (the one that has a __GP pointer) is actually a recoverable fault or not.

The names in the resident name table should not be changed as this *says* that these function will probably be called by name! The non-resident name table isn't important unless someone already calls one or more of the functions contained within it by name. If you were to change these names anyone dumping your DLL with either tdump or exehdr will be in for a shock!

The following program can be used to change all the entries (function names) in the DLL's non-resident name table to question marks! The program just has to be run once on the DLL, BUT remember to keep the output from the first run by running the program like this :

```
DLLHIDE SOUND.DRV > SOUND.DMP
```

This keeps the program's output in the file sound.dmp. If we take the DLL used in the example above and run the program on it we get this output in SOUND.DMP

```
TMS EXE File Header Utility  Version 1.00
TMS DLL File ????er Utility  Version 1.10
Copyright (C) TMS 1990-1992.  All rights reserved.
```

```
SOUND.DRV
Contents of non-resident name table for DLL
Multimedia Sound device driver.

Exports:
ord name
11   WAITSOUNDSTATE
5    SETVOICEACCENT
3    SETVOICEQUEUESIZE
8    SETVOICESOUND
10   STOPSOUND
14   GETTHRESHOLDEVENT
4    SETVOICENOTE
7    SETSOUNDNOISE
9    STARTSOUND
16   SETVOICETHRESHOLD
2    CLOSESOUND
17   DOBEEP
13   COUNTVOICENOTES
6    SETVOICEENVELOPE
1    OPENSOUND
12   SYNCALLVOICES
15   GETTHRESHOLDSTATUS
```

The listing above shows the functions that are exported (based upon the non-resident name table) from the DLL sound.drv. While that run was underway the names were replaced with strings of question marks so if we were to run DLLHIDE (this application) or, say, exehdr or tdump on the DLL again we would see this :

```
TMS EXE File Header Utility  Version 1.00
TMS DLL File ????er Utility  Version 1.10
Copyright (C) TMS 1990-1992.  All rights reserved.


SOUND.DRV
Contents of non-resident name table for DLL
?????????????????????????????????.

Exports:
ord name
11   ?????????????????
5    ????????????????
3    ???????????????????
8    ????????????????
10   ?????????
14   ???????????????????
4    ???????????????
7    ????????????????
9    ??????????
16   ???????????????????
2    ??????????
17   ??????
13   ?????????????????
6    ??????????????????
1    ?????????
```

```
12    ?????????????
15    ?????????????????
```

You can now see why I said keep the output from the first run, ie. What function's exported as ordinal 11? From the first listing we can see that it's WAITSOUNDSTATE! Here's the source code. Notice also that the description string is also given the treatment – now we don't know what the DLL does (apart from guessing from its filename – SOUND.DRV) :

The C source file :

```c
/*
** Necessary includes.
*/
#include <fcntl.h>
#include <io.h>
#include <sys\types.h>
#include <sys\stat.h>
#include <stdio.h>
#include <stdlib.h>
#include <string.h>


/*
** Necessary types.
*/
typedef unsigned short      WORD;
typedef unsigned char       BYTE;
typedef unsigned long       DWORD;
typedef int                 BOOL;
typedef struct
{
    WORD      exMagNum;
    BYTE      exLkrVer;
    BYTE      exLkrRev;
    WORD      exEntOffst;
    WORD      exEntLen;
    DWORD     exRes;
    WORD      exFlgs;
    WORD      exDatSegNum;
    WORD      exLclHpSze;
    WORD      exStkSze;
    DWORD     exCSIP;
    DWORD     exSSIP;
    WORD      exSegTblEnt;
    WORD      exModRefTblEnt;
    WORD      exNonResNmeTblSze;
    WORD      exSegTblOffst;
    WORD      exResTblOffst;
    WORD      exResNamTblOffst;
    WORD      exModRefTblOffst;
    WORD      exImpNamTblOffst;
    DWORD     exNonResNamTblOffst;
    WORD      exNumMovEntPoints;
    WORD      exShftCnt;
    WORD      exNumResSegs;
    BYTE      exTagOS;
    BYTE      exExtaEXEInfo;
```

```
   WORD      exFstLoadOffst;
   WORD      exFstLoadLen;
   WORD      exRes1;
   WORD      exWinVer;
}EXEHDR;
#define TRUE            (1)
#define FALSE           (!TRUE)
#define WINDOWSKEY      0x18   /* MZ offset.*/
#define NE              0x454E /* NE Magic. */
#define LIB_BIT         0x8000 /* bit 15.   */
#define MAX_NAME_LEN    255

/*
** Error codes.
*/
#define ERR_READ        1
#define ERR_MEM         2
#define ERR_SEEK        3
#define ERR_EXP         4
#define ERR_LIB         5
#define ERR_OLDEXE      6
#define ERR_NOTEXE      7
#define ERR_OPEN        8
#define ERR_TOOLARGE    9

/*
** Prototypes.
*/
void vProcessTable(BYTE *, WORD);
void vError(char *, char *, int);


/*
** Global stuff.
*/
static int    nFh;        /* File handle for reading DLL file. */
static BYTE * pcResTable; /* Pointer to copy of table.         */
static char * pcFile;     /* Points to current file name.      */

/*
** Program to change exported function names in a DLL's non-resident
** name table so that functions aren't visible using EXEHDR.EXE. Can
** work on wild card specs like '*.*'.
*/
void main(int argc, char ** argv)
{
   /* Ouput banner. */
   puts("TMS EXE File Header Utility  Version 1.00");
   puts("TMS DLL File ????er Utility  Version 1.10");
   puts("Copyright (C) TMS 1990-1992.  All rights reserved.");

   /* Set up stuff in case of error. */
   nFh = 0;
   pcResTable = NULL;

   if(argc < 2)
   {
       vError("Unknown", "Must give a file name.", 1);
   }
```

```
else
{
    /*
    ** For processing args. App can take wild cards like *.*.
    */
    auto int      nLoop;

    /*
    ** For each arg set pcFile to point to arg...
    */
    for(
        nLoop = 1, pcFile = *(argv + nLoop)
        ;nLoop < argc
        ;nLoop++, pcFile = *(argv + nLoop)
        )
    {
        printf("\n\n%s\n", strupr(pcFile));

        /* Open file for read/write in binary mode. */
        if((nFh = _open(pcFile, O_RDWR | O_BINARY)) != -1)
        {
            /* Used to hold the OLD exe header. */
            auto BYTE   barOldHeader[0x40];

            /* Read it in. */
            if(_read(
                    nFh
                    ,&barOldHeader[0]
                    ,sizeof(barOldHeader)
                    ) != -1
                )
            {
                /* 'MZ' is magic number of OLD exe header. */
                auto BYTE   barMag[] = {'M','Z'};

                /* Check that this file's header is an OLD exe header.*/
                if(strncmp(
                        (char *)&barOldHeader[0x0]
                        ,(char *)&barMag[0x0]
                        ,sizeof(barMag)
                        ) == 0
                    )
                {
                    /*
                    ** Check to see if this old header is a front for a new
                    ** header. Programmer's Reference Vol 4:Resources Page 69
                    */
                    if(barOldHeader[WINDOWSKEY] >= 0x40)
                    {
                        /* Go for the NEW Windows' header. */
                        if(_lseek(
                                nFh
                                ,*((DWORD *)&barOldHeader[0x3C])
                                ,SEEK_SET
                                ) != -1
                            )
                        {
                            /* Holds NEW EXE 'NE' header. */
```

```
auto EXEHDR exe;

/* Read it in. */
if(_read(nFh, &exe, sizeof(EXEHDR)) != -1)
{
    /* Is it a new EXE? */
    if(exe.exMagNum == NE)
    {
        /* Is it a library? */
        if(exe.exFlgs & LIB_BIT != 0)
        {
            /* Has it got a non-res name table? */
            if(exe.exNonResNmeTblSze != 0)
            {
                /* Go to it. */
                if(_lseek(
                        nFh
                        ,exe.exNonResNamTblOffst
                        ,SEEK_SET
                        ) != -1
                    )
                {
                    /* Init pointer - alloc memory. */
                    if(
                        (pcResTable =
                    malloc(
                            exe.exNonResNmeTblSze
                            )
                        ) != NULL
                        )
                    {
                        /* Read it all into memory. */
                        if(_read(
                                nFh
                                ,pcResTable
                                ,exe.exNonResNmeTblSze
                                ) != -1
                            )
                        {
                            /* Go an' process it. */
                            vProcessTable(
                                        pcResTable
                                        ,
                                        exe.exNonResNmeTblSze
                                        );

                            /* Re-seek to it again. */
                            if(
                                _lseek(
                                    nFh
                                    ,
                                    exe.exNonResNamTblOffst
                                    ,SEEK_SET
                                    ) != -1
                                )
                            {
                                /* Write it out. */
                                if(
                                    _write(
```

```
                            nFh
                            ,pcResTable
                            ,
                            (WORD)exe.exNonResNmeTblSze
                            ) != -1
                )
                {
                    /* Tidy up. */
                    _close(nFh);
                    nFh = 0;
                    free(pcResTable);
                    pcResTable = NULL;
                }
                else
                {
                    /* write error.*/
                    vError(
                            pcFile
                            ," Error"
                            "writing."
                                ,2
                                );
                }
            }
            else
            {
                vError(
                        pcFile
                        ," Error"
                        "seeking."
                        ,2
                        );
            }
        }
        else
        {
            vError(
                    pcFile
                    ," Error reading."
                    ,ERR_READ
                    );
        }
    }
    else
    {
        vError(
                pcFile
                ," Error getting memory."
                ,ERR_MEM
                );
    }
}
else
{
    vError(
            pcFile
            ," Error seeking."
            ,ERR_SEEK
            );
```

```
                              }
                          }
                          else
                          {
                              vError(
                                    pcFile
                                  ," Error, nothing exported."
                                  ,ERR_EXP
                                  );
                          }

                      }
                      else
                      {
                          vError(
                                pcFile
                              ," Error, not a library."
                              ,ERR_LIB
                              );
                      }
                  }
                  else
                  {
                      vError(
                            pcFile
                          ," Error, not a new exe."
                          ,ERR_OLDEXE
                          );
                  }
              }
              else
              {
                  vError(
                        pcFile
                      ," Error reading."
                      ,ERR_READ
                      );
                              }
                          }
                          else
                          {
                              vError(
                                    pcFile
                                  ," Error seeking."
                                  ,ERR_SEEK
                                  );
                          }
                      }
                      else
                      {
                          vError(
                                pcFile
                              ," Error old exe."
                              ,ERR_OLDEXE
                              );
                      }

                  }
              else
```

```
                        {
                            vError(
                                    pcFile
                                   ," Error not an exe."
                                   ,ERR_NOTEXE
                                   );
                        }
                    }
                else
                    {
                        vError(
                                pcFile
                               ,"Error reading."
                               ,ERR_READ
                               );
                    }

                _close(nFh);
                }
            else
                {
                    vError(
                            pcFile
                           ," Error opening."
                           ,ERR_OPEN
                           );
                }
        }/* Set each arg. */
    }/* arg count. */
} /* main. */



/*
** Function to actually change non-resident name table names.
**
** Passed a pointer to a memory block which contains the
** non-resident name table and the size of the table.
*/
void vProcessTable(BYTE * pResTable, WORD wSize)
{
    auto BOOL   bFlag = FALSE;

    /* Initial dec of size to account from starting from 0. */
    wSize -= 1;

    /* While we've not finished processing the name table. */
    while(*pResTable != 0x0 && wSize > 0)
    {
        auto WORD   wOrdinal;
        auto BYTE   barFuncName[MAX_NAME_LEN];
        auto BYTE * pcNameBegin;
        auto WORD   wFuncNameLen;

        /* Get length of function's (or library's) name. */
        wFuncNameLen = *pResTable;

        if(wFuncNameLen > MAX_NAME_LEN - 1)
        {
```

```
        vError(
               pcFile
              ,"Error function's name to Large."
              ,ERR_TOOLARGE
              );
}

/* Step past it. */
pResTable++;

/* Dec size accordingly. */
wSize -= 1;

/* Init pointer to name. */
pcNameBegin = pResTable;

/* Copy name to buffer. */
memcpy(barFuncName, pResTable, wFuncNameLen);

/* Null terminate name. */
barFuncName[wFuncNameLen] = 0x0;

/* bFlag FALSE until after first entry processed (name). */
if(bFlag == FALSE)
{
    /* Output some pretty stuff. */
    printf(
           "Contents of non-resident name table for DLL\n%s.\n\n"
          ,&barFuncName[0]
          );

    printf("Exports:\n");
    printf("ord\tname\n");
}

/* Step past name. */
pResTable += wFuncNameLen;

/* Dec size accordingly. */
wSize -= wFuncNameLen;

/* Read ordinal. */
wOrdinal = *(WORD *)pResTable;

/* Step past ordinal. */
pResTable += sizeof(WORD);

/* Dec size accordingly. */
wSize -= sizeof(WORD);

/*
** See if someone's put a WEP in the non-res name table!
** Don't change its name if they have.
*/
if(strcmp((char *)&barFuncName[0], "WEP") != 0)
{
    /* Change name of function to all '?'. */
    memset(pcNameBegin, '?', wFuncNameLen);
```

```
            /* If not doing first entry (mame) output it. */
            if(bFlag != FALSE)
            {
                printf("%-u\t%s\n", wOrdinal, barFuncName);
            }
        }
        else
        {
            /* Tell 'em about the WEP. */
            printf(
                    "Possible problem. WEP in non-resident name table!%s\n"
                    ,barFuncName
                    );
        }

        /* Next time output all info. */
        bFlag = TRUE;
    }
}


/*
** Error handling function. Causes the close down of the application.
*/
void vError(char * pcFileName, char * pcMessage, int nErrCode)
{
   /* Output error message. */
   printf("File -> '%s' - %s\n", pcFileName, pcMessage);

   if(nFh != 0)
   {
       _close(nFh);
   }

   if(pcResTable != NULL)
   {
       free(pcResTable);
   }

   /* Exit with errorcode. */
   exit(nErrCode);
}
```

The program works by reading in a file's exe header; in particular the file's non-resident name table (if it has one). Any non-DLL file is rejected. The non-resident name table contains the names of all functions exported by this DLL and whose names may be discarded (except those in the resident name table). A WEP is usually flagged as RESIDENTNAME. This puts the name of the function, WEP, into the resident name table so this program doesn't often see WEP functions; in fact if it does it spews out a warning to that effect – that your DLL's WEP is discardable (its name). A WEP should always be RESIDENTNAME, if it isn't you might get problems – see notes on WEPs lower down. The name table is walked (see Programmer's Reference Volume 4: Resources – Pages 69 to 81 for the makeup of the table and the exe header (also the documentation on EXEHDR is worth reading)) and patched in memory. Finally the patched name table is written back to the file (where it was read from). Simple and effective (you may use the program above without restriction by the way). OK, enough for now about some of the peripheral things about DLLs – let's get down to business!

☐ What's actually required in a DLL

Answer, it depends somewhat upon the Windows' version and the compiler you're using but essentially all a DLL requires is a Windows' Exit Procedure or WEP and an entry point which is typically called LibMain (although the **actual** entry point is called LibEntry()).

Windows' Exit Procedures (WEPs) were introduced in Windows version 3.0 to allow each DLL that hooked interrupt vectors and/or modified I/O ports to clean up when the DLL was unloaded. However, because the 3.0 WEP implementation was broken and the limitations not well documented, the use and functionality of a WEP in 3.0 was restricted.

A WEP function is a function that gets called when the library it which it belongs is being unloaded from memory. It is called by the FreeLibrary() function (Note that FreeLibrary() is called implicitly when using an import library reference to a called function) and is never called directly by an application unless that application has first used LoadLibrary() or LoadModule() etc.

Example (and minimal) WEP

```
int CALLBACK WEP(int nExitType)
{
    return 1;
}
```

nExitType can be one of the following values (defined in WINDOWS.H) – WEP_FREE_DLL or WEP_SYSTEM_EXIT. I prefer to define and prototype my WEPs as BOOL functions, ie. they return a BOOL. Windows doesn't take any notice of what the WEP returns but the SDK documentation says that the WEP should return 1; surely TRUE is better?

Microsoft's C7 Compiler can provide a default WEP if one is not provided by the programmer (the same is true for the library's entry point – LibEntry()).

Some WEP rules, which applied to Windows version 3.0, still apply to Windows version 3.1.

- All DLLs must have a WEP. Even if the WEP function doesn't do anything, it must be still be defined in the library.
- A WEP must be declared as a FAR PASCAL or CALLBACK function.

- A WEP must be exported by listing it in the EXPORTS section of the DLL's .def file. The RESIDENTNAME keyword must be associated with it (see notes on resident name table earlier). Note that it is NOT necessary to use the ordinal reference 1 – any number will do. If you see a fatal exit 409 *Out of memory loading segment* or fatal exit 403 *Invalid ordinal reference to x:y* check to make sure that your WEP is flagged as RESIDENTNAME.

- The code segment that contains the WEP must be declared PRELOAD and FIXED in the .def file. If the segment is always in memory, Windows can call the WEP without loading the code segment from disk even under low memory conditions. Because FIXED segments in a DLL are also page-locked, the WEP should be the only function in the WEP segment. Note this is only the case for 3.1 applications that must run under 3.0, ie. a *pure* 3.1 DLL's WEP may now be placed in a discardable code segment.

When the WEP is called the library's DGROUP may already have been discarded (3.0 only) so any literal or static data may have been lost before the WEP is called. It is important therefore to check that the DGROUP segment exists before attempting to access any data in it! It is also possible for the DLL's WEP to be called before the DGROUP is created (3.0 only) (even before the library's LibEntry() entry point function is called), again it is important that a WEP check for the presence of its DGROUP before accessing any static or literal data. You can check to see if DS is set to point to a valid data segment by issuing a load access rights instruction (lar) and checking the *present* bit. The DS should always contain a valid selector – what we need to determine by using lar is whether or not the segment represented by DS is in fact loaded up. To check whether or not LibEntry (and therefore LibMain()) has been called prior to the WEP being called you can set a global flag in LibMain() that is subsequently checked in the WEP (that is as long as the DGROUP hasn't gone!). Note that *lar* is a protect mode only instruction so it cannot be used in Windows 3.0 real mode. The following code extract shows what should be done to protect a non-existent DGROUP in 3.0 WEPs.

```
mov      cx,wSeg       ;Get the DGROUP selector.
lar      ax,cx         ;Load its access rights.
jnz      SEG_Bad       ;If LAR fails, this is a bad selector.
test     ax,8000h      ;Is this segment present?
jz   SEG_Bad           ;No, selector is bad - oops.
```

A WEP function needs to be exported – by fashion, or convention, it is given an ordinal value of one. It is also flagged RESIDENTNAME which ensures that the name of the function (WEP) is kept in memory at all times. The WEP function is called by name and so the name needs to be available. If the name of the function were not made resident at all times it may of course be discarded. If it has been discarded and an attempt is made to unload the library the library's non-resident name table must be loaded. If there is insufficient memory to load the name table the WEP function cannot be called – a fatal exit occurs at this point! Under 3.1 the WEP doesn't have to be exported as ordinal 1 but it does still require the attribute RESIDENTNAME.

A WEP in 3.0 was called on a KERNEL stack that was too small to call basically any Windows' function – even some of your own functions might have trashed the stack by declaring too many automatic variables, it was however big enough to allow the WEP to un-hook interrupts (which is what the WEP was originally designed to be used for). Essentially, under Windows 3.0 a WEP cannot call any other function (really useful!). Under 3.1 the WEP is still called on a kernel stack but that stack is now at least 4Kb in size – well big enough to call a Windows' API or DOS function etc. Note that, despite popular belief, that the WEP is not called on the stack of some terminating, or DLL freeing, task.

In 3.0 it was possible, under some low memory conditions, that the WEP could be called before the library initialisation routine LibEntry() had been called or even before the library's DGROUP had been created! In 3.1, Windows calls a WEP only if the library's entry point has been called and its DGROUP has been created. The WEP code, for DLLs written specifically for Windows version 3.1, no longer needs to track any of this itself.

In 3.0, a library's WEP could also be called more than once. In Windows version 3.1, the WEP is never called more than once.

In 3.0, the Windows' USER module was notified that a DLL was freed before the library's WEP was called. This meant that any resources (which are maintained by the USER module) created by the DLL were freed before the library's WEP was called! In 3.1 the USER module is notified after the library's WEP is called.

Some of the MS documentation is unclear as to exactly what can and can't be done under 3.1 (can WEPs be in discardable segments etc – you've already heard that they can but how can we be really sure that we've got this stuff right? We need to do some detective work! Exehdr (or tdump) to the rescue. You can confirm most of the stuff above by examining a Microsoft DLL (is this a good idea?!), for example take a look at GDI – if this has something wrong in it surely Windows would surely crash all the time? GDI's WEP is exported at ordinal location 59 in segment 1. If you look at segment 1 you'll see that it is a fixed code segment :

```
1 CODE 00001e20 07c1e 07c1e EXECUTEREAD, PRELOAD, NONCONFORMING, NOIOPL,
                            relocs, (fixed), (nondiscardable), (nonshared)
```

Doesn't this mean that your WEP ought to be configured similarly, ie. in a fixed segment like under 3.0? Take a look in USER, you'll find that USER's WEP is at ordinal 8 in segment 3; Wow – segment 3 in USER is discardable! Don't look in kernel – it doesn't (not surprising) have a WEP! Looking around Windows' own DLLs and drivers you can safely say that a DLL's WEP doesn't, apparently, have to in a fixed segment nor does it have to at ordinal reference one. If you use tdump (or DLLHIDE above) you will find however that the WEP's name has to be resident at all times so don't forget the RESIDENTNAME attribute in the .def file. For the same reason (discarding/reloading of segments like the non-resident name table) the WEP function should also be kept in a fixed code segment if you want it to run under Windows

3.0. Windows is not able to *page out* a fixed code segment so keep the WEP code segment as small as possible – ideally the WEP segment should contain just the actual WEP function (see Custom Control chapter for an example of a code segment that contains only a WEP).

Why must a DLL's WEP be in a fixed segment in 3.0, and how come it can be moveable in 3.1? Well in 3.0 this could happen when DLL D1 used DLL D2 (implicitly).

Application A1 uses two DLLs D1 and D2, library D1 uses routines in D2.
- A1 termination
- Call D2 WEP
- Free D2
- Call D1 WEP
- Possible segment not present (WEP discarded)
- Load segment containing D1's WEP
- Segment has fix up to D2 but D2 has been freed
- GPF!

The solution was to fix the WEP segments in memory. Under Windows 3.1 the following instead occurs.
- **A1 Terminating**
- Call D2 WEP
- Call D1 WEP
- Possible segment not present (WEP discarded)
- Load segment containing D1's WEP
- Segment has fix up to D2
- Free D2
- Free D1

Or put another way – in 3.0, if a DLL used another DLL (which is implicitly referenced via an import library), the first DLL's (D1) WEP function could get called after the associated DLL (D2) is freed. If the segment that contains the WEP is discarded while containing references to the associated DLL D2, Windows hangs when D1's WEP segment is reloaded. The segment would have to be reloaded as Windows would attempt to fix up any external references to the already freed DLL's functions. The fix for this problem was to keep the WEP routine in a FIXED segment so that it couldn't be discarded. In 3.1, <u>any</u> affected WEPs are called before any DLLs are freed or discarded. A WEP can therefore be placed in a discardable segment if, and only if the DLL's written explicitly for 3.1, if the DLL must also be 3.0 compatible its WEP must still be placed in a FIXED code segment. You can *mark* a DLL as 3.1 only using the resource compiler. Also, using implicit loading and freeing, you cannot assume anything about the order in which DLLs are either loaded or discarded, ie. the order in which LibMain()s and WEPs are called. A DLL's segments are discarded when its usage count hits zero – it's therefore possible to have DLLs unload (in particular) in any order.

As has now become apparent all this stuff changes (mostly) between 3.0 and 3.1 – Use GetVersion() to check the version (if writing a DLL that can be used under 3.x).

The library's entry point is (as far as most programmers are concerned) called LibMain; this however is the function that the **real** entry point routine, LibEntry() calls after it has been called. You used to have to write your own LibEntry() function (back in the bad oldays) but nowadays everyone and his dog provides one for you – usually in source form too. The LibEntry() function provided with the SDK looks like this :

```
;;;;;;;;;;;;;;;;;;;;;;;;;;;;;;;;;;;;;;;;;;;;;;;;;;;;;;;;;;;;;;;;;;;;;;;;;;;;;;;;
;
;        LIBENTRY.ASM
;
;        Windows dynamic link library entry routine
;
;   This module generates a code segment called INIT_TEXT.
;   It initializes the local heap if one exists and then calls
;   the C routine LibMain() which should have the form:
;   BOOL FAR PASCAL LibMain(HANDLE hInstance,
;                   WORD    wDataSeg,
;                   WORD    cbHeap,
;                   DWORD   ignore);      /* Always NULL - ignore */
;
;   The result of the call to LibMain is returned to Windows.
;   The C routine should return TRUE if it completes initialization
;   successfully, FALSE if some error occurs.
;
;   Note - The last parameter to LibMain is included for compatibility
;   reasons.  Applications that wish to modify this file and remove the
;   parameter from LibMain may do so by simply removing the two
;   "push" instructions below marked with "****".
;
;;;;;;;;;;;;;;;;;;;;;;;;;;;;;;;;;;;;;;;;;;;;;;;;;;;;;;;;;;;;;;;;;;;;;;;;;;;;;;;;

include cmacros.inc

externFP <LibMain>              ; the C routine to be called

createSeg INIT_TEXT, INIT_TEXT, BYTE, PUBLIC, CODE
sBegin    INIT_TEXT
assumes   CS,INIT_TEXT

?PLM=0                          ; 'C' naming
externA  <_acrtused>            ; ensures that Win DLL startup code is
linked

?PLM=1                          ; 'PASCAL' naming
externFP <LocalInit>            ; Windows heap init routine

cProc   LibEntry, <PUBLIC,FAR>  ; entry point into DLL

include CONVDLL.INC
```

```
cBegin
        push    di              ; handle of the module instance
        push    ds              ; library data segment
        push    cx              ; heap size
        push    es              ; Always NULL  ****  May remove (see above)
        push    si              ; Always NULL  ****  May remove (see above)

        ; if we have some heap then initialize it
        jcxz    callc           ; jump if no heap specified

        ; call the Windows function LocalInit() to set up the heap
        ; LocalInit((LPSTR)start, WORD cbHeap);

        xor     ax,ax
        cCall   LocalInit <ds, ax, cx>
        or      ax,ax           ; did it do it ok ?
        jz      error           ; quit if it failed

        ; invoke the C routine to do any special initialization

callc:
        call    LibMain         ; invoke the 'C' routine (result in AX)
        jmp short exit          ; LibMain is responsible for stack clean up

error:
        pop     si              ; clean up stack on a LocalInit error
        pop     es
        pop     cx
        pop     ds
        pop     di

exit:

cEnd

sEnd    INIT_TEXT

end LibEntry
```

See also various notes on LibEntry() *features* like _acrtused and on passing command line arguments to libraries in the rest of this chapter. Note that if CX does not contain 0 (CX contains whatever value is in the library's HEAPSIZE statement (in the .def file) that the SDK routine LocalInit() is called to initialise the library's local data heap. LocalInit() leaves one outstanding lock on the local heap if it is called (the heap is usually unlocked again in LibMain). For some more detail on LibEntry()'s parameters see notes at the end of this chapter.

Note that LibEntry() expects LibMain() to tidy up the stack for it, ie. although LibEntry() pushes some stuff it only pops it again if the call to LocalInit() fails. See notes towards the end of the chapter on what happens if calls to either LibMain or LibEntry() fail.

Here's a minimal 3.1 LibMain :

The C source file :

```
BOOL FAR PASCAL LibMain
(
   HINSTANCE  hInstance    // Instance handle of DLL.
  ,WORD       wDataSeg     // DS of DLL.
  ,WORD       cbHeapSize   // Heapsize from .DEF file.
  ,LPSTR      lpszCmdLine  // CommandLine.
)
{
   if(cbHeapSize != 0)     // If we have some heap unlock it.
   {
      UnlockData(0);
   }

   return TRUE;            // All OK so return TRUE.
}
```

Here we can see that LibMain unlocks the DLL's local heap if it has one – note that cbHeapSize is checked and not wDataSeg, a DLL can be passed a valid DS even if it has specified 0 in its HEAPSIZE statement. The function returns a BOOL result (Microsoft documentation says it returns an int – see note above in sample WEP code). If the library has not initialised properly, ie. something's not to your liking in LibMain() return FALSE from this function to prevent Windows from loading the library proper.

An example

The best way to find out about DLLs is to write one (We've already seen a large DLL, it was shown in the dialog box chapter and was a complete replacement for Windows' MessageBox() API). In the rest of this chapter we'll be looking at two small DLLs that are none the less quite useful. The first is a DLL that allows us to spy on messages sent to a window procedure or call-back function and the second is a profiling DLL, ie. a DLL that allows you to determine how long, say, a function call took.

The *spying DLL* first saw light of day in an application I wrote under Windows 2.x that emulated the SDK SPY application. The SDK SPY (Borland's WinSight application is a kinda *super SPY* – nice one Mike) application allows the user to peek a look at the messages that are driving a window procedure (just in case you didn't know!). The DLL shown here is a little cut down from the version used in my application back then and simply provides some message translation services to any interested window procedure or call-back function.

In order to use the DLL (which has just one public entry point) you must insert into the window procedure or call-back function a call to a function called bOutputMessage. bOutputMessage is a DLL function. The routine takes 6 parameters, and is prototyped like this :

```
BOOL _export FAR PASCAL BOUTPUTMESSAGE
(
   HWND      hWnd
```

```
  ,UINT      uMessage
  ,WPARAM    wParam
  ,LPARAM    lParam
  ,BOOL      bFullOutput
  ,LPSTR     lpcaBuffer
);
```

The first four parameters are those that are passed to the window procedure or call-back function, ie. window handle, message id, wParam and lParam. The next parameter, bFullOutput is a BOOL that is TRUE if the caller wants full or verbose output (explained later) or FALSE if the output is to be *brief*. The last parameter is a pointer to a buffer that is supplied by the caller. The buffer gets filled in by the routine via the passed pointer. The buffer contains (for full output) message information formatted exactly like that shown in SPY's client area, here's an example of what's contained in the buffer after a successful call to the routine:

```
    251C WM_GETMINMAXINFO      0000 07BF07B0
```

As you can see, very SPY like.

This is what happens in the DLL's bOutputMessage routine – Firstly the routine looks at the message ID and loads a string from its resources whose string table ID is the same as the passed message ID. It then uses wsprintf() to format this, and the other information supplied by you (window handle etc) into the buffer to which you have passed it a pointer. That's it! Upon return the user has a buffer that contains a NULL terminated string of text like that shown above. The user can do anything they want with it, maybe they'll output it to their debugging terminal or DBWIN or perhaps output it to a file? **This DLL was used to produce the message listings shown in the dialog chapter.**

The DLL's resources contains just one thing, a big(ish) string table, here's the DLL's resource script in full :

The .rc file :

```
#include "extract.h"


STRINGTABLE
BEGIN
        WM_ACTIVATE             ,"WM_ACTIVATE"
        WM_ACTIVATEAPP          ,"WM_ACTIVATEAPP"
        WM_ALTTABACTIVE         ,"WM_ALTTABACTIVE"
        WM_ASKCBFORMATNAME      ,"WM_ASKCBFORMATNAME"
        WM_BEGINDRAG            ,"WM_BEGINDRAG"
        WM_CANCELMODE           ,"WM_CANCELMODE"
        WM_CHANGECBCHAIN        ,"WM_CHANGECBCHAIN"
        WM_CHAR                 ,"WM_CHAR"
        WM_CHARTOITEM           ,"WM_CHARTOITEM"
        WM_CHILDACTIVATE        ,"WM_CHILDACTIVATE"
```

```
WM_CLEAR              , "WM_CLEAR"
WM_CLOSE              , "WM_CLOSE"
WM_COMMAND            , "WM_COMMAND"
WM_COMMNOTIFY         , "WM_COMMNOTIFY"
WM_COMPACTING         , "WM_COMPACTING"
WM_COMPAREITEM        , "WM_COMPAREITEM"
WM_CONVERTREQUEST     , "WM_CONVERTREQUEST"
WM_CONVERTRESULT      , "WM_CONVERTRESULT"
WM_COPY               , "WM_COPY"
WM_CREATE             , "WM_CREATE"
WM_CTLCOLOR           , "WM_CTLCOLOR"
WM_CUT                , "WM_CUT"
WM_DEADCHAR           , "WM_DEADCHAR"
WM_DELETEITEM         , "WM_DELETEITEM"
WM_DESTROY            , "WM_DESTROY"
WM_DESTROYCLIPBOARD   , "WM_DESTROYCLIPBOARD"
WM_DEVMODECHANGE      , "WM_DEVMODECHANGE"
WM_DRAGLOOP           , "WM_DRAGLOOP"
WM_DRAGMOVE           , "WM_DRAGMOVE"
WM_DRAGSELECT         , "WM_DRAGSELECT"
WM_DRAWCLIPBOARD      , "WM_DRAWCLIPBOARD"
WM_DRAWITEM           , "WM_DRAWITEM"
WM_DROPFILES          , "WM_DROPFILES"
WM_DROPOBJECT         , "WM_DROPOBJECT"
WM_ENABLE             , "WM_ENABLE"
WM_ENDSESSION         , "WM_ENDSESSION"
WM_ENTERIDLE          , "WM_ENTERIDLE"
WM_ENTERMENULOOP      , "WM_ENTERMENULOOP"
WM_ENTERSIZEMOVE      , "WM_ENTERSIZEMOVE"
WM_ERASEBKGND         , "WM_ERASEBKGND"
WM_EXITMENULOOP       , "WM_EXITMENULOOP"
WM_EXITSIZEMOVE       , "WM_EXITSIZEMOVE"
WM_FONTCHANGE         , "WM_FONTCHANGE"
WM_FILESYSCHANGE      , "WM_FILESYSCHANGE"
WM_GETDLGCODE         , "WM_GETDLGCODE"
WM_GETFONT            , "WM_GETFONT"
WM_GETHOTKEY          , "WM_GETHOTKEY"
WM_GETMINMAXINFO      , "WM_GETMINMAXINFO"
WM_GETTEXT            , "WM_GETTEXT"
WM_GETTEXTLENGTH      , "WM_GETTEXTLENGTH"
WM_HSCROLL            , "WM_HSCROLL"
WM_HSCROLLCLIPBOARD   , "WM_HSCROLLCLIPBOARD"
WM_ICONERASEBKGND     , "WM_ICONERASEBKGND"
WM_INITDIALOG         , "WM_INITDIALOG"
WM_INITMENU           , "WM_INITMENU"
WM_INITMENUPOPUP      , "WM_INITMENUPOPUP"
WM_INTERIM            , "WM_INTERIM"
WM_ISACTIVEICON       , "WM_ISACTIVEICON"
WM_KEYDOWN            , "WM_KEYDOWN"
WM_KEYUP              , "WM_KEYUP"
WM_KILLFOCUS          , "WM_KILLFOCUS"
WM_LBTRACKPOINT       , "WM_LBTRACKPOINT"
WM_LBUTTONDBLCLK      , "WM_LBUTTONDBLCLK"
WM_LBUTTONDOWN        , "WM_LBUTTONDOWN"
WM_LBUTTONUP          , "WM_LBUTTONUP"
WM_MBUTTONDBLCLK      , "WM_MBUTTONDBLCLK"
WM_MBUTTONDOWN        , "WM_MBUTTONDOWN"
WM_MBUTTONUP          , "WM_MBUTTONUP"
WM_MDIACTIVATE        , "WM_MDIACTIVATE"
```

```
WM_MDICASCADE              , "WM_MDICASCADE"
WM_MDICREATE               , "WM_MDICREATE"
WM_MDIDESTROY              , "WM_MDIDESTROY"
WM_MDIGETACTIVE            , "WM_MDIGETACTIVE"
WM_MDIICONARRANGE          , "WM_MDIICONARRANGE"
WM_MDIMAXIMIZE             , "WM_MDIMAXIMIZE"
WM_MDINEXT                 , "WM_MDINEXT"
WM_MDIRESTORE              , "WM_MDIRESTORE"
WM_MDISETMENU              , "WM_MDISETMENU"
WM_MDITILE                 , "WM_MDITILE"
WM_MEASUREITEM             , "WM_MEASUREITEM"
WM_MENUCHAR                , "WM_MENUCHAR"
WM_MENUSELECT              , "WM_MENUSELECT"
WM_MOUSEACTIVATE           , "WM_MOUSEACTIVATE"
WM_MOUSEMOVE               , "WM_MOUSEMOVE"
WM_MOVE                    , "WM_MOVE"
WM_NCACTIVATE              , "WM_NCACTIVATE"
WM_NCCALCSIZE              , "WM_NCCALCSIZE"
WM_NCCREATE                , "WM_NCCREATE"
WM_NCDESTROY               , "WM_NCDESTROY"
WM_NCHITTEST               , "WM_NCHITTEST"
WM_NCLBUTTONDBLCLK         , "WM_NCLBUTTONDBLCLK"
WM_NCLBUTTONDOWN           , "WM_NCLBUTTONDOWN"
WM_NCLBUTTONUP             , "WM_NCLBUTTONUP"
WM_NCMBUTTONDBLCLK         , "WM_NCMBUTTONDBLCLK"
WM_NCMBUTTONDOWN           , "WM_NCMBUTTONDOWN"
WM_NCMBUTTONUP             , "WM_NCMBUTTONUP"
WM_NCMOUSEMOVE             , "WM_NCMOUSEMOVE"
WM_NCPAINT                 , "WM_NCPAINT"
WM_NCRBUTTONDBLCLK         , "WM_NCRBUTTONDBLCLK"
WM_NCRBUTTONDOWN           , "WM_NCRBUTTONDOWN"
WM_NCRBUTTONUP             , "WM_NCRBUTTONUP"
WM_NEXTDLGCTL              , "WM_NEXTDLGCTL"
WM_NEXTMENU                , "WM_NEXTMENU"
WM_NULL                    , "WM_NULL"
WM_OTHERWINDOWCREATED      , "WM_OTHERWINDOWCREATED"
WM_OTHERWINDOWDESTROYED,   "WM_OTHERWINDOWDESTROYED"
WM_PAINT                   , "WM_PAINT"
WM_PAINTCLIPBOARD          , "WM_PAINTCLIPBOARD"
WM_PAINTICON               , "WM_PAINTICON"
WM_PALETTECHANGED          , "WM_PALETTECHANGED"
WM_PALETTEISCHANGING       , "WM_PALETTEISCHANGING"
WM_PARENTNOTIFY            , "WM_PARENTNOTIFY"
WM_PASTE                   , "WM_PASTE"
WM_POWER                   , "WM_POWER"
WM_QUERYDRAGICON           , "WM_QUERYDRAGICON"
WM_QUERYDROPOBJECT         , "WM_QUERYDROPOBJECT"
WM_QUERYENDSESSION         , "WM_QUERYENDSESSION"
WM_QUERYNEWPALETTE         , "WM_QUERYNEWPALETTE"
WM_QUERYOPEN               , "WM_QUERYOPEN"
WM_QUERYPARKICON           , "WM_QUERYPARKICON"
WM_QUERYSAVESTATE          , "WM_QUERYSAVESTATE"
WM_QUEUESYNC               , "WM_QUEUESYNC"
WM_QUIT                    , "WM_QUIT"
WM_RBUTTONDBLCLK           , "WM_RBUTTONDBLCLK"
WM_RBUTTONDOWN             , "WM_RBUTTONDOWN"
WM_RBUTTONUP               , "WM_RBUTTONUP"
WM_RENDERALLFORMATS        , "WM_RENDERALLFORMATS"
WM_RENDERFORMAT            , "WM_RENDERFORMAT"
```

```
            WM_SAVESTATE              , "WM_SAVESTATE"
            WM_SETCURSOR              , "WM_SETCURSOR"
            WM_SETFOCUS               , "WM_SETFOCUS"
            WM_SETFONT                , "WM_SETFONT"
            WM_SETREDRAW              , "WM_SETREDRAW"
            WM_SETTEXT                , "WM_SETTEXT"
            WM_SETVISIBLE             , "WM_SETVISIBLE"
            WM_SHOWWINDOW             , "WM_SHOWWINDOW"
            WM_SIZE                   , "WM_SIZE"
            WM_SIZECLIPBOARD          , "WM_SIZECLIPBOARD"
            WM_SIZEWAIT               , "WM_SIZEWAIT"
            WM_SPOOLERSTATUS          , "WM_SPOOLERSTATUS"
            WM_SYNCPAINT              , "WM_SYNCPAINT"
            WM_SYNCTASK               , "WM_SYNCTASK"
            WM_SYSCHAR                , "WM_SYSCHAR"
            WM_SYSCOLORCHANGE         , "WM_SYSCOLORCHANGE"
            WM_SYSCOMMAND             , "WM_SYSCOMMAND"
            WM_SYSDEADCHAR            , "WM_SYSDEADCHAR"
            WM_SYSKEYDOWN             , "WM_SYSKEYDOWN"
            WM_SYSKEYUP               , "WM_SYSKEYUP"
            WM_SYSTEMERROR            , "WM_SYSTEMERROR"
            WM_SYSTIMER               , "WM_SYSTIMER"
            WM_TESTING                , "WM_TESTING"
            WM_TIMECHANGE             , "WM_TIMECHANGE"
            WM_TIMER                  , "WM_TIMER"
            WM_UNDO                   , "WM_UNDO"
            WM_USER                   , "WM_USER"
            WM_VKEYTOITEM             , "WM_VKEYTOITEM"
            WM_VSCROLL                , "WM_VSCROLL"
            WM_VSCROLLCLIPBOARD       , "WM_VSCROLLCLIPBOARD"
            WM_WINDOWPOSCHANGED       , "WM_WINDOWPOSCHANGED"
            WM_WINDOWPOSCHANGING      , "WM_WINDOWPOSCHANGING"
            WM_WININICHANGE           , "WM_WININICHANGE"
            WM_YOMICHAR               , "WM_YOMICHAR"
END
```

As you can see the string table contains strings that *name* a load of Windows'
messages. The list is perhaps over complete in that it contains messages that are
undocumented and even some that disappeared when Windows 3.0 came out (being
in earlier versions of Windows or even Beta versions). The header file, extract.h,
contains the message definitions used in the string table above :

Extract.h File :

```
#define WM_NULL              0x0000
#define WM_CREATE            0x0001
#define WM_DESTROY           0x0002
#define WM_MOVE              0x0003
#define WM_SIZEWAIT          0x0004
#define WM_SIZE              0x0005
#define WM_ACTIVATE          0x0006
#define WM_SETFOCUS          0x0007
#define WM_KILLFOCUS         0x0008
#define WM_SETVISIBLE        0x0009
#define WM_ENABLE            0x000A
#define WM_SETREDRAW         0x000B
```

```
#define WM_SETTEXT                   0x000C
#define WM_GETTEXT                   0x000D
#define WM_GETTEXTLENGTH             0x000E
#define WM_PAINT                     0x000F
#define WM_CLOSE                     0x0010
#define WM_QUERYENDSESSION           0x0011
#define WM_QUIT                      0x0012
#define WM_QUERYOPEN                 0x0013
#define WM_ERASEBKGND                0x0014
#define WM_SYSCOLORCHANGE            0x0015
#define WM_ENDSESSION                0x0016
#define WM_SYSTEMERROR               0x0017
#define WM_SHOWWINDOW                0x0018
#define WM_CTLCOLOR                  0x0019
#define WM_WININICHANGE              0x001A
#define WM_DEVMODECHANGE             0x001B
#define WM_ACTIVATEAPP               0x001C
#define WM_FONTCHANGE                0x001D
#define WM_TIMECHANGE                0x001E
#define WM_CANCELMODE                0x001F
#define WM_SETCURSOR                 0x0020
#define WM_MOUSEACTIVATE             0x0021
#define WM_CHILDACTIVATE             0x0022
#define WM_QUEUESYNC                 0x0023
#define WM_GETMINMAXINFO             0x0024
#define WM_PAINTICON                 0x0026
#define WM_ICONERASEBKGND            0x0027
#define WM_NEXTDLGCTL                0x0028
#define WM_ALTTABACTIVE              0x0029
#define WM_SPOOLERSTATUS             0x002A
#define WM_DRAWITEM                  0x002B
#define WM_MEASUREITEM               0x002C
#define WM_DELETEITEM                0x002D
#define WM_VKEYTOITEM                0x002E
#define WM_CHARTOITEM                0x002F
#define WM_SETFONT                   0x0030
#define WM_GETFONT                   0x0031
#define WM_SAVESTATE                 0x0032
#define WM_GETHOTKEY                 0x0033
#define WM_FILESYSCHANGE             0x0034
#define WM_ISACTIVEICON              0x0035
#define WM_QUERYPARKICON             0x0036
#define WM_QUERYDRAGICON             0x0037
#define WM_QUERYSAVESTATE            0x0038
#define WM_COMPAREITEM               0x0039
#define WM_TESTING                   0x0040
#define WM_COMPACTING                0x0041
#define WM_OTHERWINDOWCREATED        0x0042
#define WM_OTHERWINDOWDESTROYED      0x0043
#define  WM_COMMNOTIFY               0x0044 /*Maybe also WM_ACTIVATESHELLWINDOW*/
#define WM_WINDOWPOSCHANGING         0x0046
#define WM_WINDOWPOSCHANGED          0x0047
#define WM_POWER                     0x0048
#define WM_NCCREATE                  0x0081
#define WM_NCDESTROY                 0x0082
#define WM_NCCALCSIZE                0x0083
#define WM_NCHITTEST                 0x0084
#define WM_NCPAINT                   0x0085
#define WM_NCACTIVATE                0x0086
```

```
#define WM_GETDLGCODE            0x0087
#define WM_SYNCPAINT             0x0088
#define WM_SYNCTASK              0x0089
#define WM_NCMOUSEMOVE           0x00A0
#define WM_NCLBUTTONDOWN         0x00A1
#define WM_NCLBUTTONUP           0x00A2
#define WM_NCLBUTTONDBLCLK       0x00A3
#define WM_NCRBUTTONDOWN         0x00A4
#define WM_NCRBUTTONUP           0x00A5
#define WM_NCRBUTTONDBLCLK       0x00A6
#define WM_NCMBUTTONDOWN         0x00A7
#define WM_NCMBUTTONUP           0x00A8
#define WM_NCMBUTTONDBLCLK       0x00A9
#define WM_KEYDOWN               0x0100
#define WM_KEYUP                 0x0101
#define WM_CHAR                  0x0102
#define WM_DEADCHAR              0x0103
#define WM_SYSKEYDOWN            0x0104
#define WM_SYSKEYUP              0x0105
#define WM_SYSCHAR               0x0106
#define WM_SYSDEADCHAR           0x0107
#define WM_YOMICHAR              0x0108
#define WM_CONVERTREQUEST        0x010A
#define WM_CONVERTRESULT         0x010B
#define WM_INTERIM               0x010C
#define WM_INITDIALOG            0x0110
#define WM_COMMAND               0x0111
#define WM_SYSCOMMAND            0x0112
#define WM_TIMER                 0x0113
#define WM_HSCROLL               0x0114
#define WM_VSCROLL               0x0115
#define WM_INITMENU              0x0116
#define WM_INITMENUPOPUP         0x0117
#define WM_SYSTIMER              0x0118
#define WM_MENUSELECT            0x011F
#define WM_MENUCHAR              0x0120
#define WM_ENTERIDLE             0x0121
#define WM_LBTRACKPOINT          0x0131
#define WM_MOUSEMOVE             0x0200
#define WM_LBUTTONDOWN           0x0201
#define WM_LBUTTONUP             0x0202
#define WM_LBUTTONDBLCLK         0x0203
#define WM_RBUTTONDOWN           0x0204
#define WM_RBUTTONUP             0x0205
#define WM_RBUTTONDBLCLK         0x0206
#define WM_MBUTTONDOWN           0x0207
#define WM_MBUTTONUP             0x0208
#define WM_MBUTTONDBLCLK         0x0209
#define WM_PARENTNOTIFY          0x0210
#define WM_ENTERMENULOOP         0x0211
#define WM_EXITMENULOOP          0x0212
#define WM_NEXTMENU              0x0213
#define WM_MDICREATE             0x0220
#define WM_MDIDESTROY            0x0221
#define WM_MDIACTIVATE           0x0222
#define WM_MDIRESTORE            0x0223
#define WM_MDINEXT               0x0224
#define WM_MDIMAXIMIZE           0x0225
#define WM_MDITILE               0x0226
```

```
#define WM_MDICASCADE            0x0227
#define WM_MDIICONARRANGE        0x0228
#define WM_MDIGETACTIVE          0x0229
#define WM_DROPOBJECT            0x022A
#define WM_QUERYDROPOBJECT       0x022B
#define WM_BEGINDRAG             0x022C
#define WM_DRAGLOOP              0x022D
#define WM_DRAGSELECT            0x022E
#define WM_DRAGMOVE              0x022F
#define WM_MDISETMENU            0x0230
#define WM_ENTERSIZEMOVE         0x0231
#define WM_EXITSIZEMOVE          0x0232
#define WM_DROPFILES             0x0233
#define WM_CUT                   0x0300
#define WM_COPY                  0x0301
#define WM_PASTE                 0x0302
#define WM_CLEAR                 0x0303
#define WM_UNDO                  0x0304
#define WM_RENDERFORMAT          0x0305
#define WM_RENDERALLFORMATS      0x0306
#define WM_DESTROYCLIPBOARD      0x0307
#define WM_DRAWCLIPBOARD         0x0308
#define WM_PAINTCLIPBOARD        0x0309
#define WM_VSCROLLCLIPBOARD      0x030A
#define WM_SIZECLIPBOARD         0x030B
#define WM_ASKCBFORMATNAME       0x030C
#define WM_CHANGECBCHAIN         0x030D
#define WM_HSCROLLCLIPBOARD      0x030E
#define WM_QUERYNEWPALETTE       0x030F
#define WM_PALETTEISCHANGING     0x0310
#define WM_PALETTECHANGED        0x0311
#define WM_USER                  0x0400
```

The messages in extract.h are listed in numeric order whilst those in the .rc file and listed in alphabetical order – this makes adding or finding a message given either its name or ID simple.

The *standard* Windows' messages were extracted from WINDOWS.H then *enhanced* from various sources (like the original DLL, old, and various versions, of WINDOWS.H, and the book *Undocumented Windows).*

An aside on LEX

Extracting the standard messages from WINDOWS.H up to 3.1 was quite simple as all the *WM* messages were kept together; with the 3.1 SDK Microsoft decided to group relevant functions and messages together (on the whole a good idea) making the job of extracting them a little more difficult (I wanted to extract them so that I could maintain a message list without disturbing WINDOWS.H, and also speed up compilation – you might decide in your own apps to simply include the whole of WINDOWS.H and have done with it? The resource compiler can now cope with WINDOWS.H's size!). A small hint here, if you haven't yet discovered the power of UNIX do so at your earliest convenience. By this I don't really mean load up the OS (although you could do far worse) but get to use some of the

UNIX utilities that are now available for DOS. I used a small LEX script to
extract the *WM* messages from WINDOWS.H – the script took about five
minutes to write and about 20 seconds to run; in case you're interested,
here it is (sorry no space for detail) :

```
%{

#include <stdio.h>
#include <stdlib.h>
#include <string.h>
#include <io.h>

void doit(void);
void main(void);
void vFoundVal(void);
void vFoundDef(void);

int    nLines        = 0;
int    nMessageLen   = 0;
int    bFoundMessage = 0;
char * pBuffer;

%}

%%

/* */
"#define WM_"[A-Z_]*                    vFoundDef();


[ \t]*[A-Za-z0??0-9]*                   vFoundVal();


\n                                      nLines++;


.                                       ;



%%

#define MEM      10
#define TRUE     1
#define FALSE    !TRUE
#define NORM     40


/*
** Found a string that starts with '#define WM_'.
*/
void vFoundDef(void)
{
    /*
    ** Found a WM_ message so flag it so that 'num found'
    ** routine knows to work on any bugger it gets.
    */
```

```c
            bFoundMessage = TRUE;

        /*
        ** Ouput the message remembering how many chars were in it
        ** - used to work out how to align the message ID.
        */
        nMessageLen = printf("%s", &yytext[0]);

}


/*
** Found a 'value', eg. '    0x0011'.
*/
void vFoundVal(void)
{
    /*
    ** Does this match follow the finding of a WM_ message?
    */
    if(bFoundMessage == TRUE)
    {
        /*
        ** Pointer to 'actual' characters which denote the
        ** message's value, ie. string minus white space.
        */
        auto   char * pC;

        /*
        ** Get rid of white space.
        */
        for(pC = &yytext[0]; *pC == ' ' || *pC == '\t'; pC++)
        {
            /* Nul statement. */
        }

        /*
        ** Form printf buffer. Need to form printf format string
        ** so that the message's value will be nicely aligned.
        */
        sprintf(pBuffer, "%%%ds\n", NORM - nMessageLen);

        /*
        ** Output message value.
        */
        printf(pBuffer, pC);

        /*
        ** Reset flag.
        */
        bFoundMessage = FALSE;
    }

    return;
}


void main(void)
{
    /*
```

```
    ** Get some memory for printf buffer used in vFoundVal.
    */
    if((pBuffer = calloc(MEM, sizeof(char))) != 0)
    {

        /*
        ** Call lexer - let it parse out the file.
        */
        yylex();

        /*
        ** All done so get rid of buffer.
        */
        free(pBuffer);
    }
    else
    {
        puts("Error allocating necessary memory");
    }

    return;
}
```

It did honestly take 5 minutes to write but it looks bigger here (due to all the comments which of course weren't in the original!). The Lex I used to generate the 'C' code was PCLEX 1.3 from Abraxas Software – a good product. It would have been even easier to write using AWK, another quite brilliant UNIX tool, but I was using LEX for something else at the time so I did it in that instead!

Anyway, back to the DLL! We've seen the resource script and the header file that defines the message constants; here's the source code for the DLL :

The C source file :

```
#define STRICT

/*
** Required headers.
** Master - not shown here - just prototypes  the functions below
** and #defs everything in WINDOWS.H conditional compilation
** list : #define NOCOMM, #define NOKERNEL etc. The bits that ARE
** required are selectively re-introduced below, this technique
** greatly reduces compilation time and the compilers far heap
** requirements. See also WSHL program.
*/
#include "master.h"

/*
** Turn back on stuff in WINDOWS.H that we need - all WINDOWS.H defines
** etc turned off in master.h.
*/
#undef NOKERNEL
#undef NOLSTRING
```

```
#undef NOUSER
#undef NOMEMMGR

/*
** More required headers.
*/
#include <windows.h>
#include <string.h >
#include <stdio.h  >

/*
** Misc stuff.
*/
#define BUFF_SIZE         255   /* min size of buffer provided by caller. */

BOOL _export FAR PASCAL BOUTPUTMESSAGE
(
        HWND
      ,UINT
      ,WPARAM
      ,LPARAM
      ,BOOL
      ,LPSTR
);

HINSTANCE hGetSetInstance(HINSTANCE);


/**************
** Code begins.
*/
HINSTANCE hGetSetInstance(HINSTANCE hInst)
{
   /*
   ** Used for holding the library's 'instance' handle.
   */
   static HINSTANCE hInstance;

   if(hInst != NULL)
   {
       hInstance = hInst;
   }

   return hInstance;
}




/*******************************************************************************
**

 Called by Windows when it loads this DLL. The function is called only once
 no matter how many times the library is loaded.

*******************************************************************************
*/
```

```
BOOL FAR PASCAL LibMain
(
   HINSTANCE  hInstance    // Instance handle of DLL.
  ,WORD       wDataSeg     // DS of DLL.
  ,WORD       cbHeapSize   // Heapsize from .DEF file.
  ,LPSTR      lpszCmdLine  // CommandLine.
)
{
   if(cbHeapSize != 0)     // If we have some heap unlock it.
   {
      UnlockData(0);
   }

   (VOID)hGetSetInstance(hInstance);

   return TRUE;            // All OK so return TRUE.
}




/***********************************************************************

This function outputs the details of a Windows' message that it is passed.

It is passed all the message parameters (hWnd, uMessage, wParam, lParam),
an indication of whether or not the output should be verbose and the
address of a buffer into which it should output its results.

***********************************************************************/


BOOL _export FAR PASCAL BOUTPUTMESSAGE
(
   HWND     hWnd
  ,UINT     uMessage
  ,WPARAM   wParam
  ,LPARAM   lParam
  ,BOOL     bFullOutput
  ,LPSTR    lpcaBuffer
)
{     /*
      ** Used to load message from resources.
      */
      static char carStringBuffer[BUFF_SIZE];

      /*
      ** The result of LoadString().
      */
      auto  BOOL bResult;


      /*******************************************
       *
       * Load the string  from the DLL's resources
       * that has ID uMessage - this should be the
       * same as the  message name. If the string
       * does not exist return FALSE.
```

```
          *
          */

          if((bResult = (BOOL)LoadString(
                                  hGetSetInstance(NULL)
                                  ,uMessage
                                  ,&carStringBuffer[0]
                                  ,BUFF_SIZE
                                  )) != 0
          )
          {

              /*****************************************************************
              *
              * Decide what information the caller requires and wsprintf it
              * into the caller's buffer.
              *
              */


              /*
              ** If the caller wants Message, hWnd, wParam and lParam.
              */

              if(bFullOutput == TRUE)
              {
                  wsprintf(
                          lpcaBuffer
                          ,"%-4.4X %-20s %-4.4X %-8.81X"
                          ,hWnd
                          , (LPSTR)&carStringBuffer[0]
                          ,wParam
                          ,lParam
                          );
              }

              /*
              ** The caller just wants the Message.
              */

              else
              {
                  wsprintf(
                          lpcaBuffer
                          ,"%-20s"
                          , (LPSTR)&carStringBuffer[0]
                          );
              }
          }
          else /* Couldn't get a string so set user's buffer to NULL. */
          {
              *lpcaBuffer = '\0';
          }


          return !!bResult;  // either TRUE or FALSE.

}
```

The code above is very small and quite straight forward and needs little explanation. The code first attempts to load a string from its resources which is positioned in its string table at index uMessage, ie. the message *value* is used as an index into the DLL's string table. If a string isn't found, ie. LoadString() fails then the first char in the caller's buffer is set to NULL, ie. it is 'C' string terminated. The function ultimately returns whatever LoadString() returns made BOOL, ie. LoadString() returns the number of chars copied into the buffer so this will be 0 if no string is found at index uMessage; if a string is found then LoadString() will return some positive value. This is turned into either TRUE or FALSE by using *!!* (not not) on bResult. If a string is loaded then the code examines the function's fifth parameter to ascertain whether or not full, or verbose, output is required. Full output would be something like this :

```
1E30  WM_GETMINMAXINFO      0000  07BF07B0
1E30  WM_NCCREATE           0000  140F15DE
1E30  WM_NCCALCSIZE         0000  140F15CC
1E30  WM_CREATE             0000  140F15DE
1E30  WM_SHOWWINDOW         0001  00000000
1E30  WM_WINDOWPOSCHANGING  0000  140F13BA
1E30  WM_WINDOWPOSCHANGING  0000  140F1348
```

Whereas *brief* output would be something like this :

```
WM_GETMINMAXINFO
WM_NCCREATE
WM_NCCALCSIZE
WM_CREATE
WM_SHOWWINDOW
WM_WINDOWPOSCHANGING
WM_WINDOWPOSCHANGING
```

By output I mean what's put into the caller's buffer (as yet we haven't seen an example of how this might be used). The DLL uses wsprintf() to format the required data into the caller's buffer. Note that although the DLL uses it's own buffer to load a string, that it would have been possible to use the buffer provided by the caller, ie. maybe we could specify, in our function specification, that the buffer's first char should indicate the size of the passed buffer; in that way we could have used it in the LoadString() call.

OK, how do I use the buffer's contents upon returning from the function? Well here's an example of how it might be used (another example follows the second DLL example) :

```
auto char      carBuffer[BUFF_SIZE];
auto FILE *    pFile;
auto NPSTR     pFileName;

pFileName = "TEST.MES";

if((pFile=fopen(pFileName, "a+t")) != NULL)
{
   if(BOUTPUTMESSAGE(
               hWnd
```

```
                              ,uMessage
                              ,wParam
                              ,lParam
                              ,TRUE
                              ,&carBuffer[0]
                              ) != FALSE
        )
    {
        fprintf(pFile,"%s\n",carBuffer);
    }
    else
    {
        fprintf(pFile,"Message Unknown! -> %X\n",uMessage);
    }

    fclose(pFile);
}
else
{
    MessageBox(0, "Couldn't open file!", pFileName, MB_OK);
}
```

This piece of code is taken from an application that uses the DLL; it *writes out* the buffer's contents to a file called TEST.MES and could be used, say, in a window procedure to *write out* selected messages (or all of them). Now you can use SPY to more or less the same thing, the differences are that :

- The DLL *knows* more messages than SPY does.
- It can be used to output message that occur while the window is being created (and having create time conversations with other windows).
- It can be turned on and off selectively and at will from code.

Here's the makefile.

The makefile :

```
# Decide whether or not to include debug information
!IFDEF DEBUG
CCDEB=-Zi
LKDEBUG= /CO
!ELSE
CCDEB=
!ENDIF

# -Aw not really needed as -GD implies it.
CC=cl -c -W4 -WX -AMw -GDs -Od -Zpe $(CCDEB)
LINK=link /NOD $(LKDEBUG) $(OBJ)

CCDEBUG= cl -c -W4 -AMw -GDs -Od -Zipe
OBJ=libentry.obj getmess.obj wep.obj

all: getmess.dll

# Build GETMESS.OBJ
getmess.obj: $*.c master.h mak
```

```
     $(CC) $*.c

# Build WEP.OBJ
wep.obj: $*.c mak
     $(CC) $*.c

# Build LIBENTRY.OBJ
libentry.obj: $*.asm
     masm -Mx $*,$*;

# Build GETMESS.RES
getmess.res : $*.rc
     rc -r -v $*.rc

# Build GETMESS.DLL
getmess.dll: $(OBJ) $*.def $*.res
     $(LINK) , $@,$*.map, libw mdllcew, $*.def

#    attach resources to dll
     rc -v $*.res $@

#    build dll import lib
     implib $*.lib $*.def
```

The WEP.C module (not shown) contains a minimal WEP function only. See the WEP example later in this chapter and also the Custom Control chapter.

Note that when using Microsoft's C7 that we don't need to define either _WINDOWS or _WINDLL as they're defined/implied by the compiler when using the -GD switch (as is -Aw).

Often you'll want to *name your segments* (sounds like a quiz show? 'I'll name that segment in 2 '). You do this typically when you want to award some segment a set of characteristics in the module's .DEF file. You can allow the compiler to award a default name if you like or decide to override the default with a name of your choosing. The Microsoft compiler assigns names that begin with the major part of the file name used and ends them with _TEXT, so for example, if you were compiling the code unit *switch.c* the default name assigned to the compiled obj file would be SWITCH_TEXT. If you use the -NT (name text) switch you can change the name; simply follow -NT with the required name, eg. -NT Switches etc. The segment is awarded its attributes in the module definition file using the SEGMENTS directive eg.

```
SEGMENTS
SWITCHES     MOVEABLE  DISCARDABLE...
WEP_TEXT     PRELOAD FIXED
```

The special segment _TEXT contains the application's start-up code, statically linked code etc and can also be awarded a set of characteristics :

```
SEGMENTS
SWITCHES     MOVEABLE  DISCARDABLE ...
_TEXT        FIXED ...
```

2nd Example

The next (and last, 'C' based, DLL) we'll look at is used to provide some profiling capabilities (yes I know that Windows and Microsoft (Source Profiler) provide profiling capabilities so just get off my case will ya?).

TMSTIME.DLL exports 5 functions; one is the WEP which we'll now forget.

```
WEP                    @1  RESIDENTNAME
DebugTime              @2
DebugCloseFile         @3
DebugOpenFile          @4
DebugRemoveFile        @5
```

The set of *Debug* functions provide a set of functions that may be used to profile your code, any code that is that can call a DLL. You want to know what's taking time in your Turbo Pascal Object Windows' code, use the DLL; you need to know how long a paint takes in VB, use the DLL.

The first function, *DebugTime* writes out the interval between this, and a subsequent call, to a file which is specified elsewhere (get to it in a moment). The function takes one parameter – a comment. This comment is also written out to the file. Each time DebugTime is called it writes out the current time, how many ms have passed since you last called the function, and the comment; it then *remembers* the current time in readiness for the next call made to it. The output file is formatted like this :

```
10:06:32.750  time since last call (ms) = 60   About to call Func
10:06:32.910  time since last call (ms) = 160  In Func, calling Foo
10:06:32.970  time since last call (ms) = 60   In Foo, calling End
10:06:33.460  time since last call (ms) = 490  In End.
```

The log always (not shown above) starts by stating that the time since the last call was 0ms. In the fragment above we can see that between calling DebugTime saying that we're going to call Func, and getting into Func and Calling DebugTime saying that we're going to call Foo about 160ms passed.

Before calling DebugTime we've got to open a log file (for all this great stuff to go into). The function that does this is surprisingly – DebugOpenFile. All DebugTime output is appended to the log file. This means that if you use the same log file and have multiple *timing runs* that it will grow and grow and grow! This might be just what you want so that's why it's like this. If you don't want this to happen, ie. you want the log file to contain just the information gathered during the last run, you can leave the log file name the same (in your code) but before calling DebugOpenFile call DebugRemoveFile passing to that function the same old log file name. To finish logging call DebugCloseFile – this ensures that the log file is closed (flushed etc) before the DLL is unloaded from memory.

The code for the library looks like this :

The C source file :

```c
/*
** Turn off silly warnings.
*/
#pragma warning(disable:4100)
#pragma warning(disable:4001)


#include <windows.h>

#include <time.h>
#include <stdio.h>
#include <sys\types.h>
#include <sys\timeb.h>
#include <string.h>
#include <time.h>

#include "tmstime.h"

/*
** CR/LF and NULL string terminator size.
*/
#define NEWLINENULL 3

/*
** Global (file) file pointer. Could be put
** into a function if globals are a problem.
*/
static   FILE  *  fh;

BOOL FAR PASCAL LibMain
(
   HANDLE  hModule
 ,WORD     wDataSeg
 ,WORD     cbHeapSize
 ,LPSTR    lpszCmdLine
)
{
   /*
   ** If we've got heap it's locked in
   ** LibEntry  -  test for local heap
   ** and unlock if necessary.
   */
   if(cbHeapSize > 0)
   {
     UnlockData(0);
   }

   /*
   ** Set global file handle to NULL, ie. invalid.
   */
   fh = NULL;

   /*
   ** All OK so return 'successful load'.
   */
   return TRUE;
}
```

```
/*
** WEP in with the main code - like this coz the whole library's not
** that big and is 'resident' for typically only a few moments.
*/
BOOL FAR PASCAL WEP (int nSystemExit)
{
   /*
   ** Just say 'OK'.
   */
   return TRUE;
}




/*
   ** Deletes a file whose name is passed in lpFileName. Usually used to delete
   ** a debug file prior to another run. The debug information gets appended to
   ** the debug file normally so after subsequent runs you have to look further
   ** down the debug file to find your run info.  By deleting the file prior to
   ** another run the debug file always contains info pertinent to the last run.
*/
BOOL FAR PASCAL __export DebugRemoveFile(LPSTR lpFileName)
{
   /*
   ** Holds local memory the sizeof lpFileName.
   */
   static LOCALHANDLE  h;

   /*
   ** The function's result.
   */
   static BOOL         bResult;

   /*
   ** Set result to FAIL.
   */
   bResult = FALSE;

   /*
   ** Get memory for copying data into local buffer.
   */
   h = LocalAlloc(LMEM_ZEROINIT, lstrlen(lpFileName) + 1);

   if(h != NULL)
   {
      /*
      ** Pointer to local memory.
      */
      static NPSTR npBuff;

      npBuff = LocalLock(h);

      if(npBuff != NULL)
      {
```

```
        /*
        ** Copy lpFileName to local memory.
        */
        lstrcpy(npBuff, lpFileName);

        /*
        ** Delete File. remove returns 0 for success so we NOT it
        ** for consistency in later tests.
        */
        bResult = !remove(npBuff);

        /*
        ** If we failed tell the caller.
        */
        if(bResult != TRUE)
        {
            MessageBox(
                    0
                    ,"Failed to remove file in Debug Library!"
                    ,npBuff
                    ,MB_OK
                    );
        }
        (VOID)LocalUnlock(h);
    }
    (VOID)LocalFree(h);
    }

    return bResult;
}




/*
** Closes a debug log file. Called when the debugging session ends thus
** closing the log file.
*/
BOOL FAR PASCAL __export DebugCloseFile(VOID)
{
    /*
    ** If a file is not already open return FALSE, else close file and
    ** return TRUE if file closes OK.
    */

    if(fh == NULL)
    {
        return FALSE;
    }
    else
    {
        /*
        ** fclose returns 0 for success so we NOT it
        ** for consistency in later tests.
        */
        return !fclose(fh);
    }
}
```

```
/*
** Open file log for debugging. Opens the file 'lpFileName' for debugging.
** The file is kept open until DebugCloseFile is called.
*/
BOOL FAR PASCAL __export DebugOpenFile(LPSTR lpFileName)
{
    /*
    ** Holds local memory the sizeof lpFileName.
    */
    static LOCALHANDLE h;

    /*
    ** If a file is already open return FALSE.
    */
    if(fh != 0)
    {
        return FALSE;
    }

    /*
    ** Allocate local memory to hold filename.
    */
    h = LocalAlloc(LMEM_ZEROINIT, lstrlen(lpFileName) + 1);

    if(h != NULL)
    {
        /*
        ** Pointer to local memory.
        */
        static NPSTR npBuff;

        npBuff = LocalLock(h);

        if(npBuff != NULL)
        {
            /*
            ** Copy lpFileName to local memory.
            */
            lstrcpy(npBuff, lpFileName);

            /*
            ** Open file.
            */
            fh = fopen(npBuff,"a+t");

            /*
            ** If we failed tell the caller.
            */
            if(fh == NULL)
            {
                MessageBox(
                        0
                        ,"Failed to open file in Debug Library!"
                        ,npBuff
                        ,MB_OK
                        );
```

```
            }

        (VOID) LocalUnlock(h);
        }
        (VOID) LocalFree(h);
    }

    return !!fh;
}



/*
** Output time into open debug log file. This is the main function of the
** library, ie. this function actually works out how much time has passed
** since the last call made to it, formats a message stating the delay,
** appends the user's comment (lpComment) and finally writes the whole
** thing out to a file.
**
** The output has the format :
**
** Current Time (including milliseconds), Comment, Time since last call in
ms.
**
** Returns time since last call into function.
*/
DWORD FAR PASCAL __export DebugTime(LPSTR lpComment)
{
    /*
    ** Used in _strtime.
    */
    static char         carTimeBuff   [BUFF_SIZE];

    /*
    ** Holds text that is output by the function.
    */
    static char         carResultBuff [BUFF_SIZE];

    /*
    ** Time stuff.
    */
    static DWORD        dwNewTimeInSecs;
    static DWORD        dwNewms;
    static DWORD        dwOldTimeInSecs;
    static DWORD        dwOldms;
    static DWORD        dwTimeDiff;

    /*
    ** Used in _ftime.
    */
    static struct timeb tdTime;

    /*
    ** Bytes in output buffers.
    */
    static WORD         wBytes;

    /*
```

```
** Check that a log file is open first.
*/
if(fh == NULL)
{
    MessageBox(
                0
                ,"File handle invalid!"
                ,"Debug Library!"
                ,MB_OK
                );


    return 0;
}


/*
** Do the time stuff.
*/
_ftime(&tdTime);
dwNewTimeInSecs = tdTime.time;
dwNewms = tdTime.millitm;
_strtime(&carTimeBuff[0]);
dwTimeDiff = (dwNewTimeInSecs * 1000 + dwNewms) -
             (dwOldTimeInSecs * 1000 + dwOldms);


/*
** If first time run reset elapsed time!
*/
if(dwTimeDiff == (dwNewTimeInSecs * 1000 + dwNewms))
{
    dwTimeDiff = 0;
}


/*
** Format output.
*/
wsprintf(
         &carResultBuff[0]
         ," %s.%-3u  time since last call (ms) = %lu\t"
         ,(LPSTR)&carTimeBuff[0]
         ,tdTime.millitm,dwTimeDiff
         );
/*
** Chars in buffer is...
*/
wBytes = (WORD)lstrlen(&carResultBuff[0]);


/*
** Write it out.
*/
if(fwrite(&carResultBuff[0], wBytes, 1, fh) == 0)
{
    MessageBox(
                0
                ,"Failed to write out time!"
                ,"Debug Library!"
                ,MB_OK
                );


    return 1;
```

```
    }

    if(lpComment != NULL)
    {
        static LOCALHANDLE h;

        /*
        ** Allocate local memory to hold comment.
        */
        h = LocalAlloc(LMEM_ZEROINIT, lstrlen(lpComment) + NEWLINENULL);

        if(h != NULL)
        {
            static NPSTR npBuff;

            /*
            ** Pointer to local memory.
            */
            npBuff = LocalLock(h);

            if(npBuff != NULL)
            {
                lstrcpy(npBuff, lpComment);

                wBytes = (WORD)lstrlen(lpComment);

                *(npBuff + wBytes) = '\n';

                /*
                ** Write out comment.
                */
                if(fwrite(npBuff, lstrlen(npBuff), 1, fh) == 0)
                {
                    MessageBox(
                            0
                            ,"Failed to write out comment!"
                            ,"Debug Library"
                            ,MB_OK
                            );
                }

                (VOID)LocalUnlock(h);
            }

            (VOID)LocalFree(h);
        }
    }

    /*
    ** Update old times ready for next call.
    */
    dwOldTimeInSecs = dwNewTimeInSecs;
    dwOldms = dwNewms;

    return dwTimeDiff;
}
```

The .def file :

```
LIBRARY    TMSTIME

EXETYPE    WINDOWS 3.1

PROTMODE

DESCRIPTION 'Profiling DLL.'

STUB       'WINSTUB.EXE'


CODE       MOVEABLE PRELOAD DISCARDABLE
DATA       PRELOAD SINGLE

HEAPSIZE   1024
STACKSIZE  0

EXPORTS
    WEP                @1  RESIDENTNAME
    DebugTime          @2
    DebugCloseFile     @3
    DebugOpenFile      @4
    DebugRemoveFile    @5
```

The makefile :

```
all: tmstime.dll

# note that -Asnw is the same as -ASw.
tmstime.obj: $*.c $*.h
    cl -W4 -WX -c -ASw -GDs -Zi -Od -Zpe $*.c > $*.err

libentry.obj: $*.asm
    masm -Mx $*,$*;

tmstime.dll: libentry.obj $*.obj $*.def
    link  /CO $*.obj libentry.obj, $*.dll,, libw sdllcew, $*.def
    rc $*.dll
    implib $*.lib $*.dll
```

The library uses standard 'C' library functions wherever it can so for example it uses fopen() instead of the Windows' API function OpenFile() – why? Because they're easier to use if you don't require user interaction! The library can be used by multiple clients but with a certain amount of caution. It's written in such a way that it operates on only one log file, ie. multiple clients would use one log file. This means that only one application should call DebugOpenFile. Any application can then call Debug-Time. All output remember is sent to the one log file so if you're using it with multiple apps be sure to put something in the comment to identify the caller. Also be aware that the time between calls is the time between calls made to DebugTime, ie. if one app calls DebugTime and then a second app calls DebugTime and then the first app calls DebugTime again the time shown against the third call is the time that has passed since the second call – not the first. To work out the interval between the first and third you can either add up the intervening intervals or refer to the time stamp on the left hand side of the output. It would be nice to make this truly multi-user – fancy a go? See note below on multiple instance DLLs for a cure to this library's short comings.

This DLL is very useful and I use it a lot because it doesn't require much effort to read and understand the log file, ie. it doesn't require other applications to prepare or present the log file, but most of all I use it because it works with anything that can call a DLL – which is most everything these days of course! The library can be of course combined with other DLLs; here's what happens when you use DebugTime with bOutputMessage which was shown in the previous example :

```
10:06:35.710   time since last call (ms) = 0      WM_MOUSEMOVE
10:06:35.710   time since last call (ms) = 0      WM_KEYUP
10:06:35.770   time since last call (ms) = 60     WM_PAINT
10:06:35.930   time since last call (ms) = 160    WM_NCHITTEST
10:06:35.930   time since last call (ms) = 0      WM_SETCURSOR
10:06:35.930   time since last call (ms) = 0      WM_MOUSEMOVE
10:06:36.870   time since last call (ms) = 940    WM_SYSKEYDOWN
10:06:37.30    time since last call (ms) = 160    WM_SYSKEYDOWN
10:06:37.30    time since last call (ms) = 0      WM_SYSCOMMAND
10:06:37.30    time since last call (ms) = 0      WM_CLOSE
10:06:37.30    time since last call (ms) = 0      WM_WINDOWPOSCHANGING
10:06:37.90    time since last call (ms) = 60     WM_WINDOWPOSCHANGED
10:06:37.90    time since last call (ms) = 0      WM_NCACTIVATE
10:06:37.90    time since last call (ms) = 0      WM_ACTIVATE
10:06:37.140   time since last call (ms) = 50     WM_ACTIVATEAPP
10:06:37.140   time since last call (ms) = 0      WM_KILLFOCUS
10:06:37.200   time since last call (ms) = 60     WM_DESTROY
```

bOutputMessage was used to retrieve just the name of the current message (non-verbose mode); the code in the app looks like this :

```
LRESULT _export CALLBACK LMAINWNDPROC
(
   HWND      hWnd
  ,UINT      uMessage
  ,WPARAM    wParam
  ,LPARAM    lParam
)
{
   /*
   ** Result of handling message.
   */
   auto LRESULT      lResult;

   /*
   ** Buffer for bOutoutMessage.
   */
   auto char         carBuffer[BUFF_SIZE];

   /*
   ** Flag which shows that logging has started.
   */
   static BOOL bFlag = FALSE;
```

```
#include "tmstime.h"

if(bFlag != FALSE)
{
    BOUTPUTMESSAGE(
                     hWnd
                    ,uMessage
                    ,wParam
                    ,lParam
                    ,FALSE
                    ,&carBuffer[0]
                    );
    /*
    ** Output message name.
    */
    DebugTime(carBuffer);
}

switch(uMessage)
{
    case WM_COMMAND:
        lResult = lCommandHandler(hWnd,uMessage,wParam,lParam);
        break;

    case WM_CREATE:
        {
            /*
            ** Name the log file.
            */
            auto char * pName = "TEST.LOG";

            /*
            ** Remove any old log file.
            */
            DebugRemoveFile(pName);

            /*
            ** Open log file.
            */
            DebugOpenFile(pName);

            /*
            ** Start logging.
            */
            bFlag = TRUE;

            lResult = lCreateHandler(hWnd,uMessage,wParam,lParam);
        }
        break;

    case WM_DESTROY:
        /*
        ** Finished logging.
        */
        DebugCloseFile();

        lResult = lDestroyHandler(hWnd,uMessage,wParam,lParam);
```

```
            break;

    default:
            lResult = lDefaultHandler(hWnd,uMessage,wParam,lParam);
            break;
    }
    return lResult;
}
```

This fragment is taken from a *main* window procedure. Logging starts as the WM_CREATE message is handled and stops as the WM_DESTROY message is handled, ie. logging's started by making a call to DebugOpenFile at WM_CREATE time and is terminated by making a call to DebugCloseFile as WM_DESTROY time. A flag is set (bFlag) to show that the log file has been opened successfully. DebugTime is called before the *switch on message* part of the window procedure is executed. If the flag is true – log! This log needs to be read carefully as of course one message can lead to many others!

☐ What you've seen

We have seen two libraries so far that together show you the following :

How to build a DLL using the latest C7 compiler switches, how to use resources defined in a DLL, how to name segments and handle segment attributes in a medium memory model DLL, how to build a small model DLL where everything's in one segment, how to use __export and EXPORT (more coming up on this), how to handle data (esp. strings) passed to a DLL, how to manipulate buffers belonging to the caller, how to use standard 'C' library calls in your DLLs, how to use buffered file I/O in DLLs and more! Quite a lot, I hope you agree.

☐ __export & EXPORTS

I have used __export and EXPORTS in most of the code we've seen in this book. You don't have to use EXPORTS if you're using C7 and specify that your functions are exported by using __export but you'll probably still want to use EXPORTS to prevent the linker assuming that the symbol (exported) has the following characteristics :

- **No input/output privilege**
- Shared data
- Resident name
- Has no alias

You still need a .def file irrespective of whether or not you use it to list EXPORTS. If you have no exports section in the DEF file you cannot use it to build a .LIB (import library) file – use the built DLL instead. Using EXPORTS also allows you to set up ordinal references to your exported functions and seems to be required (by the loader) when using either the -GEa (Customise Windows' entry/exit code – Load DS from

AX) or -GA (Optimise entry/exit code for protected mode Windows) compiler switches.

One reason that you might want to use __export instead of the .def file EXPORTS statement is that you can selectively (by using them both) *export* functions in the IMPLIB built .LIB file (import library). For example you could decide that certain entry points in your DLL are *private* in so much as they are undocumented and should remain hidden from view (see DLLHIDE.EXE presented earlier also). If a programmer uses exehdr or tdump to *find* hidden functions they will determine the function's arguments and write a prototype for the function in order to call it. They will then, typically, compile their code and link it with the import library you've provided for the DLL. The DLL might *export* functions via a mixture of __export and/or EXPORTS; the library's import library would, say, be built from the DLL's .def file. The .def file lists only those exports that are *public* so the resulting import library does not contain information on the *private* entry points. Result – unresolved externals when linking. Now there are several ways around this (like calling the function through the use of GetProcAddress(), or by rebuilding the import library by using the actual DLL file instead of the unavailable .def file, but at least you've tried! If you want to build an import library for your development team you can build one that includes everything that's been exported in the DLL by building it using both the .def file and .DLL files.

Whilst talking about using IMPLIB you might want to consider using IMPLIB to *rebuild* the kernel section (or all the sections) of LIBW.LIB. Why? Well, and for example, the function DebugOutput() is not defined in LIBW.LIB (the Windows' import library) but it is exported from the KERNEL module (perhaps it was exported using __export and didn't appear in the .def file for the kernel – see above). So if you want to call this function you normally have to explicitly import it which is a pain!

```
IMPORTS
    KERNEL._DebugOutput
```

or if you prefer

```
IMPORTS
    _DebugOutput = KERNEL.328
```

If you rebuild the kernel import library from the DLL itself (doesn't matter which *kernel* you choose as the output is exactly the same) the result will be that you will define DebugOutput() in the import library. I've done this with all the *standard* DLLs – GDI.EXE, USER.EXE and KRNL386.EXE. The result is that when I link I usually use GDI.LIB, USER.LIB and KERNEL.LIB instead of good olLIBW.LIB. I do this because I often experiment with entry points that are omitted from LIBW.LIB (either by accident (like DebugOutput()) or deliberately). Note that in the declaration of DebugOutput above that the function's a 'C' calling convention function; you must therefore prefix the function's name with a leading underscore and preserve the case of the name if you're using the /NOI (no ignore case) linker switch. You can combine separate import libraries using IMPLIB also so I could build my own *real*libw.lib if I wanted; all I'd have to do is make sure that I include everything I'm likely to need, for example SOUND.DRV for those funky sound functions!

> ### An aside of creating a single import library for multiple DLLs.
>
> A single import library for multiple DLLs can be created by supplying multiple .def files as input parameters to IMPLIB. You must ensure when doing this however that no exported function's defined in more than one .def file, ie. exporting a function more than once in an import library creates an unresolvable ambiguity when the Windows' loader resolves references to functions exported by other modules. For example, consider this hypothetical situation. We have two DLLs that share a common import library and additionally both export a function called Foo. Whenever an application refers to a function in a DLL, the loader resolves the reference to the function, which is known as a fix-up, to its *real* address. The *real* address is not known of course until run-time. The DLL containing the function must therefore be loaded to provide a *real* address for any of its functions. However, in our hypothetical scenario, this poses a dilemma as both DLLs contain a function called Foo; as a result the loader is left asking itself which one it should use and of course cannot solve the ambiguity? To prevent this situation from occurring IMPLIB issues an error message whenever a function's defined more than once. Therefore if DLLs share a common function they cannot share a single import library.
>
> There is one exception to this rule – the WEP. Only Windows calls the WEP procedure; therefore the WEP does not need to be defined in the import library. Multiple DLLs **may** share the same IMPORT library if the only common function definition in them is a WEP. To do this and avoid IMPLIB/WEP related errors create a series of modified .def files that do not export the WEP and use these as IMPLIB's input files :
>
> > Compile and link all the component DLLs. Use the original .def file to link each DLL. Each .def file must list the WEP in its EXPORTS section and give the function the attribute RESIDENTNAME.
> >
> > Copy the module definition files for each DLL into dummy .def files.
> >
> > Remove the WEP from the EXPORTS statement of each dummy DEF file (from this point on do not link any DLL using its dummy .def file). Removing the WEP entries prevents an IMPLIB error about multiple definitions of the WEP routine.
> >
> > Use the dummy .def files as input parameters to the IMPLIB utility.

Continuing on...

Note that __export, for applications only, removes the exported function's name from the executable; this allows your application to *hide* its call-backs and window procedures etc.

Another reason to use __export over EXPORTS is to save you reading the section on *decorated names* in the C7 documentation. In C++ function's (to support type safe linking – Huh!) names are *mangled* by the compiler to produce alternative names. This means that the name you must specify in the .def file is NOT the same as that defined in the translation unit. For example a function defined as **int __near __cdecl Foo(int)** ends up as **?Foo@@YAHH@Z**! If you didn't have the __export modifier you'd have to *discover* those names to export them! A side effect of this however is that __export implicitly states that you're going to call functions by name; after all, if you're not using EXPORTS you're not defining ordinals are you (see note below)?! Also, for a DLL __exports forces the linker to put the function's name into the resident name table, after all, the linker expects you to link by name, it therefore makes the name *available* at all times – if the DLL exports many functions with long names the resident name table can become very large – even in protect mode this is wasteful of memory! **Note – you can discover a function's ordinal using exehdr; note however that implicit ordinals may change from compile to compile!**

☐ DLL Wrappers

Sometimes it's handy to use a DLL wrapper. By this I mean to wrap up some desired functionality in a DLL. For example a lot of the standard 'C' library may be encapsulated in a DLL. Providing a DLL front end to a set of standard functions allows these functions to be shared amongst all interested applications; now you only need one copy of them in memory. You might also consider building some extensions to them and some of the existing WindowsAPIs. Take for example the function DOS3Call(). It allows you to access many of the old INT21h functions that are legal in Windows; in fact an application shouldn't use INT21h but should always access the DOS service through the DOS3Call wrapper. Well how about wrapping the wrapper (Just rappin' again)? You could build a library of *legal* DOS calls by providing some front end work to the DOS3Call function; and of course you could make the DLL user friendly by giving the individual functions friendly names such as RemoveDirectory() (INT21 function 3Ah) etc. In a way Microsoft have already *wrapped* many of their functions (see WINDOWSX.H) by providing a 'C' macro interface to some of them such as GlobalAllocPtr() of course a macro wrapper is desirable in so much that it is faster (as no call takes place) but has the disadvantage that such a *call* is not available, say, from Visual Basic.

☐ The dreaded DLL bug

If, when you're developing , you hit a bug in DLL code Windows will often take it out on the application that called the DLL, ie. say your DLL causes a GPF, often its the *using* application that will be terminated (the current task). Windows kills the application in such a way that it often result in the DLL staying resident. You now go off and take a look at your DLL code, spot and fix the bug and rebuild the DLL (all in a DOS box etc). You copy the DLL off to the SYSTEM directory and try another test. Result – the program crashes at exactly the same point as before! The reason for this is that when Windows loaded your application and saw that it needed DLL *x* it found it already had DLL *x*loaded (from the previous test), it therefore doesn't load your newly debugged code but simply increments the DLL's usage count. If you want to purge the DLL you have to exit Windows!

In Windows, each time an application loads a DLL, the module usage count for the DLL is incremented by 1, one customer = usage count 1, two customers and the usage count is 2 etc. As long as the module usage count is greater than zero, the DLL will remain in memory. The module usage count is decrement each time an application calls FreeLibrary() – this may be called implicitly if you *linked* with a library via an import library. When FreeLibrary() is called Windows determines whether the library should be discarded, ie. it tests to see if the library's usage count has hit zero yet. A DLL can also remain resident in memory after all the applications that call the DLL have terminated for one of about 3 additional reasons :

- The library name in the module definition (.DEF) file contains lowercase letters.
- FreeLibrary() is not called.
- FreeLibrary() is called from a Windows exit procedure (WEP).

Ensure that the library name in the .def file contains only uppercase letters.   An interaction between version 5.1 of the Microsoft linker and 3.0 run-time can cause Windows to increment the usage count of a loading DLL twice, rather than once! When the task closes, calling FreeLibrary() to decrement the lock count of the DLL, in the process, the lock count is not decremented to zero but to one!

The DLL may also remain in memory if the WEP in the DLL is used to free the library. As was stated earlier, a WEP in 3.0 may not actually be called (see earlier section on why this might happen). If the WEP is used to free the library, but doesn't get called, the library's usage count will obviously not be decremented – result, the library stays resident!

Here's a simple way to purge the DLL without leaving Windows – build an application to do it for you! Here are a couple of snapshots of an application called *unload.exe*:

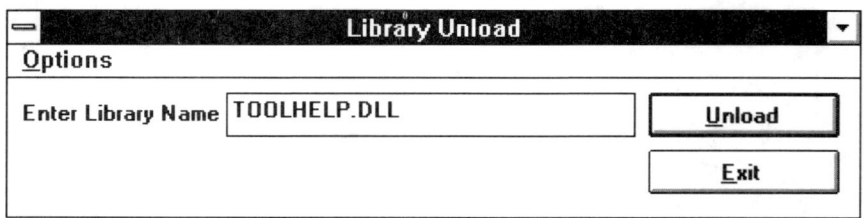

This snapshot shows the user requesting that the DLL called TOOLHELP be unloaded. When the *Unload* button is clicked the application responds like this :

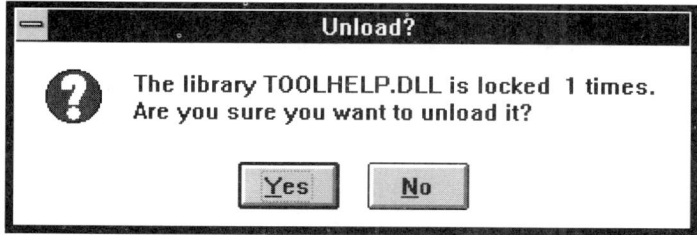

Or like this :

This application was built using Visual Basic but it could have been built with any language or environment that allow you to call DLL routines. One of the nice things about Visual Basic is that the code is so easy to read – indeed, it can almost be used as a kind of pseudo code for future 'C' or Pascal based work. *Unload's* main code is placed *beneath* the *Unload* button. When that button gets clicked the following code gets executed :

The VB source file :

```
' The unload button is called 'ModUnload' it's called
' when the pushbutton labelled 'Unload' is pressed.
Sub ModUnload_Click ()

' Handle to loaded module.
Dim hInstance As Integer

' Usage count.
Dim nModuleUse As Integer

' Name of module.
Dim LibName As String

' Used for error report.
Dim Errn As String

' Answer from MsgBox function call.
Dim OkToUnload As Integer

    ' Tidy up name shown to user.
    ' The VB expression ModuleName.Text evaluates
    ' to a string that contains the  text entered
    ' into the edit control. Ucase$ turns entered
    ' text into uppercase.
```

```
   ModuleName.Text = UCase$(ModuleName.Text)
   LibName = ModuleName.Text

   ' If nothing entered exit.
   If LibName = "" Then
ModuleName.SetFocus
Exit Sub
   End If

   ' Load the specified module up.
   hInstance = LoadLibrary(LibName)

   ' Did it work?
   If hInstance < HINSTANCE_ERROR Then

' No it didn't so find out why.
Select Case hInstance
   Case 0
     Errn = "System was out of memory, executable file was
                  corrupt, or relocations were invalid."
   Case 2
     Errn = "File was not found."
   Case 3
     Errn = "Path was not found."
   Case 5
     Errn = "Attempt was made to dynamically link to a task,
                  or there was a sharing or network-protection error."
   Case 6
     Errn = "Library required separate data segments for each task."
   Case 8
     Errn = "There was insufficient memory to start the application."
   Case 10
     Errn = "Windows version was incorrect."
   Case 11
     Errn = "Executable file was invalid. Either it was not a Windows
                  application or there was an error in the .EXE image."
   Case 12
     Errn = "Application was designed for a different operating system."
   Case 13
     Errn = "Application was designed for MS-DOS 4.0."
   Case 14
     Errn = "Type of executable file was unknown."
   Case 15
     Errn = "Attempt was made to load a real-mode application (developed
                  for an earlier version of Windows)."
   Case 16
     Errn = "Attempt was made to load a second instance of an executable
                  file containing multiple data segments that were not
   marked read-only."
   Case 19
     Errn = "Attempt was made to load a compressed executable file. The
                  file must be decompressed before it can be loaded."
   Case 20
     Errn = "Dynamic-link library (DLL) file was invalid. One of the DLLs
                  required to run this application was corrupt."
   Case 21
     Errn = "Application requires Microsoft Windows 32-bit extensions."
End Select
```

```
' Tell user why it failed.
MsgBox "Error loading (" + ModuleName.Text + "). " + Errn, 16, "Cannot Load!"
ModuleName.Text = ""
   Else
' It worked! Get module's usage count.
nModuleUse = GetModuleUsage(hInstance)

' Ask user if OK to unload. Subtract '1' from usage count for us.
' Also see if module has usage count of 1. If it has it's because this
' application's loaded it - if this is the case tell the user and unload
it.
If nModuleUse > 1 Then
    OkToUnload = MsgBox(
                        "The library "        +
                        ModuleName.Text       +
                        " is locked "         +
                        Str$(nModuleUse - 1) +
                        " times. Are you sure you want to unload
it?"
                        ,36
                        ,"Unload?"
                        )
  Else
    MsgBox "The library was not loaded previously (it is now!). It will
            now be unloaded."
            ,32
            ,"Loaded by this application"
  End If

  If OkToUnload = YES Then
    ' User (or code) said 'OK' so unload it (includes our lock).
    While GetModuleUsage(hInstance) > 0
      FreeLibrary (hInstance)
    Wend
  Else
    ' The user didn't want to unlock it so free our single lock.
    FreeLibrary (hInstance)
  End If
    End If
End Sub
```

Essentially what happens is this (if you can't be bothered to read through the code above). The application takes the name of the DLL and attempts to load it using LoadLibrary(). LoadLibrary() returns the module's instance handle (if it loaded it) or a value less than HINSTANCE_ERROR if it didn't. If it didn't load it the error is reported (the returned value denotes the error). If the library was loaded GetModuleUsage() is called. This function retrieves the usage, or lock, count for the module. If the lock count is one it's because *Unload* has loaded the library, ie. the library wasn't loaded until *Unload* loaded it! If the lock count is greater than one then the user is informed of the current lock count (roughly equates to the number of using modules although some modules will load a library a number of times!) and asked if they wish it unloaded. If they answer yes then FreeLibrary() is called until the library's usage count hits zero, ie. it is unloaded. If they answer no then the library's freed once (to undo what *Unload* did). That's it. You could code this, as I've said above, using any language or environment that can call into a DLL – I used Visual Basic because it's a dream to use when it comes to building small applications like this. Now when your program crashes due to a bug in your DLL code you can unload the DLL using *Unload* – or something like it!

☐ LpszCmdLine

You'll see from time to time the statement that the DLL's lpszCmdLine argument is not used, or *set to zero* (see comments in Microsoft's LibEntry() .asm routine shown earlier for an example), or even *set to point at arbitrary data;* well this is sometimes the case but sometimes it is not. If you load the library using LoadModule() then you can indeed use the lpszCmdLine actual parameter as a pointer to the DLL's command line arguments. Load Module's second argument is a pointer to a parameter block – which looks like this :

```
typedef
{
    WORD              wSegEnv;
    LPCSTR            lpszCmdLine;
    UINT FAR *        lpuShow;
    UINT FAR *        lpuReserved;
} LOADPARAMS;
```

Obviously lpszCmdLine is the member to use if you want to pass command line arguments to your DLL.

For more information on the actual members, and an example of their use, see the SDK documentation.

☐ Building DLLs in C++

This is not an easy one mainly because the format of a DLL, and all of its accompanying mechanics, were designed before C++ became one of the *main* language tools. Mixing DLLs and C++ is at the very best difficult to do properly and some prefer not to attempt it, or attempt it but keep the C++ under tight control (via a 'C' based wrapper) in the DLL. However, if you want to do it read on...

Classes are exported using __export – all member, and helper (friends etc) functions of the class are also exported. With C++, unlike 'C' it's an all or nothing situation, ie. you can't restrict the interface to your DLL in C++ like you can in 'C', you'll see why soon.

Static objects. Programmers who have some experience at writing DLLs in 'C' know that passing pointers to objects (variables etc) to them can be troublesome, ie. a pointer to an object declared static in one client of the DLL cannot be passed directly to another client as it now addresses arbitrary memory, or a pseudo object, in the second client's private heap or data space. If this is required the client must pass long pointers to data items instead of the more natural short pointers implicitly passed in both small and medium memory models. Also, as we all know, shared memory must be allocated *specially* in the donating client process, again this is something that is *unnatural* to C++ where often areas of storage are carved from the global heap implicitly when so called anonymous objects are created! It is tempting to think that in C++ that both instances of objects, and pointers to them, may be passed between any number of clients of the DLL irrespective of where they were created; unfortunately, due to all the implicit use of pointers within a class object this is seldom if ever the case, ie. you are almost certain to produce problems when passing any object by value between a DLL and one of its clients.

Classes must be compiled in large model (-GD -AL, link with LIBW and LDLLCEW.LIB). This adds some considerable overhead to the built DLL; reasons? Firstly it is large model (always a size hit), secondly as each member function (and all its associated friends etc) will have to exported all that prologue/epilogue code has to added to each function. Each function's name will typically be quite long (due to decoration) and will of course be flagged resident name due to the use of __export in the DLL code, result – hit, hit, hit!

The DLL's interface is made difficult because whenever you make a change to the C++ interface you will need to rebuild the DLL, even if that change is innocuous like changing a private member to be private or a one time variable definition to a const! You'll therefore also need to build a new import library (as names have certainly changed) and possibly re-build or at the very least re-link your client code. A lot of this necessary work comes directly from C++'s type safe linking mechanism discussed briefly above and in an earlier chapter.

Consider what happens if you decide that one of your C++ functions (member of a class or not) should not be passed a normal char *; instead you decide that it should be passed a const char const * (a constant pointer to a constant char). The name of the affected C++ function will now be changed, ie. it will receive a new decorated name (unlike its 'C' counterpart) to ensure type safe linking. You must therefore build a new import library (if this function is exported – as it almost certainly will be) and re-compile and link your client code – all of this just because you got the interface a little wrong. Normally we all go through numerous such changes – doing so in C++ can be costly in lost productivity due to all the rebuilding that needs to be done after the change! This if anything breaks the object orientedness of DLLs which was, in the main, to provide a set of services that could be changed without requiring any changes to be made to the client code!

Another problem is with in-lining functions. If you want your DLL to be stand-alone then you must export all your inline functions and effectively outline them! If you want to use inlines then you must ship so called interface files that include just the inline functions – now your DLL's is in two parts, the core *object* code and the inline interface support file!

The DLL's interface is also too open, ie. even the private interface to your C++ class will have to be exported, this again breaks the mold, ie. you normally only export the public entry points to your code but now, because a client application may instanciate one of your DLL C++ objects, even the object's private member functions must be available to the client application – therefore the private member functions themselves must be exported; there goes some of your abstraction, or to put it another way, how long will it take before someone calls your class's private functions directly – where did all that abstraction and protection go!? An added side effect of this last point is that the DLL code grows in size (extra code generated) and is slower (extra code requires extra time).

☐ Misc

This section contains miscellaneous stuff related to DLLs.

DLLs may use call-backs which are provided by some client task, however these call-backs require some extra work in the client code like making use of MakeProcInstance() and apparently outdated compiler switches like -Gw etc (see chapter on debugging for more on this).

The name in the LIBRARY statement should be in uppercase and match the name of the DLL file (minus extension). Naming a library with lowercase letters (or a mixture of lower and upper case letters) can cause problems if the DLL is used with version 3.0. This problem has been corrected in 3.1 (see later section for more on this). Sometimes the name needs to be put into double quotes (see reference). The name may be followed by PRIVATELIB. This means that the library may be used by only one user at a time, ie. another application attempting to link with the library will fail. Note that to use PRIVATELIB that you need a linker that is at least marked as version 5.31 (if you haven't *patched* your original C7 installation yet you're using 5.3.). If you used Link version 5.3 with PRIVATELIB you'd get a syntax error when linking, with 5.31 you don't (PRIVATELIB was added to the grammar for NAME instead of LIBRARY!). My experience of PRIVATELIB is that it doesn't work although at least now you get passed the linker! a DLL linked with PRIVATELIB and one linked without PRIVATELIB are exactly the same, ie. COMP.EXE can find no differences – OOPS, also if you include PRIVATELIB (even though it doesn't work) you'll have to build your DLL's import library using the built DLL as IMPLIB now falls or when it sees the .def file containing PRIVATELIB – double OOPS!). I can only assume that PRIVATELIB is broken or that it's equivalent to the resource compiler's -p switch. RC's -p switch was there so that under EMS memory systems a DLL could be swapped out to EMS along with its user, ie. because it only had one client it could be paged to EMS whenever the client was. The -p switch has no effect under 3.1 although DLLs compiled using -p are marked as *Private*, ie. whereas PRIVATELIB doesn't seem to have any effect -p does – when a lib created using -p is comp'ed with one that's not, comp spots the difference. You can also get exehdr to confirm that the lib's private:

```
Library:              ?????
Description:          ???????????
Operating system:     Microsoft Windows - version 3.10
```

```
Data:                    SHARED
Initialization:          Global
Private library
Initial CS:IP:           seg   1 offset 081e
Initial SS:SP:           seg   0 offset 0000
DGROUP:                  seg   2
```

The bottom line on the private lib stuff is that there doesn't seem to be a way of doing this under 3.1 unless you want to do it yourself by registering the task that loaded you as the only one that can use you – see the stuff on multiple instanciated DLLs in this chapter for more on how you might do this.

If you've used INITGLOBAL and/or INITINSTANCE in your .def files before leave them out of your Windows .def files – you're obviously an old OS/2 developer – welcome.

It is always best to keep a module's filename the same as its *real* module name. This makes the task of loading the module (or finding it) much more straight forward. Remember that a module name is not a filename, ie. to load KERNEL use just KERNEL as the module name, ie. not KRNL386.EXE (although that will work).

Libraries may be loaded three ways, explicitly using a *users* IMPORTS statement,

```
IMPORTS
    MODULE.FunctionName
    Alias1=MODULE.FunctionName [or ordinal]

example :

IMPORTS
    KERNEL._DEBUGOUTPUT
    or
    KERNEL._DebugOutput
    or
    _DEBUGOUTPUT=KERNEL._DEBUGOUTPUT
    or
    _DEBUGOUTPUT=KERNEL.328#
```

implicitly using the linker and an import library (libname.lib):

```
link /NOD module,, libname.lib,module.def
```

or dynamically using a mechanism like LoadLibrary() etc.

```
LoadLibrary()
GetProcAddress()

example :

// .DLL not required as KERNEL module always loaded. This
// is a good job as 3.1 doesn't have a KERNEL.DLL. If the
// library were not loaded we'd have to check the OS mode
```

```
    // before we loaded it up. Remember, a filename is  NOT a
    // module name.
    if((hInstance = LoadLibrary("KERNEL")) < HINSTANCE_ERROR)
    {
        // Handle error...
    }
    else
    {
        // Get DisableDOS() function. Use ordinal and
        // immediate data for  faster access and less
        // space overhead.
        lpFunc = GetProcAddress(
                                 hInstance
                               , (LPCSTR)MAKELONG(42,0)
                               );
```

This latter method is the most powerful and flexible. **Although please note that you should not use an ordinal reference to access a function where that function may not exist in the library; it is possible in such a case that the value returned from GetProcAddress() would not be 0!** If there's any doubt as to the existence of the function in the DLL get its address by using its name as this ensures that GetProcAddress() always returns the correct result, ie. 0 if the function doesn't exist else its address. Here's another example – this one uses a function's ordinal! :

```
{
    /*
    ** A MOUSEINFO structure - required by the driver's Inquire function.
    */
    typedef struct
    {
        signed          char  msExist;
        signed          char  msRelative;
        signed short int      msNumButtons;
        signed short int      msRate;
        signed short int      msXThreshold;
        signed short int      msYThreshold;
        signed short int      msXRes;
        signed short int      msYRes;
        signed short int      msMouseCommPort;
    } MOUSEINFO;

    typedef void (CALLBACK   *
MFARPROC)(MOUSEINFO NEAR *);


    auto HINSTANCE hInst;
    auto MFARPROC  fpProc;
    auto MOUSEINFO tMouse;


    /*
    ** Get a hold of the library - good idea to use MOUSE.DRV just in case
    ** the driver's not loaded  (no mouse)  - check 'usage count' to check
    ** for this.
    */
    if((hInst = LoadLibrary("MOUSE")) >= HINSTANCE_ERROR)
```

```
{
    /*
    ** Find 'Inquire' function.
    */
    if(
        (fpProc = (MFARPROC)GetProcAddress(
                                        hInst
                                        ,(LPCSTR)MAKELONG(1,0)
                                        )
        ) == NULL)
    {
        MessageBox(
                    hWnd
                    ,"Can't get 'Inquire' functions address!"
                    ,NULL
                    ,MB_OK
                    );
    }
    else
    {
        auto char carBuffer[10];

        /*
        ** Call mouse driver.
        */
        fpProc(&tMouse);

        wsprintf(&carBuffer[0], "%d", tMouse.msNumButtons);
        MessageBox(hWnd, "Buttons", &carBuffer[0], MB_OK);
    }

    FreeLibrary(hInst);
}
else
{
    MessageBox(
                hWnd
                ,"Can't load mouse driver!"
                ,NULL
                ,MB_OK
                );
}
}
```

This last example calls the mouse driver's inquire function (always provided by the mouse driver at ordinal 1) to *enquire* about the number of buttons on the installed mouse – if you ever wanted to do this and thought, after looking through GetSystemMetrics(), that you couldn't you should have looked through the DDK! The inquire function requires that you pass it a pointer to a MOUSEINFO structure (defined in DDK). The structure contains some *useful* information for Windows' applications like the number of buttons on the mouse and there's even a member that tells you where the mouse is connected, COM1 – COM4. The function must always exist in any mouse driver and be exported as *1*, ie. at ordinal position 1. This means that we can safely call it via a GetProcAddress() that uses the function's ordinal reference. The code fragment above simply outputs the number of buttons on the mouse.

A DLL's segments may be named using the -NT *segment name* compiler switch. Naming segments gives you the opportunity to individually tailor the attributes of any code in your application or DLL, it is a powerful feature. Explicitly naming segments within the DLL, keeping segment sizes to less than 16K (preferably below 4Kb – Page Size) and specifying the appropriate segment options (PRELOAD, LOADONCALL, MOVEABLE, DISCARDABLE) will lessen the module's memory requirements simplifying the task of the Windows' memory manager.

A DLL may be written so as to act for multiple clients, ie. a client task may use *private* (private to the calling task) local heap space provided in the DLL. This would be achieved like this. Each calling task has at least two unique identification tags. A task handle (TDB global memory handle), and an instance handle (DS). When you call a DLL it uses the stack of the caller; the stack is situated in the calling task's DS. Therefore by inspecting the calling task's SS register contents (which is the task's hInstance) the DLL may *find out* the identity of the calling task – of course each caller has a different SS! Similarly, the DLL could call GetCurrentTask() to find the identity of the caller. Having decided that it is possible to identify one caller from another – without the aid of the caller passing some *extra* identification parameter – the DLL can now maintain instance data for each individual client. Global memory blocks may contain a local heap (as does a task's DS which is created for it out of the global heap). A global heap object has to be initialised using LocalInit() in order for it to contain a local heap. The DLL could maintain an array of local-initialised global heap objects indexed by, say, hashing the caller's task handle. As each client calls into the library the library code (each entry point) calls a DLL routine to switch local heaps for the caller. By using a scheme such as this each client task may easily be awarded an internal (to the DLL) local heap.

DLLs can maintain data by using the local or global memory allocation routines. In most cases, memory allocated by the Windows' API GlobalAlloc() is owned by the calling task. Global memory allocated by DLLs and flagged as GMEM_DDESHARE is owned by the DLL – not the calling task. The memory is freed when the DLL is unloaded, not when any application terminates. When a function in a dynamic-link library (DLL) calls the GlobalAlloc() function without specifying the GMEM_DDESHARE flag in the wFlags parameter, the returned global memory object belongs to the currently active instance of the application that called the DLL, ie. the current task. If that instance of the application terminates, the memory is freed. If the DLL is unloaded before the application terminates, the memory remains allocated. When using local heap functions such as LocalAlloc() etc all allocations are done within the DLL's data segment (unless the DLL's got multiple local heaps allocated, say, one per calling task?). Therefore, the handles returned from these calls are only valid when utilised by the DLL. If the DLL hasn't got a local heap, ie. DS is equal to DS (in, say, a DATA NONE DLL) local allocations are taken out of the caller's local heap. Note that applications written for Windows NT may be required to free

GMEM_DDESHARE memory explicitly by calling the GlobalFree function. In other words, the system may not free GMEM_DDESHARE memory when either the DLL or the application terminates.

Note that if you're using the WEP provided by the C7 libraries that it assumes protected mode operation, for 3.0 compatibility it uses a lar instruction internally to check that the DLL's DGROUP is present. lar is a protect mode instruction only so don't use it in real mode 3.0! The C7 WEP also calls a routine in the 8087 floating point emulation library (WIN87EM.DLL). In 3.0 and under certain situations, the WIN87EM library might have been unloaded by Windows by the time the C7 WEP is called – Trap! You are advised therefore to link in your own WEP routine instead of using the WEP provided by the C7 libraries.

The *gang load* area (marked as such by TDUMP.EXE) identifies an area of the file that contains all the segments in your application that are marked as PRELOAD; these are arranged by RC into one continuos coherent section in the exe file so that the Windows' loader can perform a single read operation in order to load all of these segments into memory as the module is loaded.

When using Microsoft 'C' run-time functions, specify the model independent functions; for example: _fmemcpy, _fmemset.

The LibEntry() function is the routine that's called to truly initialise a DLL. In turn LibEntry() calls LibMain(). This last function is the function that you normally define as your DLL's initial entry point – don't forget that the *real* entry point is LibEntry() – What then do you think happens if LibEntry fails to initialise the library (read on)!? LibEntry is called as follows.

DI   Instance handle for the library.

DS   DS Selector of the DLL's data segment.

CX   Requested size, in bytes, of the initial local heap.

ES:SI   The DLL's command line arguments if called via LoadModule().

The function returns 0 to indicate that it failed to do something – perhaps it failed to initialise the DLL's local heap. If this happens then LibMain() is not called so your library initialisation code has not had a chance to do anything that might otherwise cause problems in the context that LibEntry() failed. If LibMain() or LibEntry() returns 0 then the library is not loaded. The Windows exit procedure however IS still called so remember this in the WEP, ie. Only do your library cleanup if LibMain() returned some other value than 0. You'll have to set a flag etc to check for this. You additionally might want to tell the users this? Now be careful here; if you try and create, say, a message box (in LibMain()) to inform the user that you're about to fail because XYZ etc you might cause a fatal exit! Libraries that are implicitly loaded (via linking with import libraries) or those that are loaded due to an IMPORTS .def file clause are loaded before the task loading them gets a message queue, if you try and present the users with a message box, which requires its caller to have a message queue – BANG! The message queue must exist before any code in the application, or any code running on behalf of the application (such as the DLL entry point function), can perform any operation that generates messages. Libraries that are loaded through either Load-Module() or LoadLibrary() are loaded from your code, ie. the place where you call LoadLibrary() etc is *in*your application code somewhere after WinMain(). Windows will always have created a message queue for the loading task when its WinMain() function is called – you can therefore tell the user via, say, a message box that you failed to load the library. Remember, even if LibEntry() fails the library's WEP is STILL called! To flag this has happened to the WEP (to stop it tidying up when no untidying has been done) you'll have to, once again, resort to a flag or semaphore of some sort. If LibEntry() or LibMain() returns 0 for failure then this is the value returned to the system or the calling task (whoever called LoadLibrary()). If Windows fails to load up an implicitly loaded library it will issue no visible warnings or messages – the task simply fails to start. If a task fails to load a library using LoadLibrary() then it can produce a warning message (before quitting) – LoadLibrary() will return 0 which is defined as follows in the LoadLibrary() documentation.

0 = System was out of memory, executable file was corrupt, or relocations were invalid.

Not very helpful!

LibEntry()'s parameters expanded :

DI – (Actually a module handle). Any Windows' function that requires an hInstance handle, such as MakeProcInstance(), uses the value passed in DI. If the DLL creates a window, then the instance handle of the DLL should be used in preference to that of the calling task. DLLs typically save this value in a global variable, or use a function with a *static* HINSTANCE data item.

DS –When Windows calls the entry point function, the DLL's data segment contains just static and literal data (globals, things declared static and strings etc). However, the library does not have a local heap when it is called. If you want the DLL to have a local heap it must be created using LocalInit() – see LIBENTRY.ASM for an example.

CX –The CX register's value is taken straight from the HEAPSIZE statement in the DLL's .def file. If you use LocalInit() to initialise a local heap in the data segment you can use the value in CX to specify the end of the heap (uEndAddr below) :

```
BOOL LocalInit(uSegment, uStartAddr, uEndAddr)

UINT uSegment;              /* segment to contain local heap = DS. */
UINT uStartAddr;            /* starting address for heap = 0.      */
UINT uEndAddr;              /* ending address for heap = CX.       */
```

As promised earlier here is the code for a Borland Pascal (version 7) DLL. Also shown is the source code for an application that calls the DLL, again it was written using Borland's Pascal (version 7) :

Borland Pascal source file :

```
(*
** DLL built using Borland's Pascal Version 7.
**
**
** Library name. TPW will build a .DLL for this module.
*)
library Beeper;

uses WinTypes, WinProcs;

Var
    SaveExit: Pointer;

(*
** Our 'beep beep' routine. Beeps nNumBeeps times.
*)
procedure DoBeep(nNumBeeps : integer); export;
var
    nLoop :Integer;

begin
    for nLoop := 1 to nNumBeeps do
    begin
        MessageBeep(0);
    end;
end;


(*
** Newly installed library exit (WEP type) routine.
*)
procedure LibExit; far;
begin
    (*
    ** ExitCode is defined by the system. wep_System_exit (etc)
    ** is defined in WinTypes unit.
    *)
    if ExitCode = wep_System_Exit then
    begin
        (* Here due to the Windows system closing. *)
    end
    else
    begin
        (* Here due to the library's reference count hitting 0. *)
    end;
end;


(*
** Exports...
*)
```

```
exports    DoBeep index 1;


(*
** This is equivalent to LibMain, ie. your library's init routine.
*)
begin
    (*
        ** Docs say that the old 'exit' proc's address must be preserved.
        *)
        SaveExit := ExitProc;
        ExitProc := @LibExit;
end.
```

The DLL above exports one entry point called DoBeep(). This procedure takes a single integer argument – the number of required beeps! The DLL's entry point is in the section of code above; all that happens is that the entry code registers a WEP type procedure called LibExit. ExitProc is a pointer to a function that is called (and defined) by the BPW environment when the library's about to be unloaded. Note that, unlike 'C' or C++, in BPW you can *export* any sub-routines from within the code (complete with ordinal reference).

```
(*
** Small program to show how to test a BPW built DLL. This app uses the
** WinCrt library  so  it  doesn't  need to create a window in order to
** produce output in Windows - it can just use good ol' Writeln.
*)
program Beep;

uses  WinTypes, WinProcs, WinCrt;

var
    (*
    ** Handle to a DLL.
    *)
    DLL :THandle;

    (*
    ** Procedure declaration.
    *)
    DoBeep :Procedure(x :Integer);

(*
** Program entry point.
*)
begin
    writeln('Getting Library');

    (*
    ** Load it up. Check to see if we got it.
    *)
    DLL := LoadLibrary('C:\BEEPER.DLL');
    if DLL >= 32 then
    begin
        writeln('Got library');
        (*
        ** Get routine. Check to see if we got it.
```

```
      *)
      @DoBeep := GetProcAddress(DLL, 'DoBeep');
      if @DoBeep <> nil then
      begin
          writeln('Got function');
          (*
          ** Beep, beep...
          *)
          DoBeep(10);
      end
      else
      begin
          writeln('Didn''t get function');
      end;

      (*
      ** Let library go.
      *)
      FreeLibrary(DLL);
    end;
  end.
```

The application uses LoadLibrary() (the same Load Library as used by everything else) to get a hold of the DoBeep() function exported from the library. It also does not create a window explicitly! It uses a Borland *unit* called WinCrt. This unit not only creates and maintains a window for you but also allows you to use standard Pascal writeln type output statements. Other than this, I think the program requires no further explanation!

☐ Trashing the caller's statck!

One important thing to remember about DLLs is that functions within them use the stack of the calling/using task. Any function in the DLL that uses too much stack space may therefore trash the caller's stack for them and cause a general protection fault. A DLL routine simply cannot tell how much stack space is left! One way around this problem is to switch stacks in the DLL, ie. go to a new, empty stack of a known size. 3.1 allows you to do this via two functions called SwitchStackTo() and Switch-StackBack() – these functions are described in full in the Miscellaneous chapter of this book.

☐ Searching for a DLL

The directory search order for DLLs is stated incorrectly in the 3.0 SDK documentation. The documentation states that Windows searches for DLLs in certain directories and in a certain order. It states that the order is :

- The current directory
- The Windows directory – Get**WindowsDirectory()**
- The Windows system directory – **GetSystemDirectory()**
- The directory containing the executable file. – GetModuleFileName()
- The PATH environment directories.

- Directories mapped on to a network.

'The Windows directory and *The Windows system directory* are reversed. Under 3.0 the Windows system directory is searched before the Windows directory. This means that if two versions of a DLL exist, one in each directory, that the DLL in the Windows system directory will be used in preference to the one in the Windows directory. The 3.1 SDK documentation states exactly the same search order, however, in 3.1 the order is correct, ie. given the scenario above the DLL in the Windows directory will be found first.

☐ Debug messages due to discardable segments

```
Segment was discardable under 3.0
```

If you see this debugging kernel message it means that one or more code segments of a DLL are marked as MOVEABLE and are not additionally marked as DISCARDABLE in the DLL's .def file. In 3.0 MOVEABLE code segments in a DLL were DISCARDABLE by default – to make them discardable all you had to do therefore was mark them as moveable. This has changed in 3.1 where segments must be explicitly marked DISCARDABLE to actually be discarded. The debugging kernel message warns you that what was discardable in 3.0 now isn't!

☐ LoadLibrary() returns

If the LoadLibrary() function is used to load a DLL and returns 6 the documentation states that the error is due to the library requiring separate data segments for each client task. This means that the DLL's .def file states – DATA MULTIPLE! A normal DLL only gets one data segment irrespective of the number of tasks using it so it should specify – DATA SINGLE.

☐ Floating point and DLL routines.

When an exported DLL function uses the 'C' calling convention and returns either a float, double, or long double data type the calling application will probably receive erroneous values. This problem is due to the way in which the function's result is passed back using the 'C' and PASCAL calling conventions. To cure the problem declare the called function as PASCAL, or alternatively use some other method of communicating the result back to the caller – for example get the DLL to send the result via a *sent* message or use a chunk of global heap to hold it, ie. pass back a handle to some global heap space the contains the result.

☐ Pre-loading DLLs.

Sometimes it is handy to have DLLs pre-loaded in memory, this is especially true if you're using a network or perhaps an application (that uses DLLs) that takes a significant period of time to start. This trick was used in *The Windows' Libraries for*

OS/2, or WLO (pronounced willow). WLO allowed Windows' applications to run on top of OS/2 by providing OS/2 versions of GDI, USER and KERNEL. These replacements called Presentation Manager and OS/2 *core* APIs to run the Windows' app. The first WLO app to be run required that GDI, USER and KERNEL were loaded up – something which took some time. The answer was to get these libraries pre-loaded, perhaps during OS/2 start-up itself. In WLO a small WLO'ed application was loaded which had the effect of loading the WLO libraries of course. Now, when a *real* WLO app came along the libraries (at least their module databases) were already present in memory – the bottom line was that the WLO'ed app started up much quicker.

We use this technique to pre-load some DLLs (see dialog chapter for the TMS error box DLL – this is pre-loaded in this way) including both VBRUN100.DLL and VBRUN200.DLL which are the Visual Basic run-time DLLs. We use a small non-visible Windows' application to do this which is itself loaded by using *load=* in everyones WIN.INI (the WIN.INI file is itself copied down from the network as the user logs in), ie. :

load=TMSDLLLD.EXE

The application TMSDLLLD loads a series of DLLs from a series of given (in a private INI file) paths. Also the application first checks a network based private INI file for information before using a local one (if it exists). In this way we can remotely configure all our user's machines to load certain versions of DLLs held either locally or centrally on the network. Here's the code required :

The tmsdllld.c file :

```
/* Turn off silly warnings. */
#pragma warning(disable:4100)
#pragma warning(disable:4001)


/*H*
**
** MODULE:TMSDLLLD
**
** DESC:  Loads Dlls into memory, as specified in  TMS.INI. The  section
in
**        TMS.INI to look at is [DLLs], the relevant entries in that sec-
tion
**        are LoadOnStartup= & DLLPath=.
**
*H*/


/* Strict use of types. */
#define  STRICT

#include "windows.h"
#include <stdlib.h>
#include <stdio.h>
```

```
#include <string.h>

/*
** Buffer size into which TMS.INI entry is read.
*/
#define MAX_BUFF_SIZE 255

/*
** The number of entries allowed in INI file sections.
*/
#define MAX_INI_ENTRIES 50

/*
**Max size of error message.
*/
#define MAX_ERR_SIZE  255

/*
** Used in returning from void sub-routines.
*/
#define VOID_RETURN

/*
** Predeclaration of TMS error function ....
*/
WORD FAR PASCAL wTMS_SimpleErrorBox (HWND, LPSTR);

/*
** Other predeclarations.
*/
int     PASCAL  WinMain                   (HINSTANCE, HINSTANCE, LPSTR,
int);
VOID            vParseAndLoadTmsIniEntries (HINSTANCE, const NPSTR);
VOID            vLoadDLL                   (NPSTR);
VOID            vErrorHandler             (HINSTANCE, NPSTR, UINT);




/***********************
**
** Code starts.
**
*/


int PASCAL WinMain
(
   HINSTANCE    hInstance
  ,HINSTANCE    hPrevInstance
  ,LPSTR        lpCmdLine
  ,int          nCmdShow
)
{
   /*
   ** Message structure - not used as far as it is possible to tell!
   */
   auto MSG msg;
```

```c
    /*
    ** Allow only one instance of DLL loader.
    */
    if(hPrevInstance != NULL)
    {
        return FALSE;
    }

    /*
    ** Load libs in TMSGBL.INI.
    */
    vParseAndLoadTmsIniEntries(hInstance, "G:\\GLOBAL\\LIBRARY\\TMSGBL.INI");

    /*
    ** Load libs in TMS.INI.
    */
    vParseAndLoadTmsIniEntries(hInstance, "TMS.INI");

    /*
    ** Now just yield. See also WaitMessage().
    */
    while(GetMessage(
                    &msg
                    , (HWND)NULL
                    ,NULL
                    ,NULL
                    ) == TRUE
        )
    {
        DispatchMessage(&msg);
    }

    /*
    ** Should never get to here!
    */
    MessageBeep(0);

    return msg.wParam;
}


/******************************************************************************
**

This function loads and parses two entries in the 'DLLs' section of
TMS.INI.
One entry contains a list of DLLs to pre-load, the other entry
contains a list of path names to use in locating the DLLs in the first
entry.

The entries may use any token delimiter given in pszTokenDelimiters, the
default set are a space, a comma and a semi-colon.

When the entries have been parsed attempts are made to load the first DLL
(then subsequent DLLs) using the path(s) given in DLLPath.  The order is
sequential. If after trying all the paths the  DLL has not been found, we
ask windows to do the looking.  It will look for the DLL as documented in
the windows' programmers reference under LoadLibrary().
```

```
If the DLL cannot ultimately be found we report the error. Any other error
to do with loading the DLL is also reported (again see LoadLibrary()).

*************************************************************************/

VOID vParseAndLoadTmsIniEntries
(
        HINSTANCE hInst
  ,const NPSTR    pszIniName
)
{
  /*
  ** The TMS.INI file name.
  */
  auto const NPSTR pszIniFileName = pszIniName;


  /*
  ** The section in TMS.INI in which we're interested.
  */
  auto const NPSTR pszAppNameInIni   = "DLLs";


  /*
  ** The entries in the section we're interested in.
  */
  auto const NPSTR pszDLLPathSection    = "DLLPath";
  auto const NPSTR pszDLLsToLoadSection = "LoadOnStartup";


  /*
  ** Entry defaults if entry is empty.
  */
  auto const NPSTR pszDLLPathDefault = "C:\\WIN31\\SYSTEM";
  auto const NPSTR pszDLLDefault     = "TOOLHELP.DLL";


  /*
  ** Token Delimiters.
  */
  auto const NPSTR pszTokenDelimiters = ",; ";

  /*
  ** Buffers into which the entries are read.
  */
  auto char carDLLPathsIniBuffer[MAX_BUFF_SIZE];
  auto char carDLLNamesIniBuffer[MAX_BUFF_SIZE];

  /*
  ** Used in strtok - pointers to each entry section.
  */
  auto NPSTR pszLibName;
  auto NPSTR pszPathName;

  /*
  ** Holds pointers to each entry section.
  */
  auto char * pcarLibrNames[MAX_INI_ENTRIES];
```

```
                auto char * pcarPathNames[MAX_INI_ENTRIES];

                /*
                ** Set to point at start of buffers above.
                */
                auto NPSTR pszBufferPtr;


                /*
                ** Indexes into arrays of pointers to entry sections.
                */
                auto UINT uPathNamesIndex = 0;
                auto UINT uLibrNamesIndex = 0;

                /*
                ** Used in inserting pointers to entry sections.
                */
                auto UINT uArrayIndex;

                /*
                ** Used to acquire local memory into which DLL name
                ** and path are built up.
                */
                auto UINT          uMemRequired;
                auto HLOCAL        hMem;
                auto VOID NEAR *   pMem;

                /*
                ** Flag used to indicate whether or not current path
                ** name entry has a '\' at its end.
                */
                auto BOOL bSlashFound = 0;

                /*
                ** Tell windows that we want to handle 'file not
                ** found' errors!
                */
                SetErrorMode(SEM_NOOPENFILEERRORBOX);

                /*
                ** Make sure arrays are clean - we use a NULL entry
                ** to signal when we've reached the last entry.
                */
                memset(&pcarLibrNames[0], 0x0, sizeof(pcarLibrNames));
                memset(&pcarPathNames[0], 0x0, sizeof(pcarPathNames));

                /*
                ** Load the LoadOnStartup entry.
                */
                (VOID)GetPrivateProfileString
                                        (
                                         pszAppNameInIni
                                        ,pszDLLsToLoadSection
                                        ,pszDLLDefault
                                        ,&carDLLNamesIniBuffer[0]
                                        ,MAX_BUFF_SIZE
                                        ,pszIniFileName
                                        );
```

```
/*
** Set pointer to buffer.
*/
pszBufferPtr = &carDLLNamesIniBuffer[0];

/*
** Set it to upper case.
*/
strupr(pszBufferPtr);

/*
** Reset index.
*/
uArrayIndex = 0;

/*
** Parse buffer for DLL names.
*/
while(
        (pszLibName = strtok(pszBufferPtr, pszTokenDelimiters)) != NULL &&
        uArrayIndex < MAX_INI_ENTRIES
      )
{
    pszBufferPtr = 0;
    pcarLibrNames[uArrayIndex++] = pszLibName;
}


/*
** Load the DLLPath entry.
*/
(VOID)GetPrivateProfileString
                            (
                             pszAppNameInIni
                            ,pszDLLPathSection
                            ,pszDLLPathDefault
                            ,&carDLLPathsIniBuffer[0]
                            ,MAX_BUFF_SIZE
                            ,pszIniFileName
                            );

/*
** Set pointer to buffer.
*/
pszBufferPtr = &carDLLPathsIniBuffer[0];

/*
** Set it to upper case.
*/
strupr(pszBufferPtr);

/*
** Reset index.
*/
uArrayIndex = 0;

/*
```

```
** Parse buffer for paths.
*/
while(
      (pszPathName = strtok(pszBufferPtr, pszTokenDelimiters)) != NULL &&
      uArrayIndex < MAX_INI_ENTRIES
      )
{
   pszBufferPtr = 0;
   pcarPathNames[uArrayIndex++] = pszPathName;
}

/*
** Reset indexes.
*/
uPathNamesIndex = 0;
uLibrNamesIndex = 0;

/*
** Now load 'em!
*/
while(pcarLibrNames[uLibrNamesIndex])
{
   /*
   ** Did we load it OK?
   */
   auto BOOL       bErrorStartingDLL = FALSE;

   /*
   ** The handle to the library.
   */
   auto HINSTANCE hLibraryHandle;

   /*
** While we've a path (C:\WIN31 by default).
 */
  while(pcarPathNames[uPathNamesIndex])
  {
   /*
   ** Does the path end with a slash? Set bSlashFound.
   */
   bSlashFound = *((lstrlen(pcarPathNames[uPathNamesIndex]) - 1
                 + pcarPathNames[uPathNamesIndex])) != '\\' ? TRUE : FALSE;

      /*
      ** Work out how much mem needed for path name plus filename.
      */
      uMemRequired = lstrlen(pcarLibrNames[uLibrNamesIndex]) +
                     lstrlen(pcarPathNames[uPathNamesIndex]) +
                     1                                        +
                     (UINT)bSlashFound;


      /*
      ** Get the mem.
      */
      hMem = LocalAlloc(LMEM_ZEROINIT, uMemRequired);

      /*
```

```
** If we got it...
*/
if(hMem != NULL)
{
   /*
   ** Lock it.
   */
   pMem = LocalLock(hMem);

   /*
   ** If we locked it...
   */
   if(pMem != NULL)
   {
      /*
      ** Copy the path name to it.
      */
      lstrcpy(pMem, pcarPathNames[uPathNamesIndex]);

      /*
      ** Do we need a slash or is there one given in the path?
      ** Add the slash if needed then add the lib name.
      */
      if(bSlashFound == TRUE)
      {
         lstrcat(pMem,"\\");
         lstrcat(pMem, pcarLibrNames[uLibrNamesIndex]);
      }
      else
      {
         lstrcat(pMem, pcarLibrNames[uLibrNamesIndex]);
      }

      /*
      ** Load the library.
      */
      hLibraryHandle = LoadLibrary(pMem);

      /*
      ** Set flag as to whether or not we loaded it.
      */
      bErrorStartingDLL = hLibraryHandle < HINSTANCE_ERROR ?
                     TRUE : FALSE;

      /*
      ** If we didn't load it see if the file couldn't be located

      ** or if the path was wrong.  Ignore  these errors as we've
      ** yet to check the paths given (and DLL names) in the local
      ** INI file.
      */
      if(bErrorStartingDLL)
      {
         if(((UINT)hLibraryHandle) != 2 &&
            ((UINT)hLibraryHandle) != 3)
         {
            /*
            ** The error wasn't trivial so report it.
            */
```

```
                        vErrorHandler(hInst, pMem, (UINT)hLibraryHandle);
                        bErrorStartingDLL = FALSE;
                    }
                }
                /*
                ** Get ready to through away mem.
                */
                (VOID)LocalUnlock(hMem);
            }
            else   /* Couldn't lock local mem! */
            {
                MessageBox(
                        0
                        ,"DLL Loader cannot lock required memory!"
                        ,NULL
                        ,MB_OK
                        );

                exit(254);
            }

            /*
            ** Through away mem.
            */
            (VOID)LocalFree(hMem);

            /*
            ** If we loaded it break out of this inner while loop. we
            ** don't want to try other paths (we've loaded it) and we
            ** want to keep bErrorStartingDLL as it is.
            */
            if(bErrorStartingDLL == FALSE)
            {
                break;
            }
        }
        else   /* Couldn't allocate local mem! */
        {
            MessageBox(
                    0
                    ,"DLL Loader cannot allocate required memory!"
                    ,NULL
                    ,MB_OK
                    );

            exit(255);
        }

        /*
        ** Increment path index.
        */
        uPathNamesIndex++;

    } /* while got a path name. */


/*
** Here because of a break or because we ran out of paths.
** Check bErrorStartingDLL for reason.
```

```
        */
        if(bErrorStartingDLL == TRUE)
        {
            /*
            ** Not here because of break so we haven't found DLL using
            ** paths, now try without a path so that windows looks.
            */
            if((hLibraryHandle = LoadLibrary(pcarLibrNames[uLibrNamesIndex]))<
                HINSTANCE_ERROR
                )
            {
                /*
                ** Failed ultimately so report it.
                */
                vErrorHandler(
                            hInst
                           ,pcarLibrNames[uLibrNamesIndex]
                           ,(UINT)hLibraryHandle
                           );
            }

        }

        /*
        ** Reset path names index.
        */
        uPathNamesIndex = 0;

        /*
        ** Inc DLL names index.
        */
        uLibrNamesIndex++;

    }   /* while got a lib name.                                       */



    return VOID_RETURN;
}



/******************************************************************************


This function handles errors. It may be called from :

vParseAndLoadTmsIniEntries

If vParseAndLoadTmsIniEntries fails it will call this function with a code
returned from a LoadLibrary() call. This code is used here in that in this
app's stringtable error strings are numbered according to the error code.
This means that nErrCode here refers to a LoadLibrary error and a string
resource.

The TMS standard error handler DLL is used to report any errors. This
makes the preloading of this error handler (TMSERROR.DLL) by this
application
pointless as it will be preloaded by windows when this app starts up.
```

```
********************************************************************/

VOID vErrorHandler(HINSTANCE hInst, NPSTR pszLibName, UINT uErrCode)
{
   auto char    carErrString[MAX_ERR_SIZE];
   auto NPSTR   pszLoadBuffer;
   auto UINT    uLoop = 0;

   /*
   ** Loads the specified string for this error and calls TMS err DLL
   ** to do its thing.
   */

   /*
   ** First we prepend this...
   */
   lstrcpy(&carErrString[0], "TMS DLL Loader - ");

   while(carErrString[uLoop] != NULL)
   {
      uLoop++;
   }

   /*
   ** Now load the resource error string into the buffer.
   */
   pszLoadBuffer = &carErrString[uLoop];

   if(LoadString(
                hInst
                ,uErrCode
                ,pszLoadBuffer
                ,MAX_ERR_SIZE - lstrlen(&carErrString[0])
                )
     == 0
     )
   {
      MessageBox(0, "Failed to load error msg.", "TMS DLL Loader", MB_OK);
   }
   else
   {
      auto char carTMSErrString[MAX_ERR_SIZE];

      /*
      ** Create TMS style error string from error text. Using
      ** wTMS_SimpleErrorBox() instead of wTMS_ErrorBox as we don't
      ** have a window handle.
      */
      wsprintf(
              &carTMSErrString[0]
              ,"%%%s+ %%%s+ %%2+ %%&OK+ %%&Cancel+ %%+ %%+ %%stop+ %%1+ %%modal"
              , (LPSTR)pszLibName
              , (LPSTR)&carErrString[0]
              );

      (VOID)wTMS_SimpleErrorBox (NULL,carTMSErrString);
```

```
    }

    return VOID_RETURN;
}
```

The makefile :

```
all : tmsdllld.exe

tmsdllld.exe : $*.obj $*.def $*.res
        link /CO /M $*.obj,$*.exe,$*.map,libw slibcew tmserror,$*.def
        rc -30 $*.res
        mapsym $*.map

tmsdllld.obj : $*.c makefile
        cnest < $*.c
        cl -Zi -W4 -WX -c -GAs -Zp -Od $*.c > $*.err
        type $*.err | more

tmsdllld.res : $*.rc makefile
        rc -r $*.rc
```

The .def file :

```
NAME            TMSDLLLD

DESCRIPTION     'Application which loads TMS''s default DLLs'

EXETYPE         WINDOWS 3.1

PROTMODE

STUB            'winstub.exe'

CODE  PRELOAD MOVEABLE DISCARDABLE
DATA  PRELOAD MOVEABLE MULTIPLE

HEAPSIZE    512
STACKSIZE   5120
```

The .rc file :

```
/*
** The string table's indexes are based on the codes returned by the Win-
dows'
** LoadLibrary() function. They should not be changed.
*/
STRINGTABLE
BEGIN
   0, "System was out of memory, executable file was corrupt, or
      relocations were invalid."
   2, "Could not find this file."
   3, "Path not found."
   5, "Attempt was made to dynamically link to a task, or there was a
      sharing or network-protection."
```

```
   6,  "Library required separate data segments for each task."
   8,  "There was insufficient memory to start the application."
  10,  "Windows version was incorrect."
  11,  "Executable file was invalid. Either it was not a Windows application
        or there was an error in the .EXE image."
  12,  "Application was designed for a different operating system."
  13,  "Application was designed for MS-DOS 4.0."
  14,  "Type of executable file was unknown."
  15,  "Attempt was made to load a real-mode application (developed for an
        earlier version of Windows)."
  16,  "Attempt was made to load a second instance of an executable file
        containing multiple data segments that were not marked read-only."
  19,  "Attempt was made to load a compressed executable file. The file must
        be decompressed before it can be loaded."
  20,  "Dynamic-link library (DLL) file was invalid. One of the DLLs
        required to run this application was corrupt."
  21,  "Application requires Microsoft Windows 32-bit extensions."
END
```

The application first checks the network based INI file called TMSGBL.INI for a section called [DLLs]. This section contains the entires DLLPath and LoadOnStartup. DLLPath specifies where to look and LoadOnStartup specifies what to load. When this INI file is finished with the app looks for another INI file called, plainly, TMS.INI – this will *live* on the users local drive. Again it contains the same sections as the *global* one did. If TMSDLLLD fails to load a DLL it reports the fact via a call to wTMS_SimpleErrorBox() (which was looked at in the dialog chapter). Suitable error text is retrieved from the app's resources.

Typical INI file contents :

```
/*
** This would live on the network drive in TMSGBL.INI.
*/
[DLLs]
; This section read by TMSDLLLD.EXE on windows startup
DLLPath=m:\win31,m:\win31\system
LoadOnStartup=toolhelp.dll,tmserror.dll,pxengwin.dll,vbrun200.dll,commdlg.dll


/*
** This would live in the local TMS.INI
*/
[DLLs]
; This section read by TMSDLLLD.EXE on windows startup
DLLPath=c:\win31,c:\win31\system,k:\dllextra
LoadOnStartup=toolhelp.dll,deskbut.dll,select.dll,cmdialog.vbx
```

Chapter 7

D e b u g g i n g

☐ Debugging support from the API

The first thing we'll be looking at in this chapter on debugging is what support the Windows' API gives you in your task of debugging. We won't be looking in any detail however at *debuggers* themselves like CodeView! Windows' debuggers are adequately covered in the SDK documentation whereas debugging techniques are, relatively speaking, not! We will however take a look at WDEB386, the *Kernel Debugger* later on.

Below is an extract from WINDOWS.H that lists some of the debug *type* functions structures and constants supplied by the system:

```
int  WINAPI Catch(int FAR*);
void WINAPI Throw(const int FAR*, int);

int  WINAPI ProfInsChk(void);
void WINAPI ProfSetup(int,int);
void WINAPI ProfSampRate(int,int);
void WINAPI ProfStart(void);
void WINAPI ProfStop(void);
void WINAPI ProfClear(void);
void WINAPI ProfFlush(void);
void WINAPI ProfFinish(void);
BOOL WINAPI IsBadReadPtr(const void FAR* lp, UINT cb);
BOOL WINAPI IsBadWritePtr(void FAR* lp, UINT cb);
BOOL WINAPI IsBadHugeReadPtr(const void _huge* lp, DWORD cb);
BOOL WINAPI IsBadHugeWritePtr(void _huge* lp, DWORD cb);
BOOL WINAPI IsBadCodePtr(FARPROC lpfn);
BOOL WINAPI IsBadStringPtr(const void FAR* lpsz, UINT cchMax);
typedef struct tagWINDEBUGINFO
{
    UINT    flags;
    DWORD   dwOptions;
    DWORD   dwFilter;
    char    achAllocModule[8];
    DWORD   dwAllocBreak;
    DWORD   dwAllocCount;
} WINDEBUGINFO;

BOOL    WINAPI GetWinDebugInfo(WINDEBUGINFO FAR* lpwdi, UINT flags);
BOOL    WINAPI SetWinDebugInfo(const WINDEBUGINFO FAR* lpwdi);
```

```
void     FAR _cdecl DebugOutput(UINT flags, LPCSTR lpsz, ...);

/* WINDEBUGINFO flags values */
#define WDI_OPTIONS          0x0001
#define WDI_FILTER           0x0002
#define WDI_ALLOCBREAK       0x0004
/* dwOptions values */
#define DBO_CHECKHEAP        0x0001
#define DBO_BUFFERFILL       0x0004
#define DBO_DISABLEGPTRAPPING 0x0010
#define DBO_CHECKFREE        0x0020

#define DBO_SILENT           0x8000

#define DBO_TRACEBREAK       0x2000
#define DBO_WARNINGBREAK     0x1000
#define DBO_NOERRORBREAK     0x0800
#define DBO_NOFATALBREAK     0x0400
#define DBO_INT3BREAK        0x0100

/* DebugOutput flags values */
#define DBF_TRACE            0x0000
#define DBF_WARNING          0x4000
#define DBF_ERROR            0x8000
#define DBF_FATAL            0xc000

/* dwFilter values */
#define DBF_KERNEL           0x1000
#define DBF_KRN_MEMMAN       0x0001
#define DBF_KRN_LOADMODULE   0x0002
#define DBF_KRN_SEGMENTLOAD  0x0004
#define DBF_USER             0x0800
#define DBF_GDI              0x0400
#define DBF_MMSYSTEM         0x0040
#define DBF_PENWIN           0x0020
#define DBF_APPLICATION      0x0008
#define DBF_DRIVER           0x0010

#endif  /* NOLOGERROR */
#endif  /* WINVER >= 0x030a */

void     WINAPI FatalExit(int);
void     WINAPI FatalAppExit(UINT, LPCSTR);

void     WINAPI DebugBreak(void);
void     WINAPI OutputDebugString(LPCSTR);

void     WINAPI ValidateCodeSegments(void);
void     WINAPI ValidateFreeSpaces(void);
```

You'll find the information above useful to refer to when reading through this chapter.

We'll take the functions etc in a random order starting from OuputDebugString() and DebugOutput() but that's after we take a look at *the debug libs* (the IsBad??? jobies are not covered).

☐ The Debug Libs

When you buy Microsoft's SDK for Windows it comes with an *alternative* set of core libraries called the *debug libraries,* each debug library additionally comes complete with a symbol file (unfortunately the symbols for each library's undocumented functions is missing) :

```
Name                    Extent
gdi             exe
gdi             sym
kernel                          exe
kernel                          sym
krnl286                         exe
krnl286                         sym
krnl386                         exe
krnl386                         sym
mmsystem                        dll
mmsystem                        sym
user            exe
user            sym
```

Note that you'll only have KERNEL.EXE and KERNEL.SYM if you've either used, or have, the SDK for version 3.0 (you can now remove KERNEL.EXE and KERNEL.SYM if you've made the change to 3.1).

The debugging libraries provide the Windows developer with additional features not included in the *retail v*ersion of Windows like extra error checking and error/diagnostics messages; the symbol files help you track calls into the **core** Windows' libraries.

Everyone should develop their code using the debug libraries. It's always surprises me how many so called *top* developers still develop their code without the debugging libraries installed on their systems (of course, if you're not using the Microsoft SDK you don't have the debugging libs (these are provided as part of the Visual C++ Professional V1.0 package)). How can I possibly know that? By watching what happens *in the debugging environment* when I run their applications that's how! Here's an example (name of company or product not included to save any embarrassment) taken from a commercially available application (the application was started, run for about 20 seconds (during which it was just initialising) and then closed) :

```
wn ??? USER: Missing BeginPaint() or GetUpdateRect/Rgn(fErase == TRUE) in
WM_PAINT

FatalExit code = 0x4800
Abort, Break, Exit or Ignore?
wn ??? USER: Missing BeginPaint() or GetUpdateRect/Rgn(fErase == TRUE) in
WM_PAINT

FatalExit code = 0x4800
Abort, Break, Exit or Ignore?
```

```
wn ??? USER: Missing BeginPaint or GetUpdateRect/Rgn(fErase == TRUE) in
WM_PAINT

FatalExit code = 0x4800
Abort, Break, Exit or Ignore?
err ???->USER PV_WM_ERASEBKGND+1E: Invalid HANDLE: 0x0000

FatalExit code = 0x600B
Abort, Break, Exit or Ignore?
wn ??? USER: Missing BeginPaint or GetUpdateRect/Rgn(fErase == TRUE) in
WM_PAINT

FatalExit code = 0x4800
Abort, Break, Exit or Ignore?
wn Kernel: Segment 0001 of ??? was discardable under Win 3.0

FatalExit code = 0x5000
Abort, Break, Exit or Ignore?
wn Kernel: Segment 0002 of ??? was discardable under Win 3.0

FatalExit code = 0x5000
Abort, Break, Exit or Ignore?
err ??? ENABLEMENUITEM+C: Invalid HMENU: 0x0000

FatalExit code = 0x6041
Abort, Break, Exit or Ignore?
err ???->USER PV_WM_ERASEBKGND+1E: Invalid HANDLE: 0x0000

FatalExit code = 0x600B
Abort, Break, Exit or Ignore?
wn ??? USER: Missing BeginPaint or GetUpdateRect/Rgn(fErase == TRUE) in
WM_PAINT

FatalExit code = 0x4800
Abort, Break, Exit or Ignore?
err ???->USER PV_WM_ERASEBKGND+1E: Invalid HANDLE: 0x0000

FatalExit code = 0x600B
Abort, Break, Exit or Ignore?
wn ??? USER: Missing BeginPaint or GetUpdateRect/Rgn(fErase == TRUE) in
WM_PAINT

FatalExit code = 0x4800
Abort, Break, Exit or Ignore?
wn ??? USER: Missing BeginPaint or GetUpdateRect/Rgn(fErase == TRUE) in
WM_PAINT

FatalExit code = 0x4800
Abort, Break, Exit or Ignore?
err ???->USER PV_WM_ERASEBKGND+1E: Invalid HANDLE: 0x0000

FatalExit code = 0x600B
Abort, Break, Exit or Ignore?
err ???->USER PV_WM_ERASEBKGND+1E: Invalid HANDLE: 0x0000

FatalExit code = 0x600B
Abort, Break, Exit or Ignore?
```

```
wn Kernel: GlobalReAlloc failed

FatalExit code = 0x5000
Abort, Break, Exit or Ignore?
wn Kernel: GlobalReAlloc failed

FatalExit code = 0x6061
Abort, Break, Exit or Ignore?
err ??? SELECTOBJECT+18: Invalid HGDIOBJ: 0x0000

FatalExit code = 0x6061
Abort, Break, Exit or Ignore?
err ??? SELECTOBJECT+18: Invalid HGDIOBJ: 0x0000

FatalExit code = 0x6061
Abort, Break, Exit or Ignore?
err ??? SELECTOBJECT+18: Invalid HGDIOBJ: 0x0000

FatalExit code = 0x6061
Abort, Break, Exit or Ignore?
err ??? SELECTOBJECT+18: Invalid HGDIOBJ: 0x0000

FatalExit code = 0x6061
Abort, Break, Exit or Ignore?
err ??? SELECTOBJECT+18: Invalid HGDIOBJ: 0x0000

FatalExit code = 0x6061
Abort, Break, Exit or Ignore?
err ??? SELECTOBJECT+18: Invalid HGDIOBJ: 0x0000

FatalExit code = 0x6061
Abort, Break, Exit or Ignore?
err ??? SELECTOBJECT+18: Invalid HGDIOBJ: 0x0000

FatalExit code = 0x6061
Abort, Break, Exit or Ignore?
err ??? SELECTOBJECT+18: Invalid HGDIOBJ: 0x0000

FatalExit code = 0x6061
Abort, Break, Exit or Ignore?
err ??? SELECTOBJECT+18: Invalid HGDIOBJ: 0x0000

FatalExit code = 0x6061
Abort, Break, Exit or Ignore?
wn ??? GDI:DeleteObject:Pen(1116) still selected in DC(s).

FatalExit code = 0x4400
Abort, Break, Exit or Ignore?
wn ??? GDI: Unable to deselect 1116

FatalExit code = 0x4400
Abort, Break, Exit or Ignore?
LocalFree: freeing locked object 0000:111E

FatalExit code = 0x01F0
Abort, Break, Exit or Ignore?
wn ??? USER: Missing BeginPaint or GetUpdateRect/Rgn(fErase == TRUE) in
```

```
WM_PAINT

FatalExit code = 0x4800
Abort, Break, Exit or Ignore?
wn ??? GDI: Pen not deleted: 1056

FatalExit code = 0x4000
Abort, Break, Exit or Ignore?
wn ??? GDI: Pen not deleted: 0D86

FatalExit code = 0x4000
Abort, Break, Exit or Ignore?
wn ??? GDI: Pen not deleted: 1052

FatalExit code = 0x4000
Abort, Break, Exit or Ignore?
wn ??? GDI: Pen not deleted: 12BA

FatalExit code = 0x4000
Abort, Break, Exit or Ignore?
wn ??? GDI: Pen not deleted: 1116

FatalExit code = 0x4000
Abort, Break, Exit or Ignore?
wn ??? GDI: Pen not deleted: 111E

FatalExit code = 0x4000
Abort, Break, Exit or Ignore?

FatalExit code = 0x5000
Abort, Break, Exit or Ignore?
wn ??? GDI: Pen not deleted: 116E

FatalExit code = 0x4000
Abort, Break, Exit or Ignore?
wn ??? GDI: Font not deleted: 10FE

FatalExit code = 0x4000
Abort, Break, Exit or Ignore?
wn ??? GDI: Bitmap not deleted: 1106

FatalExit code = 0x4000
Abort, Break, Exit or Ignore?
wn ??? GDI: Brush not deleted: 1162

FatalExit code = 0x4000
Abort, Break, Exit or Ignore?
wn ??? GDI: Bitmap not deleted: 1292

FatalExit code = 0x4000
Abort, Break, Exit or Ignore?
wn ??? GDI: Font not deleted: 1076

FatalExit code = 0x4000
Abort, Break, Exit or Ignore?
wn ??? GDI: Pen not deleted: 10A6
```

```
FatalExit code = 0x4000
Abort, Break, Exit or Ignore?
wn ??? GDI: Pen not deleted: 10AA

FatalExit code = 0x4000
Abort, Break, Exit or Ignore?
wn ??? GDI: Font not deleted: 12AE

FatalExit code = 0x4000
Abort, Break, Exit or Ignore?
```

When I see listings such as this appear on my debugging terminal I know that the developers of whatever application it is that I am running haven't used the debugging libraries during their development –either that or they just don't care about errors which I would find even more surprising! You might be asking yourself something like 'Why did company X ship their product when it produces all these errors and worrying warnings'? Well the answer is almost certainly that they didn't know they had all (or any) of these errors in their code because they probably develop and test using the *retail* version. It's only when you switch to the debugging libs that you see the real picture. You can get an idea now of how tolerant 3.1 really is of any badly behaving application!

How to use debug messages

Debug messages fall into three categories, trace, warning, error and lastly fatal. Each *type* of message begins with some identifying letter or letters :

TRACE message –handy stuff to output.
```
t GENERIC Trace - I feel good, ... I knew that I would yeah...!
```

WARNING message –possible problem.
```
wn GENERIC Warning - are you really sure you want me to do that?!
```

ERROR message –problem.
```
err GENERIC Error - Wow that's blow that data structure!
```

FATAL message –real bad problem.
```
fatl GENERIC Oh my goodness, I think we're gonna haaaaaannnnnggggg........!
```

The issuing module is also identified in the message (shown as ??? in the nameless-app listing above), for example, it was the module called GENERIC which caused the four example messages above to be issued to the debugging terminal.

The debug messages shown in bold in the main listing are the serious ones. From this quick test, and the debug output, we can say that the main problems with this application are that –It doesn't handle DCs and GDI objects correctly in that it has tried, at least once, to delete a GDI object that was still selected in a DC; it tries to select objects whose handle values are 0, ie. they're invalid objects, and lastly it doesn't clean up objects allocated in GDI's local heap – apart from that it's not bad!

We can confirm what the debug libraries have output about not deleting objects by peeping into GDI's local heap using Heap Walker (as GDI objects belong to GDI they're allocated in GDI's local heap space); first all we need do is pick an object and an error message. Note that in the 3.1 debugging libs there's a small bug that prevents the libs informing you that a Metafile has not been deleted from GDI's local heap. So if you use meta files –don't rely on the debug lib reports, double check you've deleted them manually.

```
FatalExit code = 0x4000
Abort, Break, Exit or Ignore?
wn ??? GDI: Bitmap not deleted: 1106
```

If we now perform a local walk on GDI's local heap and keep an eye out for this object we find that sure enough it's still allocated even though the application's long since gone!

```
┌──────────────────────────────────────────────────────────┐
│ ▭              GDI Heap (Local Walk)                      │
├──────────────────────────────────────────────────────────┤
│ Heap    Sort   Add!                                       │
├──────────────────────────────────────────────────────────┤
│ OFFSET HANDLE  SIZE FLAGS      LCK TYPE                   │
│ 82CE   0F6E      42 Moveable       Bitmap              ↑  │
│ 4172   0E1A      34 Moveable       Bitmap                 │
│ 393A   1292      34 Moveable       Bitmap                 │
│ 796A   1066      34 Moveable       Bitmap                 │
│ 5DDA   1106      34 Moveable       Bitmap                 │
│ 3B2A   0D92      34 Moveable       Bitmap                 │
│ 6A7E   0CEE      42 Moveable       Bitmap                 │
│ 3A56   1132      34 Moveable       Bitmap              ↓  │
│ 7426   0EBA      34 Moveable       Bitmap                 │
└──────────────────────────────────────────────────────────┘
```

This means that this application stresses Windows' system resources somewhat! If it were run for long enough it might even eventually stop Windows working altogether, ie. GDI's local heap might become so congested that GDI, and hence Windows, would simply have to quit on you –you get an idea that this is happening when your application (all applications) receives a WM_COMPACTING message, apps like the resource gauge shown elsewhere in this book trap this message and display a suitable warning!

Here's another debugging message complete with stack trace as reported to my debugging terminal (we'll see the code that produced this when we've examined the error message more fully) :

```
err GENERIC SHOWWINDOW+C: Invlaid HWND: 0x0000

Fatal Exit code = 0x6040
Abort, Break Exit or Ignore?
```

```
FataExit code = 0x6040
Stack trace:
KERNEL!IGROUP:ISETHANDLECOUNT+619
GENERIC!_TEXT:__nmsize+99FE
KERNEL!IGROUP:DEBUGBREAK+8D
USER!_WMGR2:SHOWWINDOW+7
GENERIC!_TEXT:MainWndProc+7F
USER!_IGROUP:GLOBALGETATONNAME+54C
GENEIC!_TEXT:WINMAIN+86
GENERIC!_TEXT:__stubmain+17
GENERIC!_TEXT:__astart+88

Abort, Break, Exit or Ignore?
```

OK, so how do you interpret these debug messages? The ability to generate debug messages is the principal feature of the debugging version of the debugging libraries. The messages identify errors caused by modules. Each message reports the type of each error and any necessary information you need to locate the error in your app. The messages normally have the following form:

```
FatalExit Code = fatalexit-code
Stack trace:
module-name!segment-name:[function-name+]address
    ....
Abort, Break, Exit or Ignore?
```

The fatalexit-code parameter identifies the type of error, in our case the fatal exit code was 0x6040 which means ERR_BAD_HWND (defined in WINDOWS.H –see extract at beginning of chapter), or that the passed window handle was invalid. This error value is generally sent by the USER module. The stack trace consists of one or more addresses representing a *chain* of return addresses running back from the function that detected the error to the function within the application that made the original call. Note:The segment and function names are available only if a symbol file (.SYM extension) exists for the given module. Otherwise, Windows displays addresses instead of names.

In the example above, the stack trace shows that the ISETHANDLECOUNT function in the KERNEL module detected the error, ie. this was as far as the error could propagate before causing the fatal exit. The error code is 0x6040 which we have already seen means invalid window handle value was used (look these up in WINSDKWH.HLP). By checking down the stack trace (top to bottom) we can see that we exited our code (module GENERIC segment _TEXT) at MainWndProc+7F; where did we go from there? Look above that line. We called ShowWindow(); ShowWindow() got 7 bytes of code executed when it called DebugBreak(). Debug-Break is used to generate an INT3 which, if we've got a debugger running, would cause the debugger to become active –ie., an error has surely been detected at this point! To take this any further we really need to go to offset 7F in MainWndProc to see what was passed to ShowWindow().

This is what the MainWndProc code looks like when viewed in CodeView with *Mixed Source and Assembler* selected :

```
LRESULT __export CALLBACK MainWndProc
(
                HWND            hWnd
                ,UINT           uMessage
                ,WPARAM         wParam
                ,LPARAM         lParam
        )
        {
09B7:01F0 8CD0                  MOV             AX,SS
09B7:01F2 C8240000             ENTER           0024,00
...
other prologue code
...


                switch(uMessage)
09B7:01FB 8B460C MOV           AX, WORD PTR [BP+0C]
09B7:01FE E9B500 JMP           02B6
                {
...
...
```

The MainWndProc code actually starts (it first instruction is at) 09B7:01F0 where the *smart* call-back prologue code begins. If we add 7F (From –GE-NERIC!_TEXT:MainWndProc+7F) to this address we should get to point in our program where we exited it and entered Windows. This was just before the error occurred. 01F0 + 7F = 026F = 09B7:026F. Let's look further down the code at that address now :

```
...
 226:           ShowWindow(hWnd, SW_SHOWNORMAL);
09B7:026A FF760E PUSH WORD PTR [BP+0E] ; BK1
09B7:026D 6A01                  PUSH 01
09B7:026F 9A1711E705            CALL 05E7:1117
```

What we see here is (at source line 226) the 'C' code ShowWindow(hWnd, SW_SHOWNORMAL);. The assembly code shows that the values passed as actual parameters to the function are hWnd, push word ptr [bp+0e], and 01, which is the value of SW_SHOWNORMAL. When these are pushed we call the function at address 05E7:1117 which from the source code we can tell is the Windows ShowWindow() function. So if this is where it all started to go wrong what can be the problem? Here's where you need to start working back from the app - Windows exit point. Here's a small extract from the 'C' source that shows the call to ShowWindow() and the *real* problem :

```
 220:   if(hWnd = NULL)
 221:   {
 222:           //...
 223:   }
 224:   else
 225:   {
 226:           ShowWindow(hWnd, SW_SHOWNORMAL);
```

```
227:   }
```

We can see from this piece of code that hWnd (passed to the function) has had zero (hWnd = NULL) assigned to it! What was almost certainly meant was a conditional test –if(hWnd == NULL)! The code above <u>always</u> results in ShowWindow() being called with a window handle value of 0!!! (Note that this could have been avoided by using -W4 -WX as at warning level 4 the compiler warns you about the assignment in a conditional expression).

☐ Abort Break Exit Ignore

What does Abort, Break, Exit or Ignore mean?

Abort means terminates Windows. Control will be passed back to DOS or to the debugger, if one was running. Break causes a breakpoint interrupt to occur, ie. an INT3 which is usually trapped by a debugger. If a debugger is running, control passes to the debugger as if you had set a breakpoint in the app's code. In this case, the CS:IP register pair point to an INT3 instruction, ie. you're usually faced with a screen full of assembler in which an INT3 is the current line. To continue execution, or to enable single-stepping, you must change the instruction pointer (IP) register to the address of the next instruction –if you don't know it you're in trouble! If you respond *Break* and no debugger is running, this option terminates Windows just as though you had responded *Abort*. *Exit* causes the application <u>only</u> to be terminated, ie. the Windows' session continues but the app is closed. Windows calls FatalAppExit() when you select this option and passes that function a pointer to the string *Terminating Application*. *Ignore* causes the error to be ignored and the app continues to run (some faults cannot be ignored, ie. a general protection violation caused by attempting to execute an invalid instruction). Lastly there are two pretty much undocumented responses you can make –SPACE and/or NEWLINE instructs the debugging libraries to re-display the debugging message. This is very helpful if the stack trace for the message is exceptionally long.

☐ What do the fatal exit codes means?

For a complete (?) list of messages output by the system search in the 3.1 SDK help file under Debugging *Messages* (print out what you find and read it –it's interesting, Oh by the way, its 23 A4 pages long!), for a list of fatal exit codes see Appendix 'C' (C.3) page 251 in the SDK's Programming Tools manual. Another good way to *get in to* the help system information on debugging is to choose *Overviews'*, *Windows Debugging Version* from WINHELP using WINSDKWH.HLP.

Some fatal exit codes are NOT documented –every version of Windows contains some of these. If you find you get a fatal exit that is not documented report the exit code to Microsoft Support or post a message querying the exit code on a good BBS like Compuserve.

☐ Going non-debug from debug and back again

Developers can switch between the debugging and non-debugging libraries by running SWITCH.BAT via either N2D.BAT (non to Debug) or D2N.BAT (debug to non); depending upon how you've set things up the whole process takes just a few seconds (see Miscellaneous chapter for a VERY small application that can be used to automate this –please!). To use the debugging libraries you need either a dumb terminal connected to your machine's AUX (usually COM1) port or an application like DBWIN (one of the sample applications shipped with the Microsoft SDK). If you use a debugging terminal set up your machine's COM1 port in your AUTOEXEC.BAT FILE so that it matches the terminal. I use an old Olivetti M15 (yes, its the one mentioned earlier!) running an MSDOS public domain terminal emulation package; the package is loaded automatically and expects data at 1200 baud, no parity bit, 8 data bits and 1 stop bit. My AUTOEXEC.BAT file contains the line @mode com1,1200,n,8,1. Ensuring that everything's megatastic!

Note that by changing the baud speed rate of the port from within Windows that you can confuse the terminal, ie. changes made in Windows can apparently affect the *real* port settings so don't go playing about with terminal (unless you want to see some interesting debug output) or the *Ports* section in control panel! I've found that using a baud speed that's greater than 2400 can cause <u>me</u> problems, I emphasise *me* here. Probably due to the software or the cables (or something) I use; I just loose it a couple of seconds after switching to say 9600 baud.

☐ Parameter Validation

3.1 debug and retail versions also perform parameter validation. Informing you that a SelectObject() on a GDI object with a handle value of 0 is an example of parameter validation. Earlier versions of Windows used to simply trust you, ie. they were gullible and believed anything you told them; if you said select this invalid object it would! The result was often that Windows would ultimately screw up in some way, perhaps even hang or GPF on you. It was easy to blame Windows of course, and in a way quite rightly, after all, shouldn't an operating system check stuff, ie. shouldn't it look before it leaps?! Microsoft got so fed up with badly behaving applications giving Windows a bad name (motto: Shit Happens) that it decided to make it harder for *bad apps* to survive, thus now we have parameter validation and apps such as Dr. Watson which can show a user that it wasn't Windows that screwed up –it was app X etc! Moral of this story? Develop using every debugging aid at your disposal; you'll produce a more robust app, users won't embarrass you by sending you Dr. Watson logs and fellow developers won't send you debugging terminal listings!

☐ interaction with the debug libs

As far as applications are concerned they interact with the debugging libraries either not at all, through a few select APIs like FatalExit() or through a structure called WINDEBUGINFO and a function called DebugOutput() which were both introduced in 3.1. The WINDEBUGINFO structure looks like this and is defined in WINDOWS.H:

```
typedef struct tagWINDEBUGINFO {
    UINT     flags;
    DWORD    dwOptions;
    DWORD    dwFilter;
    char     achAllocModule[8];
    DWORD    dwAllocBreak;
    DWORD    dwAllocCount;
} WINDEBUGINFO;
```

An application interacts most fully with the debugging libraries through this structure. The structure contains current system-debugging information for the debugging version of 3.1. The information is read using GetWinDebugInfo() and set using SetWinDebugInfo() –any task calling SetWinDebugInfo() sets the debugging library's state for the entire Windows' session and not just for the calling task. One function relies on certain system-debugging information being set before it can be used (to a degree), that function is DebugOutput() which we'll get to shortly. Here's what the WINDEBUGINFO structure's members are all about :

flag**s**

> Specifies which members of the WINDEBUGINFO structure are valid. This member can be one or more of the following values:

Value	Meaning
DI_OPTIONS	dwOptions member is valid.
WDI_FILTER	dwFilter member is valid.
WDI_ALLOCBREAK	achAllocModule, dwAllocBreak, and dwAllocCount members are valid.

dwOptions

> Specifies debugging options. This member is valid only if WDI_OPTIONS is specified in the flags member. It can be one or more of the following values:
>
> DBO_CHECKHEAP
> DBO_BUFFERFILL
> DBO_DISABLEGPTRAPPING
> DBO_CHECKFREE
> DBO_INT3BREAK
> DBO_NOFATALBREAK
> DBO_NOERRORBREAK
> DBO_WARNINGBREAK
> DBO_TRACEBREAK
>
> See later section for explanation of each constant.

dwFilter

Specifies filtering options for DBF_TRACE messages. (Normally, trace messages are not sent to the debug terminal.) This member can be one or more of the following values and is valid only if WDI_FIL-TER is specified in the flags member:

DBF_KRN_MEMMAN
DBF_KRN_LOADMODULE
DBF_KRN_SEGMENTLOAD
DBF_APPLICATION
DBF_DRIVER
DBF_PENWIN
DBF_MMSYSTEM
DBF_GDI
DBF_USER
DBF_KERNEL

See later section for explanation of each constant.

achAllocModule

Specifies the name of the application module. (This can be different from the name of the executable file.) This cannot be the name of a dynamic-link library (DLL). The name is limited to 8 characters.

dwAllocBreak

Specifies the number of global or local memory allocations to allow before failing allocation requests. When the count of allocations reaches the number specified in this member, that allocation and all subsequent allocations fail. If this member is zero, no allocation break is set, but the system counts allocations and reports the current count in the dwAllocCount member.

dwAllocCount

Current count of allocations. (This information is typically retrieved by calling the GetWinDebugInfo function.)

The achAllocModule, dwAllocBreak, and dwAllocCount just effect a single module –that module is *named* in achAllocModule (note that this is an application module name and not an EXE file name. Note also that the module name is a max of eight characters). These members can be used to ensure that an application performs correctly in out-of-memory conditions, ie. that its memory oriented exception handling is good. However dwAllocBreak affects all allocations made within the context of the module whose name appears in achAllocModule so even allocations made by the system fail once the break count is reached, ie. calls to such functions as CreateWindowEx(), CreateBrush(), and BeginPaint() may fail as well therefore this tests your exception handling wrapper placed around Windows' API calls too!

Let's just for the moment take a closer look at two of the members of WINDE-BUGINFO –dwFilter and dwOptions.

These two members can be visualised by using the Microsoft SDK sample (and VERY useful) application DBWIN.EXE; here's DBWIN's *Settings* dialog box. This application is very useful for getting a good understanding of the various WINDEBUGINFO members; indeed you can describe the effect of any member of the structure by understanding how the various structure members (and possible values) are used in DBWIN :

The diagram above shows how the dwOptions and dwFilter WINDEBUGINFO members map to the dialog's controls. The section on the left hand side maps entirely

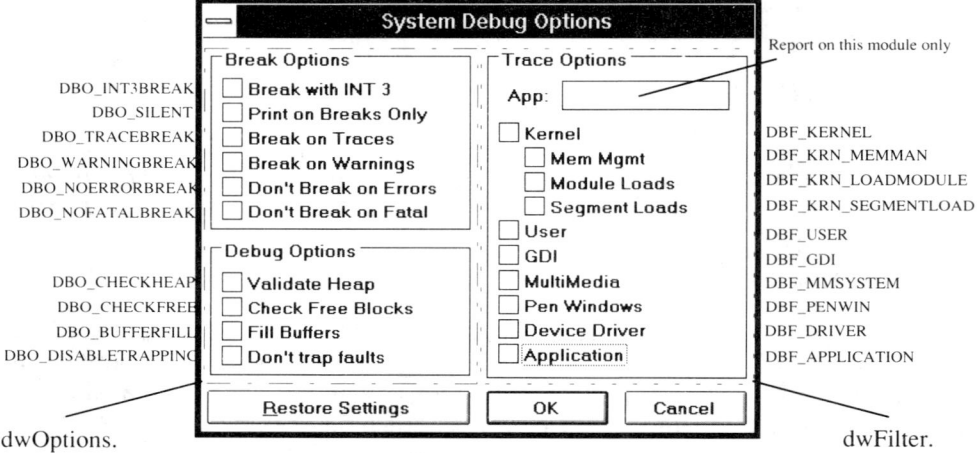

DBWIN's 'Settings...' Dialog.

to dwOptions while the section on the right maps entirely to dwFilter. The control names are not the same as the possible constant names so I have shown each constant value against the individual control that is responsible for setting/resetting it.

The *App:* field in DBWIN allows you to see only messages related to a particular application. Normally, DBWIN will display all debug messages in the system; if you enter an application's module name in this entry field, only messages for that application are displayed. You must enter the application module name as found in the application's .DEF file; note that this may be different from the file name of the application –Note that this does NOT relate to the achAllocModule member of the WINDEBUGINFO structure; note also that this control is related to DebugTaskState= [Windows] variable.

dwOptions flags are :

DBO_CHECKHEAP   0x0001

Checks the consistency of global and local heaps before every memory management call. Performs local heap checking after any LocalXXX() function call. Only affects the global heap if set as the default boot-time settings, ie. saved with File, Save Debug Settings. Only affects local heaps if set before heap is created and initialised, ie. before the application is started. This facility replaces the old WIN.INI entry shown below.

[Kernel]

EnableHeapChecking=1.

DBO_BUFFERFILL   0x0004

Fill buffers passed to Windows' APIs with 0xF9. This ensures that the supplied buffer is writeable. It also helps detect overwrite problems when supplied buffer size is not large enough –some APIs do not *know* how big the caller's buffer is, eg. GetWindowText() etc. Also note that some applications may not run with this option turned on. Reason –the supplied buffer is actually smaller than specified in the count parameter, thus causing an overwrite of application data.

DBO_DISABLEGPTRAPPING 0x0010

Disable hooking of the fault interrupt vectors such as GP and stack overflow faults (FatalExit(-1)). This option is typically not used, or useful, for normal application development because you can get many bogus traps related to parameter validation that aren't errors, also many faults would normally be handled by the system and restarted, setting this flag prevents that from happening. Result –generation of faults that would not otherwise be apparent to the developer/user. This is the same as the old WIN.INI entry show below.

[Kernel]

DisableGPTrapping=1

DBO_CHECKFREE   0x0020

Fills all freed (and free) local heap memory objects with 0xFB. All newly allocated memory is checked to ensure it's still filled with 0xFBs. This checks to see that no one has written into a free local heap memory block. To use DBO_CHECKFREE you must also specify DBO_CHECKHEAP. This facility replaces the old WIN.INI entry show below.

[Kernel]

EnableFreeChecking=1

DBO_INT3BREAK   0x0100

Break to debugger with simple INT 3 rather than a call to FatalExit(). Does not generate a stack backtrace.

DBO_NOFATALBREAK   0x0400

Does not break with *Abort, Break, Exit or Ignore* prompt if a DBF_FATAL error occurs.

DBO_NOERRORBREAK   0x0800

Does not break with *Abort, Break, Exit or Ignore* prompt if a DBF_ERROR error occurs. Also applies to invalid parameter warnings.

DBO_WARNINGBREAK   0x1000

Break with *Abort, Break, Exit or Ignore* prompt if a DBF_WARNING message occurs (normally, DBF_WARNING messages are displayed on the debugging terminal but no break occurs). Also applies to invalid parameter warnings.

DBO_TRACEBREAK   0x2000

Break with *Abort, Break, Exit or Ignore* on any DBF_TRACE message, but only if it matches the DebugFilter –**you must have something like DBF_APPLICATION | DBF_TRACE to see this work**.

DBO_SILENT   0x8000

No warning, error, or fatal messages are displayed on the debugging terminal unless a stack trace and *Abort, Break, Exit or Ignore* would occur. Note, Microsoft say 'We don't recommend the use of this flag -- it can cause you to miss or ignore many warnings that are in fact bugs that should be fixed'.

dwFilter flags are :

DBF_KRN_MEMMAN0x0001

Enables KERNEL messages related to local and global memory management.

DBF_KRN_LOADMODULE0x0002

Enables KERNEL messages related to module loading.

DBF_KRN_SEGMENTLOAD0x0004

Enables KERNEL messages related to segment loading.

DBF_APPLICATION0x0008

Enables trace messages originating from an application.

DBF_DRIVER0x0010

Enables trace messages originating from device drivers.

DBF_PENWIN0x0020

Enables trace messages originating from PENWIN.

DBF_MMSYSTEM0x0040

Enables trace messages originating from MMSYSTEM.

DBF_GDI0x0400

Enables trace messages originating from GDI.

DBF_USER0x0800

Enables trace messages originating from USER.

DBF_KERNEL0x1000

Enables any trace message originating from KERNEL. (This is a combination of DBF_KRN_MEMMAN, DBF_KRN_LOADMODULE, and DBF_KRN_SEG-MENTLOAD.)

Windows' current debugging state can be read using GetWinDebugInfo() and amended using SetWinDebugInfo() (all apart from dwAllocCount). DBWIN uses both these functions to change the debugging state/capabilities based upon a user's request.

See section on DebugOutput() for more on how to use the WINDEBUGINFO structure.

Some of the options/configurations available affect execution speed more than others. The debugging libraries are often thought of as *slow* and as a consequence many developers turn them off, ie. they switch to the non-debug libraries. The performance of the libraries can vary considerably depending upon what you want from the Windows' debugging system, ie. if you want to check the heap and have local buffers filled and checked by using DBO_CHECKHEAP and DBO_BUFFER-FILL –well, this will obviously *add* to your application's execution time as Windows is doing a lot more work behind the scenes. Bear this in mind when setting the dwOptions member of the WINDEBUGINFO structure. I often turn everything off in DBWIN to increase performance (which is the default state of the debug libs); note however that DBWIN, and the debug libs, will still report <u>any</u> warning, error or fatal error.

The debugging system always reports warnings, error, and fatal exits irrespective of the value of dwFilter. dwFilter affects only trace messages which mean by their very nature that no error has occurred and simple information only is being passed to the debugging terminal. By changing the dwOptions member you can for example specify whether or not an *error* actually causes a break, ie. an *Abort, Break, Exit or Ignore* prompt (DBO_NOERRORBREAK). You can specify that a *trace* should cause a break (DBO_TRACEBREAK), or that the system should remain on the whole silent (DBO_SILENT); each of these settings may be changed as required from running code.

If an application makes such a change the change may be made *visual* by using DBWIN's *Settings...* dialog (shown above), indeed, DBWIN's dialog is very useful for checking that the changes your application has made are the correct ones, ie. you can *see* the changes you've made by popping up DBWIN's *settings* dialog. In other words, to test your use of SetWinDebugInfo() check DBWIN's display!

☐ Static Changes

You can make a set of *default* debug settings by changing the following WIN.INI entries (or use DBWIN's *Save Debug Settings* menu item) :

[Windows]

DebugFilter=0x0008

DebugOptions=0x2000

These entries are read by Windows and used at the beginning of each new Windows' session. The default values are 0x0000. DBWIN also reads these (via a call to GetWin-DebugInfo() coz the system's already read them and used them) when it's started; so again you can *see* what's set by using DBWIN's *Settings...* dialog. Additionally DBWIN may set another [Windows] entry :

DebugTaskFilter=GENERIC

This entry is used by DBWIN to set the *App:* entry in its *Settings...* dialog. If set DBWIN only reports messages originating from, or errors caused by, the named module. When used selectively this can be used to improve system performance. **Note that if you have a debugging terminal and DBWIN that you can get two sets of debugging messages by using this feature. If you've selected, say, GENERIC as your module in** *App:* and elected to *send* debug output to *Window', but also selected everything else in Trace Options* the *real* debugging terminal will show those messages for everything other than GENERIC whilst DBWIN shows just those message for GENERIC (in its window), this feature can be very useful for seeing the system's messages for, say, loading GENERIC's resources separately to the trace messages from GENERIC.

The static settings are either created using DBWIN (or an app like it) or by using your favourite editor. The easiest way to do it is with DBWIN. Select what debugging options you require from DBWIN's *Settings...* dialog and then save those settings by selecting the *Save Debug Settings* option. You now find that DBWIN has updated WIN.INI to reflect your selections. If you want to do this using an editor you'll need the SDK docs or at the very least WINDOWS.H to determine the required values –see WINDOWS.H extract at the beginning of this chapter for all the information you require.

☐ OutputDebugString()

```
void WINAPI OutputDebugString(LPCSTR lpszOutputString);
@code sm ind =
LPCSTR lpszOutputString; /* Pointer to string to display */
```

The OutputDebugString function displays the specified character string on the debugging terminal; if a debugger is running the string may appear instead *in* the debugger. If a debugging terminal isn't running (or something like it, eg. DBWIN.EXE) then Windows will produce a system modal message box informing your user that it cannot write to device AUX. If you use this function you must have something (even a modem) connected to AUX/COM1. Actually there are a few alternatives although you probably don't want to do the second one as it involves changing your user's system configuration?

1   You can protect against using OutputDebugString() on the run-time system (where typically users don not have a suitable device attached to their COM port) by detecting the debugging version of Windows from code; use GetSystemMetrics() :

```
bDebug = GetSystemMetrics(SM_DEBUG);
...
...

if(bDebug == TRUE)
{
  OutputDebugString(...);
}
```

The call above to OutputDebugString() only takes place on a system where the Windows debugging libraries are in use.

2   You can insert the following in their SYSTEM.INI files

```
[Debug]
OutputTo=nul
```

This tells Windows to throw the debug output away.

3   Use conditional compilation on your retail build to remove them.

Just following up on 2 for a second; if you wanted to you could direct this output to a file using :

```
[Debug]
OutputTo=c:\win31\fataex.log
```

This causes Windows to log any *debug* output to the file c:\win31\fatalex.log. The file is deleted everytime Windows is restarted. It would have been better to have *older* debug information appended to this file I feel. Anyway, by using OuputTo= in your user's SYSTEM.INIs you can effectively monitor the state of your application (as they test it) –here's an example of how to do this over multiple sessions :

1   Rename the user's WIN.COM file to WIN1.COM

2   Write the following WIN.BAT batch file (amend directories etc as required) :

```
\tick "Starting Windows"          > c:\win31\start.txt
win1 %1 %2 %3
c:\win31\tick "Stopped Windows"   > c:\win31\stop.txt
type c:\win31\start.txt                    >> c:\win31\log.log
type c:\win31\fatalex.log                  >> c:\win31\log.log
type c:\win31\stop.txt                     >> c:\win31\log.log
```

This batch file effectively replaces WIN.COM for the user. The batch file makes use of a program called *tick* which outputs (to stdout) the current time and an optional comment supplied by its caller (tick's code is shown lower down). Here we see *tick* being passed *Starting Windows* etc. The output of tick is redirected to the file *start.txt* (note that any old *start.txt* will be overwritten). Windows is then started (win %1 %2 %3); up to three parameters are passed to WIN1.COM. When Windows closes down, the batch file once again gets control; it again calls tick and finally concatenates three files into the file log.log (note that any old log.log is appended to). The Windows' session start and ending times are retrieved from start/stop.txt and the contents of fatalex.log is sandwiched between them. Where does fatalex.log come from? As detailed above its created by Windows at our request; here's a very small section of SYSTEM.INI :

3.

```
[debug]
OutputTo=c:\win31\fatalex.log
```

We also need to modify WIN.INI to tell Windows what sort of output we want:

4

```
[Windows]
DebugFilter=0x0008      'Enable 'TRACE' messages from applications.
DebugOptions=0x2000     'DBO_TRACEBREAK
```

You can now place a *comment* in the log file from your code using either OutputDebugString() or DebugOutput(). If you use OutputDebugString() the output will always appear in the log file; if you choose DebugOutput() you must ensure that your beta testers are using the debugging libraries (discussed later). Typical output might look like this :

```
Wed Dec 23 04:05:15 1992
STARTING WINDOWS

wn Kernel: GlobalWire(17B6 of GDI) (try GlobalLock)
wn Kernel: GlobalWire(137F of WINOLDAP) (try GlobalLock)
wn Kernel: WINOLDAP GlobalCompact(FFFFFFFF), discarding segments

Wed Dec 23 04:05:38 1992
STOPPED WINDOWS


Wed Dec 23 04:05:55 1992
```

```
STARTING WINDOWS

wn Kernel: GlobalWire(17B6 of GDI) (try GlobalLock)
wn GENERIC Version of generic with loadsa debug info in it - sorry!
wn GENERIC hWnd=1C1C uMessage=F wParam=0 lParam=0
wn Kernel: GlobalWire(137F of WINOLDAP) (try GlobalLock)
wn GENERIC hWnd=1C1C uMessage=121 wParam=2 lParam=1008
wn Kernel: WINOLDAP GlobalCompact(FFFFFFFF), discarding segments
wn GENERIC hWnd=1C1C uMessage=212 wParam=0 lParam=0
About to try EX001001
Tried and failed! - EX001001
In Error handler -
Recursing!
Error in error handler - Oh s**t - calling static error handler.
Error in static error handler - about to fatal exit
err GENERIC  Error handler died @1005:838A, reason - recursed the stack to
death!
wn GENERIC hWnd=1C1C uMessage=101 wParam=D lParam=C01C0001
wn GENERIC hWnd=1C1C uMessage=8 wParam=1B24 lParam=0
wn GENERIC hWnd=1C1C uMessage=82 wParam=0 lParam=0

Wed Dec 23 04:06:24 1992
STOPPED WINDOWS
```

The necessary code in GENERIC to output this to the log file looked something like this :

```
OutputDebugString(lpszMessage);

DebugOutput(DBF_TRACE | DBF_APPLICATION, lpszFormatString, ...)
```

Looks like this :

```
/* Very small application to send the current time and a comment to
stdout. */
#include <time.h>
#include <stdio.h>
#include <string.h>

int main(int argc, char ** argv)
{
    auto time_t        ltime;
    auto struct tm  *  gmt;

    time(&ltime);

    gmt = gmtime(&ltime);

    printf("\n\n%s",asctime(gmt));

    /*
    ** If caller supplied a comment output it.
    */
    if(argc >= 1)
    {
        printf("%s\n\n",strupr(*(argv + 1)));
    }
    else
```

```
    {
        puts("\n");;
    }

    return 0;
}
```

The bottom line of all of this is that by using the technique outlined above you can effectively keep a watch on your Beta testers/uses using your app. You could place the log.log file on a network and monitor it, ie. if you spot that someone's been generating a interesting messages you could give 'em a call –they'll swear Big Brother's about! See texts (not in this book (apart from An aside on LEX in DLL chapter)) on using UNIX type tools like GREP, AWK and LEX to easily parse error logs such as these.

OutputDebugString() does not provide some of the niceties of DebugOutput() like formatting of arguments but when used with wsprint() (or use wvsprintf() to write your own OutputDebugString() version of DebugOutput()) provides platform independent capabilities for the outputting of messages to either a log file, DBWIN (or something like it) or a monochrome monitor or debugging terminal. Use *message*$\backslash n \backslash r$ to force a newline into the function's output.

OutputDebugString() Misc -

Note that OutputDebugString() is also part of the *standard* Windows NT API.

OutputDebugString() can also cause a system crash under 3.0 if the string to be output is longer than 270 characters and you're running CodeView –the bottom line is to make sure that your debug message is less than 270 chars long!

☐ DebugOutput()

DebugOutput() is not available on the run-time version of Windows and is therefore, unlike OutputDebugString(), quite safe to call from within your code (). The retail build has the function but all the function code does is return! It's this function that the Windows' debug libs use to report warning and errors etc to you the developer; of course, you can use them yourself to report similar warnings and errors.

To use DebugOutput() you must first import the function as it's not actually *in* the LIBW.LIB import library. The easiest way to do this is to add the following to your .def file :

```
IMPORTS
KERNEL._DebugOutput
```

Note that the imported function's name begins with a leading underscore; this is because the function's compiled using the 'C' calling convention –it has to be as it's a variadic function, ie. it's a little like printf() in that it can be passed any number of arguments of various types. You pass the function at least two parameters, a UINT and a LPCSTR. The UINT specifies the type of message to be sent to the debugging terminal. This parameter can be one of the following :

Value   Meaning

DBF_TRACE   The message reports that no error has occurred and supplies information that may simply be useful during a debugging session; **you should OR this with DBF_APPLICATION.**

DBF_WARNING   The message reports a situation that may or may not be an error, depending on the circumstances.

DBF_ERROR   The message reports an error resulting from a failed call to a Windows' function. The application continues to run.

DBF_FATAL   The message reports an error that will terminate the application.

Examples :

■DebugOutput(DBF_TRACE | DBF_APPLICATION, "Private INI entry does not exist\n");

■DebugOutput(DBF_WARNING, "Old function vInit() used - use vInitNew() instead\n");

■DebugOutput(DBF_ERROR, "Passed parameter hTab invalid - %X\n", hTab);

■DebugOutput(DBF_FATAL, "Not enough local heap space to continue!\n");

To use DBF_TRACE you MUST use DBF_TRACE together with DBF_APPLICATION, failure to do so will cause no trace message to appear on the user's debugging terminal.

Because its easy to change the system's debug settings via DBWIN or SetWinDebugInfo() It's sometime handy to write a small function to *do* all your trace output. This function ensures that *Application* tracing is turned on in the debug libs :

```
void DebugMessage(LPSTR lpszComment)
{
    /*
    ** Couple of WINDEBUGINFOs, one for the
    ** old - the other for the new.
    */
    auto WINDEBUGINFO Oldwdi;
    auto WINDEBUGINFO Newwdi;

    /*
    ** Clean new one. _fmemset used so this can be used in a DLL.
    */
    _fmemset(&Newwdi, 0x0, sizeof(WINDEBUGINFO));

    /*
    ** Set it up. WDI_FILTER is the actual minimum required
    ** in this function  - the others don't do any harm and
    ** are there for completeness only.
```

```
    */
    Newwdi.flags     = WDI_OPTIONS |
                       WDI_FILTER  |
                       WDI_ALLOCBREAK;

    /*
    ** Include this line to cause 'Abort, Retry, Exit or Ignore'
    ** on a trace.
    */
    /*
    Newwdi.dwOptions = DBO_TRACEBREAK;
    */

    /*
    ** Just interested in what the application does, if
    ** you want  to  see  stuff  for other modules like
    ** KERNEL include as appropriate.
    */
    Newwdi.dwFilter  = DBF_APPLICATION;

    /*
    ** Get the old ready to restore it.
    */
    GetWinDebugInfo(
                &Oldwdi
               ,WDI_OPTIONS |
                WDI_FILTER  |
                WDI_ALLOCBREAK
               );

    /*
    ** Set up according to new settings.
    */
    SetWinDebugInfo(&Newwdi);

    /*
    ** Output message.
    */
    DebugOutput(DBF_TRACE | DBF_APPLICATION,"%s\n",lpszComment);

    /*
    ** Restore old settings.
    */
    SetWinDebugInfo(&Oldwdi);

    return VOIDRETURN;
}
```

DebugMessage essentially *pushes* the old debugging state before setting the new debugging state so that trace messages from an application are always output. When it's output the message passed as its single parameter it *pops* the old state back again. A call to the function would look something like this :

```
DebugMessage("Creating Main Window\n");
```

We could easily expand this simple function so that you could pass it a format specification string and a set of arguments to output. This would provide a wrapper around DebugOutput() so that it always outputs trace messages from a calling application :

```
...
#include <stdarg.h>
...

VOID CDECL NEAR DebugMessageVar(LPCSTR lpszFormatString, ...)
{
    /*
    ** Couple of WINDEBUGINFOs, one for the
    ** old - the other for the new.
    */
    auto WINDEBUGINFO   Oldwdi;
    auto WINDEBUGINFO   Newwdi;

    /*
    ** Buffer into which we write our args according to
    ** lpszFormatString.
    */
    auto char           carBuffer[255];

    /*
    ** For walking the args.
    */
    auto va_list        pArg;

    /*
    ** Clean new one.
    */
    _fmemset(&Newwdi, 0x0, sizeof(WINDEBUGINFO));

    /*
    ** Set it up. WDI_FILTER is the actual minimum required
    ** in this function  - the others don't do any harm and
    ** are there for completeness only.
    */
    Newwdi.flags    = WDI_OPTIONS |
                      WDI_FILTER  |
                      WDI_ALLOCBREAK;

    /*
    ** Just interested in what the application does, if
    ** you want  to  see  stuff  for other modules like
    ** KERNEL include as appropriate.
    */
    Newwdi.dwFilter = DBF_APPLICATION;

    /*
    ** Get the old ready to restore it.
    */
    GetWinDebugInfo(
                &Oldwdi
                ,WDI_OPTIONS |
                 WDI_FILTER  |
                 WDI_ALLOCBREAK
                );
```

```
/*
** Set up according to new settings.
*/
SetWinDebugInfo(&Newwdi);


/*
** Output message.
*/
va_start(pArg, lpszFormatString);

wvsprintf(
          &carBuffer[0]
          ,lpszFormatString
          ,(LPSTR)pArg
          );

va_end(pArg);

DebugOutput(
          DBF_TRACE | DBF_APPLICATION
          ,&carBuffer[0]
          );

/*
** Restore old settings.
*/
SetWinDebugInfo(&Oldwdi);

return VOIDRETURN;
}
```

This function, DebugMessageVar, uses macros from STDARG.H to provide a *variadic* wrapper to what is essentially the earlier DebugMessage function. You can call this function like this :

```
DebugMessageVar("hWnd = %X, wParam = %X, carBuff = %s\n", hWnd, wParam,
carBuff);
```

This *is a kinda* DebugOutput() that guarantees to provide debug terminal output via DBF_TRACE –nice!

☐ Building in debug info

When you build your applications, or more importantly your DLLs (as the latter are typically shared, or used by many client tasks) try to include some debug processing. Look at the Windows SDK shipped with the Microsoft SDK and C7; it includes special debug only versions of those all important system DLLs. It would be nice if more commercially available DLLs shipped with debug versions but unfortunately not many do. Or, if you don't want to go to the trouble of shipping two versions of your DLL, ship one, but make that DLL more intelligent and useful, ie. have it do debugging dependent upon whether or not the user is using the retail or debug version of Windows.

You may *insert* debugging information into your binary in many ways; remember that one of the most efficient ways is to use DebugOutput() as it's simply a *ret* in the retail version; remember also that OutputDebugString() <u>always</u> outputs, ie. if your using it in the retail version there could be trouble with *Can't write to device AUX:* (See notes on OutputTo= earlier). You might decide to do as Microsoft do, ship some symbolic information (in their case .SYM files) with your binary; you'll probably want to stop short of including the source however! To give you a taste of what such a DLL might look like here's an example.

☐ Example

This application (STACKS.EXE) and DLL (SELECT.DLL) work together to provide the user with a means to keep any number of windows at the top of the Z order stack, ie. to keep windows *top most'. The DLL does all of the work. So much so that you often wish you could simply run* the DLL without the app! Note that if you request the source code for this book (see Misc chapter for process) that the code for this app will be different –I've added a Windows' keyboard hook filter function so that you can call up stacks via a hot key.

The application's job is to simply load the DLL and call a function in it called bSetHook. After that the app just waits; it doesn't create any windows, doesn't register any windows' classes and doesn't have a window procedure.

bSetHook() sub-classes the Windows' desktop window so that it picks up all messages being passed to the desktop window. If the user double clicks the right mouse button on the desktop window (WM_RBUTTONDBLCLK) the sub-class window procedure in the DLL captures all mouse input to the window and changes the current cursor to a combination of the IDC_ARROW cursor and a stack of windows (shown later). The user now selects a window on the desktop and clicks the left mouse button over it. Again, and as the mouse is captured, the desktop sub-class window procedure gets the WM_LBUTTONDOWN message. When it's received it calls vDoReStack which is also defined within the DLL. This function is passed the window handle of the desktop window and the lParam of the WM_LBUTTONDOWN message. vDoReStack determines which window was clicked (positional information in passed in the mouse message's lParam) using WindowFromPoint(). It then determines whether or not this window is a top-level window or not and if it's not it finds the top level window that is related to it. After it has done that it looks at that window's words to see if it is a top-most window. If it's not it is made top-most, if it is already a top-most window it is made a non-top-most window, ie. it is released and may now descend from the top of the Z order stack.

There are various things that can go wrong in this app/DLL and of course all others that you can write; the difference however between this code and the usual is that this code does something about trapping and reporting errors. These errors are either reported to the user via FatalAppExit() or to the programmer via a combination of DebugOutput(), OutputDebugString() and FatalExit(). The DLL even has a special debugging function called vDoError whose job it is to format and report errors to either the user or the programmer (or sometimes both). Before I talk about this further let's see the code. First the application source for STACKS.EXE

The stacks.c file :

```
/*
** Small application showing how to use debug support in DLLs. Also shows
** how to write an application that exists almost entirely 'in' a DLL and
** how to write an application that doesn't create a window  nor register
** a class.
**
** All this application does (effectively) is 1. stay resident and 2. call
** two DLL functions.
*/


#define STRICT


#include <windows.h>
#include "stacks.h"

#pragma warning(disable:4100)
#pragma warning(disable:4001)


#define VOIDRETURN


/*
** In SELECT.DLL.
*/
extern BOOL __export FAR PASCAL bSetHook   (VOID);
extern BOOL __export FAR PASCAL bReSetHook (VOID);

/*
** In here.
*/
int             PASCAL WinMain    (HINSTANCE, HINSTANCE, LPSTR, int);


int PASCAL WinMain
(
  HINSTANCE    hInstance
 ,HINSTANCE    hPrevInstance
 ,LPSTR        lpszCmdLine
 ,int          nCmdShow
)
{
  /*
  ** For GetMessage().
  */
  auto MSG msg;
```

```
    if(hPrevInstance == NULL)
    {
        /*
        ** Install desktop hook.
        */
        if(bSetHook() == FALSE)
        {
            MessageBox(0, "Failed to get hook", NULL, MB_OK);

            return 0;
        }

    }
    /*
    ** Only one copy should run!
    */
    else
    {
        MessageBox(
                    0
                    ,"Stacks is alreay running on the system!"
                    ,"Stacks v. 1.0 By Peter J. Morris"
                    ,MB_OK | MB_TASKMODAL
                    );

        return 0;
    }

    /*
    ** Might get a task  message etc. Note tests have shown that
    ** an application that doesn't  create a  window might still
    ** receive messages other than a WM_QUIT like  a WM_PAINT or
    ** a WM_MOUSEMOVE!!
    */
    while(GetMessage(&msg, NULL, 0, 0))
    {
        TranslateMessage(&msg);
        DispatchMessage(&msg);
    }

    /*
    ** Application closing so un-hook desktop. Probably NEVER hit,
    ** ie. as windows will have to exit to close this app down it
    ** will probably never receive a WM_QUIT message!
    */
    bReSetHook();

    return msg.wParam;
}
```

Stacks.def :

```
NAME        STACKS

DESCRIPTION  'Stacks v. 1.0 - By Peter J. Morris'
```

```
EXETYPE        WINDOWS 3.1

PROTMODE

STUB        'WINSTUB.EXE'

CODE          PRELOAD MOVEABLE DISCARDABLE
DATA          PRELOAD MOVEABLE SINGLE

HEAPSIZE      1024
STACKSIZE     5120


IMPORTS
        KERNEL._DebugOutput
```

Stacks.rc :

```
#include "stacks.h"

STACKS ICON STACK.ICO
```

Stacks.h :

```
#define STACKS 100
```

Ok, so much for the app; here's the DLL code :

Select.c :

```
/*
** Small DLL that shows how to use some of the debugging support in your
** own DLLs. This DLL allows the user  to make any visible window a top-
** most window.  It also allows top-most windows to become non-top-most.
**
**
** A DLL cannot 'run' by itself, ie. it needs a task in order to execute,
** STACKS.EXE is that application.
*/



#define STRICT


#include <windows.h>
#include <stdlib.h>
#include <string.h>
#include <toolhelp.h>
#include "select.h"

#pragma warning(disable:4100)
#pragma warning(disable:4001)
```

```
#define VOIDRETURN

/*
** DLL FatalAppExit() code.
*/
#define HOOKINGERROR (0x0001)

/*
** Used in DebugOutput().
*/
#define TRACE (DBF_TRACE | DBF_APPLICATION)

#define _MAX_MESS 250

LRESULT    __export CALLBACK    lDesktopHook              (HWND,UINT ,WPARAM
,LPARAM);
BOOL       __export FAR  PASCAL bSetHook                  (VOID);
BOOL       __export FAR  PASCAL bReSetHook                (VOID);
BOOL                FAR  PASCAL LibMain                   (HINSTANCE ,WORD
,WORD ,LPSTR);
BOOL                FAR  PASCAL WEP                       (int);
HINSTANCE           NEAR PASCAL hInstAccessDLLhInst       (HINSTANCE);
WNDPROC             NEAR PASCAL fpprocAccessOldDeskProc   (WNDPROC);
VOID                NEAR PASCAL vDoReStack                (HWND, LPARAM);
VOID
    NEAR PASCAL vDoError                      (LPCSTR ,int ,BOOL);




/*
** Basic  libmain.  Calls  hInstAccessDLLhInst
** to store the DLL's module (instance) handle.
*/
BOOL FAR PASCAL LibMain
(
   HINSTANCE    hModule
  ,WORD         wDataSeg
  ,WORD         cbHeapSize
  ,LPSTR        lpszCmdLine
)
{
   if(cbHeapSize > 0)
   {
       UnlockData(0);
   }


   (VOID)hInstAccessDLLhInst(hModule);

   return TRUE;
}
```

```
/*
** Basic wep.
*/
BOOL FAR PASCAL WEP (int bSystemExit)
{
    return TRUE;
}




/*
** Used to  store DLL's module (instance) handle. Called initially with a
** non-NULL argument from LibMain() to get it to store the handle, called
** with NULL argument to retrieve stored handle value.
*/
HINSTANCE NEAR PASCAL hInstAccessDLLhInst(HINSTANCE hInst)
{
   /*
   ** Persistent holder for instance handle.
   */
   static HINSTANCE hInstance;

   if(hInst == NULL)
   {
       if((hInst = hInstance) == NULL)
       {
           DebugOutput(
                     TRACE
                   ,"hInstAccessDLLhInst. Caller gets NULL handle.\n"
                   );
       }
   }
   else
   {
       if(hInstance != NULL)
       {
           DebugOutput(
                     TRACE
                   ,"hInstAccessDLLhInst. Overwritten instance handle.\n"
                   );
       }


       hInstance = hInst;
   }

   return hInst;
}


/*
```

```
** Used to  store Desktop's original wndproc address. See
** hInstAccessDLLhInst function for further information as this one works
** just the same way.
*/
WNDPROC NEAR PASCAL fpprocAccessOldDeskProc(WNDPROC fpProc)
{
   /*
   ** Persistent holder for wndproc address.
   */
   static WNDPROC fpOldDeskProc;

   if(fpProc == NULL)
   {
       if((fpProc = fpOldDeskProc) == NULL)
       {
           DebugOutput(
                     TRACE
                    ,"fpprocAccessOldDeskProc. Caller gets NULL wndproc.\n"
                    );
       }
   }
   else
   {
       if(fpOldDeskProc != NULL)
       {
           DebugOutput(
                     TRACE
                    ,"hInstAccessDLLhInst. Overwritten wndproc.\n"
                    );
       }

       fpOldDeskProc = fpProc;
   }

   return fpProc;
}




/*
** Set up desktop window subclassing hook.
*/
BOOL __export FAR PASCAL bSetHook(VOID)
{
   /*
   ** Window handle of desktop window.
   */
   auto HWND hWndDesktop;

   /*
   ** Get desktop window handle.
   */
   hWndDesktop = GetDesktopWindow();

   /*
```

```
** Store desktop window's old wndproc address and set up a new one.
*/
if(fpprocAccessOldDeskProc(
                                (WNDPROC)GetWindowLong(
                                                        hWndDesktop
                                                        ,GWL_WNDPROC
                                                        )
                        ) != NULL
    )
{
    SetWindowLong(
                    hWndDesktop
                    ,GWL_WNDPROC
                    ,(LONG)lDesktopHook
                    );

    return TRUE;
}
else
{
    vDoError(
            "Sub-class hook. Failed to hook desktop."
            ,HOOKINGERROR
            ,TRUE
            );

    return FALSE;
}
}




/*
** Re-Set desktop window subclassing hook.
*/
BOOL __export FAR PASCAL bReSetHook(VOID)
{
    /*
    ** Old wndproc address for desktop window.
    */
    auto WNDPROC fpOldDeskProc;


    if((fpOldDeskProc = fpprocAccessOldDeskProc(NULL)) != NULL)
    {
        SetWindowLong(
                        GetDesktopWindow()
                        ,GWL_WNDPROC
                        ,(LONG)fpOldDeskProc
                        );

        return TRUE;
    }
    else
    {
        DebugOutput(
```

```
                    DBF_WARNING
                    ,"bReSetHook. Cannot get old wndproc address.\n"
                    );

        return FALSE;
    }
}




/*
**
** Changes the Z order position of a top level window. Passed window
** handle of the desktop window and the mouse position of  an lbuttondown
** which is  generated as part of the window selection process.
*/
VOID NEAR PASCAL vDoReStack(HWND hWndDesktop, LPARAM MouseCoOrd)
{
    /*
    ** Window under mouse co-ord.
    */
    auto HWND  hWndWindow;

    /*
    ** Ultimate 'top level' window in application
    ** of which hWndWindow is a window.
    */
    auto HWND  hWndTop;

    /*
    ** Mouse location - screen relative as we're the desktop.
    */
    auto POINT tPt;

    /*
    ** Get mouse pos of lbuttondown.
    */
    tPt = MAKEPOINT(MouseCoOrd);

    /*
    ** Get a window from the pos.
    */
    hWndWindow = WindowFromPoint(tPt);

    /*
    ** Ignore if it's the desktop itself.
    */
    'if(hWndWindow == hWndDesktop)
    {
        return VOIDRETURN;
    }

    /*
    ** Get 'top' window from window clicked on.
    */
```

```
    for(
        hWndTop = hWndWindow
        ;(hWndWindow = (HWND)GetWindowWord(hWndTop, GWW_HWNDPARENT)) != NULL
        ;hWndTop = hWndWindow
        )
    {
        // Nul statememt.
    }

    /*
    ** Final check before we access selected window's words.
    */
    if(IsWindow(hWndTop))
    {
        /*
        ** Z order position.
        */
        auto HWND hWndPos;

        /*
        ** Bring it to the top - it'll re-paint here.
        */
        BringWindowToTop(hWndTop);

        /*
        ** Determine if it's already top most or not,
        ** toggle its top most state.
        */
        hWndPos = GetWindowLong(
                                hWndTop
                                ,GWL_EXSTYLE
                                ) & WS_EX_TOPMOST
                    ? HWND_NOTOPMOST
                    : HWND_TOPMOST;

        SetWindowPos(
                    hWndTop
                    ,hWndPos
                    ,0,0,0,0
                    ,SWP_NOMOVE      |
                    SWP_NOSIZE      |
                    SWP_NOACTIVATE
                    );

    }
    else
    {
        vDoError(
                "vDoReStack. Found window (%X) not valid."
                ,0
                ,FALSE
                );
    }

    return VOIDRETURN;
}
```

```
/*
** Subclassing  wndproc for desktop. Just  interested  in  two  events  -
** WM_RBUTTONDBLCLK  and WM_LBUTTONDOWN. WM_RBUTTONDBLCLK is passed on (as
** are all  other  uninteresting  events) whereas WM_LBUTTONDOWN is thrown
** away. WM_RBUTTONDBLCLK signals us that a window is about to be se-
lected,
** WM_LBUTTONDOWN might tell us it's been selected.
*/
LRESULT __export CALLBACK lDesktopHook
(
   HWND     hWnd
  ,UINT     uMessage
  ,WPARAM   wParam
  ,LPARAM   lParam
)
{
   /*
   ** Set if we've captured the mouse, ie. we're looking for a window.
   */
   static BOOL bCaptured;

   switch(uMessage)
   {
      case WM_RBUTTONDBLCLK:
         {
            /*
            ** If we're already captured ignore further double clicks.
            */
            if(bCaptured == TRUE)
            {
               break;
            }

            /*
            ** Capture mouse input to ourselves so we can track mouse.
            */
            SetCapture(GetDesktopWindow());

            /*
            ** Set 'stack' cursor. No need to keep old cursor as
            ** desktop always has IDC_ARROW cursor.
            */
            SetCursor(
                   LoadCursor(
                           hInstAccessDLLhInst(NULL)
                          ,MAKEINTRESOURCE(STACKS)
                          )
                     );

            /*
            ** Set looking flag.
            */
```

```
                    bCaptured = TRUE;
                }
            break;

        case WM_LBUTTONDOWN:

            /*
            ** If we're looking we must've found a window.
            */
            if(bCaptured == TRUE)
            {
                /*
                ** Put desktop cursor back.
                */
                SetCursor(LoadCursor(NULL, IDC_ARROW));

                /*
                ** Let go of the mouse.
                */
                ReleaseCapture();

                /*
                ** Pass mouse pos and desktop window handle to function
                ** that'll do the top-most stuff.
                */
                vDoReStack(hWnd, lParam);

                /*
                ** Re-Set looking flag.
                */
                bCaptured = FALSE;

                /*
                ** As we processed it - throw it away.
                */
                return (LRESULT)0;
            }

            /*
            ** Not looking currently so pass it on.
            */
            else
            {
            }  // FALL THROUGH;

        default:
            /*
            ** Pass on to original window procedure.
            */
            break;
    }

    /*
    ** Pass on to original window procedure.
    */
    return CallWindowProc(
                    fpprocAccessOldDeskProc(NULL)
```

```
                          ,hWnd
                          ,uMessage
                          ,wParam
                          ,lParam
                          );
}




/*
** Debugging function. This function may be called from both the debug and
** non-debug versions of Windows.
**
** The function uses TOOLHELP to get the module handle for the calling
** task, this allows the  DLL  to retrieve the task's module name so that
** for DLLs, that may have many callers, the caller's actual module name
** may be output.
** This will be of assistance in determining the actual error. This
** function does   not   use  DebugOutput(), instead   it   uses   the
** following debug type functions :
**
** FatalExit(), FatalAppExit(), OutputDebugString().
**
** If the user is using  the 'retail' version OutputDebugString() is not
** called   as   it   causes 'no device - AUX' problems. Instead
** FatalAppExit() might be used.  The 'might' depends on  the value of
** the function's third parameter.
*/

VOID NEAR PASCAL vDoError
(
    LPCSTR   lpszMessage
   ,int      nFECode
   ,BOOL     bFatal
)
{
    /*
    ** Holds calling module's full name (inc path). Static as we're a DLL
    ** and we don't want to blow the caller's stack.
    */
    static char        carModuleName[_MAX_PATH];



    /*
    ** Holds a  debugging  message.  Static as we're a DLL and we don't
    ** want to blow the caller's stack. See section on SwitchStackTo() in
    ** Miscellaneous chapter.
    */
    static char        carMaxMessage[_MAX_MESS];

    auto char          carSeperator[] = " - ";
    /*
```

```
**  Calling task's task handle.
*/
auto    HTASK       hTask;


/*
**  Used in calling toolhelp.
*/
auto    TASKENTRY   tTe;


/*
**  Pointer used in parsing caller's module name.
*/
auto    LPSTR       pcModuleName;


/*
**  Set pointer to NULL - checked against it later to see if we actually
**  got a module name from toolhelp.
*/
pcModuleName = NULL;


/*
**  Get task handle of caller.
*/
hTask = GetCurrentTask();

/*
**  Init taskentry structure.
*/
tTe.dwSize = sizeof(TASKENTRY);

/*
**  Call toolhelp. If toolhelp found info on task hTask get the task's
**  module name. Only interested in last bit (not the path) so stick a
**  '\0' in  wherever  the  last '\' is. Set pointer to point a module
**  name.
*/
if(TaskFindHandle(&tTe, hTask) != 0)
{
    GetModuleFileName(tTe.hInst, &carModuleName[0], _MAX_PATH);

    pcModuleName = _fstrrchr(&carModuleName[0], (int)'\\');

    pcModuleName++;
}

/*
**  If we got a module name pointer will not be NULL.
*/
if(pcModuleName != NULL)
{
    /*
    **  Used for keeping track of length of message.
    */
```

```
    auto int nLen;

    /*
    ** Put module name into message buffer.
    */
    _fstrncpy(&carMaxMessage[0], pcModuleName, _MAX_MESS);

    /*
    ** Get buffer's current length.
    */
    nLen = lstrlen(&carMaxMessage[0]);

    /*
    ** Concat a ' - ' to it.
    */
    _fstrncat(
            &carMaxMessage[nLen]
            ,&carSeperator[0]
            , _MAX_MESS - nLen - sizeof(carSeperator)
            );

    /*
    ** Get length again.
    */
    nLen = lstrlen(&carMaxMessage[0]);

    /*
    ** Concat message to string so far.
    */
    _fstrncpy(
            &carMaxMessage[nLen]
            ,lpszMessage
            , _MAX_MESS - lstrlen(&carMaxMessage[0])
            );
}

/*
** If the debugging version...
*/
if(GetSystemMetrics(SM_DEBUG) != 0)
{
    /*
    ** If toolhelp worked...
    */
    if(pcModuleName != NULL)
    {
        /*
        ** Send module name and message to debug terminal.
        */
        OutputDebugString(&carMaxMessage[0]);
    }
    else
    {
        /*
        ** Send message to debug terminal.
        */
        OutputDebugString(lpszMessage);
```

```c
        }

        /*
        ** CR/LF for debug terminal.
        */
        OutputDebugString("\r\n");

        /*
        ** Fatal exit with passed code - stack trace on debug terminal.
        ** FatalExit() not called in non-debug as it would produce a
        ** non-helpful message box then close down the app. If you want
        ** to close down the app call with third parameter set to TRUE.
        */
        FatalExit(nFECode);
    }

    /*
    ** Should we close?
    */
    if(bFatal == TRUE)
    {
        /*
        ** If toolhelp worked...
        */
        if(pcModuleName != NULL)
        {
            /*
            ** Let programmer/user see full message.
            */
            FatalAppExit(0, &carMaxMessage[0]);
        }
        else
        {
            /*
            ** Let programmer/user see just message.
            */
            FatalAppExit(0, &lpszMessage[0]);
        }
    }

    return VOIDRETURN;
}
```

Select.def :

```
LIBRARY       SELECT

DESCRIPTION   'Stacks DLL - By Peter J. Morris'

EXETYPE       WINDOWS 3.1

PROTMODE

STUB          'WINSTUB.EXE'

CODE          PRELOAD MOVEABLE DISCARDABLE
```

```
DATA          PRELOAD MOVEABLE SINGLE

HEAPSIZE      1024
STACKSIZE     0

EXPORTS
    WEP                       @1 RESIDENTNAME
    lDesktopHook              @2 RESIDENTNAME
    bSetHook                  @3
    bReSetHook                @4

IMPORTS
    KERNEL._DebugOutput
```

Select.rc :

```
#include "select.h"

/*
** Want the cursor to  be preloaded
** and non-discardable so that it's
** always visible quickly.
*/

STACKS CURSOR PRELOAD MOVEABLE STACK.CUR
```

Select.h :

```
#define STACKS 100
```

Stack.cur :

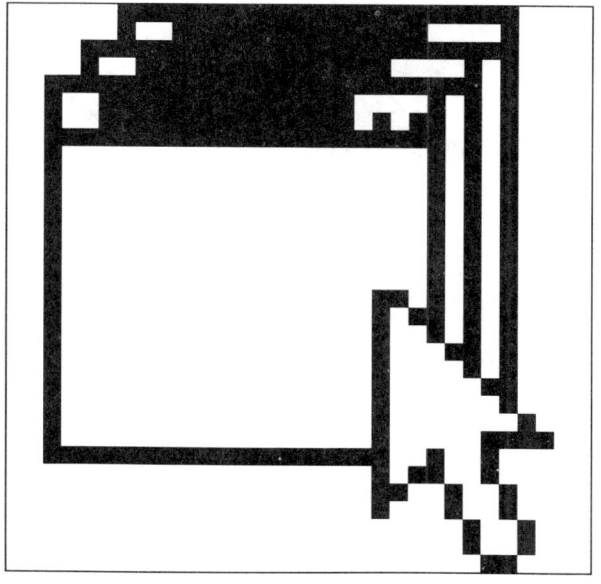

Actual Size

Stack.ico :

Actual Size

The program calls MessageBox() to report any errors to the user; it could of course have called DebugOutput() but as the application's a *user* thing, and as most users don't have a debugging terminal it's safer to use MessageBox() –after all, users are used to seeing problems reported in boxes (whoever said nice things come in small boxes!). The application calls just one DLL based function (that's our DLL –SELECT.DLL), namely bSetHook. That function returns a BOOL that is TRUE if the DLL could successfully sub-class the desktop window. Apart from that nothing should go wrong in the app.

As was mentioned earlier, the main code is in the DLL. The code uses a variety of calls to report problems and perhaps goes further than most normal code in its checking of certain things. For example, the DLL maintains two bits of global data accessed via a function call interface, ie. the data isn't really global, it's local to the functions, but it is globally available. Let's take just one of those functions apart :

```
HINSTANCE NEAR PASCAL hInstAccessDLLhInst(HINSTANCE hInst)
{
    /*
    ** Persistent holder for instance handle.
    */
    static HINSTANCE hInstance;

    if(hInst == NULL)
    {
        if((hInst = hInstance) == NULL)
        {
```

```
        DebugOutput(
                    TRACE
                    ,"hInstAccessDLLhInst. Caller gets NULL handle.\n"
                    );
        }
    }
    else
    {
        if(hInstance != NULL)
        {
            DebugOutput(
                        TRACE
                        ,"hInstAccessDLLhInst. Overwritten instance handle.\n"
                        );
        }

        hInstance = hInst;
    }

    return hInst;
}
```

This function above is used to store and access the DLL's instance handle. The function is typical of one whose main job is to restrict access to data that would otherwise have to be global to the entire source. To store something in hInstance (static in the function) you have to call the function with a non-NULL parameter value. The value passed is *set* into hInstance. To retrieve the instance handle later you call the function with a NULL parameter and it returns the stored hInstance value. Note however that the function has some helper stuff in it so that you don't call it incorrectly. If you call the function with a NULL parameter value it tests to see if the local hInstance variable is also NULL (as it would be if you hadn't previously set it) and if it is it calls DebugOutput() to pass a message to that fact to the debugging terminal –*Caller gets NULL handle*. Also, if you pass the function a non-NULL value, saying that you'd like to set hInstance (something you'd only realistically do once) it checks to see if hInstance already contains a non-NULL value, again, if it does you get a message on your debugging terminal – *Overwritten instance handle*. Note that these are just messages, ie. they're *trace* messages and there for information only. Why? Because this might not actually be an error, you might actually want a NULL value returned, or you might want to overwrite a stored hInstance value!! Also please note that the string constants are local, ie. they *live* in the DLL's data segment; you'll probably want to have these sitting in a string table in reality.

OK, so what's a real error and how is it handled? Well as the app relies on the desktop being sub-classed any failure to sub-class it is a REAL error, here's the code that attempts it :

```
BOOL __export FAR PASCAL bSetHook(VOID)
{
    /*
    ** Window handle of desktop window.
    */
    auto HWND hWndDesktop;
```

```
/*
** Get desktop window handle.
*/
hWndDesktop = GetDesktopWindow();

/*
** Store desktop window's old wndproc address and set up a new one.
*/
if(fpprocAccessOldDeskProc(
                            (WNDPROC)GetWindowLong(
                                                    hWndDesktop
                                                   ,GWL_WNDPROC
                                                   )
                            ) != NULL
    )
{
    SetWindowLong(
                   hWndDesktop
                  ,GWL_WNDPROC
                  ,(LONG)lDesktopHook
                  );

    return TRUE;
}
else
{
    vDoError(
              "Sub-class hook. Failed to hook desktop."
             ,HOOKINGERROR
             ,TRUE
             );

    return FALSE;
}
}
```

Note that if GetWindowLong() fails here that we call vDoError. Where's that? At the bottom of the DLL code :

```
VOID NEAR PASCAL vDoError
(
   LPCSTR   lpszMessage                    // Message to be output.
  ,int      nFECode                        // Error code.
  ,BOOL     bFatal                         // Do you want the app to terminate?
)
{
...
}
```

This function does several things. Firstly it's nice when coding a DLL to let the user know what application caused the problem in the DLL. As the DLL is not the using module itself it has to get the using module's name from the using module (sorry!). It gets a hold of this by first getting the task handle of the calling task. It then uses the TOOLHELP library to get the module's instance handle; to be exact, it's the TaskFind-Handle() function of tool help that does the job :

```
hTask = GetCurrentTask();

tTe.dwSize = sizeof(TASKENTRY);

if(TaskFindHandle(&tTe, hTask) != 0)
{
    GetModuleFileName(tTe.hInst, &carModuleName[0], _MAX_PATH);

    pcModuleName = _fstrrchr(&carModuleName[0], (int)'\\');

    pcModuleName++;
}
```

Having got a hold of the task handle (and the task's instance handle from TOOL-HELP) it uses GetModuleFileName() to get the full path and filename for the calling task. It finally trims this down to be just the filename using _fstrrchr() from the Microsoft 'C' library. Note that the large(ish) character arrays are declared as static so as not to crowd the caller's stack too much.

It then messes a little with the carMaxMessage buffer so that the buffer contains both the module's filename and the passed message string (carModuleName is effectively copied into carMaxMessage before this happens).

```
_fstrncpy(
        &carMaxMessage[nLen]
        ,lpszMessage
        ,_MAX_MESS - lstrlen(&carMaxMessage[0])
        );@code sm ind =
```

Then it checks to see if it's being run under the debug or non-debug version of Windows.

```
if(GetSystemMetrics(SM_DEBUG) != 0)
```

If it's the debug version it uses OutputDebugString() to send the contents of car-MaxMessage to the debugging terminal and then calls FatalExit() to give you a stack trace and an opportunity to close the app. Note that fatal exit uses the passed error code.

```
OutputDebugString(&carMaxMessage[0]);
FatalExit(nFECode);
```

If the user is using the retail version, and if we consider (as programmers) that this error is *bad* the third parameter to vDoError is very important because if it is set to FALSE (not an important enough error to terminate the program) the user sees nothing at all from this function. If bFatal is TRUE however –all hell breaks loose!

```
if(bFatal == TRUE)
{
    ...
    FatalAppExit(0, &carMaxMessage[0]);
    ...
}
```

FatalAppExit() causes the application to terminate after passing the contents of carMaxMessage to the user via a SysErrorBox(), or if you prefer, a system modal message box. Note that FatalExit() is used only if the debugging version is detected as using it on the retail version causes the app to terminate with a *standard', and non-helpful, message.*

OK, so what's the result of making a call to vDoError on each build (debug/non-debug) if, say, the bSetHook function calls it? On the debug system the first thing seen is the message sent from OutputDebugString(), note, no error code etc accompanies this message. This is followed by the call to FatalExit(). This causes the normal *Fatal Exit (?????)* message and stack trace to appear. Lastly FatalAppExit() is called; no output is produced on the debugging terminal when this function is called but a *helpful* error message is produced in the Windows screen group telling the user that the app must close now. On the retail version the only debug function called is FatalAppExit(); this operates just the same in the retail version as it does on the debug version. The DLL might also call DebugOutput() with DBF_ERROR as its first parameter if it encounters any non-terminal (sorry about the pun!) error. This has no effect in the retail version as the function simply returns when called. In the debug build however it causes a fatal exit (code 0x8000) and the *normal* stack trace to appear on the debugging terminal.

You could improve on this for forever and a day. For example you could check the return of every function that is called from the DLL and produce relevant error messages if they fail, or you could pack your code full of useful trace messages so that you can see how it's doing at anytime. Sometimes it's hard to know where to draw the line. For example, the vDoError code checks to see if TaskFindHandle() works or fails and takes remedial action if it does; but do we need to check this? Well it depends on your standards. The programmer's reference says that if the function fails it returns 0; does this mean that it *could* fail therefore? It's hard to know. Does it fail only if you give it an invalid task handle to work with? It doesn't say! I find such documentation very frustrating as the lack any *real* documentation (and our coding standards) makes me check, and deal with, any potential failure. If Microsoft said *this will only fail if you pass it an invalid task handle* I'd be safe coz GetCurrentTask() couldn't possible fail could it? Well guess what the docs say for GetCurrentTask()? *The return value is a handle to the current task if the function is successful. Otherwise it is NULL* –Damn it! Seriously, I wish Microsoft would give better docs for how and when these APIs might fail, it would make my life, and yours I suspect, much easier. It would also be very useful to know just what functions are debug aware. For example, and getting back to the point above, we might say that we don't need to check APIs for failure because they're bound to execute their own debug code (calls to DebugOutput() etc) in the event of any failure. How do we know that!? We don't, again we're forced to code even when it might not be necessary!

☐ Trappers or *Ripping Yarns*

If a series of events can go wrong, it will do so in the worst thinkable way and at the most inconvenient time – guaranteed.

Talking about TOOLHELP – you can use this library of functions to build some pretty good debugging tools like for example Dr. Watson. Watson is a good debugging tool as it provides complete information on the state of the system at the time the exception took place. I had to build a similar app for a client once who found that users closed down Watson because they didn't understand what it did; he (the client) also wanted the information in the *log* file formatted differently to that provided by Watson. The application used two TOOLHELP functions to monitor what was going on in the system –InterruptRegister() and NotifyRegister(). The first function provides for the monitoring of system interrupts; some of which signal faults in tasks. The NotifyRegister() function allows you to monitor such things as task switches, the loading/unloading of segments and *ripping* applications. Both functions require a call-back function to be defined in your monitoring application or DLL; InterruptRegister() requires the call-back to be written in assembler. The function has to be re-entrant, page-locked and must explicitly save all registers on entry (as it's re-entrant). The function is called whenever an *exception* takes place in the system. Exceptions are :

Code	Name
0	Divide Error (Division by 0)
1	Int 1
3	Int 3
6	Invalid opcode
12 (B)	Stack exception
13 (C)	General protection fault (GPF)
14 (D)	Page fault
256 (100)	Ctrl+Alt+SysRq key combination (int 256 – Used by debuggers such as CVW to switch between screens).

The Windows' SDK samples comes with an interesting example of both functions (InterruptRegister() and NotifyRegister()) called thsample; it has the required .ASM file used for defining the InterruptRegister() call-back function. The asm call-back code, which calls a 'C' function in the *main* code is easily modifiable and can be used to form the basis of an InterruptRegister() type application.

The app's NotifiyRegister() handling is not exactly verbose so let's look at a demo that shows how to use the function properly (An example of an InterruptRegister() handler follows).

A NotifyRegister() call-back looks like this :

```
BOOL __export CALLBACK NotifyRegisterCallback(wID, dwData)
```

wID is the notification code and dwData is some data (may be a pointer to something) that is relevant for the notification wID.

A notification call-back function can receive the following notifications :

Code   **NFY_UNKNOWN** (0)
Meaning   An unknown notification has been returned from KERNEL. Applications should ignore these.
dwData   Undefined

Code   NFY_LOADSEG (1)
Meaning   A segment is being loaded from an EXE (or whatever) file.
dwData   Pointer to a NFYLOADSEG.

```
typedef struct tagNFYLOADSEG
{
    DWORD     dwSize;
    WORD      wSelector;
    WORD      wSegNum;
    WORD      wType;
    WORD      wcInstance;
    LPCSTR    lpstrModuleName;
} NFYLOADSEG;
```

Code   NFY_FREESEG (2)
Meaning   A segment is being freed.
dwData   Selector of segment being freed up.

Code   NFY_STARTDLL (3)
Meaning   A DLL is being loaded. The NFYSTARTDLL structure contains information about the dynamic-link library being loaded.
dwData   Pointer to a NFYSTARTDLL.

```
typedef struct tagNFYSTARTDLL
{
    DWORD     dwSize;
    HMODULE   hModule;
    WORD      wCS;
    WORD      wIP;
} NFYSTARTDLL;
```

Code   NFY_STARTTASK (4)

Meaning   A task is being started (WinMain() etc being called).

dwData   CS:IP of the starting task.

Code   NFY_EXITTASK (5)
Meaning   A task is quitting.
dwData   The contains the program's exit code in its low byte.

Code	NFY_DELMODULE (6)
Meaning	Module being freed (Module database destroyed) –application or DLL.
dwData	The low word is a module handle of the module about to be freed.

Code	NFY_RIP (7)
Meaning	Module caused a *Rest in Peace* error. The NFYRIP structure contains information about the system when a system debugging error (RIP) occurs. The TOOLHELP StackTraceCSIPFirst() function uses the CS:IP and SS:BP values presented in this structure. The first frame in the stack always points to the FatalExit() function. The next frame points to the routine that called FatalExit(), this routine is usually a Windows' routine, ie. it's in USER, GDI, or KERNEL.
dwData	Pointer to an NFYRIP.

```
typedef struct tagNFYRIP
{
    DWORD       dwSize;
    WORD        wIP;
    WORD        wCS;
    WORD        wSS;
    WORD        wBP;
    WORD        wExitCode;
} NFYRIP;
```

Code	NFY_TASKIN (8)
Meaning	Task starting via context switch
dwData	Undefined

Code	NFY_TASKOUT (9)
Meaning	Task ending via context switch.
dwData	Undefined.

Code	NFY_INCHAR (10)
Meaning	Reply to RIP *Abort, Break, Exit or Ignore*. Call-back returns an ASCII character. If NULL is returned this is mapped to *i*, ie. ignore. Possible replies are *i* –Ignore, *e* –Exit, *b* –Break, *r* –Retry, *a* –Abort and ' ' (space) –stack trace.
dwData	Not used.

Code	NFY_OUTSTR (11)
Meaning	This event is meant to be triggered when an application or DLL uses OutputDebugString(); dwData is said to be a pointer to the string. I have not been able to confirm this however. Even after careful testing I have never received an NFY_OUTSTR event!
dwData	dwData pointer to a string to be displayed.

Code	NFY_LOGERROR (12)
Meaning	Validation error.
dwData	Pointer to an NFYLOGERROR.

```
typedef struct tagNFYLOGERROR
{
    DWORD       dwSize;
    UINT        wErrCode;
    void FAR*   lpInfo;
} NFYLOGERROR;
```

Code   NFY_LOGPARAMERROR (13)
Meaning Parameter validation error.
dwData   Pointer to an NFYLOGPARAMERROR.

```
typedef struct tagNFYLOGPARAMERROR
{
    DWORD               dwSize;
    UINT                wErrCode;
    FARPROC             lpfnErrorAddr;
    void FAR* FAR*      lpBadParam;
} NFYLOGPARAMERROR;
```

A NotifyRegister() call-back may be written in 'C' and is installed in a chain of registered call-backs. Call-backs added later (after some other application has registered its call-back) only receive notifications if the earlier call-back hasn't handled the notification. Each call-back, starting with the first registered, is passed a notification, let's say of a RIP. If that handler *handles* the notification if passes TRUE back to Windows (the caller); call-backs added after this call-back will not receive notification of the RIP. I've found that most, if not all the time, notifications should be passed on to any and all registered call-backs although we'll see in the code that in this example that is not actually the case!

The call-back is registered using NotifyRegister() and later un-registered using NotifyUnRegister().

The actual call-back used must only call functions defined in TOOLHELP, functions defined within the module where the call-back resides or PostMessage(). This means to process notifications you need a window as you'll almost certainly use PostMessage() to notify your window of notification events. The thsample application essentially ignores the data passed to the call-back in dwData; this data should be copied to a local area of memory before the application's window is informed of the event; this is because PostMessage() can cause (via task switches etc) the data to which dwData points to become invalid. You might think that the task's message queue might overflow (default size is eight messages remember) when many events occur in a short space of time? In practice this never seems to happen, ie. PostMessage() never returns FALSE (indicating that the message queue is full), either TOOLHELP/windows is being co-operative about this or else the scheduling algorithm is indeed very efficient when it comes to delivering posted messages.

The application shown below (Notify) uses NotifyRegister() to *watch* the system. It creates a window (which is shown as an icon initially) so that the notification call-back function can process an event by simply passing this window a WM_USER message.

The WM_USER message has the notification code (wID) in its wParam and dwData in its lParam. Note that this application uses DebugMessageVar, which was shown earlier, to output/report notifications to the debugging terminal.

Here's the code.

Notify.c :

```c
#define STRICT

#include <windows.h>
#include <toolhelp.h>
#include <stdarg.h>
#include <memory.h>
#include "notify.h"

#pragma warning(disable:4100)
#pragma warning(disable:4001)

#define VOIDRETURN

/*
** Handy typedefs for casts on lParam.
*/
typedef NFYLOADSEG       FAR * LS;
typedef NFYRIP           FAR * RIP;
typedef NFYSTARTDLL      FAR * SDLL;
typedef NFYLOGPARAMERROR FAR * LPE;

/*
** Union of structs and 'ordinary' data types used to pass
** information to a wndproc via PostMessage().
*/
typedef union
{
    NFYLOADSEG        LoadSeg;
    NFYRIP            Rip;
    NFYSTARTDLL       StartDLL;
    NFYLOGPARAMERROR  LogParamErr;
    DWORD             CSIP;
    BYTE              ExitCode;
    WORD              Selector;
    LPSTR             String;
    HMODULE           hModule;

} STRUCTURES;

/*
** Pointer to above.
*/
typedef STRUCTURES FAR * LPSTRUCTURES;

int            PASCAL WinMain          (HINSTANCE, HIN-
STANCE, LPSTR, int);
BOOL           NEAR PASCAL InitApplication  (HINSTANCE);
BOOL           NEAR PASCAL InitInstance     (HINSTANCE, int);
```

```
LRESULT   __export CALLBACK    MainWndProc              (HWND, UINT, WPARAM,
LPARAM);
BOOL              NEAR PASCAL bInstallNotifyHook        (HINSTANCE);
VOID              NEAR PASCAL vDeinstallNotifyHook      (VOID);
BOOL      __export CALLBACK    NotifyRegisterCallback   (WORD, DWORD);
HWND              NEAR PASCAL hAccesshWnd               (HWND);
FARPROC           NEAR PASCAL fpProcAccessThunk         (FARPROC);
VOID              NEAR CDECL  DebugMessageVar           (LPCSTR, ...);




VOID NEAR CDECL DebugMessageVar(LPCSTR lpszFormatString, ...)
{
   /*
   ** Couple of WINDEBUGINFOs, one for the
   ** old - the other for the new.
   */
   auto WINDEBUGINFO    Oldwdi;
   auto WINDEBUGINFO    Newwdi;


   /*
   ** Buffer into which we write our args according to
   ** lpszFormatString.
   */
   auto char           carBuffer[255];


   /*
   ** For walking the args.
   */
   auto va_list        pArg;


   /*
   ** Clean new one.
   */
   _fmemset(&Newwdi, 0x0, sizeof(WINDEBUGINFO));


   /*
   ** Set it up. WDI_FILTER is the actual minimum required
   ** in this function  - the others don't do any harm and
   ** are there for completeness only.
   */
   Newwdi.flags     = WDI_OPTIONS |
                      WDI_FILTER  |
                      WDI_ALLOCBREAK;


   /*
   ** Just interested in what the application does, if
   ** you want  to  see  stuff  for other modules like
   ** KERNEL include as appropriate.
   */
   Newwdi.dwFilter  = DBF_APPLICATION;


   /*
   ** Get the old ready to restore it.
   */
   GetWinDebugInfo(
```

```
                        &Oldwdi
                        ,WDI_OPTIONS |
                        WDI_FILTER |
                        WDI_ALLOCBREAK
                        );

    /*
    ** Set up according to new settings.
    */
    SetWinDebugInfo(&Newwdi);


    /*
    ** Output message.
    */
    va_start(pArg, lpszFormatString);

    wvsprintf(
                &carBuffer[0]
              ,lpszFormatString
              ,(LPSTR)pArg
              );

    va_end(pArg);

    DebugOutput(
                DBF_TRACE | DBF_APPLICATION
              ,&carBuffer[0]
              );

    /*
    ** Restore old settings.
    */
    SetWinDebugInfo(&Oldwdi);

    return VOIDRETURN;
}




/*
** Stores instace thunk.
*/
FARPROC NEAR PASCAL fpProcAccessThunk(FARPROC fpProc)
{
    static FARPROC fpProcInst;

    if(fpProc != NULL)
    {
        fpProcInst = fpProc;
    }

    return fpProcInst;
}
```

```
/*
** Stores main window's handle.
*/
HWND NEAR PASCAL hAccesshWnd(HWND hWnd)
{
    static HWND hWndStored;

    if(hWnd != NULL)
    {
        hWndStored = hWnd;
    }

    return hWndStored;
}




/*
** Installs NotifyRegister() hook.
*/
BOOL NEAR PASCAL bInstallNotifyHook(HINSTANCE hInstance)
{
    auto HTASK      hTask;
    auto FARPROC    lpfnCallBack;

    /*
    ** We require MakeProcInstance() in order to get the callback's
    ** DS correct.  Cannot  use 'Smart  Callbacks' here as TOOLHELP
    ** calls us on stack of notifying task.
    */
    if(
        (lpfnCallBack = MakeProcInstance(
                                        (FARPROC)NotifyRegisterCallback
                                        ,hInstance
                                        )
        ) != NULL
      )
    {
        fpProcAccessThunk(lpfnCallBack);

        /*
        ** Need to tell TOOLHELP's NotifyRegister() which task is
        ** installing the hook.
        */
        hTask = GetCurrentTask();

        /*
        ** Not interested in Task Switching - everything else.
        */
        return NotifyRegister(
                            hTask
                            , (LPFNNOTIFYCALLBACK)lpfnCallBack
                            ,
                            NF_RIP | NF_NORMAL | NF_TASKSWITCH
```

```
                                      );
      }
   else
   {
       return FALSE;
   }

}




/*
** De-installs NotifyRegister() hook.
*/
VOID NEAR PASCAL vDeinstallNotifyHook(VOID)
{

   NotifyUnRegister(GetCurrentTask());

   FreeProcInstance(fpProcAccessThunk(NULL));

   return VOIDRETURN;
}




/*
** NotifyRegister() hook  callback  -  called by Windows.
** Can't normally use 'Smart Callbacks (-GS) (See notes).
*/
BOOL __export CALLBACK NotifyRegisterCallback(WORD wID, DWORD dwData)
{
   /*
   ** 'Points' to our main window. Can only call other toolhelp
   ** functions and PostMessage() in here. Also called on stack
   ** of most  recently executing task  so we should use static
   ** if we can.
   */
   static HWND hWnd;

   /*
   ** Must be static as we're gonna pass its address via a PostMessage()
   ** call; if it were auto we'd loose it off the stack dude!
   */
   static STRUCTURES NFYs;

   /*
   ** What kinda notification is it?
   */
   switch(wID)
   {
       /*
       ** Use NFYs to detail information to main window procedure.
       ** This essentially  duplicates whatever dwData points to -
       ** this is  not a  waste of time however and has to be done
       ** as we  can't make use of the information  in  here as we
```

```
    ** can only call PostMessage().
    */

    case NFY_DELMODULE:
        NFYs.hModule = (HMODULE)LOWORD(dwData);
        break;

    case NFY_EXITTASK:
        NFYs.ExitCode = LOBYTE(LOWORD(dwData));
        break;

    case NFY_FREESEG:
        NFYs.Selector = LOWORD(dwData);
        break;

    case NFY_INCHAR:
        break;

    case NFY_LOGPARAMERROR:
        NFYs.LogParamErr.wErrCode      = ((LPE)dwData)->wErrCode;
        NFYs.LogParamErr.lpfnErrorAddr = ((LPE)dwData)->lpfnErrorAddr;
        NFYs.LogParamErr.lpBadParam    = ((LPE)dwData)->lpBadParam;
        break;

    case NFY_LOADSEG:
        NFYs.LoadSeg.wSelector         = ((LS)dwData)->wSelector;
        NFYs.LoadSeg.wSegNum           = ((LS)dwData)->wSegNum;
        NFYs.LoadSeg.wType             = ((LS)dwData)->wType;
        NFYs.LoadSeg.wcInstance        = ((LS)dwData)->wcInstance;
        NFYs.LoadSeg.lpstrModuleName   = ((LS)dwData)->
                        lpstrModuleName;
        break;

    case NFY_OUTSTR:
        NFYs.String = (LPSTR)dwData;
        break;

    case NFY_RIP:
        NFYs.Rip.wIP       = ((RIP)dwData)->wIP;
        NFYs.Rip.wCS       = ((RIP)dwData)->wCS;
        NFYs.Rip.wSS       = ((RIP)dwData)->wSS;
        NFYs.Rip.wBP       = ((RIP)dwData)->wBP;
        NFYs.Rip.wExitCode = ((RIP)dwData)->wExitCode;
        break;

    case NFY_STARTDLL:
        NFYs.StartDLL.hModule  = ((SDLL)dwData)->hModule;
        NFYs.StartDLL.wCS      = ((SDLL)dwData)->wCS;
        NFYs.StartDLL.wIP      = ((SDLL)dwData)->wIP;
        break;

    case NFY_STARTTASK:
        NFYs.CSIP = dwData;
        break;

    case NFY_UNKNOWN:
        return FALSE;
```

```
                break;

                /*
                ** Unrecognised notifications should NOT be handled.
                */
        default:
                return FALSE;
                break;

    }

    if((hWnd = hAccesshWnd(NULL)) != NULL)
    {
        /*
        ** We return TRUE if  we handled the notification else FALSE.
        ** I return what PostMessage() returns as it returns FALSE if
        ** our task  message queue is full - it apparently never does
        ** this in here BTW!  It would be more polite to return FALSE
        ** as then other notification handlers started after us would
        ** get the notification as well.
        */

        /* 'Who ya gonna call?...' */
        return PostMessage(
                            hWnd
                            ,WM_USER
                            ,(WPARAM)wID
                            ,(LPARAM)(LONG FAR *)&NFYs
                            );

    }
    else
    {
        /*
        ** Can't get our hWnd - maybe we haven't been created yet -
        ** return FALSE to let someone else get the notification.
        */
        return FALSE;
    }
}




/*
** App main entry point.
*/
int PASCAL WinMain
(
  HINSTANCE     hInstance
 ,HINSTANCE     hPrevInstance
 ,LPSTR         lpCmdLine
 ,int           nCmdShow
)
{
    auto MSG msg;
```

```
        msg.wParam = 0;

        /*
        ** Install NotifyRegister() hook before we do anything - if
        ** it fails exit.
        */
        if(bInstallNotifyHook(hInstance) == TRUE)
        {
            if(hPrevInstance == NULL)
            {
                if(InitApplication(hInstance) == FALSE)
                {
                    return 0;
                }
            }

            if(InitInstance(hInstance, nCmdShow) == FALSE)
            {
                return 0;
            }

            while(GetMessage(&msg, NULL, 0, 0))
            {
                TranslateMessage(&msg);
                DispatchMessage(&msg);
            }

            /*
            ** Un-install hook.
            */
            vDeinstallNotifyHook();
        }
        else
        {
            MessageBox(
                    0
                    ,"Couldn't install NotifyRegister() callback!"
                    ,NULL
                    ,MB_OK
                    );
        }

        return msg.wParam;
}




/*
** Class registration.
*/
BOOL NEAR PASCAL InitApplication(HINSTANCE hInstance)
{
    auto WNDCLASS  wc;

    wc.style          = NULL;
    wc.lpfnWndProc    = (WNDPROC)MainWndProc;
```

```
    wc.cbClsExtra       = 0;
    wc.cbWndExtra       = 0;
    wc.hInstance        = hInstance;
    wc.hIcon            = LoadIcon(NULL, IDI_APPLICATION);
    wc.hCursor          = LoadCursor(NULL, IDC_ARROW);
    wc.hbrBackground    = (HBRUSH)(COLOR_WINDOW + 1);
    wc.lpszMenuName     = MAKEINTRESOURCE(NOTIFYMENU);
    wc.lpszClassName    = "NotifyClass";

    return !!RegisterClass(&wc);
}




/*
** Window creation.
*/
BOOL NEAR PASCAL InitInstance(HINSTANCE hInstance, int nCmdShow)
{
    auto HWND hWnd;

    hWnd = CreateWindow(
                        "NotifyClass"
                        ,"NotifyRegister Window"
                        ,WS_OVERLAPPEDWINDOW
                        ,CW_USEDEFAULT
                        ,0
                        ,GetSystemMetrics(SM_CXSCREEN) / 3
                        ,GetSystemMetrics(SM_CYSCREEN) / 5
                        ,NULL
                        ,NULL
                        ,hInstance
                        ,NULL
                        );

    if(hWnd == NULL)
    {
        return FALSE;
    }

    ShowWindow(hWnd, SW_SHOWMINNOACTIVE);
    UpdateWindow(hWnd);

    /*
    ** Store hWnd.
    */
    hAccesshWnd(hWnd);

    return TRUE;
}




/*
** Main window callback (wndproc).
```

```
*/
LRESULT __export CALLBACK MainWndProc
(
   HWND     hWnd
  ,UINT     uMessage
  ,WPARAM   wParam
  ,LPARAM   lParam
)
{

   switch(uMessage)
   {
   case WM_COMMAND:
       PostMessage(hWnd, WM_CLOSE, 0, 0);
       break;


       /*
       ** Keep window nice size. Note that we can't
       ** use window's size as it's not been set yet.
       */
   case WM_GETMINMAXINFO:
       {
          auto POINT tPt;

          tPt.x = GetSystemMetrics(SM_CXSCREEN) / 3;
          tPt.y = GetSystemMetrics(SM_CYSCREEN) / 5;

          ((MINMAXINFO FAR *)lParam) -> ptMinTrackSize.x = tPt.x;
          ((MINMAXINFO FAR *)lParam) -> ptMinTrackSize.y = tPt.y;
          ((MINMAXINFO FAR *)lParam) -> ptMaxTrackSize.x = tPt.x;
          ((MINMAXINFO FAR *)lParam) -> ptMaxTrackSize.y = tPt.y;
       }
       break;

   case WM_DESTROY:
       PostQuitMessage(0);
       break;


       /*
       ** USER message sent by  NotifyCallback() handler.  Should use
       ** a  registered  message  in  case  someone  idly transmits a
       ** WM_USER message.  As we normally (in here) treat the lParam
       ** as a pointer to something this would cause problems in that
       ** we'd either trap or get erroneous information.
       */
   case WM_USER:

       /*
       ** Switch on wID code. lParam is dwData.
       */
       switch(wParam)
       {
           /*
           ** Use DebugMessageVar to format and present data nicely.
           */
```

```
case NFY_DELMODULE:
    DebugMessageVar(
                    "Del Module. hMod-%X"
                    , ((LPSTRUCTURES)lParam)->hModule
                    );
    break;

 case NFY_EXITTASK:
    DebugMessageVar(
                    "Exit Task. Code-%d"
                    , ((LPSTRUCTURES)lParam)->ExitCode
                    );
    break;

case NFY_FREESEG:
    DebugMessageVar(
                    "Free Seg. Sel-%X"
                    , ((LPSTRUCTURES)lParam)->Selector
                    );
    break;

case NFY_INCHAR:
    DebugMessageVar(
                    "Inchar"
                    );
    break;

case NFY_LOGPARAMERROR:
    DebugMessageVar(
                    "Log Param Err. wErr-%X Proc-%lX Param-%lX"
                    , ((LPE)lParam)->wErrCode
                    , ((LPE)lParam)->lpfnErrorAddr
                    , ((LPE)lParam)->lpBadParam
                    );
    break;

case NFY_LOADSEG:
    {
        auto WORD      wType;
        auto char    * pcType;
        auto LPSTR     lpszModNme;

        wType = (WORD) (((LS)lParam)->wType & 1);

        pcType = wType ? "Data" : "Code";

        /*
        ** I have occasionally had a bad string pointer in
        ** here so test it before you use it! See following
        ** notes.
        */
        lpszModNme = IsBadStringPtr(((LS)lParam)->
        lpstrModuleName, 8)
                        ? (LPSTR)"Unknown"
                        : (LPSTR)((LS)lParam)->lpstrModuleName;
```

```
                         DebugMessageVar(
                                      "Load Seg. Sel-%u SegNum-%u "
                                      "Type-%s Inst-%u Name-%s"
                                      ,((LS)lParam)->wSelector
                                      ,((LS)lParam)->wSegNum
                                      ,(LPSTR)pcType
                                      ,((LS)lParam)->wcInstance
                                      ,lpszModNme
                                      );
              }
          break;

     case NFY_OUTSTR:
          DebugMessageVar(
                           "Out str. String-%s"
                           ,((LPSTRUCTURES)lParam)->String
                           );
          break;

     case NFY_RIP:
          DebugMessageVar(
                           "Rip. IP-%u CS-%u SS-%u BP-%u Code-%X"
                           ,((RIP)lParam)->wIP
                           ,((RIP)lParam)->wCS
                           ,((RIP)lParam)->wSS
                           ,((RIP)lParam)->wBP
                           ,((RIP)lParam)->wExitCode
                           );
          break;

     case NFY_STARTDLL:
          DebugMessageVar(
                           "Start DLL. hMod-%X CS-%u IP-%u"
                           ,((SDLL)lParam)->hModule
                           ,((SDLL)lParam)->wCS
                           ,((SDLL)lParam)->wIP
                           );
          break;
     case NFY_STARTTASK:
          DebugMessageVar(
                           "Start Task. CS-%X IP-%X"
                           ,LOWORD((DWORD)lParam)
                           ,HIWORD((DWORD)lParam)
                           );
          break;

     case NFY_UNKNOWN:
          DebugMessageVar(
                           "Unknown"
                           );
          break;

     default:
          DebugMessageVar(
                           "Default. Vars-%X %lX"
                           ,wParam, lParam
                           );
```

```
                    break;

            }
        return FALSE;

    default:
        return DefWindowProc(hWnd, uMessage, wParam, lParam);
    }

    return (LRESULT)0;
}
```

Notify.def :

```
NAME        NOTIFY

DESCRIPTION  'Notify - NotifyRegister Example.'

EXETYPE     WINDOWS 3.1

PROTMODE

STUB        'WINSTUB.EXE'

CODE   PRELOAD FIXED

DATA   PRELOAD MOVEABLE MULTIPLE

HEAPSIZE    1024
STACKSIZE   5120

EXPORTS
        MainWndProc             @1
        NotifyRegisterCallback  @2


IMPORTS
        KERNEL._DebugOutput
```

Notify.h :

```
#define IDM_CLOSE   100
#define NOTIFYMENU 100
```

Notify.rc :

```
#include "notify.h"

NOTIFYMENU MENU
BEGIN
        MENUITEM "Close!", IDM_CLOSE
END
```

The makefile is not shown as it is, by and large, quite standard. There is one important change however and I'll come on to it soon.

The application uses DebugMessageVar (Shown earlier in this chapter) for all of its output. This means that its output goes to either the debugging terminal or DBWIN; it also means that it must be run under the debugging version. Here's some typical output :

```
t NOTIFY Load Seg. Sel-13671 SegNum-85 Type-Code Inst-0 Name-Unknown
t NOTIFY Exit Task. Code-87
t NOTIFY Free Seg. Sel-3557
t NOTIFY Del Module. hMod-3557
t NOTIFY Free Seg. Sel-3557
t NOTIFY Load Seg. Sel-13615 SegNum-13599 Type-Code Inst-0 Name-SPY
t NOTIFY Start Task. CS-392 IP-2C3F
t NOTIFY Start DLL. hMod-352F CS-13599 IP-1352
t NOTIFY Exit Task. Code-63
t NOTIFY Del Module. hMod-353F
t NOTIFY Free Seg. Sel-353F
t NOTIFY Del Module. hMod-353F
t NOTIFY Free Seg. Sel-353F
t NOTIFY Load Seg. Sel-13567 SegNum-2 Type-Code Inst-0 Name-STRESS
t NOTIFY Exit Task. Code-71
t NOTIFY Del Module. hMod-3547
t NOTIFY Free Seg. Sel-3547
t NOTIFY Del Module. hMod-3547
t NOTIFY Free Seg. Sel-3547
t NOTIFY Load Seg. Sel-13815 SegNum-2 Type-Data Inst-0 Name-SEND-IT
t NOTIFY Start Task. CS-392 IP-2C3F
t NOTIFY Exit Task. Code-239
t NOTIFY Del Module. hMod-2CEF
t NOTIFY Free Seg. Sel-2CEF
```

The application installs its notification hook in WinMain() before any standard application initialisation is carried out. When the apps GetMessage() loop exits the hook is un-installed.

```
int PASCAL WinMain
(
   HINSTANCE    hInstance
  ,HINSTANCE    hPrevInstance
  ,LPSTR        lpCmdLine
  ,int          nCmdShow
)
{
    auto MSG msg;

    msg.wParam = 0;

    if(bInstallNotifyHook(hInstance) == TRUE)
    {
        ... Other initialisation stuff.
        ...

        while(GetMessage(&msg, NULL, 0, 0))
        {
```

```
                    TranslateMessage(&msg);
                    DispatchMessage(&msg);
                }

            vDeinstallNotifyHook();
        }
        else
        {
            MessageBox(
                        0
                       ,"Couldn't install NotifyRegister() callback!"
                       ,NULL
                       ,MB_OK
                       );
        }

        return msg.wParam;
    }
```

bInstallNotifyHook looks like this :

```
BOOL NEAR PASCAL bInstallNotifyHook(HINSTANCE hInstance)
{
    auto HTASK          hTask;
    auto FARPROC        lpfnCallBack;

    if(
        (lpfnCallBack = MakeProcInstance(
                                        (FARPROC)NotifyRegisterCallback
                                        ,hInstance
                                        )
        ) != NULL
      )
    {
        fpProcAccessThunk(lpfnCallBack);

        hTask = GetCurrentTask();

        return NotifyRegister(
                             hTask
                             ,(LPFNNOTIFYCALLBACK)lpfnCallBack
                             ,NF_RIP | NF_NORMAL | NF_TASKSWITCH
                             );
    }
    else
    {
        return FALSE;
    }

}
```

vDeInstallNotifyHook looks like this :

```
VOID NEAR PASCAL vDeinstallNotifyHook(VOID)
{
    NotifyUnRegister(GetCurrentTask());
```

```
    FreeProcInstance(fpProcAccessThunk(NULL));

    return VOIDRETURN;
}
```

fpProcAccessThunk sets and retrieves a static variable that holds an instance thunk for the call-back. More on this shortly.

When the call-back function (NotifyRegisterCallback) is called it is passed two parameters, wID –type of notification event, and dwData –data defining the event in wID. The app simply packs the event ID and the data into a union called NFYs (type STRUCTURES) and then posts this via a WM_USER message to the main window.

```
        case NFY_RIP:
            NFYs.Rip.wIP       = ((RIP)dwData)->wIP;
            NFYs.Rip.wCS       = ((RIP)dwData)->wCS;
            NFYs.Rip.wSS       = ((RIP)dwData)->wSS;
            NFYs.Rip.wBP       = ((RIP)dwData)->wBP;
            NFYs.Rip.wExitCode = ((RIP)dwData)->wExitCode;
            break;

... other program lines.

        return PostMessage(
                        hWnd
                        ,WM_USER
                        ,(WPARAM)wID
                        ,(LPARAM)(LONG FAR *)&NFYs
                        );
```

wID is put into the WM_USER message's wParam and the address of NFYs into the lParam. **Note that NFYs has to be static here**. NFYs is of type STRUCTURES. Practically all the notification events use dData to hold some significant data, NFYs is an amalgamation of all possible dwData types.

```
typedef union
{
    NFYLOADSEG       LoadSeg;
    NFYRIP           Rip;
    NFYSTARTDLL      StartDLL;
    NFYLOGPARAMERROR LogParamErr;
    DWORD            CSIP;
    BYTE             ExitCode;
    WORD             Selector;
    LPSTR            String;
    HMODULE          hModule;

} STRUCTURES;
```

The app uses the return value of PostMessage() for its return value. TRUE means I've processed the notification so don't pass it on, FALSE means I haven't processed it so if there's another notification event handler out there –pass it on to that! Note that any NFY_UNKNOWN or any real unknown (default) case wID items force the notification call-back to return FALSE, ie. not handled. Microsoft say that this must be done to aid future compatibility. Note also on this point that each notification structure contained with NFYs has a member (dwSize) that details its size –this may be useful in the future if/when these structures change.

The main window's wndproc handling of the WM_USER message is almost the reverse of what took place in the notify call-back function. The event code (wParam now) is used in a switch statement to access the correct event handler within the WM_USER case. The data in lParam is now accessed and output to, say, DBWIN using DebugMessageVar (which is also shown in the code for completeness).

```
case NFY_RIP:
    DebugMessageVar(
                    "Rip. IP-%u CS-%u SS-%u BP-%u Code-%X"
            , ((RIP)lParam)->wIP
            , ((RIP)lParam)->wCS
            , ((RIP)lParam)->wSS
            , ((RIP)lParam)->wBP
            , ((RIP)lParam)->wExitCode
            );
    break;
```

Note that you cannot use the C700 -GA switch alone to build this application. You must use either the *old* -Gw switch or the new -GA switch TOGETHER WITH -GEe and -GEa. If you use the -GA switch the prologue code in the notification call-back will load DS from SS when it's called by the KERNEL module, unfortunately SS will hold the SS of the most recently executing task and not your DS value as is normally the case (set by the task manager in Windows). The -GEa switch is used to modify the -GA prologue so that it will work in real mode, however the code generated is more efficient than that generated by -Gw. The -GEe switch is used to force an EXPDEF record to be generated. An EXPDEF record is used by the Windows' loader to *fix up* the function's prologue so that it loads DS from AX when it's called. The actual EXPDEF record is generated by the linker and just flagged by the compiler. Normally, using *smart-call-backs* the fix-up isn't required, all the coding is done by the compiler at compile time, nothing changes at either load-time or run-time. However, in real mode the prologue code needs to be changed so that DS is loaded from the AX register. The AX register contains a valid DS for the app. MakeProcInstance() generates an *instance thunk* that contains the *real* address of the function and the DS used by the code for a given instance of the application. The two parameters to MakeProcInstance() are used to construct an instance thunk. hInstance is your task's DS and lpFunc is of course the address of your function (we'll forget reload thunks here!).

So as is now clear, we need the old *real mode* mechanism supplied by -Gw (or -GA -GEe –GEa) and an instance thunk to call the notification call-back correctly! The C700 documentation says that you cannot use -GE? with another -GE? switch. This is wrong; you must have the -GEe switch with the -GEa switch in order to have the Windows' loader change the exported function's prologue code (the three famous NOPs) so that the function expects to have DS passed to it in the AX register.

Notify sending its output to DBWIN's window.

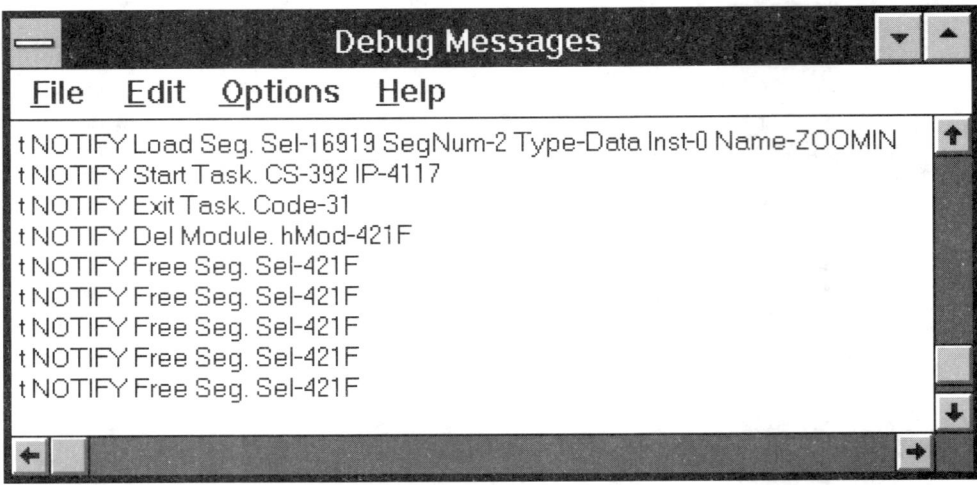

Here's an example of an InterruptRegister() handler. This example, like most other you'll find, provides a 'C' function that is called back from an assembler call-back which the real call-back as registered with Windows. First here's the assembler code:

```
Intreg.asm :

; InterruptRegister() call-back code.

?PLM    =       1       ;PASCAL style parameter handling
?WIN    =       0       ;No Windows prologue/epilogue
.286

INCLUDE CMACROS.INC
INCLUDE TOOLHELP.INC

?PLM = 0

; Defined in our main application code.
;
;WORD _cdecl CFaultHandler
;(
;       WORD    wSS,        ; pushed ss.
;       WORD    wES,        ; pushed es.
;       WORD    wDS,        ; pushed ds.
;       WORD    wDI,        ;   |
;       WORD    wSI,        ;   |
;       WORD    wBP,        ;   |
;       WORD    wSP,        ;   |
;       WORD    wBX,        ;   |
;       WORD    wDX,        ;   |
;       WORD    wCX,        ;   |
;       WORD    wOldAX,     ; pusha.
```

```
;            WORD    wOldBP,    ; pushed bp.
;            WORD    wRetIP,    ; Toolhelp IP via instance thunk.
;            WORD    wRetCS,    ; Toolhelp CS via instance thunk.
;            WORD    wRealAX,   ; For DS.
;            WORD    wFaultID,  ; Fault code.
;            WORD    wHandle,   ; ???
;            WORD    wIP,       ; Faulting instruction IP.
;            WORD    wCS,       ; Faulting instruction CS.
;            WORD    wFlags     ; Faulting flags.
;)
;
externNP CFaultHandler

?PLM = 1
; Windows' routine (Page 940 - Function reference)
;
; VOID TerminateApp(HTASK, WORD);
;
externFP TerminateApp

sBegin  CODE
        ASSUMES CS,CODE

;   ASMFaultHandler
;           Handles all faults passed to it.  Makes the processing ready
;           for a C function, then calls it.  This handler is re-entrant.
;           On entry the stack frame looks like this:
;           ------------
;SP---->|  Ret IP  | [SP + 00h] (toolhelp dll return addr via instance thunk.)
;       |  Ret CS  | [SP + 02h] (ditto...................)
;       |    AX    | [SP + 04h] (DS as called via thunk. )
;       |  FaultID | [SP + 06h] (Interrupt handler.      )
;       |  Handle  | [SP + 08h] (Internal use only.      )
;       |    IP    | [SP + 0Ah] (Faulting IP.            )
;       |    CS    | [SP + 0Ch] (Faulting CS.            )
;       |   Flags  | [SP + 0Eh] (Faulting Flags.         )
;       ------------
;
;
;           or if the fault (Exception) is INT_STKFAULT, SS and SP
;           are put on the stack first (as shown below).
;
;
;           ------------
;
;SP---->|  Ret IP  | [SP + 00h] (toolhelp dll return addr via instance thunk
;       |  Ret CS  | [SP + 02h] (ditto...................)
;       |    AX    | [SP + 04h] (DS as called via thunk. )
;       |  FaultID | [SP + 06h] (Interrupt handler.      )
;       |  Handle  | [SP + 08h] (Internal use only.      )
;       |    IP    | [SP + 0Ah] (Faulting IP.            ) iret to here to
;       |    CS    | [SP + 0Ch] (Faulting CS.            ) restart instruction.
;       |   Flags  | [SP + 0Eh] (Faulting Flags.         )
;       |    SP    | [SP + 10h] (Faulting SP.            ) Stack-low fault
;       |    SS    | [SP + 12h] (Faulting SS.            ) only.
;       ------------
;
```

```
;       Possible Actions :
;       Does a retf to toolhelp via the thunk if action is to chain on
;       to next interrupt handler. Toolhelp will call the next handler
;       installed by InterruptRegister(). There  is  always 'another'
;       handler, ie. the default handler always exists.
;
;       Calls TerminateApp(). This function will not return unless the
;       passed hTask (its first parameter) is NOT NULL (NULL means the
;       current task!) and does not identify a  valid  task.  The sub-
;       routine CFaultHandler is called in the context of the faulting
;       task,  ie. a call to GetCurrentTask() gets the  task handle of
;       the faulting task.  A call to TerminateApp(0,?) terminates the
;       faulting task.
;
;       Do an iret. This action causes the instruction that caused the
;       fault to re-start. The stack has to be cleared before this can
;       be done.
;

cProc   ASMFaultHandler, <FAR,PUBLIC>
cBegin  NOGEN

        ; Normal prologue stuff, ie. make a stack frame
        push    bp
        mov     bp,sp

        ; Save all registers
        pusha
        push    es
        push    ds
        push    ss


        ; Get DS (hInst) in ax ready for call to exported 'C' function. The
        ; register is loaded  by the instance thunk the address of which is
        ; passed to InterruptRegister() in the main 'C' code. NOTE it would
        ; be possible to load ds straight from @data and  restrict  the app
        ; to a single instance much like a DLL does.
        mov     ds,ax

; Call the CFaultHandler 'C' function:
;
; Returns : 0  = Terminate faulting task.
;           1  = Retry (restart) the faulting instruction.
;          >1  = Return to toolhelp, ie. chain to next handler.
;
; On entry to CFaultHandler the stack frame looks like this:
;       ------------
;       BP---->| Old BP  |  [BP + 00h] <-- Added by C routine
;       |        SS       |  [BP + 02h]  push ss
;       |        DS       |  [BP + 04h]  push es
;       |        ES       |  [BP + 06h]  push ds
;       |        DI       |  [BP + 08h]   |
;       |        SI       |  [BP + 0Ah]   |
;       |        BP       |  [BP + 0Ch]   |
;       |        SP       |  [BP + 0Eh]   |
;       |        BX       |  [BP + 10h]   |
```

```
;               |   DX   |  [BP + 12h]    |
;               |   CX   |  [BP + 14h]    |
;               |   AX   |  [BP + 16h]   pusha
;   Old BP---->|Old,Old BP|  [BP + 18h]   push bp
;               |  Ret IP |  [BP + 1Ah]------------------------
;               |  Ret CS |  [BP + 1Ch]           Old frame
;               |   AX   |  [BP + 1Eh]       See notes above.
;               | FaultID |  [BP + 20h]
;               | Handle  |  [BP + 22h]
;               |   IP   |  [BP + 24h]
;               |   CS   |  [BP + 26h]
;               |  Flags  |  [BP + 28h]
;               ------------
;

        ; Call the 'C' function. Return value is in ax register.
        cCall   CFaultHandler

        ; Restore some of the stuff we pushed on before the call.
        ; Don't do a popa or we'll lose ax!
        pop     ss
        pop     ds
        pop     es

        ; Decide what action should be taken now?

        ; Check for 0.
        ; ax OR'ed with ax will set the zero flag if ax is 0.
        or      ax,ax

        ; Zero so terminate faulting task.
        jz      lTerminateApp

        ; Check for 1. Zero flag set if ax IS 1.
        cmp     ax,1

        ; One so try instruction again.
        jz      lTryAgain

        ; Not zero OR one in ax so get toolhelp to try next handler by
        ; falling through lCallNextHandler.
lCallNextHandler:

        ; Restore the rest of what we pushed and do a 'far return' to
        ; toolhelp. Toolhelp will call the next registered handler.
        popa
        pop     bp
        retf


lTryAgain:
        ; Restore the rest of what we pushed and clear the stack,  ie.
        ; remove Ret IP, Ret CS, AX, FaultID and Handle. iret will
        ; then use the address of the faulting instruction.
        popa
        pop     bp
        add     sp,10
        iret
```

```
lTerminateApp:
        ; Same as above by we don't go anywhere. Tidy up stack and call
        ; TerminateApp(NULL, NO_UAEBOX) to kill the  current (faulting)
        ; task.
        popa
        pop     bp
        add     sp,10
        cCall   TerminateApp, <0,NO_UAE_BOX>


cEnd    NOGEN
sEnd
        END
```

Intreg.c :

```c
#include <windows.h>
#include <stdio.h>
#include <string.h>
#include <toolhelp.h>
#include "intreg.h"

/*
** Get rid of silly warnings.
*/
#pragma warning(disable:4100)
#pragma warning(disable:4001)

/* typedefs. */
/*
** Passed to dialog box callback from the InterruptRegister()
** callback.  Used to detail fault information for the dialog
** box to display.
*/
typedef struct
{
    WORD    wsCS;               /* CS of faulting instruction.      */
    WORD    wsIP;               /* IP of faulting instruction.      */
    WORD    wsFaultID;          /* Fault number.                    */
    WORD    wHandle;            /* Handle.                          */
    HTASK   hFaultingTask;      /* hTask of faulting application.   */
                                /* Faulting task's module name.     */
    char    carModuleName[MAX_MODULE_NAME + 1];
} DIALOGINFO, FAR * LPDIALOGINFO;

typedef const char NEAR  *       NPCSTR;

/* Prototypes. */
VOID        CALLBACK    ASMFaultHandler (VOID);
HINSTANCE   NEAR PASCAL hAccesshInstance(HINSTANCE);
HWND        NEAR PASCAL hAccesshWindow  (HWND);
HTASK       NEAR PASCAL hAccesshTask    (HTASK);
VOID        NEAR PASCAL OutError        (NPCSTR);
```

```
LRESULT CALLBACK WndProc
(
    HWND,
UINT,
WPARAM,
LPARAM
);

WORD NEAR CDECL CFaultHandler
(
    WORD,
    WORD,
    WORD,
    WORD,
    WORD,
    WORD,
    WORD,
    WORD,
    WORD,
    WORD,
    WORD,
    WORD,
    WORD,
    WORD,
    WORD,
    WORD,
    WORD,
    WORD,
    WORD,
    WORD
);


BOOL CALLBACK FaultDialogProc
(
    HWND,
    UINT,
    WPARAM,
    LPARAM
);

int PASCAL WinMain
(
    HINSTANCE,
    HINSTANCE,
    LPSTR,
    int
);




/*
** Holds application's hInstance.
*/
HINSTANCE NEAR PASCAL hAccesshInstance(HINSTANCE hInst)
```

```
{
    static HINSTANCE hInstance;

    if(hInst != NULL)
    {
        hInstance = hInst;
    }

    return hInstance;
}




/*
** Holds application's main window handle.
*/
HWND NEAR PASCAL hAccesshWindow(HWND hWnd)
{
    static HWND hWindow;

    if(hWnd != NULL)
    {
        hWindow = hWnd;
    }

    return hWindow;
}




/*
** Holds application's task handle.
*/
HTASK NEAR PASCAL hAccesshTask(HTASK hT)
{
    static HTASK hTask;

    if(hT != NULL)
    {
        hTask = hT;
    }

    return hTask;
}




/*
** Reports start-up errors.
*/
VOID NEAR PASCAL OutError(NPCSTR pszErrorStr)
{
    MessageBox(0, pszErrorStr, NULL, MB_OK);
```

```
    return;
}




/*
** Entry point.
*/
int PASCAL WinMain
(
   HINSTANCE   hInstance,
   HINSTANCE   hPrevInstance,
   LPSTR       lpszCmdLine,
   int         nCmdShow
)
{
   auto HWND       hWnd;
   auto MSG        msg;
   auto WNDCLASS   tWc;
   auto FARPROC    lpfnFault;
   auto char       carAppName[] = "IntReg";

   if(hPrevInstance == NULL)
   {
       tWc.style         = 0L;
       tWc.lpfnWndProc   = WndProc;
       tWc.cbClsExtra    = 0;
       tWc.cbWndExtra    = 0;
       tWc.hInstance     = hInstance;
       tWc.hIcon         = LoadIcon(hInstance, MAKEINTRESOURCE(INTREG));
       tWc.hCursor       = LoadCursor(NULL, IDC_ARROW);
       tWc.hbrBackground = (HBRUSH)(COLOR_WINDOW + 1);
       tWc.lpszMenuName  = NULL;
       tWc.lpszClassName = carAppName;

       if(RegisterClass(&tWc) == NULL)
       {
           OutError("Couldn't register class.");

           return 0;
       }
   }
   else
   {
      OutError("Only one instance allowed.");

      return 0;
   }

   hWnd = CreateWindow(
                       carAppName
                      ,"Interrupt Register App"
                      ,WS_OVERLAPPEDWINDOW
                      ,0
                      ,0
                      ,0
```

```
                       , 0
                       , NULL
                       , NULL
                       , hInstance
                       , NULL
                       );

    if(hWnd == NULL)
    {
        OutError("Couldn't create main window.");

        return 0;
    }


    if((lpfnFault = MakeProcInstance(
                            (FARPROC)ASMFaultHandler
                           , hInstance
                           )) != NULL
      )
    {
       if(InterruptRegister(NULL, lpfnFault) == NULL)
       {
           OutError("Couldn't install InterruptRegisterHook callback.");

           return 0;
       }
    }
    else
    {
       OutError("Couldn't get an instance thunk.");

       return 0;
    }

    /*
    ** Store away stuff for later.
    */
    hAccesshWindow(hWnd);
    hAccesshInstance(hInstance);
    hAccesshTask(GetCurrentTask());

    ShowWindow(hWnd, SW_SHOWMINNOACTIVE);
    UpdateWindow(hWnd);

    while(GetMessage(&msg, NULL, 0, 0))
    {
        TranslateMessage(&msg);
        DispatchMessage(&msg);
    }

    InterruptUnRegister(NULL);
    FreeProcInstance(lpfnFault);

    return msg.wParam;
}
```

```
LRESULT CALLBACK WndProc
(
    HWND    hWnd,
    UINT    uMessage,
    WPARAM  wParam,
    LPARAM  lParam
)
{
    switch(uMessage)
    {
            /*
            ** Don't open from iconic state.
            */
        case WM_QUERYOPEN:
            break;

        case WM_DESTROY:
            PostQuitMessage(0);
            break;

        default:
            return DefWindowProc(hWnd, uMessage, wParam, lParam);
    }
    return (LRESULT)0;
}


/*
** Part of the InterruptRegister() call-back function. Called by
** ASMFaultHandler().
** This function must be a CDECL function because if it were PASCAL
** its prologue would clear the stack  - we have to do that (to
** various degrees) in the assembler module.  Also note that this
** 'C' function can change values passed to it as if they were being
** passed in by reference, ie. the passed in values map to 'real'
** values pushed on to the stack in the assembler module!
*/
WORD CDECL CFaultHandler
(
    WORD wSS,
    WORD wDS,
    WORD wES,
    WORD wDI,
    WORD wSI,
    WORD wBP,
    WORD wSP,
    WORD wBX,
    WORD wDX,
    WORD wCX,
    WORD wAX1,
    WORD wOldBP,
    WORD wRetIP,
    WORD wRetCS,
    WORD wAX2,
    WORD wFaultID,
    WORD wHandle,
```

```
    WORD wIP,
    WORD wCS,
    WORD wFlags
)
{
  /*
  ** Re-entrancy semaphore.
  ** When things just can't get any worse  -  they will. Or -
  ** Things typically get much worse before they get better!
  */
  static BOOL       bEntered;
  /*
  ** Needed to create and process dialog box.
  */
  auto   FARPROC    lpfnDlg;
  auto   int        nResult;

  /*
  ** Hold information about the fault and faulting task.
  */
  auto   DIALOGINFO tDi;
  auto   TASKENTRY  tTe;

  /*
  ** See if we're already here, ie. been re-entered.
  ** If so, chain on to next handler.
  */
  if(bEntered != FALSE)
  {
      return IDC_CHAIN;
  }
  else
  {
      bEntered = TRUE;
  }

  /*
  ** Throw out stack faults also. NOTE: despite documentation
  ** this bit does seem to be set on a stack fault so we will
  ** handle stack faults here!
  */
  if(wFaultID & 0x8000)
  {
      return IDC_CHAIN;
  }

  /*
  ** Only trap important faults. Report these boring traps to
  ** debug system if available.
  */
  if(wFaultID == INT_CTLALTSYSRQ || wFaultID == INT_1 || wFaultID == INT_3)
  {
      DebugOutput(
              DBF_TRACE | DBF_APPLICATION
              ,"Fault %X at %04X:%04X\n"
```

```
                     ,wFaultID
                     ,wCS
                     ,wIP
                     );

    bEntered = FALSE;

    return IDC_RESTART;
}

/*
** Get info on faulting task.
*/
tTe.dwSize = sizeof(TASKENTRY);
TaskFindHandle(&tTe, GetCurrentTask());

/*
** Copy info to DIALOGINFO so that it can be
** passed to the dialog box callback.
*/
tDi.wsCS           = wCS;
tDi.wsIP           = wIP;
tDi.wsFaultID      = wFaultID;
tDi.wHandle        = wHandle;
tDi.hFaultingTask  = tTe.hTask;
lstrcpy(tDi.carModuleName, tTe.szModule);

/*
** Use the dialog box to determine what to do with the fault.
*/
lpfnDlg = MakeProcInstance(
                         (FARPROC)FaultDialogProc
                         ,hAccesshInstance(NULL)
                         );

if(lpfnDlg == NULL)
{
    return IDC_CHAIN;
}

/*
** Create dialog box - pass fault info via WM_INITDIALOG lParam.
*/
nResult = DialogBoxParam(
                         hAccesshInstance(NULL)
                         ,MAKEINTRESOURCE(IDD_DIALOG)
                         ,hAccesshWindow(NULL)
                         ,lpfnDlg
                         ,(LPARAM)(LPDIALOGINFO)&tDi
                         );

if(nResult == -1)
{
    nResult = IDC_CHAIN;
}

FreeProcInstance(lpfnDlg);
```

```
    /*
    ** Exiting handler so reset re-entrancy semaphore.
    */
    bEntered = FALSE;

    /*
    ** Pass back result to assembler module so that it can
    ** work out how to handle the fault.
    */
    return (WORD)nResult;
}


/*
** Create at request of CFaultHandler. Asks user what to do with
** the fault.
*/
BOOL CALLBACK FaultDialogProc
(
    HWND    hDlg,
    UINT    uMessage,
    WPARAM  wParam,
    LPARAM  lParam
)
{
    /*
    ** Used to set dialog control captions.
    */
    auto char carBuffer[BUFFER_SIZE];

    /*
    ** Used to position the dialog window
    ** in the center of the screen.
    */
    auto RECT tRsWindow;
    auto int  nWidth;
    auto int  nHeight;

    switch (uMessage)
    {
            /*
            ** Set up captions on dialog box and
            ** controls from fault info.
            */
        case WM_INITDIALOG:
            /* Dialog box caption set to faulting module name. */
            SetWindowText(hDlg, ((LPDIALOGINFO)lParam)->carModuleName);
            wsprintf(
                    carBuffer
                    ,"%d - Trap(%X)"
                    , ((LPDIALOGINFO)lParam)->wsFaultID
                    , ((LPDIALOGINFO)lParam)->wsFaultID
                    );

            /* Trap number. */
            SetDlgItemText(hDlg, IDC_FAULTNUMBER, carBuffer);
```

```
            wsprintf(
                    carBuffer
                   ,"%X:%X"
                   , ((LPDIALOGINFO) lParam) ->wsCS
                   , ((LPDIALOGINFO) lParam) ->wsIP
                   );

            /* CS:IP. */
            SetDlgItemText(hDlg, IDC_CSANDIP, carBuffer);
            wsprintf(carBuffer, "%X",
((LPDIALOGINFO) lParam) ->hFaultingTask);

            /* Faulting task's task handle. */
            SetDlgItemText(hDlg, IDC_HTASKFAULT, carBuffer);
            wsprintf(carBuffer, "%X", hAccesshTask(NULL));

            /* Intreg's task handle. */
            SetDlgItemText(hDlg, IDC_HTASKMAIN, carBuffer);
            wsprintf(carBuffer, "%X", ((LPDIALOGINFO) lParam) ->wHandle);

            /* Handle. */
            SetDlgItemText(hDlg, IDC_HANDLE, carBuffer);
            GetWindowRect(hDlg, &tRsWindow);

            /*
            ** Position dialog window in center of screen.
            */
            nWidth = tRsWindow.right - tRsWindow.left;
            nHeight = tRsWindow.bottom - tRsWindow.top;

            MoveWindow(
                    hDlg
                   , (GetSystemMetrics(SM_CXSCREEN) / 2) - (nWidth / 2)
                   , (GetSystemMetrics(SM_CYSCREEN) / 2) - (nHeight / 2)
                   ,nWidth
                   ,nHeight
                   ,FALSE
                   );
            break;

        /*
        ** User has selected a button. wParam has control ID.
        ** Control ID's match the required actions so all we
        ** do is return 'em.
        */
        case WM_COMMAND:
            switch (wParam)
            {
                case IDC_TERMINATE:
                case IDC_RESTART:
                case IDC_CHAIN:
                    EndDialog(hDlg, wParam);
                    break;

                default:
                    return IDC_CHAIN;
            }
```

```
            return TRUE;

        default:
            return FALSE;
    }

    return FALSE;
}
```

Inreg.rc :

```
#include <windows.h>
#include "intreg.h"

/*
** Icon.
*/
INTREG  ICON intreg.ico

/*
** Dialog box.
*/
rcinclude intreg.dlg
```

Intreg.dlg :

```
DLGINCLUDE RCDATA DISCARDABLE
BEGIN
    "INTREG.H\0"
END

IDD_DIALOG DIALOG 83, 14, 148, 69
STYLE DS_MODALFRAME | WS_POPUP | WS_CAPTION | WS_SYSMENU
FONT 10, "MS Sans Serif"
BEGIN
    CONTROL         "&Kill Task"
                    ,IDC_TERMINATE
                    ,"Button"
                    ,BS_DEFPUSHBUTTON | WS_TABSTOP
                    ,13, 54, 37, 12

    CONTROL         "&Restart"
                    ,IDC_RESTART
                    ,"Button"
                    ,WS_TABSTOP
                    ,56, 54, 37, 11

    CONTROL         "&Chain"
                    ,IDC_CHAIN
                    ,"Button"
                    ,WS_TABSTOP
                    ,99, 54, 37, 11

    CONTROL         "Fault Number"
                    ,IDC_STATIC
                    ,"Static"
```

```
                            ,SS_RIGHT | WS_GROUP
                            ,2, 2, 47, 8

CONTROL                     "CS:IP"
                            ,IDC_STATIC
                            ,"Static"
                            ,SS_RIGHT
                            ,2, 11, 47, 8

CONTROL                     "Fault hTask"
                            ,IDC_STATIC
                            ,"Static"
                            ,SS_RIGHT | WS_GROUP
                            ,2, 20, 47, 8

CONTROL                     "Host hTask"
                            ,IDC_STATIC
                            ,"Static"
                            ,SS_RIGHT | WS_GROUP
                            ,2, 29, 47, 8

CONTROL                     "Handle"
                            ,IDC_STATIC
                            ,"Static"
                            ,SS_RIGHT | WS_GROUP
                            ,2, 39, 47, 8

CONTROL                     ""
                            ,IDC_FAULTNUMBER
                            ,"Static"
                            ,SS_LEFT | WS_GROUP
                            ,59, 2, 80 ,9

CONTROL                     ""
                            ,IDC_CSANDIP
                            ,"Static"
                            ,SS_LEFT | WS_GROUP
                            ,59, 11, 80, 9

CONTROL                     ""
                            ,IDC_HTASKFAULT
                            ,"Static"
                            ,SS_LEFT | WS_GROUP
                            ,59, 20, 80, 9

CONTROL                     ""
                            ,IDC_HTASKMAIN
                            ,"Static"
                            ,SS_LEFT | WS_GROUP
                            ,59, 29, 80, 9

CONTROL                     ""
                            ,IDC_HANDLE
                            ,"Static"
                            ,SS_LEFT | WS_GROUP
                            ,59, 39, 80, 9
END
```

Intreg.def :

```
NAME            INTREG

DESCRIPTION     'Interrupt Register Handler.'

EXETYPE         WINDOWS 3.1

PROTMODE

STUB            'WINSTUB.EXE'

CODE            PRELOAD FIXED

DATA            PRELOAD MOVEABLE MULTIPLE

HEAPSIZE        1024

STACKSIZE       4096

EXPORTS
                WNDPROC
                FAULTDIALOGPROC
                ASMFAULTHANDLER

IMPORTS
                KERNEL._DebugOutput
```

Makefile info :

```
libw slibcew toolhelp
cl -AS -c -G2sw -Zi -Od -Zp -W4
```

Intreg.h :

```
/*
** General buffer (Major disaster, corporal punishment & private func-
tion!).
*/
#define BUFFER_SIZE         80

/*
** Icon resource ID.
*/
#define INTREG              200

/*
** Dialog box resource ID.
*/
#define IDD_DIALOG          100

/*
** Dialog box control IDs.
```

```
*/
#define IDC_TERMINATE      0
#define IDC_RESTART        1
#define IDC_CHAIN          2
#define IDC_STATIC        -1
#define IDC_FAULTNUMBER  300
#define IDC_CSANDIP      301
#define IDC_HTASKFAULT   302
#define IDC_HTASKMAIN    303
#define IDC_HANDLE       304
```

Intreg.ico

The application code is well documented and requires little in the way of explanation.

To use it I would suggest that you have it load before, or instead of, any other interrupt handler, ie. before Dr. Watson. The application traps faults and displays a dialog box like this :

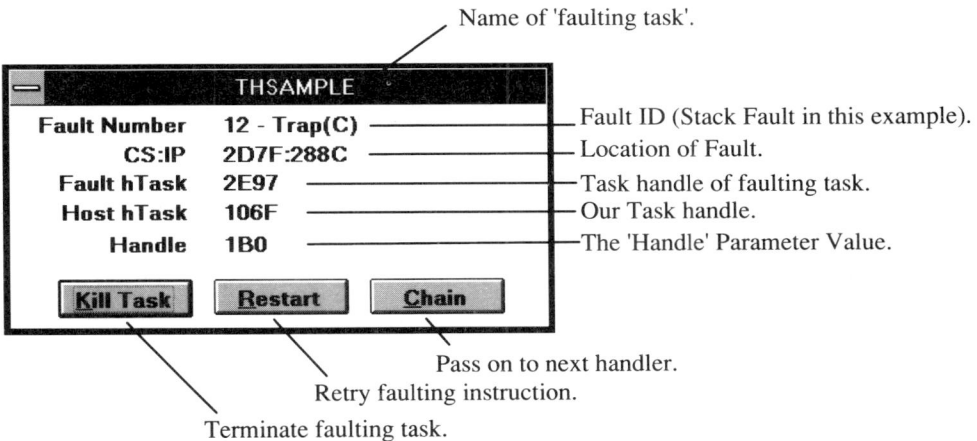

Name of 'faulting task'.

Fault ID (Stack Fault in this example).
Location of Fault.
Task handle of faulting task.
Our Task handle.
The 'Handle' Parameter Value.

Pass on to next handler.
Retry faulting instruction.
Terminate faulting task.

The whole application is modelled on the SDK TOOLHELP example so you might want to take a look at that example also. There's also a very good example of an InterruptRegister() handler in the book Undocumented Windows. The handler in there also switches stacks when it is called (as the app is called in the context of the faulting task) and uses @data to load the app's DGROUP like a DLL does (you can only do this if you allow a single instance of your application to run). Lastly, take a look at the code to DBWIN, esp. DBWIN 2 –the *enhanced* version available off Compuserve.

Intreg was tested using the SDK THSAMPLE.EXE application. Interestingly thsample has the ability to generate stack faults but the option to do so is omitted from its *Fault* menu!

☐ Dr. Watson

The *Watson* application can be used to diagnose a bug by cross-referencing the faulty line of code as reported in the log file with a mixed source/assembly language listing produced by the compiler. If you don't normally have *the doc* loaded, and generate a general protection fault in one of your apps, load it up and try the faulting app again (*if it was bad it'll be back!*) as the log file produced can be really useful in tracking down mischievous bugs.

```
GENERIC had a 'Exceed Segment Bounds (Read)' fault at GENERIC
MainWndProc+0050
$tag$A$Exceed Segment Bounds (Read)$GENERIC MainWndProc+0050$push  word
ptr es:[bx+0c]
```

The SDK *Programming Tools* manual has a detailed discussion on Dr. Watson logs and set-up. My favourite set-up is as follows :

```
[Dr. Watson]
SkipInfo=32bitregs information summary clues
ShowInfo=disassembly locals modules paramlog
DisLen=16
TrapZero=0
GPContinue=15
DisStack=100
LogFile=c:\win31\drwatson.log
```

The settings above make for the silent approach; I once did some work for a company that wanted to use Watson to log errors to a network drive without the user knowing it was being done; they even went so far as to hide Dr. Watson so that the users didn't even know that it was running. They wrote a *parasitic* app to do the job that contained a small piece of code like this :

```
switch(uMessage)
{
case WM_CREATE:
    {
        auto HWND hWndWatson;
```

```
        if((hWndWatson = FindWindow("Dr. Watson", NULL)) != NULL)
        {
            ShowWindow(hWndWatson, SW_HIDE);
        }
        else
        {
        LogToNetDrive(LogUser(), "Not running Dr. Watson");
        }
    }

    return (LRESULT)-1;

    break;
```

They had this piece of code in a start-up app which was loaded in a *Load=* line in their WIN.INI after *DRWATSON. It* tries to find, and then hide, Dr. Watson. If it fails it logs the user's name to a network drive so that the support people knew that user X wasn't running things correctly.

The Dr. Watson settings shown above mean that the log file, C:\WIN31\DRWATSON.LOG :

Does not contain information about (Skip**Info) :**
The 32 registers (32b**itregs**),
System information (info**rmation**),
The four line summary at the end of the log file (**summary**). The **clues** entry stops Watson prompting you for the summary information.

Does contain (Sho**wInfo) :**
Separate disassembly of the fault address (disasse**mbly**).
Separate stack dump of local variable and parameter values (Lo**cals**).
A list of all loaded modules (mo**dules**).
Parameter validation error logging (par**amlog**)

Disassembles 16 instructions in stack traces and the disassembly part of the failure report (Dis**Len=16**).

Does not trap (handle) divide by zero faults (Trap**Zero=0**).

Does all it can to allow faulting applications to continue (although this is sometimes more than risky) (GPContin**ue=15**).

Lastly disassembles up to 100 stack frames back from the faulting function and instruction (Dis**Stack=100**).

☐ What to look for in Watson logs

When Watson detects a general protection fault the actual fault is caused by one of the following :

1   Operation exceeded segment bounds.

2   Invalid selector.

3   Null selector.

4   Read from execute only code segment.

5   Segment not present.

6   Write to read only data segment.

7   Write to a code segment.

8   Segment wrap around.

If you get a GPF, here's what to look for :

1   This error is caused when a task tries to access memory outside the scope of a segment as described by the segment limit (size) of a selector. You should check that you are not trying to read past the end of an array or move past the end (or beginning) of a global heap object. Also check that the starting address of your read is valid?

2   This error is caused because a task has attempted to free or use a segment that wasn't there or belonged to another task. A Null selector is really a special case of an Invalid Selector.

3   This error is caused when a task tries to access memory using a selector with a value of 0 (Null). You should check that a GlobalAlloc() or GlobalLock() hasn't failed. See the selector dump in the log and check to see that ES, CS, DS etc is NOT NULL.

4   This error is caused when a task tries to read from a code segment.

5   This error is caused when a task attempts to use a segment that was *not present'.* *Check for a segment that should be fixed is actually given the FIXED* attribute. Also a GlobalAlloc() of 0 bytes may cause this error.

6   This error is caused when a task tries to write to a read only code segment. Check that you're not trying to write past the end of an array or using an invalid pointer. See also the PrestoChangoSelector() function.

7   This error is when a task tries to write to a code segment. Check for same as 7. above.

8   This error is caused when a task tries to read a code segment. Check for same as 6. above.

The Dr. Watson log file is easy to use. One of the most important parts is its stack dump. Here's a fault, written in assembler to show you how to use the stack trace information to work your way back to your faulty code.

```
LRESULT __export CALLBACK MainWndProc
(
    HWND     hWnd
  , UINT     uMessage
  , WPARAM   wParam
  , LPARAM   lParam
)
{
    switch (uMessage)
    {
    case WM_COMMAND:
        /*
        ** Generate GPF by writing to code segment!
        **
        ** This assembly means - move into a byte the value 42h.
        ** the byte is pointed to by cs:0000, ie. the first byte
        ** of code address by cs currently.
        */
        _asm{
            mov cs:[0],BYTE PTR 42h
            }
        break;

    case WM_DESTROY:
        PostQuitMessage(0);
        break;

    default:
        return DefWindowProc(hWnd, uMessage, wParam, lParam);
    }

    return (LRESULT)0;
}
```

This code attempts to write to a code segment, something that will cause a GPF as a code segment is usually flagged as execute/read only (this is confirmed by the Dr. Watson log show below). As the actual faulting code is written in assembler spotting it in a Dr. Watson log is made easier!

If you were to execute this code Dr. Watson would produce, without customisation, this report (important bits are highlighted in bold) :

```
******************************************************************************

Dr. Watson 0.80 Failure Report - Sat Jan 30 20:05:40 1993
GENERIC had a 'Code Segment (Write)' fault at GENERIC MainWndProc+0011
$tag$GENERIC$Code Segment (Write)$GENERIC MainWndProc+0011$mov     byte
ptr cs:[0000],
42$Sat Jan 30 20:05:40 1993

CPU Registers (regs)
```

```
ax=0111  bx=281c  cx=11c7  dx=0111  si=1604  di=1a9d
ip=018f  sp=15d4  bp=15dc  O- D- I+ S- Z+ A- P+ C-
cs = 1277   808364a0:097f Code Ex/R

ss = 11c7   8081f540:1f5f Data R/W
ds = 11c7   8081f540:1f5f Data R/W
es = 11c7   8081f540:1f5f Data R/W

CPU 32 bit Registers (32bit)
eax = 00000111  ebx = 0000281c  ecx = 000011c7  edx = 00000111
esi = 00001604  edi = 00001a9d  ebp = 000015dc  esp = 800115c4
fs = 0000  (        0:0000 Null Ptr
gs = 0000           0:0000 Null Ptr
eflag = 00000202


System Info (info)
Windows version 3.10
Debug build
Windows Build 3.1
Username Unknown User
Organization Unknown Organization
System Free Space 42200768
Stack base 718, top 5688, lowest 4040, size 4970
System resources:  USER: 84% free, seg 06df  GDI: 81% free, seg 0527
LargestFree 41435136, MaxPagesAvail 10116, MaxPagesLockable 2401
TotalLinear 10876, TotalUnlockedPages 2408, FreePages 1984
TotalPages 2870, FreeLinearSpace 10119, SwapFilePages 10876
Page Size 4096
9 tasks executing.
WinFlags -
  Math coprocessor
  80486
  Enhanced mode
  Protect mode


Stack Dump (stack)
```
Stack Frame 0 is GENERIC MainWndProc+0011   ss:bp 11c7:15dc

```
1277:0186  1e                push    ds
1277:0187  8e d8             mov     ds, ax
1277:0189  8b 46 0c          mov     ax, [bp+0c]
1277:018c  e9 002d           jmp     near 01bc
(GENERIC:MainWndProc+0011)
```
1277:018f 2e c6 06 0000 42   mov   byte ptr cs:[0000], 42
```
1277:0195  e9 0037           jmp     near 01cf
1277:0198  6a 00             push    00
1277:019a  9a 8c3a 039f      callf   039f:8c3a

Stack Frame 1 is USER 1:2b34              ss:bp 11c7:15f6
039f:2b2b  8c d1             mov     cx, ss
039f:2b2d  8e c1             mov     es, cx
039f:2b2f  8e d9             mov     ds, cx
039f:2b31  ff 5e 06          callf   word ptr [bp+06]
(USER:1:2b34)
039f:2b34  59                pop     cx
039f:2b35  5b                pop     bx
039f:2b36  83 f9 0f          cmp     cx, 0f
039f:2b39  75 1b             jnz     short 2b56
```

```
Stack Frame 2 is GENERIC WINMAIN+0072          ss:bp 11c7:1618
Stack Frame 3 is GENERIC __stubmain+001a       ss:bp 11c7:1626
Stack Frame 4 is GENERIC __astart+008b         ss:bp 11c7:1636
System Tasks (tasks)
Task   STACKS, Handle 1ecf, Flags 0001, Info   7680 01-20-93 11:34
   FileName C:\WIN31\STACKS.EXE
Task WINOLDAP, Handle 11bf, Flags 0001, Info  49248 03-01-92  3:10
   FileName C:\WIN31\SYSTEM\WINOA386.MOD
Task DBWINEXE, Handle 1f97, Flags 0001, Info  17920 10-02-92 11:08
   FileName C:\WINDEV\BIN\DBWIN.EXE
Task DESKCTLS, Handle 125f, Flags 0001, Info  31228 09-19-92 11:02
   FileName C:\WIN31\DESKCTLS.EXE
Task DRWATSON, Handle 1077, Flags 0001, Info  26864 03-01-92  3:10
   FileName C:\WIN31\DRWATSON.EXE
Task  PROGMAN, Handle 056f, Flags 0001, Info 115312 03-01-92  3:10
   FileName C:\WIN31\PROGMAN.EXE
Task      RES, Handle 122f, Flags 0001, Info  58116 10-03-92 10:45
   FileName C:\WIN31\RES.EXE
Task    WXSRVR, Handle 1fd7, Flags 0001, Info 17920 03-03-92 14:57
   FileName C:\C700\BIN\WXSRVR.EXE
Task  GENERIC, Handle 1ed7, Flags 0001, Info  32796 01-30-93 20:05
   FileName C:\MACHINE1\GENERIC.EXE

1> Deliberate GPF in Generic!
```

The log above shows, through the use of symbolic information retrieved by Dr. Watson, that the fault took place 11 bytes into the MainWndProc function. You could use the -Fc switch to generate a COD file and locate the exact instruction (as shown earlier in the chapter). The trace looks a little different when there's no symbolic information to be found which would typically be the case if this were not a *debug* build. Again, the important bits are highlighted (this listing is cut down to save space) :

```
*************************************************************************

Dr. Watson 0.80 Failure Report - Sat Jan 30 20:14:10 1993
GENERIC had a 'Code Segment (Write)' fault at GENERIC 2:018f
$tag$GENERIC$Code Segment (Write)$GENERIC 2:018f$mov     byte ptr
cs:[0000], 42$Sat
 Jan 30 20:14:10 1993

Stack Dump (stack)
Stack Frame 0 is GENERIC 1:018f                ss:bp 20bf:15dc
20c7:0186  1e                    push    ds
20c7:0187  8e d8                 mov     ds, ax
20c7:0189  8b 46 0c              mov     ax, [bp+0c]
20c7:018c  e9 002d               jmp     near 01bc
(GENERIC:1:018f)
20c7:018f  2e c6 06 0000 42      mov     byte ptr cs:[0000], 42
20c7:0195  e9 0037               jmp     near 01cf
20c7:0198  6a 00                 push    00
20c7:019a  9a 8c3a 039f          callf   039f:8c3a

Stack Frame 1 is USER 1:2b34                   ss:bp 20bf:15f6
039f:2b2b  8c d1                 mov     cx, ss
039f:2b2d  8e c1                 mov     es, cx
039f:2b2f  8e d9                 mov     ds, cx
```

```
039f:2b31  ff 5e 06              callf   word ptr [bp+06]
(USER:1:2b34)
039f:2b34  59                    pop     cx
039f:2b35  5b                    pop     bx
039f:2b36  83 f9 0f              cmp     cx, 0f
039f:2b39  75 1b                 jnz     short 2b56

Task  GENERIC, Handle 20e7, Flags 0001, Info   8192 01-30-93 20:13
  FileName C:\MACHINE1\GENERIC.EXE

1> Another deliberate fault!!
```

Note that here the listing requires a little more interpretation! The fault is at 2:018f, that is offset 018f in logical segment 2. Again, a COD listing can help you find the actual location (as can exehdr) but what's the segment –where's *logical segment 2*. Well the 2 refers to the order in which your segments are ordered in your .def file (assuming that you've more than one!). For example if we had the following in our def file :

```
SEGMENTS
     _TEXT MOVEABLE PRELOAD      DISCARDABLE
      FLTA MOVEABLE LOADONCALL DISCARDABLE
      FLTB MOVEABLE LOADONCALL DISCARDABLE
```

then the fault would be *in* the segment named FLTA. From this you can see that there is an implied segment number (logical segment) applied to each entry in the .def file. The first entry is called segment 1, the second 2 and so on. The segment therefore is the one called FLTA. You'd now need to refer to the make file to see which code module is called FLTA, ie. which one is compiled *cl -c .... -NT FLTA ....* The -NT (name text) compiler switch is used to *name* a segment.

The Borland equivalent of Watson is called WinSpector and in most ways it is better than Watson, in fact I'd probably go as far as to say that all of the Borland tools (except perhaps the Borland debugger) are better than their Microsoft counterparts as supplied with C7.00 and the accompanying SDK (the tools supplied with Visual C++ v. 1.0 are MUCH better) –if you're a serious Windows' developer, which I assume you are having bought this book, you should be considering buying a Borland development kit just for the tools it comes bundled with. If you're quite happy with Microsoft's 'C' compiler, as I am, you'll probably want to buy Borland Pascal (version 7 is the current version at the time of writing); I'm a great Pascal fan, especially of Borland's professional Pascal, and use it often for building DLLs –you can even build DLLs that can be accessed by DOS programs using Borland Pascal! Anyway, back to WinSpector.

☐ WinSpector

WinSpector and its utilities like DFA and BUILDSYM help you perform a post-mortem examination of UAEs, or GPFs just like Dr. Watson does. You should load it from either a WIN.INI entry (load=, run=) or as part of your start-up group. WinSpector writes a logfile to disk also like Watson which details the fault. It details the *call stack,* function names within the call stack, a disassembly of the faulting instructions, CPU register contents and general Windows' information. Also, like Watson, the log file contents can be configured so that only your favourite information is contained in the log file. The DFA Utility, WinSpector's post-processing utility, can help you utilise Turbo Debugger symbolic information to further enhance the readability of available UAE information (nice one Matt).

☐ WDEB386

The WDEB386.EXE (Kernel Debugger) is well worth a mention within this chapter even though at the beginning of it I said we'll not be looking at actual debuggers! The reason is that WDEB386 is no ordinary debugger.

WDEB386 was developed, originally as an internal tool, by Microsoft specifically to debug Windows itself, ie. it was designed *to go where no other debugger had gone before* – as a tool for developing and debugging the enhanced mode layer of Windows! It primary use to developers is to debug applications, DLLs (inc. drivers) that in some way interact with Windows at a low-level, ie. it can be used to debug a complete multitasking, protect mode system. The nature of this kind of debugger can make using it difficult and confusing in many situations and it is best left alone if you're in anyway uncertain about machine code or protect mode programming. The debugger can be used for :

- Tracing through low-level code that is *unreachable* by CodeView.
- Tracing through hardware interrupt handlers.
- Tracing through TSRs.
- Tracing through DOS device drivers.
- Viewing virtual, linear and physical memory anywhere in the system.
- Viewing descriptor tables (GDT, LDT, IDT) and the PMODE registers.
- Displaying the status of VMs.
- Monitoring interrupts and exceptions in 386 enhanced mode.
- Developing and debugging VxDs for enhanced mode.
- etc...

Motto: If your app etc is quite *normal*, stick with CodeView!

By default, the WDEB386 is installed in the C:\WINDEV directory. The file WINDE-BUG.386 is also installed during installation of the SDK installation. WINDEBUG.386 is a Virtual Device driver, or VxD, which may be resident if Windows is running in 386 enhanced mode. Its sole purpose in life is to provide a number of low-level services to debuggers, however it is not necessary for WDEB386 to function properly. WINDEBUG is copied into the Windows' system directory by the installation process, and the line *DEVICE=WINDEBUG.386* is added to the [386enh] section in the SYS-TEM.INI file.

To use WDEB386, which is also known as The Kernel Debugger, you need to be using the debug libs, sometimes called the Debugging Kernel, and a debugging terminal; note that DBWIN will not do here, a *real* debug terminal is required. The terminal is set up as 9600,n,8,1 –that is 9600 baud, no parity, eight data bits and one stop bit. We'll tell the debugger where to find the terminal explicitly when we start it up. You'll also need to build your application so that a .MAP file and relevant .SYM files are available to the debugger. Symbol files are built from map files using a utility such as MAPSYM (map to symbol) :

```
mapsym /l ????.map (Produces ????.sym)
```

All interaction with the debugger is done via the keyboard on the debugging terminal.

An aside on WIN386
Note that to use ALL the features of WDEB386 you'll also need a debug version of WIN386.EXE. WIN386.EXE is the heart of the Windows' 386 enhanced mode OS layer. It is made up of the Virtual Machine Manager, or VMM, and various *standard* VxDs – a non-debugging version ships with the *normal* retail version of Windows (without it you couldn't get to 386 Enhanced mode). Unfortunately, the debug version of WIN386 is not shipped with the SDK but with the Device Driver Kit, or DDK. Therefore to install a FULL debugging version of Windows you'll need the DDK as well as the SDK! Or to put it another way – the normal SDK *debugging version* of Windows contains debug versions of KERNEL, USER, GDI and MMSYSTEM, as well as their corresponding symbol files. The debugging version of WIN386.EXE (limited symbols provided) is available *only* as part of the DDK. In the 3.1 version of the DDK it's located in the 386\TOOLS\DE-BUG directory, whereas in the 3.0 version, it's in the VXD\TOOLS\DEBUG directory. Always make a backup of WIN386.EXE, ie. don't overwrite it with the debugging version (consider changing the batch files N2D and D2N to do this for you). To use WDEB386 with the debugging version of WIN386 you might also need to install the debugging grab*ber* –also part of the DDK. You can tell if this is required as you'll see the message *Incorrect System Version* when you start a DOS session from within Windows if you're running the debug version in 386 enhanced mode. If you see this message copy the .GR3 file from the DDK disks (\ddk\grabbers\???) to your Windows' system directory and set the line 386*Grabber=* in the boot section of SYSTEM.INI to point to it.

Let's take a simple error and work through it. Below is an extract from a modified generic.c that causes a general protection fault by attempting to write the value 42h to the address cs:[0000], ie. the code attempts to write to its own code segment. This kinda thing in protect mode causes a general protection fault to occur which will be caught by WDEB386 and the debugging kernel. The generic app was built as a medium memory model app but consists of one user supplied code module, generic.c. This module is compiled using -NT and is called SEG_GENERIC. Here's the code extract :

```
LRESULT __export CALLBACK MainWndProc
(
    HWND      hWnd
  , UINT      uMessage
  , WPARAM    wParam
  , LPARAM    lParam
)
{
    switch(uMessage)
    {
    case WM_COMMAND:
        _asm{
            mov BYTE PTR cs:[0], 42h
            }
        break;

    case WM_DESTROY:
        PostQuitMessage(0);
        break;

    default:
        return DefWindowProc(hWnd, uMessage, wParam, lParam);
    }

    return (LRESULT)0;
}
```

To debug this program using WDEB386, exit Windows and start the WDEB386 debugger like so :

```
wdeb386 /C:1 /S:krnl386.sym /V /S:generic.sym c:\win31\win.com /3 generic
```

/C:1 means send debugger output to COM1. /S:???????.sym means load these symbol tables (here we're loading the symbols for kernel and generic), /V means verbose mode (you might want to omit this switch as it does rather make WDEB386 a blabber mouth!). C:\WIN31\WIN.COM is the path to WIN.COM /3 means start Windows in enhanced mode and lastly generic is the name of our app, ie. start generic up when Windows starts.

Before Windows even starts you should start to see messages appearing on the debugging terminal. Eventually, Windows starts and so does generic.

The fault in the above code is caused when any menu item is selected in generic's main menu –it only has one menu item, *About'*. *When this is selected you'll see the normal* system modal dialog telling you that *GENERIC has caused a problem...* and asking you whether or not you want to close the application or ignore the fault. Choose close. Now you see another *normal* dialog box :

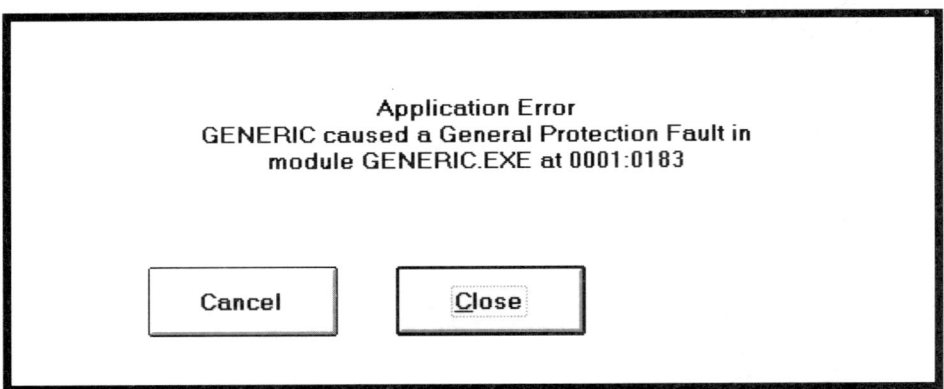

This dialog doesn't normally have the a *Cancel* button in it; it is there only because WDEB386 is loaded (although in saying this you might see it produced by other debuggers like Soft-ICE/W). Press Cancel.

At this point the debugging terminal becomes active and you enter a WDEB386 debugging session. Here's a listing of a typical session, comments are included in the listing in bold :

```
This stuff appears when the debugger is first loaded.
Kernel Debugger  Version 3.10.46 1/16/92  [80386]
These are the symbols we asked for.
Symbols linked (KERNEL)
Symbols linked (GENERIC)


..
Nothing else now appears until the debugger traps the fault.
..


Fault encountered here.
AX=00000111  BX=0000217C  CX=FFFF120F  DX=00000111  SI=00001604
DI=00001ABD
IP=00000183  SP=800115D4  BP=000015DC  CR2=00005C04  CR3=005D6  IOPL=0  F=-- --
CS=1217  SS=120F  DS=120F  ES=120F  FS=0000  GS=0000 -- NV UP EI PL ZR NA
PE NC
1217:00000183  MOV     BYTE PTR CS:[WINMAIN],42       ;'B'
CS:0000=C8

From CS:0000=C8 above we can see that this instruction means insert into
address CS:0000 the value 42, in doing so overwrite what's already there,
ie. C8. We can see also that WINMAIN is 0!

Set up debugger options we want.
#ydisaddr        Disaddr - disassembler to display the disassembly addr.
#ydisline        Disline - disassembler to display filename & linenumber of
each opcode.
#ycodebytes      Codebytes - disassembler to display code bytes along with
                 the disassembled instruction.
```

```
#y386env          Go from 32 bit to 16.

#r                See reg's as 16 bit - this is sometime easier on the eyes

AX=0111  BX=217C  CX=120F  DX=0111  SP=15D4  BP=15DC  SI=1604  DI=1ABD
IP=0183  CS=1217  DS=120F  ES=120F  SS=120F  -- NV UP EI PL ZR NA PE NC
1217:0183  MOV     BYTE PTR CS:[WINMAIN],42            ;'B'
CS:0000=C8

#y386env          Go back to 32 bit.
```

Have a general look around to see what we can see -

Dump bytes cs 1217:0183. Faulting hex code in bold.
```
#dbcs 1217:0183
1217:00000183 2E C6 06 00 00 42 E9 37-00 6A 00 9A 3A 8C 9F 03
.....B.7.j..:...
1217:00000193 E9 2D 00 FF 76 0E FF 76-0C FF 76 0A FF 76 08 FF .-
..v..v..v..
1217:000001A3 76 06 9A 70 B8 9F 03 E9-1F 00 E9 13 00 3D 02 00
v..p.........=..
1217:000001B3 75 03 E9 D4 FF 3D 11 01-75 03 E9 C3 FF E9 D3 FF
u....=..u.......
1217:000001C3 B8 00 00 BA 00 00 E9 00-00 1F 5F 5E C9 CA 0A 00
.........._^....
1217:000001D3 90 8C D0 C8 02 00 00 56-57 1E 8E D8 8B 46 0C E9
.......VW....F..
1217:000001E3 2E 00 B8 01 00 E9 41 00-83 7E 0A 01 75 03 E9 09
......A..~..u...
1217:000001F3 00 83 7E 0A 02 74 03 E9-10 00 FF 76 0E 6A 01 9A
..~..t.....v.j..
```

Dump current task state.
```
#dt
EAX=00000000 EBX=00000000 ECX=00000000 EDX=00000000 ESI=00000000
EDI=00000000
EIP=00000000 ESP=00000000 EBP=00000000 IOPL=0 -- -- -- NV UP DI PL NZ NA
PO NC
CS=0000 SS=0000 DS=0000 ES=0000 FS=0000 GS=0000  CR3=00000000
SS0=0030  ESP0=80010D88  SS1=0000  ESP1=00000000  SS2=0000  ESP2=00000000
LDTR=0000  LINK=0000  TFlags=0000  I/O Map=0068
ports trapped: 0-F,20-21,40,43,60,64,81-83,87,89-8B,A0-A1,C0,C2,C4,C6
C8,CA,CC,CE,D0,D2,D4,D6,D8,DA,DC,DE,3B4-3B5,3BA,3F8-3FE
```

**List absolute symbols in the active map(s) - from the command line that's
krnl386 and generic.**
```
#la
GENERIC:
0000 __wiobused
0000 __sized
0001 __sizec
0006 pLocalHeap
0008 pAtomTable
000A pStackTop
000C pStackMin
000E pStackBot
9876 __acrtused
9876 __acrtmsg
9876 __fptaskdata
```

```
D6D6 __aDBused
D6D6 __aDBdoswp
KERNEL:
0000 __0000h
0001 __WINFLAGS
0003 __AHSHIFT
0008 __AHINCR
0040 __0040h
A000 __A000h
B000 __B000h
B800 __B800h
C000 __C000h
D000 __D000h
E000 __E000h
F000 __ROMBIOS
F000 __F000h
```

Set up for stack trace.
```
#ka8                Display 8 stack frames (if there are eight stack frames!).
```

Show function call stack trace.
```
GENERIC:SEG_GENERIC:MainWndProc + 11
(120F,217C,0111,217C,0111,0064,0000,0000)
USER!(1) 039F:2B34
(0000,0064,0111,217C,02F5,1ABD,1217,0172)
GENERIC:SEG_GENERIC:WINMAIN + 76
(02E1,163D,120F,120E,0000,122F,0080,0001)
GENERIC:SEG_GENERIC:__stubmain + 23
(0000,0000,120F,0000,16C0,1AC4,1636,0001)
GENERIC:SEG_GENERIC:__astart + 93
(0000,0000,0000,0000,0000,0000,0000,0000)
```

Get a list of segment names - needed later maybe. Look in particular for 1217.
```
#lg
GENERIC:
1217:00000000 SEG_GENERIC
120F:00000000 DGROUP
KERNEL:
011F:00000000 IGROUP
0127:00000000 _NRESTEXT
012F:00000000 _MISCTEXT
0137:00000000 DGROUP
```

Remind ourselves of cs. SEG_GENERIC is our code segment.
```
#rcs
CS=1217
:
```

Get local descriptor entry for cs. Yep, it's code!
```
#dlcs
1217  Code    Bas=8067EA80 Lim=00000A1F DPL=3 P  RE    A  UV
```

Get symbol sandwich from current cs:ip.
```
#ln
1217:00000172 GENERIC:SEG_GENERIC:MainWndProc + 11
1217:000001D4 About - 51
```

Where did WINMAIN come from, see if we can find it? Get symbols in segment.

```
#ls seg_generic
1217:00000000 WINMAIN
1217:00000086 _InitApplication
1217:0000010E _InitInstance
1217:00000172 MainWndProc
1217:000001D4 About
1217:00000244 __wflags
1217:0000024E __astart
1217:000002EA __nomain
1217:000002F0 __stubmain
1217:0000031C __cinit
1217:000003FB _exit
1217:00000409 __exit
1217:00000418 __cexit
1217:00000429 __c_exit
1217:00000499 __ctermsub
1217:000004D6 __FF_MSGBANNER
1217:000004FA __setargv
1217:0000067C __setenvp
1217:0000070C __cintDIV
1217:00000711 __amsg_exit
1217:00000754 __wcinit
1217:00000754 __wcexit
1217:00000759 __QWINGetFocus
1217:00000759 __QWINGetSize
1217:00000759 __wgetsize
1217:00000759 __QWINMenuClick
1217:00000759 __QWINYield
1217:00000759 __QWINIsQWINin
1217:00000759 __wsetsize
1217:00000759 __wterm
1217:00000759 __QWINOpen
1217:00000759 __QWINTerm
1217:00000759 __wclose
1217:00000759 __QWINSetAboutString
1217:00000759 __QWINWrite
1217:00000759 __QWINInit
1217:00000759 __QWINClose
1217:00000759 __wmenuclick
1217:00000759 __wopen
1217:00000759 __QWINSetFocus
1217:00000759 __QWINRead
1217:00000759 __wgetfocus
1217:00000759 __QWINSetBuffSize
1217:00000759 __QWINGetBuffSize
1217:00000759 __wgetscreenbuf
1217:00000759 __QWINExit
1217:00000759 __QWINSetSize
1217:00000759 __wsetscreenbuf
1217:00000759 __wabout
1217:00000759 __wread
1217:00000759 __wsetfocus
1217:00000759 __wwrite
1217:00000760 __fptrap
1217:00000766 __NMSG_TEXT
1217:0000079D __NMSG_WRITE
1217:000007DA __myalloc
1217:00000808 __growseg
1217:00000894 __incseg
```

```
1217:000008FA __findlast
1217:0000091A __nmalloc
1217:00000976 __nfree
1217:00000990 __nrealloc
1217:000009FE __nmsize
```

Ok, we've got enough info to find the bug so...

Get back in to close app.
```
#g
```

Close down generic in Windows' session - get warning about not destroying
main window.
```
wn  USER: Window not destroyed: 217c
```

Closing down windows.
```
Symbols unlinked (GENERIC)
Symbols unlinked (KERNEL)
```

The fault is actually reported as MOV BYTE PTR CS:[WINMAIN], 42 (which is not what we expected –like where did it get WINMAIN and why was it zero!?). We can see that an attempt has been made to write to CS and now need to find out where that write took place.

Following the report there's some stuff that sets up the debugger to how I like it; following this is a general *browse about* to gain information, for example the CS is dumped (as bytes) from the faulting instruction –this might be useful in finding the error given a .COD listing. The first real bit of information however comes from the #k command. This means show a stack trace. As you can see, MainWndProc was the last function called. The *+11* is an offset, in this case this should be the offset to where things went wrong! Again, this is followed by a bit of general snooping the purpose of which is to find the segment name of the faulting segment and to confirm our suspicions about MainWndProc + 11. The next important bit is #ln. This command lists, given the loaded symbol tables, the nearest symbols to the faulting address and the name of the segment in which the code resides –again MainWndProc + 11 appears, the seg name is SEG_GENERIC. The next list, #ls, explains where the debugger got [WINMAIN] from. We know from the code that the actual faulting expression was mov BYTE PTR cs:[0], if we look at the symbols in the segment SEG_GENERIC we see that WINMAIN has an offset of 0 –thus the debugger thought that our *real* 0 referred to WINMAIN and substituted it for us –normally quite a helpful feature but maybe a little confusing this time around! Lastly, having established that the problem is in MainWndProc at offset 11 we restart the debugger so that the app may be terminated properly and debugged.

If we now go to our map file for SEG_GENERIC we can look up the nearest line number to address 0001:0183 (which is what IP was set to at the time of the fault).

Line numbers for generic.obj(generic.c) segment SEG_GENERIC

```
18 0001:0000    21 0001:0006    23 0001:000F    25 0001:0022
30 0001:0028    32 0001:003E    36 0001:0044    38 0001:005E
```

```
 39 0001:006A    40 0001:0076    42 0001:0079    43 0001:007F
  0 0001:0084    49 0001:0086    52 0001:008C    53 0001:0091
 54 0001:009B    55 0001:00A0    56 0001:00A5    57 0001:00AB
 58 0001:00BA    59 0001:00C9    60 0001:00D3    61 0001:00DE
 63 0001:00E9    64 0001:0109     0 0001:010C    70 0001:010E
 85 0001:0114    87 0001:0146    89 0001:014F    92 0001:0155
 93 0001:0160    95 0001:0168    96 0001:016E     0 0001:0171
110 0001:0172   111 0001:017D   115 0001:0183   117 0001:0189
120 0001:018C   121 0001:0193   124 0001:0196   125 0001:01AD
127 0001:01C3   128 0001:01CC     0 0001:01D2   140 0001:01D4
141 0001:01DF   144 0001:01E5   147 0001:01EB   149 0001:01FD
150 0001:0207   152 0001:020D   153 0001:0210   155 0001:0226
156 0001:022C     0 0001:0232
```

```
Program entry point at 0001:024E
```

Luckily there's a line number directly at that address, it's line 115 in GENERIC.C. If we look at that line in the source module we see :

```
Line
113    case WM_COMMAND:
114        _asm{
115                mov BYTE PTR cs:0, 42h
116            }
117        break;
```

Fault found!

You'll notice that the debugger prompts for commands with a # sign. Note that this is not always the case. The prompt actually denotes the current processor mode and can be :

- \> The processor is in real mode
- \# The processor is in protected mode
- \- The processor is in virtual 8086 mode

Note that this doesn't mean what mode Windows is running in (BTW WDEB386 can be used to debug standard mode applications etc as well as those in enhanced mode), it means what mode the processor is running in. The processor mode gives a good indication as to what code is currently executing. For example, if the prompt is a -, the code is somewhere in either DOS, the BIOS, or a DOS TSR or device driver. Whenever non-protect mode code is executed the enhanced mode layer of Windows switches the processor to virtual 86 mode to run it.

is was a simple fault, indeed one that we could have easily found using either Dr. Watson or CodeView. I hope however that in finding it with WDEB386 a little of this debugger's power and potential was revealed?

☐ Heap Walker

We had a quick look at Heap Walker elsewhere but now it's time to look at it as a debugging aid. It's particularly useful if you don't have, or for some reason can't run, the debugging libraries as it can be used to see how your application allocates memory from both the global heap and of course those ever important local heaps of GDI and USER.

The general technique for using Heap Walker is to take a snapshot of the all the heaps before you run your app and compare these later with snapshots taken when your app has terminated. If you've got the debugging libraries you'll find that most problems are reported by the libs to your debugging terminal or DBWIN's window so using Heap Walker to monitor GDI's and USER's local heaps is more or less a waste of time.

Heap Walker can save its heap info to .txt files (in your Windows' directory); this is most useful as otherwise you'd have to make notes of the state of the heaps from Heap Walker's display. The two really important heaps you'll need to watch are those belonging to GDI and USER. You'll recall that these heaps are used to *store* objects for modules, ie. a brush allocated by an app is stored in GDI's local heap. The object is considered shareable and is owned therefore by something that is persistent – GDI! When your task closes, GDI checks to see whether or not it allocated any objects. If it did, and it hasn't freed them, GDI issues a warning to the debugging terminal. You can easily see therefore when you haven't freed an object that you should have! If you haven't got the debug libs you'll need to use Heap Walker (or something like it) to see what's not been removed from the *interesting* heap. Obviously, it's going to be harder to track down the error if you've only got Heap Walker logs to go by so if you've got the debug libs – *load 'em up!*

GDI Heap (Local Walk)				
Heap	Sort	Add!		
Info	HANDLE	SIZE FLAGS	LCK TYPE	
Save		44 Free		
		44 Free		
5290		44 Free		
6F60		372 Free		
7FB8		284 Free		
5E88		44 Free		
8B0C		12 Free		
18D4		472 Free		
236C		44 Free		

Save information on Local Heap
to HW??.TXT file in Windows'
Directory.

Here are two *good* Heap Walker logs (taken by snap shoting GDI's local heap). In between these two snapshots I ran GENERIC.EXE. Note that you should leave Heap Walker running while you're using your app, and, if you can talk yourself into it, take snapshots during the run to see how your app's allocating memory in the local and global heaps.

Taken before running application :

```
Local Heap Data - sorted by Type
@code sm ind =
OFFSET HANDLE   SIZE FLAGS     LCK TYPE

  2828          304 Free
  2C00          108 Free
  236C           44 Free
  4968           16 Free
  3D8C           52 Free
  ...
  ...
  2F66   0D4A    34 Moveable      Bitmap
  499A   0CEE    42 Moveable      Bitmap
  3136   0D2A    46 Moveable      Bitmap
  ...
  ...
  42BE   0B86    30 Moveable      Brush
  2DFE   0CCE    30 Moveable      Brush
  2E8E   0CBE    30 Moveable      Brush
  369A   0B8E    30 Moveable      Brush
  166E   0D32   222 Moveable  1   DC
  3982   0C6A   214 Moveable  1   DC
  239E   0C5E   214 Moveable  1   DC
  24AA   0C56   214 Moveable  1   DC
  ...
  ...


Number Of Free Objects : 21 (5292 Bytes)
Number Of Moveable Objects : 131 (9262 Bytes)
Number Of Fixed Objects : 7 (744 Bytes)
Number Of Allocated Objects : 138 (10006 Bytes)

GDI Heap Info
HANDLE : 0527h
Percent Free : 81%

OBJECT            COUNT       SIZE

Pen                   4        104
Brush                19        622
Font                 15        658
Palette               1         26
Bitmap                7        266
Region               37       2190
DC                   11       2322
DisabledDC            0          0
MetaDC                0          0
Metafile              0          0
```

Taken after running application :

```
Local Heap Data - sorted by Type

OFFSET HANDLE   SIZE FLAGS     LCK TYPE
```

```
2828              304 Free
2C00              108 Free
236C               44 Free
4968               16 Free
3D8C               52 Free
...
...
2F66    0D4A       34 Moveable         Bitmap
499A    0CEE       42 Moveable         Bitmap
3136    0D2A       46 Moveable         Bitmap
...
...
42BE    0B86       30 Moveable         Brush
2DFE    0CCE       30 Moveable         Brush
2E8E    0CBE       30 Moveable         Brush
369A    0B8E       30 Moveable         Brush
166E    0D32      222 Moveable    1    DC
3982    0C6A      214 Moveable    1    DC
239E    0C5E      214 Moveable    1    DC
24AA    0C56      214 Moveable    1    DC
...
...


Number Of Free Objects : 21 (4012 Bytes)
Number Of Moveable Objects : 131 (9446 Bytes)
Number Of Fixed Objects : 7 (744 Bytes)
Number Of Allocated Objects : 138 (10190 Bytes)

GDI Heap Info
HANDLE : 0527h
Percent Free : 81%

OBJECT            COUNT        SIZE

Pen                   4         104
Brush                19         622
Font                 15         666
Palette               1          26
Bitmap                7         266
Region               37        2366
DC                   11        2322
DisabledDC            0           0
MetaDC                0           0
Metafile              0           0
```

Summary :

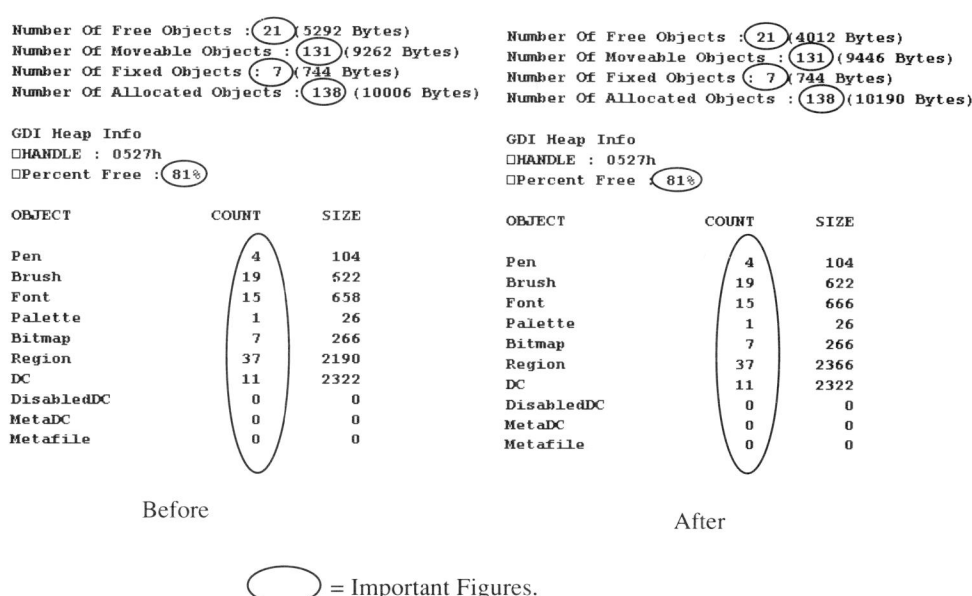

Before   After

◯ = Important Figures.

Let's see how GDI's local heap might look after an application didn't clean up properly. Here's a small code fragment that has some problems :

```
LRESULT __export CALLBACK MainWndProc
(
    HWND     hWnd
  , UINT     uMessage
  , WPARAM   wParam
  , LPARAM   lParam
)
{
    /*
    ** Holds screen DC after WM_CREATE.
    ** Released in WM_DESTROY.
    */
    static HDC hDC;

    switch(uMessage)
    {
        case WM_CREATE:
            {
                auto HMENU hMenu;

                /*
                ** Load required menu.
                */
                hMenu = LoadMenu(
```

```
                                        GetWindowWord(hWnd, GWW_HINSTANCE)
                                        ,"GenericMenu"
                                        );

                    /*
                    ** Fix to main window.
                    */
                    SetMenu(hWnd, hMenu);

                    /*
                    ** Get 'screen' DC so that we can
                    ** draw anywhere on the display.
                    */
                    hDC = CreateDC("DISPLAY", NULL, NULL, NULL);
                }
                break;

        case WM_DESTROY:
                {
                    auto HMENU hMenu;

                    /*
                    ** Get menu off main window.
                    */
                    hMenu = GetMenu(hWnd);

                    /*
                    ** Set main window menu to NULL.
                    */
                    SetMenu(hWnd, NULL);

                    /*
                    ** Get rid of menu.
                    */
                    DestroyMenu(hMenu);

                    /*
                    ** Get rid of static DC.
                    */
                    //DeleteDC(hDC);

                    PostQuitMessage(0);
                }
                break;

        default:
                return DefWindowProc(hWnd, uMessage, wParam, lParam);
    }

    return (LRESULT)0;
}
```

This piece of code is taken from a modified GENERIC.C. It creates a *screen DC* when it handles a WM_CREATE message but doesn't destroy it when it handles a WM_DESTROY message –naughty!!

Here's what GDI's local heap looks like before and after (these dumps are shortened!):

Before running the *bad app.*

```
Number Of Allocated Objects : 324 (22370 Bytes)

GDI Heap Info
HANDLE : 0527h
Percent Free : 59%

OBJECT              COUNT       SIZE

Pen                    6         156
Brush                 31        1242
Font                  50        2340
Palette                1          26
Bitmap                50        1876
Region                49        3354
DC                    20        4280
DisabledDC             1         218
MetaDC                 0           0
Metafile               0           0
```

After app termination.

```
Number Of Allocated Objects : 326 (22954 Bytes)

GDI Heap Info
HANDLE : 0527h
Percent Free : 59%

OBJECT              COUNT       SIZE

Pen                    6         156
Brush                 31        1242
Font                  50        2340
Palette                1          26
Bitmap                50        1876
Region                50        3712
DC                    21        4494
DisabledDC             1         218
MetaDC                 0           0
Metafile               0           0
```

As you can see. GDI contains two extra objects, a DC and a Region. If you've got the debug libs you'll also find the following is output :

```
wn GENERIC GDI: DC not deleted: 10AA
```

As you can see, the debug libs don't tell you about the region; this is because the left over region is as a direct result of not deleting the DC and is therefore implied.

Note that there is one type of GDI object that doesn't cause a warning message to be sent to the debugging terminal if it's not deleted – a Windows' Meta-file. This behaviour does not however constrain memory because meta files are stored in global memory objects and are freed automatically when the application terminates.

You can also use Heap Walker to test your exception handling by getting it to allocate memory. The easiest way to do this is to start your application then get Heap Walker to allocate all of memory. Now you should try and use your app (keeping an eye on the debugging terminal) –how do you handle things like CreateWindow() and CreatePen() etc failing? See also STRESS.EXE

☐ General Techniques and Miscellaneous

Checking Returns

Always check a function's returned value if that value gives an indication of a function's success or failure. For example, GetCurrentTask() can return NULL so you should check that it doesn't.

```
if((hTask = GetCurrentTask()) != NULL)
{
...
}
```

It's tempting not to check a function's return value, particularly where it seems that the function could never fail, again GetCurrentTask() might seem an ideal candidate, like when can there not be a current task?! The golden rule is that if the function reference says that a function might fail always assume it will!

Casts

Don't over cast. Casting takes away the compiler's ability to warn you of silly mistakes.

This doesn't produce a compiler warning until you get on to warning level 4! :

```
RegisterClass((LPWNDCLASS)42);
@code sm ind =
```
whereas this produces warnings at any level higher then W0!:

```
RegisterClass(42);
```

STRICT

Always allow the compiler to warn you if it can. You can help the compiler by defining STRICT in your Windows' code. #define STRICT should be the first thing in your code. Also, if you're not using -GA or -GD remember to define _WINDOWS and/or _WINDLL.

Inserting debug code into executables

Always ship two versions of your DLLs if those DLLs are to be used by other developers. Make one a debug version just like Microsoft do.

Using an exception handler (Catch & Throw)

```
int   WINAPI Catch(int FAR*);
void  WINAPI Throw(const int FAR*, int);
```

Consider using Catch() and Throw() to save and later restore a task's environment. These functions can help prevent your application having to close prematurely. They can even be used to produce error handling like that found in C++ (like using TRY).

The Catch() function is used to *capture* the current environment. The environment is saved in a an area of memory the size of a CATCHBUF. WINDOWS.H defines a CATCHBUF as an array of nine integers –the integers are used to store the system state, ie. it holds the contents of certain registers like IP, CS, SI, DI etc.

You can use Catch() and Throw() to restore your application to some stable state, ie. use it to catch errors, or even to restart the application in a certain place. For example you could use it to do the following :

```
static CATCHBUF x;

switch(uMessage)
{
case WM_COMMAND:
     switch(wParam)
     {
       case IDM_ABOUT:
           {
               auto HINSTANCE hInst;

               /*
               ** Remember where we are!
               */
               Catch(x);

               hInst = (HINSTANCE)GetWindowWord(hWnd, GWW_HINSTANCE);

               DialogBox(hInst,"AboutBox", hWnd, (DLGPROC)About);
           }
           break;

       case DOITAGAIN:

           /*
           ** Restore program to last 'remembered' position!
           */
           Throw(x, 0);
           break;
     }
     break;
```

Here the app *remembers* the state of the system just before the DialogBox() function is called. Later, in response to some more input from a menu we can hop back to the previous Catch() and do the dialog again. Of course, if the user were to pick the DOITAGAIN item before the CATCHBUF was set up we'd be in real trouble!

You can also use, despite popular belief, the 'C' run-time library functions setjmp() and longjmp(); although you only ought to use them in protect mode, ie. this is the same as the above code :

```
#include <setjmp.h>

static jmp_buf x;

switch(uMessage)
{
case WM_COMMAND:
    switch(wParam)
    {
      case IDM_ABOUT:
          {
              auto HINSTANCE hInst;

              SetJmp(x);

              hInst = (HINSTANCE)GetWindowWord(hWnd, GWW_HINSTANCE);

              DialogBox(hInst,"AboutBox", hWnd, (DLGPROC)About);
          }
          break;

      case DOITAGAIN:
          longjmp(x, 0);
          break;
    }
    break;
```

Essentially, these functions perform a non-local goto, ie. they can be used to jump to any location in your application whereas a standard goto cannot. The second parameter to Throw() (read longjmp() for Throw also) is an integer that is (apparently) returned from the Catch() function, ie. it is what Catch() will return when you do a Throw(). This can be used to determine whether or not an error condition exists, or to put it another way, it can be used to determine why Catch() is returning; is it because you've set up a CATCHBUF or because Throw() was called. Catch(), when you first call it, always returns 0; however Catch() can apparently, and at anytime, return again! When you call Throw() it appears to your code as though Catch() is returning, ie. you are returned to the point in your code following the call to Catch(), however AX now contains whatever you passed as the second parameter to Throw() (in the examples above that was always 0 as we weren't interested in knowing *why* we had apparently (or really) returned from the Catch() function. However you could check what's in AX and determine whether or not you're recovering from an error :

```
if((Result = Catch(x)) != 0)
{
switch(Result)
{
    case ERROR1:
                //Handle error 1.
                break;
```

```
        case ERROR2:
                    //Handle error 2.
                    break;

        case ......
}
```

Here we can determine that an error occurred as Catch() has apparently returned a non-zero result, ie. this CS:IP location was jumped to due to a Throw() like this :

```
If(ErrorConditionRasied())
{
Throw(x, ERROR1);
}
```

Using a .COD and/or .ASM file

Most compilers can produce mixed source and assembler files (COD in MS speak). These can be used to track down bugs (remember that utils such as Dr. Watson typically dump just assembler code, ie. no symbolic information is usually at hand). When applying optimisation take a peek at the .ASM file produced by the compiler, these are helpful for seeing what optimisations have been applied in the code generator.

Optimisations

If you detect a run-time error in your code and used the compiler's optimiser, try rebuilding and testing your app with optimisation turned off –sometimes the optimiser itself can cause problems.

Using the MAP file and SYM files

Don't forget to give your debugger every chance. Most debuggers debug better when they're given MAP and symbol files.

Fatal Exit codes and warnings

Pay attention to fatal exits and warnings. If you know a warning is not severe, ie. the debugging version will issue a warning that you know about, use DebugOutput() to inform your user that you know about the warning; additionally provide extra information on why it's generated. You'll see this happen often when using 3rd party DLLs in a development situation. If your code generates a warning that is acceptable; you can tell your user (another developer) that the warning was expected by using DebugOutput(). Additionally, tell *em why the warning's OK*.

Consider an example. You write an app that has to populate a list box with the names of all of Windows' messages; the names are to be taken from a string table. Let's say that the string table contains something like this :

```
WM_NULL"
    ...
    ...
```

```
     . . .
     WM_CREATE,              "WM_CREATE"
```

The example here uses Windows' messages as the string text and the message IDs as indexes. This means that finding the name of a message is simple. All you do is load the string that corresponds to the message ID. If you wanted to load them all, as we do, you might have something like this :

```
for(nLoop = WM_NULL; nLoop <= WM_USER; nLoop++)
{
    if(LoadString(hInstance, nLoop, &carBuffer[0], sizeof(carBuffer)))
    {
      SendMessage(hWndList, LB_ADDSTRING, 0, (LPARAM)(LPSTR)&carBuffer[0]);
    }
}
```

As not all the Windows' message slots between 0 (WM_NULL) and 0x400 (WM_USER) are filled LoadString() will periodically fail, this in turn produces a debug message :

```
wn GENERIC USER: LoadString() failed
```

A fellow developer using your DLL might be pleased to see this following such a message :

```
t GENERIC LoadString failure - attempting to load non-existent string -
this is OK.
```

Your code will need modifying very slightly to produce this helpful diagnostic :

```
bDebug = GetSystemMetrics(SM_DEBUG);
. . .
. . .
for(nLoop = WM_NULL; nLoop <= WM_USER; nLoop++)
{
    if(LoadString(
                  hInstance
                  ,nLoop
                  ,&carBuffer[0]
                  ,sizeof(carBuffer)
                  ) == 0
      )
    {
        if(bDebug == TRUE)
        {
                DebugOutput(DBF_TRACE | DBF_APPLICATION, "......");
        }
    }
    else
    {
        SendMessage(hWndList, LB_ADDSTRING, 0, (LPARAM)(LPSTR)&carBuffer[0]);
    }
}
```

Please note that the code above could have called DebugOutput() even if the debug libraries weren't loaded. The DebugOutput() function simply returns in the retail version.

Temporal Dependencies

Be aware that in Windows certain things are dependent upon order, ie. often one thing has to be done before another can succeed. As experienced developers we're used to this to a large degree, ie. we all know that before we call CreateWindow() that a particular Windows' class must exist –we know to use RegisterClass() before CreateWindow()! Such a dependency is called a temporal dependency and Windows is full of them!

Using Invalid pointers

Windows 3.0 and 3.1 made it harder to use invalid pointers, now they typically show up in as a GPF if that is they make it through the validation layer!

Invalid window/class words

Again, Windows 3.1 has made getting this wrong harder. In 3.1 you cannot store something in a class or window word that doesn't exist as you could in 3.0 and earlier. Remember to super-class an existing class if you want to add words of your own and never use words that seem to exist yet remain unused –they probably are!

Prototyping

Always use function prototypes and compile on the maximum warning level supplied by the compiler vendor. If you can, do a case sensitive link (normally although the compiler compiles case sensitive the linker ignores case!). Use the compiler's /Zg switch to generate and educate!

It's hard to retro-fit turning up the compiler's warning level, ie. you'll often just get too many warnings and will give up early! Motto: When you start a project turn the warning level up full as it's easy to cure warnings as they occur during development.

Use debug specific functions

Functions such as ValidateFreeSpaces() and ValidateCodeSegments() are seldom used, indeed a lot of programmers have never heard them even though they've been available for sometime! These functions are there to enable you to build better and more robust applications –use 'em.

Note: You'll need to add these to WIN.INI before using ValidateFreeSpaces().

[kernel]

EnableFreeChecking=1

EnableHeapChecking=1

Test with Stress etc

Test your application using whatever stressing tools are available. I have a small application that is used to fire off stress whenever I enter Windows. It ensures that I always check my application under imperfect conditions.

Explore alternative functions

Don't just use the functions provided by the *normal* system. For example, if you have the multi-media extensions loaded consider using, say, OutputDebugStr(). This function sends a debugging message directly to either the COM1 port or to a secondary monochrome display. It completely bypasses DOS so it can be used by very low level call-back functions –it can even be used to output the contents of the 386 chip's registers!

Coding Standards and Identifiers

Make sure that you code to some standard, esp. if you're part of a coding team. Also make sure that you're making the most of Hungarian Notation. My firm *The Mandelbrot Set* has coding standards for 'C', C++ and Visual Basic – these ensure that we all code to the same standard and that code written by one person can be understood by any other coder with minimal effort – if you haven't got one invest in one, it'll save a lot of time later. If you're interested, TMS sells its' coding standards (this will save you writing your own), contact me directly via email if you're interested and I'll put you on to the right person – you might even get a discount!

Source Control

Always use a source control system, esp. if you're working in a team. Microsoft have just released a Windows' hosted source control system that's not only easy to use but provides all the features you'll typically require in such a system. Installing a source control system and getting everyone to use it is really very easy – why not do it?

Make the debug build more like the retail

If you hit problems using your debugger when using the debug libs try adding the following to the [386Enh] section of SYSTEM.INI :

DebugPhysAddrs=BOOL

Where BOOL is one of either TRUE (default) or FALSE. This switch essentially creates a *debug* version of Windows that looks more like the retail version. By default when a debugger such as CodeView or WDEB386 is loaded Windows makes available the entire base physical linear memory region. When you set DebugPhysAddrs to FALSE this doesn't happen – outcome, the debugger is prevented from examining the base physical linear memory region of memory but the environment mimics that of the retail product more closely – if you have a problem in the *retail* that you don't have in the *debug* try this one – it sometimes works!

Make use of the new validation routines

```
BOOL WINAPI IsBadReadPtr(const void FAR* lp, UINT cb);
BOOL WINAPI IsBadWritePtr(void FAR* lp, UINT cb);
BOOL WINAPI IsBadHugeReadPtr(const void _huge* lp, DWORD cb);
BOOL WINAPI IsBadHugeWritePtr(void _huge* lp, DWORD cb);
BOOL WINAPI IsBadCodePtr(FARPROC lpfn);
BOOL WINAPI IsBadStringPtr(const void FAR* lpsz, UINT cchMax);
```

Don't forget IsGDIObject() also. See the *Controls* chapter for more on this API.

Use a profiler, any profiler, to help you find the bottlenecks in your code

We've seen a crude profiling DLL in the chapter on writing DLLs. Also both Microsoft and Borland ship their 'C' compilers with profiling tools. Lastly, Windows itself has profiling support built in –use it.

```
int  WINAPI ProfInsChk(void);
void WINAPI ProfSetup(int,int);
void WINAPI ProfSampRate(int,int);
void WINAPI ProfStart(void);
void WINAPI ProfStop(void);
void WINAPI ProfClear(void);
void WINAPI ProfFlush(void);
void WINAPI ProfFinish(void);
```

Look at third party debuggers

One of the most frequently used, and therefore popular, third party debuggers is Soft-ICE/W from Nu-Mega Technologies Inc. You must have seen their ads, they've got penguins splattered all over them (also see the CodeView for Windows start-up screen)! The ICE in Soft-ICE/W stands for In-Circuit Emulator. An ICE is a piece of hardware that usually plugs into where you processor used to, ie. the actual processor is removed from your machine and inserted into some remote hardware. Also, the remote hardware is typically *driven* by another PC, ie. the hardware in your machine is controlled by hardware/software running on another PC.

ICE debuggers are expensive but extremely good – there's nothing they can't cope with! A software based debugger usually has some element of an ICE debugger built into it – trouble is that rarely does one go far enough so as to be able to recover from, say, system hangs! The good news is that Soft-ICE/W seems to do just that! The Nu-Mega debugger will be most useful however to developers of rather more low-level Windows code like VxDs, DOS based TSR and device drivers – yes it can debug all of these! The one shortfall it has is that it can only be used to debug apps etc running in 386 Enhanced Mode (it therefore requires at least a 386SX or better) – if you're interested in Standard Mode only you've therefore got a problem and it'll be back to CodeView etc for you. All in all though this Nu-Mega debugger is about the most cost effective but professional debugger there is at the moment – if you're a serious developer consider getting a copy of it ASAP.

Bugs and the UI

Some bugs appear due to changes made in the user interface, ie. you change something in the UI part of your application and find that now something else doesn't work. Also some debugging requires comprehensive testing to discover – like selecting all the possible permutations of your menu items. If you want to test your app thoroughly therefore you should consider using some sort of automating tool like Microsoft's Test. This tool allows you to exercise your app and perform conformity checks etc – check it out! An inconsistency in our app's UI might also be considered a bug? For example, say you lay out you menus differently to everyone else – well isn't this a bug of sorts. Your users will have problems navigating around your application if you do this because it's different from every other Windows' application they're used to – I'd definitely call this a bug. Make sure that your user interface is conformant therefore to the Microsoft standard. See *The Windows Interface: An Application Design Guide* book that should have come with your SDK.

Wording Error Messages

How do you actually break the bad news to the user, via a message right? How much thought do you put into wording that message – very little I bet!? How often have you seen messages that look something like this :

Global lock of memory object failed. Handle 0x000, pointer 0x000:0x0000

Whilst not strictly a bug, as we generally think about them, this subject does have something to do with debugging, after all a bug possibly caused the GlobalLock() to fail. Think long and hard about how you should word bad news – remember that the user's probably not technical and that your message should convey understandable (to them) information. Imagine you're talking to this user over a beer – what words would you use to explain how a GlobalLock() could fail!? See also the dialog chapter TMSERRORBOX example.

Stress your app

Use the SDK STRESS.EXE application to put the screws on your application. See how it survives memory allocation failures, being unable to open a disk file etc. If you've not got Stress build your own. See the following functions for further information :

```
■    BOOL    WINAPI AllocMem(DWORD);
■    void    WINAPI FreeAllMem(void);
■    int     WINAPI AllocFileHandles(int);
■    void    WINAPI UnAllocFileHandles(void);
■    int     WINAPI GetFreeFileHandles(void);
■    int     WINAPI AllocDiskSpace(long,UINT);
■    void    WINAPI UnAllocDiskSpace(UINT);
■    BOOL    WINAPI AllocUserMem(UINT);
```

■   void   WINAPI FreeAllUserMem(void);

■   BOOL   WINAPI AllocGDIMem(UINT);

■   void   WINAPI FreeAllGDIMem(void);

Helpful compiler swiches

Use /f (replacement in C7.00 and C8.00 for /qc – quick compile switch) to reduce the time your application takes to be built.

Omit the *s* from -G?s to include stack probe checks in your code. You **may** see a *Stack Trashed* message box appear in Windows by including this switch when your application trashes the its stack – do this only during development.

Don't bother with the -Zr switch as the C8.00 docs (and the C7.00) say that this switch may only be used for building DOS applications (the C8.00 docs actually say that this switch will have no effect on a Windows' app).

Check out the /F switch on the linker – this FARCALLTRANSLATION switch can reduce the size and execution time of your application by converting needless far pointers into near pointers.

If you're using C8.00 make use of the modified behaviour of the -Zi switch. The way this switch is implemented in C8 means that the link will be quicker and your object files smaller. Don't delete .PDB files as they're needed by the debugger.

Chapter 8

M i s c

This chapter covers some miscellaneous stuff that would have been put in to various chapters if I'd have had time to write them proper! This whole chapter is a kinda waffle that I put together just before the final manuscript of this book went to the publisher – I apologise therefore for its sometimes wandering nature!

The first thing we'll look at is a general discussion on messaging *things*.

☐ Messages

A *posted* or *sent* Windows' message is either a direct or indirect way of calling a windows' window procedure. A sent message bypasses the task's message queue and is effectively a far call to a wndproc. If that wndproc is *in* another task then SendMessage() also causes a task switch to occur (so it's a little more than a far call to a wndproc between tasks!). A posted window's message goes via the task's message queue and is passed to the window procedure by DispatchMessage(). DispatchMessage() *waits* for the message to be processed, ie. the return value of DispatchMessage() is whatever the window procedure returned (a side effect of this is that you don't normally care what value is returned in response to a posted message – after all, you throw it away normally!). A message may also be posted to a task, ie. a message can be passed to a task rather than to a window. A good example of such a message is WM_QUIT. When you call PostQuitMessage() what effectively happens is this :

```
VOID __export FAR PASCAL PostQuitMessage(int nRes)
{
    PostAppMessage(
                    GetCurrentTask()
                ,WM_QUIT
                ,nRes
                ,(LPARAM)0
                );
}
```

PostAppMessage() is useful, in an object oriented kind of a way. A Windows' application consists of a number of objects :

- Windows (0 to n)
- A task (always 1)

- A module (at least one – and possibly more if you count DLLs used exclusively by the application)
- Some resources (0 to n)
- etc.

The task itself can be thought of as an object (you can see this reflected in modern C++ class libraries), and as such you should be able to pass it messages – you can, with PostAppMessage(). NOTE that there can not be a SendAppMessage(), after all the *app* object doesn't define a call-back function or entry point to itself apart from WinMain()!

There's no rule as to what comes via what, ie. there's nothing in the Windows SDK documentation that'll tell you which messages come via the task queue and which come via the SendMessage() API (or which come by neither route!). It rarely matters of course because sooner or later they all arrive in your window procedure. Exactly what comes via which route also changes between releases of Windows! Some messages can come from either route. Some common sense rules apply however :

- If the messsage is urgent – send it.
- If the messsage requires a reply, send it or post it depending upon the mode of synchronisation required (DDE is a good model to follow. Both methods of message passing are used in DDE).
- If the messsage carries with it some data, particularly if that data is *pointed to* – send it.

Here's more detail.

It sometimes depends on the urgency of the message and whether or not the message contains pointer type information. For example a WM_CREATE message's lParam points to a CREATESTRUCT; it therefore makes sense to create a CREATESTRUCT, get some window to use it (by sending it a WM_CREATE message), and then destroy it all at one time, ie. *send* the message and create and destroy the CREATESTRUCT around the call to SendMessage(). If you're passing some information to a window via a pointer be careful. What happens in the following code? :

```
LRESULT __export CALLBACK InAWndProc(...)
{
    switch(uMessage)
    {
            /*
            ** Pass data to remote window - data pointed to in lParam.
            */
        case UM_PASS_DATA:
            {
                auto char Name[] = "This is a name";

                PostMessage(
                        hWndRemote
                        ,UM_USERMESSAGE
                        ,0
```

```
                                       , (LPARAM) (LPSTR) &Name [0]
                                       ) ;
                    }
         }
    }
```

The intent here was to pass the address of the character array containing *This is a name* to some window via a *user* message. The information however will be lost as the string data is automatic, ie. it lives on the stack (actually a copy of the literal string is stored in DGROUP and copied onto the stack using _fmemcpy()). The message is passed using PostMessage() but by the time it is delivered the data has gone (as the auto has gone out of scope)! There are two cures to this, either declare the character array as *static* or use SendMessage() instead of PostMessage() – this one gets everyone sometime!

Because of the non-pre-emptive nature of Windows sent messages also convey some meaning of urgency, ie. if you post a message when can *the poster* ever determine that it's been received?; whereas when a message is sent it's delivered and processed before the SendMessage() API returns (unless the receiver is using ReplyMessage()). Sent messages are therefore useful for synchronising tasks (or is that windows?!). If you want two tasks to be in sync why not send a message between them?

Be careful here as sometimes Microsoft have been known to call PostMessage() synchronous and SendMessage() Asynchronous. It depends on your point of reference. A *sent* message by-passes the task's message queue and as such the message is **out of sync** with those stored in the queue! A **posted** message is appended to any messages that exist in the queue – the message is **in sync** with those in the queue! On the other hand, from a *code* perspective, a *sent* message and be thought of as a synchronous event, ie. one that can be used to determine the state of another window or task from a code sense. Also, if a message requires a response, ie. some return value other than, say (LRESULT)0, it's probably being *sent* – think about it.

For the curious, here's what happens when you start generic and immediately stop it again via Alt+F4 :-

DBWIN output :

```
    t GENERIC        From Send -> WM_GETMINMAXINFO
    t GENERIC        From Send -> WM_NCCREATE
    t GENERIC        From Send -> WM_NCCALCSIZE
    t GENERIC        From Send -> WM_CREATE
    t GENERIC        From Send -> WM_SHOWWINDOW
    t GENERIC        From Send -> WM_WINDOWPOSCHANGING
    t GENERIC        From Send -> WM_WINDOWPOSCHANGING
    t GENERIC        From Send -> WM_ACTIVATEAPP
    t GENERIC        From Send -> WM_NCACTIVATE
    t GENERIC        From Send -> WM_GETTEXT
    t GENERIC        From Send -> WM_ACTIVATE
    t GENERIC        From Send -> WM_SETFOCUS
    t GENERIC        From Send -> WM_NCPAINT
    t GENERIC        From Send -> WM_GETTEXT
```

```
t GENERIC      From Send -> WM_ERASEBKGRND
t GENERIC      From Send -> WM_WINDOWPOSCHANGED
t GENERIC      From Send -> WM_SIZE
t GENERIC      From Send -> WM_MOVE
t GENERIC      From Send -> WM_PAINT
t GENERIC      From Send -> WM_NCHITTEST
t GENERIC      From Send -> WM_SETCURSOR
t GENERIC From dispatch -> WM_MOUSEMOVE
t GENERIC      From Send -> WM_GETHOTKEY
t GENERIC From dispatch -> WM_SYSKEYDOWN
t GENERIC From dispatch -> WM_SYSKEYDOWN
t GENERIC From dispatch -> WM_SYSCOMMAND
t GENERIC From dispatch -> WM_CLOSE
t GENERIC From dispatch -> WM_WINDOWPOSCHANGING
t GENERIC From dispatch -> WM_WINDOWPOSCHANGED
t GENERIC From dispatch -> WM_NCACTIVATE
t GENERIC From dispatch -> WM_ACTIVATE
t GENERIC From dispatch -> WM_ACTIVATEAPP
t GENERIC From dispatch -> WM_KILLFOCUS
t GENERIC From dispatch -> WM_DESTROY
t GENERIC From dispatch -> WM_NCDESTROY
```

This listing shows which messages have come via the queue and which have not. To label those that bypass the queue as *sent* messages is somewhat misleading as some of them are indeed sent while others just arrive! Note that WM_QUIT is not on the list – it doesn't get passed to a window remember – it's for the task.

The code that was required to do this was :

Code :

```
LRESULT __export CALLBACK MainWndProc
(
  HWND     hWnd
 ,UINT     uMessage
 ,WPARAM   wParam
 ,LPARAM   lParam
)
{
  if(bInDispatch == TRUE)
  {
    DebugOutput(DBF_TRACE | DBF_APPLICATION, "From dispatch -> %X", uMessage);
  }
  else
  {

    DebugOutput(DBF_TRACE | DBF_APPLICATION, " From Send -> %X", uMessage);
  }

  switch(uMessage)
  {
      ... other program lines.
```

bInDispatch is set in the message loop :

```
while(GetMessage(&msg, NULL, 0, 0))
{
    TranslateMessage(&msg);

    bInDispatch = TRUE;
    DispatchMessage(&msg);
    bInDispatch = FALSE;
}
```

Some messages, like WM_INITDIALOG aren't real messages at all but come from *managers*, ie. those bits of Windows that manage a particular thing (see Dialog Box chapter for more on WM_INITDIALOG and the Dialog Box Manager). WM_PAINT also falls into this category. When a part of your window's client area needs painting a flag is set, internally somewhere, that says, 'this window needs a paint message'. Later, when your task's message queue is finally emptied, this flag is checked. If it's set, a WM_PAINT message is passed to your window – note that it is not sent via SendMessage(); it just arrives! You'll never get a posted WM_PAINT message therefore! Note that a WM_TIMER message is also not a real message and is sent when (if one needs to be sent) either GetMessage() or PeekMessage() are used on an empty task message queue.

When an app sends a message to a window belonging to another app InSend-Message() returns TRUE. You shouldn't do things that could cause blocking on the input thread here. In Windows (but not in NT) user input is serialised, ie. you can't get a mouse message until you've finished processing the last mouse message (or keyboard message). If you were therefore to bring up a modal message box in response to a sent input message you won't receive another input message! You have to finish processing the one your currently processing before another can arrive!! Also, strictly speaking, the sending application shouldn't carry on until the send message thread returns, ie. if you were to, say, send a message to another app, and that receiving app brings up a message box (blocks the thread), the original SendMessage() API call is still outstanding, ie. it won't, as yet, have returned. You could however go click on the sending app and start, say, selecting menu items of its menus! This can cause many problems, re-entrancy is just the start, deadlock follows!

When you handle a message that is being **sent** from another app, ie. you are going to block it, you should reply to that message before you block it. This sounds crazy, how can you reply to a sent message and then do something – you've passed control back to the sender haven't you? The answer is no you haven't – yet! You reply to the message using ReplyMessage(), not by returning some value. When you call Re-plyMessage() it returns immediately; its single parameter is the reply value – the value that the original app gets back from its SendMessage() call. You can now block; let's say you bring up a message box. When you do this, the sending application suddenly gets a return to its SendMessage() call. The value returned is the value you passed to ReplyMessage(). Let's say that the sending app finishes processing the reply and calls GetMessage() and yields. The receiver of the original sent message, which is now in a dialog GetMessage() loop (because a message box is a dialog box) now gets control back. Ultimately that second app finishes processing the message that was originally sent via SendMessage() from the first app and returns. The interesting question to ask at this point is where does it return to? It can't return to the first app because that app has already processed a return from the original SendMessage() call!? The answer is that it returns to Windows and not to the original app – the value you return (this is the second value returned) is therefore not used, ie. it is thrown away. You should also see the SDK documentation on QuerySendMessage() – this function can be used to determine whether or not the current message is being *sent* from the current task, something that SendMessage() doesn't do.

One of the nice things about GetMessage() is that it can be used to filter messages. Its third and fourth parameters specify a contiguous range of messages that you're interested in. If both parameters are set to the same message ID you're only interested in that one message. Message filtering like this in the message polling loop s not such a good idea – remember, not all messages come via the loop!! The best place to filter messages is in the window procedure – they all arrive there sooner or later.

PeekMessage() can also be used to retrieve messages from the task queue, in fact rumour has it that GetMessage() calls PeekMessage (I can confirm that they do use a lot of common code)?! I guess it could look something like this? :

```
BOOL WINAPI GetMessage
(
   MSG FAR *   msg
  ,HWND        hWnd
  ,UINT        nMin
  ,UINT        nMax
)
{
   if(PeekMessage(
                 msg
                ,hWnd
                ,nMin
                ,nMax
                ,PM_NOREMOVE
                ) == FALSE
     )
   {
      WaitMessage();
   }

   PeekMessage(
                 msg
                ,hWnd
                ,nMin
                ,nMax
                ,PM_REMOVE
                );

   return msg->message == WM_QUIT ? FALSE : TRUE;
}
```

PeekMessage() is usually used to process on a *non-message-basis.* Normally Windows' applications process (get the processor) whenever they have a message to process. This means that you need a message in order to run – its your packet of work if you like. This means that if you wanted to do something often, like poll a com port or something, that you have to have a steady stream of messages waiting in order to get the processor. PeekMessage() can change all that. PeekMessage(), unlike GetMessage() returns when there are no messages waiting in the task's message queue, ie. you have the processor but no message – therefore you're processing on a non-message-basis. Of course, when you have a message waiting PeekMessage() retrieves it from the queue and you can process it. This means that with PeekMessage() you can process on a non-message, and message basis – at this point you may be asking ,'**when does everything else get to run'?!!!** Before PeekMessage() comes back to you it allows other waiting tasks (those with messages in their task queues) to retrieve their messages. Note that you can prevent this from happening by specifying PM_NOYIELD! In fact by using PM_NOYIELD you can even create system-modal like states (see also bit on LockInput() later in this chapter) :

```
switch(uMessage)
{
case WM_COMMAND:
     switch(wParam)
       {
         case IDM_ENTERMODE:
             {
                 for(;;)
                 {
                     auto MSG msg;

                     if(bCancelMode == TRUE)
                     {
                         break;
                     }

                     if(PeekMessage(
                                 &msg
                                 ,NULL
                                 ,0
                                 ,0
                                 ,PM_REMOVE | PM_NOYIELD
                                 ) == TRUE
                       )
                     {
                         TranslateMessage(&msg);
                         DispatchMessage(&msg);
                     }
                 }
                 bCancelMode = FALSE;
             }
             break;

         case IDM_EXITMODE:
             bCancelMode = TRUE;
             break;
```

```
    }
    break;
```

You can use code such as this to enter a *critical section* that persists past calls to retrieve messages!

You usually see PeekMessage() used to achieve rapid polling, fast animation, or miscellaneous background processing. The alternative is to use a Windows' timer; these have limitations however. The main limitation with a timer is that it can only go off, at max, every 55ms (or so), that's about 18.2 times a second (this assumes that the system is lightly loaded and that the WM_TIMER event handler does nothing) – I wonder what two tenths of a timer message looks like! Very often that's not half fast enough. PeekMessage(), on the other hand, *comes back* (like going off in a *timer* sense) as soon as it can (the overhead is that of the function call plus whatever time PeekMessage() needs to check your task's message queue) – this assumes that no other task has any messages outstanding and also that no other task is using PeekMessage().

If you modify generic and add the following :

Global :

```
static DWORD dwTicks;
```

WinMain :

```
for(;;)
{
    if(PeekMessage(&msg, NULL, 0, 0, PM_REMOVE))
    {
        if(msg.message == WM_QUIT)
        {
            break;
        }

        TranslateMessage(&msg);
        DispatchMessage(&msg);
    }
    else
    {
        dwTicks++;
    }
}
return msg.wParam;
```

Wnd Proc :

```
case WM_CREATE:
    SetTimer(hWnd, 0, 1000, NULL);
    break;

case WM_TIMER:
    {
```

```
auto      char     carBuffer[50];
static    DWORD    dwMax;

if(dwTicks > dwMax)
{
    dwMax = dwTicks;
}

wsprintf(
         &carBuffer[0]
        ,"Ticks in last second = %lu (Max=%ld)"
        ,dwTicks
        ,dwMax
        );
```

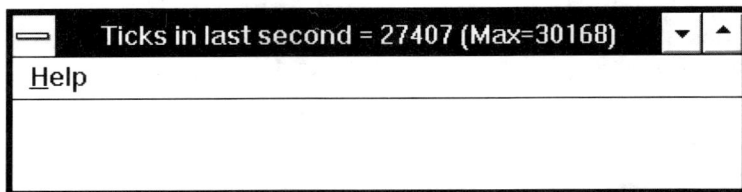

You'll find that generic's processed on a non-message basis about 30,000 times a second (depending upon how fast your machine is of course)!

By monitoring dwTicks's value once per second we can also gauge the load on the system, ie. the quieter the system the more often we get control (PeekMessage() returns) the more dwTicks gets incremented! We'll see an application that does just this in a little while.

This kind of app (a performance gauge, or as it is sometimes called, *an idle time monitor*) <u>needs</u> to process in the background all the time (if it's to give an indication of system load in real time). Normally however an application would use PeekMessage() occasionally, say, to animate a bitmap ball smoothly. Again consider the alternative to PeekMessage() – a timer. Say we had a client area that was 18 inches wide and a ball bitmap whose diameter was 1/18th the width of the client area (1 inch). If we wanted to bounce the ball from one side of the client area to the other in a second using a timer we'd have to move the ball 1 inch every 18th of a second. This stretches the timer to its limit! It would also look pretty rough as the ball would seem to flicker – we're essentially looking at an 18 frame a second movie of a moving ball! Your eyes can spot flicker quite easily below a frame rate of 25 frames per second by the way. Obviously a PeekMessage() loop (sometimes called an animation loop) would do the trick nicely. If BitBlt took zero time we could move the ball 6.E-04 inches on each return and achieve ultra smooth animation (this is like 30,000 frames a second remember!).

```
for (;;)
{
    if(PeekMessage(&msg, NULL, 0, 0, PM_REMOVE) == TRUE)
```

```
      {
        if(msg.message == WM_QUIT)
        {
            break;
        }

        TranslateMessage(&msg);
        DispatchMessage(&msg);
      }
      else
      {
        MoveBall();
      }
  }
```

However, this loop doesn't **ever** let the system go idle, ie. it always calls the function MoveBall(). MoveBall() might simply return if the program's state isn't ready for moving the ball of course. The point is that the app's busy busy busy – well Windows thinks it is!

You probably don't want to move the ball (or poll the port etc) all the time however so you should use the PeekMessage() loop only when it's required. There are several ways to this. You could use an embedded PeekMessage() loop in your code (like a modal dialog box has an embedded GetMessage() loop (as does the menu class)); or you could switch between loops in WinMain based on some sort of flag; or you could do the following :

```
for (;;)
{
    if(PeekMessage(&msg, NULL, 0, 0, PM_REMOVE) == TRUE)
    {
      if(msg.message == WM_QUIT)
      {
          break;
      }

      TranslateMessage(&msg);
      DispatchMessage(&msg);
    }
    else // No message waiting.
    {
      if(IfBallMovingRequired() == TRUE)
      {
          MoveBall();
      }
      else
      {
          WaitMessage(); // Wait for a message to be posted.
      }
    }
}
```

This loop allows the app to enter an idle state if there's no requirement to move the ball. When there is such a requirement the app can be woken up by processing a message from its message queue and returning TRUE from the function IfBallMovingRequired().

This scheme can be extended very easily. You'd *register* a function (that did something like poll a port or move a ball) with an *idle time manager*. The currently registered function will be called when the system would otherwise go idle. When no idle time processing is required you can put your app in to an idle state by calling WaitMessage(). You could of course have an array of idle time functions to call – move that ball, poll that port! Each registered function would be called in turn or even in some sort of prioritised order. What you've got now is of course another scheduler, or if you like, a pseudo multi-threading scheduler in a single app!

> On this note – have you realised that when you call SendMessage() that you're a scheduler? When the window to which your sending a message is not in your own task the Windows task manager task switches to the receiving task so that it can process the sent message correctly. When it's processed it you get control back – another task switch occurs to do this.

Allowing an application to enter an idle state is important for several reasons. Firstly your app may prevent another from doing its stuff efficiently. Consider what would happen if you had two instances of this ball moving application running and let's say that for most of the time only one will be animating its bitmap. If both instances use the first kind of loop they are both essentially taking up half of the free CPU time – the ball in either moves half the speed that it would if it were the only instance running! By using the second loop either instance gets all the spare CPU time to itself when it needs it, ie. the ball now moves twice as fast (or twice as smoothly)! Of course, <u>sometimes</u> you'll want both balls moving, the free CPU time will be divided between them and each ball will move half as fast as it would if it were the only instance running. The important word in that last bit was <u>sometimes</u>. Generally, if you don't need the spare CPU time use WaitMessage() so that some other poor sucker can have it if it wants it! The second reason why you shouldn't keep your app from going idle is that Windows relies on system idle time to do certain things such as paging optimisations, and power management on battery-powered systems (an app that remains in a PeekMessage() loop will make the system appear busy to any power management software running; this results in excessive power consumption and therefore foreshortens the time that the user can run the system). An app in a PeekMessage() loop continues to be rescheduled by the Windows scheduler, consuming CPU time and taking time away from other processes; also, in enhanced mode, the virtual machine (VM) in which Windows runs will not appear to be idle as long as an application is calling the PeekMessage() function. Therefore, to the detriment of other VMs, the Windows' VM will continue to receive a considerable fraction of the CPU's time. Lastly, in future versions, Windows will make more and more use of idle time to do background processing (designed to optimise system performance). Applications that do not allow the system to go idle will adversely affect the performance of Windows – period!

PeekMessage() can also be used to *break up* a long job. Let's say that you've written a Mandelbrot Set plotting program in Windows. Let's say further that the set takes about 5 minutes to plot. The plotting of course, like most long winded things, is done by using some sort of loop. When you enter that loop you've hogged the processor for 5 minutes. During this time the clock stops (if you've got it running), you stop receiving email, you can't task switch etc – OOPS! What you should do is make a call to PeekMessage(), say, every time you plot one pixel in the set. By calling PeekMessage() you allow other tasks to run – don't forget it. Windows is often described as a multi-tasking OS, and so it is. It is of course non-pre-emptively scheduled, BUT, as long as you write your code so that it yields control often it should run as smoothly as a pre-emptively scheduled one. Whilst on this; please don't forget that a posted message cannot be delivered in a guaranteed time frame. The posted message may in fact never arrive, it all depends on what else is running! For example. The clock application sets up a timer set to an interval of 500ms. Under normal circumstances it receives two timer events a second therefore. However, the clock does not count the passing seconds based on incoming WM_TIMER messages because a message might be delayed, or even worse, lost! Instead the clock notes the passing of time by checking the system clock, ie. the clock maintained by the PC. To put this another way – if you were to post a thousand timer messages to the clock in, say, 60 seconds, don't expect the hands to go whizzing around!

☐ Other Message Stuff

The GetMessageExtraInfo() function can be used to retrieve extra information about a message that is retrieved by GetMessage() or PeekMessage(). The extra info is message specific – I cannot find a message that has any extra info, ie. currently, for all messages, GetMessageExtraInfo() returns 0.

When a message comes via the task's message queue the actual message is a message structure. That structure contains two bits of information that are not passed on to the window procedure. The first is the position, in screen co-ordinates of the mouse when the event was generated, the second is the system time at which the event took place. Both these bits of information are accessible in the window procedure however by using GetMessagePos() and GetMessageTime(). If a window sends itself a message what will GetMessageTime() return? Will it return the time of the last event retrieved by GetMessage() or will it return the time that the SendMessage() event was generated? The answer is the latter. If you're interested in seeing how long you have to wait between an event being generated and it being subsequently delivered you can do so by subtracting GetMessageTime() from GetTickCount() (or GetCurrentTime() – same thing).

SetMessageQueue() can be used to create a larger task message queue for a given task. The default message queue size is 8. If this seems like a small amount remember that two things. An application always retrieves all of its messages before yielding control (using GetMessage()), and secondly that because Windows is non-pre-emptive that no further messages can arrive from other tasks (or Windows) until you yield control – empty your queue. Of course, you may do something in your application that could result in further messages being created and therefore added to what's already in the queue.

You can use DispatchMessage() as a kinda SendMessage()! When you retrieve a message from your message queue you dispatch to one of your windows using DispatchMessage(). You can also use DispatchMessage() to pass messages directly to other windows (just like you can with SendMessage()) by altering the message structure's *hwnd* member! Why should you want to do this? Well here's a possible reason. Let's say that you have an application that creates many windows from many classes. Let's say that you also want to handle some messages in a standard way. For arguments sake let's say that you want to trap all WM_LBUTTONDBLCLK messages passed to any window in your application because you want to activate the task list application if anyone double clicks in any of your windows. The task list is an application called TaskMan.exe – normally activated when you double click on the desktop window (or hit Ctrl + Esc). Now you could do this by altering every class window procedure thus :

```
...
case WM_LBUTTONDBLCLK:
     PostMessage(GetDesktopWindow(), uMessage, wParam, lParam);
     break;
...
```

Remember, you'll have to do this in all your class window procedures.

This approach has three disadvantages.

- You have to remember to add this code to every class window procedure.
- It duplicates code (and coding effort – see 1.).
- You can't do it for modeless dialogs unless you want to super-class the dialog class (which is easier than it might sound BTW – see dialog chapter).

If on the other hand you do this in your application :

```
...
while(GetMessage(&msg, NULL, 0, 0) == TRUE)
{
     if(msg.message == WM_LBUTTONDBLCLK)
     {
          msg.hwnd = GetDesktopWindow())
     }
     ...
     DispatchMessage(&msg);
}   `
...
```

You'll activate the task list whenever you double click in any of your windows – including any modeless dialog box window you've got up (modal dialogs have their own GetMessage() polling loop). There is one disadvantage to this method – no one expects to see it! Whenever anyone looks at your code they'll expect to see messages processed in a window procedure – not in WinMain(). This is a convention thing and can be overcome by documenting each window procedure code :

```
...
case WM_LBUTTONDBLCLK:
    // NEVER GET HERE - MESSAGE FILTERED IN WINMAIN.
    break;
...
```

However this has all the disadvantages talked about earlier, ie. duplication of code etc.

Note that there is another difference between these two approaches. DispatchMessage() waits for the message to be processed – it's as though DispatchMessage() is really SendMessage() in disguise? Maybe it even looks like this!? :

```
LRESULT WINAPI DispatchMessage
(
    MSG FAR * lpMsg
)
{
    return SendMessage(
                        lpMsg->hwnd
                       ,lpMsg->message
                       ,lpMsg->wParam
                       ,lpMsg->lParam
                       );
}
```

You can carry on re-writing APIs like this all day – try it, it's very enlightening!

Another couple of uses for PeekMessage().

Firstly it can be used to see if you're about to lose the CPU, ie. the Windows' scheduler is about to pass the baton to another task. Use a normal GetMessage() loop but include in the loop a PeekMessage() call. After you dispatch the message test the message queue to see if it's empty using PeekMessage() – use PM_NOREMOVE in the call. If PeekMessage() comes back FALSE you know that once you call GetMessage() again you'll lose the processor. You could at this point <u>send</u> yourself a WM_USER message. This message means *Hey, we're about to go to sleep*!

First some defines :

```
#define UM_PROCESSOR WM_USER
#define LOOSING      1
#define NOTLOOSING   2
```

Modified GetMessage Loop :

```
while(GetMessage(&msg, NULL, 0, 0))
{
auto BOOL bProc;
```

```
        TranslateMessage(&msg);
        DispatchMessage(&msg);

        bProc = PeekMessage(&msg, NULL, 0, 0, PM_NOREMOVE);

        if(IsWindow(hMainWnd) && !bProc)
        {
            SendMessage(
                        hMainWnd
                        ,UM_PROCESSOR
                        ,LOOSING
                        ,0
                        );
        }
    }
}
```

Modified WndProc :

```
case UM_PROCESSOR:
    switch(wParam)
    {
        case LOOSING: // about to lose processor.
            MessageBeep(0);
            break;

    }
    break;
```

By the way, I can't think of a use for this – if you can please let me know!

You might have to be a little more careful doing this kind of thing by the way as not all messages work as messages! For example the WM_PAINT message, as has been stated elsewhere, isn't the same as other messages – certainly it doesn't *live* in your task message queue (it's an internal flag); what does this mean? Well it means for starters that PeekMessage() will return FALSE even though you still have a paint message outstanding *in your message queue!* You could flush the queue of the outstanding WM_PAINT message by using UpdateWindow() however. Well how do you know whether or not you should call UpdateWindow()? Well it doesn't really matter when you call this function because if you haven't got a WM_PAINT message waiting it simply returns. If you **really** want to detect whether or not you've got a WM_PAINT message waiting you could use GetUpdateRect() passing NULL in the function's second parameter, the function will return TRUE if you've got a WM_PAINT message waiting! WM_TIMER messages are very similar to WM_PAINT messages in that they too don't live in your task's message queue. A WM_TIMER message is generated (if one should be) by using PeekMessage() and/or GetMessage() on a empty task message queue!

Also PeekMessage() can be useful for flushing a task's queue. I once built an application that could pass messages to any window in the system via either

PostAppMessage(), PostMessage() or SendMessage() (also CallWindowProc()). Sometimes the sending app was required to **post** hundreds of messages; it also had to achieve total transmission before yielding control in the traditional sense. The app was able to do the job – thanks to PeekMessage(). First the transmitting app used PostMessage() to fill the destination task's message queue. When PostMessage() returned FALSE, indicating that the destination task's queue was full, PeekMessage() was used in one of two ways. Firstly the transmitting app could simply call PeekMessage() for itself when PostMessage() return FALSE. This allowed the other task to empty its task queue. Secondly the transmitting app could empty the receiving task's queue for it, ie. it *Peek*ed its queue and called DispatchMessage() for the other task – in fact GetMessage() would have done except for the fact that the transmitting app needed to know when to commence transmitting; this was easily done with PeekMessage() of course because when the receiving app's queue was emptied it returned FALSE. When it did the transmission could start all over again! All this of course could apply to your own task's message queue – if using PostMessage() to pass loadsa messages, use PeekMessage() to ease the burden!

Lastly, PeekMessage() can be used to examine the queue's contents entirely, and can even enable selective retrieval and re-ordering of the queued messages! It works like this. Firstly created an array of eight MSG structures (MSG tarMessages[8]). Then, retrieve all the queued messages using PeekMessage() with PM_REMOVE set. Arrange each message in the array. When PeekMessage() returns FALSE, which should occur before the array gets full, you have retrieved all waiting messages. At this point you still have the processor and you have no messages in your queue. You can now scan the retrieved messages and do anything you like with them. For example you could send some on to your window procedure using DispatchMessage(). You could change any of their values (perhaps hwnd to eventually pass the message to some other window). You could even swap some of them around or throw them away completely. When you've finished playing with them you can put them back in the queue using PostMessage(). At this point you once again call good old GetMessage() to retrieve them and pass them, via DispatchMessage(), to your windows!! P.S. By experimenting with this technique you can discover just what gets queued and in what order!

Using DefWindowProc() directly. Very often tasks send themselves message to get something done – perhaps they might send themselves a WM_SETTEXT message to change their caption etc. This is quite a natural thing to do in Windows – it being object oriented and all. Very often, if the message is meant to make Windows do something it can be passed directly to the system by calling DefWindowProc(). This saves the overhead of the function call to SendMessage() and of course the time taken by SendMessage() to deliver the message. Let's take the WM_SETTEXT message again for an example. There's nothing stopping you from doing this :

```
case WM_COMMAND:
    switch(wParam)
    {
            /* Set caption text. */
```

```
        case UM_SETTITLE:
                return DefWindowProc(hWnd, WM_SETTEXT, 0, (LPSTR)"Hello");
                break;
    . . . .
    . . . .
```

Instead of this :

```
case WM_COMMAND:
        switch(wParam)
        {
                /* Set caption text. */
            case UM_SETTITLE:
                return SendMessage(hWnd, WM_SETTEXT, 0, (LPSTR)"Hello");
                break;
    . . . .
    . . . .
```

By the way, you could also use CallWindowProc() instead of SendMessage(), ie. :

```
    return CallWindowProc(MainWndProc, hWnd, WM_SETTEXT, 0, (LPSTR)"Hello");
```

Don't try this outside of Windows 3.x's protect mode!!!!

It's sometimes also useful to take over control of the task's message loop in modal dialog boxes. Remember that modal dialogs usually use a GetMessage() loop of their own. If you do take over the loop, say, at WM_INITDIALOG time be sure to call IsDialogMessage() – see dialog chapter for more on IsDialogMessage().

You can also use GetQueueStatus() and GetInputState() to peek into the message queue. GetQueueStatus() can tell you what type of messages exist in the queue. GetInputState() can be used to see if a keyboard or mouse message has been generated. Both these functions are typically faster than either PeekMessage() and/or GetMessage() so you should use them if you can.

The last message *thing* we'll take a quick look at is SetMessageQueue(). This function can be used to increase the size of your task's message queue. You can set the queue size up to a maximum of 120, ie. it can contain 120 posted messages! You should change your task's queue size before you receive any messages. The reason for this is that the existing message queue, complete with its contents is destroyed before the new one is created, ie. you could lose messages! You should set the message queue size therefore when the queue is empty (check with PeekMessage()) or before any messages are posted to your task (a good time is before any window is created). If SetMessageQueue() fails you now have no queue! What ever you do don't call GetMessage() if this should happen – if you do you'll never get control back because you can never get a posted message (note that such a task can get control back by being *sent* a message). You should call SetMessageQueue() again but this time request a smaller queue! If the function always fails you should tell your user that the app has failed and exit using FatalExit() or FatalAppExit() – don't use PostQuitMessage()!!

OK. Getting back to a previous point that you could monitor the load on the CPU using PeekMessage(). Here's an application that can do just that – it's called *Perf Meter* (which is short for *Performance Meter*). I wish you could see this guy run – it's <u>real</u> interesting!

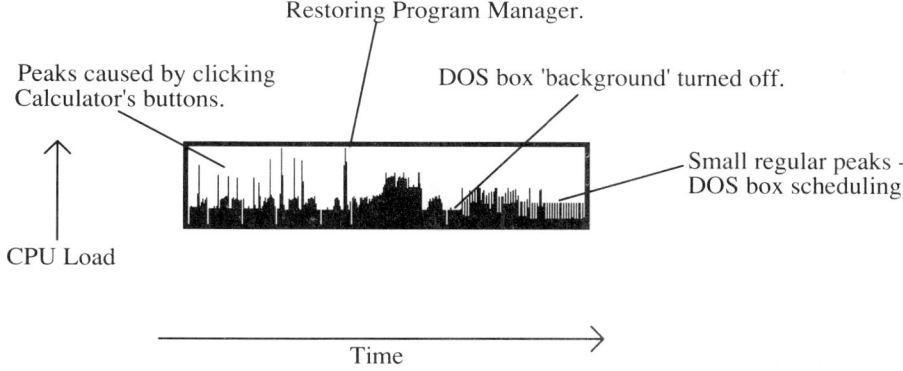

Restoring Program Manager.

Peaks caused by clicking
Calculator's buttons.

DOS box 'background' turned off.

Small regular peaks -
DOS box scheduling.

CPU Load

Time

Here's another interesting shot of it. This one should give you a feel for how fast the app scrolls its client area) :

Windows' "Clock" ticking.

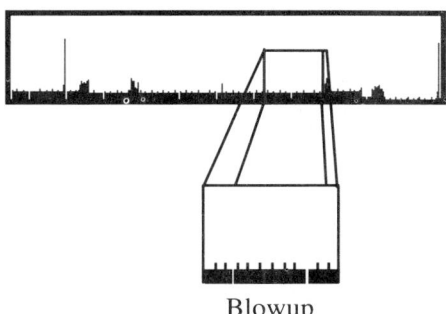

Blowup

And a couple more :

Typing in 'Word'.   Caret in 'Word' flashing.

Focusing 'Word'.

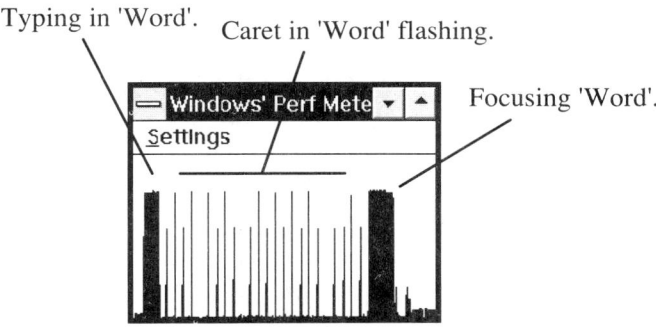

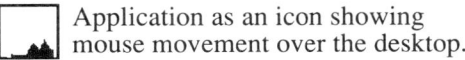
Application as an icon showing
mouse movement over the desktop.

The application works as described above in the discussion of using PeekMessage()
to gauge system CPU load. The application source code is shown below.

```
Perf.c :

#define STRICT

#include <windows.h>
#include <stdlib.h>
#include <string.h>
#include "perf.h"


/*
** Get rid of silly warnings.
*/
#pragma warning(disable:4100)
#pragma warning(disable:4001)

#define VOID_RETURN                 /* Coding standards stuff. */

/*
** Used to get a hold off min/max info stuff.
*/
typedef MINMAXINFO FAR * LPMINMAXINFO;

/*
** Critical! if TIMERTICKSTOSAMPLE is too great nTickCount could
** overflow! Same could happen if SAMPLERATE is too great (big).
*/
#define TIMERTICKSTOSAMPLE 10    /* WM_TIMER event number to sampl. (ave).
*/
#define SAMPLERATE          75   /* Millisecs per timer tick (ave & pump).
*/

#define WAITTIME            5000  /* WAITTIME / 1000 secs delay the average
*/

/*
** Timer IDs.
*/
#define CALCAVERAGE 0            /* Average calc timer.  */
#define ENGINE      1            /* Engine (pump) timer. */
#define WAIT        2            /* 'Wait' timer.        */

/*
** Incremented in PeekMessage() loop. Use to see how
** busy the system is.
*/
static int  nTickCount;

/*
** Holds the average number of increments of nTickCount there
** have been in a timer period (SAMPLERATE).
*/
static int  nAverage;
```

```
/*
** Used in INI file processing.
*/
#define BUFFERSIZE 50

/*
** The 'Please wait' modeless dialog box handle.
*/
static HWND hWndDialog;

/*
** Used for INI file stuff.
*/
static const char carINIFileName[] = "PERF.INI";
static const char carSection    [] = "Performance Meter";
static const char carShow        [] = "Show";
static const char carPosition    [] = "Position";
static const char carOptions     [] = "Options";
static const char carEmpty       [] = "";


/***********************************************
*
* Code begins.
*
*/



/*
** Either adds or removes the caption, sysmenu,
** min & max boxes and window menu from window.
*/
VOID NEAR PASCAL vDoNoCaption
(
   HWND     hWnd
 ,UINT     uMessage
 ,WPARAM   wParam
 ,LPARAM   lParam
)
{
   /*
   ** Holds hWnd's window style for manipulation.
   */
   auto    DWORD dwStyle;

   /*
   ** Used to hold the window's menu whilst it's
   ** removed from the window.
   */
   static  HMENU hMenu;

   /*
   ** Get window's current normal style bits.
   */
   dwStyle = GetWindowLong(hWnd, GWL_STYLE);

   /*
```

```
** Has it got a caption already (test WS_SYSMENU for this!)?
*/
if(!!(dwStyle & WS_SYSMENU))
{
    /*
    ** YES - so remove it all, Ha ha ha hahhhh!
    */

    /*
    ** Save menu away in static and re-set
    ** window's menu to nothing.
    */
    hMenu = GetMenu(hWnd);
    SetMenu(hWnd, NULL);

    /*
    ** Frig  window  styles so  to remove the
    ** stuff we don't want. NOTE: MUST re-add
    ** WS_BORDER here.
    */
    dwStyle &= ~WS_CAPTION;
    dwStyle &= ~WS_SYSMENU;
    dwStyle &= ~WS_MINIMIZEBOX;
    dwStyle &= ~WS_MAXIMIZEBOX;
    dwStyle |=  WS_BORDER;

}
else
{
    /*
    ** NO - so put it all back again.
    */

    /*
    ** Restore menu from static.
    */
    SetMenu(hWnd, hMenu);

    /*
    ** Frig once more!
    */
    dwStyle |= WS_CAPTION;
    dwStyle |= WS_SYSMENU;
    dwStyle |= WS_MINIMIZEBOX;
    dwStyle |= WS_MAXIMIZEBOX;
    dwStyle |= WS_BORDER;
}

/*
** Stuff the style bits back and force a re-paint of the
** non-client  stuff  using  DrawMenuBar() - not alot of
** people know about that!
*/
SetWindowLong(hWnd, GWL_STYLE, dwStyle);
DrawMenuBar(hWnd);

return VOID_RETURN;
}
```

```
/*
** Handles the selection of 'our' syscommand item. NOTE that
** it doesn't have  to  return DefWndProc as our main window
** proc replies  0  for us - all system menu handling causes
** DefWndProc to return 0 - who  cares anyway, like it's not
** as though someone were watching you know!
*/
VOID NEAR PASCAL vDoSysCommand
(
   HWND     hWnd
  ,UINT     uMessage
  ,WPARAM   wParam
  ,LPARAM   lParam
)
{
   if(wParam == IDM_ONTOP)
   {
      /*
      ** Get the WM_COMMAND handler to do this.
      */
      SendMessage(hWnd, WM_COMMAND, wParam, 0);
   }
   else
   {
      /*
      ** All other system menu stuff handled here.
      */
      DefWindowProc(hWnd, uMessage, wParam, lParam);
   }

   return VOID_RETURN;
}




/*
** Handles the processing of a WM_GETMINMAXINFO message.
*/
VOID NEAR PASCAL vDoMinMaxInfo
(
   HWND     hWnd
  ,UINT     uMessage
  ,WPARAM   wParam
  ,LPARAM   lParam
)
{
   auto LPMINMAXINFO lpMinMaxInfo;
   auto int          nScreenWidth;
   auto int          nScreenHeight;

   lpMinMaxInfo = (LPMINMAXINFO)(lParam);

   /*
```

```
   ** Make the window max/min reasonable. Can't let
   ** the  window get too big or the app will think
   ** that Windows will have stopped!
   */
   nScreenWidth  = GetSystemMetrics(SM_CXSCREEN);
   nScreenHeight = GetSystemMetrics(SM_CYSCREEN);

   lpMinMaxInfo->ptMaxTrackSize.x = nScreenWidth  / 3;
   lpMinMaxInfo->ptMaxTrackSize.y = nScreenHeight / 4;

   lpMinMaxInfo->ptMinTrackSize.x = nScreenWidth  / 6;
   lpMinMaxInfo->ptMinTrackSize.y = nScreenHeight / 10;

   return VOID_RETURN;
}




/*
** Either places window (hWnd) on top or releases
** it from being on top of all other windows.
*/
VOID NEAR PASCAL vDoWindowOnTop
(
   HWND     hWnd
 , UINT     uMessage
 , WPARAM   wParam
 , LPARAM   lParam
)
{
   /*
   ** Holds system menu - we have to check, and change
   ** the 'Always On Top' item.
   */
   auto HMENU hSysMenu;

   /*
   ** Checked state.
   */
   auto BOOL  bCheck;

   /*
   ** Get working copy of system menu.
   */
   hSysMenu = GetSystemMenu(hWnd, FALSE);

   /*
   ** Is item checked?
   */
   if(
      GetMenuState(
                  hSysMenu
                 ,wParam
                 ,MF_BYCOMMAND
                 ) &
      MF_CHECKED
     )
```

```
{
    /*
    ** YES - we want to uncheck it, set flag to FALSE.
    */
    bCheck = FALSE;

    /*
    ** Change window extended style bits accordingly.
    */
    SetWindowPos(
                hWnd
                ,HWND_NOTOPMOST
                ,0
                ,0
                ,0
                ,0
                ,SWP_NOMOVE | SWP_NOSIZE
                );
}
else
{
    /*
    ** NO - we want to check it, set flag to TRUE.
    */
    bCheck = TRUE;

    /*
    ** Change window extended style bits accordingly.
    */
    SetWindowPos(
                hWnd
                ,HWND_TOPMOST
                ,0
                ,0
                ,0
                ,0
                ,SWP_NOMOVE | SWP_NOSIZE
                );

}

/*
** Make change to item's checked state.
*/
CheckMenuItem(
                hSysMenu
              ,wParam
              ,MF_BYCOMMAND   |
               bCheck         ?
               MF_CHECKED     :
               MF_UNCHECKED
               );

return VOID_RETURN;
}
```

```
/*
** Program entry point.
*/
int PASCAL WinMain
(
   HINSTANCE    hInstance
  ,HINSTANCE    hPrevInstance
  ,LPSTR        lpCmdLine
  ,int          nCmdShow
)
{
   auto MSG msg;

   if(hPrevInstance == NULL)
   {
      if(InitApplication(hInstance) == FALSE)
      {
         return 0;
      }
   }
   else
   {
      MessageBox(
                0
               ,"The Windows' performance meter is already\n"
                "running on your system. It doesn't make sense\n"
                "to have two copies of it running!"
               ,"Perf-Meter Running!"
               ,MB_OK
               );

      return 0;
   }

   if(InitInstance(hInstance, nCmdShow) == FALSE)
   {
      return 0;
   }

   /*
   ** Use PeekMessage() loop instead of  GetMessage() as we want
   ** to 'time' and  animate quicker that we could do it  with a
   ** timer. NOTE: Could not have used GetTickCount() to do this.
   */
   for(;;)
   {
      if(PeekMessage(&msg, NULL, NULL, NULL, PM_REMOVE) == TRUE)
      {
         if(msg.message == WM_QUIT)
         {
            break;
         }
         else
         {
            TranslateMessage(&msg);

            DispatchMessage(&msg);
```

```
            }
        }
        else
        {
            /*
            ** No one has a message so we get the prossor (BG speak).
            */
            nTickCount++;
        }
    }

    return msg.wParam;
}




/*
** Application init.
*/
BOOL NEAR PASCAL InitApplication
(
    HINSTANCE   hInstance
)
{
    auto WNDCLASS  wc;

    /*
    ** We want this 'thing' to draw as quickly as is possible
    ** so having our own DC and aligning the window in memory
    ** is good.
    */
    wc.style            = CS_OWNDC            |
                          CS_BYTEALIGNCLIENT |
                          CS_DBLCLKS          |
                          CS_HREDRAW          |
                          CS_VREDRAW;

    wc.lpfnWndProc      = (WNDPROC)MainWndProc;
    wc.cbClsExtra       = 0;
    wc.cbWndExtra       = 0;
    wc.hInstance        = hInstance;

    /*
    ** We want the perf-meter to work as an icon so NULL here.
    */
    wc.hIcon            = NULL;

    wc.hCursor          = LoadCursor(NULL, IDC_ARROW);
    wc.hbrBackground    = GetStockObject(GRAY_BRUSH);
    wc.lpszMenuName     = MAKEINTRESOURCE(PERFMENU);
    wc.lpszClassName    = MAKEINTATOM(PERFCLASS);


    return RegisterClass(&wc);
}
```

```c
/*
** Instance init.
*/
BOOL NEAR PASCAL InitInstance
(
   HINSTANCE   hInstance
  ,int         nCmdShow
)
{
   auto HWND hWnd;

   /*
   ** Size the window in accordance with MINMAXINFO handling.
   */
   hWnd = CreateWindow(
                       MAKEINTATOM(PERFCLASS)
                      ,"Windows' Perf Meter"
                      ,WS_OVERLAPPED   |
                       WS_BORDER       |
                       WS_THICKFRAME   |
                       WS_MINIMIZEBOX  |
                       WS_MAXIMIZEBOX  |
                       WS_SYSMENU      |
                       WS_CAPTION
                      ,CW_USEDEFAULT
                      ,0
                      ,GetSystemMetrics(SM_CXSCREEN) / 3
                      ,GetSystemMetrics(SM_CYSCREEN) / 4
                      ,NULL
                      ,NULL
                      ,hInstance
                      ,NULL
                      );


   return hWnd != NULL ? TRUE : FALSE;
}




/*
** Our beloved monolithic wndproc!
*/
LRESULT __export CALLBACK MainWndProc
(
   HWND     hWnd
  ,UINT     uMessage
  ,WPARAM   wParam
  ,LPARAM   lParam
)
{
   /*
   ** Holds our DC for as long as the window is around.
   */
```

```
static HDC      hDC;

/*
** Current size of the client arear.
*/
static RECT     rsClient;

/*
** Are we dynamically working out the average AND the
** the checked state of the relevant menu item.
*/
static BOOL     bCheck;

switch(uMessage)
{
   case WM_COMMAND:
        switch(wParam)
        {
                /*
                ** User's selected 'Always on top'.
                */
            case IDM_ONTOP:
                {
                    vDoWindowOnTop(hWnd, uMessage, wParam, lParam);
                }
                break;

                /*
                ** User's selected 'About'.
                */
            case IDM_ABOUT:
                {
                    /*
                    ** Use a message box for an about box.
                    */
                    MessageBox(
                            hWnd
                            ,"Perf-Meter for Windows. By\n"
                            "Peter J. Morris (C) 1993."
                            ,"About Perf-Meter..."
                            ,MB_OK | MB_TASKMODAL
                            );
                }
                break;

                /*
                ** User's selected 'No Title'.
                */
            case IDM_NOCAPTION:
                {
                    vDoNoCaption(hWnd, uMessage, wParam, lParam);

                }
                break;

                /*
                ** User's selected 'Adjust meter dynamically'.
                **
```

```
                    ** Dynamically work out average so that we can
                    ** see  what  effect  this  app  has  on system
                    ** performance.
                    */
               case IDM_USENEWAVE:
                    {
                        /*
                        ** Holds copy of window's menu.
                        */
                        auto    HMENU    hMenu;

                        /*
                        ** Holds original average. Static so that we
                        ** can  restore it if  this item is selected
                        ** again.
                        */
                        static  int     nOldAverage;

                        /*
                        ** Do menu stuff.
                        */
                        hMenu = GetMenu(hWnd);


                        if(
                           GetMenuState(
                                       hMenu
                                      ,wParam
                                      ,MF_BYCOMMAND
                                      ) &
                            MF_CHECKED
                          )
                        {
                            /*
                            ** It's checked at the moment...
                            */
                            bCheck = FALSE;

                            /*
                            ** Restore old average.
                            */
                            nAverage = nOldAverage;

                            /*
                            ** Get a new window ext based on old
                            ** average.
                            */
                            PostMessage(hWnd, UM_RECALC, 0, 0);

                        }
                        else
                        {
                            /*
                            ** It's not checked at the moment...
                            */
                            bCheck = TRUE;

                            /*
```

```
                                   ** Save old average.
                                   */
                                   nOldAverage = nAverage;

                           }

                   CheckMenuItem(
                                   GetMenu(hWnd)
                                   ,wParam
                                   ,MF_BYCOMMAND  |
                                   bCheck         ?
                                   MF_CHECKED     :
                                   MF_UNCHECKED
                                   );
               }
       }

       /*
       ** Get re-draw.
       */
       InvalidateRect(hWnd, NULL, TRUE);
       break;

case WM_CREATE:
       /*
       ** Simply  post ourselve a message telling us that we're
       ** ok to  start doing  stuff. Sometimes doing stuff, say
       ** to your window's menu, in the WM_CREATE handler seems
       ** to fail!  The window  will be entirely stable however
       ** in the UM_START handler.
       */
       PostMessage(hWnd, UM_START, 0, 0);
       break;

case WM_DESTROY:
       /*
       ** Ignored by Windows (OWNDC) but here for good practice.
       */
       ReleaseDC(hWnd, hDC);

       /*
       ** Release timer.
       */
       KillTimer(hWnd, ENGINE);

       /*
       ** Die!
       */
       PostQuitMessage(0);
       break;

       /*
       ** Adjust  size  of  window  according  to  screen  size.
       ** NOTE  that  the  window  size  is critical, ie. if the
       ** window size is too big (and the sample rate too small)
       ** then the system appears  to  be  infinately  busy  due
       ** to  the  time  taken to do the bit blt scroll. If this
       ** happens  reduce  the  size  of  the window or decrease
```

```
       ** the  sample  rate.  Reducing  the  sample  rate  means
       ** that the window will scroll slower also.
       */
case WM_GETMINMAXINFO:
       vDoMinMaxInfo(hWnd, uMessage, wParam, lParam);
       break;


       /*
       ** If menu is selected assume that it screws up the
       ** display - force redraw.
       */
case WM_MENUSELECT:
       if(LOWORD(lParam) == -1 && HIWORD(lParam) == 0)
       {
           InvalidateRect(hWnd, NULL, TRUE);
       }
       break;


       /*
       ** HITTEST handling so that the window can be moved
       ** even if it's lost its caption.
       */
case WM_NCHITTEST:
       if(
           (DefWindowProc(
                        hWnd
                       ,uMessage
                       ,wParam
                       ,lParam
                       ) == HTCLIENT)

          &&

           !(GetWindowLong(hWnd, GWL_STYLE) & WS_SYSMENU)
          )
       {
           return HTCAPTION;
       }
       else
       {
           return DefWindowProc(hWnd, uMessage, wParam, lParam);
       }
       break;


       /*
       ** Re-work window extent when re-sized.
       */
case WM_SIZE:
       PostMessage(hWnd, UM_RECALC, 0, 0);
       break;


       /*
       ** Do sys command handler.
       */
case WM_SYSCOMMAND:
       vDoSysCommand(hWnd, uMessage, wParam, lParam);
       break;
```

```
case WM_TIMER:
    {
        switch(wParam)
        {
                /*
                ** This timer is set in UM_START. It allows
                ** the system enough time  to become quiet.
                ** This is  esp important if the perf-meter
                ** is started, say, from a  startup group.
                */
            case WAIT:
                /*
                ** Kill this timer and start 'calc' timer off.
                */
                KillTimer(hWnd, wParam);
                SetTimer(hWnd, CALCAVERAGE, SAMPLERATE, NULL);
                break;

                /*
                ** Draws the perf-meter display according
                ** to nAverage and nTickCount.
                */
            case ENGINE:
                {
                    /*
                    ** If  punter  wants to 'take this app
                    ** into  account  then we  should work
                    ** out a new average, ie. this routine
                    ** wasn't  running  when we worked out
                    ** the  average  before so we'd better
                    ** time it in here and adjust nAverage.
                    ** bCheck decides.
                    */
                    if((nAverage < nTickCount) && bCheck)
                    {
                        /*
                        ** nTickCount adjusted so undate
                        ** window ext etc.
                        */
                        nAverage = nTickCount;
                        SendMessage(hWnd, UM_RECALC, 0, 0);
                    }

                    /*
                    ** Draw the line. NOTE: that even though
                    ** we're  using ANISO we'll draw 'up' as
                    ** we set the window ext before.
                    */
                    MoveTo(hDC, 0, 0);
                    LineTo(hDC, 0, nAverage - nTickCount);

                    /*
                    ** Scroll the client area.
                    */
                    ScrollWindow(hWnd, 1, 0, NULL, NULL);

                    /*
```

```
                          ** Re-set ticks.
                          */
                          nTickCount = 0;

                  }
                  break;

              /*
              ** Works out an average number of 'ticks' per
              ** timer  event. Used  to  determine how many
              ** ticks occur when the system's quiet.
              */
          case CALCAVERAGE:
              {
                  /*
                  ** Holds count of WM_TIMER events.
                  */
                  static int   nSecCount;

                  /*
                  ** Reset tick count coz it will have been
                  ** incremented by  now and  we need it at
                  ** zero to get a good average!
                  */
                  if(nSecCount == 0)
                  {
                      nTickCount = 0;
                  }

                  /*
                  ** Inc how many times we've been called.
                  */
                  nSecCount++;


                  /*
                  ** Have we reached the required number to
                  ** get a good sample?
                  */
                  if(nSecCount == TIMERTICKSTOSAMPLE)
                  {
                      /*
                      ** Average per WM_TIMER event was
                      ** ...
                      */
                      nAverage = (nTickCount / TIMERTICKSTOSAMPLE);

                      /*
                      ** Adjust by 10%.
                      */
                      nAverage += nAverage / 10;

                      /*
                  ** Kill  this timer  as we're done with it and
                  ** create a new one to actually drive the app.
                      */
                      KillTimer(hWnd, wParam);
                      SetTimer(hWnd, ENGINE, SAMPLERATE, NULL);
```

```
                                /*
                                ** Re-set ticks.
                                */
                                nTickCount = 0;

                                /*
                        ** Signal 'ready to process' and  update window
                        ** ext etc, ie. force app to re-calc window ext
                            ** based on current ave.
                            */
                            SendMessage(hWnd, UM_RECALC, 0, 0);
                            SendMessage(hWnd, UM_SETUP, 0, 0);
                    }
                }
                break;
        }
    }
    break;

    /*
    ** Do caption processing.
    */
case WM_NCLBUTTONDBLCLK:     // FALL THRU.
case WM_LBUTTONDBLCLK:
    PostMessage(hWnd, WM_COMMAND, IDM_NOCAPTION, 0);
    break;

    /*
    ** Adjust average.
    */
case WM_NCRBUTTONDBLCLK:     // FALL THRU
case WM_RBUTTONDBLCLK:
    if(GetKeyState(VK_SHIFT) & 0x8000)
    {
        nAverage -= nAverage / 10;
    }
    else
    {
        nAverage += nAverage / 10;
    }
    break;

    /*
    ** Closing so write out interesting stuff to INI file. Done
    ** here because the window still exists at this point.
    */
case WM_QUERYENDSESSION:     // FALL THRU.
case WM_CLOSE:
    {
        auto char              carBuffer[BUFFERSIZE];
        auto WINDOWPLACEMENT   wp;
        auto RECT              rsWindow;

        /*
        ** Init windowplacement. NOTE: could have used
        ** IsZoomed() and IsIconic() to this stuff.
        */
```

```
        wp.length = sizeof(WINDOWPLACEMENT);

        /*
        ** Get 'show' state and write it out to INI file.
        */
        GetWindowPlacement(hWnd, &wp);

        wsprintf(carBuffer, "%u", wp.showCmd);

        WritePrivateProfileString(
                                   carSection
                                  ,carShow
                                  ,carBuffer
                                  ,(LPCSTR)carINIFileName
                                  );

        /*
        ** Get window size and pos and write it out to INI file.
        */
        GetWindowRect(hWnd, &rsWindow);

        wsprintf(
                 carBuffer
                ,"%d,%d,%d,%d"
                ,rsWindow.top
                ,rsWindow.left
                ,rsWindow.right  - rsWindow.left
                ,rsWindow.bottom - rsWindow.top
                );

        WritePrivateProfileString(
                                   carSection
                                  ,carPosition
                                  ,carBuffer
                                  ,(LPCSTR)carINIFileName
                                  );

        /*
        ** Get top-most and 'title' state and write it out
        ** to INI file.
        */
        wsprintf(
                 carBuffer
                ,"%d,%d"
                ,!!(GetWindowLong(hWnd, GWL_EXSTYLE) & WS_EX_TOPMOST)
                ,!!(GetWindowLong(hWnd, GWL_STYLE)   & WS_SYSMENU)
                );

        WritePrivateProfileString(
                                   carSection
                                  ,carOptions
                                  ,carBuffer
                                  ,(LPCSTR)carINIFileName
                                  );

        return DefWindowProc(hWnd, uMessage, wParam, lParam);
    }
break;
```

```
        /*
        ** Private message (could have used WM_SIZE) to work out
        ** required window extent.
        */
case UM_RECALC:
        /*
        ** Changing size (or average) so work out window ext etc.
        */
        {
            /*
            ** Get our current size.
            */
            GetClientRect(hWnd, &rsClient);

            /*
            ** Set up co-ordinates (window) so that positive y
            ** goes up and that max window height = average.
            */
            SetWindowExt(hDC, rsClient.right, -nAverage);
            SetWindowOrg(hDC, 0, nAverage);

            /*
            ** Map window to viewport and map viewport to client area.
            */
            SetViewportOrg(hDC, 0, 0);
            SetViewportExt(hDC, rsClient.right, rsClient.bottom);
        }
        break;

        /*
        ** Private message used to retrieve stuff from INI file.
        */
case UM_SETUP:
        {
            /*
            ** INI stuff read into here.
            */
            auto char   carBuffer[BUFFERSIZE];

            /*
            ** Used in strtok calls.
            */
            auto char * pcEntry;

            /*
            ** Window positional info.
            */
            auto int    nTop    = 0;
            auto int    nLeft   = 0;
            auto int    nRight  = 0;
            auto int    nBottom = 0;

            /*
            ** Get window position and size from INI file.
            */
            GetPrivateProfileString(
                                    (LPCSTR)carSection
```

```
                              , (LPCSTR) carPosition
                              , (LPCSTR) carEmpty
                              , carBuffer
                              , sizeof (carBuffer)
                              , (LPCSTR) carINIFileName
                              );

/*
** Parse it and set size and pos.
*/
pcEntry = carBuffer;

if(lstrcmp(pcEntry, "") != 0)
{
    auto char * pcTok;
    auto int    nLoop = 0;

    while((pcTok = strtok(pcEntry, ",")) != NULL)
    {

        /*
        ** Keep strtok going.
        */
        pcEntry = NULL;

        /*
        ** Count of tokens found.
        */
        nLoop++;

        if(nLoop == 1)
        {
            nTop = atoi(pcTok);
        }
        else
        if(nLoop == 2)
        {
            nLeft = atoi(pcTok);
        }
        else
        if(nLoop == 3)
        {
            nRight = atoi(pcTok);
        }
        else
        if(nLoop == 4)
        {
            nBottom = atoi(pcTok);
        }
        else
        {
            /*
            ** Ignore any further positions.
            */
        }

    }
```

```
                    if(nRight && nBottom)
                    {
                        SetWindowPos(
                                    hWnd
                                    ,NULL
                                    ,nLeft
                                    ,nTop
                                    ,nRight
                                    ,nBottom
                                    ,SWP_NOZORDER
                                    );

                    }
            }

            /*
            ** Get list of optons from INI file.
            */
            GetPrivateProfileString(
                                    (LPCSTR)carSection
                                    ,(LPCSTR)carOptions
                                    ,(LPCSTR)carEmpty
                                    ,carBuffer
                                    ,sizeof(carBuffer)
                                    ,(LPCSTR)carINIFileName
                                    );

            pcEntry = carBuffer;

            if(lstrcmp(pcEntry, "") != 0)
            {
                auto char * pcTok;
                auto int    nLoop = 0;

                while((pcTok = strtok(pcEntry, ",")) != NULL)
                {
                    /*
                    ** Keep strtok going.
                    */
                    pcEntry = NULL;

                    /*
                    ** Count of tokens found.
                    */
                    nLoop++;

                    /*
                    ** This is the 'on-top' entry.
                    */
                    if(nLoop == 1)
                    {
                        if(atoi(pcTok) == 1)
                        {
                            SendMessage(
                                        hWnd
                                        ,WM_SYSCOMMAND
                                        ,IDM_ONTOP
```

```
                                                ,0
                                                );
                                        }
                                }
                                else

                                /*
                                ** This is the 'no title' entry.
                                */
                                if(nLoop == 2)
                                {
                                        if(atoi(pcTok) == 0)
                                        {
                                                SendMessage(
                                                                hWnd
                                                                ,WM_COMMAND
                                                                ,IDM_NOCAPTION
                                                                ,0
                                                                );

                                        }
                                }
                                else
                                {
                                        /*
                                        ** Ignore any further options.
                                        */
                                }
                        }
                }


                ShowWindow(
                        hWnd
                        ,GetPrivateProfileInt(
                                                carSection
                                                ,carShow
                                                ,SW_SHOWNORMAL
                                                ,carINIFileName
                                                )
                        );

        UpdateWindow(hWnd);

        /*
        ** Main window init'ed OK here so get rid of modeless,
        ** but system modal dialog box.
        */
        DestroyWindow(hWndDialog);

        }
        break;

case UM_START:
        {
        /*
        ** Holds copy of system menu.
        */
```

```
        auto HMENU hSysMenu;


    /*
** Create modeless dialog box telling the user that perf-meter
** is initialising. CreateDialog() returns immediately.
*/
    if((hWndDialog = CreateDialog(
                                  (HINSTANCE)GetWindowWord
                                  (hWnd
                                  ,GWW_HINSTANCE
                                                                  )
                                  ,MAKEINTRESOURCE(IDD_HELLODIALOG)
                                  ,hWnd
                                  ,(DLGPROC)DialogProc
                                  )) != NULL
      )
    {
        /*
        ** If we  got  the  modeless  dialog  window make it
        ** system modal. This allows perf-meter to calculate
        ** on a quiet system, ie. the  user  cannot make the
        ** system  busy  if there's  system modal window up;
        ** if they could it would confuse  perf-meter. Could
        ** have used LockInput() here.

        */
        SetSysModalWindow(hWndDialog);
    }
    else
    {
        /*
        ** Couldn't create dialog so close.
        */
        PostMessage(hWnd, WM_CLOSE, 0, 0);
    }


    /*
    ** Wait WAITTIME / 1000 seconds before doing anything -
    ** lets  the  whole  system settle down and gives us a.
    ** quiet system to work with.
    **
    ** If we can't get a  timer  tell the user and exit the
    ** application.
    */
    if(SetTimer(hWnd, WAIT, WAITTIME, NULL) == 0)
    {
        MessageBox(
                   hWnd
                   ,"Not enough timers to run this application.\n"
                   "Close an application and try again."
                   ,"Unable to start!"
                   ,MB_OK | MB_ICONSTOP
                   );

        PostMessage(hWnd, WM_CLOSE, 0, 0);
    }
```

```
                    /*
                    ** Get our OWNDC here.
                    */
                    hDC = GetDC(hWnd);


                    /*
                    ** Set up stuff  we want in DC here. We want
                    ** the drawing to be simple and proportional
                    ** so use ANISO mapping.
                    */
                    SetMapMode(hDC, MM_ANISOTROPIC);


                    /*
                    ** Insert item into system menu.
                    */
                    hSysMenu = GetSystemMenu(hWnd, FALSE);

                    InsertMenu(
                                hSysMenu
                              ,IDM_SWITCHTO
                              ,MF_BYCOMMAND | MF_STRING
                              ,IDM_ONTOP
                              ,"Always On &Top"
                              );


               }
               break;

        default:
               return DefWindowProc(hWnd, uMessage, wParam, lParam);
     }
     return (LRESULT)0;
}



/*
** Modeless dialog  callback. This dialog informs the user that Perf-Meter
** is initialising. This dialog's window is also made system modal so that
** the user is prevented from  making  the system busy while perf-meter is
** analysing the 'quiet' system.
*/
BOOL __export CALLBACK DialogProc
(
   HWND     hDlg
  ,UINT     uMessage
  ,WPARAM   wParam
  ,LPARAM   lParam
)
{
   if(uMessage == WM_INITDIALOG)
   {
      /*
      ** Used for positioning the dialog window in the
      ** center of the screen.
      */
      auto RECT rsWindow;
      auto int  nScreenWidth;
```

```
        auto int   nScreenHeight;

    /*
    ** Calculate and position the dialog in the center of the screen.
    */
    GetWindowRect(hDlg, &rsWindow);
    nScreenWidth  = GetSystemMetrics(SM_CXSCREEN);
    nScreenHeight = GetSystemMetrics(SM_CYSCREEN);

    MoveWindow(
            hDlg
           ,(nScreenWidth  - (rsWindow.right  - rsWindow.left)) / 2
           ,(nScreenHeight - (rsWindow.bottom - rsWindow.top))  / 2
           ,rsWindow.right  - rsWindow.left
           ,rsWindow.bottom - rsWindow.top
           ,FALSE
           );
    }

    /*
    ** 'Say' that we don't handle ANY messages - the DM will look after
    ** the dialog for us!
    */
    return FALSE;
}
```

Perf.h :

```
/*
** Menu item IDs.
*/
#define IDM_ABOUT      100
#define IDM_USENEWAVE  200
#define IDM_NOCAPTION  300
#define IDM_ONTOP      0xF000 - 1
#define IDM_SWITCHTO   0xF130

/*
** Private message IDs.
*/
#define UM_SETUP       WM_USER + 1
#define UM_RECALC      WM_USER + 2
#define UM_START       WM_USER + 3


/*
** Resource and class IDs.
*/
#define PERFMENU          101
#define PERFICON          102
#define PERFCLASS         103
#define IDD_HELLODIALOG   104

/*
** Function prototypes.
*/
```

```
#if !defined RC_INVOKED


VOID            PASCAL NEAR vDoNoCaption     (HWND,UINT ,WPARAM ,LPARAM );
VOID            PASCAL NEAR vDoSysCommand    (HWND,UINT ,WPARAM ,LPARAM );
VOID            PASCAL NEAR vDoMinMaxInfo    (HWND,UINT ,WPARAM ,LPARAM );
VOID            PASCAL NEAR vDoWindowOnTop   (HWND,UINT ,WPARAM ,LPARAM );
BOOL            PASCAL NEAR InitApplication (HINSTANCE);
BOOL            PASCAL NEAR InitInstance    (HINSTANCE,int);
int             PASCAL      WinMain          (HINSTANCE,HINSTANCE,LPSTR,int);
LRESULT __export CALLBACK   MainWndProc      (HWND,UINT ,WPARAM ,LPARAM );
BOOL    __export CALLBACK   DialogProc       (HWND,UINT ,WPARAM ,LPARAM );


#endif
```

Perf.rc :

```
#include <windows.h>
#include "perf.h"

/*
** Icon for app. Not used in app directly.
*/
PERFICON ICON PERF.ICO

/*
** Menu.
*/
PERFMENU MENU
BEGIN
    POPUP "&Settings"
    BEGIN
        MENUITEM "Adjust &meter dynamically",       IDM_USENEWAVE
        MENUITEM "&No Title",                        IDM_NOCAPTION
        MENUITEM SEPARATOR
        MENUITEM "&About Perf-Meter...",            IDM_ABOUT
    END
END


DLGINCLUDE RCDATA DISCARDABLE
BEGIN
    "PERF.H\0"
END

IDD_HELLODIALOG DIALOG PRELOAD 120, 62, 161, 61
STYLE DS_MODALFRAME | WS_POPUP | WS_VISIBLE | WS_CAPTION | WS_SYSMENU
CAPTION "Perf-Meter By Peter J. Morris"
FONT 8, "MS Sans Serif"
BEGIN

        CONTROL
          "Perf-Meter is initialising. During this time "
          "(About 5 seconds) your machine will be effectively unresponsive."
          ,-1
          ,"Static"
```

```
              ,SS_CENTER | WS_GROUP
              ,24
              ,9
              ,116
              ,51
END
```

Perf.def :

```
NAME        PERF WINDOWAPI

DESCRIPTION   "Windows Performance Meter by Peter J. Morris."

EXETYPE      WINDOWS 3.1

PROTMODE

STUB         'WINSTUB.EXE'

CODE   DISCARDABLE  MOVEABLE  PRELOAD          EXECUTEONLY
DATA   MOVEABLE               PRELOAD  SINGLE  READWRITE

HEAPSIZE      1024
STACKSIZE     5000

EXPORTS
       MainWndProc   @1
       DialogProc    @2
```

Perf.ico :
Not Shown – any icon will do.

As was mentioned before the code listings, this application uses a PeekMessage()
loop. It uses the loop for one thing – to gauge system load. When the application starts
up it creates a modeless dialog box. This modeless dialog is made system modal to
make sure that nothing else can happen in the system.

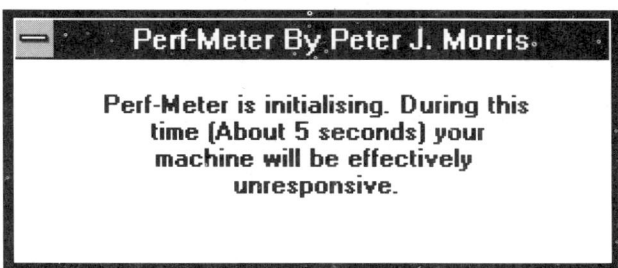

Once this is done the application uses a PeekMessage() loop and a Windows' timer
to count ticks, ie. to see how many times PeekMessage() returns in a quiet system
between successive timer ticks (it does this over several timer intervals to get an
average). Once it's done this it knows that on a quiet system the average number of

ticks in a timer interval will be *x*. It then kills itself (the timer) and starts another timer off whose purpose is two fold. Firstly this second timer *moves* the scrolling client area, ie. it gives the app the impetus to do the scroll. Secondly it is used to once again count PeekMessage() returns. The number of returns is plotted against the average returns calculated by the first timer. The window used in the plotting has been set with the MM_ANISOTROPIC mapping mode and has the Y axis turned upside down, ie. plotting against it means drawing *up*. The windows' window extent is set to the average number of ticks as calculated by the first timer. The origin of the window is set to be aligned with the bottom of the window's client area via the window's viewport, ie. the viewport is set to the whole of the client area and the window is set to be *x* (little x) units in Y which points *up*; it's origin is set so that it aligns with the bottom left pixel in the client area of the window.

The window also has its own DC and has class styles set which are designed to speed up drawing on most devices. Each time the second timer goes off the number of PeekMessage() returns is plotted against the average by using MoveTo() and LineTo() (PatBlt() would have been faster). When this line is draw the whole of the window's client area is scrolled one pixel to the right using ScrollWindow() and the cycle is ready to repeat.

The application also has code that is used to turn the window's caption on and off, position the window when it has no caption by clicking and dragging in the window's client area, making the window a top-most window, handling WM_GETMINMAX-INFO messages, and finally saving and restoring the window's state and position in an INI file. The whole effect is based on the behaviour of the Windows' clock application. The private INI file contents look like this :

```
[Performance Meter]
Show=1
Position=651,800,203,76
Options=1,0
```

To see what does what – see the code. This app also uses some of its own private messages; each private message ID begins with UM_, ie. USER MESSAGE.

☐ Command-line arguments & environment variables

A windows application gets its command line arguments through one of two mechanisms. We all know about lpszCmdLine. This parameter to WinMain contains all the command line args space separated :

If lpszCmdLine points to -> "this is a set of command line args". The arguments are :

"this"
"is"
"a"
"set"

"of"
"command"
"line"
"args"

These are best parsed using a function such as strtok (large or compact model) or _fstrtok (all models). The following piece of code prints out (to DBWIN's window or the debugging terminal) a complete list of the application's command line arguments.

```
#include <string.h>

int PASCAL WinMain
(
   HINSTANCE    hInstance
  ,HINSTANCE    hPrevInstance
  ,LPSTR        lpszCmdLine
  ,int          nCmdShow
)
{
   auto MSG msg;
   auto LPSTR lpArg;

   while((lpArg = _fstrtok(lpszCmdLine, " ")) != NULL)
   {
      lpszCmdLine = NULL; // Keep _fstrtok() going.

      // No cast necessary on lpArg - it's a long pointer already!
      DebugOutput(
                  DBF_TRACE | DBF_APPLICATION
                 ,"Arg = %s"
                 ,lpArg
                 );

   }
   ....
```

The command line args are also available via __argv and __argc as shown in the code snippet below :

```
int PASCAL WinMain
(
   HINSTANCE    hInstance
  ,HINSTANCE    hPrevInstance
  ,LPSTR        lpszCmdLine
  ,int          nCmdShow
)
{
   auto MSG msg;

   extern char ** __argv;
   extern int     __argc;

   auto int nLoop;

   for(nLoop = 0; nLoop < __argc; nLoop++)
   {
      // Cast required on *(__argv + nLoop) as normally this is a short pointer.
```

```
        DebugOutput (
                    DBF_TRACE | DBF_APPLICATION
                    ,"%s"
                    , (LPSTR)*(__argv + nLoop)
                    );
    }
    ...
```

Note that this latter method provides one bit of information not available through lpszCmdLine – argv[0], or the name of the application including its full path name; this can be very useful. This piece of information is available through other means by the way. By the way, argv[0] under 3.0 was the name of the actual kernel (file) used in the Windows session, ie. it was either KERNEL.EXE, KRNL286.EXE or KRNL386.EXE.

Environment variables. These again can be accessed two ways; firstly there's the _environ way :

```
int PASCAL WinMain
(
   HINSTANCE    hInstance
  ,HINSTANCE    hPrevInstance
  ,LPSTR        lpszCmdLine
  ,int          nCmdShow
)
{

   auto MSG msg;

   extern char ** _environ;

   while(*(_environ) != NULL)
   {

      DebugOutput (
                    DBF_TRACE | DBF_APPLICATION
                    ,"Env Var = %s"
                    , (LPSTR)*(_environ++)
                    );
   }
   ...
```

This outputs the following to DBWIN's window on my system :

```
t GENERIC Env Var = COMSPEC=C:\COMMAND.COM
t GENERIC Env Var = BLASTER=A220 I7 D1 T4
t GENERIC Env Var = PATH=C:\WINDEV\MDK;C:\C700\BIN;F:\BIN;C:\WIN31;C:\SYSTEM
t GENERIC Env Var = LIB=C:\windev\MDK\lib;C:\C700\LIB;C:\C700\MFC\LIB;F:\LIB
t GENERIC Env Var = INCLUDE=C:\windev\MDK\include;C:\C700\INCLUDE
t GENERIC Env Var = HELPFILES=C:\SYSTEM\HELP\*.HLP
t GENERIC Env Var = INIT=C:\C700\INIT;G:\INIT
t GENERIC Env Var = TMP=D:\
t GENERIC Env Var = ASMEX=G:\SAMPLES
t GENERIC Env Var = PROMPT=$e[0m[$e[1;33m$p$e[0m]$_$g
t GENERIC Env Var = BPATH=;c:\brief\macros
t GENERIC Env Var = BHELP=c:\system\help
```

```
t GENERIC Env Var = BFILE=c:\brief\state.rst
t GENERIC Env Var = BBACKUP=c:\brief\backup
t GENERIC Env Var = BCC="!cl -c %s.c"
t GENERIC Env Var = BPACKAGES=c:r
t GENERIC Env Var = BFLAGS=-i1201255Mtz -mPJM -mrestore -Dega -D101key -p -cl,1,1,3,3
t GENERIC Env Var = BTMP=D:\
t GENERIC Env Var = TEMP=D:\
t GENERIC Env Var = QH=\SYSTEM\HELP\*.HLP
t GENERIC Env Var = DIRCMD=/OGN/L
t GENERIC Env Var = SOUND=C:\SBPRO
t GENERIC Env Var = windir=C:\WIN31
```

Then there's get GetDOSEnvironment() :

```
int PASCAL WinMain
(
   HINSTANCE    hInstance
  ,HINSTANCE    hPrevInstance
  ,LPSTR        lpszCmdLine
  ,int          nCmdShow
)
{

    auto MSG msg;
    auto LPSTR lpEnviron;

    for(
        lpEnviron = GetDOSEnvironment()
      ;*lpEnviron != NULL
      ;lpEnviron += lstrlen(lpEnviron) + 1
      )
    {
      DebugOutput(
                  DBF_TRACE | DBF_APPLICATION
                 ,"Env Var = %s"
                 ,lpEnviron
                 );
    }
    ...
```

This produces output which is identical to the previous example.

Note that both __argv AND __argv have **two** leading underscores and that _environ has just the one.

> The environment variable *windir* can be used from a DOS application to ascertain whether or not Windows is currently running. This saves you having to use INT 2F etc.

Here's a simple example of a program that uses _environ, __argc and __argv all at the same time.

From the debugging chapter we saw that you can switch between the debug and non-debug versions of Windows by running the batch files N2D.BAT and D2N.BAT from DOS, ie. you exit Windows and run the appropriate batch file. If this could be more automated then maybe more people would use it – here's a way to do just that, check this program out :

ExecIt.c :

```
#define STRICT

#define BUFF_SIZE 100

#include <windows.h>
#include <string.h>

#pragma warning(disable:4100)
#pragma warning(disable:4001)

int PASCAL WinMain
(
   HINSTANCE    hInstance
  ,HINSTANCE    hPrevInstance
  ,LPSTR        lpCmdLine
  ,int          nCmdShow
)
{
   /*
   ** Args, arg count and environment.
   */
   extern char **   __argv;
   extern int       __argc;
   extern char **   _environ;

   /*
   ** Any arg given?
   */
   if( __argc <= 1 || __argc > 2)
   {
       MessageBox(
               0
              ,"ExecIt - not enough parameters.\n"
               "Usage : ExecIt 'Batch file name'."
              ,NULL
              ,MB_OK
              );
   }
   else
   {
       /*
       ** Give the command processor some environment to work with.
       */
       auto char    carEnv[] = "/E:1024 /C ";

       /*
       ** Build up command line to command.com in here.
       */
       auto char    carBuffer[BUFF_SIZE];

       /*
```

```
        ** Points to command.com.
        */
        auto LPSTR   lpEnv;


        /*
        ** Command.com always first environment variable. Get it
        ** and set pointer to it.
        */
        lpEnv = _fstrrchr(*_environ,(int)':');
        lpEnv--;

        /*
        ** Copy arg into buffer with environment setting stuff.
        */
        lstrcpy(&carBuffer[0], &carEnv[0]);
        lstrcat(&carBuffer[0], *(__argv + 1));

        /*
        ** Dooooo - It!
        */
        ExitWindowsExec(lpEnv, &carBuffer[0]);

    }

    return 0;
}
```

ExecIt.def :

```
NAME        EXECIT WINDOWSAPI

DESCRIPTION 'Windows App Which Runs Batch Files.'

EXETYPE     WINDOWS 3.1

PROTMODE

STUB        'WINSTUB.EXE'

CODE   PRELOAD MOVEABLE DISCARDABLE

DATA   PRELOAD MOVEABLE MULTIPLE


HEAPSIZE    1024
STACKSIZE   5120
```

ExecIt.rc :

```
100 ICON notsafe.ico
200 ICON safe.ico
```

This very small application allows you to automate the running of any batch file by defining an icon/entry in any Program Manager group. In particular I use it to run N2D.BAT and D2N.BAT.

N2D

D2N

I have the two icons above in my SDK group. Each icon is used, together with ExecIt.exe to change between the debug and non-debug version of Windows. Here's how D2N's properties etc are defined in the Program Manager :

Program Item Properties

Description: **D2N**

Command Line: C:\WINDEV\BIN\EXECIT.EXE D

Working Directory: C:\

Shortcut Key: None

☐ Run Minimized

OK

Cancel

Browse...

Change Icon...

Help

From the code above, we're telling *execit* to start COMMAND.COM, and then tell it, COMMAND.COM that is, to run D2N.BAT (in the snap shot above you can just make out the beginning of D2N.BAT). The application finds COMMAND.COM's location by accessing the first environment variable. DOS shells/boxes will always have COMSPEC defined as the first environment variable so we don't have to go looking for it – it's always the one at the top (**Note that this is no longer necessarily true using MS-DOS 6. You might find that *Config* is the first environment variable!**). It then creates a buffer that contains :

/E:1024 /C D2N

This is used as an argument to COMMAND.COM, it tells it to create a 1Kb environment and then to run D2N. The whole thing is exec'ed by ExitWindowsExec(), this API is used to close down Windows, run a program or batch file and then re-start Windows. The whole process of switching between debug and non-debug takes about 15 seconds and one double click!

☐ Stubs

A Windows' stub is an executable that typically runs in DOS when an attempt is made to start a Windows' application from a DOS session (either DOS box or *real* DOS). Typically the code in the stub produces a message like this, 'This program requires

Microsoft Windows'. In this instance the stub code is simply ordinary DOS code that gets executed in the DOS session. A Windows' application is usually (because you can build a Windows' app that doesn't have a stub) made up of two executables – the old app, or stub and the NE app, ie. the Windows' application proper.

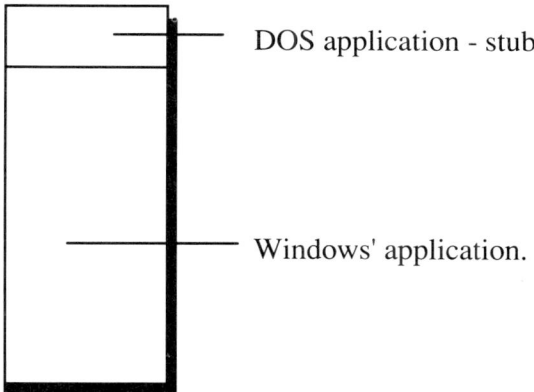

DOS application - stub.

Windows' application.

See the programmers reference on the format of a New Executable for more on this (also see DLL chapter in this book).

The stub code can be any ordinary DOS executable. This allows us do some nice tricks. For example you could write a dual mode application. Consider writing both DOS and Windows based file-find applications. These two individual applications can be *made one* by attaching the DOS file find to the Windows' file find via the stub mechanism – dual mode application. When the user runs the *single* executable from DOS they get a DOS based file-finder, and when they run the same executable from within Windows they get a Windows' file-finder!! It is also possible to write multi-platform stubs, ie. one that can run under Presentation Manager, OS/2 text mode, DOS and Windows but we won't go into the details here.

OK, we've seen DOS stubs for Windows' apps but how about Windows' stubs for DOS apps!? Or to put it another way – you can also create a **Windows'** stub for a DOS based application!

Isn't annoying when you run a DOS app under Windows thinking that it's a Windows' application (I think so). The _default.pif file describes the attributes of the DOS app and Windows attempts to run it. This means that a DOS box will appear full screen (unless you've altered _default.pif) obliterating the Windows' screen – everything needs to re-paint when the DOS box is closed down! However, you could write a Windows stub and attach it to the DOS application so that when it is run from within Windows the user is informed, via a window, that this application is a DOS application! This is done by attaching the DOS application to a Windows' application stub. When the user runs the application from within Windows they get the Windows stub telling them that this is a DOS application; when they run it under DOS they get the *real* app, ie. the stub !

Here's a first go at a Windows' stub that works like this :

Wstub.c :

```c
/*
** Get rid of silly warnings.
*/
#pragma warning(disable:4100)
#pragma warning(disable:4001)

/*
** A 'Windows' stub  for a DOS app! Add  this  stub to  your  DOS app and
** if the user tries to run it from Windows instead of the usual 'DOS box
** opening to run the applicaton you'll get a Window shown that tells you
** what you've done! Insert the  name of your DOS app in the 'STUB' entry
** in WSTUB.DEF and  change  the name of the module 'NAME' to the name of
** the DOS app, once the app has  been  built rename it from wstub.exe to
** whatever your DOS was called.
*/

/* e.g. :_
**
** name TEST
**
** STUB 'TEST.EXE'
*/

#define  STRICT

#define  WIDTH 75
#include <windows.h>
#include <string.h>

#define DEGREES(X) (X) * 10

LRESULT __export CALLBACK WndProc         (HWND, UINT, WPARAM, LPARAM);
LRESULT __export CALLBACK SubClassWndProc (HWND, UINT, WPARAM, LPARAM);
int PASCAL WinMain                        (HINSTANCE, HINSTANCE, LPSTR, int);

FARPROC lpPrevProc;

int PASCAL WinMain
(
  HINSTANCE     hInstance
 ,HINSTANCE     hPrevInstance
 ,LPSTR         lpszCmdline
 ,int           nCmdShow
)
{
  auto    HWND        hWnd;
  auto    MSG         msg;
  auto    WNDCLASS    wc;

  auto char carClassName[] = "WINDOWSSTUB";

  wc.style        =   (WORD)CS_HREDRAW | CS_VREDRAW;
  wc.lpfnWndProc  =   (WNDPROC)WndProc;
  wc.cbClsExtra   =   0;
```

```
    wc.cbWndExtra      =    0;
    wc.hInstance       =    hInstance;
    wc.hIcon           =    NULL;
    wc.hCursor         =    LoadCursor(NULL,IDC_ARROW);
    wc.hbrBackground   =    COLOR_WINDOW + 1;
    wc.lpszMenuName    =    NULL;
    wc.lpszClassName   =    &carClassName[0];

    if(!RegisterClass(&wc))
    {
        return 0;
    }

    if ((hWnd=CreateWindow(
                        &carClassName[0]
                        ,"MS-DOS App!"
                        ,WS_BORDER   |
                        WS_POPUP    |
                        WS_VISIBLE  |
                        WS_CAPTION  |
                        WS_SYSMENU
                        , (GetSystemMetrics(SM_CXSCREEN)  / 2) -
                        ((GetSystemMetrics(SM_CXSCREEN)  / 2) / 2)
                        , (GetSystemMetrics(SM_CYSCREEN)  / 2) -
                        ((GetSystemMetrics(SM_CYSCREEN)  / 4) / 2)
                        ,GetSystemMetrics(SM_CXSCREEN)   / 2
                        ,GetSystemMetrics(SM_CYSCREEN)   / 4
                        ,NULL
                        ,NULL
                        ,hInstance
                        ,NULL
                        )) == NULL
        )
    {
        return 0;
    }

    ShowWindow(hWnd, SW_SHOWNORMAL);

    UpdateWindow(hWnd);

    while(GetMessage(&msg, NULL, 0, 0))
    {
        TranslateMessage(&msg);
        DispatchMessage(&msg);
    }

    return msg.wParam;
}


LRESULT __export CALLBACK WndProc
(
  HWND     hWnd
 ,UINT     uMessage
 ,WPARAM   wParam
```

```
,LPARAM  lParam
)
{
   static HINSTANCE   hInst;
   static RECT        rsClient;
   auto   HWND        hWndChild;
   auto   PAINTSTRUCT ps;
   auto   HFONT       hFont;
   auto   LOGFONT     lf;


   extern char ** __argv;

   static char carMessage[100];


   switch(uMessage)
   {
      case WM_PAINT:

            BeginPaint(hWnd,&ps);

            lf.lfHeight             = 50;
            lf.lfWidth              = 10;
            lf.lfEscapement         = DEGREES(5);
            lf.lfOrientation        = DEGREES(0);
            lf.lfWeight             = FW_HEAVY;
            lf.lfItalic             = 1;
            lf.lfUnderline          = 0;
            lf.lfStrikeOut          = 0;
            lf.lfCharSet            = DEFAULT_CHARSET;
            lf.lfOutPrecision       = OUT_DEFAULT_PRECIS;
            lf.lfClipPrecision      = CLIP_DEFAULT_PRECIS;
            lf.lfQuality            = 1;
            lf.lfPitchAndFamily     = DEFAULT_PITCH | FF_DONTCARE;
            lstrcpy(lf.lfFaceName, "Arial");

            hFont=CreateFontIndirect(&lf);

            if(hFont != NULL)
            {
              SelectObject(ps.hdc, hFont);
            }

            lstrcpy(&carMessage[0], _fstrrchr(*(__argv), '\\') + 1);
            lstrcat(&carMessage[0], " Is a DOS applicaton!");

            SetBkMode(ps.hdc, TRANSPARENT);

            /*
            ** Draw the same caption using different colors -
            ** makes it twinkle!
            */
            SetTextColor(ps.hdc, RGB(255, 0, 0));
            DrawText(
                    ps.hdc
                    ,&carMessage[0]
                    ,-1
                    ,&rsClient
```

```
                     ,DT_SINGLELINE | DT_VCENTER | DT_CENTER
                     );

          SetTextColor(ps.hdc, RGB(0, 255, 0));
          DrawText(
                  ps.hdc
                 ,&carMessage[0]
                 ,-1
                 ,&rsClient
                 ,DT_SINGLELINE | DT_VCENTER | DT_CENTER
                 );

          SetTextColor(ps.hdc, RGB(0, 0, 255));
          DrawText(
                  ps.hdc
                 ,&carMessage[0]
                 ,-1
                 ,&rsClient
                 ,DT_SINGLELINE | DT_VCENTER | DT_CENTER
                 );

          SetTextColor(ps.hdc, RGB(0, 0, 0));
          DrawText(
                  ps.hdc
                 ,&carMessage[0]
                 ,-1
                 ,&rsClient
                 ,DT_SINGLELINE | DT_VCENTER | DT_CENTER
                 );

       EndPaint(hWnd, &ps);
       break;

   case WM_CREATE:
       hInst=((LPCREATESTRUCT)lParam)->hInstance;

       GetClientRect(hWnd, &rsClient);

       hWndChild=CreateWindow("BUTTON"
                              ,"OK"
                              ,WS_CHILD | BS_DEFPUSHBUTTON
                              ,(rsClient.right / 2) - (WIDTH / 2)
                              ,(rsClient.bottom / 3) * 2
                              ,WIDTH
                              ,30
                              ,hWnd
                              ,(HMENU)IDOK
                              ,hInst
                              ,NULL);

       ShowWindow(hWndChild, SW_SHOWNORMAL);

       UpdateWindow(hWndChild);

       SetFocus(hWndChild);

       lpPrevProc=(FARPROC)GetWindowLong(hWndChild, GWL_WNDPROC);

       SetWindowLong(hWndChild, GWL_WNDPROC, (LONG)SubClassWndProc);
```

```
                    rsClient.bottom = rsClient.bottom - (rsClient.bottom / 3);

                break;

        case WM_COMMAND:
            if(wParam==IDOK)
            {
               DestroyWindow(hWnd);
            }
            break;

        case WM_DESTROY:
            SetWindowLong(hWndChild,GWL_WNDPROC,(LPARAM)lpPrevProc);
            PostQuitMessage(0);
            break;

        default:
            return DefWindowProc(hWnd, uMessage, wParam, lParam);
    }
    return 0L;
}




LRESULT __export CALLBACK SubClassWndProc
(
  HWND      hWnd
 ,UINT      uMessage
 ,WPARAM    wParam
 ,LPARAM    lParam
)
{
   switch(uMessage)
   {
       case WM_KEYDOWN:

            if(wParam == VK_RETURN || wParam == VK_SPACE)

            PostMessage(
                    GetParent(hWnd)
                   ,WM_COMMAND
                   ,GetWindowWord(hWnd,GWW_ID)
                   ,0
                   );
            break;

       default:
            return CallWindowProc(
                              (WNDPROC)lpPrevProc
                             ,hWnd
                             ,uMessage
                             ,wParam
                             ,lParam
                             );
            break;
```

```
   }
}
```

Wstub.rc

```
/* Nothing. */
```

Wstub.def

```
NAME            TEST  WINDOWSAPI  ; Needs changing.

DESCRIPTION     'Windows' SHELL program'

EXETYPE         WINDOWS 3.1

PROTMODE

STUB            'test.exe' ; Change this to the name of your .EXE DOS app.

DATA            PRELOAD MOVEABLE MULTIPLE
CODE            PRELOAD MOVEABLE

HEAPSIZE        4096
STACKSIZE       2048

EXPORTS         WndProc @1
```

To use this Windows' stub you attach a DOS application to it. The DOS application's name is placed in the STUB entry in wstub's .def file. You should also change the module name of wstub to the same as the DOS application name (see above).

For example. Let's say that we have a DOS app called test.exe. Here's test's source :

```
main()
{
}
```

Big app huh??!!

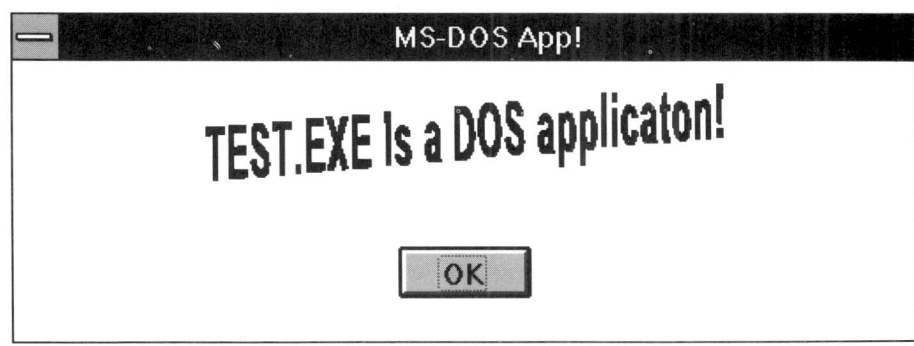

We compile and link this into test.exe. We then alter wstub's .def file as shown above. and re-link wstub. Finally we delete test.exe and rename wstub.exe to test.exe – done. When you run this test.exe from DOS the DOS application runs. When you run test.exe from Windows the Windows' stub runs. The Windows' stub produces the window shown on the previous page.

You get the idea?

Note that this app also shows – sub-classing, some font handling and using __argv[0] etc.

The stub can also, when used in the regular way, be made to start Windows and the application if Windows isn't running. I apologise for some of the identifiers in this DOS code; the application was written under very strict coding standard naming conventions :

```
/******************************************************************************


    Replacement WINSTUB.EXE for windows apps. This stub will start windows and
    an application simply by typing the application's name at the DOS prompt.
    parameters may also be passed on the DOS command line to the windows app.

    It will also output a message to your users when they close down windows.

    The message is pointed to by 'glprnpszExit', appended to the end of this
    string is the name of the app in lower case with the first character in
    upper case.

    pr = private
    au = auto
    st = static

    bl = block
    gl = global
    fi = pr = file

    compile and link line - uses C7 W4 and either real or implict real lib.

    cl -AS -W[4,3] -c stub.c
    link stub,,,slibce[r],nul


    ******************************************************************************/

#include<stdio.h>
#include<string.h>
#include<stdlib.h>
#include<memory.h>
#include<ctype.h>

#define private static

void        *       vpZmalloc(int);
char const *        npsAddString        (char const *, char const * const, int);
void                vStartWinAndApp     (char const * const, char const * const);
```

```
char const *           const npszAppNameFirstUpper  (char * const);
int                    main                         (int, char **);

private char const * const glprnpszTrying     = "Trying to start Windows and";
private char const * const glprnpszWindows    = "WIN";
private char *             glprnpszExitString = "Next time remember to run "
                                                "Windows before running";



/******************************************************************************

 Alloc memory 'space' initialised and NULL terminated.

 PASSED : aublnNumbytes = number of bytes to allocate.
 RETURNS: void pointer to allocated heap space.

******************************************************************************/

void * vpZmalloc(int aublnNumbytes)
{
   const   char    SPACE = (char)0x20;
   auto    void *  aublvpMem;

   aublvpMem=(void *)calloc(aublnNumbytes, sizeof(char));
   memset(aublvpMem, SPACE, aublnNumbytes - 1);

   return aublvpMem;
}



/******************************************************************************

 Adds a string pointed to by npsSourceString to a buufer pointed to by
 npsDest, copies nSourceLength bytes over then returns the pointer npsDest
 incremented so as to point over a space character.

 PASSED : pointer to destination buffer, pointer to source buffer, number of
          bytes to copy.
 RETURNS: incremented pointer to destination.

******************************************************************************/

char const * npsAddString
(
   char const *        npsDest
  ,char const * const  npsSourceString
  ,int                 nSourceLength
)
{
   strncpy((char *)npsDest, npsSourceString, nSourceLength);

   return npsDest += strlen(npsSourceString) + 1;
}
```

```
/******************************************************************************

 Starts windows and  the app, this is pointed  to by npszAppString and we
use
 a system call to do it. if this fails we call fprintf() to report  the er-
ror
 else we call, when windows has shut down, fprintf with a message saying
what
 ever you like

 ******************************************************************************/


void vStartWinandApp
(
   char const * const   npszAppString
  ,char const * const   npszArg0
)
{
   auto char const * const aublnpszString =

   npszAppNameFirstUpper((char * const)npszArg0);

   fprintf(stdout, "%s %s\n\n", glprnpszTrying, aublnpszString);

   if(system(npszAppString) != 0)
   {
      fprintf(
             stderr
            ,"Error executing - \"%s\"\nusing 'system',errno=%d, check C7
      documentation.\n"
            ,npszAppString
            ,errno
            );
   }
   else
   {
      fprintf(stdout, "%s %s", glprnpszExitString, aublnpszString);
   }

   return;
}




/******************************************************************************
Capitalises the first char of our app's name and returns a pointer to it

 ******************************************************************************/

char const * const npszAppNameFirstUpper(char * const npszAppName)
{
   auto char * aublnpszString;
```

```
   aublnpszString = strrchr(npszAppName, (int)'\\');

   aublnpszString++;

   strlwr(aublnpszString);

   *aublnpszString = (char)toascii((int)*aublnpszString);

   *aublnpszString = (char)toupper((int)*aublnpszString);

   return (char const * const)aublnpszString;
}




/**********************************************************************




 Main - works out how much memory is in the argv array of char pointers as
 strings plus 'WIN' plus all the spaces and a NULL terminator. calls
 vpZmalloc to allocate the memory then adds the strings 'WIN' and
 argv strings to it. adds a null to the end of it and uuper cases it then
 causes windows to start with the app and arguments passed in lpszCmdLine
 to the windows app. finally it frees the memory.

 **********************************************************************/


int main(int argc, char ** argv)
{
   auto int           aublnStrlen;
   auto int           aublnLoop;
   auto void      *   aublvpMem;
   auto char const *  aublnpszChar;

   for(
        aublnLoop = aublnStrlen=0
      ;aublnLoop < argc
      ;aublnLoop++
      )
   {
      aublnStrlen += strlen(*(argv + aublnLoop));
   }

   aublnStrlen += argc;
   aublnStrlen += strlen(glprnpszWindows);
   aublnStrlen++;

   aublvpMem = vpZmalloc(aublnStrlen);

   if(aublvpMem != NULL)
   {
      aublnpszChar = (char *)aublvpMem;

      aublnpszChar = npsAddString(
```

```
                                       aublnpszChar
                                      ,glprnpszWindows
                                      ,strlen(glprnpszWindows)
                                      );

        for(aublnLoop = 0; aublnLoop < argc; aublnLoop++)
        {
            aublnpszChar = npsAddString(
                                       aublnpszChar
                                      ,(char const * const)*(argv + aublnLoop)
                                      ,strlen(*(argv + aublnLoop))
                                      );
        }

        vStartWinandApp(strupr((char *)aublvpMem), *argv);

        free(aublvpMem);

        return 0;
    }
    else
    {
        fprintf(stderr, "Error\n\n");

        return 1;
    }
}
```

This application produces the following message when run from DOS :

```
 Trying to start Windows and ??????
```

where ?????? is the name of the executable you have just run.

When Windows is finally terminated the application produces this message :

```
 Next time remember to run Windows before running ??????
```

Of course these messages/actions could be anything you want but a message such as *Thanks for using ??????* always looks good.

Of course, the best way to run a Windows' app under a DOS box under Windows (!) is to simply have it start in Windows, ie. if you attempt to run a Windows' app in a DOS box currently you run the DOS stub – what you really want is for the app to start in Windows!? The WXServer app that ships with C7.00 can be used to get somewhere near to this ideal but it still requires the user to *know* that application X is a Windows' application (you can get the DOS stub to exec WXServer itself however!). This was where I was going to present a method for doing this but for various reasons (mostly commercial (and some technical)) it has not been included. If you're interested in doing this, contact me for a chat.

☐ Other Windows' Development Languages and Methods

This section talks about alternative languages and methods that can be employed to develop Windows applications – it's a very brief look! In fact the only method that has an example is Visual Basic (which is the first alternative we'll look at); all the others are just described.

Visual Basic

I guess the very first language discussed has to Visual Basic! When I first started writing this book VB didn't exist in any form. At the time of going to press it exists as V 2.0 and there's even a DOS version of it available!

VB has, in my opinion, completely revolutionised the way that a lot of Windows' applications are written. At one time of course the only way you could write a Windows' application was to write it in C using a Microsoft 'C' compiler! Well times have changed and this is no longer the case, however, I still personally feel that Microsoft's tools are second to none and that for the majority of applications a good 'C' compiler is still essential. There are also some thing's that you have to do in 'C', ie. things that are so low-level that no 4GL type of environment provides ways of doing them (nor should it). A good grounding in what is, and what's not possible, and a good knowledge of the SDK and 'C' are still required therefore to write fast *flash* apps.

Visual Basic is an object based development system. By this I mean that all Visual Basic items are objects. Some are visual, ie. they can be seen at run time, whilst others are visible only at design time. What's design/run time? A VB app is designed in a design-time environment (see below) and executes in a run-time environment. Typical objects are Windows themselves (called *forms* in VB speak), controls such as push buttons, list boxes etc, timers, file system objects and pictures; there's even an *App* object. Each one of these objects (except App in the list above) can be positioned at design time. Each object responds to a set of events (messages); for example the form may respond to a resize event (WM_SIZE message). You write code that handles these events – just like you're used to writing C code to handle messages currently. Also, each object has a set of properties that can be set to various values (some can only be changed at design time whilst others can only be changed at run time, ie. at various times some properties are *read-only*). Typical properties are the *Interval* property on a timer object (how many milliseconds elapse between each successive timer event is generated), the *Width* property on a form (window width) etc. Lastly, objects can also have *methods* applied to them. A typical method might be the *Print* method. When this method is applied to a form the form object prints itself!

Let's knock up a clock application in VB.

The app will display the current time in its caption. The app will also resize itself so that only its caption is visible and allow only one instance of itself to run.

Here we go :

The Visual Basic Design Time Environment

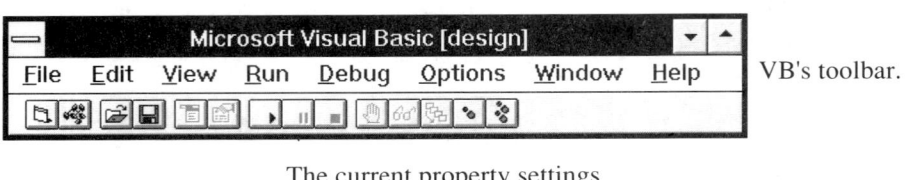

VB's toolbar.

The current property settings
of the currently selected object.

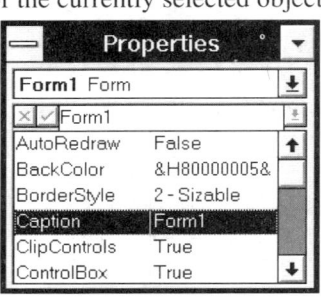

The project list.

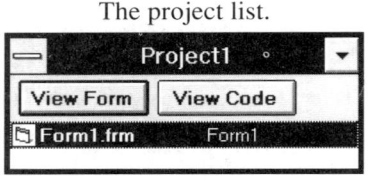

The 'toolbox'
this shows you
the objects that
can be dropped
into a form.

The first window (form) in your application

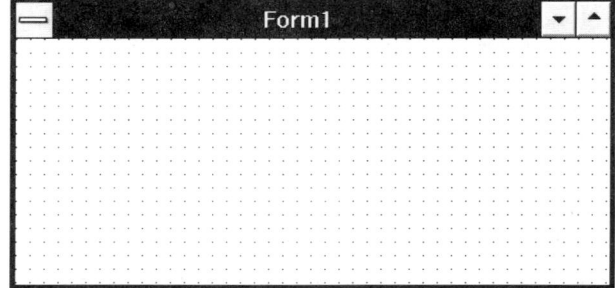

The first thing we'll do is add a timer control to the form. The timer control looks like a stop-watch in the toolbox. Just click it in the toolbox and draw it into the form.

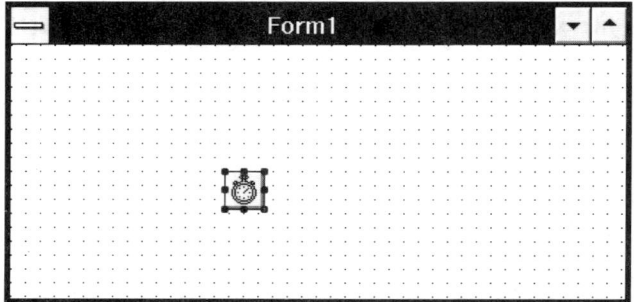

The timer object is not visible at run-time, only at design time.

Every object in VB has a name attached to it, just like every integer you declare in your C code has a name attached to it that identifies it from any other integer. The name of course allows you to reference the object whenever you need it. The VB timer object above will have been given a default name of Timer1 – we'll leave it at that.

We need to set up some of the timer's properties now so let's see what properties it has. The *Properties* list shown above shows the properties, and their current settings, for the currently selected object – that's still the timer. Here's the list :

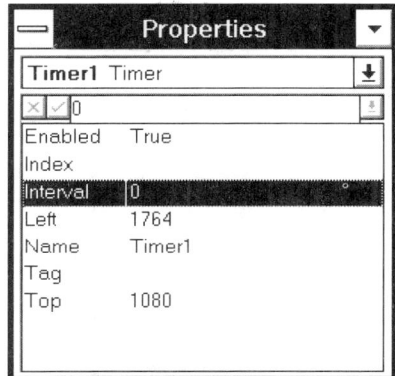

As you can see, the object name is a property – so we could change it. We need to change just the *interval* property for now. We'll set that to 1000 for 1000 milliseconds. That's the length of time that must elapse between timer events being generated. *Top* and *Left* are the position of the object on the form in TWIPS. *Enabled* determines if the timer's working or not. *Index* is used when dealing with control arrays and *Tag* is a very handy property that can be set to any arbitrary data – like private window words!

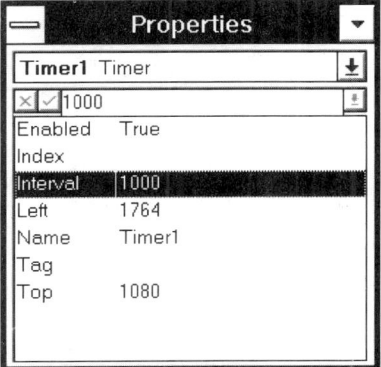

We need now to say what should happen when each timer event is generated. The timer object itself receives these timer events. We get to see, and write, event code for a given object by double-clicking on the object itself. When you double click on an object a *code* window opens up. Here's what happens when we double click on the timer object :

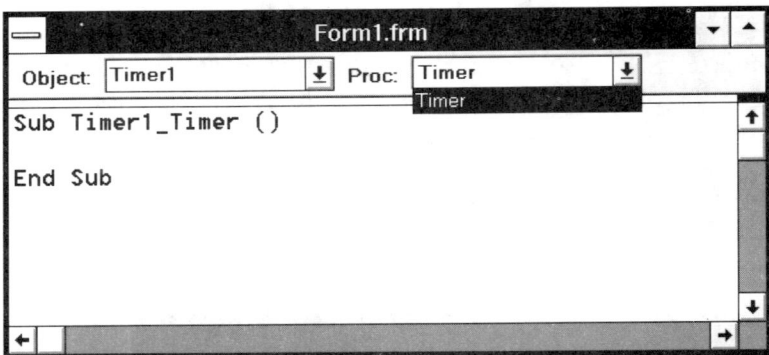

The window above is the coding window for the timer object. Each event handler takes the form of a sub-routine. The naming convention used to name the sub-routines is ObjectName_EventName. Here we can see that this sub-routine handles the *Timer* event for the *Timer1* object. The combo on the right lists all the events that this object can handle. As you can see the list has just one entry – Timer.

Now we need to write some code :

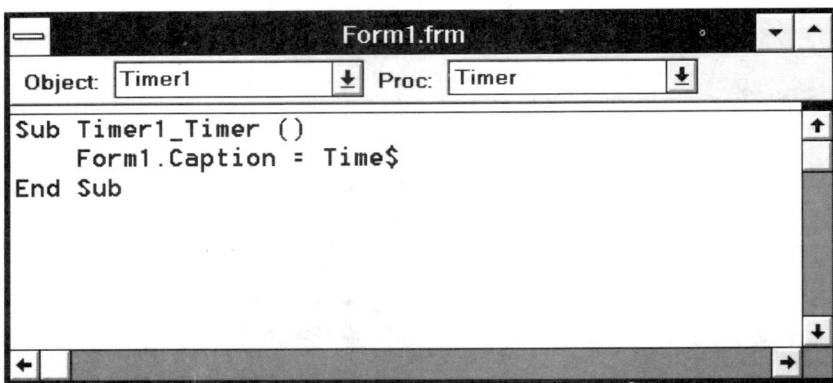

The code *says* – on each timer event set the *Caption* property of the object *Form1* to whatever the call to Time$ returns. Time$ is a procedure that's built into VB; it returns the current time as a string. The Form1 object is the form shown earlier. In VB's design-time environment you're always given the first form. The Caption property of Form1 is what appears in the title of the Form1 window. You'll see from the earlier figure that it's currently *Form1*. At this point let's try out the app. If you hit the F5 key (like CodeView's *Go* key) the application will run – note that we don't have to compile it! It looks like this if we run it.

OK. Now we'll tell the window to re-size itself so that only the caption is visible. To do this we'll write some code that's executed when the form is created, or in VB speak – Loaded.

If we double click the main form window we'll get the following code window :

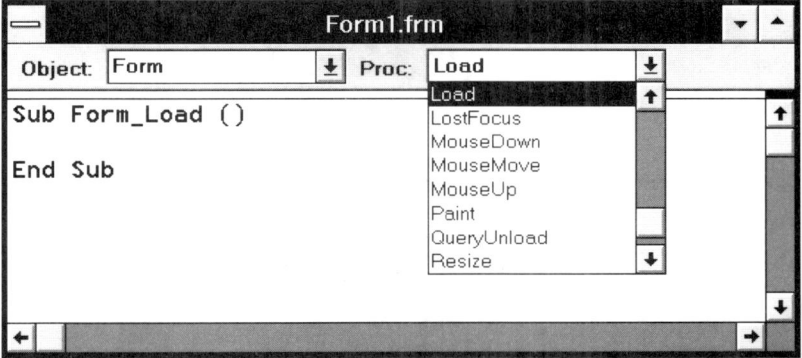

Note that this is the coding window for the Form1 object. Again, the event list combo box has been dropped down so that you can see <u>some</u> of the events that the form object can handle. The event shown above, *Load*, is executed whenever the form is loaded (created).

We need to add some code in here to tell the main form window to resize itself when it's created :

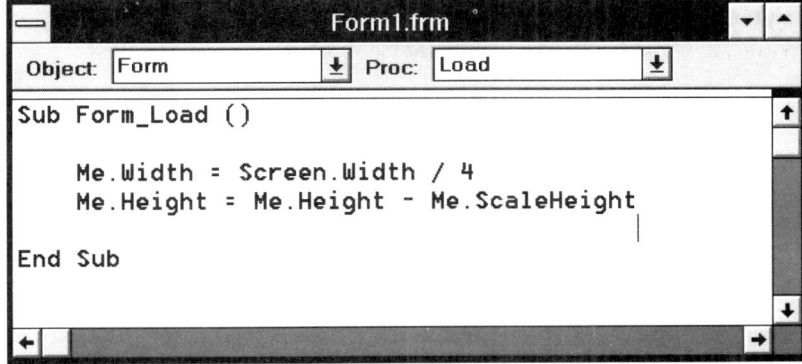

This code *says* – when you're created make your size one quarter that of the screen width. Make your height your external height minus your internal height (like Window Rect minus Client Rect). *Me* refers to the current form. Height and Width are properties of any form object. Note that you address properties like you address structure members in 'C' – ie. with a dot. The screen object is a special object that VB creates for you. This is a kind of GetSystemMetrics() object if you like.

If we run the app now it looks like this :

Now there's something wrong with the *look* of this window? Ah yes – it can be resized! We don't really want that as someone could do this :

We need to alter the *Border Style* property of the form and tell it that we don't want a resizable border :

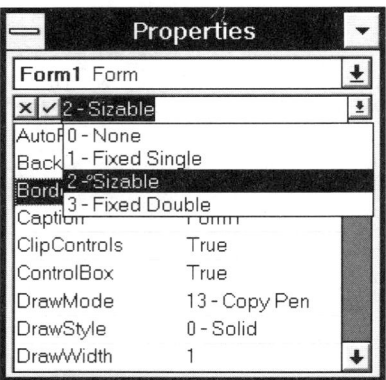

Here's the property list for the main form. We can see that from the border styles available *Fixed Double* is the most suitable so we should select it :

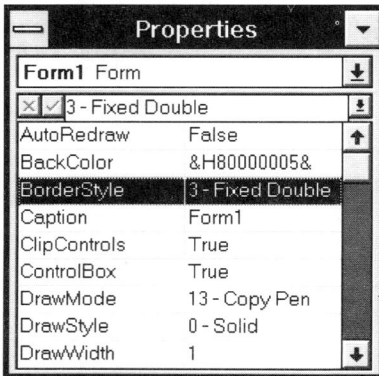

Now when we run the application it looks like this :

Much better. What have we left to do. Oh yes – We must prevent the user from running more than one instance of the app. To do this we access another *special* object called the *App* object in the form's *Load* event handler :

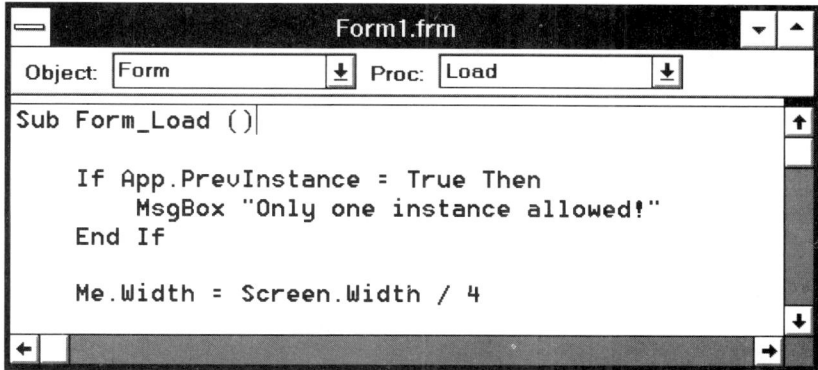

Here we're saying – If the App object's *PrevInstance* property is set to True then produce the message box shown below. The PrevInstance property of the App object is set to True if there's already an instance of this application running. Here's the message box :

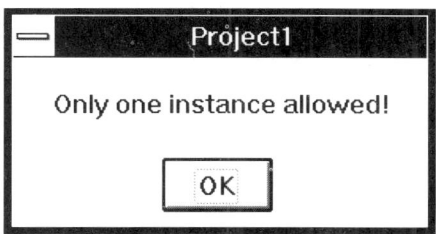

The last thing to do now is to make the VB app into an executable (.EXE file). This is done in just a couple of seconds by selecting MakeEXE File ... off VB's *File* menu. There you have it, a clock app! Total lines of code written = 6 !!! How many lines of 'C' would it have taken you then?

Of course VB does a lot more than this – so much so in fact that many companies (TMS (the one I work for) included) are doing near complete commercial development in it!

One of the greatest features of VB (and now Visual C++ V1.0) is its ability to use third party add on controls, ie. specialised controls written by independent software vendors. The VB professional tool kit comes with a set of these add-on controls for you to use :

Standard & Custom Controls.

Some of the custom controls
are labelled up.

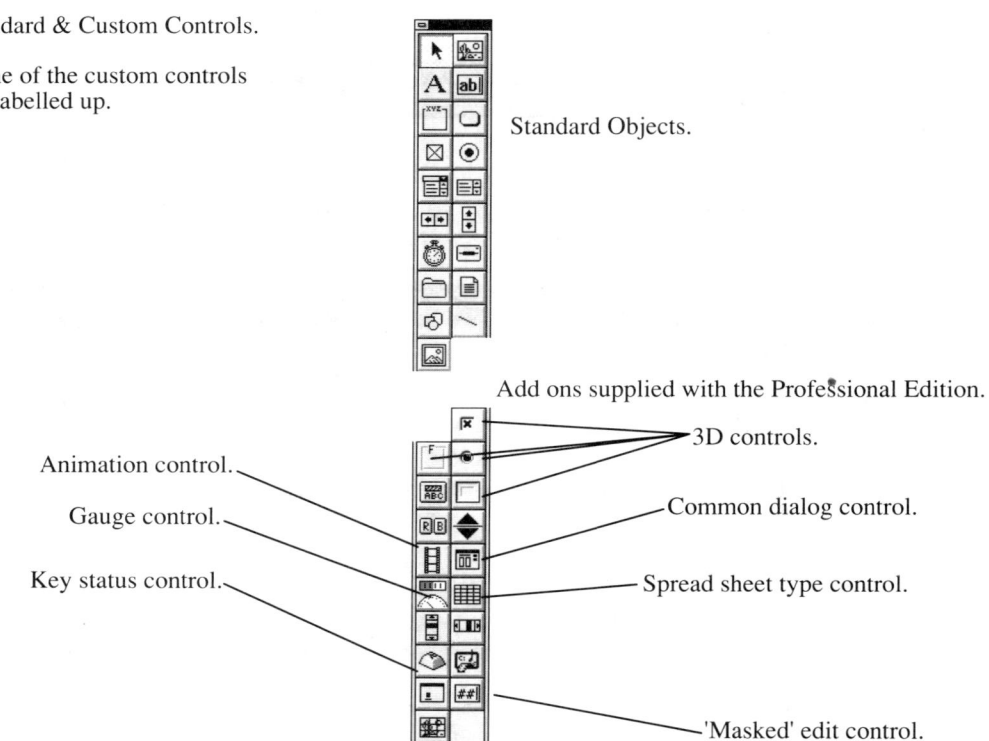

Standard Objects.

Add ons supplied with the Professional Edition.

3D controls.

Animation control.

Gauge control.

Key status control.

Common dialog control.

Spread sheet type control.

'Masked' edit control.

Other commercially available controls help you build and access databases (one of
the best is QE VB from Pioneer Software – very good), do Windows' coms (there's
actually a standard Pro tool kit control that does this), set *hooks* sub-class windows
etc, etc. There's even a control that will let you build neural networks!

Visual C++ V1.0 (or C8.00).

This is Microsoft's *new* visual development environment for the die-hard C and/or
C++ programmer. Visual C++ 1.0 is also known as C8.00 as that's the version of the
C/C++ compiler bundled in the product (you can run C8.00 outside of Windows).

```
Microsoft (R) C/C++ Optimizing Compiler Version 8.00
Copyright (c) Microsoft Corp 1984-1993. All rights reserved.

usage: cl [ option... ] filename... [ -link linkoption... ]
```

Visual C++ is really the Windows hosted front end to the compiler engine :

A Snap-shot of the Professional Edition Program Manager Group.

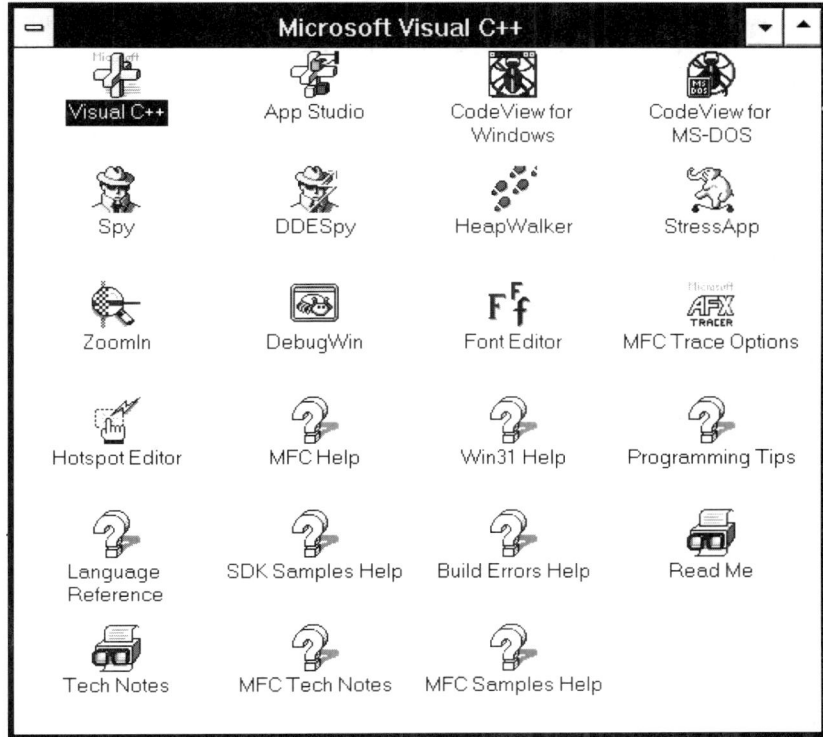

The environment includes a Borland R*esource Workshop* type product called the App Stud*io*. It also has, as do most MS products nowadays, a W*izard*, ie. a semi-intelligent property that can assist the user in creating some aspect of the application.

The App Studio is the bit of Vis C where you can drop Visual Basic custom controls into your application (everyone's heard that it can use 'em by now), ie. you insert them into a dialog box and build things like this :

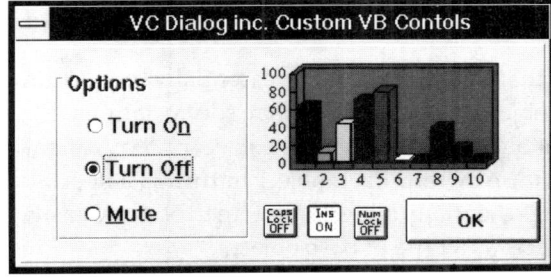

I like the App Studio and the compiler (although I use it from DOS currently), I don't like MFC 2 nor do I feel at ease with the rest of the Visual C++ environment, ie. the editor etc – it might grow on me, I shall have to see.

SmallTalk

Smalltalk is the object oriented, GUI, hosted language developed at Xerox PARC. It is based on the *cosmic* object approach to object oriented programming, ie. everything in it is derived from an object called *Object*. Objects communicate by passing messages. As you know, conventional Windows' objects also communicate using messages so the approach is one that existing Windows programmers take to with comparative ease.

Smalltalk, like Visual Basic is a development system that is truly Windows hosted, ie. object manipulation and project testing is done entirely within the Windows' environment. Before VB came along I used Smalltalk/V Windows from DIGITALK to write a number of small, yet quite sophisticated applications; these days I prefer to do it in VB simply because I can use ultra sophisticated add-on controls easily.

Smalltalk/V Windows does allow you to do something that VB doesn't however – port your code without changes to, say, Presentation Manager.

One of the big problems with Smalltalk is getting resources. By this I don't mean dialogs etc, I mean programmers with any experience in the language – they're as rare as rocking horse shit!

> A joke : This is true – honest. I went into a BIG bookstore in London once and asked in the technical section if they had a book on SmallTalk. I was told, 'no they didn't, but they did have one on making polite dinner conversation'

C++.

Now becoming a main-stream development language. C++ is a kinda super-set of 'C', or as some die-hards would have it called – *Bastardised 'C'*! Again, like Smalltalk, C++ is an object oriented language. Objects in C++ are instances of classes (now there's a familiar word). Classes have abstraction applied to them. This means a class contains data and functionality or if you prefer (as I do) state and method. Also like Smalltalk C++ allows inheritance and polymorphism, or if you prefer late – binding. Like window/class words again to a large degree (like a Ph.D.!).

This means that a complex object is essentially broken down into smaller special cases of simpler objects (now doesn't that sound familiar?). For example a 747 Aircraft object might be derived from a base object called AirCraft and an intermediate object called FixWingAirCraft. Each object in turn is a special case of a more basic object. Late-binding essentially allows a system to be more easily extended by treating newly derived objects as a type of base object.

Again, take the 747 above. Suppose you were to build a air-port insurance valuation system that needed to know the replacement cost of each aircraft currently resident at the airport. It would be nice to build the valuation system so that given any arbitrary aircraft the valuation system can retrieve the replacement cost of the actual aircraft. Late-binding allows you to treat all special cases of AirCraft (the base object of all special cases of aircraft like a 747) as AirCraft, ie. you can ask each object how much it's worth but treat all aircraft as a base AirCraft type. However, each actual object *knows* what it is (747, Glider, Piper Warrior etc) and responds appropriately and not as an AirCraft object – just to say that again; each object responds as the kind of object it is rather than as the type of object to which you have a reference. This allows you to add a new type of aircraft to the system at any time and still run the valuation software without any modification. The key point here is that objects *know* what they are and respond accordingly.

C++, like SmallTalk is one of those languages well suited to Windows' programming and to existing Windows' programmers – it models the GUI quite nicely. Unlike SmallTalk however, and because it's based on that well know portable assembler called 'C', you can break into objects (their private bits) without too much trouble. See also the remarks I made about C++'s suitability as a DLL authoring tool in, where else but, the DLL chapter.

By the way, don't think that using C++ means that you MUST use classes etc, you could use it simply as *a better 'C'*, ie. use the bits that you think are cool, for example. Declaring variables etc where they're used, using the *double slash* as a comment marker, using in-line functions, using the *const* keyword (ie. getting *real* constants), giving function arguments default values etc etc. In other words, you don't HAVE to be using MFC V2.0 etc to use C++, you can use it now and learn about the language as you get used to it.

Class Libraries for C++

C++ really comes into its own however when used with a class hierarchy like Microsoft's MFC, Borland's OWL (a real hoot!), ZApp, Zinc, Win++, Glockenspiel's CommonView or XVT's (formerly API Inc.) XVT etc (also see book list for Windows++). A class library is a collection of pre-written C++ classes (object definitions – not objects) that may or may not come with source. Typically complex tasks like printing are taken care of for you by the class library. Object orientation is all about programming by citing the differences between one object and the next, eg. explaining how a control window is different to (a special case of) a normal window. Classes allow you to modify them by inheriting and modifying some base class's behaviour – your class is a kinda base class but it's different in these ways .... If an object can be verbalised as a kinda something else then that something else, if it exists as an object already, is an ideal candidate to inherit behaviour from in the definition of the new object.

CommonView from Glockenspiel was a good class framework (eventually) and allowed applications to be ported easily from one environment to another, say from Windows to OSF Motif! frameworks such as MFC don't allow this (unless you want to do a lot of the work). Another good class library/framework is XVT. XVT originally had just a 'C' binding – it now has a C++ binding, ie. XVT now has classes. XVT also allows you to port, or migrate, code easily from one environment to another. XVT was also chosen as *base technology* for the IEEE P1201.1 GUI API standards group – I know coz I was there! This means that potentially XVT is the one to watch if you're ever going to port from one environment to another – check it out.

ToolBook

Another interesting development environment is Asymetrix's ToolBook and Multi-Media ToolBook (V1.5). Asymetrix was founded by Paul Allen – that's the guy who with Bill Gates founded Microsoft! ToolBook is also Object Oriented in that it comes with a language called OpenScript, that has object oriented extensions, and pre-defined objects. Users can simply cut and paste these objects into their applications or build new ones using OpenScript. NOTE – ToolBook developers are called *Authors*. ToolBook (esp. Multi-Media ToolBook) is designed to help you build those applications that are usually very difficult to build; sounds good – On-line Presentations, Interactive Training Aids, Hypermedia Documents and Application Prototypes etc. Some of its best features are that it !–

- Provides a clear, simple and effective implementation of DDE, ie. it is *well connected*.
- Allows users to access external DLL functions, ie. it connects to the outside world.
- Has very powerful *string* handling ('get last word of text... etc).
- Provides integral hypertext and flat-file database functions.
- Provides animation and graphic manipulation.
- Provides speed and flexibility in both designing and programming a solution.

Like VB, ToolBook applications respond to certain events, like keyboard events, mouse events etc. The event handling code is typically written in OpenScript. Tool-Book also has the notion of a class hierarchy. The language is quite simple to master and learn and very complex applications can built quite quickly. The only problem I find with ToolBook is that its use is a little too specialised to make it a tool that I would use daily.

Borland's Pascal 7 with Objects

I'm a great and long lasting fan of Pascal – so much so that I often doubt my sanity for writing in 'C' and C++ as I do! The latest release of Borland's Pascal, version 7, is a real treat. I use it almost entirely for writing DLLs as I prefer to do the UI stuff in VB or SmallTalk. What more can I say – buy it – it's great!

Macro Languages

Don't knock 'em. I've recently finished working with a company that has just completed an amazing Word for Windows customisation project that was done almost entirely using Word's own basic (rumour has it that future version of Microsoft's application products will have an even more powerful version of basic (as will VB) called object basic). The problem, or is it a positive thing, is that macro languages such as Word Basic can only really be used to modify the behaviour of the product in which they reside, ie. you wouldn't want to try and write a spreadsheet application using Word Basic! On the whole however they can be used where you might normally go for your regular expression parser etc – ie, Word Basic is well suited to manipulating text etc, whilst Excel's is very good at handling numeric data etc.

Application Generators

You could also use products that generate code ('C', C++, MFC or CommonView based C++ etc). I'd steer clear of these for several reasons. Normally they can only generate a *shell* of an application – you still have to do the real work. Also the code is usually for some reason not acceptable. Lastly, they're expensive and usually non-customisable (you can't change the code that's generated). They are pretty good however as learning aids, ie. if you want to see how to do a modeless dialog box using MFC – generate some code and take a look. Of course you could always look in a book!

WINIO (or WINDOS)

This is a library of functions that allow you to write Windows' applications using more normal standard 'C' functions like main(), printf(), getchar() etc. It also provides real nice features like scrolling displays that you don't have to write any code to get and persistent windows, ie. windows that maintain their contents over re-paints, again you don't have to do this work WINIO does it all for you. I'm not sure if you can buy this library or not? I got my copy with the book Undocumented Windows (Schulman, Maxey & Pietrek – Addison Wesley ISBN 0-201-60834-0). The book's fab but it was well worth buying just to get hold of WINIO – it's really good for knocking up small applications quickly and easily if you've got a good 'C' programming background. It's recently been ported to Win32s by Andrew Schulman so it's good for doing cross platform development too!

SQL Windows

This product from Gupta is a little like SmallTalk and Visual Basic in that it's an entirely Windows hosted development environment. SQL Windows' advantage over the other two is in its database handling. SQL Windows' is VERY database aware; it even has controls (a little like QEVB has) that are used for handling database data. Another nice feature is its folding editor (you either love or hate these). A folding editor is an editor which allows you to hide blocks in what's called a fold. For example you might have a function called Foo() that is rather large and is obscuring other code. The answer is to fold up Foo() so that it all but disappears.

Assembler

If you really want it to be fast and small use assembler. Surprisingly there are quite a few Windows developers out there using assembly language to ensure that their offering is smallest and fastest. The down side of using assembler is that it's non-portable and would therefore take some effort to say port it to Windows NT running on a MIP's processor! If you're thinking of using assembler try to see if it would be better applied in small doses, ie. can certain parts only be written in assembler? Also, try to use a set of macros to aid you, eg. CMARCOS.INC

Microsoft's Access

If the app you're building has to acquire and then manipulate data you probably ought to check out Access. I've no hands-on experience of this product (at the time of writing it's been out for about a month) but I've recently come into contact with people that have – to a man, they think is wonderful.

Porting Tools

How about porting your DOS code to Windows – how can this be done. Well there are several ways, painful and less-painful! Check out the *Quick Win* libs that come with the C7 compiler – compile -Mq and see how far you get. The quick win libs can provide a DOS application with a Windows interface that looks like the DOS app's. Here's a very simple app :

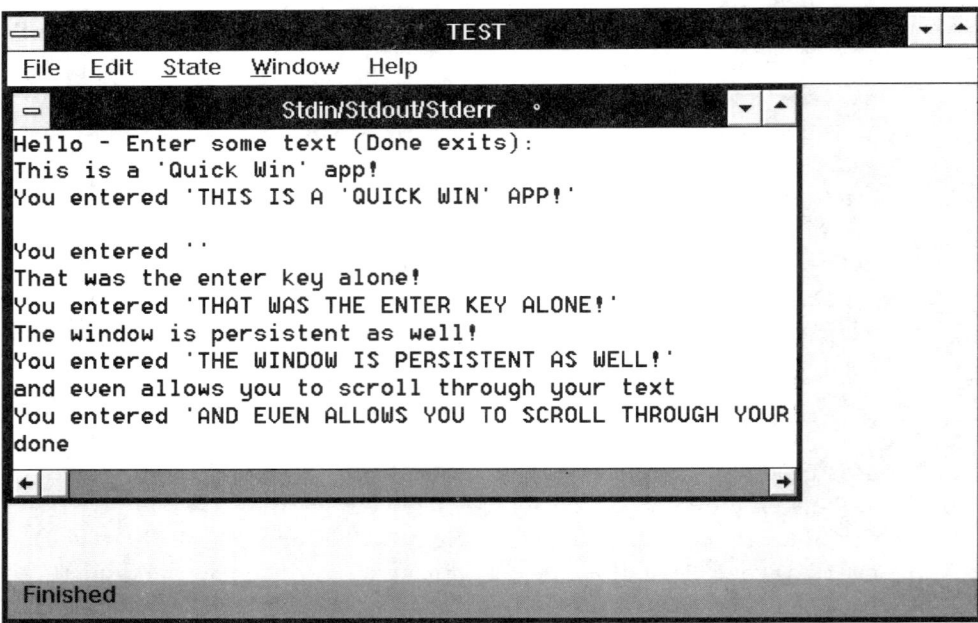

This application, as you can see, is an MDI application, it has a full menu and even a nice icon. The application reads entered text and displays it. Entering *Done* terminates the app. Again, the text window is persistent, ie. the text within it is maintained and re-painted as necessary by the Quick Win libraries. Also the text can be scrolled in both X and Y – all done for you by Quick Win. The code used to produce this app was this :

```
main()
{
   auto int   x;
   auto char car[100];

   puts("Hello - Enter some text (Done exits):");

   while(strcmpi(gets(&car[0]), "Done") != 0)
   {
       printf("You entered '%s'\n", strupr(&car[0]));
   }
}
```

Small isn't it?! Note that it uses functions such as printf() puts() and gets() and has a main() instead of WinMain()! The app was simply compiled cl -Mq test.c.

If you wanted to have more control over the front end you might look at a product like GUI Assist (From MicroMini). This product allows you to define (in fact you have to write it) a Windows interface for any text mode DOS application (using something like VB). You then link your Windows' app to your existing DOS app via MicroMini DLL routines, in other words MicroMini is responsible for starting your DOS app (usually in an iconised state) and linking it with the Windows' app. Information entered into the Windows' app is sent via MicroMini's DLL routines to the DOS app (you do this by calling the necessary DLL routines). The DOS app responds and the response is read from the virtual DOS machine's screen by MicroMini (again, under you direction) and made available to the Windows' app – which then probably displays it! For some complex DOS apps, esp. if those apps have truly dynamic screens, this approach requires a lot of work, indeed you might be better re-writing your code as Windows' code, however it does work for a large number of apps and is well worth considering as a potential *fast-track* route to Windows' migration.

☐ Properties vs. Words

A question I see posted on BBS system like Compuserve very often is, 'Should I use window words rather than window's properties as I've heard that properties are much slower to access than words are?'.

Window, and class words, are indeed efficient. A single access to SetWindowWord() and GetWindowWord() on my machine takes about 0.02 of a millisecond! In other words 10,000 accesses to both functions would take about 200ms total – now that's pretty fast (by the way – the far call overhead to these functions is in the order of 0.0055ms the pair). These figures are pretty much constant; small variations only. When using properties the speed of the calls to SetProp() and GetProp() depends upon the amount of work done in performing the string search internally, ie. the longer the string that identifies the property is, surprise surprise, the longer the call takes. If I use single character strings to identify properties a call to SetProp() GetProp() takes 0.075ms – that's 0.055ms slower than a call to the SetWindowWord() GetWindow-Word() pair. If the string length is increased to, say, 4 characters a pair of calls to SetProp() GetProp() takes 0.099ms. If the string length is increased to, say, 16 characters (which is probably the maximum you'd ever use) each pair takes 0.20ms – quite a bit slower than SetWindowWord() GetWindowWord()!

When you're trying to decide which method to use you must however remember that 0.20ms is typically not a long time! In fact unless you're doing about 10000 accesses all at once (which I was to get these figures) it's not really noticeable at all!

The bottom line is if you want to do it the fastest way possible use the Set???Word()/Get????Word() functions. If you're not that bothered (knowing that a single pair access takes just 0.20ms (or 0.10ms for a individual call to either GetProp() or SetProp() – that's one tenth of one thousandth of a second) then go ahead and use properties.

☐ SwitchStackTo() & SwitchStackBack()

These functions allow an application or DLL to change the stack of a task. They're typically used however in DLLs only for two reasons.

- DLLs normally run with DS not equal to SS.

They're even compiled with the -Aw switch so that warnings result when you take the address of a frame variable. You're therefore more likely to run into less problems if you change SS relative to DS in a DLL. That brings us on to the second reason.

- Because DLLs run on the stack of the caller they have no control over the size of the caller's stack – or how much stack is left.

A DLL could therefore trash the stack of the caller quite easily – it doesn't know how much stack space is left on the stack after all! For example, consider a DLL function that used recursion to traverse some kind of *tree* data structure. Recursion is a stack killer as we all know and so this kind of function is somewhat dangerous if it resides in a DLL because, unlike in an application, the function cannot know how much stack space is left to work with. The answer is to create a new stack for your DLL function to use of a known size! This is where SwitchStackTo() and SwitchStackBack() come in.

These functions can also be used in applications; here's an example of how to use 'em in an app. This code fragment is taken from a modified generic.c :

```
// Helper function.
VOID Warn(VOID * p)
{
}

LRESULT __export CALLBACK MainWndProc(...
...
{
    switch(uMessage)
    {
    case WM_COMMAND:
        switch(wParam)
        {
```

```
        case IDM_ABOUT:
            {
                auto    HINSTANCE   hInst;

                auto    HGLOBAL     hGlobal;
                auto    VOID FAR *  pGlobal;
                auto    UINT        uDS;

                static HWND         hWndLocal;

                hWndLocal = hWnd;

                hGlobal = GlobalAlloc(LMEM_ZEROINIT, 10000);
                pGlobal = GlobalLock(hGlobal);

                uDS = SELECTOROF(pGlobal);

                SwitchStackTo(uDS, 10000, sizeof(WORD));

                MessageBox(hWndLocal, "Stack Switched", NULL, MB_OK);

                Warn((void *)&hWnd);

                hInst = (HINSTANCE)GetWindowWord(hWndLocal, GWW_HINSTANCE);

                DialogBox(hInst, "AboutBox", hWndLocal, (DLGPROC)About);

                SwitchStackBack();

                GlobalUnlock(hGlobal);
                GlobalFree(hGlobal);
            }
            break;
    }
    break;
```

This code is almost OK but there is a bug in it – can you spot it before it's revealed?

The stack is switched remember by SwitchStackTo(). Note that the code between SwitchStackTo() and SwitchStackBack() uses hWndLocal. hWndLocal is a static variable that contains the value of hWnd as passed to MainWndProc(); well why not just use hWnd? The reason is because hWnd is passed on the stack right – and we switch stacks, ergo – hWnd is not available to the code that's running on the new stack! Note that if we were to use hWnd (the automatic variable) that we wouldn't get any warning from the compiler – after all it doesn't know that the stack's been switched. Note also that if we told the compiler that SS was not equal to DS by including the -Aw switch that we still wouldn't get a warning! Again, the compiler assumes, as hWnd was passed as a parameter to the function that it is available, ie. it doesn't know that it went *walk-about* when we called that SwitchStackTo() function! See the function Warn()? that function is declared as taking a NEAR VOID * (small model app) and we pass it the address of hWnd – now that DOES create a warning if we use -Aw because we've taken the address of a stack frame variable and passed it to a function that might well assume that the NEAR address it's been passed is some offset from DS – which it's not! Of course, if we actually accessed hWnd via a FAR pointer we'd be OK as long as the address of hWnd were taken before the stack got switched. If we took the address as a far pointer address after the stack gets changed we're in deep *****. The compiler knows that hWnd is on the stack and forms the address from the current SS value and some offset – OOPS, SS, at the time the Warn() function's called, is not the same as it was when the function was entered, ie. hWnd is on the old stack and we've passed a far pointer to the function that is made up of the new SS plus some offset!!!! Now for the error in the code above – did you spot it? The problem is with hInst. This is an automatic variable (this is by the way where using the *auto* really helps). Later, when the stack's been switched, hInst is assigned to :

```
hInst = (HINSTANCE)GetWindowWord(hWndLocal, GWW_HINSTANCE);
```

The compiler knows the offset to hInst on the stack and inserts into that location whatever

```
GetWindowWord(hWndLocal, GWW_HINSTANCE)
```

returns. However, remember that we've changed stacks here! SS is now not the same as it was when the function got called. hInst is therefore inserted into our *clean* stack at *New SS* :&hInst! The code that relies on hInst still happens to work because, luckily the offset to hInst lies beyond the used part of the new stack – more by luck than judgement however!

When swapping stacks remember to *save off* any automatic items (stack variables) in static variables – these will be available when the stack is changed. Always access these static copies – never access the passed or *auto* variables unless it's by FAR pointers that were initialised prior to swapping the stack. Here's the code tidied up :

```
// Helper function.
VOID Warn(VOID * p)
{
}


LRESULT __export CALLBACK MainWndProc
(
    HWND     hWnd
    ,UINT    uMessage
    ,WPARAM  wParam
    ,LPARAM  lParam
)
{
    switch(uMessage)
    {
    case WM_COMMAND:
        switch(wParam)
        {
            case IDM_ABOUT:
                {
```

```
/*
** These 'autos' are OK because they're used before
** and after the stack is swapped.
*/
auto    HGLOBAL      hGlobal;
auto    VOID FAR *   pGlobal;
auto    UINT         uDS;

/*
** We need hInst and hWndLocal after the stack is
** swapped so we make them static.
*/
static HINSTANCE    hInst;
static HWND         hWndLocal;

/*
** SAVE hWnd before loosing it on the old stack.
*/
hWndLocal = hWnd;

/*
** Allocate new 10kb stack.
*/
hGlobal = GlobalAlloc(LMEM_ZEROINIT, 10000);

/*
** Lock it to get sel:offset.
*/
pGlobal = GlobalLock(hGlobal);

/*
** Get sel - this will be the new stack's SS.
*/
uDS = SELECTOROF(pGlobal);

/*
** Switch stacks here. Stack end is one WORD from
** 0 (ie. sizeof(WORD) or two bytes away).
*/
SwitchStackTo(uDS, 10000, sizeof(WORD));

MessageBox(hWndLocal, "Stack Switched", NULL, MB_OK);

/*
** Cause compiler warning about taking address of frame
** variable - this would have caused a warning before
** the stack was swapped as well - use -Aw to get the
** warning.
*/
Warn((void *)&hWnd);

/*
** Use hInst and hWndLocal;
*/
hInst = (HINSTANCE)GetWindowWord(hWndLocal, GWW_HINSTANCE);

/*
** Use hInst and hWndLocal;
```

```
                      */
                      DialogBox(hInst, "AboutBox", hWndLocal, (DLGPROC)About);

                      /*
                      ** Get back to old stack. Note that any return value is
                      ** preserved, ie. AX & DX are preserved here.
                      */
                      SwitchStackBack();

                      /*
                      ** Blow up stack as we're now on the old stack again.
                      */
                      GlobalUnlock(hGlobal);
                      GlobalFree(hGlobal);
                  }
              break;

        }
        break;
```

GlobalAlloc() is used above to allocate a 10Kb chunk of global memory that will act
as the new stack segment for the application. We have to lock the memory down with
GlobalLock() first however. The pointer returned by GlobalLock() consists of a 16 bit
selector and a 16 bit offset. We use the selector part (using SELECTOROF()) in the call
to SwitchStackTo(). We also need to pass that function two offsets – the offset of the
beginning of the stack in bytes (which is 10,000) and the offset of the top of the stack,
ie the last WORD that can be used in the stack – this is not zero as any *pushed* WORD
value would overflow the stack – it's set to sizeof(WORD), ie. 2. The stack looks like
this :

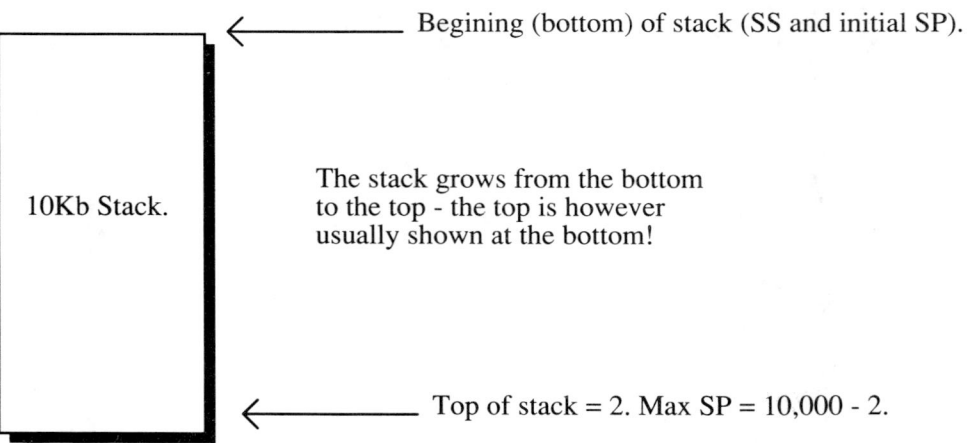

Begining (bottom) of stack (SS and initial SP).

10Kb Stack.

The stack grows from the bottom
to the top - the top is however
usually shown at the bottom!

Top of stack = 2. Max SP = 10,000 - 2.

Here's the dialog box produced by the above code :

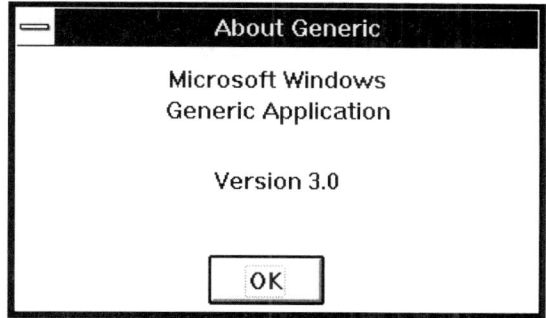

Here's the dialog's template :

```
AboutBox DIALOG 22, 17, 144, 75
STYLE DS_MODALFRAME | WS_CAPTION | WS_SYSMENU
CAPTION "About Generic"
BEGIN
    CTEXT "Microsoft Windows"     100,       0,  5, 144,  8
    CTEXT "Generic Application"   101,       0, 14, 144,  8
    CTEXT "Version 3.0"            -1,       0, 34, 144,  8
    DEFPUSHBUTTON "OK"           IDOK,     53, 59,  32, 14,        WS_GROUP
END
```

Why am I showing you all this? 'Coz there's still a potential nasty here!

There is still, potentially, a problem with this last piece of code. The code is currently being created using -GAs, ie. smart-call-backs are used. This means that any exported function that gets called will load DS from whatever it finds in SS – well the code works, ie. it produces the dialog box etc, so what's the problem? Well the dialog box call-back currently looks like this :

```
BOOL __export CALLBACK About
(
   HWND     hDlg
  ,UINT     uMessage
  ,WPARAM   wParam
  ,LPARAM   lParam
)
{
   switch(uMessage)
   {
       case WM_INITDIALOG:
           return TRUE;

       case WM_COMMAND:
           if(wParam == IDOK || wParam == IDCANCEL)
           {
               EndDialog(hDlg, TRUE);
               return TRUE;
           }
           break;
```

```
    }

        return FALSE;
}
```

Note that this call-back does not access any static data, ie. no data that it uses is stored in the app's default data segment. Data like IDCANCEL is held in the code as immediate data and data such as hDlg is passed on the stack. When this call-back executes it loads DS to whatever SS currently is, remember, from the code above, that SS now points to a new stack segment! This means DS points to the same new stack segment and not the app's DS!! Good job it doesn't use any static data – it wouldn't get it! Let's change this code a little to introduce some local data into the frame (just the first few lines are shown) :

```
BOOL __export CALLBACK About
(
    HWND     hDlg
   ,UINT     uMessage
   ,WPARAM   wParam
   ,LPARAM   lParam
)
{
    static char a[]="Hello";
    auto   char b[]="Goodbye";

    switch(uMessage)
    {
        case WM_INITDIALOG:
            SetWindowText(GetDlgItem(hDlg, 100), a);
            SetWindowText(GetDlgItem(hDlg, 101), b);
            return TRUE;
```

This piece of code tries to change the text used in two of the dialog's static controls. When it's actioned the dialog produced looks like this :

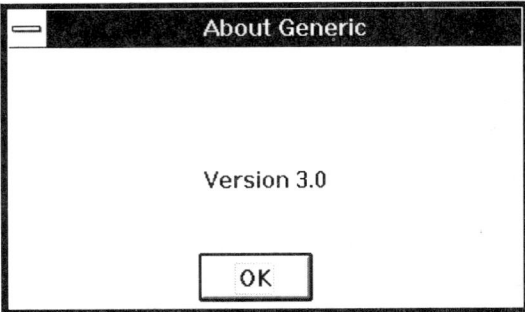

Errrrr, like where'd my text go! Well the text is all held in the app's DS, even if the array is declared as an auto the literal data (between the quotes) is held in the application's DGROUP (and copied to the stack using _fmemcpy()). The app's DS register is set to whatever SS is; SS points to, more-or-less, a big chunk of memory filled with NULLs. In effect what happens here is that the string offsets used in the code point to NULL data (there's a better than even chance also the *a* itself is NULL), ie. NULL terminated strings – result = no text appears!!

What we need to do is to tell the *About* function to ignore what's in SS and load the DS from somewhere else. MakeProcInstance() to the rescue!! No, it's not dead yet, good ol' MPI is still required (see the DLL chapter for another situation that still requires MPI). Here's how we can modify the code in MainWndProc to use MakeProcInstance() :

```
case IDM_ABOUT:
    {
        static HINSTANCE  hInst;
        static FARPROC    lpAbout;

        auto    HGLOBAL   hGlobal;
        auto    VOID FAR * pGlobal;
        auto    UINT      uDS;

        static HWND       hWndLocal;

        hWndLocal = hWnd;

        hGlobal = GlobalAlloc(LMEM_ZEROINIT, 10000);
        pGlobal = GlobalLock(hGlobal);

        uDS = SELECTOROF(pGlobal);

        SwitchStackTo(uDS, 10000, sizeof(WORD));

        MessageBox(hWndLocal, "Stack Switched", NULL, MB_OK);

        Warn((void *)&hWnd);

        hInst = (HINSTANCE)GetWindowWord(hWndLocal, GWW_HINSTANCE);

        lpAbout = MakeProcInstance((FARPROC)About, hInst);

        DialogBox(hInst, "AboutBox", hWndLocal, (DLGPROC)lpAbout);

        FreeProcInstance(lpAbout);

        SwitchStackBack();

        GlobalUnlock(hGlobal);
        GlobalFree(hGlobal);
    }
    break;
```

Important lines etc are shown in bold face. Note that lpAbout is static (see notes above for why it must be static). If we re-compile and run this we get the same dialog as before! :-

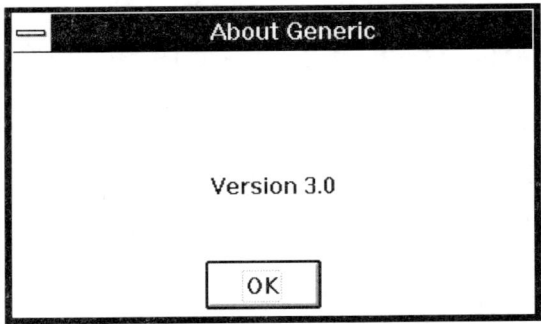

We still need to tell the compiler not to generate smart-call-backs, ie. although we built, and called *About* through, an instance thunk, the About function's prologue code still loaded DS from SS! If we replace -GAs with -Gws in the app's make file we'll get this :-

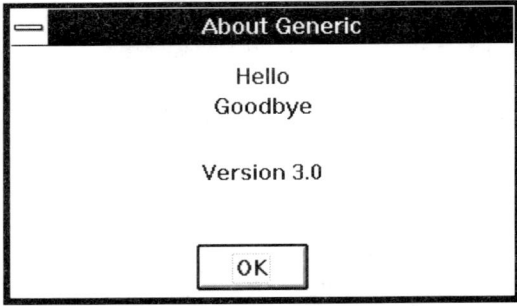

And that is just about what we wanted in the first place!

As I said at the beginning of this section, these functions are typically used in DLLs, remember however that all the problems discussed above still exist even in a DLL, ie. save autos you're passed in statics (or some dynamic heap space – as long as you save the handle in a static). Switching stacks can have many side-effects, some of which we've seen here; but often the increase in stack space is well worth the effort.

Just on the subject of SS not equal to DS in an application; please note that you can switch DS almost as easily as you can switch SS. An app's DS is set to point to the app's local heap which is located in its default data segment. Well just as you can have multiple stacks using SwitchStackTo() you can have multiple local heaps too. The way you do it to use LocalInit() on a segment allocated from the global heap. LocalInit() is used to initialise a global heap object (or part of it) so that it contains a logical local heap, ie. LocalAlloc() calls are allowed on it. Here's some code that will do the trick :

First allocate and prepare the global heap object :

```
HGLOBAL NEAR PASCAL CreateLocalHeap(UINT uSize)
{
    auto HGLOBAL hMem;
```

```
        uSize += 16;

        if((hMem = GlobalAlloc(
                           GMEM_MOVEABLE |
                           GMEM_ZEROINIT
                           ,(DWORD)(uSize)
                           )) != NULL
          )
        {
            auto UINT uStartAddr;
            auto UINT uEndAddr;
            auto WORD wSeg;

            wSeg = SELECTOROF(GlobalLock(hMem));

            uStartAddr = 16;
            uEndAddr   = (UINT)GlobalSize(hMem) - 1;

            (VOID)LocalInit(wSeg, uStartAddr, uEndAddr);

            GlobalUnlock(hMem);
            GlobalUnlock(hMem);

            return hMem;
        }
        else
        {
            return (HGLOBAL)0;
        }

    }
```

This first function is passed the number of accessible bytes required in the local heap. Note that it has 16 added to it. Windows requires these extra 16 bytes to manage the local heap; they are positioned at the beginning of the heap – as we require uSize bytes to be accessible we have to add 16 to uSize as 16 bytes will be lost to the local heap memory manager. GlobalAlloc() is used to allocate the actual segment. Then LocalInit() is used to initialise the heap. Note that the starting address is 16, ie. the 17th byte into the local heap. The ending size is given by GlobalSize(hMem) -1 (as we started counting at 0). Lastly, if all went well, hMem is returned.

To access the local heap we have to switch our current DS to SELECTOROF(hMem). Here's a piece of code which does this :

```
LRESULT __export CALLBACK MainWndProc
(
  HWND      hWnd
 ,UINT      uMessage
 ,WPARAM    wParam
 ,LPARAM    lParam
)
{

    switch(uMessage)
    {
```

```
case WM_COMMAND:
    switch(wParam)
    {
        case IDM_ACCESS:
            {
                auto HGLOBAL hMem;

                /*
                ** Get local heap 16,000 bytes big.
                */
                if((hMem = CreateLocalHeap(16000)) != NULL)
                {
                    auto WORD   wSel;
                    auto HLOCAL hLocMem;
                    auto PSTR   pLocMem;

                    /*
                    ** Now switch to it.
                    */
                    wSel = SELECTOROF(GlobalLock(hMem));

                    _asm
                    {
                        push  ds        // save old DS.
                        mov   ax, wSel  // get new DS into AX.
                        push  ax        // push new DS.
                        pop   ds            // get new DS into DS.
                    }

                    /*
                    ** Perform local heap allocation on new local heap.
                    */
                    if((hLocMem = LocalAlloc(
                                            LMEM_ZEROINIT
                                            ,1000
                                            )) != NULL
                      )
                    {
                        /*
                        ** Get local heap pointer...
                        */
                        pLocMem = LocalLock(hMem);

                        //... Use local heap object here.

                        /*
                        ** Finished with new local heap now. Free it.
                        */
                        LocalUnlock(hLocMem);
                        LocalFree(hLocMem);

                    }
                    else
                    {
                        // Handle error.
                    }
```

```
                                /*
                                ** Restore old DS.
                                */
                                _asm pop  ds

                                /*
                                ** Destroy segment holding new local heap.
                                */
                                if(DestroyLocalHeap(hMem))
                                {
                                }
                                else
                                {
                                    // Handle error.
                                }
                        }
                        else
                        {
                            // Handle error.
                        }


                    }
                    break;
            }
            break;

        case WM_DESTROY:
            PostQuitMessage(0);
            break;

        default:
            return DefWindowProc(hWnd, uMessage, wParam, lParam);
    }

    return (LRESULT)0;
}
```

DestroyLocalHeap() simply calls GlobalFree() after it calls GlobalUnlock() for as many times as the object is currently locked.

☐ Finding out window info

If you want to find out information about a window use functions like GetWindowLong(), GetWindowWord(), GetClassWord(), GetWindow(), GetWindowText() and GetClassName() etc. When these functions are brought together they may be used to produce SPY like applications. Here's a really crude example which shows a little of this :

```
LRESULT __export CALLBACK MainWndProc
(
    HWND     hWnd
   ,UINT     uMessage
   ,WPARAM   wParam
```

```
      ,LPARAM   lParam
   )
   {
      static HWND hWndFound;
      static BOOL bCap;

      switch(uMessage)
      {
      case WM_LBUTTONDOWN:
          SetCapture(hWnd);
          bCap = TRUE;
          break;

      case WM_MOUSEMOVE:
          {
            if(bCap != FALSE)
            {
                auto   POINT tPt;
                static HWND  hWndLast;

                ClientToScreen(hWnd, (LPPOINT)&lParam);

                tPt = MAKEPOINT(lParam);

                hWndFound = WindowFromPoint(tPt);

                if(hWndLast != hWndFound)
                {
                    ProcessWindow(hWndFound);

                    hWndLast = hWndFound;
                }
            }

          }
          break;

      case WM_LBUTTONUP:
          ReleaseCapture();
          bCap = FALSE;
          break;

      case WM_DESTROY:
          PostQuitMessage(0);
          break;

      default:
          return DefWindowProc(hWnd, uMessage, wParam, lParam);
      }

      return (LRESULT)0;
   }
```

The replacement wndproc above allows us to point and click on any visible window on the desktop. It uses SetCapture() to capture all mouse input to itself to do this. When we select a window by clicking on it the function ProcessWindow() is called. This function currently looks like this :

```
#define DO(x) DebugOutput(DBF_TRACE | DBF_APPLICATION, x)

VOID ProcessWindow(HWND hWnd)
{
    auto LONG lhWndStyle;
    auto WORD wClassStyle;
    auto char carClassName [50];
    auto char carWindowName[50];

    GetWindowText(hWnd, &carWindowName[0], 50);
    GetClassName (hWnd, &carClassName [0], 50);

    DO(&carWindowName[0]);
    DO(&carClassName [0]);

    lhWndStyle  = GetWindowLong(hWnd, GWL_STYLE);
    wClassStyle = GetClassWord (hWnd, GCW_STYLE);

    // WINDOW STUFF ─────────────

    DO("WINDOW STYLES");

    if(lhWndStyle & WS_POPUP)
        DO("Popup");
    else
    if(lhWndStyle & WS_CHILD)
        DO("Child");
    else
        DO("Overlapped");

    if(lhWndStyle & WS_CLIPSIBLINGS)
        DO("Clipsiblings");

    if(lhWndStyle & WS_CLIPCHILDREN)
        DO("ClipChildren");

    if(lhWndStyle & WS_VISIBLE)
        DO("Visible");

    if(lhWndStyle & WS_DISABLED)
        DO("Disabled");

    if(lhWndStyle & WS_MINIMIZE)
        DO("Minimised");

    if(lhWndStyle & WS_MAXIMIZE)
        DO("Maximised");

    if(lhWndStyle & WS_CAPTION)                  /* WS_BORDER | WS_DLGFRAME    */
        DO("Caption");

    if(lhWndStyle & WS_BORDER)
        DO("Border");

    if(lhWndStyle & WS_DLGFRAME)
        DO("Dlgframe");

    if(lhWndStyle & WS_VSCROLL)
```

```
        DO("Vscroll");

if(lhWndStyle & WS_HSCROLL)
    DO("Hscroll");

if(lhWndStyle & WS_SYSMENU)
    DO("Sysmenu");

if(lhWndStyle & WS_THICKFRAME)
    DO("Thickframe");

if(lhWndStyle & WS_MINIMIZEBOX)
    DO("Minimise box");

if(lhWndStyle & WS_MAXIMIZEBOX)
    DO("Maximise box");

if(lhWndStyle & WS_GROUP)
    DO("Group");

if(lhWndStyle & WS_TABSTOP)
    DO("Tabstop");

// EX WINDOW STUFF ──────────

DO("EXTENDED WINDOW STYLES");

lhWndStyle = GetWindowLong(hWnd, GWL_EXSTYLE);

if(lhWndStyle & WS_EX_DLGMODALFRAME)
    DO("Dlgmodalframe");

if(lhWndStyle & WS_EX_NOPARENTNOTIFY)
    DO("Noparentnotify");

if(lhWndStyle & WS_EX_TOPMOST)
    DO("Topmost");

if(lhWndStyle & WS_EX_ACCEPTFILES)
    DO("Acceptfiles");

if(lhWndStyle & WS_EX_TRANSPARENT)
    DO("Transparent");

// CLASS STUFF ──────────

DO("CLASS STYLES");

if(wClassStyle & CS_VREDRAW)
    DO("Vredraw");

if(wClassStyle & CS_HREDRAW)
    DO("Hredraw");

if(wClassStyle & CS_KEYCVTWINDOW)
    DO("Keycvtwindow");

if(wClassStyle & CS_DBLCLKS)
```

```
        DO("Dblclks");

    if(wClassStyle & CS_OWNDC)
        DO("OwnDC");

    if(wClassStyle & CS_CLASSDC)
        DO("ClassDC");

    if(wClassStyle & CS_PARENTDC)
        DO("ParentDC");

    if(wClassStyle & CS_NOKEYCVT)
        DO("Nokeycvt");

    if(wClassStyle & CS_NOCLOSE)
        DO("Noclose");

    if(wClassStyle & CS_SAVEBITS)
        DO("Savebits");

    if(wClassStyle & CS_BYTEALIGNCLIENT)
        DO("Bytealignclient");

    if(wClassStyle & CS_BYTEALIGNWINDOW)
        DO("Bytealignwindow");

    if(wClassStyle & CS_GLOBALCLASS)
        DO("Globalclass");

    DO("");
    DO("");
}
```

It gets the window's style, extended style and class style and outputs information about it to the debugging terminal via DebugOutput(). For all its crudeness it still can be quite useful; and what's more easily extended to provide more and more information about any given window – like its parent window hierarchy perhaps? Here's a typical output when the window selected is the main window of the *Perf-Meter* application shown earlier :

```
t GENERIC Windows' Perf Meter
t GENERIC #103
t GENERIC WINDOW STYLES
t GENERIC Overlapped
t GENERIC Clipsiblings
t GENERIC Visible
t GENERIC Caption
t GENERIC Border
t GENERIC Thickframe
t GENERIC EXTENDED WINDOW STYLES
t GENERIC Topmost
t GENERIC CLASS STYLES
t GENERIC Vredraw
t GENERIC Hredraw
t GENERIC Dblclks
t GENERIC OwnDC
```

```
t GENERIC Bytealignclient
```

And here's another when it's run over the print manager :

```
t GENERIC Print Manager
t GENERIC PrintManager
t GENERIC WINDOW STYLES
t GENERIC Overlapped
t GENERIC Clipsiblings
t GENERIC ClipChildren
t GENERIC Visible
t GENERIC Minimised
t GENERIC Caption
t GENERIC Border
t GENERIC Dlgframe
t GENERIC Hscroll
t GENERIC Sysmenu
t GENERIC Thickframe
t GENERIC Minimise box
t GENERIC Maximise box
t GENERIC Group
t GENERIC Tabstop
t GENERIC EXTENDED WINDOW STYLES
t GENERIC Acceptfiles
t GENERIC CLASS STYLES
t GENERIC Dblclks
```

☐ Byte Alignment

There are two quite badly documented and widely misunderstood class styles, CS_BYTEALIGNCLIENT and CS_BYTEALIGNWINDOW. Here's the info on them! When you *byte align* a window or a window's client area you are essentially allowing Windows to perform certain optimisation when it draws in either the window or the client area. The CS_BYTEALIGNCLIENT and CS_BYTEALIGNWINDOW styles *say* that the window, or the client area, should be positioned in *X* on a byte boundary. An application that uses any of the *blit* functions to move, copy or otherwise transfer pixels from one window to another window, or from a source area in a window in to a destination area in the same window, should set the CS_BYTEALIGNWINDOW or CS_BYTEALIGNCLIENT flag when registering the window classes involved. Note that some of these blits are done for you by Windows or implicitly by you. For example, when you move a window or pull down a menu you cause Windows to bit blit.

By aligning the window or client area on byte boundaries, the application can be assured that *blit* operations occur on byte aligned areas of the window (byte aligned means aligned with video memory). Blitting operations carried out on byte aligned areas are notably faster than blitting operations on areas that are not byte aligned. Note that on some hardware that there is little or no improvement when byte aligning (Packed Pixel devices = no benefit). The application we saw earlier, Perf-Meter, is a good example of an application that would (and does) benefit from byte aligning its client area. This application uses ScrollWindow() to cause a bit block transfer of pixels from one segment of its client area to another. If you look at the code for the application you'll see that it uses CS_BYTEALIGNCLIENT to improve the speed of the transfer. The application's aligned on the desktop on a byte boundary, that is to say that its client area will be aligned in X on a pixel whose position is exactly divisible by eight, eg. 8, 16, 24 etc :

Blowup of Perf-Meter's Desktop/Window Alignment

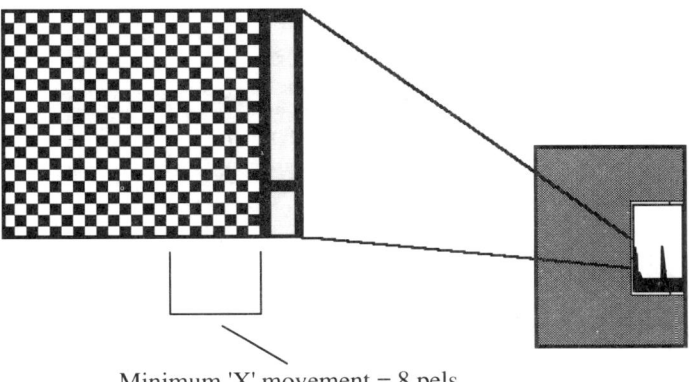

Minimum 'X' movement = 8 pels.

CS_BYTEALIGNWINDOW takes precedence over CS_BYTEALIGNCLIENT so you should not use these styles together – what you'll get is CS_BYTEALIGNWINDOW. Use CS_BYTEALIGNCLIENT if you are moving, or otherwise processing, areas of your window's client area with any bit block transfer functions. Use CS_BY-TEALIGNWINDOW to improve re-draw performance when the window is moved or if using bit block transfer functions to draw in any of the window's non-client area. You can use a mixture also, ie. these class *properties* are variable at run-time.

Here's a little app that demonstrates the effects of byte aligning :

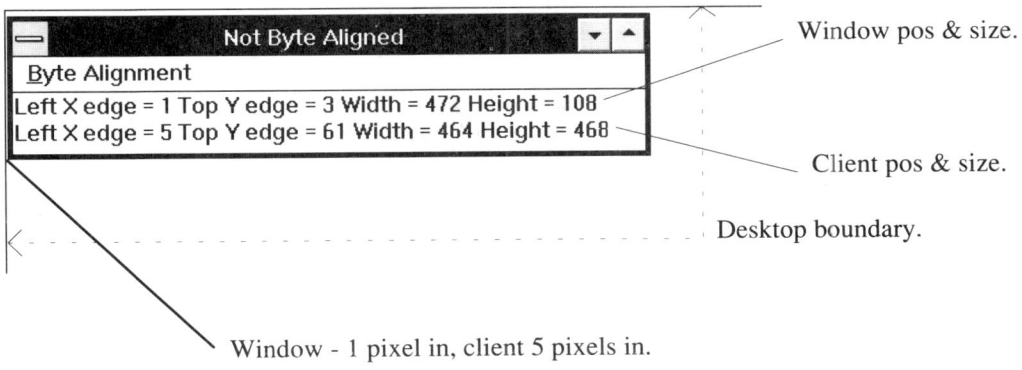

The application shown above demonstrates byte aligning. It may be set to byte align its window or client area. It additionally displays, in screen co-ordinates, both its window and client area positions (relative to the screen origin and in terms of the screen co-ordinate system, ie. pixels). In the figure above neither the window nor client is byte aligned – the Windows' class used was registered using NULL as a style. The app allows us to select either client area byte alignment, window byte alignment, both (which is really window byte alignment) or no byte alignment.

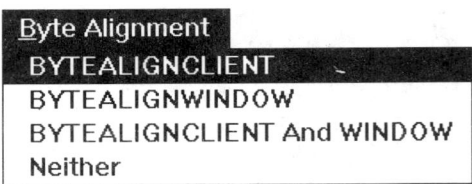

If we select window byte alignment this is what we'll get :

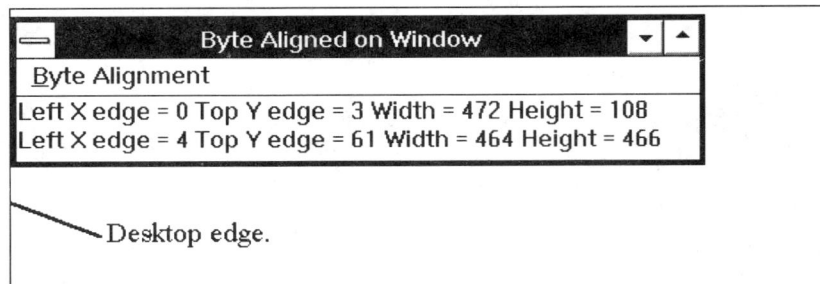

Note that the window is now adjusted so that it is aligned on pixel 0 in X. If we move the window less than four pixels to the right and drop it, it will spring back to the position shown above. If we move it more than 4 pixels (say 5) and drop it, it will *hop* right to align itself 8 pixels in from the screen boundary (see not below on side effect of this behaviour) :

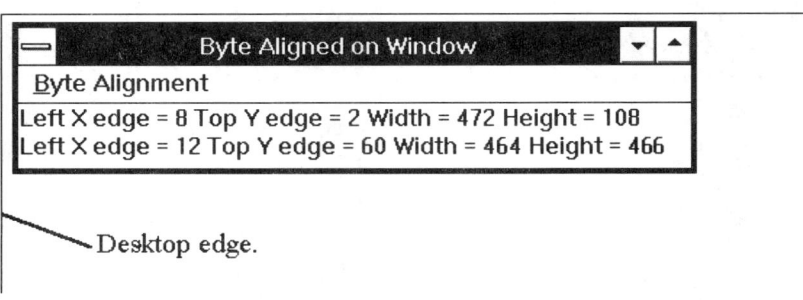

Note that the client area has not up until now been byte aligned. If we elect to byte align the client area and try and move the window in any direction (just clicking its caption bar will do) we'll see that the client area now becomes byte aligned :

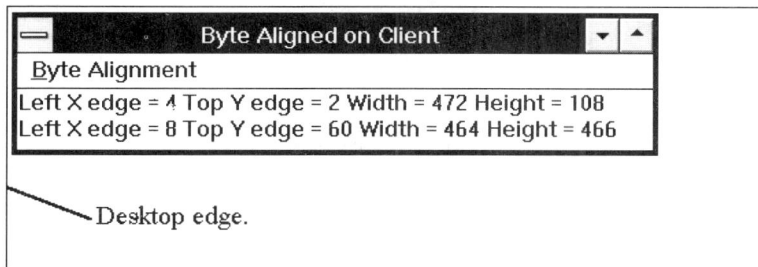

Desktop edge.

Note that *aligning* the window or client does not effect the position of the window or client in Y nor the width and/or height of the window or client area.

Here's the *guts* of the code behind the demo app :

```
LRESULT CALLBACK MainWndProc(...)
{
    ...
    ...
    case WM_COMMAND:
        {
            auto WORD wClassStyle;
            auto PSTR pcCaption;

            wClassStyle = GetClassWord(hWnd, GCW_STYLE);

            wClassStyle &= ~CS_BYTEALIGNCLIENT;
            wClassStyle &= ~CS_BYTEALIGNWINDOW;

            switch(wParam)
            {
                case IDM_CLIENT:
                    wClassStyle |= CS_BYTEALIGNCLIENT;
                    pcCaption = "Byte Aligned on Client";
                    break;

                case IDM_WINDOW:
                    wClassStyle |= CS_BYTEALIGNWINDOW;
                    pcCaption = "Byte Aligned on Window";
                    break;

                case IDM_BOTH:
                    wClassStyle |= CS_BYTEALIGNWINDOW;
                    wClassStyle |= CS_BYTEALIGNCLIENT;
                    pcCaption = "Byte Aligned on Window & Client";
                    break;

                case IDM_NEITHER:
                    pcCaption = "Not Byte Aligned";
```

```
                    break;
                }
                SetClassWord(hWnd, GCW_STYLE, wClassStyle);
                SetWindowText(hWnd, pcCaption);
            }
            break;

    case WM_MOVE:
            {
                auto RECT rsWindow;
                auto RECT rsClient;
                auto char carBuffer[100];
                auto HDC  hDC;

                hDC = GetDC(hWnd);

                GetWindowRect(hWnd, &rsWindow);
                GetClientRect(hWnd, &rsClient);

                ClientToScreen(hWnd, (LPPOINT)&rsClient.left);
                ClientToScreen(hWnd, (LPPOINT)&rsClient.right);

                wsprintf(
                        &carBuffer[0]
                       ,"Left X edge = %d Top Y edge = %d Width = %d Height = %d"

                       ,rsWindow.left
                       ,rsWindow.top
                       ,rsWindow.right - rsWindow.left
                       ,rsWindow.bottom - rsWindow.top
                       );

                TextOut(hDC, 0, 0, &carBuffer[0], lstrlen(&carBuffer[0]));

                wsprintf(
                        &carBuffer[0]
                       ,"Left X edge = %d Top Y edge = %d Width = %d Height = %d"
                       ,rsClient.left
                       ,rsClient.top
                       ,rsClient.right - rsClient.left
                       ,rsClient.bottom - rsClient.top
                       );

                TextOut(hDC, 0, 20, &carBuffer[0], lstrlen(&carBuffer[0]));

                ReleaseDC(hWnd, hDC);
            }
            break;
    ...
    ...
```

Be aware of one small feature of using either of these styles. It is possible when using them (especially CS_BYTEALIGNWINDOW) to have the window move entirely off screen. When the window *hops* to align with the next byte boundary it might align with a byte boundary that is off screen!! This will only happen when you move the window across the screen to the right hand edge of the desktop – with the window off the screen the user cannot *get a hold* of it with the mouse to move it back!

☐ Using const instead of #define

Make use of const instead of using the pre-processor's macro substitution directive – #define. By using const debuggers such as CodeView can supply symbolic information on the constant being used, eg. you could watch BUFFERSIZE in only one of the following examples :

```
#define BUFFERSIZE 100

// cannot easily find out how big BUFFERSIZE is in CV.
static char carBuffer[BUFFERSIZE];
```

alternative -

```
const int BUFFERSIZE = 100;

// can easily find out how big BUFFERSIZE is in CV.
static char carBuffer[BUFFERSIZE];
```

☐ Large Model Applications & Multiple Instances

It is possible, using C7.00, to build and run large model applications a number of times, ie. to run multiple instances of true large model applications. Take for example the generic application. If you were to change -AS to -AL and link with LLIBCEW.LIB instead of SLIBCEW.LIB you'd have a large model application.

If we modify the code so that each instance of this generic alters a static data item we can also prove that each instance accesses its own individual data item :

```
LRESULT __export CALLBACK MainWndProc
(
   HWND     hWnd
  ,UINT     uMessage
  ,WPARAM   wParam
  ,LPARAM   lParam
)
{
   switch(uMessage)
   {

   case WM_KEYDOWN:
      {
         static  int     nCount;
         auto    char    carBuffer[100];

         nCount++;

         wsprintf(carBuffer, "%d", nCount);

         SetWindowText(hWnd, carBuffer);
      }
      break;
```

This bit of code counts the number of times the main window in generic receives a

WM_KEYDOWN message and alters the window's caption to show the running total so far. Here's two instances of it running:

Multiple instances of a large model Generic.

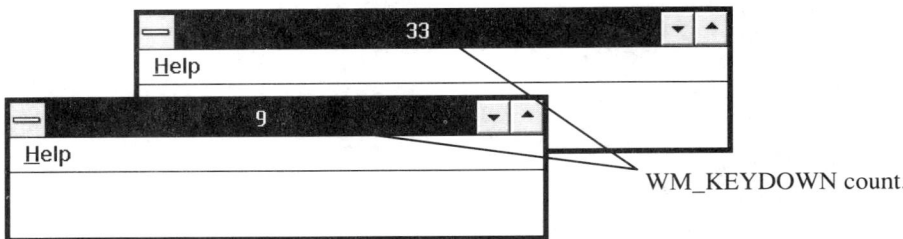

WM_KEYDOWN count.

Here's a Heap Walker's view of things :

```
┌─────────────────────────────────────────────────────────────────────┐
│ ─                    HeapWalker- (Main Heap)                    ▼  ▲ │
├─────────────────────────────────────────────────────────────────────┤
│ File   Walk   Sort   Object   Alloc   Add!                          │
├─────────────────────────────────────────────────────────────────────┤
│ ADDRESS   HANDLE   SIZE LOCK    FLG HEAP OWNER    TYPE              ↑ │
│ 80B55680  316E       96                  GENDRV   Private             │
│ 80AB4840  2CE6      3168      D          GENERIC  Code!GENERIC_TEXT (1)│
│ 809FBA80  2B56      6752           Y     GENERIC  DGroup              │
│ 809F9020  2ABE      6752           Y     GENERIC  DGroup              │
│ 809F7000  3306       352                 GENERIC  Module Database     │
│ 809FD4E0  2F56      4096                 GENERIC  Private             │
│ 809FAA80  37FE      4096                 GENERIC  Private             │
│ 809F8820  36C6       512      D          GENERIC  Resource Menu       │
│ 0005EF40  20B7       512 P1   F          GENERIC  Task                │
│ 0005F260  36CF       512 P1   F          GENERIC  Task                │
│ 8073D760  1FAE     11552      D          GRABBER  Code 1              │
│ 808A6900  1FFE       320                 GRABBER  Module Database     │
│ 808A71C0  1B96      2848                 HEAPWALK Code 1              │
│ 8089E620  1B8E      3136                 HEAPWALK Code 2            ↓ │
└─────────────────────────────────────────────────────────────────────┘
```

In Heap Walker above we can see that each instance of generic has a DGROUP segment, additionally each has a small (size 512 bytes) fixed segment (the task database). This small dataseg would be here even if this were a small model application. Bottom line, no problem using large model if you've only got one *real* data segment.

The problem with large model and data segments begins when you try and run multiple instances of an application with more than one data segment! We can force this in generic like this :

```
LRESULT __export CALLBACK MainWndProc
(
    HWND      hWnd
   ,UINT      uMessage
   ,WPARAM    wParam
   ,LPARAM    lParam
)
{
```

```
switch(uMessage)
{

case WM_KEYDOWN:
    {
        static int  FAR nCount;    // Force FAR data item. This will end
                                   // up in its own data segment!
        auto   char     carBuffer[100];

        nCount++;

        wsprintf(carBuffer, "%d", nCount);

        SetWindowText(hWnd, carBuffer);
    }
    break;
```

When we try to run more than one instance of this version we get the following message appearing in DBWIN :

```
wn Kernel: Error 10 loading generic.EXE
```

Only one instance allowed! The reason for this is that we have forcefully produced an extra data segment. Windows is unable to build, and keep track, of this secondary data segment for later instances and so refuses to allow any subsequent instances to run. It will however allow secondary instances to run if we tell it that this other data segment contains read only code – each instance could then share the one copy. Read only code is like a resource, ie. because it is read only Windows allows multiple instances to share it – no single instance changes it so what harm can come of it? If we could tell Windows therefore that this data seg contains read only data we'll be laughing! Well, we can do just that using the following in our .def file:

```
DATA  PRELOAD MOVEABLE MULTIPLE READONLY
```

This tells Windows that all our data is read only. We of course actually know that it is not but Windows believes us! We can now run multiple instances of this app and share a data segment between them! The screenshot on the next page shows what Heap Walker's display looks like now; note the highlighted secondary segment. Note also that it is 32 bytes in size (the minimum size for a global heap object).

The code we saw earlier **does** change the data item contained within this secondary data segment (nCount)! What happens here is that the item is changed *in* each instance, ie. there is only one copy of nCount and each application can read and write to it. Each instance's nCount variable is exactly how the last tasked instance left it because they're one in the same variable!!! This might be of some use to you as it's a pretty interesting and easy way of doing inter-instance coms via shared data!!

It is possible to force this far data into DGROUP by the way. Each instance would then run with its own private copy of nCount. If you want to do this be aware that there are even tools out there to help you do it – see Compuserve for more information.

There is no way to get multiple instances of a large model app that has more than one data segment (extras NOT marked as read-only) though.

```
┌─────────────────────────────────────────────────────────────────────┐
│ ═     ₒ                HeapWalker- (Main Heap)               ₒ    ▼ ▲ │
├─────────────────────────────────────────────────────────────────────┤
│ File   Walk   Sort   Object   Alloc   Add!                           │
├─────────────────────────────────────────────────────────────────────┤
│ ADDRESS   HANDLE   SIZE LOCK      FLG HEAP OWNER     TYPE             │
│ 00075360  327E       96                    GENDRV    Private        ↑ │
│ 00075300  28B6       96                    GENDRV    Private          │
│ 80B55680  316E       96                    GENDRV    Private          │
│ 80737FC0  095E     3104        D           GENERIC   Code!GENERIC_TEXT (1) │
│ 0005F6C0  36C6       32                    GENERIC   Data             │
│ 80B90540  2336     6752              Y     GENERIC   DGroup           │
│ 80B83080  1926     6752              Y     GENERIC   DGroup           │
│ 000627A0  37FE      352                    GENERIC   Module Database  │
│ 00062B00  34F6     4096                    GENERIC   Private          │
│ 00063DA0  24BE     4096                    GENERIC   Private          │
│ 00062900  0966      512        D           GENERIC   Resource Menu    │
│ 0005F260  20B7      512 P1     F           GENERIC   Task             │
│ 0005EF40  2B57      512 P1     F           GENERIC   Task             │
│ 8073D760  1FAE    11552        D           GRABBER   Code 1         ↓ │
│ 000.6000  1EEE      220                    GRABBER   Module Database   │
└─────────────────────────────────────────────────────────────────────┘
```

☐ Using DOS3Call

DOS3Call() is the way *into* DOS interrupt 21h for Windows' programmers. Despite what the programmer's function reference says, 'DOS3Call() may be called from an application written in "C" '; however DOS3Call() does require some assembly code (which can be *in-line* in your 'C' code) as it requires that certain registers are set-up prior to you calling it – you'll also need to *read* some registers when it comes back most likely.

You'll need a good'ish DOS reference to use this function as you'll need to know how to set up the required registers prior to the call and which ones to read upon its return.

Here's an example. Ever seen those applications that put the current time into the right hand edge of the menu bar? We'll here's an application that does just that! It uses DOS function 2Ch to find the current time and *set's* this, using SetMenuBarTime, into the menu bar. It looks like this :

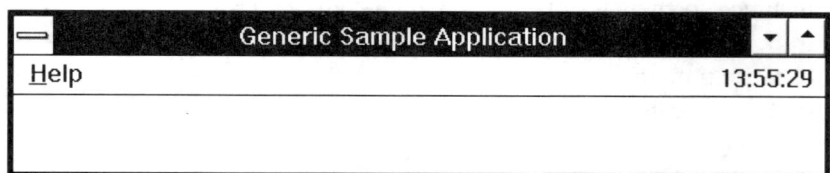

```
┌─────────────────────────────────────────────────────────────────────┐
│ ═                   Generic Sample Application                   ▼ ▲ │
├─────────────────────────────────────────────────────────────────────┤
│ Help                                                        13:55:29 │
├─────────────────────────────────────────────────────────────────────┤
│                                                                      │
│                                                                      │
└─────────────────────────────────────────────────────────────────────┘
```

Here's the code required; first the code to get the time via DOS3Call():

```
LRESULT __export CALLBACK MainWndProc
(
   HWND     hWnd
  ,UINT     uMessage
  ,WPARAM   wParam
  ,LPARAM   lParam
)
{
    switch(uMessage)
    {
       case WM_CREATE:
            /*
            ** Ask for a one second tick.
            */
            if(SetTimer(hWnd, 0, 1000, NULL) == 0)
            {
                MessageBox(hWnd, "Not enough timers!", NULL, MB_OK);
                return (LRESULT)-1;
            }
            break;

       case WM_TIMER:
            {
                /*
                ** Holds hours, minutes and seconds.
                */
                auto BYTE bHours;
                auto BYTE bMinutes;
                auto BYTE bSeconds;
                auto char carBuffer[100];

                /*
                ** Get Time MSDOS INT 21 function 2CH.
                */
                _asm
                {
                    mov ah, 2ch
                }

                /*
                ** Do DOS interrupt.
                */
                DOS3Call();

                /*
                ** Store result of DOS interrupt.
                */
                _asm
                {
                    mov bHours,   ch
                    mov bMinutes, cl
                    mov bSeconds, dh
                }

                /*
                ** Format time string buffer.
                */
                wsprintf(
```

```
                             &carBuffer[0]
                             ,"%02d:%02d:%02d"
                             ,bHours
                             ,bMinutes
                             ,bSeconds
                             );

                /*
                ** Output time right justified on menu bar.
                */
                SetMenuBarTime(hWnd, &carBuffer[0]);
            }
            break;


        case WM_DESTROY:
            /*
            ** Tidy up.
            */
            KillTimer(hWnd, 0);
            PostQuitMessage(0);
            break;
```

INT21h function 2Ch returns the current hours in CH, minutes in CL, seconds in DH and hundredths in DL. We don't use the hundredths! There are two bits of assembly required. First we load up AH with the DOS function we require – 2Ch:

```
    _asm
    {
        mov ah, 2ch
    }
```

Following that we make the call to DOS3Call().

```
    /*
    ** Do DOS interrupt.
    */
    DOS3Call();
```

You'll have to prototype this function as it's not in WINDOWS.H :

```
VOID FAR PASCAL DOS3Call(VOID);
```

When DOS3Call() comes back we use some more assembly to store away the result of the call.

```
    /*
    ** Store result of DOS interrupt.
    */
    _asm
    {
        mov bHours,   ch
        mov bMinutes, cl
        mov bSeconds, dh
    }
```

That's all there is to using the function. To draw the time in the menu bar we call SetMenuBarTime. Here's that function :

```
/*
** Set time string lpTimeBuffer into menu bar of window hWnd.
*/
VOID NEAR PASCAL SetMenuBarTime(HWND hWnd, LPSTR lpTimeBuffer)
{
    auto HDC     hDC;
    auto RECT    rsWindow;
    auto WORD    wTextLen;
    auto WORD    wTextHeight;
    auto int     nX;
    auto DWORD   dwTextDimensions;
    auto int     nMenuHeight;
    auto int     nLen;

    static int   nXpos;
    static int   nYpos;


    /*
    ** Could have done this using SetTextAlign().
    */


    /*
    ** Is everything OK? NOTE: the order of these logical tests is
    ** VERY important. The GetWindowDC() call must be last else if
    ** it were say first we would probably always allocate a DC -
    ** if we were then to find out we were iconic we'd essentially
    ** return without releasing the DC!
    */
    if(
        IsWindow(hWnd)                          &&
        IsIconic(hWnd) == FALSE                 &&
        (hDC = GetWindowDC(hWnd)) != NULL
      )
    {
        /*
        ** Get text length.
        */
        nLen = lstrlen(lpTimeBuffer);

        /*
        ** Find out how big our window is.
        */
        GetWindowRect(hWnd, &rsWindow);

        /*
        ** If we haven't set the text pos before do it now.
        */
        if(nYpos == 0 && nXpos == 0)
        {
            /*
            ** Find out how big our text is.
            */
            dwTextDimensions = GetTextExtent(
```

```
                                        hDC
                                        ,lpTimeBuffer
                                        ,nLen
                                        );

        /*
        ** Get length of text and adjust it
        */
        wTextLen = LOWORD(dwTextDimensions);
        wTextLen += (wTextLen / nLen);

        /*
        ** Get the text height.
        */
        wTextHeight = HIWORD(dwTextDimensions);

        /*
        ** Get the menu height.
        */
        nMenuHeight = GetSystemMetrics(SM_CYMENU);

        /*
        ** Work out ypos and adjust it.
        */
        nYpos = GetSystemMetrics(SM_CYCAPTION) +
                GetSystemMetrics(SM_CYFRAME);
        nYpos += (nMenuHeight - wTextHeight) / 2;

        /*
        ** Work out xpos.
        */
        nXpos = GetSystemMetrics(SM_CXBORDER) +
                GetSystemMetrics(SM_CXFRAME)  +
                wTextLen;
    }

    /*
    ** Work out releative xpos based on window size.
    */
    nX = rsWindow.right - rsWindow.left - nXpos;

    /*
    ** Make sure we're using the correct background color
    ** for drawing on the menu.
    */
    SetBkColor(hDC, GetSysColor(COLOR_MENU));

    /*
    ** Draw it.
    */
    TextOut(hDC, nX, nYpos, lpTimeBuffer, nLen);

    /*
    ** Tidy up.
    */
    ReleaseDC(hWnd, hDC);
  }
}
```

☐ Message crackers

Firstly, if you want to know everything about message crackers read WIN-DOWSX.TXT as supplied with the MS SDK.

Message crackers allow an application to do two things.

- Handle messages in a type safe and portable way.
- Keep things tidy and consistent.

Message crackers are macros defined in an include file called WINDOWSX.H. This file doesn't just contain the message cracker macros but whole loads more. Read WINDOWSX.TXT for more information. Referring back to chapters 1 & 2 I said that most Windows' applications follow the old design. One of those old design habits is putting everything in one place in a window procedure, ie. handling all messages for a given class window in its class-window procedure – messy! Really we ought to be handling particular messages using message handling functions. This helps keep the window procedure tidier and therefore makes it both easier to read and to maintain. Message crackers help you do this (they actually insist). They also allow you to forget about the size and positions of various items passed with the message in its parameters. For example, when using the crackers you don't have to know that when you handle a WM_COMMAND message that wParam contains the window handle of the control or menu item identifier and that the HIWORD of the lParam could be a notification code etc.

The macros were designed to make it easier for you to move to a 32 bit Windows API by hiding what was in where via a portable set of re-definable macros. For example, let's take the WM_COMMAND message again. If this message is sent from a control, as say a dialog box notification type WM_COMMAND message, the lParam's LOWORD will contain a window handle to the control and its HIWORD will contain a notification code (BN_CLICKED) etc. In 32 Windows all old 16 bit handles become 32 bits wide as do all the message parameters like wParam. Here though we can see a problem. In 16 bit Windows the lParam (already 32 bits) holds a handle and a WORD value; if the handle was to be made 32 bits wide there'd be no room for the notification code! Something has to change! Well what changes is where certain items are placed in the parameters. Taking our WM_COMMAND example again; in 32 bit windows the parameters are as follows. The lParam contains either NULL, if the message is from a menu item, or a window handle if the message is from a control! Obviously, 16 bit applications that expect the wParam to contain a window handle will be in for a shock when they get ported to 32 bit Windows! A solution to this problem (which only effects a few messages by the way) is to use the message cracker macros. These macros unpack the message's parameters and pass them to a previously defined handler function. The macros are platform specific, ie. they're re-written for 16 and 32 bit Windows so that the handler function gets what it expects!

Each cracker is defined in WINDOWSX.H, here's the definition of the WM_COMMAND message cracker :

```
/* void Cls_OnCommand(HWND hwnd, int id, HWND hwndCtl, UINT codeNotify); */
#define HANDLE_WM_COMMAND(hwnd, wParam, lParam, fn) \
(fn)((hwnd), (int)(wParam), (HWND)LOWORD(lParam), (UINT)HIWORD(lParam)), 0L)
```

Each cracker has a comment with it which details what the handler function associated with it should look like (note that the function name is not important). Here we can see that the handler function looks like this :

```
LRESULT NEAR PASCAL OnCommand
(
   HWND     hWnd
 , int      nID
 , HWND     hWndControl
 , UINT     nNotify
)
{
...
}
```

To use a WM_COMMAND handler in your application you'd define a function that looked like this. Then in your window procedure code you'd put the following where you'd normally (!) have you WM_COMMAND handling in-line code :

```
case WM_COMMAND:
     return HANDLE_WM_COMMAND(
                              hWnd
                            , wParam
                            , lParam
                            , OnCommand
                            );
```

This is expanded to this by the pre-processor :

```
(OnCommand)((hWnd), (int)(wParam), (HWND)LOWORD(lParam), (UINT)HIWORD(lParam)), 0L);
```

It's a function call to your OnCommand() handler function!

There's another alternative notation you could use :

```
HANDLE_MSG(hWnd, WM_DESTROY, OnDestroy);
```

This notation saves you having to insert the normal case statements into your window procedure code, ie. it expands to a case statement :

```
case (WM_DESTROY): return (((OnDestroy))((hWnd)), 0L);
```

A replacement window procedure may contain any mixture of these styles as shown below :

```
LRESULT __export CALLBACK MainWndProc
(
   HWND     hWnd
 , UINT     uMessage
 , WPARAM   wParam
```

```
      ,LPARAM    lParam
   )
   {
      switch(uMessage)
      {
           /*
           ** Conventional handler.
           */
      case WM_CREATE:
           break;

           /*
           ** First type of message cracker.
           */
      case WM_COMMAND:
           return HANDLE_WM_COMMAND(
                                      hWnd
                                     ,wParam
                                     ,lParam
                                     ,OnCommand
                                     );

      /*
      ** Second type of message cracker.
      */
      HANDLE_MSG(hWnd, WM_DESTROY, OnDestroy);

      default:
           return DefWindowProc(hWnd, uMessage, wParam, lParam);
      }

      return (LRESULT)0;
   }
```

Here are the handlers for WM_COMMAND and WM_DESTROY messages :

```
LRESULT NEAR PASCAL OnCommand
(
   HWND     hWnd ·
  ,int      nID
  ,HWND     hWndControl
  ,UINT     nNotify
)
{

   switch(nID)
   {
     case IDM_ABOUT:
          {
              if(nNotify == BN_CLICKED)
              {
                  auto HINSTANCE hInst;

                  hInst = (HINSTANCE)GetWindowWord(
                                                  hWnd
                                                 ,GWW_HINSTANCE
                                                 );

                  DialogBox(
```

```
                                hInst
                                ,"AboutBox"
                                ,hWnd
                                , (DLGPROC)About
                                );
                    }
            }
            break;
    }

    return (LRESULT)0;
}


LRESULT NEAR PASCAL OnDestroy
(
    HWND      hWnd
)
{
    PostQuitMessage(0);

    return (LRESULT)0;
}
```

To use a cracker you should look it up in WINDOWSX.H to see what prototype the handler function should have. Then you define the handler and insert the required type of message cracker you prefer into the window procedure code – that's all there is to it! For a complete discussion of message crackers see the file WINDOWSX.TXT supplied with the SDK.

☐ Finding System Info

How do you build dialogs like that found in the Program Manager (see snapshots below)? Well the functions you'll probably want to look at are :

- GetVersion()
- GetWinFlags()
- GlobalCompact()
- GetSystemMetrics()
- And the TOOLHELP functions MemManInfo() and SystemHeapInfo()

Here's an example of the code that's required to build dialogs such as those shown below :

```
BOOL __export CALLBACK About
(
    HWND      hDlg
    ,UINT     uMessage
    ,WPARAM   wParam
    ,LPARAM   lParam
)
{
```

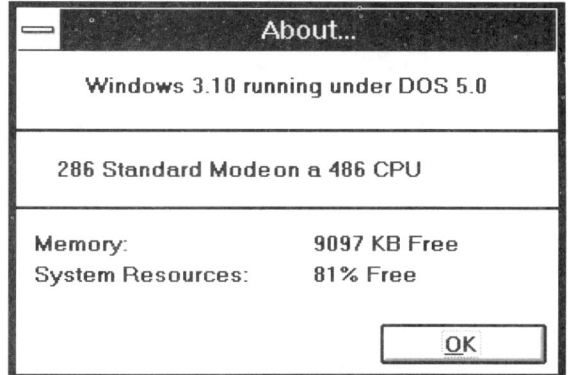

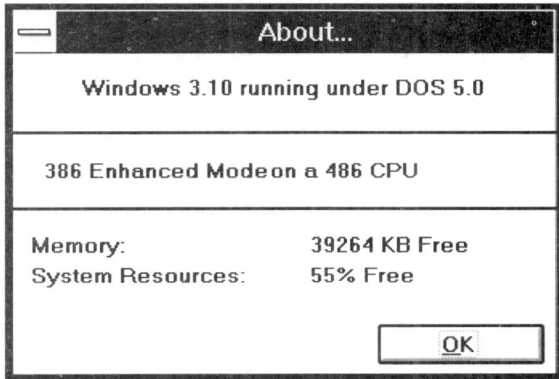

```
switch(uMessage)
{
    case WM_INITDIALOG:
        {

            /*
            ** Find CPU type.
            */
            {
                #define GWF_CPUMASK     0x000E

                auto char  * pcCPUName;
                auto DWORD   dwFlags;
                auto char    car486[]     = "on a 486 CPU";
                auto char    car386[]     = "on a 386 CPU";
                auto char    car286[]     = "on a 286 CPU";
                auto char    carUnknown[] = "Unknown";

                dwFlags = GetWinFlags();

                switch((dwFlags & GWF_CPUMASK))
                {
                    case WF_CPU486:
                        pcCPUName = &car486[0];
                        break;

                    case WF_CPU386:
                        pcCPUName = &car386[0];
```

```
                            break;

            case WF_CPU286:
                    pcCPUName = &car286[0];
                    break;

            default:
                    pcCPUName = &carUnknown[0];
                    break;
    }

    SetDlgItemText(hDlg, IDC_CPU, pcCPUName);
}


/*
** Find Windows' mode.
*/
{
    #define GWF_MODEMASK        0x0030

    auto char   * pcModeName;
    auto DWORD    dwFlags;
    auto char     carStandard[] = "286 Standard Mode";
    auto char     carEnhanced[] = "386 Enhanced Mode";
    auto char     carUnknown[]  = "Unknown";

    dwFlags = GetWinFlags();

    switch((dwFlags & GWF_MODEMASK))
    {
        case WF_WIN286:
                pcModeName = &carStandard[0];
                break;

        case WF_WIN386:
                pcModeName = &carEnhanced[0];
                break;

        default:
                pcModeName = &carUnknown[0];
                break;
    }

    SetDlgItemText(hDlg, IDC_MODE, pcModeName);
}


/*
** Find DOS & Windows versions.
*/
{
    auto char   carBuffer[BUFF_SIZE];
    auto DWORD  dwVer;
    auto WORD   wWinVer;
    auto WORD   wDOSVer;

    dwVer   = GetVersion();
```

```
        wWinVer = LOWORD(dwVer);

        wDOSVer = HIWORD(dwVer);

        wsprintf(
                &carBuffer[0]
                ,"Windows %u.%u running on DOS %u.%u"
                ,LOBYTE(wWinVer)
                ,HIBYTE(wWinVer)
                ,HIBYTE(wDOSVer)
                ,LOBYTE(wDOSVer)
                );

        SetDlgItemText(
                    hDlg
                    ,IDC_DOS_WINDOWS
                    ,&carBuffer[0]
                    );
}

/*
** Find GDI/USER heap free space.
*/
{
    auto char        carBuffer[BUFF_SIZE];
    auto SYSHEAPINFO shi;

    shi.dwSize = sizeof shi;

    SystemHeapInfo(&shi);

    wsprintf(
            &carBuffer[0]
            ,"%u%% Free"
            ,min(
                shi.wUserFreePercent
                ,shi.wGDIFreePercent
                )
            );

    SetDlgItemText(
                hDlg
                ,IDC_HEAPS
                ,&carBuffer[0]
                );
}

/*
** Find memory free.
*/
{
    auto char        carBuffer[BUFF_SIZE];
    auto MEMMANINFO mmi;

    mmi.dwSize = sizeof(mmi);

    MemManInfo(&mmi);
```

```
                        wsprintf(
                                &carBuffer[0]
                                ,"%lu KB Free"
                                ,mmi.dwLargestFreeBlock / 1000
                                );

                        SetDlgItemText(hDlg, IDC_MEM, carBuffer);

                }

        }
        return TRUE;

    case WM_COMMAND:
        if(wParam == IDOK || wParam == IDCANCEL)
        {
            EndDialog(hDlg, TRUE);
            return TRUE;
        }
        break;

    }

    return FALSE;
}
```

Here's the dialog template used above (note that given the code and the template that the .h file #defines for the controls are irrelevant) :

```
IDM_ABOUT DIALOG 56, 31, 150, 104
STYLE DS_MODALFRAME | WS_CAPTION | WS_SYSMENU
CAPTION "About..."
FONT 8, "MS Sans Serif"
BEGIN
    CONTROL         "CPU is .........."
                    ,IDC_CPU, "Static"
                    ,WS_GROUP
                    ,71, 34, 74, 8

    CONTROL         "Memory is ..........."
                    ,IDC_MEM, "Static"
                    ,WS_GROUP
                    ,82, 58, 67, 8

    CONTROL         "&OK"
                    ,IDOK
                    ,"Button"
                    ,BS_DEFPUSHBUTTON | WS_GROUP | WS_TABSTOP
                    ,101, 88, 46, 13

    CONTROL         "DOS/WIN vers ..........."
                    ,IDC_DOS_WINDOWS, "Static"
                    ,SS_CENTER | WS_GROUP
                    , 3, 7, 144, 8
```

```
CONTROL            "Resources ............"
                   ,IDC_HEAPS
                   ,"Static"
                   ,WS_GROUP
                   ,82, 68, 67, 8

CONTROL            "Memory:"
                   ,-1
                   ,"Static"
                   ,WS_GROUP
                   ,5, 58, 71, 8

CONTROL            "System Resources:"
                   ,-1
                   ,"Static"
                   ,WS_GROUP
                   ,5, 68, 72, 8

CONTROL            ""
                   ,IDC_MODE
                   ,"Static"
                   ,SS_RIGHT | WS_GROUP
                   ,4, 34, 67, 8

CONTROL            ""
                   ,103
                   ,"Static"
                   ,SS_BLACKRECT
                   ,0, 25, 150, 1
END
```

Note that each section of code, ie. each bit that *really* does something, is a self contained compound statement allowing you to cut and paste it more easily into your own code. Other things to note about the code –

- The only useful field in the MEMMANINFO structure in standard mode is dwLargetsFreeBlock.

- GlobalCompact() does not use virtual memory when calculating free space.

- GetVersion() has always returned the DOS version, ie. it's always returned a DWORD.

☐ Tarting it up!

Ever feel that the good ol' GUI isn't really as graphical as it could (or is that should) be? If the answer is YES then why not do something about it! Sometimes the graphical capabilities of the GUI, whichever one it is, are just not exploited to the full. More often than not however it because there's no precedent for doing so, ie. as long as your app looks like all the others what more could/should you do? You must remember that it's generally a good idea for all Windows' apps to look and feel the same!

Well here's an *example* for you to think about. How many times have you selected a font, tried it and then rejected it? I do it all the time – possible because I have too many fonts on my system! The reason a font's rejected is usually because it doesn't fit, ie. it's unsuitable; of course you can't tell that until you've selected it and tried it – very frustrating! The answer seems obvious; why not show the user the font before they select it!? Here's what I mean; take a look at the snap-shot shown below. This once again is a modified *generic*. The only difference between this generic and the *normal* one is that this one's got a *Fonts* menu which is shown in a dropped down state. Please note that the fonts available are actually shown in the menu!

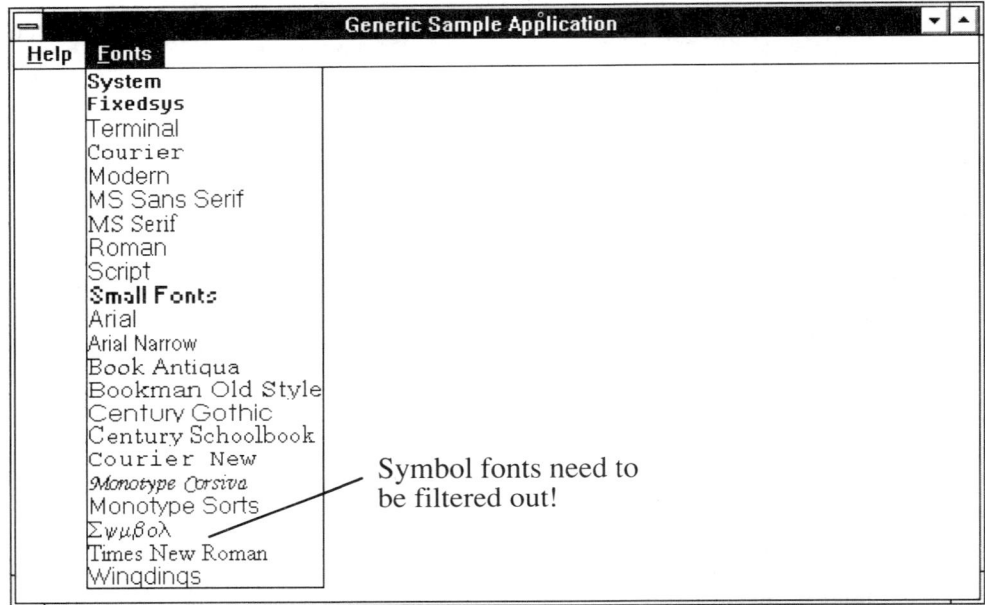

Seeing fonts!

The fonts shown are those available under 3.1 – there's quite a few aren't there?!!

The user can now see what fonts are available before they make a selection. This is a good example of applying a simple small thing that can make all the difference! You could even include a menuitem that allows the user to alter the style of the text shown, ie. items to italicise or embolden the text etc. You could also discriminate between those fonts that are scaleable and those that are not, or even better, just list those that the printer also supports; or maybe just the True-Type fonts – the list seems endless!

The application above uses owner draw menu items to do what it does. These items are those that you, the programmer, draws in. You can have anything in them, including of course text showing actual fonts! The implementation shown below is crude – just knocked up you might say, so please don't use it as a template – think of a better way to do it (also see notes following the code on using a list box instead)!

Here's the necessary code fragments :

The main window's wndproc :

```c
LRESULT __export CALLBACK MainWndProc
(
   HWND     hWnd
  ,UINT     uMessage
  ,WPARAM   wParam
  ,LPARAM   lParam
)
{
    switch(uMessage)
    {
        /*
        ** Signal ready t'go.
        */
    case WM_CREATE:
        PostMessage(hWnd, WM_USER, 0, 0);
        break;

        /*
        ** Make each item 'biggest'.
        */
    case WM_MEASUREITEM:
        ((MEASUREITEMSTRUCT FAR *) lParam) -> itemHeight = MaxHeight;
         ((MEASUREITEMSTRUCT FAR *) lParam) -> itemWidth  = MaxWidth  + 10;
        break;

    case WM_USER:
        {
          auto HDC   hDC;
          auto HMENU hPop;

          /*
          ** For enum stuff.
          */
          hDC  = GetDC(hWnd);
          hPop = CreateMenu();

          /*
          ** Find out about current fonts.
          */
          EnumFontFamilies(
                        hDC
                       ,NULL
                       ,(FONTENUMPROC)fntEnumProc
                       ,MAKELONG(hDC, hPop)
                       );

          /*
          ** New menu populated with rubbish, now add it to main menu.
          */
          AppendMenu(
                    GetMenu(hWnd)
                   ,MF_ENABLED | MF_POPUP
                   ,(UINT)hPop
                   ,"&Fonts"
                   );
```

```
              /*
              ** Clean up.
              */
              ReleaseDC(hWnd, hDC);

              /*
              ** Show new menu bar item.
              */
              DrawMenuBar(hWnd);
          }
          break;

      case WM_DRAWITEM:
          {
          auto     int      nID;
          auto     HFONT    hf;
          static   LOGFONT  LF;

              /*
              ** 'Switch' on operation required -
              ** Draw, set focus, or highlight.
              */
              if(((DRAWITEMSTRUCT FAR *)lParam)->itemAction == ODA_DRAWENTIRE)
                {
                  /*
                  ** Get item ID.
                  */
                  nID = ((DRAWITEMSTRUCT FAR *)lParam)->itemID;

                  /*
                  ** Set required facename into logfont.
                  */
                  lstrcpy(LF.lfFaceName, FontNames[nID]);

                  /*
                  ** Create a font based on logfont, ie. facename.
                  */
                  hf = CreateFontIndirect(&LF);

                  /*
                  ** Select it into DC provided as part of
                  ** WM_DRAWITEM message.
                  */
                  hf = SelectObject(
                                    ((DRAWITEMSTRUCT FAR *)lParam)->hDC
                                   ,hf
                                   );

                  /*
                  ** Now draw the name of the facename in a font
                  ** of the facename!
                  */
                  DrawText(
                           ((DRAWITEMSTRUCT FAR *)lParam)->hDC
                          ,FontNames[nID]
                          ,-1
                          ,&(((DRAWITEMSTRUCT FAR *)lParam)->rcItem)
                          ,DT_SINGLELINE   |
```

```
                                    DT_VCENTER      |
                                    DT_LEFT
                                    );

                    /*
                    ** Get rid of font.
                    */
                    hf = SelectObject(
                                        ((DRAWITEMSTRUCT FAR *)lParam)->hDC
                                        ,hf
                                        );
                    DeleteObject(hf);

            }
            else
            {
                /*
                ** Highlighting or selecting menu item so just invert it.
                */
                InvertRect(
                        ((DRAWITEMSTRUCT FAR *)lParam)->hDC
                        ,&(((DRAWITEMSTRUCT FAR *)lParam)->rcItem)
                        );
            }


        }
        break;

    case WM_DESTROY:
        PostQuitMessage(0);
        break;

    default:
        return DefWindowProc(hWnd, uMessage, wParam, lParam);
    }

    return (LRESULT)0;
}
```

The *enum* callback :

```
int CALLBACK __export fntEnumProc
(
   LOGFONT    FAR *    lpLF
  ,TEXTMETRIC FAR *    lpTM
  ,int                 nFT
  ,LPARAM              lParam
)
{
   auto   HDC    hDC;
   auto   HMENU  hPop;
   static int    nLoop;

   /*
   ** Packed 'user' params.
   */
   hDC  = (HDC)LOWORD(lParam);
```

```
    hPop = (HMENU)HIWORD(lParam);

    /*
    ** Keep track of max width and height.
    */
    MaxWidth = (WORD)max(
                MaxWidth
                ,LOWORD(
                        GetTextExtent(
                                hDC
                                ,lpLF->lfFaceName
                                ,lstrlen(lpLF->lfFaceName)
                                )
                    )
                );

    MaxHeight = (WORD)max(
                MaxHeight
                ,HIWORD(
                        GetTextExtent(
                                hDC
                                ,lpLF->lfFaceName
                                ,lstrlen(lpLF->lfFaceName)
                                )
                    )
                );
    /*
    ** Store away face name.
    */
    lstrcpy(FontNames[nLoop], lpLF->lfFaceName);

    /*
    ** Add a new owner draw for each item. nLoop is the key here as
    ** it's our signal in our WM_DRAWITEM handler to each facename.
    */
    AppendMenu(hPop, MF_ENABLED | MF_OWNERDRAW, nLoop++, NULL);

    return 1;
}
```

Some Global stuff :

```
/*
** Array of arrays of char to
** store facenames for later.
*/
static char FontNames[500][100];

/*
** Max width and height of menu-item.
*/
static WORD     MaxWidth;
static WORD     MaxHeight;
```

The main wndproc first starts doing its stuff when it sees a WM_CREATE message. It posts itself a WM_USER message so that it can do some start-up stuff once everything's up-dated and stable etc. When it receives the WM_USER message it enumerates the fonts on the machine and stores them in a global array of arrays of char. This is about the crudest bit, ie. it's not dynamic nor is it DGROUP friendly! After that it adds the *Fonts* menu to the window's main menu and waits.

The enum call-back adds a menu item for each font (note that EnumFontFamilies() has NULL for its second parameter) enumerated. No text actually gets added; the system simply *knows* that there's a number of owner draw items associated with the popup menu. There is one piece of information that gets added – that's nLoop's current value, ie. the control, or menu ID, gets added. Each ID is later treated as an index into the global array of face names. One last thing is done in the enum proc. A watch is kept on the length (and, although not as important, height) of each string, ie. each face name's length is calculated; these are used later to size the menu, ie. to make the face name text fit into the menu in a consistent manner.

At this point (pretty much) the main window appears complete with the *Fonts* menu. When the user selects the Fonts menu Windows, for each entry in the menu, passes the main window call-back two message, a WM_MEASUREITEM and a WM_DRAWITEM. The measureitem is Windows' way of asking us how big the item is; we reply the same for all items – the biggest width and height we saw in the enum call-back. The drawitem handler is where it all happens. For each drawitem message we look up the face name associated with the menu item (its ID is passed as part of the drawitem message's parameters), create a font based on that face name and draw the actual face name into the item using DrawText(). If the item's being selected, ie. not drawn, we simply invert it using InvertRect().

Note that we haven't worked out whether or not the list (the menu) is too big! That is to say, when we add all these items we don't worry about whether or not the menu spills off the top and bottom of the screen (as it will do if it were big enough!)! This easily happens when dealing with a large number of fonts. I have a machine that has 250 outline fonts installed and it causes this kind of menu severe grief. We ought to build in some menu-bar-breaks etc if we're dealing with a large number of fonts! We might also want to make some decision as to whether or not the menu should contain all these *nice* face names if the number of fonts is greater than some fixed number because drawing them all, ie. creating, drawing with and destroying all these fonts takes some time?

An alternative to menu bar breaks is to produce a scrollable list. It is possible also to add a scroll bar to a menu! I did this once just to see how it could be done. The idea is along the lines of, a menu is simply a list of items so why not, like a list box, show just some of the items and allow the user to scroll through the list as they see fit?! It especially makes sense when there's a large number of items as Windows' menus can grow in size beyond the screen size! The typical answer to this kind of problem is to put the items in a list box which itself is contained in a dialog box (like the *More*

Windows' menu item produces in an MDI app), but an alternative is to let the user scroll the menu instead – OK it's not CUA but it's nice! I did it by adding a child window scrollbar to the menu window (see chapter on windows for how to find a menu window); you could however I guess show a list box as a popup window underneath a menu bar menu item when it's selected :

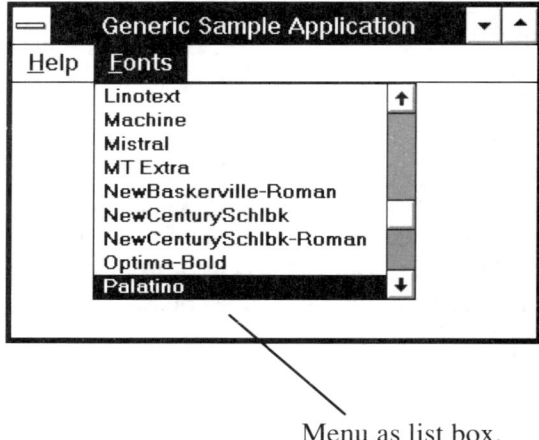

Menu as list box.

Here's an example of what I mean! Here we're essentially doing away with the dialog box and just using the list box – NOTE that this one's not owner draw, but it could be! Another way to look at this example is to say it's a kind of combo box!?

Here's another example showing a scrollbar in a real menu as talk about above :

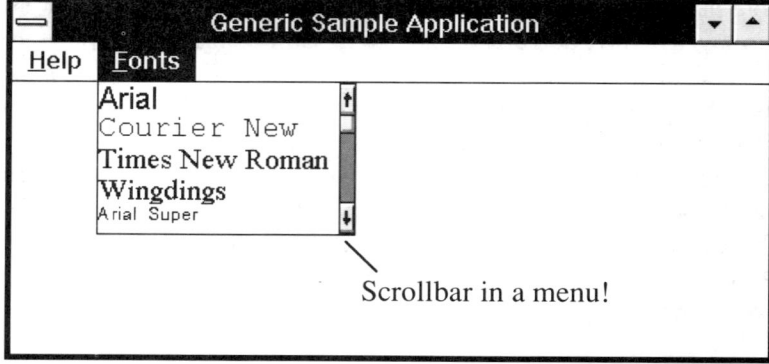

Scrollbar in a menu!

Please note that code examples of how to actually do these tricks is not included (for various reasons beyond my control); the idea here therefore is to simply stimulate you!

☐ **Waiting for the Bus**

Windows applications are non-pre-emptively scheduled whilst DOS processes are pre-emptively scheduled (in 386 Enhanced mode) – Windows is a multi-tasking operating system! When two processes want to communicate synchronously they'll therefore need some kind of semaphore mechanism, ie. they need to wait on some kind of a signal. Typically the mechanism employed is message based, ie. I start a process which in starting signals to me that it's started – I now wait. When the second process has completed, doing whatever its been doing, it signals to me that it's completed and I continue. This kind of signalling is rather messy to facilitate and is somewhat limited, ie. you need to exec a task that knows to tell you that its started/ended, you'll need calls to APIs like FindWindow() and/or SendMessage(), and some static data as a flag etc etc. You also need a Windows' window in both process. The main limiting factor is however that you can't *do it* at all with DOS processes, ie. you can't wait for a DOS process to complete and, even if you could, it couldn't signal you via a Windows' message that it had!!

Well there's an alternative. Every process in Windows is of course a task, even a DOS process has a task ID/handle. Let's say now then that you want to start a process and wait until that process had completed before doing something else – a kind of WinExecAndWait() is required. You can't simply use WinExec() (or anything like it) as you're executing either a Windows' or DOS process that will be scheduled along with you, ie. WinExec() comes back immediately and both the parent and child process run concurrently (well they seem to be concurrent!). If we could exec a process, find its task ID/handle and wait until that task ID/handle becomes invalid (task close down) we might be able to do this! Here's some code taken from a cut down generic that shows how to do just that :

The MainWndProc :

```
LRESULT  __export CALLBACK MainWndProc
(
    HWND     hWnd
  ,UINT     uMessage
  ,WPARAM   wParam
  ,LPARAM   lParam
)
{
    switch(uMessage)
    {
        case UM_EXECWAIT:
            {
                auto HINSTANCE hAppInst;
                auto char      carBuffer[50];

                if(LoadString(
                            GetWindowWord(hWnd, GWW_HINSTANCE)
                        ,(UINT)wParam
                        ,&carBuffer[0]
                        ,sizeof(carBuffer)
                        ) != 0
```

```
                    &&           /* sequence point. */

    (hAppInst = (HINSTANCE)WinExec(
                                  &carBuffer[0]
                                  ,1
                                  )) >= HINSTANCE_ERROR
    )

/*
** Start task.
*/
{
    auto TASKENTRY tTe;
    auto BOOL      bOK;
    auto HTASK     hTask;

    tTe.dwSize = sizeof(TASKENTRY);

    /*
    ** Find task handle from hInstance for started task.
    */
    for(
        hTask = NULL, bOK = TaskFirst(&tTe)
      ;bOK
      ;bOK = TaskNext(&tTe)
    )
    {
        if(tTe.hInst == hAppInst)
        {
            /*
            ** Found it!
            */
            hTask = tTe.hTask;

            break;
        }
    }

    /*
    ** If we found task handle for started task...
    */
    if(hTask != NULL)
    {
        auto MSG msg;

        /*
        ** Disable our  window  preventing user from
        ** using  it further. An alternative to this
        ** is to hide it using ShowWindow() -
        ** ShowWindow(hWnd, SW_HIDE);
        */
        EnableWindow(hWnd, FALSE);

        /*
        ** While started task is running...
        */
        while(IsTask(hTask) != FALSE)
```

```
                    {
                        /*
                        ** Yield and wait.
                        */
                        WaitMessage();

                        /*
                        ** Got a message so flush queue and yield.
                        */
                        while(PeekMessage(
                                         &msg
                                         ,NULL
                                         ,0
                                         ,0
                                         ,PM_NOREMOVE
                                         ) == TRUE
                             )
                        {
                            /*
                            ** No need to use TranslateMessage()
                            ** as we can't get keyboard input.
                            */
                            DispatchMessage(&msg);
                        }
                    }

                    /*
                    ** Started task has gone so enable our window. If
                    ** hiding - ShowWindow(hWnd, SW_SHOWNORMAL);
                    */
                    EnableWindow(hWnd, TRUE);

                    /*
                    ** Switch to it.
                    */
                    SetActiveWindow(hWnd);
                }
            }
        }
        break;

    case WM_COMMAND:
        switch(wParam)
        {
            case IDM_CALC:
            case IDM_DOS:
            case IDM_MINE:
                PostMessage(hWnd, UM_EXECWAIT, wParam, 0);
                break;
        }
        break;

    case WM_DESTROY:
        PostQuitMessage(0);
        break;

    default:
```

```
                   return DefWindowProc(hWnd, uMessage, wParam, lParam);
      }

   return (LRESULT)0;
}
```

The .rc file :

```
#include <windows.h>
#include "generic.h"

GenericMenu MENU
BEGIN
    POPUP        "&Run"
    BEGIN
        MENUITEM "Run &Calc",    IDM_CALC
        MENUITEM "Run &DOS",     IDM_DOS
        MENUITEM "Run &WinMine", IDM_MINE
    END
END

STRINGTABLE
BEGIN
    IDM_CALC,  "CALC.EXE"
    IDM_DOS,   "DOSPRMPT.PIF"
    IDM_MINE,  "WINMINE.EXE"
END
```

The include file :

```
#define IDM_CALC 100
#define IDM_DOS  200
#define IDM_MINE 300

#define UM_EXECWAIT WM_USER
```

The MainWndProc() processes a new *user* message – UM_EXECWAIT. UM_EXECWAIT is our WinExecAndWait routine coded as a message. This message is posted to the window by the window's WM_COMMAND handler. The WM_COMMAND handler simply passes on the ID of the selected menu item in the UM_EXECWAIT message.

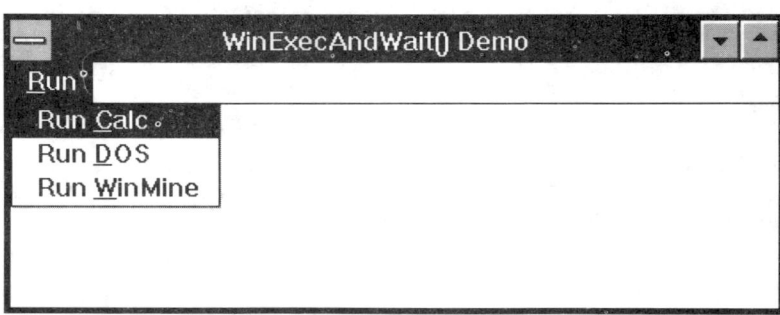

The UM_EXECWAIT message processing is as follows :

We take the menu id, which is passed in the message's wParam, and load a string from the app's string table that has this ID. We then try a WinExec() on that string. If either the LoadString() or WinExec() fails we simply break out of the UM_EXECWAIT handler.

```
if(LoadString(
             GetWindowWord(hWnd, GWW_HINSTANCE)
           ,(UINT)wParam
           ,&carBuffer[0]
           ,sizeof(carBuffer)
           ) != 0


           &&

   (hAppInst = (HINSTANCE)WinExec(
                              &carBuffer[0]
                           ,1
                           )) >= HINSTANCE_ERROR
   )
```

Once the app has been started we find its task handle by using its instance handle. The app's instance handle ID is returned from WinExec() and stored in hAppInst as shown above. Next TOOLHELP is used to turn the instance handle into a task handle via TaskFirst() and TaskNext() :

```
for(
     hTask = NULL, bOK = TaskFirst(&tTe)
    ;bOK
    ;bOK = TaskNext(&tTe)
 )
 {
     if(tTe.hInst == hAppInst)
     {
         hTask = tTe.hTask;

         break;
     }
 }
```

Once we've located the started task's task handle we disable the parent process's window and enter a loop that tests to see if the started task's task handle is still valid. If it is we call WaitMessage(). When any message arrives the message queue is flushed by using PeekMessage() and the loop begins all over. The WaitMessage() call is to allow other apps to process on idle time (note that by using WaitMessage() in the loop that we'll need a message to *wake up*, luckily it will automatically get this). If you run Perf-Meter (shown earlier) and selectively remove/add this call in the code above you'll *see* the difference it makes –

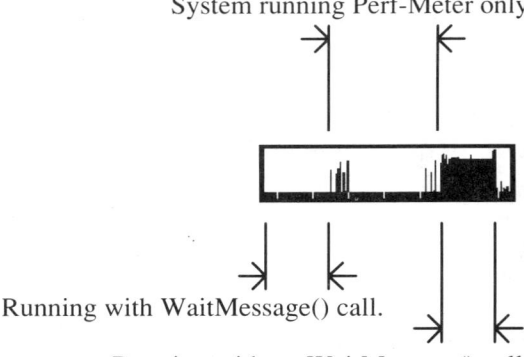

System running Perf-Meter only.

Running with WaitMessage() call.

Running without WaitMessage() call.

When the child process has terminated IsTask() returns false and the loop exits. At this point the parent process's window is re-enabled :

```
EnableWindow(hWnd, FALSE);

while(IsTask(hTask) != FALSE)
{
    WaitMessage();

    while(PeekMessage(
                    &msg
                    ,NULL
                    ,0
                    ,0
                    ,PM_NOREMOVE
                    ) == TRUE
        )
    {
        DispatchMessage(&msg);
    }
}

EnableWindow(hWnd, TRUE);
```

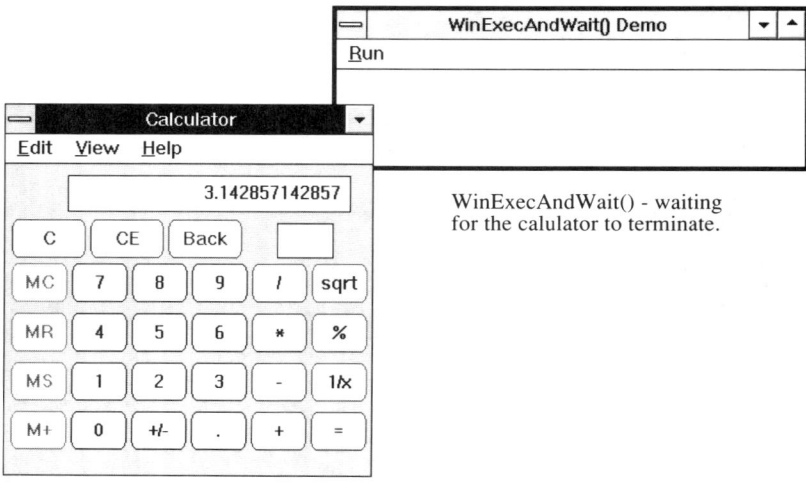

WinExecAndWait() - waiting for the calulator to terminate.

The overall effect of this is quite useful. You can now, using this technique, exec and wait for **any** executable process to complete – even a DOS box! You could also modify the app so that you can wait on a DLL being unloaded!!

We use the code above mostly to exec DOS processes that run batch processing commands. The Windows' application that execs them typically processes the data that's built by the batch process. We also use a variation of this code to automate running some troublesome apps, ie. apps that sometimes run OK but on some occasions stall. The executing app *knows* how long each task should take and can terminate it and re-try it via this mechanism – the stalled app is terminated using TerminateApp() by the way.

Another way to SetSysModalWindow().

The 3.1 function LockInput() can be used to impose a system modal state upon a window. The function is used in a sandwich, ie. you use it the first time to impose the state, process in the system modal state, then use the function again to remove the state. GetSysModalWindow() will return the window handle passed to the LockInput() function, ie. the affected window is made truly system modal.

The End

Well it's here, the end of the book that is. I hope you've enjoyed it and consider it money well spent.

If you'd like to give me some feedback (or hire me!) please do so by either emailing me directly or writing to me. You can email at – **100016,2751** which is via (Compuserve) or at **100017.2751@compuserve.com** over the internet. If you'd like to write to me the address is :

Dr. Peter J. Morris.
The Mandelbrot Set.
Mandel House,
Nostle Road,
Northleach,
Gloucestershire.
GL54 3PF.
Great Britain.

As was noted elsewhere in the book (I seem to remember!), most of the sources from the book are available from me directly. Please contact me for details using either of the methods mentioned above.

Well, it accompanied me around the world (I've worked on this book in Australia,

Various locations around the US including Honolulu, on the last three vacations I've had, in hotels too numerous to mention and on many planes and trains to/from other locations both at home and abroad) but now it's done – I can relax! Wait, what's just arrived in the mail – Hmmmm, this looks interesting (no rest for the wicked).

I've just got two last things to say :

**Be excellent to each other
and
PARTY ON DUDES!**

Appendices

☐ **Comscan Source.**

Comscan.l (from chapter 2).

This is a UNIX lex type script. You need lex to build the Comscan 'C' source. If you don't have lex to hand download one of the many public domain versions of it from any handy, good, BBS system.

```
%{

/* COMSCAN. Author Peter J. Morris (TMS internal - 2.0). */

#include <stdio.h>
#include <stdlib.h>
#include <string.h>
#include <io.h>

unsigned short int bFuncCommentFound;
unsigned short int bHeadCommentFound;
unsigned short int lines;

void tok(void);
void test(void);
void nl(void);
void Ordinary(void);
void FunctionCommentBegin(void);
void FunctionCommentEnd(void);
void HeaderCommentBegin(void);
void HeaderCommentEnd(void);
void DoBanner(void);

%}

%%

"\/*F*"[*]*         FunctionCommentBegin();

[*]*"*F*\/"         FunctionCommentEnd();

"\/*H*"[*]*         HeaderCommentBegin();

[*]*"*H*\/"         HeaderCommentEnd();

\n                  nl();

.                   Ordinary();

%%
```

```c
void main(int argc, char ** argv)
{
   auto char          *        npucAuCmdLneFlgs    = *(argv+1);
   auto char const * const npucCoAuVldToks     = "/-";
   auto char          *        npucAuSnglTok;
   auto int                    bSilent             = 0;


   if(argc > 1)
   {
      strupr(npucAuCmdLneFlgs);

      while((npucAuSnglTok = strtok(npucAuCmdLneFlgs,npucCoAuVldToks)) != 0)
        {

          npucAuCmdLneFlgs = (char *)0;

          switch(*npucAuSnglTok)
            {
             case 'S':
                 bSilent   = 1;
                 break;

             default:
                 printf("Unrecognised flag -%c, exiting.\n",*npucAuSnglTok);
                 exit(1);
                 break;
          }
      }              /* end while. */
   }                 /* end if. */

   if(bSilent != 1)
   {
      DoBanner();
   }

   lines = 1;
   yylex();

}


void DoBanner(void)
{
         puts("COMSCAN - C 'special comment detector'");
         puts("TMS (C) 1991-3. All rights reserved.\n");
         puts("Scans input file for comments that mark functions and");
         puts("module headers. These begin with /*F*, /*H* and end");
         puts("with *F*/, *H*/ respectively.\n");
         puts("The comment 'lives' within these tokens. For example");
         puts("the following is a legal function comment:-\n");
         puts("/*F***************************************************");
         puts("*");
         puts("* This is a function comment.");
         puts("*");
         puts("*F*/\n");
         puts("The contents of the comment is output together with some");
         puts("line number information as to where the comment is positioned");
```

```
                puts("within the source module.");
                puts("Usage: COMSCAN [Flags] < filename.");
            puts("The only flag recognised is -S for silent running (no banner).");
}


void Ordinary(void)
{
        if(bFuncCommentFound || bHeadCommentFound)
        {
                printf("%c",yytext[0]);
        }
}

void nl(void)
{
        lines++;
        if(bFuncCommentFound || bHeadCommentFound)
        {
                ECHO;
                printf("%3d ",lines);
        }
}


void FunctionCommentBegin(void)
{
        printf("\n\n\nFunction Comment\n%3d ",lines);
        bFuncCommentFound = 1;
}


void FunctionCommentEnd(void)
{
        bFuncCommentFound = 0;
}


void HeaderCommentBegin(void)
{
        printf("\n\n\nHeader Comment\n%3d ",lines);
        bHeadCommentFound = 1;
}


void HeaderCommentEnd(void)
{
        bHeadCommentFound = 0;
}
```

Makefile.

```
all : lexyy.exe

lexyy.c : comscan.l
```

```
lexyy.exe : lexyy.c
        cl -W3 lexyy.c > comscan.err
        del comscan.exe
        ren lexyy.exe comscan.exe
        ..\pclex comscan.l
```

☐ DefDlgProc.

DefDlgProc() referenced in the dialog box chapter.

```
/*-------------------------------------------------------------------------
*/
/*
*/
/*  DefDlgProc() -
*/
/*
*/
/*-------------------------------------------------------------------------
*/

LRESULT API IDefDlgProc(HWND hwnd, WORD message, WPARAM wParam, LPARAM lParam)
{
    HWND hwndT1;
    HWND hwndT2;
    BOOL result;

    ((PDLG)hwnd)->resultWP = 0L;
    result = FALSE;
    //
    // Call the dialog proc if it exists
    //
    if (((PDLG)hwnd)->lpfnDlg == NULL ||
            !(result = CallDlgProc(hwnd, message, wParam, lParam)))
        {

        // Make sure window still exists.
        if (!IsWindow(hwnd))
        {
           DebugErr(DBF_ERROR, "Dialog window destroyed in dialog callback");
            goto ReturnIt;
        }

        switch (message)
        {
        case WM_ERASEBKGND:
            FillWindow(hwnd, hwnd, (HDC)wParam, (HBRUSH)CTLCOLOR_DLG);
            return((LRESULT)(LONG)TRUE);

        case WM_SHOWWINDOW:
            // If hiding the window, save the focus. If showing the window
            // by means of a SW_* command and the fEnd bit is set, do not
            // pass to DWP so it won't get shown.
            //
```

```
        if (!wParam)
            SaveDlgFocus(hwnd);
        else if (LOWORD(lParam) && pdlg->fEnd)
            break;
        return(DefWindowProc(hwnd, message, wParam, lParam));

case WM_SYSCOMMAND:
    //
    // If we're minimizing and a dialog control has the focus,
    // save the hwnd for that control
    //
    if ((int) wParam == SC_MINIMIZE)
        SaveDlgFocus(hwnd);
    return(DefWindowProc(hwnd, message, wParam, lParam));

case WM_ACTIVATE:
    if (fDialog = (wParam != 0))
        RestoreDlgFocus(hwnd);
    else
        SaveDlgFocus(hwnd);
    break;

case WM_SETFOCUS:
    if (!pdlg->fEnd && !RestoreDlgFocus(hwnd))
        DlgSetFocus(GetFirstTab(hwnd));
    break;

case WM_CLOSE:
    // Make sure cancel button is not disabled before sending the
    // IDCANCEL.  Note that we need to do this as a message instead
    // of directly calling the dlg proc so that any dialog box
    // filters get this.
    //
    hwndT1 = GetDlgItem(hwnd, IDCANCEL);
    if (hwndT1 && TestWF(hwndT1, WFDISABLED))
        MessageBeep(0);
    else
        PostMessage(
                    hwnd
                    ,WM_COMMAND
                    ,(WPARAM)IDCANCEL
                    ,MAKELPARAM(hwndT1, BN_CLICKED)
                    );
    break;

case WM_NCDESTROY:
    fDialog = FALSE;        /* clear this flag */

    // Make sure we are going to terminate the mode loop, in case
    // DestroyWindow was called instead of EndDialog.  We'll RIP
    // in DialogBox2.
    //
    ((PDLG)hwnd)->fEnd = TRUE;

    if (!(hwnd->style & DS_LOCALEDIT))
    {
        if (((PDLG)hwnd)->hData)
        {
```

```
                    GlobalUnlock(((PDLG)hwnd)->hData);

                    ReleaseEditDS(((PDLG)hwnd)->hData);
                    ((PDLG)hwnd)->hData = NULL;
                }
            }

            // Delete the user defined font if any
            if (((PDLG)hwnd)->hUserFont)
            {
                DeleteObject((HANDLE)((PDLG)hwnd)->hUserFont);
                ((PDLG)hwnd)->hUserFont = NULL;
            }

            // Always let DefWindowProc do its thing to ensure that
            // everything associated with the window is freed up.
            //
            DefWindowProc(hwnd, message, wParam, lParam);
            break;

        case DM_SETDEFID:
            if (!(((PDLG)hwnd)->fEnd))
            {
                // Make sure that the new default button has the highlight.
                // We need to ignore this if we are ending the dialog box
                // because hwnd->result is no longer a default window id but
                // rather the return value of the dialog box.
                //
                // Catch the case of setting the defid to null or setting
                // the defid to something else when it was initially null.
                //
                CheckDefPushButton(hwnd,
                    (((PDLG)hwnd)->result
                     ? GetDlgItem(hwnd, ((PDLG)hwnd)->result) : NULL),
                    (wParam
                     ? GetDlgItem(hwnd, (int) wParam) : NULL) );
                ((PDLG)hwnd)->result = (int)wParam;
            }
            return((LRESULT)(DWORD)TRUE);

        case DM_GETDEFID:
            if (!((PDLG)hwnd)->fEnd && ((PDLG)hwnd)->result)
                return(MAKELRESULT(((PDLG)hwnd)->result, DC_HASDEFID));
            else
                return(0L);

        case WM_NEXTDLGCTL:
            // This message is so TAB-like operations can be properly handled
            // (simple SetFocus won't do the default button stuff)
            //
            hwndT2 = hwndFocus;
            if (LOWORD(lParam))
            {
                if (hwndT2 == NULL)
                    hwndT2 = hwnd;

                // wParam contains the hwnd of the ctl to set focus to
                hwndT1 = (HWND)wParam;
            }
```

```
        else
        {
            if (hwndT2 == NULL)
            {
                // Set focus to the first tab item.
                hwndT1 = GetFirstTab(hwnd);
                hwndT2 = hwnd;
            }
            else
            {
                // If window with focus not a dlg ctl, ignore message.
                if (!IsChild(hwnd, hwndT2))
                    return((LRESULT)(LONG)TRUE);

                // wParam = TRUE for previous, FALSE for next
                hwndT1 = GetNextDlgTabItem(hwnd, hwndT2, (BOOL)wParam);
            }
        }
        DlgSetFocus(hwndT1);
        CheckDefPushButton(hwnd, hwndT2, hwndT1);
        return((LRESULT)(LONG)TRUE);

case WM_ENTERMENULOOP:
case WM_LBUTTONDOWN:
case WM_NCLBUTTONDOWN:
    //
    // PLEASE NOTE: The following code is a VERY UGLY compatibility
    // hack.  NEVER write code that looks at the window proc address
    // in order to determine the window type.  The following code will
    // not work with subclassed combo or edit controls.
    //
    if (hwndT1 = hwndFocus)
    {
        if (hwndT1->pcls->lpfnWndProc == ComboBoxCtlWndProc)
        {
            // If user clicks anywhere in dialog box and a combo box (or
            // the editcontrol of a combo box) has the focus, then hide
            // it's listbox.
            //
            SendMessage(hwndT1, CB_SHOWDROPDOWN, FALSE, 0L);
        }
        else
        {
            if (hwndT1->pcls->lpfnWndProc == EditWndProc &&
              hwndT1->hwndParent->pcls->lpfnWndProc==ComboBoxCtlWndProc)
            {
                SendMessage(hwndT1->hwndParent,CB_SHOWDROPDOWN, FALSE, 0L);
            }
        }
    }
    return(DefWindowProc(hwnd, message, wParam, lParam));

case WM_GETFONT:
    return (LRESULT)(DWORD)(WORD)((PDLG)hwnd)->hUserFont;

// We don't want to pass the following messages to DefWindowProc:
// instead, return the value returned by the dialog proc (FALSE)
//
case WM_VKEYTOITEM:
```

```
        case WM_COMPAREITEM:
        case WM_CHARTOITEM:
        case WM_INITDIALOG:
            break;

    default:
        return(DefWindowProc(hwnd, message, wParam, lParam));
    }
}

ReturnIt:
    // These messages are special cased in an unusual way: the return value
    // of the dialog function is not BOOL fProcessed, but instead it's the
    // return value of these messages.
    //
    if (message == WM_CTLCOLOR ||
        message == WM_COMPAREITEM ||
        message == WM_VKEYTOITEM ||
        message == WM_CHARTOITEM ||
        message == WM_QUERYDRAGICON ||
        message == WM_INITDIALOG)
    {
        return((LRESULT)(DWORD)result);
    }

    return(((PDLG)hwnd)->resultWP);
}

BOOL SaveDlgFocus(HWND hwnd)
{
    if (hwndFocus && IsChild(hwnd, hwndFocus) && !((PDLG)hwnd)->hwndFocusSave)
    {
        ((PDLG)hwnd)->hwndFocusSave = hwndFocus;
        RemoveDefaultButton(hwnd, hwndFocus);
        return(TRUE);
    }
    return(FALSE);
}

BOOL RestoreDlgFocus(HWND hwnd)
{
    BOOL fRestored = FALSE;

    if (((PDLG)hwnd)->hwndFocusSave && !TestWF(hwnd, WFMINIMIZED))
    {
        if (IsWindow(((PDLG)hwnd)->hwndFocusSave))
        {
            CheckDefPushButton(hwnd, hwndFocus, ((PDLG)hwnd)->hwndFocusSave);
            SetFocus(((PDLG)hwnd)->hwndFocusSave);
            fRestored = TRUE;
        }

        ((PDLG)hwnd)->hwndFocusSave = NULL;
    }
    return(fRestored);
}
```

☐ **DefWindowProc.**

DefWindowProc() referenced in the dialog box chapter and elsewhere in the book.

```
/*-------------------------------------------------------------------------------
*/
/*
*/
/*  DefWindowProc() -
*/
/*
*/
/*-------------------------------------------------------------------------------
*/

LRESULT API IDefWindowProc(HWND hwnd, WORD message, WPARAM wParam, LPARAM lParam)
{
    int      i;
    HBRUSH   hbr;
    HWND     hwndT;

    switch (message)
    {
    case WM_NCCREATE:
// If WS_HSCROLL or WS_VSCROLL, initialize storage for scroll positions.
//
// NOTE: Scroll bar storage and text storage will be freed automatically
// by Windows during CreateWindow()
//
if (TestWF(hwnd, (WFHSCROLL | WFVSCROLL)))
{
    // Initialize extra storage for

    if (InitPwSB(hwnd) == NULL)
      return((LONG)FALSE);
}
// Store window text if present.
//
return((LRESULT)(LONG)DefSetText(hwnd, ((LPCREATESTRUCT)lParam)->lpszName));

    case WM_NCCALCSIZE:
//
// wParam = fCalcValidRects
// lParam = LPRECT rgrc[3]:
//        lprc[0] = rcWindowNew = New window rectangle
//    if fCalcValidRects:
//        lprc[1] = rcWindowOld = Old window rectangle
//        lprc[2] = rcClientOld = Old client rectangle
//
// On return:
//        rgrc[0] = rcClientNew = New client rect
//    if fCalcValidRects:
//        rgrc[1] = rcValidDst = Destination valid rectangle
//        rgrc[2] = rcValidSrc = Source valid rectangle
//
CalcClientRect(hwnd, (LPRECT)lParam);
break;
```

```
   case WM_NCHITTEST:
//
// Determine what area the passed coordinate is in.
//
return((LRESULT)(DWORD)FindNCHit(hwnd, (LONG)lParam));

   case WM_NCPAINT:
//
// Do non-client area drawing.
//
DWP_DoNCPaint(hwnd, (HRGN)wParam);
break;

   case WM_NCACTIVATE:
//
// Do non-client drawing in response to
// activation or deactivation.
//
DWP_DoNCActivate(hwnd, (BOOL)wParam);
return (LRESULT)(DWORD)TRUE;

   case WM_CANCELMODE:
//
// Terminate any modes the system might
// be in, such as scrollbar tracking, menu mode,
// button capture, etc.
//
DWP_DoCancelMode(hwnd);
break;

   case WM_SETTEXT:
// Set the new text and redraw the caption or icon title window.
//
DefSetText(hwnd, (LPCSTR)lParam);
DWP_RedrawTitle(hwnd);
break;

   case WM_GETTEXT:
//
// If the buffer size is > 0, copy as much of the window text as
// will fit (making sure to zero terminate the result).
//
if (wParam)
{
    if (hwnd->hName)
        return (LRESULT)(LONG)TextCopy(hwnd->hName, (LPSTR)lParam, (int)wParam);

    // No string: make sure we return an empty string.
    //
    ((LPSTR)lParam)[0] = 0;
}
return (0L);

   case WM_GETTEXTLENGTH:
//
// Just return the length of the window text (excluding 0 terminator)
//
if (hwnd->hName)
    return((LRESULT)(LONG)lstrlen(TextPointer(hwnd->hName)));
```

```
   return(0L);

     case WM_PAINT:
     case WM_PAINTICON:
   DWP_Paint(message, hwnd);
   break;

     case WM_ERASEBKGND:
     case WM_ICONERASEBKGND:
   return (LRESULT)(LONG)DWP_EraseBkgnd(hwnd, message, (HDC)wParam);

     case WM_SYNCPAINT:
   //
   // This message is sent when SetWindowPos() is trying
   // to get the screen looking nice after window rearrangement,
   // and one of the windows involved is of another task.
   // This message avoids lots of inter-app message traffic
   // by switching to the other task and continuing the
   // recursion there.
   //
   // wParam          = flags
   // LOWORD(lParam) = hrgnClip
   // HIWORD(lParam) = hwndSkip  (not used; always NULL)
   //
   // hwndSkip is now always NULL.
   //
   // NOTE: THIS MESSAGE IS FOR INTERNAL USE ONLY! ITS BEHAVIOR
   // IS DIFFERENT IN 3.1 THAN IN 3.0!!
   //
   DoSyncPaint(hwnd, NULL, ((WORD)wParam | DSP_WM_SYNCPAINT));
   break;

     case WM_SYSCOMMAND:
   SysCommand(hwnd, (int)wParam, lParam);
   break;

     case WM_ACTIVATE:
   //
   // By default, windows set the focus to themselves when activated.
   //
   if ((BOOL)wParam)
       SetFocus(hwnd);
   break;

     case WM_SETREDRAW:
   //
   // Set or clear the WS_VISIBLE bit, without invalidating the window.
   // (Also performs some internal housekeeping to ensure that window
   // DC clip regions are computed correctly).
   //
   DWP_SetRedraw(hwnd, (BOOL)wParam);
   break;

     case WM_WINDOWPOSCHANGING:
   //
   // If the window's size is changing, and the window has
   // a size border (WS_THICKFRAME) or is a main window (WS_OVERLAPPED),
   // then adjust the new width and height by sending a WM_MINMAXINFO message.
   //
```

```
#define ppos ((WINDOWPOS FAR *)lParam)
if (!(ppos->flags & SWP_NOSIZE))
    AdjustSize(hwnd, &ppos->cx, &ppos->cy);
#undef ppos
break;

  case WM_WINDOWPOSCHANGED:
//
// If (!(lpswp->flags & SWP_NOCLIENTMOVE)
//    send WM_MOVE message
//
// If (!(lpswp->flags & SWP_NOCLIENTSIZE)
//    send WM_SIZE message with wParam set based on
//    current WS_MINIMIZED/WS_MAXIMIZED style.
//
// If DefWindowProc() is not called, WM_MOVE and WM_SIZE messages
// will not be sent to the window.
//
HandleWindowPosChanged(hwnd, (WINDOWPOS FAR *)lParam);
break;

  case WM_CTLCOLOR:
//
// Set up the supplied DC with the foreground and background
// colors we want to use in the control, and return a brush
// to use for filling.
//
switch (HIWORD(lParam))
{
case CTLCOLOR_SCROLLBAR:
    //
    // Background = white
    // Foreground = black
    // brush = COLOR_SCROLLBAR.
    //
    SetBkColor((HDC)wParam, RGB(255, 255, 255));
    SetTextColor((HDC)wParam, RGB(0, 0, 0));
    hbr = sysClrObjects.hbrScrollbar;

    // The scroll bar color may be dithered, so unrealize it.
    //
    UnrealizeObject(hbr);
    break;

default:
    //
    // Background = COLOR_WINDOW
    // Foreground = COLOR_WINDOWTEXT
    // Brush = COLOR_WINDOW
    //
    SetBkColor((HDC)wParam, sysColors.clrWindow);
    SetTextColor((HDC)wParam, sysColors.clrWindowText);
    hbr = sysClrObjects.hbrWindow;
}
return((LRESULT)(DWORD)(WORD)hbr);

  case WM_SETCURSOR:
//
// wParam  == hwndHit == hwnd that cursor is over
```

```
// lParamL == codeHT  == Hit test area code (result of WM_NCHITTEST)
// lParamH == msg      == Mouse message number (may be 0)
//
// Strategy: First forward WM_SETCURSOR message to parent.  If it
// returns TRUE (i.e., it set the cursor), just return.  Otherwise,
// set the cursor based on codeHT and msg.
//
return (LRESULT)(LONG)DWP_SetCursor(hwnd, (HWND)wParam,
        LOWORD(lParam), HIWORD(lParam));

    case WM_MOUSEACTIVATE:
//
// First give the parent a chance to process the message.
//
hwndT = GetChildParent(hwnd);
if (hwndT)
{
    i = (int)(DWORD)SendMessage(hwndT, WM_MOUSEACTIVATE,
        wParam, lParam);

    if (i != 0)
        return (LRESULT)(LONG)i;
}

// If the user clicked in the title bar, don't activate now:
// the activation will take place later when the move or size
// occurs.
//
if (LOWORD(lParam) == HTCAPTION)
    return((LRESULT)(LONG)MA_NOACTIVATE);

return((LRESULT)(LONG)MA_ACTIVATE);

    case WM_SHOWWINDOW:
//
// If we are being called because our owner window is being shown,
// hidden, minimized, or un-minimized, then we must hide or show
// show ourself as appropriate.
//
// This behavior occurs for popup windows or owned windows only.
// It's not designed for use with child windows.
//
if (LOWORD(lParam) != 0 && (TestwndPopup(hwnd) || hwnd->hwndOwner))
{
    // The WFHIDDENPOPUP flag is an internal flag that indicates
    // that the window was hidden because its owner was hidden.
    // This way we only show windows that were hidden by this code,
    // not intentionally by the application.
    //
    // Go ahead and hide or show this window, but only if:
    //
    // a) we need to be hidden, or
    // b) we need to be shown, and we were hidden by
    //    an earlier WM_SHOWWINDOW message
    //
    if ((!wParam && TestWF(hwnd, WFVISIBLE)) ||
        (wParam && !TestWF(hwnd, WFVISIBLE) && TestWF(hwnd, WFHIDDENPOPUP)))
    {
        // Remember that we were hidden by WM_SHOWWINDOW processing
```

```
        /.
        ClrWF(hwnd, WFHIDDENPOPUP);
        if (!wParam)
            SetWF(hwnd, WFHIDDENPOPUP);

        ShowWindow(hwnd, (wParam ? SW_SHOWNOACTIVATE : SW_HIDE));
    }
}
break;

    case WM_NCLBUTTONDOWN:
    case WM_NCLBUTTONUP:
    case WM_NCLBUTTONDBLCLK:
    case WM_NCMOUSEMOVE:
//
// Deal with mouse messages in the non-client area.
//
DWP_NCMouse(hwnd, message, wParam, lParam);
break;

    case WM_KEYDOWN:
// Windows 2.0 backward compatibility:
// Alias F10 to the menu key
// (only for apps that don't handle WM_KEY* messages themselves)
//
if ((WORD)wParam == VK_F10)
    fF10Status = TRUE;
break;

    case WM_SYSKEYDOWN:
// Is the ALT key down?
if (HIWORD(lParam) & SYS_ALTERNATE)
{
    // Toggle only if this is not an autorepeat key
    //
    if ((HIWORD(lParam) & SYS_PREVKEYSTATE) == 0)
    {
        if (((WORD)wParam == VK_MENU) && (!fMenuStatus))
            fMenuStatus = TRUE;
        else
            fMenuStatus = FALSE;
    }

    fF10Status = FALSE;

    DWP_ProcessVirtKey((WORD)wParam);
}
else
{
    if ((WORD)wParam == VK_F10)
    {
        fF10Status = TRUE;
    }
    else
    {
        if ((WORD)wParam == VK_ESCAPE)
        {
            if (GetKeyState(VK_SHIFT) < 0)
            {
```

```
                SendMessage(hwnd, WM_SYSCOMMAND,
                    (WPARAM)SC_KEYMENU, (LPARAM)(DWORD)MENUSYSMENU);
            }
        }
    }
}
break;

    case WM_KEYUP:
    case WM_SYSKEYUP:
// Press and release F10 or ALT. Send this only to top-level
// windows, otherwise MDI gets confused.  The fix in which
// DefMDIChildProc() passed up the message was insufficient in the
// case a child window of the MDI child had the focus.
//
if ( ((WORD)wParam == VK_MENU && (fMenuStatus == TRUE)) ||
     ((WORD)wParam == VK_F10 && fF10Status) )
{
    SendMessage(GetTopLevelWindow(hwnd), WM_SYSCOMMAND,
        (WPARAM)SC_KEYMENU, 0L);
}
fF10Status = fMenuStatus = FALSE;
break;

    case WM_SYSCHAR:
// If syskey is down and we have a char... */
fMenuStatus = FALSE;

if ((WORD)wParam == VK_RETURN && TestWF(hwnd, WFMINIMIZED))
{
    // If the window is iconic and user hits RETURN, we want to
    // restore this window.
    //
    PostMessage(hwnd, WM_SYSCOMMAND, (WPARAM)SC_RESTORE, 0L);
    break;
}

if ((HIWORD(lParam) & SYS_ALTERNATE) && wParam)
{
    if ((WORD)wParam == VK_TAB || (WORD)wParam == VK_ESCAPE)
        break;

    // Send ALT-SPACE only to top-level windows.
    if (((WORD)wParam == MENUSYSMENU) && (TestwndChild(hwnd)))
        SendMessage(hwnd->hwndParent, message, wParam, lParam);
    else
        SendMessage(
                    hwnd
                    ,WM_SYSCOMMAND
                    , (WPARAM)SC_KEYMENU
                    , (LPARAM)(DWORD)(WORD)wParam
                    );
}
else
{
    // Ctrl-Esc produces a WM_SYSCHAR, but should not beep
    if ((WORD)wParam != VK_ESCAPE)
        MessageBeep(0);
}
```

```
break;

  case WM_CLOSE:
//
// Default WM_CLOSE handling is to destroy the window.
//
DestroyWindow(hwnd);
break;

  case WM_QUERYOPEN:
  case WM_QUERYENDSESSION:
return((LRESULT)(LONG)TRUE);

  case WM_ISACTIVEICON:
return ((LRESULT)(DWORD)(BOOL)(TestWF(hwnd, WFFRAMEON) != 0));

  case WM_CHARTOITEM:
  case WM_VKEYTOITEM:
//
// Return -1 to cause default processing
//
return((LRESULT)-1L);

  case WM_DRAWITEM:
#define lpdis   ((LPDRAWITEMSTRUCT)lParam)
if (lpdis->CtlType == ODT_LISTBOX)
    LBDefaultListboxDrawItem(lpdis);
#undef  lpdis
break;

  case WM_GETHOTKEY:
return((LRESULT)(LONG)DWP_GetHotKey(hwnd));
break;

  case WM_SETHOTKEY:
return((LRESULT)(LONG)SetHotKey(hwnd, (WORD)wParam));
break;

  case WM_QUERYDRAGICON:
return((LRESULT)(DWORD)(WORD)DWP_QueryDragIcon(hwnd));
break;

  case WM_QUERYDROPOBJECT:
//
// If the application is WS_EX_ACCEPTFILES, return TRUE.
//
if (TestWF(hwnd, WEFACCEPTFILES))
    return (LRESULT)(DWORD)TRUE;

return (LRESULT)(DWORD)FALSE;

  case WM_DROPOBJECT:
return (LRESULT)(DWORD)DO_DROPFILE;

  }   // end switch
  return(0L);
}
```

B o o k l i s t

Here's a list of some of the books that I have on Windows' programming (some of these aren't actually Windows' programming books but are none the less quite useful) – all have been useful at some time or another (the extra useful ones are marked with a *). Some of these books are quite old, some may even be out of print for all I know - some certainly have later editions! The books appear in random order :

*Undocumented Windows.

Addison Wesley.
Andrew Schulman, David Maxey, Matt Pietrek.
ISBN 0-201-60834-0

Writing Windows' Device Drivers.

Daniel A. Norton.
Addison Wesley.
ISBN 0-201-57795-X

Windows Programming PowerPack.

Jeffrey D. Clark.
Sams.
ISBN 0-672-30129-6

*Windows 3 Developers Workshop.

Richard Wilton.
Microsoft Press.
ISBN 1-55615-244-2

*Windows API Bible.

James L.Conger.
The Waite Group.
ISBN 1-878739-15-8

*Programming Windows.

Charles Petzold.
Microsoft Press.
ISBN 1-55615-264-7

*Windows++.

Paul Dilascia.
Addison Wesley.
ISBN 0-201-60891-X

Windows 3: A Devleloper's Guide.

Jeffrey M. Richter.
M&T Books.
ISBN 1-55851-164-4

*Peter Norton's Windows 3.0 Power Programming Techniques.

Peter Norton & Paul Yao.
Bantam.
ISBN 0-553-34940-6

Programming With Windows.

Farrell.
Que.
ISBN 0-88022-299-9

*Windows Programmer's Guide to Serial Communications.

Timothy S. Monk.
Sams.
ISBN 0-672-30030-3

Windows System Programming.

Peter Wilken and Dirk Honekamp.
Abacus.
ISBN 1-55755-116-2

Advanced Windows Programming.

Martin Heller.
Wiley.
ISBN 0-471-54711-5

Developing Windows 3 Applications.

Brent Rector.
Sams.
ISBN 0-672-22802-5

*Windows 3.0 Programming Primer.
(In my opinion - not really a primer, more a collection of handy sub-routines)

Alan Southerton.
Addison Wesley.
ISBN 0-201-55078-4

*Windows Programmers Guide to DLLs And Memory Management.

Mike Klien.
Sams.
ISBN 0-672-30236-5

C Programmer's Guide to Microsoft Windows 2.0.

Carl Townsend.
Sams.
ISBN 0-672-22621-9

Microsoft Windows Program Development.

Michael Hyman.
MIS.
ISBN 0-943518-34-2

| Windows Programming Secrets. | Kris Jamsa. McGraw-Hill. ISBN 0-07-881262-3 |

| *Graphics Programming under Windows. | Myers & Doner. Sybex. ISBN 0-89588-448-8 |

| *Introduction to Windows Programming. | Guy Quedens & Pamela S. Beason. Scott Foresman IBM Computer Books. ISBN 0-673-38058-0 |

| Programmer's Guide To Windows. | Durant, Carlson & Yao. Sybex. ISBN 0-89588-496-8 |

Additionally you might like to get :-

| Windows NT. | Helen Custer. Microsoft Press. ISBN 1-55615-481-X |

| Win32 Application Programming Interface. The Programmer's Reference Volumes 1 & 2. | Microsoft Press. ISBN 1-55615-497-6 & ISBN 1-55615-498-4 |

See also the books on 'C' listed in Chapter1.

Alphabetically supported list of Windows' function prototypes.

```
int          WINAPI AbortDoc(HDC);
int          WINAPI AccessResource(HINSTANCE,HRSRC);
ATOM         WINAPI AddAtom(LPCSTR);
int          WINAPI AddFontResource(LPCSTR);
VOID         WINAPI AdjustWindowRect(RECT FAR*,DWORD,BOOL);
VOID         WINAPI AdjustWindowRectEx(RECT FAR*,DWORD,BOOL,DWORD);
UINT         WINAPI AllocDStoCSAlias(UINT);
HGLOBAL      WINAPI AllocResource(HINSTANCE,HRSRC,DWORD);
UINT         WINAPI AllocSelector(UINT);
VOID         WINAPI AnimatePalette(HPALETTE,UINT,UINT,const PALETTEENTRY FAR*);
LPSTR        WINAPI AnsiLower(LPSTR);
UINT         WINAPI AnsiLowerBuff(LPSTR,UINT);
LPSTR        WINAPI AnsiNext(LPCSTR);
LPSTR        WINAPI AnsiPrev(LPCSTR,LPCSTR);
VOID         WINAPI AnsiToOem(const char _huge*,char _huge*);
VOID         WINAPI AnsiToOemBuff(LPCSTR,LPSTR,UINT);
LPSTR        WINAPI AnsiUpper(LPSTR);
UINT         WINAPI AnsiUpperBuff(LPSTR,UINT);
BOOL         WINAPI AnyPopup(VOID);
BOOL         WINAPI AppendMenu(HMENU,UINT,UINT,LPCSTR);
BOOL         WINAPI Arc(HDC,int,int,int,int,int,int,int,int);
UINT         WINAPI ArrangeIconicWindows(HWND);
```

```
HDWP         WINAPI BeginDeferWindowPos(int);
HDC          WINAPI BeginPaint(HWND,PAINTSTRUCT FAR*);
BOOL         WINAPI BitBlt(HDC,int,int,int,int,HDC,int,int,DWORD);
BOOL         WINAPI BringWindowToTop(HWND);
int          WINAPI BuildCommDCB(LPCSTR,DCB FAR*);
```

```
BOOL         WINAPI CallMsgFilter(MSG FAR*,int);
LRESULT      WINAPI CallNextHookEx(HHOOK,int,WPARAM,LPARAM);
LRESULT      WINAPI CallWindowProc(FARPROC,HWND,UINT,WPARAM,LPARAM);
```

```
LRESULT      WINAPI CallWindowProc(WNDPROC,HWND,UINT,WPARAM,LPARAM);
int          WINAPI Catch(int FAR*);
BOOL         WINAPI ChangeClipboardChain(HWND,HWND);
BOOL         WINAPI ChangeMenu(HMENU,UINT,LPCSTR,UINT,UINT);
VOID         WINAPI CheckDlgButton(HWND,int,UINT);
BOOL         WINAPI CheckMenuItem(HMENU,UINT,UINT);
VOID         WINAPI CheckRadioButton(HWND,int,int,int);
HWND         WINAPI ChildWindowFromPoint(HWND,POINT);
BOOL         WINAPI Chord(HDC,int,int,int,int,int,int,int,int);
int          WINAPI ClearCommBreak(int);
VOID         WINAPI ClientToScreen(HWND,POINT FAR*);
VOID         WINAPI ClipCursor(const RECT FAR*);
BOOL         WINAPI CloseClipboard(VOID);
int          WINAPI CloseComm(int);
LRESULT      WINAPI CloseDriver(HDRVR,LPARAM,LPARAM);
HMETAFILE    WINAPI CloseMetaFile(HDC);
VOID         WINAPI CloseSound(VOID);
VOID         WINAPI CloseWindow(HWND);
int          WINAPI CombineRgn(HRGN,HRGN,HRGN,int);
HCURSOR      WINAPI CopyCursor(HINSTANCE,HCURSOR);
HICON        WINAPI CopyIcon(HINSTANCE,HICON);
HMETAFILE    WINAPI CopyMetaFile(HMETAFILE,LPCSTR);
VOID         WINAPI CopyRect(RECT FAR*,const RECT FAR*);
int          WINAPI CountClipboardFormats(VOID);
int          WINAPI CountVoiceNotes(int);
HBITMAP      WINAPI CreateBitmap(int,int,UINT,UINT,const VOID FAR*);
HBITMAP      WINAPI CreateBitmapIndirect(BITMAP FAR* );
HBRUSH       WINAPI CreateBrushIndirect(LOGBRUSH FAR*);
VOID         WINAPI CreateCaret(HWND,HBITMAP,int,int);
HBITMAP      WINAPI CreateCompatibleBitmap(HDC,int,int);
HDC          WINAPI CreateCompatibleDC(HDC);
HCURSOR      WINAPI CreateCursor(HINSTANCE,int,int,int,int,const VOID FAR*,const VOID
             FAR*);
HDC          WINAPI CreateDC(LPCSTR,LPCSTR,LPCSTR,const VOID FAR*);
HWND         WINAPI CreateDialog(HINSTANCE,LPCSTR,HWND,DLGPROC);
HWND         WINAPI CreateDialogIndirect(HINSTANCE,const VOID FAR*,HWND,DLGPROC);
HWND         WINAPI CreateDialogIndirectParam(HINSTANCE,const VOID
             FAR*,HWND,DLGPROC,LPARAM);
HWND         WINAPI CreateDialogParam(HINSTANCE,LPCSTR,HWND,DLGPROC,LPARAM);
HBITMAP      WINAPI CreateDIBitmap(HDC,BITMAPINFOHEADER FAR*,DWORD,const VOID

             FAR*,BITMAPINFO FAR*,UINT);
HBRUSH       WINAPI CreateDIBPatternBrush(HGLOBAL,UINT);
HBITMAP      WINAPI CreateDiscardableBitmap(HDC,int,int);
HRGN         WINAPI CreateEllipticRgn(int,int,int,int);
HRGN         WINAPI CreateEllipticRgnIndirect(const RECT FAR*);
HFONT        WINAPI CreateFont(int,int,int,int,int,BYTE,BYTE,BYTE,BYTE,BYTE,BYTE
             ,BYTE,BYTE,LPCSTR);
HFONT        WINAPI CreateFontIndirect(const LOGFONT FAR*);
HBRUSH       WINAPI CreateHatchBrush(int,COLORREF);
HDC          WINAPI CreateIC(LPCSTR,LPCSTR,LPCSTR,const VOID FAR*);
HICON        WINAPI CreateIcon(HINSTANCE,int,int,BYTE,BYTE,const VOID FAR*,const VOID
             FAR*);
HMENU        WINAPI CreateMenu(VOID);
HDC          WINAPI CreateMetaFile(LPCSTR);
HPALETTE     WINAPI CreatePalette(const LOGPALETTE FAR*);
HBRUSH       WINAPI CreatePatternBrush(HBITMAP);
HPEN         WINAPI CreatePen(int,int,COLORREF);
HPEN         WINAPI CreatePenIndirect(LOGPEN FAR*);
```

```
HRGN        WINAPI CreatePolygonRgn(const POINT FAR*,int,int);
HRGN        WINAPI CreatePolyPolygonRgn(const POINT FAR*,const int FAR*,int,int);
HMENU       WINAPI CreatePopupMenu(VOID);
HRGN        WINAPI CreateRectRgn(int,int,int,int);
HRGN        WINAPI CreateRectRgnIndirect(const RECT FAR*);
HRGN        WINAPI CreateRoundRectRgn(int,int,int,int,int,int);
BOOL        WINAPI CreateScalableFontResource(UINT,LPCSTR,LPCSTR,LPCSTR);
HBRUSH      WINAPI CreateSolidBrush(COLORREF);
HWND        WINAPI CreateWindow(LPCSTR,LPCSTR,DWORD,int,int,int,int,HWND,HMENU
            ,HINSTANCE,VOID FAR*);
HWND        WINAPI CreateWindowEx(DWORD,LPCSTR,LPCSTR,DWORD,int,int,int,int,HWND
            ,HMENU,HINSTANCE,VOID FAR*);
```

```
VOID        WINAPI DebugBreak(VOID);
VOID FAR    CDECL  DebugOutput(UINT,LPCSTR,...);
LRESULT     WINAPI DefDlgProc(HWND,UINT,WPARAM,LPARAM);
LRESULT     WINAPI DefDriverProc(DWORD,HDRVR,UINT,LPARAM,LPARAM);
HDWP        WINAPI DeferWindowPos(HDWP,HWND,HWND,int,int,int,int,UINT);
LRESULT     WINAPI DefFrameProc(HWND,HWND,UINT,WPARAM,LPARAM);
LRESULT     WINAPI DefHookProc(int,WPARAM,LPARAM,HHOOK FAR*);
LRESULT     WINAPI DefHookProc(int,WPARAM,LPARAM,HOOKPROC FAR*);
LRESULT     WINAPI DefMDIChildProc(HWND,UINT,WPARAM,LPARAM);
LRESULT     WINAPI DefWindowProc(HWND,UINT,WPARAM,LPARAM);
ATOM        WINAPI DeleteAtom(ATOM);
BOOL        WINAPI DeleteDC(HDC);
BOOL        WINAPI DeleteMenu(HMENU,UINT,UINT);
BOOL        WINAPI DeleteMetaFile(HMETAFILE);
BOOL        WINAPI DeleteObject(HGDIOBJ);
VOID        WINAPI DestroyCaret(VOID);
BOOL        WINAPI DestroyCursor(HCURSOR);
BOOL        WINAPI DestroyIcon(HICON);
BOOL        WINAPI DestroyMenu(HMENU);
BOOL        WINAPI DestroyWindow(HWND);
int         WINAPI DialogBox(HINSTANCE,LPCSTR,HWND,DLGPROC);
int         WINAPI DialogBoxIndirect(HINSTANCE,HGLOBAL,HWND,DLGPROC);
int         WINAPI DialogBoxIndirectParam(HINSTANCE,HGLOBAL,HWND,DLGPROC,LPARAM);
int         WINAPI DialogBoxParam(HINSTANCE,LPCSTR,HWND,DLGPROC,LPARAM);
VOID        WINAPI DirectedYield(HTASK);
LONG        WINAPI DispatchMessage(const MSG FAR*);
int         WINAPI DlgDirList(HWND,LPSTR,int,int,UINT);
int         WINAPI DlgDirListComboBox(HWND,LPSTR,int,int,UINT);
BOOL        WINAPI DlgDirSelect(HWND,LPSTR,int);
BOOL        WINAPI DlgDirSelectComboBox(HWND,LPSTR,int);
BOOL        WINAPI DlgDirSelectComboBoxEx(HWND,LPSTR,int,int);
BOOL        WINAPI DlgDirSelectEx(HWND,LPSTR,int,int);
BOOL        WINAPI DPtoLP(HDC,POINT FAR*,int);
VOID        WINAPI DrawFocusRect(HDC,const RECT FAR*);
BOOL        WINAPI DrawIcon(HDC,int,int,HICON);
VOID        WINAPI DrawMenuBar(HWND);
int         WINAPI DrawText(HDC,LPCSTR,int,RECT FAR*,UINT);
```

```
BOOL        WINAPI Ellipse(HDC,int,int,int,int);
BOOL        WINAPI EmptyClipboard(VOID);
BOOL        WINAPI EnableCommNotification(int,HWND,int,int);
BOOL        WINAPI EnableHardwareInput(BOOL);
BOOL        WINAPI EnableMenuItem(HMENU,UINT,UINT);
BOOL        WINAPI EnableScrollBar(HWND,int,UINT);
BOOL        WINAPI EnableWindow(HWND,BOOL);
BOOL        WINAPI EndDeferWindowPos(HDWP);
VOID        WINAPI EndDialog(HWND,int);
int         WINAPI EndDoc(HDC);
int         WINAPI EndPage(HDC);
VOID        WINAPI EndPaint(HWND,const PAINTSTRUCT FAR*);
BOOL        WINAPI EnumChildWindows(HWND,WNDENUMPROC,LPARAM);
UINT        WINAPI EnumClipboardFormats(UINT);
int         WINAPI EnumFontFamilies(HDC,LPCSTR,FONTENUMPROC,LPARAM);
int         WINAPI EnumFontFamilies(HDC,LPCSTR,FONTENUMPROC,LPSTR);
int         WINAPI EnumFonts(HDC,LPCSTR,OLDFONTENUMPROC,LPARAM);
int         WINAPI EnumFonts(HDC,LPCSTR,OLDFONTENUMPROC,LPSTR);
BOOL        WINAPI EnumMetaFile(HDC,HMETAFILE,MFENUMPROC,LPARAM);
int         WINAPI EnumObjects(HDC,int,GOBJENUMPROC,LPARAM);
int         WINAPI EnumObjects(HDC,int,GOBJENUMPROC,LPSTR);
int         WINAPI EnumProps(HWND,PROPENUMPROC);
BOOL        WINAPI EnumTaskWindows(HTASK,WNDENUMPROC,LPARAM);
BOOL        WINAPI EnumWindows(WNDENUMPROC,LPARAM);
BOOL        WINAPI EqualRect(const RECT FAR*,const RECT FAR*);
BOOL        WINAPI EqualRgn(HRGN,HRGN);
int         WINAPI Escape(HDC,int,int,LPCSTR,VOID FAR*);
LONG        WINAPI EscapeCommFunction(int,int);
int         WINAPI ExcludeClipRect(HDC,int,int,int,int);
int         WINAPI ExcludeUpdateRgn(HDC,HWND);
BOOL        WINAPI ExitWindows(DWORD,UINT);
BOOL        WINAPI ExitWindowsExec(LPCSTR,LPCSTR);
BOOL        WINAPI ExtFloodFill(HDC,int,int,COLORREF,UINT);
BOOL        WINAPI ExtTextOut(HDC,int,int,UINT,const RECT FAR*,LPCSTR,UINT,int
            FAR*);
```

```
VOID        WINAPI FatalAppExit(UINT,LPCSTR);
VOID        WINAPI FatalExit(int);
int         WINAPI FillRect(HDC,const RECT FAR*,HBRUSH);
BOOL        WINAPI FillRgn(HDC,HRGN,HBRUSH);
ATOM        WINAPI FindAtom(LPCSTR);
HRSRC       WINAPI FindResource(HINSTANCE,LPCSTR,LPCSTR);
HWND        WINAPI FindWindow(LPCSTR,LPCSTR);
BOOL        WINAPI FlashWindow(HWND,BOOL);
BOOL        WINAPI FloodFill(HDC,int,int,COLORREF);
int         WINAPI FlushComm(int,int);
int         WINAPI FrameRect(HDC,const RECT FAR*,HBRUSH);
BOOL        WINAPI FrameRgn(HDC,HRGN,HBRUSH,int,int);
VOID        WINAPI FreeLibrary(HINSTANCE);
BOOL        WINAPI FreeModule(HINSTANCE);
VOID        WINAPI FreeProcInstance(FARPROC);
```

```
BOOL        WINAPI FreeResource(HGLOBAL);
UINT        WINAPI FreeSelector(UINT);
```

```
HWND        WINAPI GetActiveWindow(VOID);
DWORD       WINAPI GetAspectRatioFilter(HDC);
BOOL        WINAPI GetAspectRatioFilterEx(HDC,SIZE FAR*);
int         WINAPI GetAsyncKeyState(int);
HLOCAL      WINAPI GetAtomHandle(ATOM);
UINT        WINAPI GetAtomName(ATOM,LPSTR,int);
LONG        WINAPI GetBitmapBits(HBITMAP,LONG,VOID FAR*);
DWORD       WINAPI GetBitmapDimension(HBITMAP);
BOOL        WINAPI GetBitmapDimensionEx(HBITMAP,SIZE FAR*);
COLORREF    WINAPI GetBkColor(HDC);
int         WINAPI GetBkMode(HDC);
UINT        WINAPI GetBoundsRect(HDC hDC,RECT FAR*,UINT);
DWORD       WINAPI GetBrushOrg(HDC);
BOOL        WINAPI GetBrushOrgEx(HDC,POINT FAR*);
HWND        WINAPI GetCapture(VOID);
UINT        WINAPI GetCaretBlinkTime(VOID);
VOID        WINAPI GetCaretPos(POINT FAR*);
BOOL        WINAPI GetCharABCWidths(HDC,UINT,UINT,ABC FAR*);
BOOL        WINAPI GetCharWidth(HDC,UINT,UINT,int FAR*);
BOOL        WINAPI GetClassInfo(HINSTANCE,LPCSTR,WNDCLASS FAR*);
LONG        WINAPI GetClassLong(HWND,int);
int         WINAPI GetClassName(HWND,LPSTR,int);
WORD        WINAPI GetClassWord(HWND,int);
VOID        WINAPI GetClientRect(HWND,RECT FAR*);
HANDLE      WINAPI GetClipboardData(UINT);
int         WINAPI GetClipboardFormatName(UINT,LPSTR,int);
HWND        WINAPI GetClipboardOwner(VOID);
HWND        WINAPI GetClipboardViewer(VOID);
int         WINAPI GetClipBox(HDC,RECT FAR*);
VOID        WINAPI GetClipCursor(RECT FAR*);
HGLOBAL     WINAPI GetCodeHandle(FARPROC);
VOID        WINAPI GetCodeInfo(FARPROC,SEGINFO FAR*);
int         WINAPI GetCommError(int,COMSTAT FAR* );
UINT        WINAPI GetCommEventMask(int,int);
int         WINAPI GetCommState(int,DCB FAR*);
UINT        WINAPI GetCurrentPDB(VOID);
DWORD       WINAPI GetCurrentPosition(HDC);
BOOL        WINAPI GetCurrentPositionEx(HDC,POINT FAR*);
HTASK       WINAPI GetCurrentTask(VOID);
DWORD       WINAPI GetCurrentTime(VOID);
HCURSOR     WINAPI GetCursor(VOID);
VOID        WINAPI GetCursorPos(POINT FAR*);
HDC         WINAPI GetDC(HWND);
HDC         WINAPI GetDCEx(register HWND,HRGN,DWORD);
DWORD       WINAPI GetDCOrg(HDC);
HWND        WINAPI GetDesktopWindow(VOID);
int         WINAPI GetDeviceCaps(HDC,int);
DWORD       WINAPI GetDialogBaseUnits(VOID);
int         WINAPI GetDIBits(HDC,HBITMAP,UINT,UINT,VOID FAR*,BITMAPINFO FAR*,UINT);
int         WINAPI GetDlgCtrlID(HWND);
```

```
HWND        WINAPI GetDlgItem(HWND,int);
UINT        WINAPI GetDlgItemInt(HWND,int,BOOL FAR* ,BOOL);
int         WINAPI GetDlgItemText(HWND,int,LPSTR,int);
LPSTR       WINAPI GetDOSEnvironment(VOID);
UINT        WINAPI GetDoubleClickTime(VOID);
BOOL        WINAPI GetDriverInfo(HDRVR,DRIVERINFOSTRUCT FAR*);
HINSTANCE   WINAPI GetDriverModuleHandle(HDRVR);
UINT        WINAPI GetDriveType(int);
int         WINAPI GetEnvironment(LPCSTR,VOID FAR*,UINT);
HWND        WINAPI GetFocus(VOID);
DWORD       WINAPI GetFontData(HDC,DWORD,DWORD,VOID FAR*,DWORD);
DWORD       WINAPI GetFreeSpace(UINT);
UINT        WINAPI GetFreeSystemResources(UINT);
DWORD       WINAPI GetGlyphOutline(HDC,UINT,UINT,GLYPHMETRICS FAR*,DWORD,VOID
            FAR*,const MAT2 FAR*);
BOOL        WINAPI GetInputState(VOID);
int         WINAPI GetInstanceData(HINSTANCE,BYTE*,int);
int         WINAPI GetKBCodePage(VOID);
int         WINAPI GetKerningPairs(HDC,int,KERNINGPAIR FAR*);
VOID        WINAPI GetKeyboardState(BYTE FAR* );
int         WINAPI GetKeyboardType(int);
int         WINAPI GetKeyNameText(LONG,LPSTR,int);
int         WINAPI GetKeyState(int);
HWND        WINAPI GetLastActivePopup(HWND);
int         WINAPI GetMapMode(HDC);
HMENU       WINAPI GetMenu(HWND);
DWORD       WINAPI GetMenuCheckMarkDimensions(VOID);
int         WINAPI GetMenuItemCount(HMENU);
UINT        WINAPI GetMenuItemID(HMENU,int);
UINT        WINAPI GetMenuState(HMENU,UINT,UINT);
int         WINAPI GetMenuString(HMENU,UINT,LPSTR,int,UINT);
BOOL        WINAPI GetMessage(MSG FAR*,HWND,UINT,UINT);
LPARAM      WINAPI GetMessageExtraInfo(VOID);
DWORD       WINAPI GetMessagePos(VOID);
LONG        WINAPI GetMessageTime(VOID);
HMETAFILE   WINAPI GetMetaFile(LPCSTR);
HGLOBAL     WINAPI GetMetaFileBits(HMETAFILE);
int         WINAPI GetModuleFileName(HINSTANCE,LPSTR,int);
HMODULE     WINAPI GetModuleHandle(LPCSTR);
int         WINAPI GetModuleUsage(HINSTANCE);
COLORREF    WINAPI GetNearestColor(HDC,COLORREF);
UINT        WINAPI GetNearestPaletteIndex(HPALETTE,COLORREF);
HWND        WINAPI GetNextDlgGroupItem(HWND,HWND,BOOL);
HWND        WINAPI GetNextDlgTabItem(HWND,HWND,BOOL);
HDRVR       WINAPI GetNextDriver(HDRVR,DWORD);
HWND        WINAPI GetNextWindow(HWND,UINT);
UINT        WINAPI GetNumTasks(VOID);
int         WINAPI GetObject(HGDIOBJ,int,VOID FAR*);
HWND        WINAPI GetOpenClipboardWindow(VOID);
WORD        WINAPI GetOutlineTextMetrics(HDC,UINT,OUTLINETEXTMETRIC FAR*);
UINT        WINAPI GetPaletteEntries(HPALETTE,UINT,UINT,PALETTEENTRY FAR*);
HWND        WINAPI GetParent(HWND);
COLORREF    WINAPI GetPixel(HDC,int,int);
int         WINAPI GetPolyFillMode(HDC);
int         WINAPI GetPriorityClipboardFormat(UINT FAR*,int);
UINT        WINAPI GetPrivateProfileInt(LPCSTR,LPCSTR,int,LPCSTR);
int         WINAPI GetPrivateProfileString(LPCSTR,LPCSTR,LPCSTR,LPSTR,int,LPCSTR);
FARPROC     WINAPI GetProcAddress(HINSTANCE,LPCSTR);
UINT        WINAPI GetProfileInt(LPCSTR,LPCSTR,int);
```

```
int          WINAPI GetProfileString(LPCSTR,LPCSTR,LPCSTR,LPSTR,int);
HANDLE       WINAPI GetProp(HWND,LPCSTR);
DWORD        WINAPI GetQueueStatus(UINT);
BOOL         WINAPI GetRasterizerCaps(RASTERIZER_STATUS FAR*,int);
int          WINAPI GetRgnBox(HRGN,RECT FAR*);
int          WINAPI GetROP2(HDC);
int          WINAPI GetScrollPos(HWND,int);
VOID         WINAPI GetScrollRange(HWND,int,int FAR*,int FAR*);
DWORD        WINAPI GetSelectorBase(UINT);
DWORD        WINAPI GetSelectorLimit(UINT);
HGDIOBJ      WINAPI GetStockObject(int);
int          WINAPI GetStretchBltMode(HDC);
HMENU        WINAPI GetSubMenu(HMENU,int);
COLORREF     WINAPI GetSysColor(int);
HWND         WINAPI GetSysModalWindow(VOID);
LONG         WINAPI GetSystemDebugState(VOID);
UINT         WINAPI GetSystemDirectory(LPSTR,UINT);
HMENU        WINAPI GetSystemMenu(HWND,BOOL);
int          WINAPI GetSystemMetrics(int);
UINT         WINAPI GetSystemPaletteEntries(HDC,UINT,UINT,PALETTEENTRY FAR*);
UINT         WINAPI GetSystemPaletteUse(HDC);
DWORD        WINAPI GetTabbedTextExtent(HDC,LPCSTR,int,int,int FAR*);
BYTE         WINAPI GetTempDrive(char);
int          WINAPI GetTempFileName(BYTE,LPCSTR,UINT,LPSTR);
UINT         WINAPI GetTextAlign(HDC);
int          WINAPI GetTextCharacterExtra(HDC);
COLORREF     WINAPI GetTextColor(HDC);
DWORD        WINAPI GetTextExtent(HDC,LPCSTR,int);
BOOL         WINAPI GetTextExtentPoint(HDC,LPCSTR,int,SIZE FAR*);
int          WINAPI GetTextFace(HDC,int,LPSTR);
BOOL         WINAPI GetTextMetrics(HDC,TEXTMETRIC FAR*);
int FAR*     WINAPI GetThresholdEvent(VOID);
int          WINAPI GetThresholdStatus(VOID);
DWORD        WINAPI GetTickCount(VOID);
DWORD        WINAPI GetTimerResolution(VOID);
HWND         WINAPI GetTopWindow(HWND);
BOOL         WINAPI GetUpdateRect(HWND,RECT FAR*,BOOL);
int          WINAPI GetUpdateRgn(HWND,HRGN,BOOL);
DWORD        WINAPI GetVersion(VOID);
DWORD        WINAPI GetViewportExt(HDC);
BOOL         WINAPI GetViewportExtEx(HDC,SIZE FAR*);
DWORD        WINAPI GetViewportOrg(HDC);
BOOL         WINAPI GetViewportOrgEx(HDC,POINT FAR*);
BOOL         WINAPI GetWinDebugInfo(WINDEBUGINFO FAR*,UINT);
HWND         WINAPI GetWindow(HWND,UINT);
HDC          WINAPI GetWindowDC(HWND);
DWORD        WINAPI GetWindowExt(HDC);
BOOL         WINAPI GetWindowExtEx(HDC,SIZE FAR*);
LONG         WINAPI GetWindowLong(HWND,int);
DWORD        WINAPI GetWindowOrg(HDC);
BOOL         WINAPI GetWindowOrgEx(HDC,POINT FAR*);
BOOL         WINAPI GetWindowPlacement(HWND,WINDOWPLACEMENT FAR*);
VOID         WINAPI GetWindowRect(HWND,RECT FAR*);
UINT         WINAPI GetWindowsDirectory(LPSTR,UINT);
HTASK        WINAPI GetWindowTask(HWND);
int          WINAPI GetWindowText(HWND,LPSTR,int);
int          WINAPI GetWindowTextLength(HWND);
WORD         WINAPI GetWindowWord(HWND,int);
DWORD        WINAPI GetWinFlags(VOID);
```

```
ATOM          WINAPI GlobalAddAtom(LPCSTR);
HGLOBAL       WINAPI GlobalAlloc(UINT,DWORD);
DWORD         WINAPI GlobalCompact(DWORD);
ATOM          WINAPI GlobalDeleteAtom(ATOM);
DWORD         WINAPI GlobalDosAlloc(DWORD);
UINT          WINAPI GlobalDosFree(UINT);
ATOM          WINAPI GlobalFindAtom(LPCSTR);
VOID          WINAPI GlobalFix(HGLOBAL);
UINT          WINAPI GlobalFlags(HGLOBAL);
HGLOBAL       WINAPI GlobalFree(HGLOBAL);
UINT          WINAPI GlobalGetAtomName(ATOM,LPSTR,int);
DWORD         WINAPI GlobalHandle(UINT);
VOID FAR*     WINAPI GlobalLock(HGLOBAL);
char FAR*     WINAPI GlobalLock(HGLOBAL);
HGLOBAL       WINAPI GlobalLRUNewest(HGLOBAL);
HGLOBAL       WINAPI GlobalLRUOldest(HGLOBAL);
VOID          WINAPI GlobalNotify(GNOTIFYPROC);
UINT          WINAPI GlobalPageLock(HGLOBAL);
UINT          WINAPI GlobalPageUnlock(HGLOBAL);
HGLOBAL       WINAPI GlobalReAlloc(HGLOBAL,DWORD,UINT);
DWORD         WINAPI GlobalSize(HGLOBAL);
VOID          WINAPI GlobalUnfix(HGLOBAL);
BOOL          WINAPI GlobalUnlock(HGLOBAL);
BOOL          WINAPI GlobalUnWire(HGLOBAL);
VOID FAR*     WINAPI GlobalWire(HGLOBAL);
char FAR*     WINAPI GlobalWire(HGLOBAL);
BOOL          WINAPI GrayString(HDC,HBRUSH,GRAYSTRINGPROC,LPARAM,int,int,int,int,int);
```

H

```
long          WINAPI _hread(HFILE,VOID _huge*,long);
long          WINAPI _hwrite(HFILE,const VOID _huge*,long);
VOID          WINAPI HideCaret(HWND);
BOOL          WINAPI HiliteMenuItem(HWND,HMENU,UINT,UINT);
VOID          WINAPI hmemcpy(VOID _huge*,const VOID _huge*,long);
```

I

```
HFILE         WINAPI _lclose(HFILE);
HFILE         WINAPI _lcreat(LPCSTR,int);
LONG          WINAPI _llseek(HFILE,LONG,int);
HFILE         WINAPI _lopen(LPCSTR,int);
UINT          WINAPI _lread(HFILE,VOID _huge*,UINT);
UINT          WINAPI _lwrite(HFILE,const VOID _huge*,UINT);
VOID          WINAPI InflateRect(RECT FAR*,int,int);
BOOL          WINAPI InitAtomTable(int);
BOOL          WINAPI InSendMessage(VOID);
BOOL          WINAPI InsertMenu(HMENU,UINT,UINT,UINT,LPCSTR);
int           WINAPI IntersectClipRect(HDC,int,int,int,int);
BOOL          WINAPI IntersectRect(RECT FAR*,const RECT FAR*,const RECT FAR*);
VOID          WINAPI InvalidateRect(HWND,const RECT FAR*,BOOL);
VOID          WINAPI InvalidateRgn(HWND,HRGN,BOOL);
VOID          WINAPI InvertRect(HDC,const RECT FAR*);
```

```
BOOL       WINAPI InvertRgn(HDC,HRGN);
BOOL       WINAPI IsBadCodePtr(FARPROC);
BOOL       WINAPI IsBadHugeReadPtr(const VOID _huge*,DWORD);
BOOL       WINAPI IsBadHugeWritePtr(VOID _huge*,DWORD);
BOOL       WINAPI IsBadReadPtr(const VOID FAR*,UINT);
BOOL       WINAPI IsBadStringPtr(const VOID FAR*,UINT);
BOOL       WINAPI IsBadWritePtr(VOID FAR*,UINT);
BOOL       WINAPI IsCharAlpha(char);
BOOL       WINAPI IsCharAlphaNumeric(char);
BOOL       WINAPI IsCharLower(char);
BOOL       WINAPI IsCharUpper(char);
BOOL       WINAPI IsChild(HWND,HWND);
BOOL       WINAPI IsClipboardFormatAvailable(UINT);
BOOL       WINAPI IsDBCSLeadByte(BYTE);
BOOL       WINAPI IsDialogMessage(HWND,MSG FAR*);
UINT       WINAPI IsDlgButtonChecked(HWND,int);
BOOL       WINAPI IsGDIObject(HGDIOBJ);
BOOL       WINAPI IsIconic(HWND);
BOOL       WINAPI IsMenu(HMENU);
BOOL       WINAPI IsRectEmpty(const RECT FAR*);
BOOL       WINAPI IsTask(HTASK);
BOOL       WINAPI IsWindow(HWND);
BOOL       WINAPI IsWindowEnabled(HWND);
BOOL       WINAPI IsWindowVisible(HWND);
BOOL       WINAPI IsZoomed(HWND);
```

```
BOOL       WINAPI KillTimer(HWND,UINT);
```

```
VOID       WINAPI LimitEmsPages(DWORD);
VOID       WINAPI LineDDA(int,int,int,int,LINEDDAPROC,LPARAM);
BOOL       WINAPI LineTo(HDC,int,int);
HACCEL     WINAPI LoadAccelerators(HINSTANCE,LPCSTR);
HBITMAP    WINAPI LoadBitmap(HINSTANCE,LPCSTR);
HCURSOR    WINAPI LoadCursor(HINSTANCE,LPCSTR);
HICON      WINAPI LoadIcon(HINSTANCE,LPCSTR);
HINSTANCE  WINAPI LoadLibrary(LPCSTR);
HMENU      WINAPI LoadMenu(HINSTANCE,LPCSTR);
HMENU      WINAPI LoadMenuIndirect(const VOID FAR*);
HINSTANCE  WINAPI LoadModule(LPCSTR,LPVOID);
HGLOBAL    WINAPI LoadResource(HINSTANCE,HRSRC);
int        WINAPI LoadString(HINSTANCE,UINT,LPSTR,int);
HLOCAL     WINAPI LocalAlloc(UINT,UINT);
UINT       WINAPI LocalCompact(UINT);
UINT       WINAPI LocalFlags(HLOCAL);
HLOCAL     WINAPI LocalFree(HLOCAL);
HLOCAL     WINAPI LocalHandle(UINT);
HLOCAL     WINAPI LocalHandle(VOID NEAR*);
BOOL       WINAPI LocalInit(UINT,UINT,UINT);
VOID NEAR* WINAPI LocalLock(HLOCAL);
```

```
char NEAR*    WINAPI LocalLock(HLOCAL);
HLOCAL        WINAPI LocalReAlloc(HLOCAL,UINT,UINT);
UINT          WINAPI LocalShrink(HLOCAL,UINT);
UINT          WINAPI LocalSize(HLOCAL);
BOOL          WINAPI LocalUnlock(HLOCAL);
BOOL          WINAPI LockInput(HANDLE,HWND,BOOL);
VOID FAR*     WINAPI LockResource(HGLOBAL);
char FAR*     WINAPI LockResource(HGLOBAL);
HGLOBAL       WINAPI LockSegment(UINT);
BOOL          WINAPI LockWindowUpdate(HWND);
VOID          WINAPI LogError(UINT,VOID FAR*);
VOID          WINAPI LogParamError(UINT,FARPROC,VOID FAR*);
BOOL          WINAPI LPtoDP(HDC,POINT FAR*,int);
LPSTR         WINAPI lstrcat(LPSTR,LPCSTR);
int           WINAPI lstrcmp(LPCSTR,LPCSTR);
int           WINAPI lstrcmpi(LPCSTR,LPCSTR);
LPSTR         WINAPI lstrcpy(LPSTR,LPCSTR);
LPSTR         WINAPI lstrcpyn(LPSTR,LPCSTR,int);
int           WINAPI lstrlen(LPCSTR);
```

```
FARPROC       WINAPI MakeProcInstance(FARPROC,HINSTANCE);
VOID          WINAPI MapDialogRect(HWND,RECT FAR*);
UINT          WINAPI MapVirtualKey(UINT,UINT);
VOID          WINAPI MapWindowPoints(HWND,HWND,POINT FAR*,UINT);
VOID          WINAPI MessageBeep(UINT);
int           WINAPI MessageBox(HWND,LPCSTR,LPCSTR,UINT);
BOOL          WINAPI ModifyMenu(HMENU,UINT,UINT,UINT,LPCSTR);
DWORD         WINAPI MoveTo(HDC,int,int);
BOOL          WINAPI MoveToEx(HDC,int,int,POINT FAR*);
BOOL          WINAPI MoveWindow(HWND,int,int,int,int,BOOL);
int           WINAPI MulDiv(int,int,int);
```

```
DWORD         WINAPI OemKeyScan(UINT);
VOID          WINAPI OemToAnsi(const char _huge*,char _huge*);
VOID          WINAPI OemToAnsiBuff(LPCSTR,LPSTR,UINT);
int           WINAPI OffsetClipRgn(HDC,int,int);
VOID          WINAPI OffsetRect(RECT FAR*,int,int);
int           WINAPI OffsetRgn(HRGN,int,int);
DWORD         WINAPI OffsetViewportOrg(HDC,int,int);
BOOL          WINAPI OffsetViewportOrgEx(HDC,int,int,POINT FAR*);
DWORD         WINAPI OffsetWindowOrg(HDC,int,int);
BOOL          WINAPI OffsetWindowOrgEx(HDC,int,int,POINT FAR*);
BOOL          WINAPI OpenClipboard(HWND);
int           WINAPI OpenComm(LPCSTR,UINT,UINT);
HDRVR         WINAPI OpenDriver(LPCSTR,LPCSTR,LPARAM);
HFILE         WINAPI OpenFile(LPCSTR,OFSTRUCT FAR*,UINT);
BOOL          WINAPI OpenIcon(HWND);
int           WINAPI OpenSound(VOID);
```

```
VOID        WINAPI OutputDebugString(LPCSTR);
```

```
BOOL        WINAPI PaintRgn(HDC,HRGN);
BOOL        WINAPI PatBlt(HDC,int,int,int,int,DWORD);
BOOL        WINAPI PeekMessage(MSG FAR*,HWND,UINT,UINT,UINT);
BOOL        WINAPI Pie(HDC,int,int,int,int,int,int,int,int);
BOOL        WINAPI PlayMetaFile(HDC,HMETAFILE);
VOID        WINAPI PlayMetaFileRecord(HDC,HANDLETABLE FAR*,METARECORD FAR*,UINT);
BOOL        WINAPI Polygon(HDC,const POINT FAR*,int);
BOOL        WINAPI Polyline(HDC,const POINT FAR*,int);
BOOL        WINAPI PolyPolygon(HDC,const POINT FAR*,int FAR*,int);
BOOL        WINAPI PostAppMessage(HTASK,UINT,WPARAM,LPARAM);
BOOL        WINAPI PostMessage(HWND,UINT,WPARAM,LPARAM);
VOID        WINAPI PostQuitMessage(int);
UINT        WINAPI PrestoChangoSelector(UINT,UINT);
VOID        WINAPI ProfClear(VOID);
VOID        WINAPI ProfFinish(VOID);
VOID        WINAPI ProfFlush(VOID);
int         WINAPI ProfInsChk(VOID);
VOID        WINAPI ProfSampRate(int,int);
VOID        WINAPI ProfSetup(int,int);
VOID        WINAPI ProfStart(VOID);
VOID        WINAPI ProfStop(VOID);
BOOL        WINAPI PtInRect(const RECT FAR*,POINT);
BOOL        WINAPI PtInRegion(HRGN,int,int);
BOOL        WINAPI PtVisible(HDC,int,int);
```

```
BOOL        WINAPI QueryAbort(HDC,int);
BOOL        WINAPI QuerySendMessage(HANDLE,HANDLE,HANDLE,LPMSG);
```

```
int         WINAPI ReadComm(int,VOID FAR*,int);
UINT        WINAPI RealizePalette(HDC);
BOOL        WINAPI Rectangle(HDC,int,int,int,int);
BOOL        WINAPI RectInRegion(HRGN,const RECT FAR*);
BOOL        WINAPI RectVisible(HDC,const RECT FAR*);
BOOL        WINAPI RedrawWindow(HWND,const RECT FAR*,HRGN,UINT);
ATOM        WINAPI RegisterClass(const WNDCLASS FAR*);
UINT        WINAPI RegisterClipboardFormat(LPCSTR);
UINT        WINAPI RegisterWindowMessage(LPCSTR);
VOID        WINAPI ReleaseCapture(VOID);
int         WINAPI ReleaseDC(HWND,HDC);
BOOL        WINAPI RemoveFontResource(LPCSTR);
BOOL        WINAPI RemoveMenu(HMENU,UINT,UINT);
```

```
HANDLE       WINAPI RemoveProp(HWND,LPCSTR);
VOID         WINAPI ReplyMessage(LRESULT);
BOOL         WINAPI ResizePalette(HPALETTE,UINT);
BOOL         WINAPI RestoreDC(HDC,int);
BOOL         WINAPI RoundRect(HDC,int,int,int,int,int,int);
```

S

```
int          WINAPI SaveDC(HDC);
DWORD        WINAPI ScaleViewportExt(HDC,int,int,int,int);
BOOL         WINAPI ScaleViewportExtEx(HDC,int,int,int,int,SIZE FAR*);
DWORD        WINAPI ScaleWindowExt(HDC,int,int,int,int);
BOOL         WINAPI ScaleWindowExtEx(HDC,int,int,int,int,SIZE FAR*);
VOID         WINAPI ScreenToClient(HWND,POINT FAR*);
BOOL         WINAPI ScrollDC(HDC,int,int,const RECT FAR*,const RECT FAR*,HRGN,RECT
             FAR*);
VOID         WINAPI ScrollWindow(HWND,int,int,const RECT FAR*,const RECT FAR*);
int          WINAPI ScrollWindowEx(HWND,int,int,const RECT FAR*,const RECT FAR*,
             HRGN, RECT FAR*, UINT);
int          WINAPI SelectClipRgn(HDC,HRGN);
HGDIOBJ      WINAPI SelectObject(HDC,HGDIOBJ);
HPALETTE     WINAPI SelectPalette(HDC,HPALETTE,BOOL);
LRESULT      WINAPI SendDlgItemMessage(HWND,int,UINT,WPARAM,LPARAM);
LRESULT      WINAPI SendDriverMessage(HDRVR,UINT,LPARAM,LPARAM);
LRESULT      WINAPI SendMessage(HWND,UINT,WPARAM,LPARAM);
int          WINAPI SetAbortProc(HDC,ABORTPROC);
HWND         WINAPI SetActiveWindow(HWND);
LONG         WINAPI SetBitmapBits(HBITMAP,DWORD,const VOID FAR*);
DWORD        WINAPI SetBitmapDimension(HBITMAP,int,int);
BOOL         WINAPI SetBitmapDimensionEx(HBITMAP,int,int,SIZE FAR*);
COLORREF     WINAPI SetBkColor(HDC,COLORREF);
int          WINAPI SetBkMode(HDC,int);
UINT         WINAPI SetBoundsRect(HDC,const RECT FAR*,UINT);
DWORD        WINAPI SetBrushOrg(HDC,int,int);
HWND         WINAPI SetCapture(HWND);
VOID         WINAPI SetCaretBlinkTime(UINT);
VOID         WINAPI SetCaretPos(int,int);
LONG         WINAPI SetClassLong(HWND,int,LONG);
WORD         WINAPI SetClassWord(HWND,int,WORD);
HANDLE       WINAPI SetClipboardData(UINT,HANDLE);
HWND         WINAPI SetClipboardViewer(HWND);
int          WINAPI SetCommBreak(int);
UINT FAR*    WINAPI SetCommEventMask(int,UINT);
int          WINAPI SetCommState(const DCB FAR*);
HCURSOR      WINAPI SetCursor(HCURSOR);
VOID         WINAPI SetCursorPos(int,int);
int          WINAPI SetDIBits(HDC,HBITMAP,UINT,UINT,const VOID FAR*,BITMAPINFO
             FAR*,UINT);
int          WINAPI SetDIBitsToDevice(HDC,int,int,int,int,int,int,UINT,UINT,
VOID         WINAPI SetDlgItemInt(HWND,int,UINT,BOOL);
VOID         WINAPI SetDlgItemText(HWND,int,LPCSTR);
VOID         WINAPI SetDoubleClickTime(UINT);
int          WINAPI SetEnvironment(LPCSTR,const VOID FAR*,UINT);
UINT         WINAPI SetErrorMode(UINT);
HWND         WINAPI SetFocus(HWND);
UINT         WINAPI SetHandleCount(UINT);
```

```
VOID          WINAPI SetKeyboardState(BYTE FAR* );
int           WINAPI SetMapMode(HDC,int);
DWORD         WINAPI SetMapperFlags(HDC,DWORD);
BOOL          WINAPI SetMenu(HWND,HMENU);
BOOL          WINAPI SetMenuItemBitmaps(HMENU,UINT,UINT,HBITMAP,HBITMAP);
BOOL          WINAPI SetMessageQueue(int);
HMETAFILE     WINAPI SetMetaFileBits(HGLOBAL);
HMETAFILE     WINAPI SetMetaFileBitsBetter(HGLOBAL);
UINT          WINAPI SetPaletteEntries(HPALETTE,UINT,UINT,const PALETTEENTRY FAR*);
HWND          WINAPI SetParent(HWND,HWND);
COLORREF      WINAPI SetPixel(HDC,int,int,COLORREF);
int           WINAPI SetPolyFillMode(HDC,int);
BOOL          WINAPI SetProp(HWND,LPCSTR,HANDLE);
VOID          WINAPI SetRect(RECT FAR*,int,int,int,int);
VOID          WINAPI SetRectEmpty(RECT FAR*);
VOID          WINAPI SetRectRgn(HRGN,int,int,int,int);
RSRCHDLRPROC  WINAPI SetResourceHandler(HINSTANCE,LPCSTR,RSRCHDLRPROC);
int           WINAPI SetROP2(HDC,int);
int           WINAPI SetScrollPos(HWND,int,int,BOOL);
VOID          WINAPI SetScrollRange(HWND,int,int,int,BOOL);
UINT          WINAPI SetSelectorBase(UINT,DWORD);
UINT          WINAPI SetSelectorLimit(UINT,DWORD);
int           WINAPI SetSoundNoise(int,int);
int           WINAPI SetStretchBltMode(HDC,int);
LONG          WINAPI SetSwapAreaSize(UINT);
VOID          WINAPI SetSysColors(int,const int FAR*,const COLORREF FAR*);
HWND          WINAPI SetSysModalWindow(HWND);
UINT          WINAPI SetSystemPaletteUse(HDC,UINT);
UINT          WINAPI SetTextAlign(HDC,UINT);
int           WINAPI SetTextCharacterExtra(HDC,int);
COLORREF      WINAPI SetTextColor(HDC,COLORREF);
int           WINAPI SetTextJustification(HDC,int,int);
UINT          WINAPI SetTimer(HWND,UINT,UINT,TIMERPROC);
DWORD         WINAPI SetViewportExt(HDC,int,int);
BOOL          WINAPI SetViewportExtEx(HDC,int,int,SIZE FAR*);
DWORD         WINAPI SetViewportOrg(HDC,int,int);
BOOL          WINAPI SetViewportOrgEx(HDC,int,int,POINT FAR*);
int           WINAPI SetVoiceAccent(int,int,int,int,int);
int           WINAPI SetVoiceEnvelope(int,int,int);
int           WINAPI SetVoiceNote(int,int,int,int);
int           WINAPI SetVoiceQueueSize(int,int);
int           WINAPI SetVoiceSound(int,DWORD,int);
int           WINAPI SetVoiceThreshold(int,int);
BOOL          WINAPI SetWinDebugInfo(const WINDEBUGINFO FAR*);
DWORD         WINAPI SetWindowExt(HDC,int,int);
BOOL          WINAPI SetWindowExtEx(HDC,int,int,SIZE FAR*);
LONG          WINAPI SetWindowLong(HWND,int,LONG);
DWORD         WINAPI SetWindowOrg(HDC,int,int);
BOOL          WINAPI SetWindowOrgEx(HDC,int,int,POINT FAR*);
BOOL          WINAPI SetWindowPlacement(HWND,const WINDOWPLACEMENT FAR*);
BOOL          WINAPI SetWindowPos(HWND,HWND,int,int,int,int,UINT);
HHOOK         WINAPI SetWindowsHook(int,HOOKPROC);
HOOKPROC      WINAPI SetWindowsHook(int,HOOKPROC);
HHOOK         WINAPI SetWindowsHookEx(int,HOOKPROC,HINSTANCE,HTASK);
VOID          WINAPI SetWindowText(HWND,LPCSTR);
WORD          WINAPI SetWindowWord(HWND,int,WORD);
VOID          WINAPI ShowCaret(HWND);
int           WINAPI ShowCursor(BOOL);
VOID          WINAPI ShowOwnedPopups(HWND,BOOL);
```

```
VOID         WINAPI ShowScrollBar(HWND,int,BOOL);
BOOL         WINAPI ShowWindow(HWND,int);
DWORD        WINAPI SizeofResource(HINSTANCE,HRSRC);
HANDLE       WINAPI SpoolFile(LPSTR,LPSTR,LPSTR,LPSTR);
int          WINAPI StartDoc(HDC,DOCINFO FAR*);
int          WINAPI StartPage(HDC);
int          WINAPI StartSound(VOID);
int          WINAPI StopSound(VOID);
BOOL         WINAPI StretchBlt(HDC,int,int,int,int,HDC,int,int,int,int,DWORD);
int          WINAPI StretchDIBits(HDC,int,int,int,int,int,
BOOL         WINAPI SubtractRect(RECT FAR*,const RECT FAR*,const RECT FAR*);
BOOL         WINAPI SwapMouseButton(BOOL);
VOID         WINAPI SwapRecording(UINT);
VOID         WINAPI SwitchStackBack(VOID);
VOID         WINAPI SwitchStackTo(UINT,UINT,UINT);
int          WINAPI SyncAllVoices(VOID);
BOOL         WINAPI SystemParametersInfo(UINT,UINT,VOID FAR*,UINT);
```

T

```
LONG         WINAPI TabbedTextOut(HDC,int,int,LPCSTR,int,int,int FAR*,int);
BOOL         WINAPI TextOut(HDC,int,int,LPCSTR,int);
VOID         WINAPI Throw(const int FAR*,int);
int          WINAPI ToAscii(UINT,UINT,BYTE FAR*,DWORD FAR*,UINT);
BOOL         WINAPI TrackPopupMenu(HMENU,UINT,int,int,int,HWND,const RECT FAR*);
int          WINAPI TranslateAccelerator(HWND,HACCEL,MSG FAR*);
BOOL         WINAPI TranslateMDISysAccel(HWND,MSG FAR*);
BOOL         WINAPI TranslateMessage(const MSG FAR*);
int          WINAPI TransmitCommChar(int,char);
```

U

```
int          WINAPI UngetCommChar(int,char);
BOOL         WINAPI UnhookWindowsHook(int,HOOKPROC);
BOOL         WINAPI UnhookWindowsHookEx(HHOOK);
BOOL         WINAPI UnionRect(RECT FAR*,const RECT FAR*,const RECT FAR*);
VOID         WINAPI UnlockSegment(UINT);
BOOL         WINAPI UnrealizeObject(HGDIOBJ);
BOOL         WINAPI UnregisterClass(LPCSTR,HINSTANCE);
int          WINAPI UpdateColors(HDC);
VOID         WINAPI UpdateWindow(HWND);
```

V

```
VOID         WINAPI ValidateCodeSegments(VOID);
VOID         WINAPI ValidateFreeSpaces(VOID);
VOID         WINAPI ValidateRect(HWND,const RECT FAR*);
VOID         WINAPI ValidateRgn(HWND,HRGN);
UINT         WINAPI VkKeyScan(UINT);
```

```
VOID        WINAPI WaitMessage(VOID);
int         WINAPI WaitSoundState(int);
HWND        WINAPI WindowFromPoint(POINT);
UINT        WINAPI WinExec(LPCSTR,UINT);
BOOL        WINAPI WinHelp(HWND,LPCSTR,UINT,DWORD);
int         PASCAL WinMain(HINSTANCE,HINSTANCE,LPSTR,int);
UINT        WINAPI WNetAddConnection(LPSTR,LPSTR,LPSTR);
UINT        WINAPI WNetCancelConnection(LPSTR,BOOL);
UINT        WINAPI WNetGetConnection(LPSTR,LPSTR,UINT FAR*);
int         WINAPI WriteComm(int,const VOID FAR*,int);
BOOL        WINAPI WritePrivateProfileString(LPCSTR,LPCSTR,LPCSTR,LPCSTR);
BOOL        WINAPI WriteProfileString(LPCSTR,LPCSTR,LPCSTR);
int FAR     CDECL  wsprintf(LPSTR,LPCSTR,...);
int         WINAPI wvsprintf(LPSTR,LPCSTR,const VOID FAR*);
```

```
VOID        WINAPI Yield(VOID);
```

Useful Macros from WINDOWS.H

```
#define LOBYTE(w)                 ((BYTE)(w))
#define HIBYTE(w)                 ((BYTE)(((UINT)(w) >> 8) & 0xFF))
#define LOWORD(l)                 ((WORD)(DWORD)(l))
#define HIWORD(l)                 ((WORD)((((DWORD)(l)) >> 16) & 0xFFFF))
#define MAKELONG(LOW, HIGH)       ((LONG)(((WORD)(LOW)) | (((DWORD)((WORD)(HIGH))) <<

                                  16)))
#define max(a,b)                  (((a) > (b)) ? (a) : (b))
#define min(a,b)                  (((a) < (b)) ? (a) : (b))
#define MAKELPARAM(LOW, HIGH)     ((LPARAM)MAKELONG(LOW, HIGH))
#define MAKELRESULT(LOW, HIGH)    ((LRESULT)MAKELONG(LOW, HIGH))
#define MAKELP(sel, off)          ((void FAR*)MAKELONG((off), (sel)))
#define SELECTOROF(lp)            HIWORD(lp)
#define OFFSETOF(lp)              LOWORD(lp)
#define GlobalDiscard(h)          GlobalReAlloc(h, 0L, GMEM_MOVEABLE)
#define LockData(DUMMY)           LockSegment((UINT)-1)
#define UnlockData(DUMMY)         UnlockSegment((UINT)-1)
#define LocalDiscard(h)           LocalReAlloc(h, 0, LMEM_MOVEABLE)
#define UnlockResource(h)         GlobalUnlock(h)
#define MAKEINTRESOURCE(i)        ((LPCSTR)MAKELP(0, (i)))
#define MAKEINTATOM(i)            ((LPCSTR)MAKELP(0, (i)))
#define MAKEPOINT(l)              (*((POINT FAR*)&(l)))
#define RGB(r,g,b)                ((COLOR-
REF)(((BYTE)(r)|((WORD)(g)<<8))|(((DWORD)(BYTE)(b))<<16)))
#define GetRValue(rgb)            ((BYTE)(rgb))
#define GetGValue(rgb)            ((BYTE)(((WORD)(rgb)) >> 8))
#define GetBValue(rgb)            ((BYTE)((rgb)>>16))
#define PALETTERGB(r,g,b)         (0x02000000L | RGB(r,g,b))
#define PALETTEINDEX(i)           ((COLORREF)(0x01000000L | (DWORD)(WORD)(i)))
```

Alphabetically sorted list of WINDOWS.H structures.

A

```
typedef struct tagABC
{
    int     abcA;
    UINT    abcB;
    int     abcC;
} ABC;
```

B

```
typedef struct tagBITMAP
{
    int         bmType;
    int         bmWidth;
    int         bmHeight;
    int         bmWidthBytes;
    BYTE        bmPlanes;
    BYTE        bmBitsPixel;
    void FAR*   bmBits;
} BITMAP;
```

```
typedef struct tagBITMAPCOREHEADER
{
    DWORD   bcSize;
    short   bcWidth;
    short   bcHeight;
    WORD    bcPlanes;
    WORD    bcBitCount;
} BITMAPCOREHEADER;
```

```
typedef struct tagBITMAPCOREINFO
{
    BITMAPCOREHEADER bmciHeader;
    RGBTRIPLE              bmciColors[1];
} BITMAPCOREINFO;
```

```
typedef struct tagBITMAPFILEHEADER
{
    UINT    bfType;
```

```
    DWORD   bfSize;
    UINT    bfReserved1;
    UINT    bfReserved2;
    DWORD   bfOffBits;
} BITMAPFILEHEADER;
```

```
typedef struct tagBITMAPINFO
{
    BITMAPINFOHEADER bmiHeader;
    RGBQUAD             bmiColors[1];
} BITMAPINFO;
```

```
typedef struct tagBITMAPINFOHEADER
{
    DWORD   biSize;
    LONG    biWidth;
    LONG    biHeight;
    WORD    biPlanes;
    WORD    biBitCount;
    DWORD   biCompression;
    DWORD   biSizeImage;
    LONG    biXPelsPerMeter;
    LONG    biYPelsPerMeter;
    DWORD   biClrUsed;
    DWORD   biClrImportant;
} BITMAPINFOHEADER;
```

C

```
typedef struct tagCBTACTIVATESTRUCT
{ ·
    BOOL    fMouse;
    HWND    hWndActive;
} CBTACTIVATESTRUCT;
```

```
typedef struct tagCBT_CREATEWND
{
    CREATESTRUCT FAR* lpcs;
    HWND    hwndInsertAfter;
} CBT_CREATEWND;
```

```
typedef struct tagCLIENTCREATESTRUCT
```

```
{
    HMENU   hWindowMenu;
    UINT    idFirstChild;
} CLIENTCREATESTRUCT;

typedef struct tagCOMPAREITEMSTRUCT
{
    UINT        CtlType;
    UINT        CtlID;
    HWND        hwndItem;
    UINT        itemID1;
    DWORD       itemData1;
    UINT        itemID2;
    DWORD       itemData2;
} COMPAREITEMSTRUCT;

typedef struct tagCOMSTAT
{
    BYTE status;
    UINT cbInQue;
    UINT cbOutQue;
} COMSTAT;

typedef struct tagCOMSTAT
{
    BYTE fCtsHold   :1;
    BYTE fDsrHold   :1;
    BYTE fRlsdHold  :1;
    BYTE fXoffHold  :1;
    BYTE fXoffSent  :1;
    BYTE fEof       :1;
    BYTE fTxim      :1;
    UINT cbInQue;
    UINT cbOutQue;
} COMSTAT;

typedef struct tagCREATESTRUCT
{
    void FAR* lpCreateParams;
    HINSTANCE hInstance;
    HMENU     hMenu;
    HWND      hwndParent;
    int       cy;
    int       cx;
    int       y;
    int       x;
    LONG      style;
    LPCSTR    lpszName;
    LPCSTR    lpszClass;
    DWORD     dwExStyle;
} CREATESTRUCT;
```

D

```
typedef struct tagDCB
{
```

```
    BYTE Id;
    UINT BaudRate;
    BYTE ByteSize;
    BYTE Parity;
    BYTE StopBits;
    UINT RlsTimeout;
    UINT CtsTimeout;
    UINT DsrTimeout;

    UINT fBinary       :1;
    UINT fRtsDisable   :1;
    UINT fParity       :1;
    UINT fOutxCtsFlow  :1;
    UINT fOutxDsrFlow  :1;
    UINT fDummy        :2;
    UINT fDtrDisable   :1;

    UINT fOutX         :1;
    UINT fInX          :1;
    UINT fPeChar       :1;
    UINT fNull         :1;
    UINT fChEvt        :1;
    UINT fDtrflow      :1;
    UINT fRtsflow      :1;
    UINT fDummy2       :1;

    char XonChar;
    char XoffChar;
    UINT XonLim;
    UINT XoffLim;
    char PeChar;
    char EofChar;
    char EvtChar;
    UINT TxDelay;
} DCB;

typedef struct tagDEBUGHOOKINFO
{
    HMODULE        hModuleHook;
    LPARAM         reserved;
    LPARAM         lParam;
    WPARAM         wParam;
    int            code;
} DEBUGHOOKINFO;

typedef struct tagDELETEITEMSTRUCT
{
    UINT        CtlType;
    UINT        CtlID;
    UINT        itemID;
    HWND        hwndItem;
    DWORD       itemData;
} DELETEITEMSTRUCT;

typedef struct
{
    int     cbSize;
    LPCSTR  lpszDocName;
    LPCSTR  lpszOutput;
```

```
}   DOCINFO;

typedef struct tagDRAWITEMSTRUCT
{
    UINT       CtlType;
    UINT       CtlID;
    UINT       itemID;
    UINT       itemAction;
    UINT       itemState;
    HWND       hwndItem;
    HDC        hDC;
    RECT       cItem;
    DWORD      itemData;
} DRAWITEMSTRUCT;

typedef struct tagDRIVERINFOSTRUCT
{
    UINT       length;
    HDRVR      hDriver;
    HINSTANCE  hModule;
    char       szAliasName[128];
} DRIVERINFOSTRUCT;

typedef struct tagDRVCONFIGINFO
{
    DWORD    dwDCISize;
    LPCSTR   lpszDCISectionName;
    LPCSTR   lpszDCIAliasName;
} DRVCONFIGINFO;
```

E

```
typedef struct tagENUMLOGFONT
{
    LOGFONT elfLogFont;
    char    elfFullName[LF_FULLFACESIZE];
    char    elfStyle[LF_FACESIZE];
} ENUMLOGFONT, FAR* LPENUMLOGFONT;

typedef struct tagEVENTMSG
{
    UINT    message;
    UINT    paramL;
    UINT    paramH;
    DWORD   time;
} EVENTMSG;
```

F

```
typedef struct tagFIXED
{
    UINT    fract;
    int     value;
```

```
} FIXED, FAR* LPFIXED;
```

G

```
typedef struct tagGLYPHMETRICS
{
    UINT    gmBlackBoxX;
    UINT    gmBlackBoxY;
    POINT   gmptGlyphOrigin;
    int     gmCellIncX;
    int     gmCellIncY;
} GLYPHMETRICS, FAR* LPGLYPHMETRICS;

typedef struct tagHANDLETABLE
{
    HGDIOBJ objectHandle[1];
} HANDLETABLE;
```

H

```
typedef struct
{
    int  wStructSize;
    int  x;
    int  y;
    int  dx;
    int  dy;
    int  wMax;
    char rgchMember[2];
} HELPWININFO;

typedef struct tagHARDWAREHOOKSTRUCT
{
    HWND    hWnd;
    UINT    wMessage;
    WPARAM  wParam;
    LPARAM  lParam;
} HARDWAREHOOKSTRUCT;
```

K

```
typedef struct tagKERNINGPAIR
{
    WORD wFirst;
    WORD wSecond;
    int  iKernAmount;
} KERNINGPAIR, FAR* LPKERNINGPAIR;
```

L

```
typedef struct tagLOGBRUSH
{
    UINT     lbStyle;
    COLORREF lbColor;
    int      lbHatch;
} LOGBRUSH;

typedef struct tagLOGFONT
{
    int     lfHeight;
    int     lfWidth;
    int     lfEscapement;
    int     lfOrientation;
    int     lfWeight;
    BYTE    lfItalic;
    BYTE    lfUnderline;
    BYTE    lfStrikeOut;
    BYTE    lfCharSet;
    BYTE    lfOutPrecision;
    BYTE    lfClipPrecision;
    BYTE    lfQuality;
    BYTE    lfPitchAndFamily;
    char    lfFaceName[LF_FACESIZE];
} LOGFONT;

typedef struct tagLOGPALETTE
{
    WORD         palVersion;
    WORD         palNumEntries;
    PALETTEENTRY palPalEntry[1];
} LOGPALETTE;

typedef struct tagLOGPEN
{
    UINT     lopnStyle;
    POINT    lopnWidth;
    COLORREF lopnColor;
} LOGPEN;
```

M

```
typedef struct
{
    UINT    versionNumber;
    UINT    offset;
} MENUITEMTEMPLATEHEADER;

typedef struct
{
    UINT    mtOption;
    UINT    mtID;
    char    mtString[1];
} MENUITEMTEMPLATE;
```

```
typedef struct tagMAT2
{
    FIXED   eM11;
    FIXED   eM12;
    FIXED   eM21;
    FIXED   eM22;
} MAT2, FAR* LPMAT2;

typedef struct tagMDICREATESTRUCT
{
    LPCSTR   szClass;
    LPCSTR   szTitle;
    HINSTANCE hOwner;
    int      x;
    int      y;
    int      cx;
    int      cy;
    DWORD    style;
    LPARAM   lParam;
} MDICREATESTRUCT;

typedef struct tagMEASUREITEMSTRUCT
{
    UINT     CtlType;
    UINT     CtlID;
    UINT     itemID;
    UINT     itemWidth;
    UINT     itemHeight;
    DWORD    itemData;
} MEASUREITEMSTRUCT;

typedef struct tagMETAFILEPICT
{
    int     mm;
    int     xExt;
    int     yExt;
    HMETAFILE hMF;
} METAFILEPICT;

typedef struct tagMETAHEADER
{
    UINT    mtType;
    UINT    mtHeaderSize;
    UINT    mtVersion;
    DWORD   mtSize;
    UINT    mtNoObjects;
    DWORD   mtMaxRecord;
    UINT    mtNoParameters;
} METAHEADER;

typedef struct tagMETARECORD
{
    DWORD   rdSize;
    UINT    rdFunction;
    UINT    rdParm[1];
} METARECORD;

typedef struct tagMINMAXINFO
```

```
{
    POINT ptReserved;
    POINT ptMaxSize;
    POINT ptMaxPosition;
    POINT ptMinTrackSize;
    POINT ptMaxTrackSize;
} MINMAXINFO;

typedef struct tagMOUSEHOOKSTRUCT
{
    POINT    pt;
    HWND     hwnd;
    UINT     wHitTestCode;
    DWORD    dwExtraInfo;
} MOUSEHOOKSTRUCT;

typedef struct tagMSG
{
    HWND        hwnd;
    UINT        message;
    WPARAM      wParam;
    LPARAM      lParam;
    DWORD       time;
    POINT       pt;
} MSG;

typedef struct tagMULTIKEYHELP
{
    UINT    mkSize;
    BYTE    mkKeylist;
    BYTE    szKeyphrase[1];
} MULTIKEYHELP;
```

N

```
typedef struct tagNCCALCSIZE_PARAMS
{
    RECT    rgrc[3];
    WINDOWPOS FAR* lppos;
} NCCALCSIZE_PARAMS;

typedef struct tagNCCALCSIZE_PARAMS
{
    RECT    rgrc[2];
} NCCALCSIZE_PARAMS;

typedef struct tagNEWTEXTMETRIC
{
    int     tmHeight;
    int     tmAscent;
    int     tmDescent;
    int     tmInternalLeading;
    int     tmExternalLeading;
    int     tmAveCharWidth;
    int     tmMaxCharWidth;
    int     tmWeight;
```

```
    BYTE     tmItalic;
    BYTE     tmUnderlined;
    BYTE     tmStruckOut;
    BYTE     tmFirstChar;
    BYTE     tmLastChar;
    BYTE     tmDefaultChar;
    BYTE     tmBreakChar;
    BYTE     tmPitchAndFamily;
    BYTE     tmCharSet;
    int      tmOverhang;
    int      tmDigitizedAspectX;
    int      tmDigitizedAspectY;
    DWORD    ntmFlags;
    UINT     ntmSizeEM;
    UINT     ntmCellHeight;
    UINT     ntmAvgWidth;
} NEWTEXTMETRIC;
```

O

```
typedef struct tagOFSTRUCT
{
    BYTE cBytes;
    BYTE fFixedDisk;
    UINT nErrCode;
    BYTE reserved[4];
    char szPathName[128];
} OFSTRUCT;

typedef struct tagOUTLINETEXTMETRIC
{
    UINT        otmSize;
    TEXTMETRIC otmTextMetrics;
    BYTE        otmFiller;
    PANOSE      otmPanoseNumber;
    UINT        otmfsSelection;
    UINT        otmfsType;
    int         otmsCharSlopeRise;
    int         otmsCharSlopeRun;
    int         otmItalicAngle;
    UINT        otmEMSquare;
    int         otmAscent;
    int         otmDescent;
    UINT        otmLineGap;
    UINT        otmsCapEmHeight;
    UINT        otmsXHeight;
    RECT        otmrcFontBox;
    int         otmMacAscent;
    int         otmMacDescent;
    UINT        otmMacLineGap;
    UINT        otmusMinimumPPEM;
    POINT       otmptSubscriptSize;
    POINT       otmptSubscriptOffset;
    POINT       otmptSuperscriptSize;
    POINT       otmptSuperscriptOffset;
    UINT        otmsStrikeoutSize;
```

```
    int     otmsStrikeoutPosition;
    int     otmsUnderscorePosition;
    int     otmsUnderscoreSize;
    PSTR    otmpFamilyName;
    PSTR    otmpFaceName;
    PSTR    otmpStyleName;
    PSTR    otmpFullName;
} OUTLINETEXTMETRIC, FAR*
LPOUTLINETEXTMETRIC;
```

P

```
typedef struct tagPAINTSTRUCT
{
    HDC  hdc;
    BOOL fErase;
    RECT rcPaint;
    BOOL fRestore;
    BOOL fIncUpdate;
    BYTE rgbReserved[16];
} PAINTSTRUCT;

typedef struct tagPALETTEENTRY
{
    BYTE    peRed;
    BYTE    peGreen;
    BYTE    peBlue;
    BYTE    peFlags;
} PALETTEENTRY;

typedef struct tagPANOSE
{
    BYTE    bFamilyType;
    BYTE    bSerifStyle;
    BYTE    bWeight;
    BYTE    bProportion;
    BYTE    bContrast;
    BYTE    bStrokeVariation;
    BYTE    bArmStyle;
    BYTE    bLetterform;
    BYTE    bMidline;
    BYTE    bXHeight;
} PANOSE, FAR* LPPANOSE;

typedef struct tagPOINT
{
    int x;
    int y;
} POINT;

typedef struct tagPOINTFX
{
    FIXED x;
    FIXED y;
} POINTFX, FAR* LPPOINTFX;
```

R

```
typedef struct tagRASTERIZER_STATUS
{
    int    nSize;
    int    wFlags;
    int    nLanguageID;
} RASTERIZER_STATUS;

typedef struct tagRECT
{
    int left;
    int top;
    int right;
    int bottom;
} RECT;

typedef struct tagRGBQUAD
{
    BYTE    rgbBlue;
    BYTE    rgbGreen;
    BYTE    rgbRed;
    BYTE    rgbReserved;
} RGBQUAD;

typedef struct tagRGBTRIPLE
{
    BYTE    rgbtBlue;
    BYTE    rgbtGreen;
    BYTE    rgbtRed;
} RGBTRIPLE;
```

S

```
typedef struct tagSEGINFO
{
    UINT offSegment;
    UINT cbSegment;
    UINT flags;
    UINT cbAlloc;
    HGLOBAL h;
    UINT alignShift;
    UINT reserved[2];
} SEGINFO;

typedef struct tagSIZE
{
    int cx;
    int cy;
} SIZE;

typedef struct tagTEXTMETRIC
{
    int    tmHeight;
    int    tmAscent;
```

```
    int     tmDescent;
    int     tmInternalLeading;
    int     tmExternalLeading;
    int     tmAveCharWidth;
    int     tmMaxCharWidth;
    int     tmWeight;
    BYTE    tmItalic;
    BYTE    tmUnderlined;
    BYTE    tmStruckOut;
    BYTE    tmFirstChar;
    BYTE    tmLastChar;
    BYTE    tmDefaultChar;
    BYTE    tmBreakChar;
    BYTE    tmPitchAndFamily;
    BYTE    tmCharSet;
    int     tmOverhang;
    int     tmDigitizedAspectX;
    int     tmDigitizedAspectY;
} TEXTMETRIC;


typedef struct tagTTPOLYCURVE
{
    UINT    wType;
    UINT    cpfx;
    POINTFX apfx[1];
} TTPOLYCURVE, FAR* LPTTPOLYCURVE;


typedef struct tagTTPOLYGONHEADER
{
    DWORD   cb;
    DWORD   dwType;
    POINTFX pfxStart;
} TTPOLYGONHEADER, FAR* LPTTPOLYGONHEADER;
```

```
typedef struct tagWINDEBUGINFO
{
    UINT    flags;
    DWORD   dwOptions;
```

```
    DWORD   dwFilter;
    char    achAllocModule[8];
    DWORD   dwAllocBreak;
    DWORD   dwAllocCount;
} WINDEBUGINFO;


typedef struct tagWINDOWPLACEMENT
{
    UINT  length;
    UINT  flags;
    UINT  showCmd;
    POINT ptMinPosition;
    POINT ptMaxPosition;
    RECT  rcNormalPosition;
} WINDOWPLACEMENT;


typedef struct tagWINDOWPOS
{
    HWND  hwnd;
    HWND  hwndInsertAfter;
    int   x;
    int   y;
    int   cx;
    int   cy;
    UINT  flags;
} WINDOWPOS;


typedef struct tag1WNDCLASS
{
    UINT      style;
    WNDPROC   lpfnWndProc;
    int       cbClsExtra;
    int       cbWndExtra;
    HINSTANCE hInstance;
    HICON     hIcon;
    HCURSOR   hCursor;
    HBRUSH    hbrBackground;
    LPCSTR    lpszMenuName;
    LPCSTR    lpszClassName;
} WNDCLASS;
```

Index

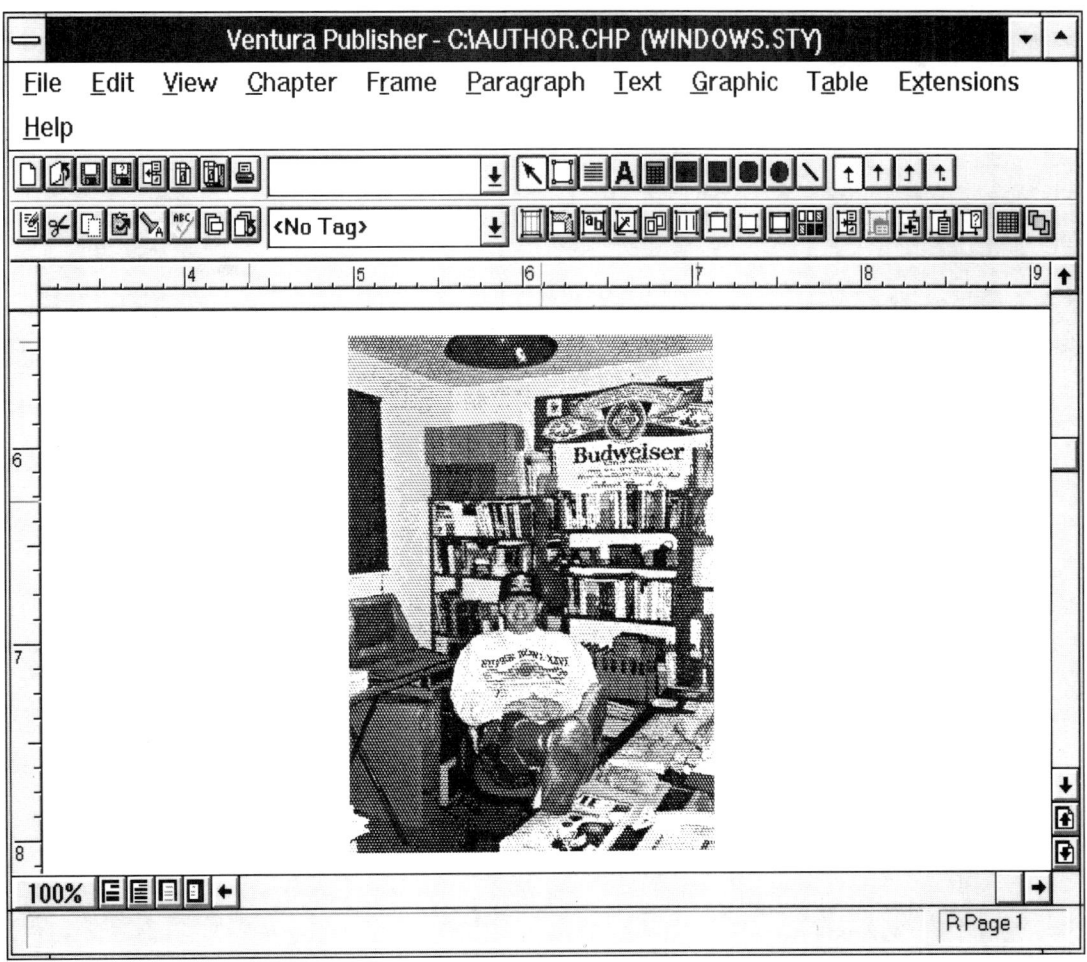

Peter J. Morris Ph.D., F.I.A.P., M.I.D.P.M., F.I.Diag.E, has worked with Windows since 'the early days'. Morris has been involved in Windows' programming since its inception and is well known to many Windows' programmers in the industry. Morris was a founding member of the IEEE P1201 GUI standards group where he concentrated on areas such as standardising the GUI API and Drivability. He has also worked with other standards groups like ANSI's X3J11 ('C') and X3J16 (C++) groups. Morris, a one time member of Microsoft's Consulting Services group now works as a freelance consultant in the UK. He can be contacted via electronic mail on CIS 100016,2751 or through the Internet on 100017.2751@Compuserve.com